Sweet Peas, Suffragettes and Showmen

Events that changed the world in the

RHS HALLS

SWEET PEAS, SUFFRAGETTES AND SHOWMEN

Events that changed the world in the

RHS HALLS

René Dee

PHILLIMORE

2011

Published by

PHILLIMORE & CO. LTD

Andover, Hampshire, England

www.phillimore.co.uk

ISBN 978-1-86077-665-6

For Geoff who gave me the opportunity.

Contents

Acknowledgements

There are many people and organisations that have helped me with my research and information during the past seven years that have led to this book, so I acknowledge them all here with sincere and grateful thanks. Without them, my book, and the extraordinary history revealed, would not have been possible, or as complete.

Firstly, I would like to thank several enlightened colleagues who recognised the value and importance of this book when I first proposed it in 2004. These include Suzanne Mitchell and Susannah Charlton who both acted as RHS Publishers during their time at the RHS, and Brent Elliott in his capacity as Librarian. The subsequent support received from Brent Elliott, Chris Brickell, Andrew Sells, Martin Slocock and Lawrence Banks in support of my bursary application to the RHS Bursaries Advisory Committee was invaluable. My thanks must also go to Bill Simpson, Chairman of this Committee, that approved my application.

However, my special thanks is directed to Brent Elliott, who as Librarian of the RHS Lindley Library, and a work colleague at the time, gave me full support and access to the RHS Halls archives in 2003. This was the start of my journey in compiling the event listings from which my further research was able to be carried out. It includes a visit to British Library Newspapers, Colindale, with him in 2003. My thanks also go to him for reading my first early chapters, my chapter on the RHS Flower Shows, and his important feedback. He also allowed me access to the RHS Council Minutes much later in his capacity as Archivist and, via Lucy Waite, permission to publish a number of photographs, letters and documents from the RHS archives in order to illustrate the book. These include several images from his own book: *The Royal Horticultural Society A History 1804-2004*, published by Phillimore & Co. Ltd, 2004, © The Royal Horticultural Society, 2004.

In the same vein, my thanks goes to Roisin Duffy, and Julian Agostini from Mash Media who arranged for me to have access to their *Exhibition Bulletin* archives, originally published by Peter Cole. This filled many gaps in my event listings during the '60s-'80s in particular.

John Glanfield, who wrote a similar history of Earl's Court and Olympia, published in 2003, spurred me on from the very beginning, gave me moral support, and gave me valuable archive resources information.

Suzanne Barshall from the Craft Guild of Chefs in Richmond, Surrey, very kindly allowed me access to their archives in 2004, which contained very early references and material relating to the Universal Cookery & Food Exhibition. I thank her, and The Guild, for the subsequent permission to reproduce some of these in my book.

Renée Anderson, Learning Centre Manager, Victoria Centre at Westminster Kingsway College, Vincent Square, also kindly gave me access to her archives, photos, and similar UC&FE catalogue material, as well as documents from *Food & Cookery & the Catering World*, which I gratefully acknowledge.

Ann Hatherill has been supportive from the very start in helping me with the history of the Society of Model and Experimental Engineers (S.M. & E.E.) and The Model Engineer Exhibition. As archivist of the S.M. & E.E., Ann gave me considerable assistance leading to the Centenary Exhibition and, latterly, for this book. In particular, I must thank her for the original photos and personal mementos of her father, the late Bill Carter.

John Holman, Editor, British Philatelic and Postmark Bulletins, Royal Mail kindly sent me a history of STAMPEX and introduced me to Bill Tonkin. Bill Tonkin gave me valuable information from his personal collection, and from archives of the Exhibition Study Group, of which he was a leading member. He was also very helpful to me in the early stages of putting together the Centenary Exhibition I organised at the RHS Lawrence Hall in 2004.

Similarly, I have to thank both Francis and Charles Kiddle for helping me with that event, and for letting me use their APEX material and the brochure cover I have also reproduced in the book. Many of the rare poster labels that I own were sourced by Charles Kiddle of World Poster Stamps from far-flung corners of the world, and have been invaluable in my further research.

Michael Furnell provided me with copies of *Stamp Collectors' Fortnightly* and *The Stamp Lover* in connection with some of the major philatelic exhibitions. He also gave me information about his own *Homefinders* New Homes Shows of the 1970s.

I am also very grateful to Michael Sefi, Keeper of the Royal Philatelic Collection, who has given me valuable and precise information concerning the Royal Family's involvement with the 1906 and 1912 philatelic exhibitions that are referred to in the book, and also in connection with his own relative, Alexander Sefi.

Jill Brill from the 'National Badminton Museum', Milton Keynes, was also an early supporter from 2004, and the provider of original material from her museum, together with copies of *The Badminton Gazette* depicting photos of early matches in the Hall. These are shown on pages 174-5.

Marion Petersen from Westbank, B.C., Canada, kindly wrote to me and supplied me with personal recollections of her time spent as a member of the Westminster Choral Society.

Similarly, Sheila Cutler from Brighton, Sussex, took me to the unique 'Bergman Österberg Union Archive' located in the original part of Madame Österberg's Physical Training College in Dartford, now integrated into the University of Greenwich, and shared with me her own personal recollections as a student there. Rosemary Moon, representing the University and the Archive, kindly gave me permission to reproduce unique photos showing the Hall being used for a display in it, as well as a photo of Madame Österberg herself. These are shown on pages 125-7.

My thanks to Paul Hughes who supplied me with a constant flow of information about the Applied Arts and Handcrafts Exhibitions, scans of catalogues, dates, anecdotes and other very useful information.

David Sheppard, who ran the *Daily Mail* Picture Library in 2003, kindly gave me access to it where I was able to find more unique photos of early *Daily Mail* Schoolboy's Own and Ski Exhibitions. Seven years later, Danny Howell of Solo Syndication, also based at Northcliffe House, Derry Street, London, helped me track these down again and allowed me to use them on behalf of the *Daily Mail*. These are shown on pages 189-91 and 192.

Michelle Payne, from The National Children's Wear Association of Great Britain and Ireland kindly sent me front covers of several of their Junior Fashion Fair Catalogues, and supplied dates for many of the 60 shows they organised. The 1953 cover is shown on page 151.

Photographs shown on pages 39, 110, 143, 150, 169, 200, 201, 210, 212 and 274 are credited to 'collection/Getty Images'.

Photographs shown on pages 117, 122, 160, 168 and 226 are credited to 'Press Association Images'.

Photographs shown on pages 153 and 260 are credited to 'Mirrorpix'.

Photograph shown on page 41 is credited to '*Manchester Daily Express* SSPL'.

Photograph shown on page 159 is credited to 'National Media Museum/SSPL'.

Roger Edwards, Editor, *Health & Strength* magazine helped put me in touch with Ron Tyrrell and David Webster who both supplied me with key information and images about the Health & Strength League and New Health Society events, as well as personal anecdotes and new information in this area. One of the images is shown on page 167.

I am grateful to Colin Walker from Walker Toys, a Boy Scout historian and author of the website 'Scouting Milestones' at www.scoutingmilestones.freeserve.co.uk who responded to my call in 2004 to RHS Members to recall what they could of past events in the Halls. Colin provided hitherto unknown information about the role Boy Scouts had played in the Halls prior to King George VI's Coronation.

There were many who helped me piece together the dog and cat Championship Shows history; some providing black and white photos and others, new information. Firstly, my thanks to Kellie Snow, Assistant Librarian, The Kennel Club who provided me with scans of very early show catalogues, and much later to Ciarra Farrell. My thanks also to Julia May, Archivist at The Governing Council of the Cat Fancy, Lorna Taylor of the Kensington Kitten & Neuter Cat Club, Miss J. Beeson of The Governing Council of the Cat Fancy, Ted Jones of Wickford, Essex, and Marc Henrie, of London W12 for their catalogues and photographs. Marc Henrie's photographs are shown on page 35.

Thank you to the ladies who took part in the reminiscence group sessions organised by Kate Ferguson of the Abbey Centre in Great Smith Street, London in 2004. Their memories provided several anecdotes about the children in the local community, and how they saw the events in the Halls. My thanks also to Stephen McClelland, Chairman of the Vincent Square Residents' Association, who let me have a copy of the booklet sponsored by them entitled *About Vincent Square*, written by Alicia C. Percival in 1981, from which useful local knowledge has also been gained.

Lawrence Napper from EAS, University of East Anglia, Norwich, working on the British Cinema History Research Project, provided me with several articles from the February 1921 *Kinematograph Weekly* about the 1921 Cinema Accessories and Musical Appliances Exhibition.

Peter Stubbs from www.edinphoto.org.uk was of great assistance in helping me chart the Photographers' Association Congresses and Photo Fairs held between 1910 and 1933. His research at the National Library of Scotland and the *British Journal of Photography* were most profitable.

The Archives and Rare Books Division of the London School of Economics Library gave me valuable insights into The Primrose League, the Independent Labour Party, The Labour Party, James Keir Hardie, Emmeline Pankhurst, *The Clarion* and, Clarion Van Movement. I acknowledge their permission and that of 'Independent Labour Publications' for me to reproduce the ILP Reception Dance Programme ILP/5/1924/27 shown on page 90.

The Robert Farnon Society website at www.rfsoc.org.uk gave me good information about Cyril Stapleton & His Show Band, as well as others showbands of the period. Louise from Hammer Films, Paul Welsh (Film Historian) and Roy Skeggs from Elstree Studios all helped trace information about the Michael Carreras produced Hammer Films relating to Cyril Stapleton & His Show Band.

Roger Lee from www.billiardsandsnookerarchive.co.uk gave me a great deal of information on the 1947 Snooker Championship between Joe Davis and Horace Lindstrum, including permission to reproduce the photographs shown on pages 177 and 178.

XII   SWEET PEAS, SUFFRAGETTES AND SHOWMEN

Thank you also to Eleanor Fleetham from the BBC Written Archives Centre who helped me locate the 1982 BBC Proms Programme from Richard Farr of BBC Proms, and my thanks to Richard for providing this and allowing me to reproduce it, on behalf of the BBC.

Jo Elsworth, Keeper of the Theatre Collection at the University of Bristol and Louise Matter, also from the University, originally found the Old Vic Circle Invitation cards that I displayed in 2004, and now have been given permission to publish here under their Copyright: 'Royal Victoria Hall Foundation; Courtesy of the University of Bristol Theatre Collection.'

My thanks to Hilary Davies and all the staff at the City of Westminster Archives Centre who assisted me at various times, and where I was able to use their online research websites such as COPAC, *The Times*, and other newspapers, from which a great deal of information was gleaned from many national and regional newspapers which I have quoted from throughout. The Centre gave me permission to reproduce from their own archives the two St Margaret's Musical Society concert invitation cards shown on page 16, Ref: 2391/23 and 24. They also directed me to Dr Tony Trowles, Librarian of Westminster Abbey, who gave me access to the *St Margaret's Parish Magazines* from 1901-6 that gave me information about St Margaret's Musical Society, and their concert performances.

Beverley Cook, Curator, Social & Working History, The Department of History Collections at the Museum of London assisted me in 2004 and subsequently helped me secure permissions to publish three images, nos 82.232/409, 50.82/1775 and 79.222/2b. from their Collection shown on pages 263, 82 and 201 respectively under their © Museum of London.

The British Library gave permission for four images to be reproduced from their archives: g.176a The Magpie Madrigal Society,1886-1911 shown on page 17; RB.23.b.6374 1913 Military Bazaar Front Cover of Catalogue; RB.23.b.6374 1913 Military Bazaar inside page shown on page 118 and on page 120 © The British Library-Hairdressers' Weekly Journal, 28 October 1922 pages 2132 & 2141. shown on pages 155 and 156.

Rachael Johnson of The Wellcome Library, London arranged permission to reproduce the first promotional literature produced by the RHS for its new Hall in 1904 shown on page 7, and also the Chemists' Exhibition March sheet music cover shown on page 41 from their archives WA/MMM/CO/Ear/821 Box 60. I was also able to gain references to other items relating to the London Medical and New Health Society Exhibitions.

Gail Cameron, Curator of The Women's Library, London Metropolitan University gave me valuable assistance in 2004, and again assisted in securing permission for me to publish five images Ref. Nos 5FWI/I/11 Posters – Handicraft Exhibition New Hall 1938 and 745.5 WOM Women and their Work catalogue May 1915 shown on pages 149 and 146.

Doug Stimson of the Science Museum Library, Swindon, kindly let me have four images of The Travel Exhibition brochure Ref: 91 TRAVEL (LONGSML) 1SML that are shown on pages 47, 49, 51 and 52.

Thank you to John Kemp of the *Sunday Times* Wine Club who sent me an early issue of *The Wine Times* shown on page 233.

Thank you to Peter Anslow and Graham Wilson for checking through my drafts of references to their International Ski Shows and Mind Body Spirit Festivals, respectively. Thank you also to Don Baldwin and Diana Balfour of Photographica for their help and assistance concerning their photographic collectors' club and fair.

Alan G. Wheeler kindly responded to my call for memories and mementos in 2003 with information about his visits to several exhibitions in the Halls.

Derek Connell took an early interest in my 2004 Centenary Exhibition and provided philatelic covers of STAMPEX events. Subsequently, he helped me with identification of Public Health Shows at the Royal Agricultural Hall, Islington from his collection of poster stamps.

David Bache of 'David Bache Photography' has kindly consented to his images shown on pages 290 and 291 being reproduced.

Oliver Murray, photographer, has kindly consented to his images on page 289 being reproduced.

Richard Cooke, photographer, at www.rcphotographer.co.uk has kindly consented to his images on pages 245, 300 and the Frontispiece being reproduced.

Patrick White of 'Apollo Photographers Limited', at www.apollophotographers.co.uk has kindly consented to his image on page 14 being reproduced.

Jon Enoch of Jon Enoch Photography at www.jonenoch.com has kindly consented to his image on page 273 being reproduced.

Jerry Munson, photographer, Tel: 807 7403, took the photo shown on page 256 in 1991, on behalf of the RHS when I was there. I have tried locating him to obtain his consent to reproduce this here, but have been unsuccessful in tracing him. However, I acknowledge his copyright.

Dr Steve Richardson of Tarvin, Cheshire, kindly sent me scans of the 1907-28 Model Engineer catalogue covers in 2005, and I subsequently obtained high resolution versions of these from Tony Griffiths of www.lathes.co.uk.

Olly Croft from British Darts Organisation kindly let me have details and catalogue covers of Darts tournaments that had been staged in the Halls, as did Andy Scott from Portsmouth.

John Montgomery, Librarian at the Royal United Services Institute (RUSI), was very kind in helping me find references for the history of the London Scottish Regiment, and also of the influence Madame Österberg had in the physical training methods of the British Army.

Ray Phillips, Head of Information Services Development, The King's Fund, London kindly directed me to the Wellcome Library for references on the New Health Society and Sir William Arbuthnot Lane.

I was lucky enough to have access to the Royal College of Midwives Archives in Portland Place in 2003 before they moved these, and here I found a copy of the Nurses and Midwives Yearbook (1910) that gave valuable information about the 3rd Annual Nursing & Midwifery Conference & Exhibition held that year.

The National Honey Show website www.honeyshow.co.uk provided useful and complementary information to already known history, and in relation to their tenancies in the RHS Halls. I acknowledge their copyright to this information.

Rebecca Evans from the British Dental Trade Association in Chesham, Buckinghamshire, kindly sent me copies of catalogues for dental trade exhibitions held in the 1950s.

Mike Pearl of Prestbury, Macclesfield sent me a card of the 19th Eucharistic Congress that led to me finding the whole set, and Miriam Power, Archivist at Westminster Cathedral, kindly helped me with information about the Congress itself. Simon Hargreaves from Sheffield sent me two STAMPEX philatelic items that led me to finding many others on ebay and via the fairs in the Halls.

References to the Baptist Missionary Society and George Grenfell in Chapter 3 are courtesy of Wholesome Words at www.wholesomewords.org and I acknowledge their copyright to these.

References to Shooting Clubs and Competitions in Chapter 5 are courtesy of www.nsra.co.uk and I acknowledge their copyright to these.

Thank you to Geoffrey Pocock for allowing me to use the photo of Roger Pocock from his book, *One Hundred Years of the Legion of Frontiersmen … Soldiers, Spies and Counter Spies, Sacrifice and Service to the State*, shown on page 53.

Other information and material supplied that has helped me with the production of this book was received from David and Maggie Davis, organisers of the Picture Postcard Shows, Mr and Mrs Alfred Ennis of Littlestone, New Romney, who kindly donated archive photographs and cuttings from *Kent Farmer* and *Kent Cob* when he took part at the Schoolboy's Own Exhibitions in 1951 and 1955 as part of the Kent National Farmers Union. Douglas McClary from Exeter also responded to my 2004 call to RHS Members to recall other events they had been to in the Halls. He sent me his recollections of the various Pigeon Shows he had attended transforming his involvement from local events to National competition. Among items he sent me were a number of Pigeon Racing and Show photos, catalogues, news-cuttings and a prize card which I gratefully acknowledge. Bob Ball also sent me his recollections of past events attended as a schoolboy.

Last, but by no means least, are my respective PAs, including Susan Stone, Philippa Murray, Joanne Lear and Fleur Gatfield, who all helped me with the painstaking research carried out while I was still at the RHS.

All exhibition and event catalogues, invitation cards, stamp covers, illustrations etc have been collected by me personally via a variety of sources, not least of which is Ebay.

Every effort has been made to trace and acknowledge the copyright of illustrations and photos. If any have been overlooked this has been unintentional and I would be pleased to hear from the copyright holder.

Foreword

René Dee was Managing Director responsible for the RHS Halls & Conference Centre in London, during a period of 17 years from 1991 to 2008. He directed and oversaw major redevelopment and change to the Lindley Hall (Old Hall), the Lawrence Hall (New Hall), and the Conference Centre that generated substantial income to support the Society.

In the course of that time, and especially following the organisation of the Lindley Hall Centenary Exhibition he staged in 2004, he became fascinated by their history. Most RHS Members will think of the Halls mainly as the venues for the Flower Shows that, originally, were held fortnightly. They have, in fact, played a much wider role in London's social history.

This book shows that they witnessed many of the most important changes in 20th-century life. They hosted among many others, suffragette meetings, landmark political events, pioneering medical and nursing conferences, academic and professional examinations, soldiers waiting to go to war; as well as championship dog, cat, rabbit, and pigeon shows. More than 7,000 events have been held in them over ten decades, since the Lindley Hall was opened in 1904 by King Edward VII and Queen Alexandra, and the Lawrence Hall by Princess Mary in 1928.

The Halls are buildings of great historic and architectural interest, and indeed the Lawrence Hall is one of London's iconic Art Deco buildings, being the first in London to use pre-stressed concrete arches in its construction, and winning a RIBA Gold Medal for it.

This scholarly work is written in a lively way, superbly illustrated, and will be of interest to a wide range of readers. It is a wonderful contribution to one of the more fascinating byways of the RHS's distinguished history.

Elizabeth Banks
President: Royal Horticultural Society

List of Subscribers

10-11 Carlton House Terrace
Matthew Adams
Julian Agostini
Donald G. Baldwin
Elizabeth Banks
Lawrence Banks
Sally de Beaumont
Bedford College
Bergman Österberg Union
Paula Bevin
Chester Boyd
Chris Brickell
British Racing & Sports Car Club
S.A. Buxton
Sir Richard Carew Pole
Jackson Clark
Nigel Collett
Linda Collier
Paul Colson
Derek Connell
Corinthian-Casuals F.C.
Suzanne Currell-Barshall
Custard Communications
Sheila Cutler
Jo and Pete Danks
Rob Davidson
Eileen Margaret Dee
Matthew Frederick Dee
John Durden
Dr Brent Elliott
Tom and Mary Kay Eyerman

Paul Richard Ferrari
Roger Fox
Myriam Fröesch-Burnand
Bruno Garselis
Governing Council of the Cat Fancy
Marietjie Grose
Allyson Hargreaves
Ann Hatherill
Lisa Hatsfield, Chairman,
    Unique Venues of London
Peter Hazzard
Donald Hearn
Robert L. Hungerford
David Jamilly
Daniele Kaspar
Michel et Elhem Kaspar
Mr and Mrs Brian Kennedy
The Kennel Club
Charles Kiddle
Joanne Lear
Roger Lee
Maugie Lyons
Sharon and Myron Mahendra
Mash Media Group Ltd
Ambrosia Matsetse-Chisonta
Frank and Jackie McGrath
Stuart Medhurst
Carole Anne Mehta
Dinsa Fredoon Mehta
Farah-Lisette Mehta
Rustam-Marc Mehta

Russell Morgan
Philippa Murray
National Badminton Museum,
    Milton Keynes, England
National Philatelic Society
    (formerly the Junior Philatelic Society)
The Old Vic
One Great George Street
Karin Parkinson
Sarina Patel
Mathew J. Perkins
Roy W. Perrett GCFA
Gary Peters
Myriam Powers,
    Archivist, Westminster Cathedral
Jane and Gerard Rosenberg
Searcys
Michael Sefi
Andrew Sells
Michael Sharp

Alex Simm
Bill Simpson
Martin Slocock
Peter Smale
Society of Genealogists
Stamp Lover
Adele Summers
Bill Tonkin
Justin Trevellyan
Chris and Tania Tribe
David Tribe
Maria Tribe
John Trory
Di and Jim Vale
Selwyn Veater
Vincent Square Residents' Assocation
Air Vice-Marshal David Walker OBE, MVO
HRH The Countess of Wessex
Westminster Kingsway College
Christopher Yates

Introduction

The *Compact Oxford English Dictionary* defines a hall as 'a large room for meetings, concerts etc.' This is certainly an equally compact definition but it is the 'etc' that leaves the door open to further enquiry and speculation as to what else this may include. The answer, unquestionably, is anything and everything that can fit into the said space that meets the objectives of the owner and those wanting to use it. Like theatres, halls act as spaces where people play out their lives and where drama exists. What takes place inside them also reflects what goes on outside. Decisions are taken and actions are made in them that can change the world. Like a theatre or circus 'Big Top', the hall is also always changing its 'performances' and attracts new audiences for each one. In effect, the hall owner is in show business, but is rarely in a position to stage one. This places him in a good position to observe from a distance. I was privileged to be in this position for 17 years managing two of London's finest halls, the Royal Horticultural Society Halls. Research I carried out over 10 years revealed just what they have seen pass through their doors since 1904, that brought them to life and made them, not simply halls but more a way of life.

Hall owners have always built their halls in a multiplicity of sizes, configurations and architectural styles for an equally diverse range of uses. Many of the City livery halls, commercial exhibition halls, halls of entertainment, local authority halls and those of the many learned societies, institutions and associations to whom they belong were also built with a single purpose of meeting their respective organisation's primary needs. Since then, many have adapted their application and usage because of changed circumstances within their own organisations, the economic conditions of the day, or both. The Royal Horticultural Society and its Halls have not been immune to this process of change.

Classic exhibition halls and structures such as Paxton's original Crystal Palace at Hyde Park and the subsequent one at Sydenham; the White City Palaces, Earls Court and Olympia, Alexandra Palace, Wembley, the Royal Agricultural Hall and the Royal Albert Hall were, or have all become, recognisable landmarks, and recognised equally for hosting memorable exhibitions and events on a grand scale. The Great Exhibition of the Works of Industry of all Nations in 1851 at the Crystal Palace, opened by Queen Victoria, was only one of many unapologetic imperial and nationalistic statements made using the hall as a means of showcasing them. Often, the architectural design of the building was as important as the

event taking place inside it. This was certainly true for the last great exhibition held on the South Bank of London in 1951, the Festival of Britain, which gave us the legacy of the Royal Festival Halls, amongst others.

The British Empire Exhibitions of 1924 and 1925 at Wembley, and the fine arts and industry themes that had been led and exampled by the French and Continental genre of 'Expositions Universelles', continued to satiate the public demand that they should

The Great Exhibition of the Works of Industry of all Nations – external view and season ticket.

entertain, as much as educate. Over 32 million people visited the 1889 Paris *Exposition* and over 48 million in 1900. Our own 1851 exhibition attracted just over six million and in 1924 The British Empire Exhibition attracted just over 21 million, albeit over different time frames. Many of the classic events resulting from these have endured over a century of changed social order, life styles, interests and attitudes. The Ideal Home Exhibition, Crufts Dog Show, the annual Motor and Boat Shows are those that most easily come to mind when thinking of enduring events that remain fixtures in some of these halls.

Queen Victoria Diamond Jubilee commemorative silk. HM Queen Victoria was the Society's first Royal Patron from 1837-1901.

"HER COURT WAS PURE; HER LIFE SERENE;
GOD GAVE HER PEACE; HER LANDS REPOSED;
A THOUSAND CLAIMS TO REVERENCE CLOSED
IN HER AS MOTHER, WIFE, AND QUEEN."   TENNYSON.

But there were many other smaller and equally important halls in and around London that thrived and hosted an eclectic mix of events from the mid-19th to the early 20th centuries. The Royal Aquarium (where Central Hall Westminster now stands) and Caxton Hall in Westminster; the Egyptian Hall, St James Hall, the Princes' Hall and Dorland Hall in and around Piccadilly; the Prince's Skating Rink, Knightsbridge; the Queen's Hall, Langham Place; the Essex Hall, Strand; the Lyric Hall, Great Portland Street; the Æolian Hall in Bond Street; the Memorial Hall in Farringdon Street, and the many City livery halls were but a few. The Royal Horticultural Halls on Vincent Square and Elverton Street, Westminster rank as importantly among these, not simply for their architectural styles, but also for the events that took place inside them and the sustained duration of their use for over a century to the present day. By 1911, it was specifically and photographically depicted as a primary attraction, alongside Westminster Cathedral, Victoria Street, Church House and Westminster School in the most important travel guide of the time, Baedeker's 1911 edition of *London and its Environs*.

The history of The Royal Horticultural Society and its distinguished accomplishments in the fields of horticulture and gardening are already well documented, including the many and regular flower shows held in its London Halls. Dr Brent Elliott, its eminent Historian, Librarian, and Archivist wrote a definitive book on the Society's history that was published in 2004 to mark the year of its Bicentenary.

However, what has never been fully documented nor revealed before now is the rich, fascinating, and important history of the non-horticultural events, and those involved with them that have taken place in their Halls since the opening of the first one, on Vincent Square, by King Edward VII and Queen Alexandra on 22 July 1904. The second Hall, an Art-Deco marvel of its day built on Elverton Street, was opened by HRH Princess Mary on 26 June 1928. The paradox is that these Halls, although built specifically for the RHS, have never simply been repositories for their own regular flower, fruit and vegetable shows and conferences, or those of its Affiliated Societies. More especially, they have been home to a diverse mix of more than 7,000 historically, politically, socially and culturally important events that mirrored life and its continuous change in London and Great Britain through 10 decades up to the present day. My book, therefore, concentrates on this aspect of their, hitherto, unrevealed use; the events that were staged in them; the extraordinary people involved with them, and our ability to observe and note through them, as catalysts, the changing face of the way we have lived, thought and developed over this period.

Millions of people and many generations of men, women and children have made the determined journey to reach them from far and wide; to walk through their turnstiles to be entertained, educated, exhorted, lectured, preached at, examined, filmed, sold to, entreated, amazed and shocked. They have danced, sung, acted, prayed, demonstrated, celebrated, commemorated, exercised, boxed, played musical instruments, driven model cars, bought classic cars, ridden model railways, sailed model boats, indulged in their hobbies and pastimes, listened to political and religious leaders, attended conventions, meetings, conferences and assemblies, witnessed new inventions, fashions and technology, traded and bartered, paraded their cats and dogs, rabbits and pigeons, displayed cage birds, poultry, fish and small livestock, reunited as clubs, trained and waited to go to war, fired small arms, watched sporting tournaments, played snooker, badminton, darts, bowls and chess, skied and skateboarded through a kaleidoscope of history, as changing as any chameleon can be.

There were dark and unsettling times during two world wars, political upheavals, a General Strike, recessions, financial crises and the constant battles for social change to improve the lot of the poor, the ill and the dispossessed. Trade Union and socialist activity and the struggle for women's emancipation were strong threads that were being woven through defining events that took place in these Halls. But, there were also stable and sensible times, exhilarating and fun times that changed people's lives and influenced the direction they chose to continue in. Love was found and lost at balls, dances, whist drives, reunions and concerts. Careers were catapulted, or short-circuited, at the many academic and professional examinations that were held in the Halls from as early as 1905 and, until the advent of television, the events that took place in them were a regular and important medium for social intercourse, education and entertainment.

ROYAL HORTICULTURAL SOCIETY

OPENING OF THE
SOCIETY'S NEW HALL
BY
H·M·THE KING
FRIDAY JULY 22ND
1904

LEFT *Front cover of the brochure for the official opening of what is now called the Lindley Hall, Vincent Square.*

I

The Birth of a Hall

From Concept to Realisation

Baron Henry Schröder (1824-1910). Director of Schröder's Bank, and benefactor of the Vincent Square Hall.

Edwin Stubbs (c.1870-1918). Architect of the Lindley Hall, Vincent Square.

The idea that the RHS should consider a new exhibition hall of its own was originally put forward by King Edward VII (then the Prince of Wales) when he opened its Temple Flower Show on London's Embankment in 1890. The RHS had been residing in offices at 117 Victoria Street, Westminster, since 1888 and held its fortnightly flower shows in the London Scottish Volunteer Rifles Corps Drill Hall at 59 Buckingham Gate, just off Victoria Street. A new hall would provide the Society with a venue for its horticultural shows, and a home for its library and staff.

The overall agreement and lease was personally secured and financed by Baron Sir Henry Schröder, a prominent RHS Council Member, and later transferred to the Society in July 1902 (the year of King Edward VII's coronation). It also brought with it, although not until some years later, a brand new street to allow for the extra traffic that would be generated from its use. This followed an agreement secured from the Ecclesiastical Commissioners, whose land it was, and who imposed a condition that 'it would be necessary to construct a new street 40 feet in width between Horseferry Road and Bell Street, south of Ship Court'. This was to be Elverton Street.

Victoria Street was already an established business and political hub in Westminster, so it is not surprising that as the Hall emerged many organisations in and around it, including Westminster Cathedral and Westminster Abbey, watched with interest and made enquiries as to its potential use. The Society appointed Mr Edwin J. Stubbs as architect and he took account of the need for the building to have maximum flexibility as a multi-purpose venue, not simply one to accommodate plants and flowers, providing a 'Minstrel's' Gallery, two Annexes, a separately configured lecture theatre and three meeting rooms. The Hall could seat 1,250, its annexes 200 each, the lecture theatre 250, the RHS Council Room 150, and the three committee rooms 240 between them. He also ensured that it would comply with the London County Council music and dancing licensing regulations for public buildings so that it could be let for these purposes as well. However, he could not have known just how flexible and versatile his Hall would need to be across the next century, nor the issues that would arise as a result.

This manifested itself almost immediately, as the Society itself was, from the very start, always a minority occupier of the Hall. The overheads to run it, and the later second Hall, were high and the RHS had to achieve the maximum occupancy possible to provide the necessary income to maintain the fabric of the

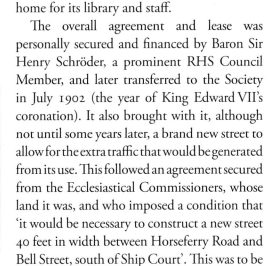

building and its infrastructure which, over time, inevitably deteriorated through regular use. From the very beginning the RHS faced strong competition from a number of other halls and establishments in and around London, as it still does today. It will be noted later that the necessary occupancy and income generation were not always successfully achieved and the long-term viability of the Halls was seriously questioned on a number of occasions throughout their history. It was not until 1987 that a separate Limited Liability Company was incorporated as a wholly owned subsidiary of the Society to run the Halls at 'arms length' on strictly commercial lines.

Grand Opening

The foundation stone of the Hall was laid by the Princess of Wales on 4 August 1903. It was built at a cost of £40,000 (£3.58 million at today's value), King Edward VII having contributed 100 guineas (£9,500) and the Prince of Wales 50 guineas (£4,750). The RHS Council formally

LEFT *Postcard of King Edward VII's Coronation, 26 June 1902. HM King Edward VII was the Society's 3rd Royal Patron from 1904 to 1910.*

BELOW *Photo of the exterior of the Lindley Hall, 1904.*

agreed that the Hall be named 'The Royal Horticultural Hall' on 8 March 1904. (See box at end of Chapter.)

The Hall was officially opened by King Edward VII and Queen Alexandra, the Society's patron, accompanied by HRH Princess Victoria, on 22 July 1904; this also marked The Society's Centenary, albeit four months later than the precise date. A list of distinguished guests had been invited, including the Home Secretary, Aretas Akers-Douglas, representing Arthur Balfour's Conservative government, and the

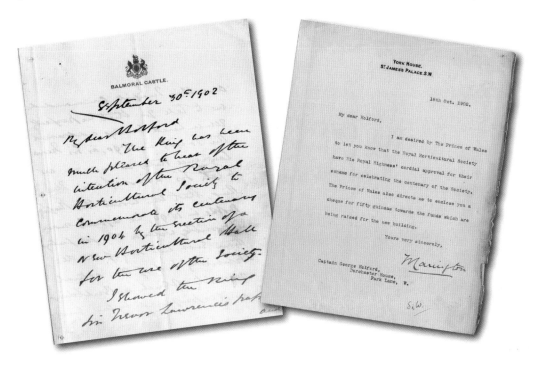

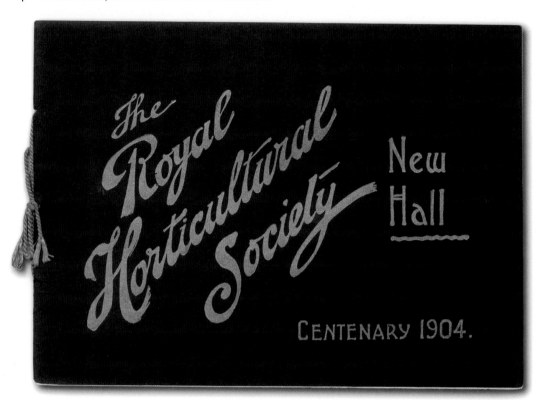

The Royal Horticultural Society New Hall CENTENARY 1904.

LEFT　*The fundraising Centenary brochure cover for the Lindley Hall.*

mayors of several London boroughs. While they waited for the King and Queen to arrive they were entertained by Lieutenant Charles Godfrey's String Band. A guard of honour of the Cadet Corps of the boys of Westminster School was stationed at the main entrance to the Hall and detachments of the London Scottish Volunteer Rifle Corps were posted at the approach of the main entrance. The royal party were received at the entrance by the Royal Horticultural Society's 8th President, Sir Trevor Lawrence; Sir John Llewelyn (a vice-president), Baron Sir Henry Schröder (chairman of the building committee), Mr J. Gurney-Fowler (chairman of the appeals committee) and other prominent members of the RHS Council. They

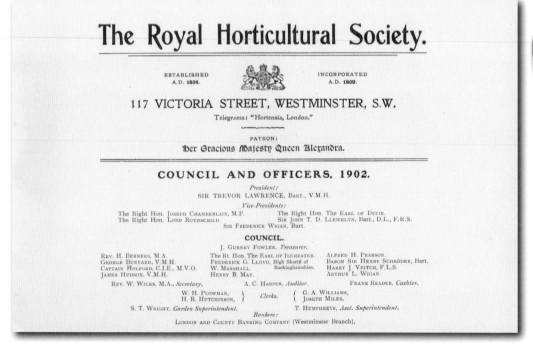

LEFT　*Council and Officers of the RHS in 1902, from the fundraising Centenary brochure.*

ABOVE　*Metal badge for the Royal Horticultural Society, c.1900.*

RIGHT *Queen Alexandra commemorative silk, 1902. HM Queen Alexandra was the Society's 2nd Royal Patron from 1901 to 1925.*

were directed to a raised dais erected in the centre of one side of the building covered with crimson baize and a large Indian carpet.

Save for the palms at the back of the platform nothing in the way of decoration was attempted, but the fine proportions, spacious area and light appearance of the Hall produced a favourable impression.

The President, Sir Trevor Lawrence, read an address, and in replying His Majesty said:

I am very glad that you have at length obtained a suitable Hall for your beautiful and interesting shows, and adequate accommodation for your library and for the performance of the official work of the Society, and it is with great pleasure that the Queen and I are here today to declare these new buildings open. We are also pleased to be able to congratulate the Society on having acquired the garden to which you allude and for which you are indebted to the goodness of Sir Thomas Hanbury (this was Wisley Garden in Surrey). The Queen and myself wish that every success may attend the opening of this new Hall and its adjoining premises, and that the Centenary which we are celebrating this year may prove to be the occasion of an accession of prosperity to the Royal Horticultural Society. I have much pleasure in declaring this Royal Horticultural Hall – this magnificent Hall – open.

Four days later, on 26 July, the Society's first horticultural event in the Hall took place: the fortnightly flower show was held in conjunction with the National Carnation and Picotee Society. The National Rose Society, the Sweet Pea and the National Potato Societies were also early Affiliated Societies of the RHS to use the new Hall.

Even after the Hall had been opened, a good deal of work still remained to be done on the offices, lecture-room and library. However, it was completed before the end of the year; on 20 August, Mr Stubbs was instructed to have the floor dressed with boiled oil at the cost not exceeding £20!

RIGHT *Sir John James Trevor Lawrence (1831-1913), 8th President of the RHS, 1885-1913.*

The First Lettings

The RHS considered the letting of its Hall to external organisations an integral part of its activities because the prime purpose of the Hall, to host its own flower shows, was limited. (The flower shows, although run fortnightly from 26 July 1904, were only one-day events until March 1913. An extra day was added after this date and two-day events continued until 1987, after which they became monthly). Reference to this had been made in Baron Sir Henry Schröder's report presented to the King on opening the Hall. The reference was short, but clear, when he said, 'The main purpose is the holding of our Fortnightly Shows but, other interests have not been lost sight of, and we have reason to believe that the Hall will often be in demand for numerous other purposes.' Indeed, on 3 May 1904 a letting circular had been approved and on 14 June the RHS recorded

its first enquiry, from The Westminster Choral Society regarding a series of three concerts the following winter.

The Council itself reviewed and decided upon those who applied to use the Hall via its then Secretary, the Rev. W. Wilks. The Council Meeting Minutes of that year reveal this very clearly, especially when the Conditions and Regulations and Charges for Letting the Hall were published in the Society's first publicity brochure for it. These reflected the proposed flexibility of their use, and the types of events anticipated were clearly described, including the use of a piano.

A Scale of Charges showed a complex menu of options to hire both the Hall and its Annexes for a 'Meeting, Concert, Lecture or Entertainment in aid of the funds of any Charitable or Philanthropic Society or Institution, during the day, for a half-day, or

Opening of the Lindley Hall by HM King Edward VII and HM Queen Alexandra, accompanied by HRH Princess Victoria, on 22 July 1904.

an evening (9 till 1, or 2 till 6).' [These were £7 7 shillings (£657) £4 4 shillings (£376) and £10 10 shillings (£939) respectively. 'For any other purpose for one day and evening to midnight' the charge was £26 5 shillings (£2,348) and just £21 (£1,878) per day and evening to midnight in a series. If it was required for the day only (9 till 6) this was reduced to £15 15 shillings (£1,409); for a half-day only (9 till 1, or 2 till 6), £10 10 shillings (£939). There was also a separate charge for an evening terminating before midnight and one lasting after midnight. Finally, 'For Concert rehearsals, &c., and for preparing for Bazaars, &c., to take place in the Hall' charges were reduced by half. A 25 per cent discount was also available to charities, although the Council at its 19 April meeting that same year had decided that this should not be advertised! An equally complex set of rates was set out for the Lecture Theatre and the three additional meeting rooms located on the first floor.]

As a sign that interest from outside was definitely beginning to take place, the RHS Council at its 18 October meeting reported that they had been approached by The London Coliseum to be allowed to 'piece and fix stage scenery in the Hall'. This was declined! On 1 November it was agreed to pay 10 per cent commission on receipt of completed contracts, when applicable. Framed pictures of the Hall were given to Messrs Unite, to display for exhibitions to possible hirers. This must have been one of the very first promotional efforts by the RHS to sell their Hall to external third parties that were non-horticultural Societies. Then on 15 November the Council noted that a letter from the Social Bureau had been received proposing to undertake the sole letting of the Hall on commission. The Council decided to keep control of the letting process for the present. However, when they were also later approached by Keith Prowse in 1907 they then agreed that they should handle their Hall lettings on a similar basis. Finally, on 13 December, just short of five months after opening, agreement was reached by Council 'to allow political and other meetings to be held in the Hall, irrespective of party, creed etc.' The rationale was that, in effect, 'representing a

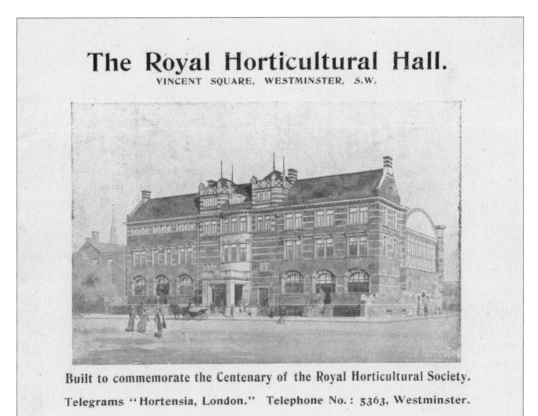

First promotional brochure produced (1904) to sell the Lindley Hall commercially to a non-horticultural, and external audience.

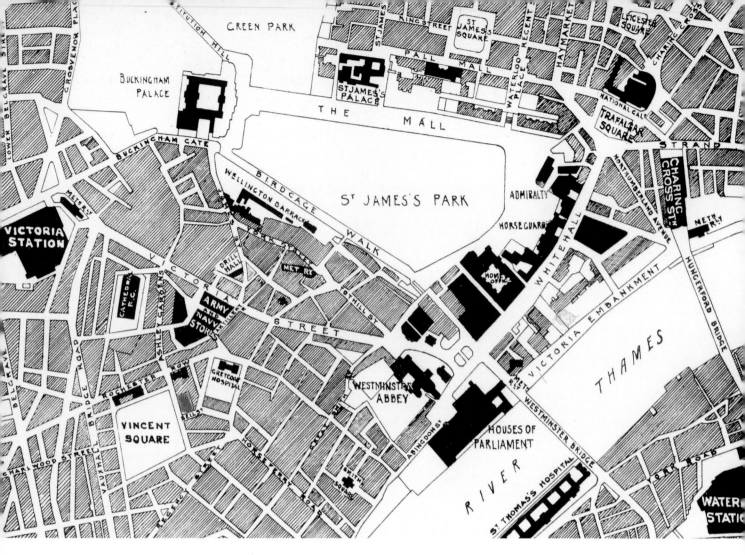

private Society numbering amongst its Fellows all possible varieties and shades of thought, the Council should maintain an absolutely neutral attitude'. This certainly proved that the Society was willing for the Hall to act as a commercial venue and open to everyone, although this was to prove testing at times, given that events held by some organisations were beginning to shake the establishment foundations of the day and were willing to be unruly, disruptive and sometimes violent.

One of the first main non-horticultural users of the Hall in 1905 described it in the following terms: 'The Royal Horticultural Hall, where our Exhibition is to be held during the first week of May 1905, is situate in a commanding position on the north side of Vincent Square, at the corner of Bell Street. This building is better adapted for our purpose than any place previously hired by us and, constructed expressly for exhibitions. The ground floor having a superficial area of about

13,000 square feet, and being provided with a splendid glass roof, besides a glass front at the east end, and four round headed windows. Communicating with this hall by a private staircase are four rooms on the first floor. Herein it is proposed to hold the 16th Universal Cookery & Food Exhibition. The floor is laid with wood blocks and the walls are of white stone-like plaster with solid oak dado all round. Gas and additional electric light cables are laid on, but the cost of fittings and current and gas must be paid for by the several exhibitors requiring their use. The first floor is similarly fitted, with the exception of the upper part of the walls, which are coloured a quiet shade of green. The hall is also fitted with most modern appliances for ventilation and lighting, and the existence of a raised music gallery will be of great assistance to the Executive, saving the Association considerable expense.' It went on to add, 'The Hall is equidistant from Victoria and St James's Park Stations on the District

Railway, the electrification of which is now proceeding rapidly towards completion. The most direct route for pedestrians is via Ashley Gardens; and omnibuses run from all parts to Parliament Square (Westminster Abbey) and Victoria.'

To illustrate the immediate impact that the new hall had on its neighbours and future clients in Westminster, all of the following organisations used the RHS Hall in the first decades and beyond. The Labour Party, based at 28 Victoria Street with J. Ramsay MacDonald as Secretary, held meetings and receptions there. The Westminster Conservative Association was at 64 Victoria Street with Louis

Henry Hayter as their Secretary and they held several events there also. The Primrose League was also based at the same address. The Conservative & Unionist Central Office was based in Palace Chambers, Bridge Street, and held a Reception to the Prime Minister, Ramsay MacDonald, on 16 November 1928, when G.H. Edwards was its Honorary Secretary. The Society of Working Men's Rifle Clubs, that would become the National Small-Bore Rifle Association in 1947, was first based at 17 Victoria Street.

Most of the Colonial Offices were based in Victoria Street including the Commonwealth of Australia. The Agent Generals for Victoria and South Australia, as well as British Columbia, Nova Scotia and Prince Edward Island, attended the official opening of the Hall in 1904. British Columbia would hold its own exhibition in it in November 1909. The Agents General for Western Australia, Queensland and Tasmania were at Nos 72, 15 and 1 Victoria Street respectively. The Agent General for the Cape of Good Hope was at 100 Victoria Street. Most were involved in the International Philatelic Exhibition held in the Hall between 23 May and 1 June 1906. They all took part in a remarkable Travel Exhibition and, the first of its kind, under extensive patronage from prominent Council Members of The Royal Geographical Society and many other distinguished polar, African and international explorers, held in the 'Hall and Grounds' between 18 May and 8 June 1907.

Additionally, the Cape of Good Hope Agent General had played a major role in the setting up of an extraordinary exhibition called the South Africa Products Exhibition. This had been mounted by an Executive Committee representing all parts of South Africa and opened by King Edward VII and Queen Alexandra on 23 February 1907. The South Africa Products Exhibition offices were at Belgravia Chambers, 72 Victoria Street.

The Navy League & Boys Naval Brigade was based at 13 Victoria Street. On 21 October 1905, the Navy League and the British and Foreign Sailors' Society organised

BELOW The Illustrated Daily Post-card of Nelson Centenary celebrations in London, 1905, showing the Lindley Hall being used for 'musical celebration'.

THE ILLUSTRATED
Daily Post-card

LISHED AT   39-40, SHOE LANE
                                E.C.

No. 1   OCT 21   1905   Price ½d.

CENTENARY CELEBRATION.

8 a.m. National Flags hoisted in Trafalgar Square.

2. 30. p.m. Public Service in Square.

3. 45. p.m. Musical Celebration at Horticultural Hall, Westminster.

Night. Naval Banquet a Criterion.

„ Concerts at Albert Hall and Crystal Palace.

Fireworks at Earls Court.

Sunday :— Special Services in Cathedrals and Churches.

KEEP EVER GREEN

the Memory

OF

NELSON.

TRAFALGAR.   1805-1905.

the Nelson Centenary Celebrations in London that were fêted almost on the same scale as any Coronation. A series of events were organised by them throughout the day in London in Trafalgar Square, the Albert Hall, Earl's Court and Crystal Palace. The RHS Hall was also chosen for musical celebrations to be held in them starting at 3.45 p.m. These were organised by the women's branch of the League and the Hall was bedecked with the flags of Nelson's famous signal, 'England expects that every man will do his duty'. Patriotic naval songs of England were sung and their origins explained by Sir Frederick Bridge, one of London's best known musicians, conductor of the Royal Choral Society and organist at Westminster Abbey. An *Illustrated Daily Postcard* was issued to commemorate the day and this denotes these events on it.

The Army & Navy Co-operative Society Ltd and its Stores (later to become House of Fraser) as exclusive as any club, and a nostalgic link between the service men abroad and their families at home, was based at 105 Victoria Street and became one of the first organisations to offer the RHS and its clients a catering service.

In 1905, the Universal Cookery & Food Association was based at 329 Vauxhall Bridge Road, near Victoria Station, but later moved to 110 Victoria Street. The UC&FA had run an annual exhibition for 13 years prior to the opening of the Hall, and in 1904 this had been held in the Albert Hall but, in May 1905, it transferred to the RHS Hall where it would stay for the next 20 years. The connection between the UC&FA and the RHS became very strong due to a variety of factors. Mr W. Burdett-Coutts, a Westminster MP who had attended the official opening of the Hall in 1904, had also been President of the UC&FA in that year. Clearly, he must have reflected then on the space and configuration offered by the Hall, its Lecture Theatre and meeting rooms, as well as the proximity of the Hall to their offices. Secondly, being able to host this prestigious event in his constituency, Westminster, must also have been very appealing.

The National Anti-Vivisection Society (originally founded in 1875 in Victoria

THE NELSON CENTENARY.
The Nelson Celebration
in Trafalgar Square,
London, October 21st, 1905.

Nelson Centenary post-card, 1905.

Street, as the Victoria Street Society, by Miss Francis Power Cobbe, a great humanitarian, social reformer and active feminist) were at 92 Victoria Street and held their AGM in the Hall on 17 May 1906, the same year in which the government of the day appointed the Second Royal Commission on Vivisection. Lord Llangattock was President and chaired the meeting. His wife, Lady Llangattock, would also frequent the Hall on a number of occasions in her capacity as an active supporter of worthy causes. She was also an avid collector of Nelson memorabilia and this can be seen

Nelson Centenary post-card, 1905.

undoubtedly have also played a part in the later approaches to hire the Hall by a variety of women's suffrage organisations, including the National Union of Women's Suffrage Societies (also based in Victoria Street at No.25) the National Women's Social and Political Union and the breakaway Women's Freedom League. Archbishop Bagshaw, Lord Coleridge and The Venerable Basil Wilberforce (Archdeacon of Westminster) were also active supporters of the Society and present at the meeting. Another important women's organisation, The Women's Institute, who also had offices at 92 Victoria Street, would hold some of their earliest handicraft exhibitions in the Hall in the 1920s. The Association of Headmistresses was based at the same address in 1905, and the Association of Chambers of Commerce of the UK also resided in Victoria Street.

Our Dumb Friends' League (founded in 1897 and later to become The Blue Cross in 1958) were also based in Victoria Street and had been involved principally with providing better conditions for London's horses that plied its streets remorselessly and, in 1900, had provided the first horse ambulance for use on London's streets. In 1906, they opened the Victoria Animal Hospital based at Shepherd House, Hugh Street, to provide veterinary care to the animals of poor people. G. Blackwell Snr, The Cats' and Dogs' Friend – 'Where you can get Buttock Steak at 2d. (75p) per lb and Rump Steak at 2½d. (93p) per lb., fresh cut from the joints, while others carry inferior meat round the streets in baskets for hours, exposed to all kinds of weather' – was located at 27 Rochester Row in 1908. Well-heeled Dog Societies and Clubs with their 'High Society' members that organised hundreds of their Championship Shows in the Hall during half a century often raised funds for Our Dumb Friends' League through these events. After the First World War the League ran annual fund-raising Fairs and Bazaars of their own in the Hall over a 20-year period and gained Royal Patronage.

Many events involved the aristocracy of the period, including Royalty, whose patronage

today at the Museum in Monmouth. Most notably she was present one month later at a grand bazaar and floral fête in aid of the Royal Waterloo Hospital for Children and Women and, in June 1911, at a Coronation Bazaar held two weeks before King George V's Coronation. Their son, Charles Stewart Rolls, would visit the same Hall in 1907 in his capacity as one of the prime movers of a remarkable Travel Exhibition held there.

Francis Cobbe's membership of the executive council of the London National Society for Women's Suffrage would

National Anti-
Vivisection Meeting
announcement
in The Times,
16 May 1906.

THE ANNUAL MEETING
of the

NATIONAL

ANTI-VIVISECTION

SOCIETY

Will be held on
THURSDAY, MAY 17th, 1906, at the
ROYAL HORTICULTURAL HALL
Vincent-square, Westminster.

The President,
The Right Hon. LORD LLANGATTOCK,
will take the Chair at 8.30 p.m.,
supported by
ARCHBISHOP BAGSHAWE,
EARL of HADDINGTON,
LORD ERNEST HAMILTON,
LORD COLERIDGE, K.C.,
The HON. STEPHEN COLERIDGE,
The VENERABLE BASIL WILBERFORCE (Archdeacon of
Westminster),
The RIGHT HON. T. BURT, M.P.,
F. A. CHANNING, Esq., M.P.,
R. C. LEHMANN, Esq., M.P.,
and others.

Speakers :
GEORGE GREENWOOD, Esq., M.P.,
J. M. ROBERTSON, Esq., M.P.,
D. M. SMEATON, Esq., M.P.,
JOHN HODGE, Esq., M.P.,
R. L. EVERETT, Esq., M.P.,
and others.

For Reserved Seats apply to the Secretary, at the Society's Offices
92, VICTORIA-STREET, WESTMINSTER.

National Anti-
Vivisection Meeting
announcement
in The Times,
16 May 1906.

was seen as vital and was regularly given. Indeed they became regular visitors to them, often simply visiting unannounced, but also attending in an official capacity to open them formally. This was a time of great philanthropy, and fundraising was central to many events that supported needy causes of the day, the poor, orphan children, redundant and disabled soldiers, new hospitals, abused women and animals, medical research and those charitable institutions that championed these and other causes. The military, the Church, the political parties and the factions of the day were regularly involved in helping to bring about, or aid, social changes in one form or another. It was these organisations that provided both the mainstay of early events and the audiences with them. Good flexible facilities, close to the seats of their powerbases and in Westminster, were vital. Many MPs and Ministers also lived very close by. We will also see that many of the Society's own officers and trustees, including its presidents, held positions of influence in the military, political and business domains that helped bring events into the Halls.

As in life, some events were transitory or fleeting, never to be seen again after the first one had taken place. One-off events would always be so. However, with regular events, errors of judgement in timing, misconceived concepts, insufficient promotion, lack of organisational skills, or business acumen were reasons then, and now, for stalled or failed events. But, for those that understood their markets and audiences well, many were destined to endure for periods between five and 50 years with a few still running today after 100 years, albeit in different configurations and run by different organisations.

The media and publications of the day, including *The London Illustrated News*, *The Graphic* and the local *Westminster & Pimlico News*, covered the events in the Hall extensively. *The Times* Court Circular gave details of the movements of the Royal Family and the aristocracy concerning their involvement with events in the Hall. They also listed all the events that took place in the Royal Institutions, Societies, Academies and Institutes in London, including the RHS. *The Observer, Daily Telegraph, Daily Mirror, Daily Express, Evening News, The Manchester Guardian* and other papers regularly listed them in their 'London Amusements' sections alongside London Theatres, Concert Halls together with the other principal Exhibition Halls of the time such as Earls Court, Olympia, Crystal Palace and the Royal Agricultural Hall. Both *Pathé* and *Movietone News* filmed newsreels at many events from the 1920s, and other smaller independent film makers also did so much earlier. A number of media titles also sponsored and, in some cases, ran their own events. The *Daily Mirror* 'Fair of Fashions' that opened on 26 June 1909 and the *Daily Express* 'Women and Their Work' that took place 1-7 May 1915 were two that were held in the RHS Hall. However, the *Daily Mail* 'Ideal Home Exhibition' that began at Olympia on 9 October 1908 must rate as the best example of them all. Although the RHS Hall was not finally chosen for this event by its then Advertising Manager, Mr Wareham Smith – credited with conceiving this landmark show – he did originally hold a tenancy for it to be launched in the Hall in November that year.

However, he did launch several other exhibitions in the Hall, including the *Daily Mail* 'British & Irish Lace Exhibition' on 9-14 March of the same year. The first comprehensive event of its kind, this event brought to the Hall lace makers at work from Honiton, Norfolk, Buckinghamshire, Bedfordshire, Carrickmacross, Limerick, Youghal, Malmesbury and Devonshire. Honi-

ton lace makers had become legendary, mainly as a result of having been commissioned to make the flounce, veil and trimmings for Queen Victoria's wedding dress, something that had taken 200 people nine months to complete. The highlight of the show was the original model of the first bobbin net Lace Machine, made in 1809 by John Heathcote, having been brought down from Nottingham Castle Museum, itself in the centre of the hand-made lace making industry. Historic lace items such as Oliver Cromwell's christening robe and a pair of mittens worn by Mrs Malcolm Drummond's great-grandmother at the famous Waterloo Ball were also there. The main purpose of the exhibition was to showcase and promote British and Irish manufacturing expertise in this area that competed with its Continental rivals. The principal stores of the day, including Ponting's of Kensington High Street and D.H. Evans of Oxford Street, supported the event with special displays throughout the event. The Duchess of Somerset opened the show.

The first decade of the Hall's operation was a great success with an extraordinary amount and range of events taking place in it, so much so that, before the decade was out (at the Society's 3 March 1908 Council Meeting), it was seriously giving consideration to the possibility of acquiring more land to the north-east of the existing hall, for a second one to be built. A committee consisting of Sir Albert Rollit, Mr Britney and The Treasurer was appointed to look into it and report back. However, mainly due to the First World War, it would be a further 20 years before a second hall would open its doors for business.

The names used for the two RHS Halls standing today have changed a number of times since the first one opened on Vincent Street in July 1904. Known as the New Hall before it was built, it was formally called the Royal Horticultural Hall on opening, until 1928 when it then changed to become the Old Hall. This was as a result of the second hall on Elverton Street opening that was, in turn, called the New Hall. In 1991, the Halls were named Hall 1 and Hall 2 when applied to their commercial and non-horticultural use. The RHS continued to use the names Old and New respectively for their flower shows in them until 2002, when the names changed again, following extensive changes to the Old Hall. The Old Hall/Hall 1 was renamed as the Lindley Hall. The New Hall/Hall 2 name was also changed at the same time to become the Lawrence Hall. The Lindley and Lawrence Halls are the names now universally applied for all uses in them by the RHS to the present day. Jointly, they were known as the Royal Horticultural Halls until 1991, except for a brief period in the 1980s when they were branded the Westminster Exhibition Centre for their non-horticultural commercial use only. From 1991 to the present day they have been known as the Royal Horticultural Halls & Conference Centre.

II

First Shows

Let There be Music

The earliest recorded non-horticultural event to take place in the RHS Hall was a musical concert on 23 November 1904, given by St Margaret's Musical Society (aka St Margaret's Choral Society), one of four excellent choral groups that gave performances in the Hall during the next six years. St Margaret's Musical Society was a body of choral and instrumental performers drawn entirely from the St Margaret's Parish of Westminster and formed in 1901 by the Rev. Jocelyn Perkins. He was the Rector of St Margaret's Church, Westminster and a Sacristan and Minor Canon of Westminster Abbey. He became their first President and was also their principal conductor. The Society had started with 80 choral singers only but, by the time of their third public concert given in Caxton Hall in May 1904, they had grown to 140 and had also formed their own orchestra. At their fourth performance, and the first time in the RHS Hall in November 1904, they performed Part One of 'Messiah', Schumann's 'Advent Hymn' and a version of Psalm xxiii for tenor solo by Dr Walford Davies. According to the report in *The Times* the next day, the Hall 'was well filled'. On 10 March 1905, they returned to perform a Grand Sacred Concert, including 'The Woman

of Samaria' by Sterndale Bennett and 'The Sound of War' by T. Tertius Noble, organist of York Minster. The March 1905 edition of *St Margaret's Parish Magazine* records that this concert was attended by 1,200 and 'the most successful of the many concerts given'. Then on 5 June that same year they staged a Grand Operatic Concert of Mendelssohn's 'Loreley' and Gounod's 'Faust'. At this performance their orchestra and chorus comprised almost 300 performers and both were again conducted by the Rev. Jocelyn Perkins. Each performance could be booked for one shilling (£4.50). They performed a further series of Grand Concerts in the Hall until July 1908 and returned as St Margaret's Philharmonic Society in January 1911.

The Magpie Madrigal Society (founded in 1886 as The Magpie Minstrels) was another important and established group that gave regular performances throughout London. In 1889 HRH Princess Louise, Duchess of Argyll had become President of The Magpie Minstrels, subsequently attending the practices and taking part in the concerts, some of them held in aid of charitable causes. Princess Christian attended a concert in the RHS Hall on 16 May 1906 when funds were raised for the Metropolitan Association for

S. MARGARET'S MUSICAL SOCIETY.

Grand Operatic Concert,

ROYAL HORTICULTURAL SOCIETY'S HALL,

VINCENT SQUARE, WESTMINSTER.

TUESDAY, JUNE 6, 1905, at 8 p.m.

Mendelssohn's "**Loreley,**"   *Gounod's* "**Faust.**"

MISS ELEANOR FELIX.
MISS ETHEL BEVANS.
MR. VIVIAN BENNETTS.
MR. HARRY DEARTH.

Conductor = Rev. JOCELYN PERKINS, M.A.

Reserved Seat - -   BAND & CHORUS OF NEARLY
ONE SHILLING.   **300** PERFORMERS.   P. T. O.

S. Margaret's Musical Society.

GRAND SACRED CONCERT,

ROYAL HORTICULTURAL SOCIETY'S HALL,

VINCENT SQUARE, WESTMINSTER,

FRIDAY, MARCH 10th, 1905, at 8 p.m.

MISS EVA HARDY.   MISS ENID GABELL.
MR. ALFRED PINNINGTON.
MR. WILLIAM FORINGTON.

THE WOMAN OF SAMARIA *(Sterndale Bennett).*
THE SOUND OF WAR *(Mr. T. Tertius Noble,*
Organist of York Minster).
Mr. T. TERTIUS NOBLE will conduct his own work.

Conductor—REV. JOCELYN PERKINS, M.A.

Reserved Seat = = = ONE SHILLING.
P. T. O.

Befriending Young Servants! Princess Louise Augusta of Schleswig-Holstein also later gave her patronage and attended another of their concerts in the Hall on 1 May 1907 when the proceeds were donated to the Hammersmith and Fulham District Nursing Association.

To have listened to 16th- and 17th-century Madrigals, Motets, Chansons, Villanelles and other works, some composed by modern composers of the day including Sir Hubert Parry, Ralph Vaughan-Williams, Dr Walford Davies and Gustav Holst, in that new hall must have been rather special. Parry returned to the

Hall on 12-17 February 1912 as Minister of the Congregational Church, Seaford, Sussex, to perform an extraordinary work he had arranged and written, entitled 'The Historical Pageant of Non-conformity'. Parry was to become renowned for composing the music to Blake's poem in 1916 that is now known as *Jerusalem*. He would also later conduct another of his renowned works in the Hall on 12 October 1920, 'The Mayflower Pageant', accompanied by almost 1,000 performers, a choir of 750 and an orchestra. Reviews in *Musical World* of the Bach Choir's 65th concert

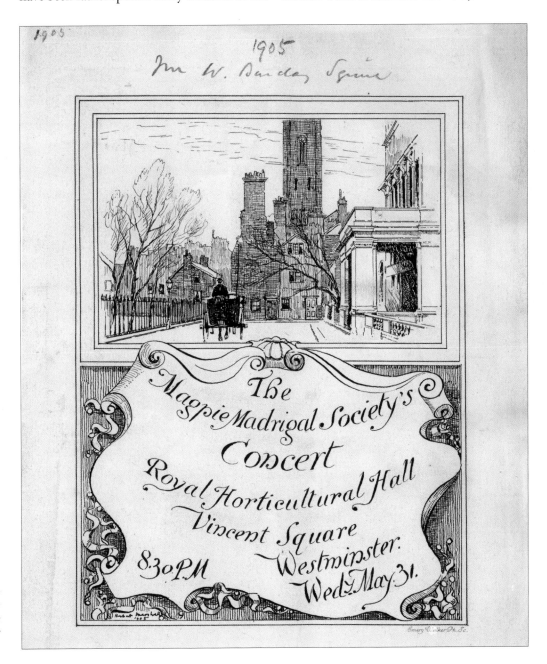

held there on 28 January 1905 were positive, recording that 'the audience had the pleasure of listening to the Bach Choir (founded in 1876) over which Dr Walford Davies presided with his usual skill'. Walford had studied under Parry at The Royal School of Music and, in 1898, he became Organist of Middle Temple Church. Later, in 1927, he took up the position of Organist of St George's Chapel, Windsor Castle and in 1934 was appointed Master of the King's Music, following the death of Sir Edward Elgar. From 1915 to the present day the Bach Choir used another hall close by, Westminster Cathedral's Hall, to practise in, and I would often hear them when I used to walk along Ambrosden Avenue to and from my own Hall on Vincent Square between 1991 and 2008.

The Llanelli Choir was a Male Voice Welsh Choir numbering 230, and on 14 November 1907 it travelled down to Windsor and London for a series of concerts. Two of those took place in the Hall, one of which was attended by one of Wales's best known politicians at the time, and a future Prime Minister, David Lloyd George. He was then President of the Board of Trade in Sir Henry Campbell-Bannerman's Liberal government, but would return to the Hall on many occasions in many guises over the next 30 years, including as an avid beekeeper and heather-honey producer at the National Honey Show in 1937 and 1938. The audience was packed with Welshmen living in London. The concert included the stirring 'Men of Harlech' and Sir Hubert Parry's hymn, 'Aberystwyth'. By contrast, 'Deutchland über alles', 'Song of the Vikings' and the late Prince Consort's hymn, 'Gotha', were also sung. The Choir was conducted by the renowned Welsh

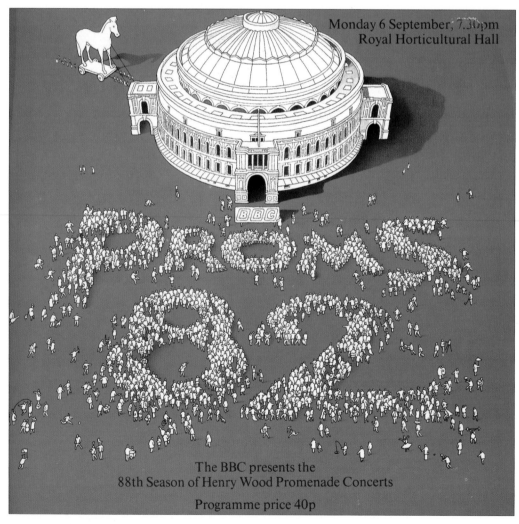

Monday 6 September, 7.30pm
Royal Horticultural Hall

The BBC presents the
88th Season of Henry Wood Promenade Concerts

Programme price 40p

BBC Proms '82 – the 88th Season of Henry Wood Promenade Concerts at the Lindley Hall, 6 September 1982.

musician, Mr John Thomas, who had given his first London Concert of Welsh music in 1862 and formed the London Welsh Choral Union in 1871. He had also been appointed harpist to Queen Victoria and a teacher of the harp at the Royal Academy in the same year.

Other orchestral and choral societies to use the Hall during this period were the English Ladies' Orchestral Society and the Westminster Choral Society. The latter (formed in 1886) performed many oratorios and many famous soloists, including Isobel Baillie, the Scottish soprano, and Kathleen Ferrier, the outstanding contralto, sang with this Society. Marion Petersen was also a member of the Westminster Choral Society between 1946 and 1952, after which she emigrated to Canada. Her recollection of Kathleen Ferrier was given to me as follows: 'Once, while practising 'The Dream of Gerontius', the door to the auditorium opened, a woman came in, walked down the centre aisle, took a seat, then listened to the singing. The first pages of the choral singing completed, we were suddenly astonished to hear a voice carrying on the solo until the choir came in once more. This continued to the end of the final bar of that part of the work. The lady in the auditorium, singing without music from her seat, was Kathleen Ferrier. She had come to help with the practice, so that we would be used to singing with her in the performance. I have never known any other soloist appear, other than at the final rehearsal. She seldom used music, as she knew the music by heart, she was a kind, friendly, and most completely natural person. She was an outstanding contralto, whose meteoric rise to international fame, was, sadly, cut all too short by her death at the early age of forty two.'

Then in 1953, the London Coronation Choir that sang at Queen Elizabeth II's Coronation in Westminster Abbey on 2 June booked the Hall from 15-19 June for a Choral Concert. Even later still, on 6 September 1982, during the 88th Season of Henry Wood Promenade Concerts, the first UK performance of Pierre Boulez's *Répons* was held in the same Hall and broadcast on BBC TV's Arena programme, and on Radio 3.

This was a very different performance that involved the electro-acoustic treatment of the natural, amplified and transformed sounds of the soloists as well as alternation between collective and individual play. Those who came to listen to this did not have the comfort of fixed seating, but had to sit on cushions on the floor! The 'Two Interpretations' were performed by Ensemble Inter Contemporain directed by the composer, who also gave a talk on his work. This new musical work had been commissioned by the Southwest German Radio for the Donaueschingen Festival and first given on 18 October 1981 by the same performers with the collaboration of the Experimental Studio of the Heinrich Strobel Foundation of Southwest German Radio. In the BBC Programme for this Promenade Concert it stated that 'Pierre Boulez has said that *Répons* is an example of the latest stage in his interest in writing procedures distinctly deriving from mediaeval music'. Early musical instruments would also come to the RHS, much later in 1973, in the form of a regular Early Musical Instruments Exhibition that corresponded with the rapidly growing and increasingly popular Early Music Festival that was being held in York at the time, but would spread throughout Britain and become internationally renowned.

Chefs and Cookery

As has already been referred to, the 16th Universal Cookery & Food Exhibition organised by the Association of the same name was secured by the RHS and held in its new hall on 2-5 May 1905. This was to prove highly significant and a hugely important moment that secured more exposure and promotion to a very wide group of influential people than could have been achieved by normal forms of promotion. From this one event, it can confidently be said that the Hall became instantly attractive to a huge audience of gentry, politicians, military and church leaders involved with organising events in their own given fields of interest and involvement. The next 10 years of activity

FAR LEFT   *Postcard for the 18th Universal Cookery & Food Exhibition at the Lindley Hall, 5-9 November 1907.*

LEFT   *Schedule for the 17th Universal Cookery & Food Exhibition at the Lindley Hall, 27 November–1 December 1906.*

BELOW   *Prizes, Displays and Competition notices, and floor plan for the 17th Universal Cookery & Food Exhibition, 27 November–1 December 1906.*

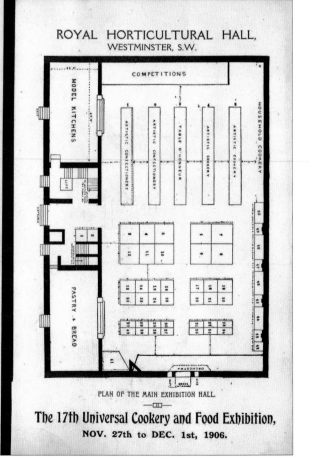

reflect the strong and direct links from those involved with this event.

This was the greatest cooking exhibition of its kind, represented by the world's best chefs including the renowned Frenchman, Georges Auguste Escoffier, then chef to the Carlton Club who was reverently referred to as 'the Emperor of Chefs and Chef to the Emperors'; M.J. Ménager, chef to King Edward VII; M. Cedard, chef to the Prince of Wales (and later as King George V); the famed Swiss culinary specialist, C. Herman Senn, whose Maison Comestible at 329, Vauxhall Bridge Road, Victoria had been established in 1883 (and where the UCFA were first based); the Dutchman, Iwan W. Kriens (who would later become Head Master of the Westminster Technical Institute's Hotel and Restaurant School and lived at 44 Vincent Square); and chefs from the best hotels and restaurants across Europe including, in London, *The Goring Hotel* in

BELOW Senn's Culinary Specialities advertisement, 1906. C.H. Senn was a Swiss, who ran the Universal Cookery & Food Association as its Managing Director, and General Secretary, from the same address as his own culinary business.

Belgravia, the *Hotel Cecil* in the Strand, the *Charing Cross Hotel*, the *Criterion* and *Café Monico* restaurants in the West End. Mr Feltham, chef to the late Queen Victoria, also attended. The exhibition was opened by HRH The Duke of Connaught and welcomed by its President, W. Burdett-Coutts, MP. Among the distinguished chefs and guests was the RHS President, Sir Trevor Lawrence.

By the time of the 22nd Exhibition in 1911, Cesar Ritz had opened his hotel in 1906 and the *Waldorf Astoria* opened in 1908. The 22nd Exhibition was again opened by the Duke of Connaught, one of eight Royal Family Patrons, including Queen Maud of Norway. Interestingly, by then, Sir Trevor Lawrence had also become a patron. Other Patrons consisted of 11 Dukes and Duchesses, three Marquess and Marchionesses, 15 Earls, 11 Countesses, one Dowager, 33 Lords and Ladies, one Baron and

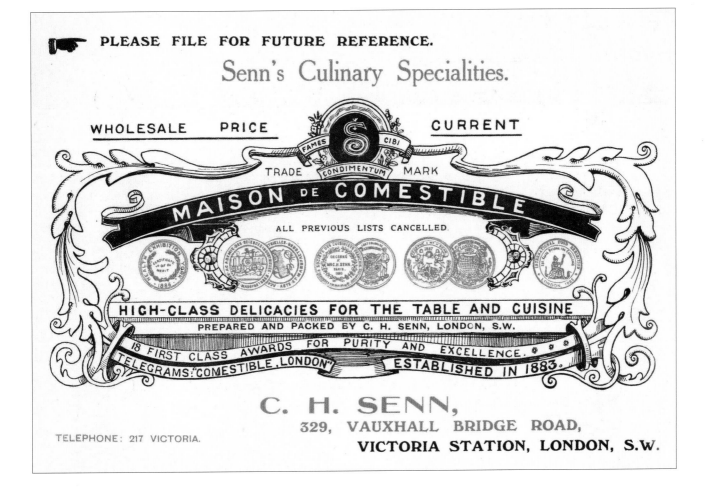

16 C   H.R.H. THE DUKE OF CONNAUGHT.   ROTARY PHOTO. E.C.

Baroness, one Viscount and Viscountess, 29 worldwide Ambassadors, 27 Knights of the Realm, seven MPs, 48 military officers from Field-Marshals to Captains (including Field-Marshal Earl Roberts, V.C. and Lt.-General Sir John French) four Mayors and three Lord Mayors, including the Lord and Lady Mayoress of London. The Worshipful Company of Cooks (whose history reaches back to the reign of Edward VI) and The Committee of the National Training School of Cookery were some of the organisations that had also become patrons. Another 25 non-titled individuals were also named as such. Queen Alexandra was Chief Patroness.

Part of the reason for such an august list of patrons was the role its philanthropic vice-president, the Baroness Angela Burdett-Coutts, had played in the formation of the Association back in 1885. Described as England's wealthiest woman on receipt of her grandfather Coutts's banking inheritance in 1837, she had given away almost three million pounds of her money as scholarships, endowments and a wide range of philanthropic

causes by the time she died in 1906. A close confidante of Queen Victoria, she also had strong friendships and connections with Herbert Gladstone, Lord Salisbury, Sir Henry Stanley and Dr Livingstone (the renowned African explorers), Lord Wolsely, Lord Roberts, Lord Kitchener and the great actor, Sir Henry Irvine.

One of her most prominent projects was in helping to found and fund the Ragged School Union and Shaftesbury Society with Lord Shaftesbury in 1844. The Ragged School Union first used the RHS Hall on 28 December 1908 when 1,000 poor children from these London schools were treated to a dinner paid for by funds raised by other children of the Children's Sunbeam Society in South Australia, on the Foundation Day anniversary of Australia. The Ragged School Union had representatives in British Columbia, Canada, Jamaica, New York, New Zealand, South Africa and Tasmania. One of the London schools, The One Tun Ragged School founded in 1853, was located very close to the Hall in Old Pye Street and remained as such until 1930. Other projects of hers involved the Temperance Society, the National Society for the Prevention of Cruelty to Children and the Columbia Road Market in the East End of London where she did much to relieve the abject poverty and poor conditions that she confronted there. Charles Dickens, who was one of her close friends, dedicated his book, *Martin Chuzzlewit*, to her for the work she had done in the East End. She funded a home for former prostitutes, created soup kitchens, working-class housing schemes and the building of Anglican churches. In Ireland she helped to promote the fishing industry by starting schools, providing boats and advancing £250,000. She was also very interested in supporting overseas missionary and nursing exploits across the British Empire, as well as projects for Dyak and Aboriginal communities in Borneo and Australia, respectively, providing cotton gins in Nigeria as well as helping Turkish peasants and refugees from the 1877 Russo-Turkish

Postcard of Prince Arthur, Duke of Connaught (1850-1942). HRH Prince Arthur opened the first Universal Cookery & Food Exhibition to take place in the Lindley Hall on 2 May 1905. He would also later become the 7th Royal Patron of the Royal Horticultural Society from 1924 to 1942.

War. As a result of some of these, she also became associated with Florence Nightingale and Louisa Twining.

She had been given a tract of land by the Dean and Chapter of Westminster on an area known as Devil's Acre, to use as the site for a new parish dedicated to St Stephen. (The name of Devil's Acre could partly have been ascribed to Vincent Square – widely believed to have been used as a plague pit where many thousands of Londoners who succumbed to this appalling disease in 1665 were laid beneath it.) On this land, with further encouragement from Charles Dickens, she built St Stephen's Church in Rochester Row, very near to where the Society's new Hall would be built 54 years later. She dedicated St Stephen's in memory of her father, Sir Francis Burdett, MP. At the time of the opening of the RHS Hall its vicar, the Rev. W.H. Twining, was present.

She also built a school on this land and contributed to the United Westminster Almshouses, both also situated in Rochester Row. The Burdett-Coutts CE Primary School had accommodation for 989 pupils in 1903, and she felt very strongly that her school should prepare young people as well as possible to meet the challenges that they would later face. In fact, many went out to the colonies to start new lives. One ex-pupil became the Prime Minister of Australia!

In 1893, she built the Westminster Technical Institute on Vincent Square, which would later have the RHS Hall built right next to it. It would become an integral part of the Universal Cookery & Food Association's objective in helping young men and women to train as cooks and chefs, by providing the first scholarships of their kind at what became known as the London County Council Cookery Technical School from 1910, following her presentation of the Institute to the Council free of charge. This remained the only establishment in the UK teaching professional cookery until the mid-1940s, although the Soho School of Cookery, founded by Crosse and Blackwell, also existed. It also later became a facility that was used in tandem with their annual exhibitions and other events staged in the RHS Hall. Now

known as Westminster Kingsway College, it is the premier catering and hospitality college in the UK, and continues the Burdett Coutts and UC&FA initiative to help young men and women achieve careers in the fields of culinary arts and hospitality, with alumni such as Sophie Wright, Jamie Oliver and Ainsley Harriott.

So, from the above, it can be seen that Baroness Burdett-Coutts had a very real involvement and interest in the development of this area in which the RHS would build its first Hall. Bringing the Universal Cookery & Food Association's annual exhibitions to it, via her husband, and the career opportunities it offered young men and women at the Institute next door, would, therefore, have been very appealing. The stated aims of the Association were certainly in line with the philanthropic objectives of the Baroness because, although the primary aim was to maintain the highest standards of artistic cookery, they were also very focused in

Iwan Kriens, Head Master of the Westminster Technical Institute's Hotel and Restaurant School (now known as Westminster Kingsway College) with pupils, c.1936. The Institute and School was located next door to the Lindley Hall on Vincent Square. Iwan Kriens also became a Managing Director of the Universal Cookery & Food Exhibition, and one of the first catering contractors to the RHS.

seeking to awaken public interest in the art of cookery and place it in a position worthy of its increasingly vital importance to the improvement of the National Health. A lofty statement, but backed up by free lectures and lessons given by competent teachers to the poor and working class in various parishes in the poorer parts of London. This included distributing recipes for inexpensive dishes and awarding cookery and confectionery scholarships for men and women. Had she lived long enough to hear it, she would have been delighted when, in 1912, the exhibition was attended by J.A. Pease, MP, President of the Board of Education, who was reported in *The Times* as saying that 'the government realised the importance of cookery in the households of the country, and that the exhibition would materially assist the Board of Education in their work'. Six years earlier, in 1906, school dinners had been first introduced, mainly in response to complaints by the military about what they felt were undernourished and sub-standard Boer War recruits. However, 96 years later Jamie Oliver was still trying to influence government to change what he saw as bad cooking habits in schools, and by the masses!

It should also be noted that their annual exhibitions were not run for profit. If any profits were made, these were devoted to educational and charitable purposes and towards their Benevolent Fund. At the 1907 event profits were made and these went to 'The Fresh Air Fund' and the 'Lord Mayor's Cripples' Fund'. The Fresh Air Fund was run by St Margaret's Parish, Westminster, and enabled the poor to be provided with a changed environment from the city out into the country where they could rest and recuperate, in order to return re-invigorated to continue their working lives. Almost 60 years later, between 4-7 October 1966, clean air had become a cause championed by the National Society for Clean Air at Field House, Breams Buildings, London SE15, when they staged their International Clean Air Exhibition in the RHS New Hall.

A great deal of voluntary work in connection with hospitals and other charitable and educational institutions was carried out by the UC&FA with thousands of pounds devoted to it. Cookery competitions were also organised from time to time amongst cookery pupils at elementary schools, and Army and Navy, and Mercantile Marine cooks. This covered subjects such as Invalid Cookery, Hospital Dietary, Vegetarian and Meatless Fare.

At the 1911 exhibition, seven executive committees organised the exhibits and competitions and these were in the following Groups. The

BELOW *Bird's eye view of a Section of the Domestic Cookery Group in the Lindley Hall at the 23rd Universal Cookery & Food Exhibition, 1912, from* Food and Cookery and The Catering World, *December 1912.*

LEFT *Back cover of the 17th Universal Cookery & Food Exhibition, 1906.*

Commercial Group, Domestic Cookery Group, Army and Navy Group, Culinary Group, Artistic Confectionery Group, Bakery Group and Competitive Demonstrations. The members of these Groups represented a very broad and comprehensive cross-section of the industry. Mr Otto Richard Goring, Proprietor of *The Goring Hotel*, was on the Commercial and Competitive Demonstrations Committees. He had opened his new hotel, situated just a stone's throw away from Victoria Station, in March 1910, and claimed to be the first hotel in the world to have private bathrooms and central heating in every bedroom. They cost 7s. 6d. (£32.81) then but are a lot more now, although during their Centenary celebrations in 2010 they offered their rooms at these original rates! The hotel became world-renowned in April 2011, when Kate Middleton and her family stayed prior to her marriage to Prince William.

Mr F.W. Goodenough from the Gas Light & Coke Company was also on the Commercial Group. His company was based in Horseferry Road and was an important exhibitor that would become a regular one at a variety of new shows and exhibitions at the Hall over the

next 10 years, in particular. The revolutionary introduction of gas for lighting, cooking and heating to London homes, hospitals, hotels and other properties was to have a significant effect on people's lives and had begun in earnest about 1840, but it was back in 1812 when the newly formed Gas Light & Coke Company had been given a charter to first supply Westminster Bridge with gas lighting from its Bankside gas works. At the UC&FA Exhibition they displayed an impressive range of new gas appliances for use in the kitchen. These included Sugg's Criterion Gas Kitchen, Fletcher's Gas-heated Smoothing Iron Heater and Irons, and Still's Metropole Toaster and Hot Closet! The Culinary Group Committee consisted of leading chefs from, amongst others, Gatti's Royal Adelaide Gallery Restaurant (founded by Italian immigrant ice-cream maker and confectioner, Carlo Gatti), the Athenæum Club, Pall Mall, and Café Monico in Tichbourne Street. Predictably, the Army & Navy Group included the Army & Navy Stores on Victoria Street, but also *St Ermin's Hotel* in Caxton Street, close by. The Domestic Cookery Group had the most

RIGHT *Pamphlet used by Ch. Herman Senn at demonstration on The Art of Omlette Making, given at the Lindley Hall, 28 November 1906. Senn was also chef of the Reform Club.*

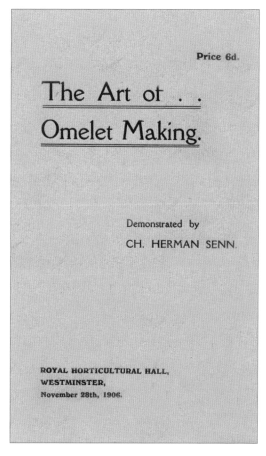

Price 6d.

The Art of . . Omelet Making.

Demonstrated by
CH. HERMAN SENN.

ROYAL HORTICULTURAL HALL,
WESTMINSTER,
November 28th, 1906.

LEFT *Silver and bronze medals presented to competition winners at the Universal Cookery & Food Exhibitions during the period, 1911-13. These include the 1911 Special Prize Silver Medal and Ribbon presented by The Countess of Bective, and the 1911 Silver Medal presented by The Gas Light and Coke Company for 'Economy for Cooking by Gas'. The medal struck to celebrate the Centenary of The Gas Light and Coke Company, 1812-1912, is also shown.*

was sponsored by Messrs Elders & Fyffes) and 'Omlet Competitions – to prepare two Omlets, one cheese and one tomato with three eggs only allowed for each Omlet'; Herman Senn, the Association's Managing Director and General Secretary, had previously given demonstrations at the Hall on 28 November 1906, supported by his pamphlet entitled *The Art of Omlet Making*.

He also delivered an address at the Hall in September 1913 on the subject of 'Ignorance in Cooking Vegetables'. The *Daily Express* reported him saying that, 'So far as the typical English cuisine is concerned, it cannot be stated that the average English cook displays as much acquaintance with those delicious and appetising vegetables as does the Continental cook, who prepares them with so much skill and delicacy'. He went on to say, 'We are far too conservative in this country, and the sooner we induce our family cooks to be more enterprising in this respect the sooner the struggle for greater variety of vegetables and better ways of cooking will be overcome'. *Plus ça change!*

Extensive awards were made in the form of Grand Prix Special Prizes, Challenge Shields, Orders of Merit, Gold, Silver and Bronze Medals, cash prizes, Diplomas and Certificates of Merit in all Groups for the best exhibits, demonstrations and contributions. The Special Prize Awards were made from organisations and institutions such as The Lords of the Admiralty, The London Press Exchange, The Gas Light & Coke Company, *The Goring Hotel*, Messrs Nestlé and Anglo-Swiss Condensed Milk, Mr W. Burdett-Coutts, MP, and The Geneva Association of Hotel and Restaurant Employees.

Exhibitors included well known brands and products such as Bovril, Brooke Bond, Cerebos, Marmite and Nestlé, but also other organisations such as the Nautical School of Cookery, London Docks, the *Daily Express* Paper Bag Cookery Department, the London Vegetarian Association, the State of San Paulo (Brazil) Pure Coffee Company and Charles Zolper, Chef, King of Spain Hotel, Aachen, Germany. Regular 'revolutionary' demonstrations by 'an

representatives, mainly from training schools and Polytechnics around the country, but also including Westminster Hospital and The Royal Hospital, Chelsea.

Within the first six Groups, 103 exhibits were presented ranging from 'A Coburg Loaf' (now simply known as a Cob); 'An Assortment of Fondant Simple, Fondant Fourrés, and Fruits Farces'; 'One Three-tier Wedding Cake – dummies permitted, piping only'; 'An Invalid Tray – to contain a dish of fish or meat, light pudding or jelly or custard, and two beverages, including beef tea or a soup (this was open only to Trained Nurses)' and, 'A Complete-laid Luncheon Dinner or Supper Table, not less than six dishes nor more than eight to be exhibited on small tables. Hors-d'Œuvre and Sweet Course only count as one dish in their respective course'.

In the Competitive Demonstrations Group these ranged from 'Tea Table Competitions' (for ladies only); 'Fowl Cooking Competition – to prepare and cook a Poulet Sauté Parmentier'; 'Three best dishes made from Bananas' (this

Catalogue cover for the 27th Universal Cookery & Food Exhibition at the Lindley Hall, 22-6 October 1923, showing HM Queen Alexandra as Chief Patroness.

expert chef' were given of the *Daily Express* paper-bag offerings that included, Chicken Fricassee, Mackerel with Maître d'hôtel butter and Tomato Pasties. I would have liked to have been there to witness these and the expressions on people's faces when they first saw them. Imagine also the wafting aromas of all these dishes circulating around the Hall and the mouth watering desire to eat most of them.

Throughout the exhibition visitors and exhibitors were entertained by Herr Meny's Blue Hungarian Band. Herr Meny had been a not infrequent entertainment choice by many event organisers before this, and was to remain so for many in the future. In 1905, he even specially composed the 'Chemists' Exhibition March' that was dedicated to the British & Colonial Druggist, organisers of the annual Chemists' Exhibition that first came to the RHS Hall in that year. It was certainly considered necessary that any exhibitions, or public event of this kind, would include daily entertainment and this ranged from military bands to those comparable with Herr Meny's Bands. Apart from his Blue Hungarian Band, Herr Meny could offer his customers a further choice of his White Hungarian Band, as well as his White and Blue Viennese Bands (at the 1906 International Philatelic Exhibition Keith Prowse & Co. Ltd, Band and Entertainment Agency, had been sole agents for the Blue Viennese Band). An extensive repertoire of music was played including 'Under the Austrian Eagle', a March by Wagner; 'Anahuac', a Mexican Caprice of Herr Meny's own composition; 'Pomp and Circumstance Grand March' by Elgar, and 'Nigger's Birthday' a Two-Step by Lincke – the latter, a choice that would obviously not be countenanced today. The catering provided in the restaurant at the 1911 show was by Searcy, Tansley & Co., now known as Searcy's 1847, after the date they first started in business. However, their founder, John Searcy, exhibited in his own name as early as 1884 at the International Health Exhibition in the Royal Horticultural Society's Kensington Gardens. Searcy's are still active and in business, and promote themselves as the 'Connoisseur's Connoisseur'.

One last anecdote before leaving this remarkable annual event that stayed in the Hall until 1925, when it then moved to larger premises at Olympia, is the story of an ex-Reform Club Chef who has been rightly featured in The Florence Nightingale Museum at St Thomas's Hospital. Alexis Sayer volunteered his services at the Crimea in March 1855 after seeing a soldier's letter in *The Times* asking how best to cook Army rations. His valuable contribution was the much needed re-organisation of their hospital kitchens, the invention of new dishes from standard rations, the appointment of proper cooks and the design of more efficient utensils. These included a 'Scutari teapot' and a portable cooking stove that, with minor changes, is still being used to the present day. It is tempting to speculate that the Baroness and Florence Nightingale discussed Sayer's exploits and that this spurred the development of the UC&FA, especially since Herman Senn was also a Reform Club chef. The Universal Cookery & Food Association changed its name in 1965 to become the Cookery & Food Association. Later still, they changed its name to adopt that of its most active Division, and became the Craft Guild of Chefs. They still represent this industry sector admirably.

Pets, Poultry and Livestock

On 4 April 1873 Mr S.E. Shirley, MP, from Warwickshire, called together the National Dog Club Committee, and a discussion ensued that resulted in 12 gentlemen meeting at No 2 Albert Mansions, Victoria Street, London. This meeting marked the founding of the Kennel

Postcard of HM Queen Alexandra and HRH Princess Victoria with their dogs. Queen Alexandra was Patron of The Ladies' Kennel Association and Princess Victoria was President.

Club that provided for the intense interest held by the Victorian aristocracy of breeding and exhibiting dogs of all kinds. The best known dog show of all is, of course, 'Crufts', started by Charles Cruft in 1886 at the Royal Aquarium, Westminster when he was still working with Spratt's. The Royal Agricultural Hall, Islington then became the chosen venue for many years and 'Crufts' is still running today, now under the auspices of The Kennel Club, to whom it was sold in the early 1940s. In 1905, HRH The Duke of Connaught was President of the Kennel Club and the King, its Patron. Both had seen the Hall and it seems very likely that they would have felt that it would be ideal for their own more exclusive Championship Shows. Most members of the Royal Family, and especially the King and Queen, entered their own dogs into Championship Shows. King Edward VII favoured Thibet Sheep-Dogs and had entered these into shows when he had been Prince of Wales.

The first recorded event in the RHS Hall took place on 6 April 1905 when the Ladies' Kennel Association Championship Show took place. Their Patron was HRH Queen Alexandra and its President was HRH Princess Helena Victoria. This was the start of regular Championship Shows staged in the Hall by many different Clubs and Societies (more than 170 in 51 years) representing all manner of breeds. The last show to have taken place was for the Poodle Club on 8 October 1955. In 1906 the 4th Annual French Bulldogs, Griffons Bruxellois and Pekingese Championship Show was held on 30 March and then on 7 December the Toy Dog Society Show was staged.

This prompted a rather cutting article to be written in the *Daily Express* the following day under the heading, 'The Toy Dog's Social Mission'. The article highlighted the lavish attention, money and food heaped on these lucky animals by their rich owners, but also noted that, 'If their owners did not spend the 100 Guineas (£9,500) that they paid to the breeders of these animals it is possible that the children of those workmen and tradesmen might have to drink watered down milk if the wealthy mistress ceased to buy the dogs from

The Bystander, September 19, 1906   609

Toy Dogs No Longer!
"MINIATURE BULLDOGS" ON SHOW AT WESTMINSTER

Mrs. Edgar Waterlow's Nuthurst Doctor
First, Open Class, and Champion

Bouledogues Francais
Mrs. Theo. Becker's Jules Pluvia, 1st Champion

Some interesting points were noted at the show of the London Bulldog Society at the Horticultural Hall last week. For one thing, the name of the dogs is no longer to be "toy" dogs, but "miniature bulldogs," the reason being that they are, from various causes, getting nearer the true bulldog type. The specimen above (Nuthurst Doctor) is sufficiently convincing as a case in point. Mrs. Waterlow's fine exhibit possesses the full, round chest of the ideal bulldog. A change, too, has come in the matter of ears. The "bat ear," which had been developed by "toy" bulldogs, thanks to their being bred so largely in France, has now, after the liberal introduction of English blood, developed into the crumpled ear of the English bulldog. The above two photographs illustrate the difference between the two kinds of ears.

Judging the Special Novice Class

the breeder'. The earlier comment made was that, 'Pretty as it is to see these little animals resting on their silk cushions, hung about with satin curtains; graceful as the ways of the little creatures are, when they eat and drink the excellent foods provided for them by their infatuated owners, it is difficult to avoid making a mental contrast with the inferior lot of those little animals which roam about the streets of our poorer quarters, and do not sleep upon silk cushions, nor feed upon the best of diet – the little human animals.'

The Express had a point, as even stray dogs in London had been given better consideration

ABOVE *Article from* The Bystander, *19 September 1906 reporting on the 15th Annual London Bulldog Society Championship Show that took place in the Lindley Hall on 13 September 1906.*

than their human counterparts in many instances, especially when Battersea Dogs and Cats Home had been founded in 1860. This famous rescue centre celebrated its 150th anniversary in March 2010, having taken in more than three million dogs and cats during the period.

Perhaps it was not surprising, therefore, that the organisers of these early dog (and cat) shows soon tied in with Our Dumb Friends' League to raise funds to support those creatures less fortunate than their own. Even later still after the First World War in 1922, Our Dumb Friends' League (later to become Blue Cross) held the first of their own fundraising Bazaars in the Hall with, again, the Royal Patrons and aristocracy of the day officially opening and attending them. In 1931, it was Miss Amy Johnson, the aviator,

who opened their Christmas Fair. At the two-day Christmas Fair in 1928, Colonel M.W. Douglas, late of the Indian Civil Service, where he had been responsible for the administration of the Andaman Islands, applied his skills as Secretary of the League and proudly announced that their latest achievement, an all-night service of treatment at the Animals Hospital in Hugh Street, Victoria with a qualified veterinary surgeon on duty, had been put in place. By then, the League was taking in 15,000 'patients' a year into this hospital. The thorny issue of vivisection that was hotly debated at the time and still now, was put aside by Colonel Douglas who was quoted by the *Daily Express* as saying, 'We do not bother about controversies on vivisection and anti-vivisection. Our job is purely practical.' A view that was not readily countenanced by all, and

BELOW *Article from The Daily Graphic, 29 October 1909, reporting on the 18th London Bulldog Society Championship Show that took place in the Lindley Hall on 28 October 1909.*

The judging ring.

Waiting their turn to enter the ring. THE LONDON BULLDOG SOCIETY'S ANNUAL SHOW, OPENED AT THE ROYAL HORTICULTURAL HALL, WESTMINSTER, YESTERDAY. The judges' examination. (See page 20.)

at the National Small Livestock Association's 1st National Championship Show, also held in the Hall 11-16 November 1946, many of the small animals that were used for vivisection research were on display. Here were golden hamsters, red, white and blue mice, lilac and chocolate brown rabbits and Himalayan cavies. In reporting this event, *The Times* made the point that, 'They not only make pleasant pets, but are also of use in research laboratories for the testing of milk for children and vitamin foods.'

However, dogs and dog shows did cause problems from the Society's neighbours when, at their Council Meeting on 11 June 1907, it

was reported that, 'Miss Murray Smith, the owner of St George's House opposite the Hall on Elverton Street, had complained of the noise made by dogs in the Hall at night before dog shows took place the following day'. Without any form of sound insulation, they would have made a racket! The *Daily Express* report of the National Terrier Club Championship, held on 15 January that same year, gives a clue as to the extent and justification of the complaint. Under the headline, 'Record Exhibition of Terriers', the correspondent reported that, 'Nearly seven hundred terriers barked, whined, yelped and smiled in the Royal Horticultural Hall yesterday. Hundreds of dog

ABOVE LEFT
Catalogue cover of the Championship Joint Show for French Bulldogs, Brussels Griffons, Pekingese and Pomeranians, that took place in the Lindley Hall on 8 April 1908.

ABOVE   *Catalogue cover of The Bulldog Club's Championship Show that took place in the Lindley Hall on 25 May 1921.*

experts inspected the stalls and discussed the points of Airedale terriers, dandie dinments, Scottish terriers, Irish terriers, Welsh terriers, Skye terriers, wire-hair fox terriers, Bedlington terriers, West Highland white terriers, and smooth fox terriers, and here and there in big rings fanciers from all parts of the country led their dogs round and round under the eye of the judge in a sort of semi-canine barn dance'. The experts were described variously as 'a comfortable looking country clergyman, a trim young lady in tight-fitting tailor-made clothes and a group of military-looking young men in cloth caps'. 'A delightful smooth fox terrier, Jack Hall, the property of Mr J.C. Tinne' won the first prize followed by Lady Eva Heathcote's Scotch terrier, Hinton Hamish.

Lady Eva Heathcote also displayed cats in Championship cat shows. Famous clubs such as the Southern Counties Cat Club, National Cat Club, Governing Council of the Cat Fancy and the Kensington Kitten & Neuter Cat Club held their own Championship Shows (over 37 of them) in the Halls until July 1992. The very first official cat show had been held at the Crystal Palace, Sydenham on 13 July 1871. By 1976, the Supreme Cat Show, organised by the Governing Council of the Cat Fancy, had become as large and prestigious a show as its counterpart dog show, Cruft's. On 9 January 1908, the Southern Counties Cat Club opened with 500 entries in 92 classes, in aid of the Mansion House Crippled Children's Fund. At the 8 January 1914 Southern Counties Cat Club's Grand Championship Show, the *Daily Express* reported under a headline of 'Trimmed for the Latest Fashions' that 'one of the entrants wore a handsome stole and muff of its own fur. Its coat had been so deftly trimmed (much as a poodle is shaved) that it looked like one of those

BELOW *Letter from The Ladies' Kennel Association requesting information for their 'members dog show', 3 February 1919.*

BELOW RIGHT *Catalogue cover of The Fox Terrier Club's Thirty-Eighth Championship Show that took place in the Lindley Hall on 20 January 1921.*

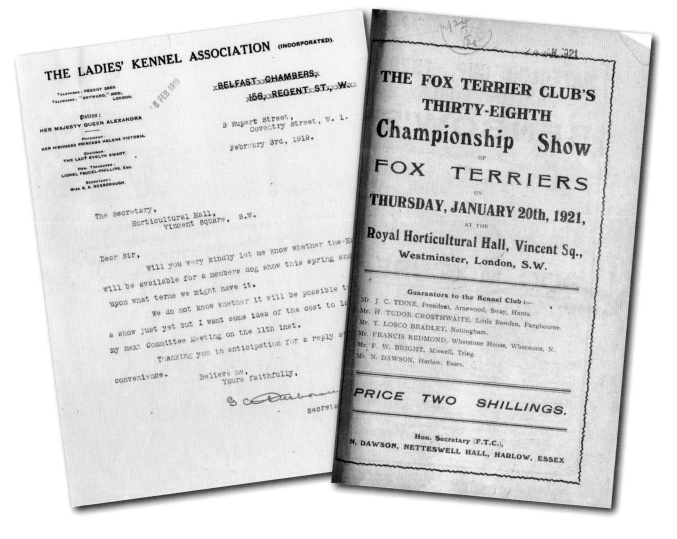

smart Bond Street models of seal musquash worn with a bushy wolf stole and muff.' It continued with 'A snow-white beauty had a collarette of black fur which was reminiscent of those elegant white fox opera cloaks which are such a craze this winter. The modes for yellow fox were no less well exemplified by large golden-coated tabbies.' At its 50th Anniversary Show in the same Hall held on 2 February 1954, not much had changed with *The Times* reporting that, 'Apart from a few kittens who have not yet learned all the aristocratic assumptions that their lineage entitles them to make, the sons and daughters of proud dynasties turned their backs on admirers, curled up, closed their eyes in restless dreams, and drew what comfort they could from cot blankets folded round hot water bottles!'

Real fur, in the form of rabbit, would also later appear in the Hall in 1928 and 1929 when the British Fur Rabbit Society held their annual Rabbit & Fur Shows there. This was one set of animals that Miss Murray could be sure of not being disturbed by as they sat in their hutches, row upon row; perfect examples of decorum. The *Daily Express* reported that, 'White-smocked attendants moved with unhurried tread, a spinning-wheel turned peacefully in one corner, and the centre of the room was filled with hutch upon hutch of magnificent fur-producing rabbits. There were chinchillas, coats from whose skins were exhibited in the hall; there were beaver and beige coloured bunnies, while Flemish giants startled by their size and silver-blacks by their novelty. All behaved themselves admirably betraying only by a twitching nose – caused perhaps by the all-pervading rabbit smell? – the fact that they were alive. Most magnificent, I thought were the pink-eyed Angoras, covered with tremendous coats of white fur.'

On 28 May 1908, the Pomeranian Club's Second Annual Show was staged at the London Scottish Volunteer Rifles Corps Drill Hall at 59 Buckingham Gate – the same Hall in which the RHS had staged its own fortnightly flower shows between March 1888 and 1904. Dog shows and many other events had been held in this Drill Hall since 1886 when it first opened

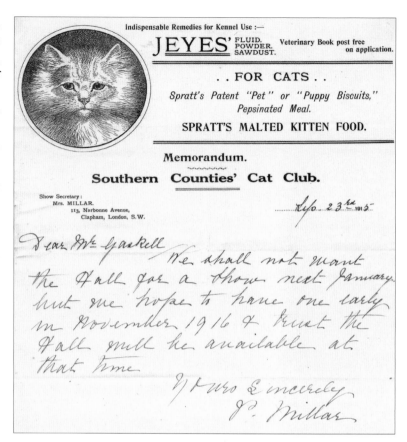

LEFT   *Catalogue cover for the Coronation Championship Cat Show (All Breeds), organised by the Governing Council Cat Fancy in the Lawrence Hall on 9 October 1953.*

RIGHT *Catalogue cover for The Show of the Coronation Year, organised by The Kensington Kitten & Neuter Cat Club in the Lindley Hall on 31 July 1953.*

FAR RIGHT *Catalogue cover for The National Cat Club's Fifty Ninth Championship Show (All Breeds) in the Lawrence Hall on 7 December 1955.*

BELOW *Photos of the 43rd and 46th The Kensington Kitten & Neuter Cat Club's Shows in the Lawrence Hall in August 1978 and 1981. The 1981 Show took place on 1 August and was named 'Royal Celebration Show', to mark the wedding of HRH the Prince of Wales to Lady Diana Spencer.*

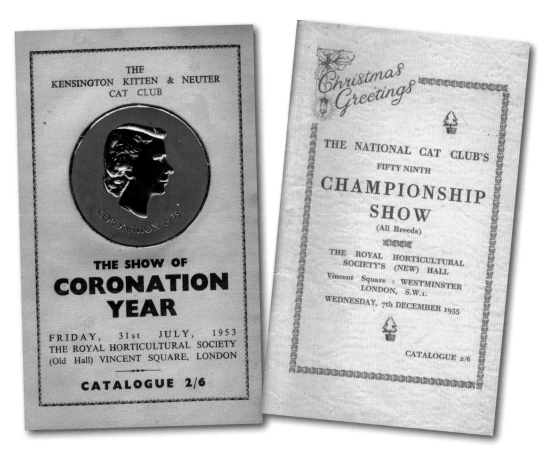

and doubtless, this also acted as a conduit for them to move to the RHS. Further strong links with the London Scottish Regiment and its Drill Hall would evolve during the next 20 years. It was badly damaged by German bombs during the First World War, but later repaired. However, in 1985 it was demolished and the London Scottish Regiment built a new Drill Hall even closer to RHS, right next to its second Hall in Elverton Street.

By November 1913, The Ladies' Kennel Association held one of their most successful

shows at the RHS Hall. *The Times* reported that, 'The entry of 1,030 is the largest ever received, and included many well-known prize-winners. Of these, 183 were Pekingese; 71 Griffons Bruxellois; 64 Pomeranians; 57 Highland white terriers; 44 bulldogs; 39 Cairn-terriers and 15 Fox-terriers but, there were also Old English Sheep-Dogs, Great Danes, Poodles, Irish Setters, Samoyedes and Dachshunds. Foreign breeds included Pyrenean mountain dogs, Persian gazelle hounds, Tibet spaniels and Lhasa terriers. Then, on 3 February 1925 the first annual Winter Show of the Alsatian League & Club of Great Britain took place in the Hall and among them, Claus of Seale, the Prince of Wales's dog.

As interesting were the aristocratic ladies that brought them. The *Illustrated London News* had a regular full-page pictorial in each issue featuring Ladies and their dogs entitled, 'The Woman's Cult of the Dog'. It was clearly important to be seen in Society with the right dog beside you. The following were just a few of those present at these shows. Lady Edward Spencer-Churchill was a regular exhibitor at the Pet Dog Society Championships Shows. So was Lady Sybil Grant. She was the eldest child of Lord Rosebery who had been Prime Minister in 1894. Her mother was the former Hannah de Rothschild, at one time reputed to be the richest woman in England. Lady Sybil was the first person in England to breed the rare Pyrenean Mountain dog, and had also succeeded in breeding a rare strain of dog, the Shetland Toy, which she saved from extinction. By 1914, she had also become one of the leading literary figures of the day – one of her novels being published by Mills & Boon! Lady Kathleen Pilkington had become the 1st President of the French Bulldog Club of England in 1903, following her earlier involvement in setting up the Toy Bulldog Club, but she also was a great supporter of Irish Wolfhounds. Her other passion was collecting foreign birds and was reputed to have one of the best collections in England. Her legacy to dog lovers remains in the Perpetual

Trophy of The Lady Pilkington Memorial Teaset for 'Best in Show', still presented today at the Ladies' Kennel Association National Championship Show. Fanny Wilson became Princess Alexis Dolgorouki by marrying Prince Alexis Dolgorouki, a Chamberlain to the Tsar of Russia. They married when they were both aged 50, part in the Russian Embassy Chapel and part at St Margaret's Church, Westminster. They were great socialites and commissioned Sir Edwin Lutyens to build a house in Taplow called Nashdon – meaning in Russian, 'our home'. Lady Dorothy D'Oyly Carte also exhibited and married Rupert D'Oyly Carte in 1907, five years after he had taken over his late father's role as Chairman of The Savoy

Photo of a woman wearing a Chinchilla coat next to a Chinchilla rabbit at The British Fur Rabbit Society's Rabbit & Fur Show in the Lindley Hall on 12-15 December 1928.

ABOVE *Photograph from an article in* The Tatler *reporting on the Pekingese Club Dog Show, held in aid of Belgian Refugees in the Lindley Hall on 27 January 1915.*

ABOVE RIGHT *Photo of 'Care of Welham', worth over £2,000 at the 1st Annual Winter Show of the Alsatian League & Club of Great Britain held in the Lindley Hall on 3 February 1925.*

Photo of, 'Blistrud of Sears', owned by Mrs M.E. Willoughby of Southampton at the Alsatian League & Club of Great Britain's Championship Show held in the Lindley Hall on 6 February 1930.

Group which included the *Savoy Hotel, Claridges*, the *Berkeley Hotel, Simpsons-in-the-Strand* and *The Grand Hotel*, Rome. He also sustained the famous Gilbert and Sullivan operas his father had successfully promoted and managed.

Another, Corinna Katherine Vereker became Lady Gort when she married her second cousin Lord Gort in February 1911. Gort was then a Lieutenant in the Grenadier Guards and was in charge of the NCO's detailed to bear the coffin and attend the catafalque at King Edward VII's funeral. He later became a highly distinguished soldier during the First World War when he was awarded the Military Cross in 1915, the Distinguished Service Order and Bar in 1917, the Victoria Cross in 1918 and a second Bar to his DSO in 1919. He continued his extraordinary military career rising to become Military Secretary to the War Minister and Chief of the Imperial General Staff, both in 1937. At the outbreak of the Second World War he was given command of the British Expeditionary Force, made an ADC to King George VI in 1940, and later held posts as Governor of Gibraltar and Malta.

Miss Smith's complaint was not the first received as a result of the Society's activities in the Hall and it would by no means be the last. The first recorded complaint had been noted by Council at its 26 June 1906 Meeting, following 'A Grand Bazaar and Floral Fête'

in aid of the Royal Waterloo Hospital for Children and Women, attended by HRH The Duchess of Albany and the Prince and Princess Alexander of Teck. The disturbance concerned was the result of 'hammering and going on all night' when the stalls were being built. In those days shell scheme stands were unavailable and everything had to be put together by carpenters and other tradesmen which was inevitably noisy, especially in the dead of night in a very quiet area of Westminster.

One thing that Stubbs, the architect, had not built into his design for the Hall was

any sound proofing, and in 1920 another complaint from their neighbours was recorded by the RHS Council that, this time, involved noise made by cockerels! When the National Utility Poultry Society (then based at 3 Vincent Square) applied for a tenancy for their 2nd Show in December 1921, the RHS Council agreed to it taking place expressly on the basis that only pullets were exhibited, and not cockerels. The sound of cockerels raising the roof at dawn over Vincent Square could be viewed as romantic, but clearly the residents didn't see it like that. No concern was shown about the fact that daily demonstrations were given at this show on 'the killing and trussing of table poultry by Mr Campbell, a one-armed ex-Service man', as reported in *The Times* on 7 December 1921.

Easton & Robertson, architects for the RHS's subsequent Hall on Elverton Street that opened in 1928, did not really learn from this either. Both Halls were, in effect, giant greenhouses with light-giving glass roofs. With increasing residential developments around the Halls, and increasing concerns from their new occupants, managing noise disturbance would become a priority. In 1993, I found myself in Horseferry Magistrates Court, following a complaint from Nicholas Winterton, MP to Westminster City Council, about noise that had disturbed him during a weekday awards function for *The Grocer* magazine, but on this occasion from the 2nd Hall in Elverton Street, next door to where Mr Winterton lived.

The Grand Bazaar held in June 1906, already referred to and one of many being staged in the Hall during this period, was a great success, and widely reported because of the important cause it was supporting, defraying the cost of the new hospital building. Hospitals were very much in the front line at this time and in need of support, so this and many similar events were strongly supported by Royalty, the gentry, the Church, politicians and the military. Sir Trevor Lawrence, the RHS President, donated £200 (£17,886) to the St Bartholomew's Hospital Rebuilding Fund in 1906, and in the Court Circular of *The Times* on 21 February 1906 it

was announced that 'Princess Christian has, upon the invitation of the Duchess of Albany, become a patroness of the Royal Waterloo Hospital Bazaar and Floral Fête.' The same Circular also announced that Princess Christian had also consented to become patron of the National Association for the Feeble Minded, an organisation involved with another important annual medical exhibition and conference that was staged in the Hall for 30 years up to 1939.

JEYES' DOG BOOK

THIS BOOK of 40 pages is a mine of information of value to all owners and breeders of dogs.

In addition to these more or less common dog troubles, many more serious diseases are dealt with. There is also a breeding table.

ABSCESSES, CYSTS, ULCERS
CANKER IN THE EAR
COLDS, BRONCHITIS, PNEUMONIA
CUTS, WOUNDS, ETC.
DERMATITIS, ECZEMA
DIARRHŒA, DYSENTRY
DISTEMPER, INFLUENZA
FLATULENCE, WIND
FLEAS, LICE, TICKS
GASTRITIS, WORMS
SKIN DISEASES, RINGWORM
SORE FEET

This valuable book written by a well-known Veterinary Surgeon will be sent post free on application to

JEYES' SANITARY COMPOUNDS CO. LTD.,
MILLBROOK, CHIGWELL, ESSEX.

Jeyes' Dog Book *advertisement in the 13th The Scottish Terrier Club's Championship Show catalogue held in the Lindley Hall on 28 February 1947.*

Nursing, Midwives and Medical

The developments being made at that time for the greater recognition and status of nurses and midwives, via important conferences and medical exhibitions of this kind, were taking place in the RHS Hall through the increasingly strong connections being made with the key representatives within these and other areas. On the day of the Bazaar opening the royal party was met by the Bishop of London, Sir George Chubb (Chairman of the Hospital Committee) and the Lady Mayoress. Also present was Arthur Stanley, MP (Honorary Treasurer), who in 1916 as Sir Arthur Stanley established the Royal College of Nursing with

Photo of 3rd Annual Nursing & Midwifery Conference & Exhibition, held in the Lindley Hall on 28-30 April 1910.

Dame Sarah Swift and in 1927 was president of the Incorporated Association of Hospital Officers, and opened their fourth annual Congress that ran alongside the first Hospitals and Institutions Exhibition, both held in the RHS Hall. The royal party the Princess of Wales, the Queen of Spain and the Queen-Mother of the Netherlands – all presided at the stalls and sold many of the articles that they had provided. These included a large collection of Indian toys, dolls, souvenir fans and personally embroidered linen, cushions and covers.

On 27 April 1910, the 3rd Nursing & Midwifery Conference & Exhibition took

Poster for the 3rd Annual Nursing & Midwifery Conference & Exhibition, opened by HRH Princess Christian of Schleswig-Holstein, held in the Lindley Hall on 27-30 April 1910. The Conference was held in the London County Council Technical Institute (now known as Westminster Kingsway College) next door to the Hall.

place. The exhibition itself was in the Hall, but the conference was held in the London County Council Institute next door. It had transferred from the Grafton Galleries in Bond Street and the Cavendish Rooms in Mortimer Street where it had been held in the previous two years. This had been organised by Mr Ernest Schofield, from the British & Colonial Druggist Company, then based at 22-4 Great Portland Street. His company, that also produced a publication of the same name, had been serving the pharmaceutical and druggist trades since 1886. They had also been organising annual Chemist Society Exhibitions since 1894, and first brought this into the RHS Hall in 1905. It had been Burroughs Wellcome & Co. that had revolutionised the way that pharmaceuticals were produced by deciding to machine manufacture their own compressed pills that, hitherto, had been largely made by pestle and

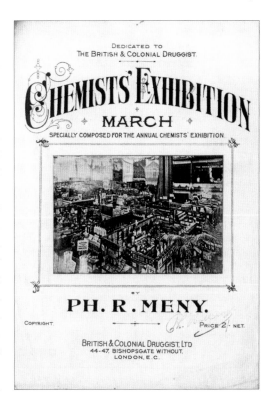

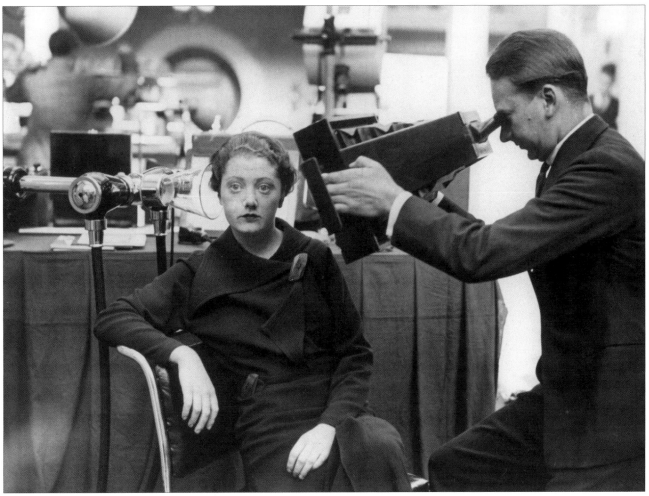

mortar. This was when very few manufacturing pharmacists existed. Silas Burroughs died of pneumonia in 1895 leaving Henry Wellcome to forge ahead with his worldwide enterprise, becoming the leading figure in the British Pharmaceutical industry. By the time of the 1931 London Medical Exhibition, Burroughs Wellcome & Co. (The Wellcome Foundation) were exhibiting 250 of their products. Henry Wellcome came to see Thomas E. Sedgwick, Assistant Secretary of the RHS, in June 1905 to talk about a tenancy for a Historical Medicine Exhibition that he was interested in launching. This does not appear to have gone ahead. However, Schofield did launch the first London Medical Exhibition that year in the Hall. Both shows would continue in the RHS Hall for many years – the London Medical Exhibition until November 1962. The RHS Hall would also become a centre for pioneering new dental and optical trade exhibitions, as a result. These early medical and nursing events would lead to major national and international medical congresses covering the fields of nursing, midwifery, medicine, surgery, pharmacology and physiology. One such event that Schofield also organised, and was described by *The Times* as 'probably the largest Health Exhibition ever held in the World', took place at the Imperial Institute in August 1913 and ran in tandem with the 17th International Congress of Medicine opened by Prince Arthur of Connaught on behalf of the King at the Royal Albert Hall. Prince Arthur also opened the 1st Hospitals and Institutions Exhibitions at the RHS in 1927, already referred to, and also organised by Schofield.

HRH Princess Christian of Schleswig-Holstein, acting in her capacity as Patron to The Midwives' Institute and Trained Nurses' Club, formally opened the 1910 Nursing & Midwifery Conference & Exhibition. As has already been noted, she had also recently become Patron to the National Association for the Feeble Minded and one of the main conference subjects was 'Mental Nursing & 'Feeble-Minded Unmarried Mothers in Workhouses'. Other topics covered were

'Nursing in Un-separated Workhouses, and Reference to the Report of the Royal Commission on the Poor Laws', 'State Registration of Trained Nurses' and 'The Living Wage for Midwives in Rural Districts – The Poor Mother'. Among the speakers at the Conference were prominent Doctors and Matrons from hospitals around the country, Dr E.B. Reckitt of Reckitt & Coleman, and representatives of respective Associations and bodies such as the Workhouse Nursing Association, Royal British Nurses' Association and the National Association of Midwives. Lady Acland spoke of the friction that existed in some rural districts between doctors and midwives, and Dr Bygott strongly objected to the system adopted by some county nursing associations that did not

Exhibition programme for the 4th Annual Nursing & Midwifery Conference & Exhibition, held in the Lindley Hall on 4-7 April 1911. The Conference was held in the London County Council Technical Institute (now known as Westminster Kingsway College) next door to the Hall, as it had been in 1910.

Photo of nurse, c.1912.

allow midwives to attend illegitimate births. Dr Bernard Hollander strongly deprecated the use of alcohol for any mental cases, and recommended that nurses should never drink in the presence of their patients! By the time of the 6th Conference and Exhibition in 1913, the executive committees for nursing and midwives contained 34 Matrons from all of the main London hospitals and infirmaries, as well as from Birmingham, Sheffield, Cardiff and Leicester. In 1914, the principal theme taken up was 'surgery in the slums' where a slum apartment (either in a city or remote country district) was reconstructed and depicted 'before and after its transformation by a trained nurse into an operating room'. The 'State Registration of Nurses' was still the headline subject for the conference but, unsurprisingly, 'Women's Work in War' was also there. The last Nursing & Midwifery Conference & Exhibition held in the RHS Hall took place in 1939, opened by Princess Marie Louise who had become its Patron. By then, it had changed to be under the promotional mantle of *Nursing Mirror and Midwives Journal*.

The backdrop to the importance of these conferences and exhibitions was that, even though The Midwives' Institute existed to represent midwives and midwifery (its original aims were to 'raise the efficiency and improve the status of midwives and to petition parliament for their recognition') and, in 1902, it had been successful in having the first Midwives' Act for England and Wales passed, it still faced what would be a further 17-year petitioning process to provide the necessary statutory provisions for training and training grants by local supervisory bodies.

Childbirth in the late 19th century and early 20th was often difficult and dangerous. Maternal mortality stood at around 500 per 100,000 births compared with approximately 12 per 100,000 today. In 1903, the maternal mortality rate was only negligibly lower than that of 1847. In Westminster, out of 3,185 infants born, 370 died before the age of one. Few women had access to trained attendants in childbirth and many of the poor had to depend on local untrained midwives. Like surgeons of an earlier age, prior to the 1902 Act, they were untrained, unqualified and uncertified. Any woman, or for that matter, any man could practise midwifery. Some practitioners were prostitutes who were reputedly paid in gin.

Nurses were facing similar issues of recognition and status. However, unlike their midwifery colleagues, they had an extraordinary and protracted battle over 30 years to secure government recognition of their professional status which finally arrived in November 1919, as the Registration Act 1919. Seen as part of the overall suffrage issue by many women, nurses' demands were seen by government (and by many doctors) as a threat, and it continued to take the view that their work should be seen as philanthropic.

This had not been helped by the attitude of no less an establishment figure than Florence Nightingale who was opposed to any form of public registration for nurses and acted accordingly to prevent it. She believed that nursing was a vocation and an art, and should only be followed by those who had a 'calling'. Queen Alexandra, Princess Christian and Princess Louise appeared not to fully support Florence Nightingale's view and, instead, were very pro-active in supporting the progress

Photo from the 18 February 1939 issue of Nursing Mirror *of HRH Princess Marie Louise opening the 29th Hospitals, Nursing, Midwifery & Public Health Exhibition and Conference as Patron, held in the Lawrence Hall. This was organised by* Nursing Mirror Ltd, and Midwives Journal *and held on 13-17 February 1939.*

A BOUQUET FOR PRINCESS MARIE LOUISE

when she attended the opening on Monday of the Twenty-Ninth Hospitals, Nursing, Midwifery and Public Health Exhibition and Conference at the New Horticultural Hall, Westminster. Her Highness is Patron of the Exhibition.

Poster labels used for advertising the respective annual Chemists' Exhibitions held in the Lawrence Hall during the years 1931-5.

and development of nurses in this way via the patronages they could, and did, bestow on many nursing organisations and events.

The British Journal of Nursing Supplement on 28 April 1910 described who would be taking part in the 3rd Nursing & Midwifery Conference & Exhibition. Amongst other exhibitors were, 'Bovril Ltd (of international reputation), Cadbury Bros. (of pure cocoa fame), Coleman and Co., Keen Robinson (the friend of the monthly nurse and midwife), J.S. Fry and Sons (whose chocolate is eagerly sought for), Gas Light and Coke Co. (whose gas fires are now indispensable in nursing homes and private homes) and W.H. Bailey and Son, at whose stand, and in whose Oxford Street establishment, the midwife who cannot find what she needs must be hard to please.'

Meanwhile, medical progress was in evidence, and the *Daily Express* in its 7 May 1907 report of the 13th Chemists' Exhibition at the Hall wrote, 'A veritable armoury of all that shields man and destroys man's enemies proves that

A selection of bottle/tube labels from Cameron's Pharmaceutical Chemist, Seaford, East Sussex, England.

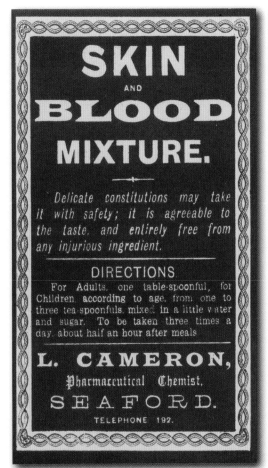

SKIN
AND
BLOOD
MIXTURE.

Delicate constitutions may take it with safety; it is agreeable to the taste, and entirely free from any injurious ingredient.

DIRECTIONS.

For Adults, one table-spoonful, for Children according to age, from one to three tea-spoonfuls, mixed in a little water and sugar. To be taken three times a day, about half an hour after meals.

L. CAMERON,
Pharmaceutical Chemist,
SEAFORD.

TELEPHONE 192.

CAMERON'S
SUNBURN
LOTION,

FOR WHITENING AND SOFTENING
THE SKIN.

Removes and prevents all Roughness, Redness of the Hands or Face, leaving the Skin delicately soft, smooth and white.

SOLE MANUFACTURERS:
L. CAMERON & SON,
Pharmacists,
BROAD STREET, SEAFORD.

SHAKE THE BOTTLE.

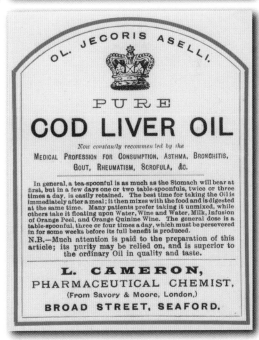

OL. JECORIS ASELLI.

PURE
COD LIVER OIL

Now constantly recommended by the
MEDICAL PROFESSION FOR CONSUMPTION, ASTHMA, BRONCHITIS, GOUT, RHEUMATISM, SCROFULA, &c.

In general, a tea-spoonful is as much as the Stomach will bear at first, but in a few days one or two table-spoonfuls, twice or three times a day, is easily retained. The best time for taking the Oil is immediately after a meal; it then mixes with the food and is digested at the same time. Many patients prefer taking it unmixed, while others take it floating upon Water, Wine and Water, Milk, Infusion of Orange Peel, and Orange Quinine Wine. The general dose is a table-spoonful, three or four times a day, which must be persevered in for some weeks before its full benefit is produced.

N.B.—Much attention is paid to the preparation of this article; its purity may be relied on, and is superior to the ordinary Oil in quality and taste.

L. CAMERON,
PHARMACEUTICAL CHEMIST,
(From Savory & Moore, London,)
BROAD STREET, SEAFORD.

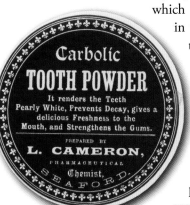

Carbolic
TOOTH POWDER
It renders the Teeth Pearly White, Prevents Decay, gives a delicious Freshness to the Mouth, and Strengthens the Gums.

PREPARED BY
L. CAMERON,
PHARMACEUTICAL
Chemist,
SEAFORD.

the science of the present day is indeed living science. It bears most encouraging witness to the fact that we are gaining rapidly on the ills and diseases which dog our steps through life. Particularly interesting is the exhibit of the by-products of the slaughter house. One of these, Suprarenelin, staunches the flow of blood at a cut or wound.' At the later May 1910 Exhibition the *Daily Express* reported on a series of novel medicines and preparations with equally novel claims. 'A phosphorus food which glows with a dazzling blue light in the dark was the chief feature of the Chemists' Exhibition. It is contended that the new food will make new men, and giants will walk about the land', was one claim. Another was, 'A non-inflammable benzoline, Securetine, is shown for cleaning dresses and gloves. If the liquid is poured into the hand and a match applied the flame fizzles out as if it were dipped in water. It is an absolutely dry shampoo'. But perhaps the one that brings a smile to the face in the knowledge that man's vanity was as strong then as it is today was the

'Birch Tree hair lotion, which it is claimed prevents the hair from falling out, and makes new hair grow with extraordinary rapidity'.

At the October 1905 London Medical Exhibition small pieces of Opium made from Yorkshire poppies, and pills coated with 22-carat gold leaf, had been displayed in the Hall. And at the 1910 Exhibition, equally exotic products were being displayed. The *Daily Express* reported on this and wrote, 'A vegetable antiseptic has been evolved from the Duke of Edinburgh rose which is made up into small aromatic lozenges. These, when dissolved in the mouth, wage relentless war against the countless millions of those bacilli which set up the conditions known as 'cold in the head'. The reporter also noted, 'Bottled Mud, imported from the Spanish springs of La Toja, and strongly recommended for rheumatism, gout, anæmia, neurasthenia, and many other diseases and complaints. Henceforward, it will be possible for a sufferer from, say, acute rheumatism to avoid a long and frequently costly sojourn at a Continental spring or spa and to enjoy a mud bath 'cure' in his own bed.'

These exhibitions were aimed mainly at doctors, chemists and all those involved in the medical profession, but the general public was also allowed into the Chemists' Exhibition in 1907, where almost 100 principal druggists and druggists' sundriesmen from throughout the UK exhibited. As an inducement for them to attend, the organisers had given those chemists that came from outside London, rebates from the cost of their return fares to London, and all London chemists that lived within a four-mile radius of the Hall had their cab fares paid. The general public who did visit were clearly not the poor, but the well to do and rising middle classes who could afford to take long and frequently costly sojourns to Continental springs or spas. However, both of these shows organised by Ernest Schofield were considered revolutionary and changed the way medical products and medicine had previously been brought to the attention of the medical practitioners who prescribed them to their patients. Hitherto, new information about pills, lotions, medication and remedies had

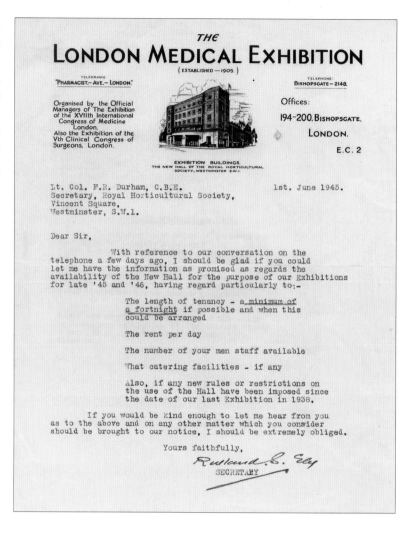

been mainly distributed by hand to individual doctors and chemists. Doctors in London had never before been offered an exhibition where they could so conveniently find everything they wanted in one place.

In September 1909, another 'professional trade show' where a special series of demonstrations and lectures took place is also recorded for the first time in the Hall. Billed by *The Times* as the 'International Dental Exhibition', they reported that, 'The exhibition comprises a remarkable display of dental instruments, chiefly of British manufacture. A complete set of the various patterns of teeth manufactured numbers no fewer than 1,008.' This was organised by the Society of Extractors and Adapters of Teeth and was held annually until 1912 that became the Incorporated Dental Society, who went on to stage landmark dental exhibitions in the Hall until 27 August 1915. In 1913,

Letter from The London Medical Exhibition to the Secretary of the RHS requesting prospective tenancies, dated 1 June 1945.

the *Daily Express* reported that, 'An important proposal to add a dental panel to the existing machinery of the Insurance Act, with a view to combating the alarming deterioration in teeth by providing State insurance patients with free dentistry, is being eagerly discussed among members of the Incorporated Dental Society, who are holding their annual congress at the Horticultural Hall, Westminster. *The Express* understands that Mr Lloyd George has already been approached on the subject by members of the Dental Society and has held out hopes that dentistry may be added to the present insurance benefits in 1915 and 1916.' However, credit for bringing greater awareness of the Dental trade, and the way in which it worked, must be given to Ernest Schofield who had seized the moment in April 1906 by organising the first exhibition of its kind in London at the Cavendish Rooms in Mortimer Street, called the Dental Surgeons' Exhibition. The dates of 23-7 April were also exactly the same as those he had confirmed with the RHS for his 12th Chemist Society's Exhibition and, clearly, promoted them together. Interestingly, his wife would take over his mantle during the First World War by organising an important National Welfare and Economy Exhibition that was the first event to be staged in the new London County Council's County Hall on London's South Bank, held between June and August of 1917.

Travel and Exploration

Significantly different was The Travel Exhibition, the first of its kind staged in London, held 18 May-8 June 1907. This was organised by A. Staines Manders of 75 Chancery Lane, London, who had already been connected with many exhibitions in Australia and New Zealand (Sydney, Garden Palace, 1879); (Melbourne, 1880-1 & 1888); (Adelaide, 1881 & 1887); (Perth, 1882); (Christchurch, 1882) plus the Colonial and Indian (London, 1886 & 1905) and the Health, Food and Hygiene Exhibition (London, 1906). The Colonial and Indian Exhibition of 1886 had taken place in the Royal Horticultural Society's then Gardens (behind the Albert Hall), to commemorate Queen Victoria's Golden Jubilee – in fact she opened the exhibition herself. The exhibition was a huge success with an attendance of over five and half million. It also made a profit of £34,643 (£3.27 million) that was used to set up London's Imperial Institute after which Arthur Balfour, the future Conservative Prime Minister between 1902 and 1905, served on the committee that established Imperial College. In 1910 Manders organised the International Pure Food and Allied Trades Exhibition at the RHS Hall, clearly as a result of his involvement in the 1906 Health Show. In 1914 Manders was also involved in the London International Rubber and Allied Trades Exhibition that was initially booked in the Hall in 1908, but later cancelled and transferred to Olympia because it had been oversubscribed. Later still, following the First World War, Manders wrote a book intended for 'ANZAC, Canadians and all other soldiers of the Empire' entitled, *Colonials Guide to London*.

The theme of his Travel Exhibition at the RHS Hall in 1907 continued to reflect

Catalogue cover for the Travel Exhibition, held in the Lindley Hall on 18 May-8 June 1907. The Exhibition was opened by the Chairman of its Executive Committee, Colonel W.J. Bosworth on 18 May 1907.

CATALOGUE

OF THE

TRAVEL EXHIBITION

18TH MAY TO 8TH JUNE 1907,

HELD AT THE

ROYAL HORTICULTURAL HALL,

VINCENT SQUARE, WESTMINSTER.

Opened by

COLONEL W. J. BOSWORTH,

ON SATURDAY, 18TH MAY 1907.

Mitchell Hughes and Clarke, Printers, 140 Wardour Street, London, W.

3 Pence

Britain's past exploratory and colonial exploits, but also highlighted the pioneering new ways of aviation, and of travelling by motor car and caravan. The 5th Annual Exhibition of Motor Vehicles had been held at Olympia just six months earlier, cars were being raced on Blackpool's famous front and an indication of how relevant these new developments were becoming to the aristocracy, and those who could afford them, may be seen from the Court Circular of *The Times* on 10 January 1911 that warranted the announcement that, 'Lady Garvagh is leaving town tomorrow for a motor-car tour on the Riviera.' By this time, of course, the motor car was becoming popular and the days of opposition to it, led mainly from the horse, harness and coach building interested parties, was waning. Opposition had been most vociferous from horse-breeders and representations by several MPs were made in Parliament. Mr Burdett-Coutts, MP had been one of these! At the turn of the century cars numbered just a few thousand. By 1934 that number had shot up to two million.

However, in 1907 the most accessible and widely used method of travelling for most was still by horse and cart or carriage, but cycling was also widespread and the Cyclists' Touring Club (CTC), another organisation based in Victoria Street, at No. 47, was also at the Travel Exhibition offering advice and support, special hotel tariffs and unique touring facilities. [It was also at this event that the first evidence of the use of an external floral contractor was made by the RHS, rather than use flowers it could produce itself at its garden in Wisley, Surrey. This remains the case to this day and highlights a misconception that many event organisers have that the RHS acts in the same way as a florist. The contractor was Stroud & Co., Decorative Florists, who were aptly based at 182 Green Lanes, Finsbury Park. They were appointed floral decorators at many London exhibitions held at the Royal Agricultural Hall, Olympia, Earl's Court and the RHS Hall.][1]

1   Floral contractor

Here was an exhibition that was very largely supported by prominent Council and other Members of The Royal Geographical Society, itself the embodiment of exploration across the globe, and 18 Associations and Clubs, including the Royal Automobile Club of Britain and Ireland, the Æronautical Society of Great Britain, the Polyglot Club, the Railway Club, the National Camping Club and the Imperial South Africa Association. More than 100 of Britain's most dedicated explorers, pioneers, geographers, colonialists and aristocrats had become Patrons and advisers to the exhibition. The President of the Alpine Club, the Premier of New Zealand, the Director of Royal Gardens, Kew and the Poet Laureate of the day, Alfred Austin, were also included in this roll call. One such member was Colonel Sir Thomas Hungerford Holdich who, as a military surveyor, had travelled to many parts of the world, and in India to Rajputana, Bhutan, Central India, Central Provinces, the North West Frontier Province, Waziristan, Baluchistan and Kashmir.

The Chairman of the Executive Committee was Colonel W.J. Bosworth. He was The Automobile Association's first Chairman (founded just two years earlier) and had been issued with the very first AA Badge, No.1, in April 1906. Notable Vice-Presidents of the

ABOVE   *Pamphlet cover of PART 2 from a series of sketches at the Colonial and Indian Exhibition, 1886, by John Dimsdale. The Exhibition had taken place on the site of the Royal Horticultural Society's Gardens in Kensington to commemorate Queen Victoria's Golden Jubilee.*

RIGHT   *Page from the 1907 Travel Exhibition catalogue showing the President, Vice-Presidents, and Executive Committee.*

RIGHT   *Enamel badge of The Camping Club of Great Britain & Ireland, 1901. They were exhibitors at the 1907 Travel Exhibition.*

Travel Exhibition, London, 1907.

President.

SIR GILBERT PARKER, D.C.L., M.P.

Vice-Presidents.

HIS HIGHNESS THE AGA KHAN, G.C.I.E. (Bombay).
THE RIGHT HON. THE EARL OF ASHBURNHAM.
THE RIGHT HON. THE EARL OF DARTMOUTH.
THE RIGHT HON. THE EARL OF LONSDALE.
LORD MONTAGUE OF BEAULIEU.
THE HON. ARTHUR STANLEY, M.V.O., M.P.
THE HON. C. S. ROLLS, M.A.
COLONEL SIR CLEMENT M. ROYDS, C.B.
COLONEL SIR THOS. HUNGERFORD HOLDICH, K.C.M.G., etc.
  (Council Royal Geographical Society).
SIR WILLIAM J. BELL, LL.D., J.P., etc.
SIR E. NOEL WALKER, K.C.M.G.
SIR JOHN FURLEY, C.B., D.L.
SIR HENRY SETON-KARR, C.M.G.
SIR M. M. BHOWNAGGREE, K.C.I.E.
SIR T. V. S. ANGIER.
COLONEL C. E. YATE, C.S.I., C.M.G.
MAJOR B. BADEN POWELL.
MAJOR ARTHUR HAGGARD.
CAPTAIN FREDERICK G. JACKSON.
CAPTAIN R. MUIRHEAD COLLINS, C.M.G. (Representing the Commonwealth of Australia).
ALGERNON E. ASPINALL, Esq. (West India Committee).
GEORGE CAVE, Esq., K.C., M.P.
CHARLES BRIGHT, Esq., F.R.S.E.
S. F. EDGE, Esq.
CHARLES JARROTT, Esq.

Executive Committee.

COLONEL W. J. BOSWORTH (Chairman).
SIR WILLIAM J. BELL, LL.D., etc.
SIR E. NOEL WALKER, K.C.M.G.
THE HON. C. S. ROLLS, M.A.
COLONEL C. E. YATE, C.S.I., C.M.G.
CAPTAIN FREDERICK G. JACKSON.

Madrid and Paris-Vienna. In the latter, travelling at a speed of around 75 mph, he crashed into a tree. In 1898, Rolls became one of the founder members of the Automobile Club (later commanded to become the RAC by King Edward VII) and in 1900 he won the *Daily Mail* 'Thousand Miles Reliability Trial'. In 1902, he exhibited his cars for the first time at the Agricultural Hall under the name of Charles S. Rolls & Co. He was also a founder member of the Aero Club in 1901 and a keen balloonist and aviator who, tragically, died flying a Wright Brothers plane in 1910. He had been the first person to fly a double crossing of the Channel, and also the first Briton to die in an aviation accident. Extraordinarily, his famous Rolls-Royce Company saw its final demise on 6 June 1998, when it was sold by Vickers to German car manufacturer, VW, in the very same Hall that he had visited 91 years earlier at the Travel Exhibition. His grandson attended and was violently opposed to the sale, but lost to a majority of the shareholders assembled in the Hall who accepted the Board's proposal to do so.

Lord Montague famously took King Edward VII for a ride in his new four-cylinder 12hp Daimler for what he later claimed in 1926 to be 'if not his first, at any rate for the second time he had ever been in a car'. If we are to believe the claim made by Charles Rolls that King Edward VII's first ride in a motor car was in his own, then his second was in Lord Montague's car. More memorable and important a ride was T.E. Lawrence's triumphant entrance into Damascus in an open-topped Rolls-Royce on 1 October 1918, although somewhat more grubby and sand-blown than ideally should have been for such an occasion.

Another Vice-President, and also a keen aviator and balloonist, was Major Baden Baden-Powell, brother of Chief Scout, Lord Baden-Powell. (By coincidence, in May 1900 he had been a member of the relief forces at the 'Relief of Mafeking' that had secured his brother's safety who had been under siege up to that time.) In 1902, he became President of

event were The Aga Khan, Lord Montague of Beaulieu and Charles Stewart Rolls. Rolls, whose partnership with Frederick Henry Royce had begun in 1904 and became formally known as Rolls-Royce in 1906, also produced the first 'Silver-Ghost' model that year. Rolls had bought his first car in 1896 and subsequently entered in a number of races, notably the Paris-Ostend, Bordeaux-Biarritz, Paris-Berlin, Paris-the Æronautical Society and, in 1908, went to France to fly with Wilbur Wright and was present at many of the major pioneer balloon ascents taking place in Europe and the USA at that time. He had visited the Zeppelin works in Germany and had prophesied their military use of Zeppelins against Britain in a time of future war, one that was to become a catastrophic reality, but was derided by his peers and the governments of the period before the First World War. It is not surprising, therefore, that the exhibition also featured the Spencer Brother's Captive Hot-Air Balloon, tethered in 'the Grounds' at the rear of the Hall. Visitors could take advantage of six ascents an hour to a height of 1,000 feet during the day and evening at a cost of five shillings (£19.70) – this was additional to the one shilling (£4) exhibition admittance fee. I'm not sure what the neighbours thought about that! It must have been a wonderful experience as the London skyline at that period would not have been impaired by later modern buildings and construction. Some of London's first aerial maps had been plotted from balloons. Also at the rear of the Hall was a 'portable swimming tent', 18ft by 12ft, holding 3,000 gallons of water displayed, and demonstrated, by the Army & Navy Stores. Whether you could dive into the pool from the balloon was not clear!

A flying machine of a very different kind on display was The Frost and Hutchinson Experimental Flying Machine. This had wings constructed of artificial feathers, arranged anatomically and mechanically on the natural principles of a bird's wing. The catalogue entry for this dubious contraption stated that, 'This machine has been worked under power, and has given promising results … a small syndicate is required to carry on the experiments, primarily as research and sport, and secondly to develop suitable commercial results.' Like Baden-Powell he was rebutted by the War Office when he offered his own patent to the Secretary of State for War. The reply he received was unequivocal and said, 'The nation does not intend to adopt aerial navigation as a means of warfare'. How appallingly short-sighted and wrong they were at that time. By the time of the Second World War they had learnt from the error of their ways but, at a terrible cost in the First World War that could have been avoided had they listened to these early pioneers of flight. In fact, it would be an Italian pilot, Lieutenant Giulio Gavotti, who was the first person to conduct the first ever air raid in November 1911 in Libya, when he literally threw out by hand small bombs from his biplane.

Someone whose flying machine was not on display, but who had claimed to have flown a 'heavier than air machine' 10 years before the Wright Brothers was Sir Hiram Maxim. His legendary 'Maxim Flyer' first flight at Baldwyn's Park in the Borough of Bexley in July 1894 was watched by the Prince of Wales, Rudyard Kipling and Sir Arthur Conan Doyle. H.G. Wells had also been there and later, in his Science Fiction masterpiece, 'The War of the Worlds' depicted a Martian flying machine not dissimilar to Maxims. However, Maxim became better known for his Maxim Machine Gun that had first been used by Britain's colonial forces in the Matabele War in 1893-4. In one engagement, 50 soldiers fought off 5,000 Matabele warriors with just four Maxim guns. His notoriety with both inventions enabled his place among the other patrons of the Travel Exhibition, but it would be interesting to know which one was considered the most important. His visit to the Hall during the Travel Exhibition would not be his last as he was later to return in October 1909 to open officially the 3rd Annual Model Engineer Exhibition that had been launched in the Hall two years before in 1907. His talents as a mechanical engineer and weapons designer were passed on to his son, Hiram Percy Maxim, who invented the 'Maxim Silencer' a suppressor for firearms (patented in 1909) and a muffler for gasoline engines. However, he was better known for his early amateur radio experiments in America, where he lived.

Captain Frederick George Jackson was an arctic explorer who, in 1893-4, had explored the Tundra in arctic Lapland and Russia and, in 1894-7, commanded the Jackson-Harmsworth expedition that explored Franz Josef Land.

Jackson proved that Franz Josef Land was an archipelago, not a continent, as had been suspected. His chance encounter in 1896 with Fridtjof Nansen and F.H. Johansen, who were returning by sledge from their attempted journey to the North Pole, probably saved their lives. In later years Jackson became a well-known African traveller so was also well qualified to become a member of the Travel Exhibition's Executive Committee. One of the exhibits was his Polar exhibition equipment. Also on show and, as important, were the relics of the late Antarctic Expedition of Captain Scott lent by Petty Officer Ernest E. Joyce who had accompanied Scott in 'Discovery'. These included a rather macabre display of the teeth of the last sledge dogs that died on Scott's Furthest South Journey. Having said that, Damien Hurst's recent art forms have extended whatever boundaries existed since then.

The Army & Navy Stores displayed a variety of leather Medicine Cases (Tin Lined) – (I have seen a similar one on display in Zanzibar's Museum used by African explorer,

Dr Livingston.) Bellamy's Chair, or Litter, with Sun Awning complete, could also be purchased for travelling in the African Bush for the sum of £5 17s. 6d. (£525). A helpful diagram showed how two African Porters would carry this on their heads by way of poles that stretched forwards and backwards from the chair itself. Piggott Brothers and Co. Ltd was also there offering an array of tenting for exploring, surveying, mining or engineering. The RHS would later enjoy a long association with Piggott's as they supplied them with their own tent and marquee requirements, at their Chelsea Flower Shows, in particular. Dr Jaeger's 'Outfits for Abroad' were also advertised with the statement that a Diploma had been awarded for a Gold Medal in recognition of their 'Sanitary Woollen System', a claim no longer used in their marketing today!

McDoddies were based in Bermondsey and produced British Vegetable Preserves (Dry). They had a display of over 20 varieties and claimed that these had been selected, among many others, by Lieut. Shackleton,

RIGHT *Page from the 1907 Travel Exhibition catalogue showing Army & Navy Co-Operative Society, Ltd, camp equipment, 'For Travelling in the African Bush'.*

FAR RIGHT *Page from the 1907 Travel Exhibition catalogue showing Piggott Brothers and Co. Ltd, tents and equipment, 'For Exploring, Surveying, Mining, Engineering, etc'.*

Commander for the South Pole Exhibition that would set sail aboard 'Nimrod' from Lyttelton, New Zealand on New Year's Day, 1908 and would become known as the British Antarctic Expedition 1907-9. The extent to which this fired the imagination among the public can be gauged by the fact that some 30,000 people gathered to wave them off.

Also, probably for the first time ever, was a public display by members of the legendary Legion of Frontiersmen with many artefacts, native implements and curios that they had gathered from far-flung corners of the globe during their travels. Formed by Roger Pocock only one year earlier in 1904, the Frontiersmen were to be 'the eyes and ears of the Empire in times of War' and came close to becoming the first official British intelligence gathering and counter-intelligence organisation. They were also to become famous as the first British troops into action in 1914.

The Legion was limited to veterans discharged from the Forces, and men who had been trained by work and travel 'in wild countries or at sea'. It went on to explain that, 'these men, who have lived by the trades of travel, are well fitted for service as a Field Intelligence Corps. Although officially recognised, the Legion is a self-governing and self-supporting society on which the sun never sets, because its membership extends throughout the world. Although started entirely without capital, at the end of the first year, 23 March last, the Corps was able to put 1,000 men into the field. 29 men have been cowboys or stock riders, 20 have been sailors and 33 have served in engineering trades.' The description is wonderfully romantic and sums up the atmosphere of the period where young men (and women) set out across continents to explore, discover and forge new trails and writers such as John Buchan, Rudyard Kipling and Rider Haggard fuelled their readers' imaginations with stories of adventure and derring-do. Indeed, the Canadian Emigration Department were also there to encourage people to develop the land and become 'Homesteaders'. (My Swiss ancestors did exactly that in 1904, and the postcards they sent back from the small towns and communities of Margo and Invernay, Saskatchewan, that they joined and helped develop, look not much different from a 'Wild West' Cowboy film set.) It had been Roger Pocock's experience in Canada serving in North-West Mounted Police (the forerunner to the Royal Canadian Mounted Police) that had formed the basis of the Legion's uniform, but more importantly, his far wider-ranging ideas for service to the State were more advanced than Baden Powell's Boy Scout movement. However, Pocock could not compete with Baden Powell's national hero status that eclipsed these.

Prince Louis of Battenberg became one of the founders of the Legion in 1905

Page from the 1907 Travel Exhibition catalogue showing three exhibitors, including the legendary 'The Legion of Frontiersmen.'

28   TRAVEL EXHIBITION, 1907.

36. THE AGENT-GENERAL FOR THE CAPE OF GOOD HOPE, 100 Victoria Street, Westminster, London, S.W. Photographs, Pictures, Pamphlets illustrating the Cape Colony and Cape Government Railways.

37. CANADIAN GOVERNMENT EMIGRATION DEPARTMENT, 11 and 12 Charing Cross, London, W.C.—Specimens of Canadian Grain, Fruit, Minerals, Views of Canada, etc., in charge of a Canadian Government Official, who will supply information and advice. Publications descriptive of Canada, and Maps, may be obtained free of charge at the Stand.

———

A Collection of Coloured Prints depicting Travel in the Early Days by the Royal Mail Coaches have been kindly lent by JOSEPH GREGO, Esq., and are distributed in different parts of the Exhibition. Title is attached to each Print.

———

A Collection of Early Railway Photographs and Oil Paintings, lent by A. R. BELL, Esq., "The Locomotive Magazine," London.

NOTE.—These pictures are not numbered, but will be found in various parts of the building, with full title on each.

———

THE LEGION OF FRONTIERSMEN is an Eye and Ear Department to assist His Majesty's Forces in time of War. It is limited to veterans discharged from the Forces, and men who have been trained by work and travel in wild countries or at sea. These men, who have lived by the trades of travel, are well fitted for service as a Field Intelligence Corps. Although officially recognized, the Legion is a self-governing and self-supporting society on which the sun never sets, because its membership extends throughout the world. Although started entirely without capital, at the end of the first year, March 23rd last, the Corps was able to put 1000 men into the field. Taking the records at random of 100 men it has been found that they hold 19 commissions and 85 decorations. That 29 men have been cowboys or stock riders, 20 have been sailors, 33 have served in the engineering trades. There are five frontier qualifications per man, and the average age is only 33. It is natural that such a corps of travellers, any squadron of which can furnish men who know all trades and countries and many languages, should be exhibiting at the Travel Exhibition. A few carefully selected exhibitors are able to display here the appliances of travel and the hunting trophies which illustrate all the great wild regions. A member of the Legion will be present at the Exhibition to furnish further details to enquirers.

The Committee beg to acknowledge the assistance rendered to the Exhibition by the Legion. Many interesting Exhibits have been lent by the Members, and will be found in different parts of the Building.

and his granddaughter, The Countess Mountbatten of Burma is the present Patron of the renamed Legion of Frontiersmen of the Commonwealth. Many men of influence and power either belonged to The Legion or were strongly supportive of it, from Arthur Conan Doyle to Edgar Wallace. Lord Lonsdale became its first President and he was also one of the 24 Vice-Presidents of The Travel Exhibition.

The name Frederick Courteney Selous is legendary amongst those who have a love of Africa, and Tanzania in particular. There, the world's largest game reserve is named after him, and in 1982 UNESCO named it a World Heritage Site. Selous went out to Africa and set himself up as a professional game hunter at the age of 20. His name appears frequently in the definitive *Rowland Ward's Records of Big Game* that listed the full details of game bagged by the Big Game Hunters of the period from size of horns to country and region where they were shot. Tanzania was a German colony at the time. He was epitomised as the British colonial gentleman and big game hunter, eulogised by President Roosevelt who accompanied him on game hunts, and believed also to have been the person on whom Rider Haggard's *Allan Quatermain* was based. However, he was also a naturalist and prolific author of repute and a memorial bust of him in the main hall of the Natural History Museum, London, bears testament to that. At the age of 64, at the start of the First World War in 1915, he was recruited by a Frontiersman, Colonel Daniel Patrick Driscoll, into the 25th Fusiliers in East Africa fighting the Germans along the coast between Mombasa and Dar Es Salaam. Colonel Driscoll did so because of the specific knowledge and expertise Selous had of the region.

Selous claimed that he never carried out any service for the Legion of Frontiersmen itself, but the connections were certainly there in 1907 when Selous also agreed to become a patron of the Travel Exhibition together with another big game hunter, Sir Henry Seton-Karr, and Major Arthur Haggard who were vice-presidents. Seton-Karr later became Chairman of the Executive Council of the Legion. The last word goes to Rudyard Kipling who wrote

enigmatically, 'There's a legion that never was listed that carries no colours or crest, but split in a thousand detachments, is breaking the road for the rest'. It is highly likely that Kipling also visited Mander's first Travel Exhibition, and by November that year he had been named as one of the vice-presidents for a greatly expanded and newly named, 'World's Touring, Sport, Pastimes, and Travel Exhibition' to be held at Olympia in July the following year.

Empire

The extravagant and extraordinary Delhi Durbar of 1903, that had been held to commemorate the coronation of King Edward VII and Queen Alexandra as Emperor and Empress of India, lasted for two weeks and had been meticulously arranged by Lord Curzon, Viceroy of India. This had certainly reinforced Britain's colonial position and strength in India. However, by 1907 the British Empire was beginning to show signs of strain and almost frantic efforts were being made in many quarters to sustain it. The social and working conditions of the British working classes at home were also under strain, and deemed more important than the Empire by those factions that sought to bring about radical change. One of the ways in which the public were reminded of its greatness, and could celebrate it as a national holiday, was the annual occasion of Empire Day on 24 May. This had emerged in the late 1890s in Canada when it was proposed that all schools should celebrate Queen Victoria's birthday with patriotic celebrations. However, it was not officially named as such until 1904 and, remarkably, lasted until 1958, after which it became British Commonwealth Day and then simply Commonwealth Day, as it is known today. I still have photos of my father at his school in London where all the children dressed in a variety of costumes and attire representing the diverse nationalities from the Colonies that made up the Empire. Postcards of mass drill displays and pageants held on Empire Day were produced in their hundreds of thousands for distribution around the world.

One of the organisations that sought to stimulate further the interest of the British Empire in the youth of the day was the Empire Education Fund, and on 18 July 1907 it staged a major exhibition in the RHS Hall of about 40,000 pictures depicting life in India and the British colonies. The Hall was split into sections where views were shown on 'automatic electrical magic lanterns' and this was opened by The Lord Mayor of London, William Purdie Treloar.

From 23 February–16 March 1908 another remarkable event took place that involved one the British Empire's most important colonies, South Africa. This was the South African Products Exhibition, opened by Their Majesties King Edward VII and Queen Alexandra. Large and enthusiastic crowds had lined the whole of the route to welcome the King and Queen and their Royal Party that included the Prince and Princess of Wales, Princesses Christian,

LEFT   Silk bookmark celebrating HM Queen Victoria's Golden Jubilee as 'Queen of an Empire on which the sun never sets!'

RIGHT   1915 and 1916 Overseas Club Certificates presented on 24 May, Empire Day, to those children who 'had helped send some comfort and happiness to the brave sailors and soldiers of the British Empire fighting to uphold Liberty, Justice, Honour and Freedom in the Great War'.

BELOW   Delhi Coronation Durbar admission ticket to the Durbar Amphitheatre, on 1 January 1903, signed by the British Foreign Secretary, H.S. Barnes.

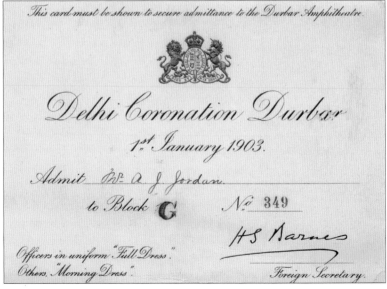

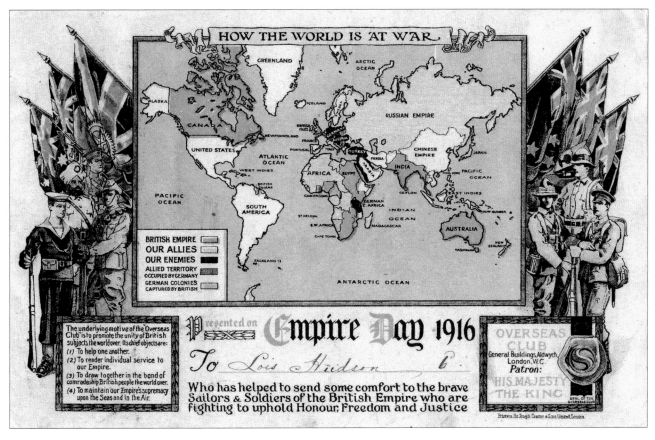

Victoria and Louise and the Duke of Argyll, driving in state from Buckingham Palace to the Hall. Westminster City Council had decorated the entire route with flags and bunting, and at the entrance to Victoria Street two large banners had been hung emblazoned with the words, 'The City of Westminster greets the King and Queen'.

This was an event that, in the Foreword of its Official Catalogue, had as its main aim the hope that it would 'tend in some degree to draw closer the union with the Mother Country and with each other the various

ABOVE AND RIGHT *Postcards issued for the South African Products Exhibition held in the Lindley Hall on 23 February– 16 March 1907. Opened by Their Majesties King Edward VII and Queen Alexandra.*

states which form the magnificent appanage of the Empire of South Africa.' It went on to say, 'Unhappily, throughout her chequered history, South Africa has been associated as much with Bellona as with Ceres, and too often the ploughshare had to be neglected for the sword. But a new era of peace and brotherhood has dawned. Progress in the arts of peace has received a new impetus, and South Africans commend to the attention of the Home Folk this Exhibition of their products in the confident hope that the realisation of the present will be immeasurably surpassed by the potentialities of the future.'

The Executive Committee consisted of the primary representatives for South Africa's five Colonial Governments – the Cape, the Transvaal, Natal, the Orange River Colony, and Rhodesia. Its Chairman was Captain Pieter C. Van Blommestein Bam, a Dutchman who had fought with the British forces in South Africa and whose initiative it had been. This had followed a visit he had made to Canada, where he had seen how the efforts to promote that country and their products had been a

success. An article in *South Africa*, a weekly journal distributed to all 'interested in South African Affairs', reported on a meeting held in the Great Hall of the *Cannon Street Hotel* in December 1906 that, 'Captain Bam impressed upon those present that both the British and the Dutch in South Africa were determined in their minds that there were to be no politics in the matter.' In fact, following its run at the Hall in London it moved to Amsterdam, Holland.

Much later, he was also to play an important part in the eventual realisation of the World's

Catalogue cover and internal pages for the South African Products Exhibition held in the Lindley Hall, 23 February to 16 March 1907.

most extensive and important imperial exhibition ever staged, the British Empire Exhibition, in 1924-5. Initial proposals for this had been put forward by the British Empire League as far back as 1902 with a suggested title of the Imperial Exhibition. However, things did not progress very quickly so, in November 1910, two years after his South Africa Products Exhibition, Bam, together with the Canadian high commissioner, Lord Strathcona (who had raised Lord Strathcona's Horse, a private unit of Canadian soldiers, during the Second Boer War) and exhibition impresario, Imre Kiralfy, jointly re-invigorated this effort to coincide with the Prince of Wales' coming of age in 1915 – only to be further delayed by the First World War, and organisational problems that stalled this until 1924 and 1925, when it was subsequently considered to have been too late. Even that most iconic of British Empire flag bearers, Rudyard Kipling, who

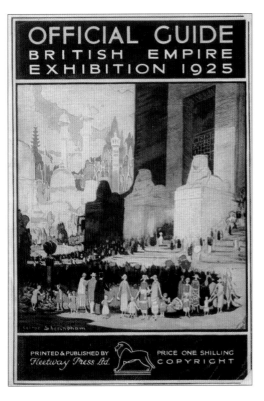

Metal badge, and pair of ceramic souvenir military shells for the 1924 British Empire Exhibition held at the White City, London.

had been asked to name all the roads on the Wembley site to reflect his own well known writings of Empire, could not save what ended up a financially embarrassing situation with overall attendances well down on what had been expected. This was seen as a final signal by many that the British Empire would never regain its former glory, nor see an imperial display like it ever again.

However, it must be remembered that in May 1902, the Boer War had only recently ended, so Bam's initiative with the South African Products Exhibition was an important step in the rebuilding process, and both governments had agreed upon its

ABOVE   *Postcard for 1909 Imperial International Exhibition, White City, London.*

LEFT   *British Empire Exhibition, White City, London, Torchlight and Searchlight Tattoo ticket, and poster label, 1924.*

RIGHT   *Silks of Boer War Generals, Sir Redvers Buller and Lord Kitchener, 1907. Buller was Commander of the force that relieved Ladysmith. Lord Kitchener of Khartoum, as he was known following the Battle of Omdurman in Sudan, played a key role during the 2nd Boer War in support of Lord Roberts.*

WOVEN IN PURE SILK.

WOVEN IN PURE SILK

The Daily Mirror

THE MORNING JOURNAL WITH THE SECOND LARGEST NET SALE.

No. 1,037.   Registered at the G. P. O. as a Newspaper.   TUESDAY, FEBRUARY 26, 1907,   One Halfpenny.

ACTUAL PHOTOGRAPH OF THE KING KNIGHTING SIR PIETER BAM.

A remarkable and unique photograph of the knighting of Captain Pieter Canzius van Blommerstein Bam by King Edward at the Royal Horticultural Hall, Westminster, when the exhibition of South African products was opened. Captain Bam is a Dutchman, and fought with the British forces in South Africa. The photograph shows the King laying a sword on Captain Bam's shoulder. The photograph is a reproduction of an enlargement from a bioscope picture taken by the Warwick Trading Company, and is now being shown at the Palace Theatre, Shaftesbury-avenue, W. Inset is Sir Pieter Bam.—(Elliott and Fry.)

LEFT *The* Daily
Mirror *front page
photo of HM King
Edward VII knighting
the Chairman of the
Executive Committee
of the South African
Products Exhibition,
Captain Pieter Canzius
Blommerstein van
Bam, in the Lindley
Hall on the opening
day of the Exhibition,
23 February 1907. The
Exhibition was open
23 February–
16 March 1907.*

THE ILLUSTRATED LONDON NEWS, MARCH 2, 1907. 342

THE SOUTH AFRICAN PRODUCTS EXHIBITION, OPENED BY THE KING.

PHOTOGRAPHS BY TOPICAL, EXCEPT THE CENTRE AND PORTRAITS, WHICH ARE BY VANDYK.

1. A MODEL OF CALEDON CHURCH IN EVERLASTING FLOWERS.   2. NATAL ART: A BOUQUET MADE OF FISH-SCALES.   3. THE MAGNIFICENT FAN PRESENTED TO THE QUEEN.
4. THE KING PERFORMING THE OPENING CEREMONY.
5. IMAGES AND IMPLEMENTS MADE BY NATAL NATIVES.   6. A GENERAL VIEW OF THE EXHIBITION.

The South African Products Exhibition was opened by the King and Queen on February 23 at the Horticultural Society's Hall, Westminster. Their Majesties were received by the Earl of Elgin, Captain Pieter Van Bam, member of the Cape Legislative Assembly; Sir Thomas Fuller, senior Agent-General; and other members of the Executive Committee, whose portraits are here given. Sir Thomas Fuller presented the Address, and after the King had replied, declaring the Exhibition open, his Majesty knighted Captain Van Bam. The King accepted from the people of South Africa a wonderful walking-stick of rhinoceros horn, and the Queen a superb fan of ostrich-feathers mounted in South African gold.

RIGHT   *The
Illustrated London
News of 2 March 1907
showing photos of the
South African Products
Exhibition in the
Lindley Hall.*

General view of the South African Industries Exhibition, opened by the King

The Bystander *magazine of 6 March 1907 showing photos of the South African Products Exhibition in the Lindley Hall.*

importance and significance. Knowing that Joseph Chamberlain who, during his tour of South Africa in 1902 and 1903 as Colonial Secretary, had played such a strong part in helping to reconcile the Boers with the British, while also recognising the importance of South Africa to the British Empire, I cannot help speculating as to whether, in his RHS Vice President's role, he played a part in this important event being held in the RHS Hall. And, perhaps it was not surprising (although it was surprising to those who were there) that, at the opening ceremony in the Hall, the King spontaneously knighted Captain Van Bam on the spot with a sword borrowed from a naval officer standing nearby with the words, 'Rise up, Sir Pieter'. The *Daily Mirror* of the next day devoted its entire front page to this with a still photo from a cinematographic film taken by film makers, Warwick Trading Company, at the ceremony. Within 3½ hours of it having been taken, it was being shown to a large matinee audience at the Palace Theatre on Shaftesbury Avenue.

To this day, I do not know of another London Hall where this has taken place. The King and his family were, by now, well acquainted with the Hall so probably felt 'at home' in it or, perhaps, the delight he expressed on receiving a rhinoceros horn walking stick, and the ostrich feather fan mounted in South African gold for the Queen, tipped the balance! The only other public knighting of this kind I know of is later, in 1910, at the opening of the statue of Queen Victoria outside Buckingham Palace, when King George V also knighted on the spot its renowned sculptor, Thomas Brock.

The Victoria League was an independent, non-political organisation set up to promote 'a closer union between the different parts of what was then the British Empire by the interchange of information and hospitality and by co-operation in any practical scheme tending to foster friendly understanding and good fellowship within the Empire.' It had been spearheaded by Lady Edward Cecil and Miss Balfour, the Prime Minister's sister, in April 1901. This had been largely in response to

the bitterness that had taken place during the Boer War. Rudyard Kipling called The League 'the organisation of sympathy'. Some of the League's earliest requests for practical work came from South Africa – for help in tending war graves, in raising funds to alleviate distress among British refugees, and for comforts for Boer women and children in detention camps. Midway through the Exhibition, the League organised an 'At Home' Reception in the Hall which *The Times* reported nearly 1,000 people attended.

In 1906, the future Queen Mary, then Princess of Wales, had become Patron of The League. Strangely, she is not reported as having attended the Reception but the Princesses Christian and Louise Augusta did, together with a very strong representation of influential supporters including Miss Balfour and Lady Edward Cecil. Winston Churchill was also there, recently elected as a Liberal Member of Parliament for North West Manchester. This followed the Liberal government win in 1906, but it was more likely to have been his exploits as a war correspondent during the Boer War in South Africa that had secured his invitation.

On display in the Exhibition was a vast array of exhibits including 'Fowl from the Veldt' in the form of two fully grown stuffed ostriches and chickens. Wine, brandy, tobacco, maize, honey, chutney, wool, mohair and ostrich feathers from the Cape; fruit of all kinds, tea, coffee, rubber, timber, coal, Kaffir Corn, animal skins and native curios from Natal; gold, diamonds, coal, copper, tin, asbestos, building stones, iron ores, cotton, cereals and salt from Transvaal and similar products from both Rhodesia and Orange River were also presented.

The Aberdeen Line of Direct Steamers advertised in the exhibition catalogue, 'crossings from London to Natal and East Africa' with the reassuring message that it was 'the only Line going south of the Equator fitted with Wireless Telegraphy'. Potentially, less confidence-boosting were other Lines such as Houlder who also advertised their cargo ships, but without any reference to W.T. 1st Class to Durban with Aberdeen cost 'From 29 guineas (£2,658)'

...TISH EXHIBITION LONDON 1908: "SALUTATION"

LEFT AND BELOW RIGHT *Postcard of the 1908 Franco-British Exhibition of Science, Arts and Industry, and Garden Club poster label. The Exhibition was held at White City, London. It was opened on 14 May 1908 by HM King George V, and closed in October of the same year. It was also where the 1908 London Olympics took place.*

and 2nd Class 'From £22.10 (£1,190)'. Fortunately, the wireless telegraphy was open to both classes. Dinneford's Magnesia was also on hand in the event of 'Acidity of the Stomach, Headache, Heartburn, Indigestion, Sour Eructations and Bilious Affections' – all conditions that could obviously be experienced in South Africa, as well as in the homeland and should be prepared for. Sutton & Sons, 'The King's Seedsmen' of Reading, both advertised and had a stand, displaying their roots, crops and seeds. The now sumptuously refurbished and five-star *Langham Hotel* in Portland Place was advertised as a 'Family Hotel of the First Order'. Both Perrier and Malvern Waters advertised their health-giving properties and Spratts offered Dog Cakes, Chicken Meal, Bird Seeds and Parrot Food – 'Obtainable throughout the World'.

Regrettably, one incident marred the Exhibition. The *Daily Express* reported on 14 March that a daring robbery had taken place. 'Two ingots of gold, worth £1,000 (£88,460), were stolen on Tuesday evening. The ingots were safe in an ebony and glass case, forming one of the principal exhibits on a stall in the Cape Colony section.' It went on to say that, 'They were in the special charge of an attendant, who also answered enquiries about a stall on the opposite side of the aisle.

A tall man in a long mackintosh examined them closely, and at the same moment, another visitor called the attendant, and asked about the price for some tobacco on the stall opposite. The man in the mackintosh strolled away and at 9.35 a.m. ingots and case had vanished'. The gold was of particular interest because this was claimed to have been the first gold crushed in British Bechuanaland. They never found the person who took them but, reading through accounts of other exhibitions of the period, it seems that thefts of this kind were not uncommon.

An almost identical one took place at the Franco-British Exhibition of Science, Arts and Industry held on the 140-acre Great White City and Stadium at Shepherds Bush, London between May and October 1908. The exhibition had been at the initiative of the British and French Chambers of Commerce in London, to reinforce the 'Entente Cordiale' which had been signed by Britain and France in 1904. The RHS had also contributed to its organisation. Interestingly, it was where the suggestion of constructing a Channel tunnel to link the two countries was first mooted. It was reported in the *Daily Express* that, on 21 October, 'A daring theft of two platinum ingots, valued at £1,000 (£88,460), has taken place at the Franco-British Exhibition. The

ingots were stolen from a glass showcase in the British section of the Machinery Hall'. It went on to say that, 'Only two bars of platinum were missing, although the case contained exhibits valued at more than £15,000 (£1,33 million).' Clearly, high value items on display at exhibitions such as these had been identified as vulnerable and 'easy pickings' for those who had a great deal of time to study the daily routines of the Hall and venue staff, and could identify the holes in their security. History repeated itself more recently during the Millennium Exhibition at the Dome when a daring raid to steal the gold on display there was attempted but, on that occasion, successfully prevented.

LEFT *Souvenir of the Latin-British Exhibition, one of the last two events held at the Great White City in Shepherd's Bush.*

III

Important Early Themes

The Church and Religion

Photo of Papal Legate to the 19th Eucharistic Congress, His Eminence Cardinal Vincent Vannutelli, Bishop of Palestrina. The Congress took place in London on 10-13 September 1908. The opening meeting and several others, took place in the Lindley Hall.

If what had been seen in the Halls in the first three years of its commercial operation can be regarded as exotic, spectacular and important, what would come to the Hall on 10-13 September 1908 would be no less so, but in a totally different way. No better example exists to highlight the contrast between the Hall's original and primary use and this event, the 19th Eucharistic Congress, regarded then by the whole Catholic world as 'the greatest religious triumph of its generation'. It also brought into focus a serious blunder made by Mr Asquith's Conservative government of the day that resulted in a universal tirade of condemnation across the political and religious divide from all factions of the media.

Eucharistic Congresses are gatherings of ecclesiastics and laymen for the purpose of celebrating and glorifying the Holy Eucharist and of seeking the best means to spread its knowledge and love throughout the world. The Real Presence of Jesus Christ in the Eucharist is one of the principal dogmas of the Catholic Faith and is, therefore, of paramount importance. The belief is that, as the most precious treasure that Christ has left to His Church, the Eucharist is at the centre of Catholic worship and the source of Christian piety.

In the history of the 19 Congresses that had started in Lille, France in 1881, none had taken place in England and more than 350 years had elapsed since a Pope's Legate (let alone the Pope himself) had been seen in England. It would be another 74 years before the first pontiff to visit Britain, Pope John Paul II, would visit Britain on 28 May 1982, and 104 years before the first State Visit to Britain by a pontiff, Pope Benedict XVI, would be made on 16 September 2010. Once the decision had been taken to hold the 19th Eucharistic Congress in London the Pope designated Cardinal Vincent Vannutelli as his Legate to attend the sessions of this new Congress. With him came six other Cardinals, 14 Archbishops, 90 Bishops and a host of priests. No such gathering of ecclesiastics had ever been seen outside Rome in modern times. Over 25,000 adults and 20,000 children took part in it and, on 9 September, the Congress was solemnly opened in Westminster Cathedral in conjunction with the Archbishop's Conference held in the RHS Hall. The regular sessions began the next day on Thursday 10 September. Three daily 'Section A' meetings in English also took place in the RHS Hall chaired by Archbishop Bourne

EUCHARISTIC CONGRESS, London, 1908.
The Great Procession, Sunday, September 13th.

AND OVERLEAF *Set of postcards issued to commemorate the 19th Eucharistic Congress, London on 10-13 September 1908, showing meetings held the in the Lindley Hall, the Great Procession and the Children's Procession.*

EUCHARISTIC CONGRESS, London, 1908.   Opening Meeting at Horticultural Hall.

EUCHARISTIC CONGRESS, London, 1908.   Sectional Meeting at Horticultural Hall.

EUCHARISTIC CONGRESS. London, 1908. Children's Procession.—Boys entering Westminster Cathedral

EUCHARISTIC CONGRESS, London, 1908. The Great Procession, Sunday, September 13th.

EUCHARISTIC CONGRESS, London, 1908. The Children's Procession entering Westminster Cathedral.

EUCHARISTIC CONGRESS, London, 1908.   Archbishop Bourne addressing a Meeting at the Horticultural Hall.

of Westminster. Others such as 'Section B' (also in English) took place at the London Scottish Drill Hall and the 'Section C' meetings (in French) took place in the newly named Caxton Hall, formerly Westminster town hall. The official account that recorded the description of the RHS Hall during the Sessions staged in it described it as follows:

> 10 a.m. witnesses the filling of the spacious Horticultural Hall, a magnificently lighted oblong building with vaulted glass roof. The platform which occupies the greater part of the width of the Hall is backed by a rich drapery of red silk and velvet canopy in the centre of which are the Papal Arms. The front of the platform is gracefully decorated with alternating white and yellow flowers with an abundance of green supplied by ferns and plants. Large panels around the higher walls display the arms of the visiting Cardinals and Bishops, that of the Cardinal Legate being on the right and that of His Grace of Westminster on the left of the Papal Arms. A magnificent triptych to the left of the audience of Our Blessed Lady with the Holy Child, attended by angels with musical instruments gives an appearance of permanency to the decorations. Beautifully printed hangings fill the panels between the pillars, emblematic of the Holy Eucharist sheaves of wheat bordered with garlands of grapes, supporting medallions with the type of the Blessed Sacrament, are on all the panels with appropriate Scripture texts.

This must have been an extraordinary scene to witness and, once again, ample evidence of the 'open to all races and creeds' policy that the RHS had fervently expressed before opening its Hall. As much later evidence of this I can't help recalling and juxtaposing this scene with one I personally witnessed 85 years later when, on 20 March 1992, pictures of Iran's prior Shi'i Religious Leader, Ayatollah Khomeini, were prominently displayed all around its walls in a celebration of Iran's New Year that had been organised by their Embassy in London.

On the afternoon of the fourth day of the 19th Eucharistic Congress a procession of 20,000 Catholic children gathered from the schools in and around the metropolis to walk through Westminster, ending in the Cathedral for an address to be delivered by Cardinal Logue and Benediction by the Cardinal Legate. Because not all the children could fit into the Cathedral many were sent to the RHS Hall that afternoon and also to the Drill Hall in Buckingham Gate where they were kept amused until Cardinal Logue was able to come and speak to them.

The culmination of the Congress was planned to have been another mass procession through Westminster's streets carrying the Blessed Sacraments for all to see. However, owing to a protest and public clamour against this, made principally by the societies composing the Protestant Alliance, Mr Asquith, the Prime Minister, sent an '11th hour' formal request to Archbishop Bourne on behalf of 'His Majesty's Government', for all elements of ecclesiastical decoration to be eliminated and, in particular, the abandonment of carrying the Sacraments, in accordance with the Catholic Emancipation Act of 1829. This decision was scrupulously obeyed but overwhelmingly castigated by the media because full details of the procession had been submitted to the Home Office long before and not rejected until then. It was strongly felt that Mr Asquith had only changed his mind due to the strong lobbying of the Protestant Alliance.

Media reports in *The Times, Daily News, Daily Telegraph, Daily Chronicle, The Spectator* and *The Standard* gave vent to their views. The *Telegraph* reported on 14 September, 'It is impossible to write in terms other than those of the strongest condemnation of the conduct of the government with respect to yesterday's Procession of the Blessed Sacrament, which was to have brought to a conclusion the proceedings of the Eucharistic Congress. They have once more displayed their characteristic weakness and irresolution, their susceptibility to pressure, and their readiness to make concessions to the clamour of a few extremists.' *The Standard* wrote, 'The Catholic Emancipation Act of 1829 is quite clear that, such exercise in public of the rites and ceremonies of the Roman Catholic Church is against the law. Everybody, whose judgement is unbiased by bigotry will admit that this restriction is no longer either necessary or expedient.' *The Daily Chronicle* said, 'We regret, then, that any action whatsoever was taken by the government. A great many persons will applaud the Prime Minister's action. These Roman Catholics, they will say, are becoming too arrogant. It was high time they were reminded that England is a Protestant country. In all seriousness we ask, was the reminder necessary? Is our Protestantism so feeble that it needs to be artificially encouraged by a government interdict on a religious procession?'

The procession was a huge success, in spite of the government. Many thousands of people lined the route and cheered. Special trains had been laid on for them to come from all parts of the country and others came from abroad. *The Report of the Nineteenth Eucharistic Congress* published by Sands and Company in 1909 describes that 'The Procession was led by a master of ceremonies, followed by 800 servers of the Guild of St Stephen in their cassocks and cottas, ranks upon ranks of religious and secular priests, the Canons in their mozaettas, the striking robes of the Greek Uniate clergy, the Abbots of the religious orders, the double line of Bishops and Archbishops from around the world attended by their chaplains – all leading up in the most striking way to the imposing person of the Legate in his splendid Cardinal's robes, followed by his train bearer and attended by his suite and guard of honour. Eight peers of the realm with other gentlemen of distinction and two members of the French Senate formed a distinguished escort to the noble and ascetic Prince of the Church, who overtopped them all in stature. At a little distance behind followed the other Cardinals, each a blaze of colour in his robes of royal purple which to our eyes is practically scarlet, and each attended by his chaplain and train-bearer. Then another master of ceremonies, walking alone, drew attention to the coming of the Archbishop of Westminster in his violet cappa magna; and finally the rear-guard was formed by a dense array of Monsignori of various grades, the lesser 'porporati', who, with many distinguished members of the laity, brought the procession to a seemly close. The culmination to the procession that had walked through Ashley Place, Carlisle Place, Francis Street, Stillington Street, Rochester Row, Artillery Row, Howick Place, Ashley Gardens, Francis Street and Ambrosden Avenue took place in front of the great western doorways of the church where everyone had returned to and amassed.'

Whilst it had not been possible to parade the Eucharist in the street a last-minute agreement with the Home Office the night before allowed that its public benediction could be made within the walls of the Cathedral and so it was that, 'on the sound of bugles in salute and, from the topmost heights of the Cathedral tower the Cardinal Legate appeared on the balcony bearing the Sacred Host and, with tears streaming from his eyes he blessed the faithful, first of all from the main entrance, and then from the north and south loggias of the building. Every space, window and gallery that could be secured as a vantage point to witness this extraordinary event was taken.' It is clear from the accounts given that for those who witnessed it, they would have placed it as importantly a moment in their lives as when later generations would witness the first man to land on the moon and remembered the day as strongly as when later generations still would also remember where they were when President Kennedy was shot.

The final comment is left to the Pope who sent a special letter to the Archbishop of Westminster after the event saying that, although it had been the first of its kind in England, it should be looked upon as the greatest of all. Looking at what followed in later years in Northern Ireland and elsewhere, as we continue on our path of observing history through the eyes of our Hall, I am forced to take the view that man does not easily learn from it.

It should be noted, however, that the Congress was not the first time that the Hall had been requested by the Church, or other religious groups and faiths, and that the land upon which the Hall had been built was owned by the Ecclesiastical Commissioners. The RHS Council Minutes for 28 March 1905 record that they had been approached by Westminster Chapel to use the Hall for 13 Sunday Services during July, August and September that same year. This Chapel, only a few yards from the London Scottish Drill Hall on Buckingham Gate, had been going through hard times with diminishing congregations up until the arrival of a greatly gifted Welsh preacher and former schoolmaster, Dr George Campbell Morgan, in 1904. Dr Morgan had travelled extensively in the USA as a Bible teacher alongside the great American evangelist, D.L. Moody, and managed to revive its fortunes. Westminster Chapel still thrives today. However, it would appear that these did not take place in the Hall because the RHS Council recorded much later in their 22 June 1909 Meeting Minutes that, 'Application for a Sunday afternoon meeting by the Baptist Missionary Society was declined because the Hall had never before been let on a Sunday, on the grounds that one day of rest in seven is necessary to every member of staff'.

This appears to have changed by 1912 because, at the RHS Council Meeting of 17 December that year, a letter was read out from Miss Murray Smith complaining this time of 'the disturbance to her tenants in St Georges House during the night and on Sundays by work going on in the Hall.' She requested, 'for night and Sunday work to be prohibited'. Legal opinion was sought and the Society was advised to take every possible step to 'diminish the nuisance complained of by Miss Murray Smith'. The Society replied to Miss Smith that, 'all possible steps would be taken to prevent noises being made at night and that Sunday work will only be done when absolutely imperative, and only then with every thoughtful consideration for the comfort of Residents in St Georges House.' It was clear by this reply that Sunday working was necessary and here to stay.

However, the Baptist Missionary Society, in conjunction with the Congo Balolo

Mission, the American Baptist Mission Union, the Swedish Missionary Society, and the Congo Reform Association were allowed to book and stage an extraordinary exhibition on 18-27 September that year entitled, the Congo Exhibition. At this event, a family of four Congolese natives had been brought over and were displayed daily in their traditional hut in the Hall to depict the conditions of daily life in this part of Africa and to stir the consciences of those who visited into supporting the work of the Society and its associate Missions to bring

Postcard commemorating the 21st Eucharistic Congress held in Montreal, Canada on 7-11 September 1910. The card refers to the London Congress held in 1908.

about change for the Congolese people. The Exhibition had a political, as well as a social objective. The 'Congo question' was one that had been brought to the fore by Edmond Dene Morel and Roger Casement, founders of the Congo Reform Association. They were appalled at the way King Leopold of Belgium had abused the powers he had been given as a result of the 1885 Congress of Berlin to administer and improve the lot of the Congo and its peoples. Leopold plundered the country for rubber in particular and, in doing so, chalked up a human toll of staggering proportions. People who resisted were beaten, tortured, mutilated or killed. Writer Algis Valiunas described the situation as 'wickedness triumphant'. Another well-known writer, Arthur Conan Doyle, had met with Morel in 1909 and, most probably at the Congo Exhibition in the Hall, when he was motivated by 'a burning indignation, which is the best of all driving power' to write his book, *The Crime of the Congo*, in just eight days. Morel and Casement were also the inspiration for the central characters in Doyle's *The Lost World*.

Through its many missionaries that had devoted themselves to their cause, the Baptist Missionary Society had been working to this end for the past 30 years. The most important of these had been George Grenfell, a visionary Baptist leader who thought of himself as a successor to John the Baptist and applied himself in a remarkable way towards missionary exploration and the establishment of mission stations in the Congo as 'Centers of Light'. Livingstone and Stanley, through their own explorations and exploits, had brought to the attention of the British public the 'Dark Continent of Africa' with its active slave trade, tribal wars and brutal customs. On 14 May 1877, just three months before Stanley and his shattered expedition reached Boma at the mouth of the Congo, another devoted Baptist, Robert Arthington, offered the Baptist Society £1,000 (£95,000) for the purpose of taking 'the blessed light of the gospel' to the Congo region. With astounding vision he wrote: 'I hope we shall soon have a steamer on

the Congo, to carry the gospel eastward, and south and north of the river, as the way may open, as far as Nyangwe.' The Society did not act immediately, but were later prompted to do so by the publication of Stanley's letter in the *Daily Telegraph*, 17 September 1877.

Early in 1878 Grenfell was already in Africa and on his way along the bank of the Congo. 'So,' as stated by C.H. Patton in *The Lure of Africa*, 'the Baptists were the first to see and to seize the great opening made by Stanley's explorations.' Grenfell encountered almost insuperable difficulties. But finally, after 13 attempts, after splashing through many swamps and tramping through grass often 15 feet high, after frequent perilous escapes from savages and after one of his companions had been severely wounded, he passed the cataracts and reached Stanley Pool, in February 1881. By means of the vast system of waterways created by the Congo and its numerous tributaries, some twenty or twenty-five million people could be reached. Canoes were available but they were both slow and dangerous. Hippopotami often upset them, after which crocodiles feasted upon the occupants. The solution of the problem was a steamer, as had been suggested several years earlier by Robert Arthington, who had provided £1,000 (£95,000) toward its construction and £3,000 (c.£285,000) toward its perpetual maintenance. 'I believe the time is come when we should place a steamer on the Congo River, where we can sail north-eastward into the heart of Africa for many hundred miles uninterruptedly and bring the glad tidings of the everlasting gospel to thousands of human beings who now are ignorant of the way of life and of immortality.'

Leaving his wife behind in the Congo, Grenfell returned to England where he supervised the construction of the *Peace*, a screw steamer 78 feet in length and drawing 12 inches of water. After it had been tested on the Thames, it was taken apart, put in 800 packages weighing 65 pounds each and shipped to the mouth of the Congo. It took a thousand men to carry the vessel and necessary food supplies up the river and past the rapids to Stanley Pool. Grenfell had brought with him a young missionary engineer whose special assignment was to put the vessel together and then keep it in good running order. Soon after reaching African soil, he fell sick and died. Two other engineers were promptly sent out from England, but both of them also died within a few weeks.

So it fell to Grenfell himself to undertake the enormous task of putting the ship together. This he successfully achieved and, on its maiden voyage, covered 1,200 miles reaching a point half way to Stanley Fall while also exploring several of the chief tributaries. During his travels through many of the village he visited, he was shocked at the way people lived their lives and their practices. He categorised six practices that he felt were either definitely a part of their religious system, or an expression of depravity out of which their religion was powerless to lift them. These were burial murders, witchcraft cruelties, slave raiding, cannibalism, sensuality, and sadistic methods of punishment. He resolved to change this through conversion to Christianity.

Grenfell had been badly disillusioned by the Belgian's administration of the Congo Free State. Knowing the savagery and chaos of native rule, he expected a great improvement from the rule of the Belgians and assisted them in many ways, notably by serving in 1891 as a capitol Commissioner to settle the southern boundary of the State. However, even prior to this, he had begun to have grave misgivings, as he saw the Belgians tightening their grip on the Congo with King Leopold ruling as if it were his personal properly. Ironically, it had been Henry Stanley who had earlier been employed by Leopold to negotiate and secure control over tribal lands for him between 1879 and 1884. It was 1890 when Grenfell's own misgivings were realised, and the Belgian authorities commandeered the *Peace* to further their own schemes. Grenfell's subsequent protests in England were so strong that the steamer was restored and the Belgian King bestowed

on him in Brussels much later on the insignia of 'Chevalier of the Order of Leopold'. His self-deprecating response to this was to describe himself, 'like a barn door with a brass knocker'.

Grenfell died on his beloved steamer at Bapoto on 1 July 1906. He had been the first person to steam up the Congo and explore many of its tributaries and The Royal Geographical Society had awarded him a Gold Medal for doing so in 1886. It was, therefore, hugely significant that one of the many exhibits in the RHS Hall for the Baptist Missionary Society's exhibition was a portion of the bow of his steamer, *Peace*. Apart from having been the home of George Grenfell and his wife throughout their time in the Congo, it had also been used by Stanley in the Emin Pasha relief expedition.

Other religious meetings and faiths to use the Halls included the Annual Meeting of the Society for the Propagation of the Gospel in Foreign Parts, presided by The Archbishop of Canterbury that took place on 29 April 1909. The Bishops of St Albans, Salisbury, Kingston and Rangoon, Bishop Johnson, Bishop Morley and Bishop Taylor-Smith were also present. This Society had received its charter from King William III in 1701, and would later celebrate its 250th anniversary on 17 June 1951 at St Paul's Cathedral attended by HM The Queen. The Catholic Truth Society also met in the Old Hall for their Emancipation Centenary meeting on 12 April 1929 with Cardinal Bourne presiding. The Watch Tower Bible Society (Jehovah's Witnesses) also used the Hall for one of their meetings on 29 April 1908. This organisation had originated in the USA in 1872 under Charles Taze Russell who predicted that Christ's second coming would be in 1914. The 9th Church of Christ Scientists held a Christian Science Lecture in the New Hall on 24 November 1928, and in May 1952 and 1953 it was The Plymouth Brethren who came to the Halls. Also known as the Exclusive Brethren and Taylorites, they practised a doctrine of 'separation from iniquity', or separation from sin.

Repro postcard and photo of Emmeline Pankhurst (1858-1928), Honorary Secretary, National Women's Social & Political Union, c.1908.

The Sphere *magazine front cover of 12 December 1908, depicting the suffragette disturbance caused at a meeting of the Women's Liberal Federation at the Royal Albert Hall.*

Women and Politics

Political and social ferment was rife in the decade before war broke out in 1914. The women's suffrage movement was at the forefront of this. Just like the nurses and midwives seeking recognition of their status, the battle of attaining enfranchisement for women had already been taking place for many years. Unlike the nurses and midwives who continued to battle with government for their own specific objectives through orderly and constitutionally political processes, there were some women who lost patience with their reliance on men, and politicians in government in particular, to bring about the change they sought, i.e. the right to vote. These women decided to become militant to achieve what they really wanted. The precedent had already been set by successive generations of working men in the 19th century when their own violent struggle throughout it had led to them being able to vote. However, even in the late 1880s approximately only 4.5 million men out of a total of 27.5 million in England and Wales were empowered to vote.

It was Emmeline Pankhurst and her daughters, Christabel and Sylvia, who first took on the governments of the day between 1903-14 with a persistently militant campaign that brought them and thousands of their colleagues into direct conflict with the authorities, involving regular violent treatment and harassment. More than one thousand were imprisoned and many received severe jail sentences in Strangeways and Holloway Prisons, among others in the country. One of these was Ada Flatman, who in a BBC archive recording made c.1946 recalled first being motivated by the 'Suffragette' cause at a very early meeting in the Horticultural Hall when Emmeline Pankhurst spoke. She also recalled her subsequent arrest and incarceration in Holloway Prison, as well as her heckling of cabinet ministers such as 'Mr Birrell' (Augustine Birrell), who was known to oppose the notion of granting women the vote. The Women's Social and Political Union (W.S.P.U.) was formed in Emmeline Pankhurst's house in Manchester on 10 October 1903. It would later become the National Women's Social and Political Union (N.W.S.P.U.) to differentiate between a breakaway group that had continued to use the same W.S.P.U. name until November 1908 when it changed to become known as the Women's Freedom League (WFL). Both groups classed themselves as militant but the WFL refused to attack persons or property other than ballot papers.

THE SPHERE

AN ILLUSTRATED NEWSPAPER FOR THE HOME

Volume XXXV. No. 464.   { REGISTERED AT THE GENERAL POST OFFICE AS A NEWSPAPER }   London, December 12, 1908.   [WITH SUPPLEMENT]   Price Sixpence.

DRAWN BY H. M. PAGET AT THE ALBERT HALL
THE SUFFRAGETTES' CROWNING EFFORT—THE ATTEMPT TO STOP MR. LLOYD GEORGE'S SPEECH AT THE ALBERT HALL

On Saturday afternoon (December 5) the militant Suffragettes attempted to wreck the mass meeting arranged by the Women's Liberal Federation, the body which is attempting to gain a vote for women by peaceful means. Mr. Lloyd George had only uttered a few sentences when he was interrupted by Miss Helen Ogston, daughter of the Professor of Surgery at Aberdeen University. She resisted ejection with a dog whip, which she used freely on the men who attempted to remove her. Beyond can be seen the Chancellor of the Exchequer waiting for the storm to subside. A description by an eye-witness will be found on another page

However, not all women were supportive of their campaigns or actions and they also found themselves in direct conflict with the other more traditional non-militant suffragist groups. Ironically, these groups increased their membership and influence substantially as a direct result of the heightened awareness of the primary issues the militant groups achieved. One of these, the National Women's Liberal Federation, had been cleverly established by William Gladstone's Liberal government in 1887. The Federation confidently promised that, by allying themselves with the Liberal Party politicians within a party political system, women would soon secure the right to vote. However, this was regarded with great scepticism by Emmeline Pankhurst and, at best, a sop to women to keep them under control and at bay. The omens had not been good when, in 1884, shortly after Mr Gladstone had come to power with his Liberal government he had ensured that an independent women's suffrage bill failed to be heard in Parliament.

The RHS first allowed a W.S.P.U. 'women only' meeting to be held in its Hall on 23 January 1907 (probably the meeting that Ada Flatman attended) at the start of their 1907 campaign. This preceded by three weeks the first of their notorious 'Women's Parliament' meetings held in Caxton Hall throughout their long campaign until 1915 when the First World War broke out. (Ironically, Caxton Hall, situated on the corners of Caxton and Palmer Streets, just off Victoria Street, had originally been built as Westminster's town hall and its foundation stone laid by none other than The Baroness Burdett-Coutts on 29 March 1882. One can't help wondering what stance she would have taken on the militant campaigns of the Suffragist movement – most of them planned in this Hall.) However, it is likely that Emmeline Pankhurst had first been introduced to the RHS

Original leaflet No.24, to warn, 'Against Woman Suffrage – Some Reasons', published by the National League for Opposing Woman Suffrage, Caxton House, Tothill Street, Westminster, under the authorship Grace Saxon Mills, c.1908.

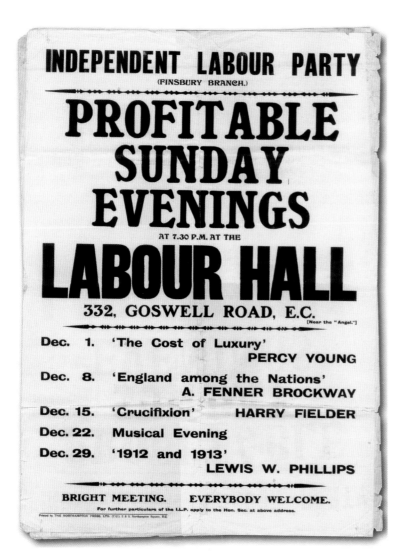

INDEPENDENT LABOUR PARTY
(FINSBURY BRANCH.)

PROFITABLE SUNDAY EVENINGS

AT 7.30 P.M. AT THE

LABOUR HALL

332, GOSWELL ROAD, E.C.
[Near the "Angel."]

Dec. 1. 'The Cost of Luxury'
                              PERCY YOUNG

Dec. 8. 'England among the Nations'
                              A. FENNER BROCKWAY

Dec. 15. 'Crucifixion'   HARRY FIELDER

Dec. 22. Musical Evening

Dec. 29. '1912 and 1913'
                              LEWIS W. PHILLIPS

BRIGHT MEETING.   EVERYBODY WELCOME.
For further particulars of the I.L.P. apply to the Hon. Sec. at above address.
Printed by THE NORTHAMPTON PRESS, LTD. (T.U.), 2 & 3, Northampton Square, E.C.

Independent Labour Party poster advertising a meeting at the Labour Party Hall, 332 Goswell Road, EC, c.1912.

Hall on 15 February 1906 when Keir Hardie, MP (her lover), then acting as Chairman of the Independent Labour Party, hosted a Reception and Social Evening there to the 'Labour Representation Committee, Other Socialist Members of Parliament and the Delegates to the Labour Representation Conference'. The programme proudly proclaimed 'The World for the Workers' at its head and songs such as 'Sons of Labour', 'England Arise' and the 'Marseillaise' were sung. The notations against each *to be sung by all present* left no one in doubt as to the need to do so (ILP pamphlets of the period were entitled, 'The Peril of Poverty', 'Fighters for Freedom', 'Socialism and Teetotalism', 'The Christ that is To Be' and 'Who Owns the Land?'). Addresses were given by Keir Hardie, J. Ramsay MacDonald and others. Emmeline had been a member of the National Administrative

Council of the I.L.P. since April 1904 and in July of that same year had been asked to 'draft a bill on Women's Suffrage to be introduced into Parliament by Keir Hardie'. This bill, eventually prepared for Parliament on 14 November 1906, was thwarted by not being heard and was a huge blow to both Pankhurst and Hardie. It led to a demonstration on 22 November held in the RHS Hall, to demand the enfranchisement of women. Earlier in the year, they had suffered another blow because at the 5 April 1906 NAC meeting it was resolved that Mrs Pankhurst be elected as the ILP representative at the planned Prime Minister's Deputation, in spite of an objection made by Ramsay MacDonald. There was clearly real concern from the Committee and it was raised again at a later meeting. Then, at their 27 April 1906 meeting, they resolved that 'Mrs Pankhurst be withdrawn as the I.L.P. representative of the planned Deputation to the Prime Minister'. Keir Hardie tried hard to save her, but to no avail, and by June 1906, Ramsay MacDonald had also taken over the I.L.P. NAC Chair.

Pankhurst was still a member of the I.L.P. NAC on 22 November 1906 when she is next recorded as speaking at a demonstration in the Hall organised by the Metropolitan District Council of the I.L.P. in support of women's suffrage at which Keir Hardie presided. He drew attention to the Bill that was before the House of Commons and urged its supporters to continue their actions, that he felt had achieved more in the past 12 months than at any time before, if women were to become voters at the next general election. Two resolutions were adopted at the meeting. The first was moved by Mr Walsh MP who called for the immediate release of all the women imprisoned in Holloway Prison. This was seconded by Mrs Barras of the Women's Co-operative Guild and supported by both Mrs Despard and Mr Walter B. McLaren. The second from Mrs Pankhurst, made on behalf of the W.S.P.U., called on the government to enfranchise women at once. In doing so she reminded her audience that for the sake of 'the cause' she had contributed all three of her daughters to prison during the year, with

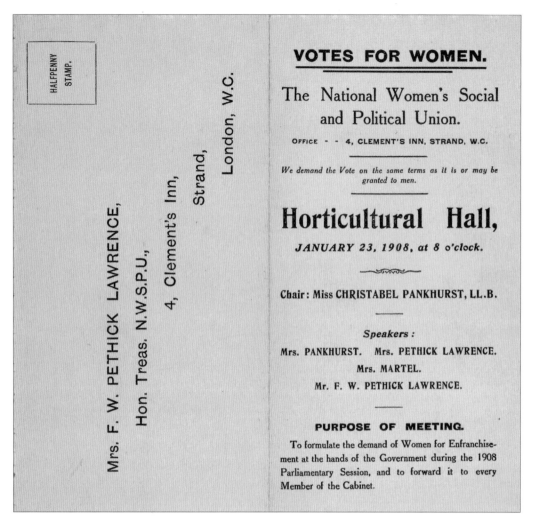

The National Women's Social and Political Union advance programme notice for a meeting at the Lindley Hall on 23 January 1908. Miss Christabel Pankhurst, LLB, was in the Chair.

one of them also serving a second term. This was seconded by Mrs Stanbury of the Central Society for Women's Suffrage and supported by Mr Snowden, MP Subsequently, her increasingly active role with the N.W.S.P.U. and a reduced position of influence on the NAC of the I.L.P. resulted in her departure from the I.L.P. at the 4 October Meeting, a year later. The minutes of that meeting record simply that, 'Mrs Pankhurst had resigned her membership of the Party'.

The next time she came to the RHS Hall was on 23 January 1908 under her own representation as the N.W.S.P.U. This meeting was chaired by Christabel Pankhurst. Christabel, her mother, Emmeline and Mr and Mrs Pethick Lawrence all delivered speeches, but Mrs Nellie Alma Martel, who was on the programme to do so, was unable to attend as she was campaigning in Ross. She and Emmeline

had been at the Newton Abbot by-election just seven days earlier and had taken a severe physical beating from a group of clay cutters wearing red Liberal rosettes and were both still suffering from this. Emmeline is recorded as 'limping in' to the meeting. The N.W.S.P.U. motto was: 'We demand the Vote on the same terms as it is, or may be, granted to men.' The purpose of the meeting was 'To formulate the demand of Women for Enfranchisement at the hands of the government during the 1908 Parliamentary Session, and to forward it to every Member of the Cabinet.' There is no evidence or record of whether this meeting was unruly or disruptive but, only six days before, suffragettes had chained themselves to railings as a diversion for Mrs Drummond to try to enter 10 Downing Street to interrupt a Cabinet Meeting. Then on 6 February 1909 Emmeline Pankhurst led a militant march to the House of Commons, following a W.S.P.U. meeting in the Hall, was arrested and sentenced to 14 days' imprisonment, in lieu of a fine. However, her fine was paid the next day by 'unknown person'. This was reported in the *Suffragette* on 7 February.

The Women's Exhibition in May 1909 was especially important to Sylvia Pankhurst at the start of her WSPU movement when this exhibition (that probably could have been held in the RHS Hall), was held at the Prince's Skating Rink, Knightsbridge. Although the exhibition consisted of the normal displays and activities associated with women of that period, it was overtly suffragist and revolutionary in many ways.

There is no doubt that the suffragettes posed a dilemma for the RHS where the implementation of its Halls letting policy was concerned. The RHS had become strongly supported by, and connected with, Royalty, the governments of the day and the establishment at large. To allow militant non-establishment organisations such as the W.S.P.U. into their Hall must have raised eyebrows in some quarters. Among the 26 members of the executive committee of the Women's Liberal Federation were Mrs Lloyd

George and Mrs Winston Churchill. Members of government such as Sir Edward Grey were also regular visitors to the Society's flower shows and he lived close by at One Queen Anne's Gate (now a prestigious Conference Centre of the same name).

One incident that took place on 3 November 1908, reported in the *Daily Mirror* the next day, gives a clue as to why this was the case. It was at the formal opening of the 19th Universal Cookery & Food Exhibition, by now a well established and important fixture in the Hall, that the suffragettes probably damaged their own position with the RHS by 'constantly harassing' and subjecting The President of the Board of Trade, Lord Carrington, to 'a persistent series of interruptions' when he tried officially to open the exhibition. *The Mirror* went on to say that, 'Many suffragettes had to leave the building hurriedly under the escort of a friendly constable before the Cabinet Minister could get a courteous hearing'.

Another incident took place much later on 16 December 1911 involving Gladstone's creation, the Women's Liberal Federation, which the militant suffragettes had despised for so long, even though it had broken away from the more

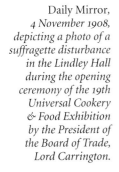

Daily Mirror, 4 November 1908, depicting a photo of a suffragette disturbance in the Lindley Hall during the opening ceremony of the 19th Universal Cookery & Food Exhibition by the President of the Board of Trade, Lord Carrington.

moderate group, the Women's National Liberal Federation (WNLF). But, the tide looked as though it was beginning to turn and it was at this meeting in the Hall that David Lloyd George, Chancellor of the Exchequer, and Sir Edward Grey, Foreign Secretary, gave impassioned speeches that addressed the beginning of the campaign leading to securing the franchise to women, through an amendment of the 1912 Reform Bill. This was ironic given that Sir Edward Grey, about to become a member of the new Liberal government in 1905, had refused to countenance any question of women's suffrage when he was faced with the question, 'Will the Liberal government give votes to women'. This was posed to him by Christabel Pankhurst and Annie Kenney at a meeting in the Free Trade Hall in Manchester on 13 October 1905, after which they were imprisoned.

Perhaps, it was not surprising, therefore, that both men were assaulted on arrival at the RHS Hall by militant suffragettes who rushed towards them shouting 'Traitors' and who threw pamphlets at them. As a further indication of the concern that was felt from the threats posed by disruptions and unruly behaviour, everyone admitted to the meeting (even the reporters) had to sign an undertaking not to ask questions or interrupt. Mrs Eva McLaren, a renowned Liberal and feminist who had herself once been arrested and prosecuted for failing to pay her taxes in protest that women were unable to vote, presided over the meeting and read a welcome letter from their President, Rosalind, Countess of Carlisle. The countess was a strenuous worker in support of many philanthropic causes, and also fervently active in the temperance movement (dubbed 'The Radical Countess') who had been unable to attend. However, she did preside at a later Council Meeting in May 1913, when Lady Aberconway, who as Mrs Charles McLaren had been largely instrumental in forming the WLF together with Eva McLaren, amongst others, also attended. Lady Aberconway was described in her obituary in *The Times* on 12 January 1933 as one of the greatest horticulturists in Europe, having inherited the Bodnant estate in North Wales from her father, and transformed its gardens into one of the finest in the United Kingdom. She lived to see her son, Henry, 2nd Baron Aberconway become the 12th President of the RHS, having already served on its Council from 1923-7. She would have been even more delighted to have seen her grandson, Charles, 3rd Baron Aberconway become the 14th President of the RHS in 1961, having already served on its Council from 1955.

Addressing the December 1911 meeting, Eva McLaren described Sir Edward Grey and David Lloyd George as 'the fighting champions of the women's suffrage cause.' However, on driving away from the Hall, a man assaulted David Lloyd George by throwing a leather dispatch box through his car window, striking him on the face and inflicting several bruises and a wound under his left eye. Allan Ross McDougal, aged 19, was sentenced to two months' imprisonment with hard labour, as a result!

Only one further meeting of theirs, on 7 March 1912, is recorded as having taken place in the Hall, between February 1909 and January 1913, in spite of this being the height of their activity when they held many meetings in town-halls and other halls throughout London to rally support. However, Emmeline Pankhurst, her daughter Sylvia and Mrs Drummond did hold a packed meeting in the Hall on 28 January 1913 that reflected their increasing frustration at the government's obvious continued reluctance to pass a Suffrage bill. At this meeting, *The Times* reported that, 'Mrs Pankhurst, who was in the chair, referring to the Parliamentary position of the Suffrage question said: 'We knew, and we have information which assures us, that the whole plot was decided long ago, even to the Speaker's ruling. We know that the Prime Minister knew what was going to be done days before it was done. But what is our answer to this treachery? Militancy.' And it was militancy that immediately followed this meeting when Sylvia Pankhurst and Mrs Drummond led a group of women to the House of Commons to demand a meeting with Lloyd George there and then. He refused and offered to meet them the following morning, but they refused to wait and were arrested because they would not move on. They were taken to Cannon-row police station.

The RHS Council Minutes during this period do bring to light the issues they faced in dealing with the militant suffragettes. It was eventually at their 9 September 1913 Council Meeting that a memorandum, written by the Secretary, the Rev. W. Wilks, 'for the careful and important consideration of the President and Members of the Council', reminded them of their policy to respect 'a strictly non-political attitude in the matter of the Hall lettings and that the Council should maintain an absolutely neutral attitude'. This memo had been prompted by a letter sent to him from the N.W.S.P.U. drawing attention to this policy and because he had been put in a position on several occasions where it had been made clear to him by members of the Council that the Hall should not, in future, be hired to Emmeline Pankhurst's N.W.S.P.U. After deliberation, the Council carried by seven votes to two to continue to accept further N.W.S.P.U. applications for hire, 'as long as propriety and decorum were maintained'. Not so lucky were the Communist Party, as Brent Elliott points out in his book, *The Royal Horticultural Halls: A History*, 'In 1926 the Communist Party was refused permission to rent the Hall for "welcoming certain of their members when they are released after imprisonment for sedition".'

As an interesting postscript to the Pankhursts and their involvement with the RHS Hall, Sylvia Pankhurst, many years later on 22 July 1946, wrote to the Society on behalf of the Princess Tsahai Memorial Hospital Fund, whose patrons were the Emperor (Haile Selassie) and Empress of Ethiopia and their daughter, to request the hire of it for a memorial bazaar. Sylvia, at this period of her life, had been very heavily involved in supporting the Ethiopian Emperor against fascist aggression from Mussolini and had become Editor of the *New Times and Ethiopian Post*. She retired to Ethiopia in the mid-1950s and died there in 1960. There is no record of the Bazaar having been held in the RHS Hall, but her letter to the Society remains.

The Society's concerns about the Pankhursts' militant group seem also to have been equally shared with the other militant group, the Women's Freedom League, because, following a lecture on 'Some Economic Aspects of the Women's Suffrage Movement' by Reginald

Letter dated 22 July 1946, from Sylvia Pankhurst to the RHS requesting a tenancy for a Memorial Bazaar, on behalf of the Princess Tsahai Memorial Hospital Fund.

Princess Tsahai Memorial Hospital Fund

Patrons:
THEIR IMPERIAL MAJESTIES THE EMPEROR AND EMPRESS OF ETHIOPIA.
H.I.H. PRINCESS TENAGNE WORK HAILE SELASSIE OF ETHIOPIA.
Chairman: LORD WINSTER.
Bankers: NATIONAL PROVINCIAL BANK, LTD.,
Bloomsbury Square Branch, New Oxford House, W.C.1.

All Donations to be sent to—
Hon. Treasurer:
LORD HORDER
c/o Messrs. H. REYNOLDS & CO.
Hon. Chartered Accountant.
1. Bloomsbury Court, W.C.1.

Overseas Donations to LORD HORDER
c/o Messrs. H. Reynold's & Co.
through any branch of
BARCLAYS BANK abroad.
(Dominions, Colonial and Overseas.)

Correspondence only to—
Hon. Secretary:
E. SYLVIA PANKHURST.
3, Charteris Road, Woodford, Essex.
BUCkhurst 2461.

ESP/AB   22nd July, 1946.

The Manager,
Royal Horticultural Society,
Vincent Square,
London, S.W.1.

Dear Sir,

We intend to hold a Bazaar on behalf of the Princess Tsahai Memorial Hospital in November and should be glad to know if you could let us have your Hall for this purpose, what vacant dates you have, what your charge would be ~~~~~~~~ from 10 a.m. to 8 p.m., 10 a.m. to 7 p.m., 10 a.m. to 6 p.m., what the difference would be if we only had the Hall from 11 a.m., and what the charge would be for a second day from 2 p.m. to 6 p.m., 7 p.m., or 8 p.m.

Faithfully yours,

E. SYLVIA PANKHURST.

John Campbell, held on 10 February 1909, they resolved later that month to decline further applications from them also. However, once again they subsequently relented (probably after similar pressure had been brought to bear on the hapless Secretary) and did accept other meetings to be held on 10 February the following year and in March 1912. One has to bear in mind that all around the Society in Westminster there were regular demonstrations and meetings that caused public order to be severely challenged. Indeed, the National Union of Women's Suffrage Societies was based at 25 Victoria Street under the direction of Mrs Henry Fawcett and Mrs Eva McLaren with the objective to form a Women's Suffrage Society in every county and borough. They held 'at homes' twice a month and the Women's Freedom League held their own at Buckingham Street weekly. Emmeline Pankhurst also lived at the home of one of her youngest married sisters at 5 Vincent Square for brief periods. She would, of course, have been very familiar with Rochester Row police station on the other side of the square, where many of her colleagues fighting the suffragette cause appeared to face charges in the small court within the station, following their arrest in Parliament Square, or the immediate locality. Such was the concern by government that at the opening of Parliament in February 1908 some 4,000 constables and mounted police were deployed along the route where the King would drive to open it, where normally there would have only been around 2,500. Many of the mounted police came from Rochester Row police station that had been a 'Police Horse Patrol Station' since 1869.

Women were not the only gender taxing the RHS policies. The Right To Work National Council, a body proclaiming no political bias that concerned itself with 'matters pertaining to unemployment', applied to use the Hall in 1906. Its executive committee was chaired by the prominent Socialist and Independent Labour Party members George N. Barnes and J. Ramsay MacDonald with Kier Hardie also a member. Consideration was given to this at the RHS Council's 6 November meeting but, clearly facing a similar dilemma,

no decision was made. They then declined letting applications from the Right To Work National Council on 26 January 1909 and 26 January 1910. No reasons were recorded as to why, but this organisation was also militant in their pursuit of securing better conditions of employment throughout the country. However, on 16 February 1909, the day of the opening of Parliament, and as part of a four-day demonstration organised by the Right to Work National Council described in the *Daily Express* as 'the scene of the most menacing Socialist demonstrations ever organised in the metropolis', the Hall was used to marshal at least 8,000 unemployed women and children from all over the country who had marched from Cavendish Square through London. At the Hall they were provided with a meal before deputations of them went on to the House of Commons to see the members that represented the constituencies they had come from. According to the *Manchester Guardian*, 'not less than 16,000' unemployed men, women and children had marched through London to coincide with the opening of Parliament. A group of suffragettes also joined in, headed by Mrs Despard who, with her other ladies, helped serve 'a mug of milk and a bag of cakes to at least 8,000 tired and hungry women and children who filed into the Hall'. Organised by the chief Socialist and Labour societies that included the Socialist Democratic Party, the Independent Labour Party, the Labour Representation Association and the Right to Work Committees, a meeting also took place in the Hall that demanded, 'all public business be obstructed until the unemployed question receives attention from the government.'

Four years earlier, in April 1905, the RHS Council had agreed to allow the Westminster Constitutional Association to hold a ticket meeting at £15 15s. (£1,409) subject to £50 (£4,472) being deposited as 'cautious money' against any claim for damage to the Society's property. Even though this was a Conservative Association based in Westminster there was obviously still an expectation that unruly and riotous behaviour may occur that could cause damage to the Hall.

And, on the evening of 15 April 1911, the London Cab-drivers' Union held a mass meeting of their members in the Hall to agree upon a reply to an ultimatum issued by their masters, the Motor Cab Proprietors' Association. The Union had asked all Motor Cab drivers in London to take their cabs home at 6 p.m. that evening before attending the meeting, and *The Times* advised their readers that, as a result, there could be a shortage of these! Here was a classic confrontation between union and proprietor that has continued to

this day. The proprietors had unilaterally decided that the drivers should pay the petrol tax of an additional 1½d (54p) per gallon for all petrol used, or an increase in fares before any discussions had taken place. The meeting unanimously passed two resolutions to 'cease work in the event that any new system, which in our opinion is prejudicial to the public and drivers alike, is put into effect before the findings of the recently appointed committee is made', and that, 'the taxi drivers of London should be paid a daily wage'. Motor Hansoms, as they had originally been named in 1904 when only three of them existed, had increased rapidly in the intervening years and by 1910 there were 5,070. In the same year, the last horse-drawn omnibus ran its final journey from London Bridge. Taxis cost, on average, £350 (£30,625) to purchase, but the average daily earnings of each cab were about £1 3s. 1d. (£101) of which the driver's percentage worked out at 5s.9½d. (£25.50). From this they had to deduct 2s. (£8.75) per day for petrol, and the pennies they had to pay for admission to railway stations. This left them a net daily sum of 15s. 3½d. (£67.08).

RHS Application for Hire Agreement made with the National Amalgamated Union of Shop Assistants & Clerks, dated 1 May 1926, for a May Day Dance and Rally with subsequent hand-written note on it!

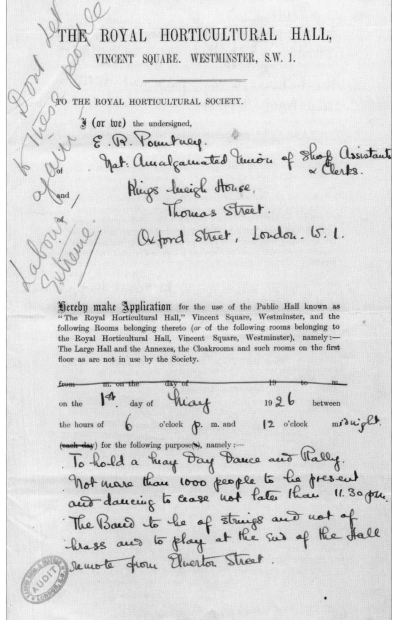

The last word on this goes to whoever wrote across the RHS contract that had been drawn up for a May Day Dance and Rally for the National Amalgamated Union of Shop Assistants & Clerks on 1 May 1926. Scrawled in heavy pencil, and clearly written after the event with feeling were the words, 'Don't let to these people again – Labour Extreme.' One assumes that it was the words of the then RHS Secretary, Col. F.R. Durham. However, taking into account the dire outcome of the negotiations relating to the miners' strike that had broken down that day between Stanley Baldwin's Conservative government and the General Council of the TUC, the timing of this rally and dance rendered it prone to trouble. This was the day the TUC announced The General Strike of 1926, starting on 3 May. One thousand union members, coming to the Hall having heard this news, would have produced a volatile situation. It is no wonder that a fervent rally, coupled with ample liquor in the Royal Horticultural Society's Hall, would have been very tempting to many to treat the occasion almost as the French did when storming the Bastille!

At least the RHS Council had already added a written clause into their contract for this event, that dancing should 'cease not later than 11.30 p.m. and that the Band [as there always was at a dance or social occasion of this nature] was to be of strings, and not of brass, and to play at the end of the Hall.' Dances, reunions and social events of this nature had been held regularly since 1907 by other trades unions, notably the Teachers Union, the National Cyclists' Union, the National Print Workers Union, The National Society of Operative Printers' Assistants (NATSOPA), the London Union of Training Colleges, the socialist London Clarion Van and *Daily Herald* League movements, the Workers' Travel Association, and the Cabdrivers' Benevolent Association. The London Clarion Van Movement, supported by the leading Labour and Socialist Organ, *The Clarion*, was part of a wider Clarion fellowship that encompassed Clarion Cycling, Swimming, Gardening, Photographic, and Handicraft Clubs and Guilds. In 1908 *The Clarion* claimed a circulation of 'over 80,000 weekly' and that 'more than any other influence it has been instrumental in bringing the question of Socialism so prominently before the public'. The London Clarion Vanners, or Clarionettes, as they were also called were the early socialist missionaries spreading their gospel and securing new members from the districts they visited. By 1908, and within three years of fundraising, they had 'nearly £400 (£35,384) – to build and equip two Clarion Vans, the finest vehicles of their kind in existence, and organised a Van Propaganda, which for effectiveness declines to accept a second place to any in the kingdom.' Their annual London fundraising social events, New-Year Reunions, Concerts and Dances, whist drives, and meetings were held in the RHS Hall for 21 years between 1908 and 1933. Some were also promoted by the *Daily Herald* League that had similar objectives. During the General Strike of 1926 it published *The British Worker*, in full

support of it. Archbishop Bourne called it, 'A sin against God'. The London Labour Party held its own annual reunion and dance at the Hall for 14 years between 1924 and 1938 and after the Second World War on several occasions up to 1950 in conjunction with the Fabian Society. Even they had to pay a £50 (£2,223) deposit on each booking because of the rule that stated, 'A deposit is required when the Hall is taken by or for any political purpose, party or organisation. This will be returned provided no damage is done to the building, or its equipment, the Council of the RHS being sole judges of such damage.' They were, of course, well aware by then of the ferment that could arise between the political parties and the factions that arose from them. One such faction was the 'Ginger Club'. *The Times* reported on 16 February 1927 that it was 'composed of self-styled rebels in the political Labour Party and the trade union movement, inaugurated at a birthday party given by Mr George Lansbury at the Horticultural Hall on Monday'. One of those present, Mr A.J. Cook, said, 'that of all the agreements supposed to have been made for the miners (post General Strike) not one would be honoured or kept for a moment longer than it was bound to be'. He then announced a new slogan for the Ginger Club: 'Capitalism cannot be mended; it must be ended.' The Rev. William Wilks, who acted as the Society's first Secretary between 1880 and 1920, had to deal with much of the unruly behaviour and difficult conditions of some of these events. However, he also reveals potential unruliness from another quarter in a note back to Miss M.E. Dalrymple Hay who had enquired about a tenancy for a Display by The Boys' Naval Brigade in October 1916. Miss Dalrymple was The B.N.B.'s Hon. Secretary, and had also acted as Secretary to the Colonial Nursing Association for 12½ years up to 1913. In her note to Wilks she made the point that the Brigade had 'sent over 100 officers – 1,400 boys into H.M Services since the commencement of the war'. In a PS to his reply to her, Wilks wrote, 'You should have some form of ticket admission otherwise all the little gamins of the neighbourhood are

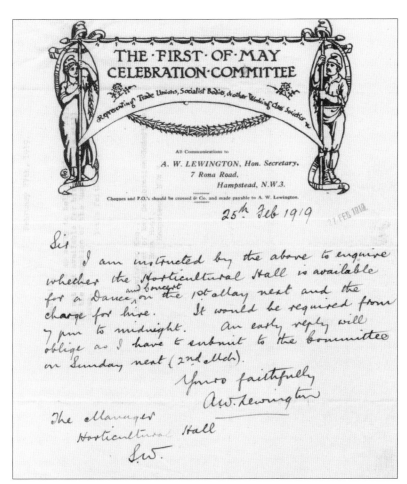

apt to get in and some may be exceedingly undesirable.' Indeed, in 2004, when I ran some reminiscence groups of local residents who had been to the events in the Halls as children, one lady explained that when she had been a 'nipper' she knew the Commissionaire on the door, and he would let her in to see what kind of show was inside! Many of the local children also used to run errands to raise money, either for tuck, or to get into the shows.

The birth of The Parliamentary Labour Party as we know it today took place on 15 February 1906 at the Methodist Memorial Hall in London's Farringdon Street during the day. It was followed by their Independent Labour Party (Great Britain) Metropolitan District Council Reception to the Labour Representation Committee, and other socialist Members of Parliament and parliamentary candidates, in the RHS Hall that evening. Prior to its formation earlier that day, the Labour Party had simply been a loose-knit association called the Labour Representation Committee formed on 27-8 February 1900. (Exactly 100 years later, on 28 February 2000, the Labour Party returned to the RHS Hall, where they

held part of their Centenary Celebration.) Its new leader, and the principal architect of the socialist movement, Keir Hardie, was elected but he would resign two years later in 1908 to devote much of his time campaigning for votes for women and assisting Sylvia Pankhurst, with whom he was still romantically linked. He was no stranger to militant confrontation in the cause of women's enfranchisement and had, in fact, already been arrested for his campaigning at an early suffragette meeting in London. He had fought for Socialism and its many causes all his life, having worked in the mines for 17 years until he was 24. He then devoted himself to journalism and was elected to the Lanarkshire Miners' Union. He both edited and owned the weekly 'Labour Leader', the official organ of the I.L.P. and became its first Chairman in 1893. Famously, Keir Hardie sent a shudder of horror through the Mother of all Parliaments by presenting himself at the bar of the House in 1892 when he took the oath, on his election as a Member for North-West Ham, clad in the costume of his class – a blue serge double-breasted jacket and waistcoat, fawn-coloured trousers, a striped flannel shirt with a coloured scarf tied round its collar in a sailor knot and a blue Scotch cap!

On 19 July 1906 the Labour Party held another reception in the Hall, this time their Inter-Parliamentary Reception following its Conference of Representatives of the Socialist and Labour Parties of the Parliaments of Europe that had, on that occasion, been held in Essex Hall on the Strand, London. This Conference and Reception was hosted by James Ramsay MacDonald and attended by some forty of their Continental friends including Jean Jaurés, Leader of the French Socialist Party, August Bebel, a German Social Democrat and one of the founders of what is known today as the SPD, M. Anikine, a member of the Russian *Duma*, and Emile Vandervelde, President of The International Socialist Bureau in Belgium. At the Conference Mr Anikine had urged the necessity of protesting in the Parliaments of all the civilised countries, 'against the crimes of the Tsar's Government'. He would later become a primary figure in the

INDEPENDENT LABOUR PARTY
London & Southern Counties Divisional Council.
International Reception, Sept. 27th, 1924
HORTICULTURAL HALL.

DANCE PROGRAMME.

1. One Step.................March of the Mannikins
2. Fox Trot................Maybe
3. Fox Trot................I love you
4. Waltz....................Just a girl that men forget
5. Fox Trot...............Linger awhile
6. Waltz....................A kiss in the dark
7. Fox Trot...............Japanese Sunset
8. Lancers.................Operatica
9. One Step....... ....Scottish Medley
INTERVAL.
10. One Step ....American Medley
11. Fox Trot...............Pasadena
12. Fox Trot...............12 o'clock at night
13. Waltz....................When the lights are low
14. Fox Trot ....The One I love
15. Lancers.................Idaho
16. Waltz....................What'll I do
17. Fox Trot...............Night in the woods
18. One Step...............If all the girls
    Extras
    M.Cs. : FRED HAGGER & E. V. LLOYD.
West End I.L.P. Orchestra Conductor, Leonard Pearce.

LEFT   *Dance programme for the Independent Labour Party, London & Southern Counties Divisional Council for an International Reception held in the Lindley Hall, on 27 September 1924.*

BELOW   *The National Trade Union and Labour Party Liaison Committee's brochure for the Labour Party Centenary Celebration, held in the Lawrence Hall on, 28 February 2000.*

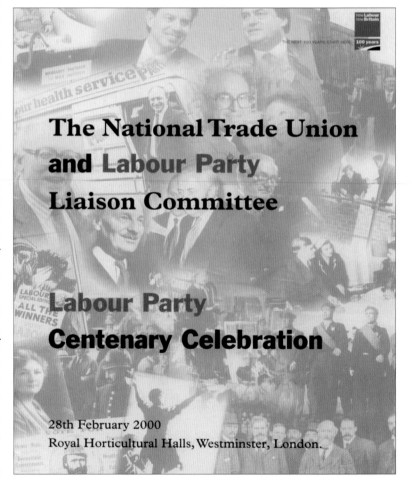

The National Trade Union and Labour Party Liaison Committee

Labour Party Centenary Celebration

28th February 2000
Royal Horticultural Halls, Westminster, London.

Revolution that led to the overthrow of the Tzar and his family.

At the complete opposite end of the political divide was The Tariff Reform League, a protectionist pressure group formed of radicals from the Conservative and Unionist Party that supported Joseph Chamberlain's crusade to support preferential treatment of tariffs for the Colonies and greater imperial consolidation. This had been hotly debated within the Party and differing views existed outside The League. However, on 7 February 1908 at its Annual Conference in the Hall, chaired by Viscount Ridley, 1,200 delegates from all over the country attended to support the reform of fiscal policy and, as such, the Conservative and Unionist Party's first constructive policy supported by Mr Balfour. As Brent Elliott in his definitive book, *The Royal Horticultural Society: A History 1804-2004*, explains: 'The free enterprise policies of the Gladstone years gave way to an increasing acceptance

THE LABOUR PARTY.

A RECEPTION

to the Socialist and Labour Members of Foreign Parliaments, in connection with the International Socialist Commission, will be held at the Horticultural Hall, Vincent Square, Westminster, S.W., on

THURSDAY, JULY 19th, 1906,

from 8 to 11 p.m.

ADMISSION 1/-

RT HON. J. CHAMBERLAIN

Postcard of the Rt. Hon. Joseph Chamberlain (1836-1914) who acted as a Vice-President of the RHS between the turn of the century until his death in July 1914, but was also active in the Hall where meetings of his Tariff Reform League were held.

the maintenance of religion, the Constitution, and the Imperial ascendancy of the British Empire. The Ladies' Grand Council of the Primrose League, whose first president was Fanny, Duchess of Marlborough in 1844, was in turn succeeded by Lady Salisbury, Lady Gwendolen Cecil, and Miss Balfour, sister of the Rt. Hon. A.J. Balfour, MP, who became president in 1903. Notable among the members of the executive committee of the Ladies' Grand Council were Lady Gwendolen Cecil, extra-president; the Countess of Jersey, Countess Dowager of Ancaster, vice-presidents; and the Lady Louise Loder, the Lady Llangattock, and the Lady Knightley of Fawsley, all indefatigable political workers and hostesses. No formal women's suffrage associations existed with the Grand Council. The opinions of the Primrose dames on the subject were divided and they were allowed individual freedom of choice and action where this was concerned.

On 16 May 1905 and 9 May 1906 the Hall had been host to another political party for the Liberal Social Council Receptions that followed their annual meetings. In May 1905 Arthur Balfour's Conservative Party was still in power and the Liberals would have to wait until 5 December that year before proclaiming themselves as the new government. So, in attendance at the May Reception amongst many others was Mr Herbert Henry Asquith, MP (the future Liberal Prime Minister who would take over after Sir Henry Campbell-Bannerman's death in 1908), Mr James Bryce, MP who would serve as Chief Secretary for Ireland from 1905-6, Mr Herbert Gladstone, MP, the youngest son of William Gladstone who had been born in Downing Street and would become the new Home Secretary, Sir Arthur Hayter, MP, who had chaired the Public Accounts Committee for the past four years and Mr Haldane, MP, who from 1905-12 would become Secretary of State for War, and Viscount Haldane in 1911.

The following year, the 1906 Liberal Social Council 'At Home' Reception was hosted by its president, The Countess of Crewe, in order to meet The Prime Minister, Sir Henry

of protectionism – a trend associated in great part with the Society's own Vice-President, Joseph Chamberlain (who held this office from the turn of the century until his death in July 1914). During the dark days of 1916, the question of the post-war economy was under earnest discussion, and the RHS took part in a Parliamentary committee on the imposition of protective tariffs on imports. In the autumn of 1917, the majority of Council voted that, after the war, all the Society's energies should be devoted to the reorganisation and development of British Horticulture and our Horticultural Trade.'

This trend had also been strongly supported by The Primrose League, another staunchly conservative group that first used the Hall on 18 February 1909 when the St George's Habitation General Meeting took place. The habitations of the Primrose League numbered about one thousand, and consisted of men and women members, designated knights, dames, and associates. The primary work of the habitations was to increase the number of members and instruct them in the principles and objects of the League; the chief ones being

Campbell-Bannerman. This followed its annual meeting held at Caxton Hall during the day. *The Times* reported that, 'Nearly 5,000 invitations had been issued and the (RHS) hall was thronged. The invited guests included all the members of the government, Liberal peers and Liberal members of Parliament, the members of all the metropolitan Liberal associations and of the Liberal Social Council. The guests were received by Lady Crewe, Lady Chesterfield, Lady Wimborne, Lady Burghclere, Lady Leconsfield, Lady Marjorie Sinclair, Lady Carrington and others. The band of the Coldstream Guards played during the evening.'

The Countess of Crewe was the second daughter of the Earl of Rosebery, the former Liberal Premier, and her mother was the daughter and heiress of the late Baron Meyer de Rothchild. In the summer of 1904 at a ball held in their town residence, Crewe House

Daily Mirror, 21 October 1908, depicting a photo of Mrs Winston Churchill, and the Lord Mayor of Westminster, opening a Bazaar in aid of the Robert Browning Settlement in Walworth in the Lindley Hall. This was her first public appearance since her marriage to Winston Churchill in St Margaret's Church, Westminster, on 12 September 1908.

in Curzon Street, Mayfair, one of their guests was 29-year-old Winston Churchill and this is where he first met his future wife, 19-year-old Clementine Hosier. On 21 October 1908 in the RHS Hall, she would make her first public appearance in London since her marriage, on the occasion of the opening of a Bazaar in aid of the Robert Browning's Settlement at Walworth. Sir Winston had married Clementine Hozier at St Margaret's Church in Westminster less than a month before on 12 September, so it was both touching and fitting that when she entered the Hall, escorted by the Mayor of Westminster, it was to the strains of the 'Wedding March'.

The *Daily Express* reported that, advancing to the edge of the platform, Mrs Churchill said, 'I want to thank you very much for the kind reception you have given me. I can assure you I am very glad to be here, and I feel much honoured in taking part in such an interesting and important event in the life of the Robert Browning Settlement in Walworth. I have heard of its wonderful and varied work by the little book Mrs Stead kindly sent me. It has told me of the Browning Bethany Homes for Old People, of the country holidays, of the girls' clubs and the boys' brigade, of the coffee tavern, of the lovely little gardens, and of the countless other efforts to make life brighter and happier for those who live in one of the poorest and one of the most crowded districts of London.'

The district concerned was Walworth in the Borough of Southwark and Mrs Stead was the wife of the Rev. Francis Herbert Stead who had arrived at the Robert Browning Settlement in Walworth as its Warden in 1895. He had been horrified at the poverty and conditions he found there and set about bringing about many positive changes to people's lives, but to old people in particular. Through his remarkable campaigning he is credited as having brought about the very first Old Age Pensions Act passed by Lloyd George as Chancellor of the Exchequer under the Asquith government in August 1908. This gave pensions of between 1s. and 5s. (£4.42 and £22.12) a week to some half a million men and women over 70 who did not earn more than 12s. (£53.08) a week. The Bazaar at the Hall that Mrs Churchill opened to raise funds for the Walworth Settlement was held just two months after this landmark piece of legislation was brought in and focused a great deal of additional attention on the plight of the poor and much-needed funds, as a result.

Hobbies and Pastimes

Philatelic Superlatives

The first public exhibition of stamps was held in London, in 1890, to celebrate the Jubilee of Uniform Penny Postage. This was opened by Prince Alfred, Duke of Edinburgh (Duke of Saxe-Coburg-Gotha) who was an enthusiastic stamp collector; portions of HRH's collection figured among the exhibits. Later, in the same year as the 1890 Exhibition he became Honorary President of The Philatelic Society, London – a position he held until his death. The Society was granted the right to call itself 'The Royal Philatelic Society, London' late in 1906.

The International Philatelic Exhibition, held in the RHS Hall on 23 May to 1 June 1906, was only the fourth show of international rank to be held in Britain, and was equally notable for its exhibitors, as well as its exhibits. Its patron, the Prince of Wales, who had become President of The Philatelic Society, London in May 1896 (and had also opened the second Philatelic Exhibition, held in 1897) was both a visitor to it, and an exhibitor. He displayed a portion of the contents of his magnificent collection that is now known as the Royal Philatelic Collection and, in particular, what is still the rarest and most valuable stamp in the world, the Mauritius 1847, 2d. Blue. This had then fetched the record price of £1,450 (£129,674) at public auction. Its value today has to be counted in seven figures! The stamps at the exhibition were insured for £300,000 (£26.83 million), but it was acknowledged in the catalogue's Introduction by Edward B. Evans that, should the stamps be destroyed, this sum would not cover their replacement. HRH Prince Edward

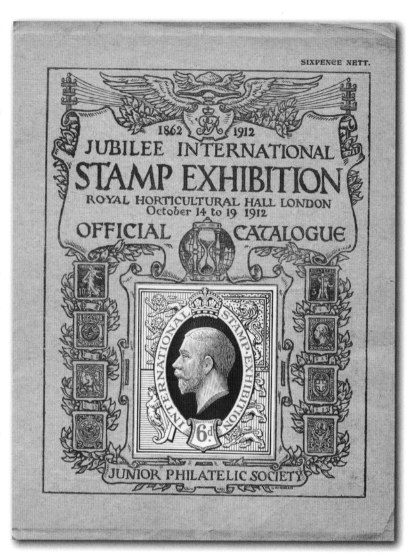

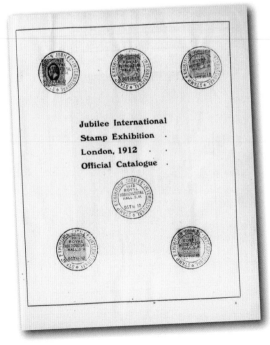

Official Catalogue of the 1862-1912 Jubilee International Stamp Exhibition, organised by the Junior Philatelic Society held in the Royal Horticultural Hall on 14-19 October 1912, showing the 'Ideal' stamps cancelled with the Exhibition's official postmark on them.

Official Catalogue of the 1906 International Philatelic Exhibition organised by the Philatelic Society, London, held in the Lindley Hall on 23 May-1 June 1906. HRH The Prince of Wales was President of the Philatelic Society, London, and Patron of the Exhibition. The Rt. Hon. Austen Chamberlain, MP, PC, was one of five Vice-Patrons. His brother, Joseph Chamberlain, was a Vice-President of the Royal Horticultural Society at this time.

Michael Sefi, Keeper of the Royal Philatelic Collection, attended a Reception during the Centenary Exhibition I staged in the Lawrence Hall in September 2004 of that year, partly in recognition of this. One of his relatives, Alexander J. Sefi, had also exhibited a specialised collection of stamps from Kashmir at the 1862-1912 Jubilee International Stamp Exhibition in the same Hall, and was to become a Partner in the renowned stamp dealer, Sefi, Pemberton & Co. who also published the monthly *Philatelic Journal of Great Britain*. Sefi went on to publish the first standard work on the study of philately entitled *An Introduction to Advanced Philately*, the first edition of which was published in 1926 (second edition 1932) by Rowley & Rowley. His firm also exhibited at the 1930 *Daily Mail* Schoolboy's Exhibition stand 15b in the Lawrence Hall, where they introduced their new 'Philatelic Microscope'. In 1933, Alexander Sefi became a signatory to the coveted Roll of Distinguished Philatelists (and died in 1934).

The Postmaster-General at the time of the 1906 exhibition and his three predecessors were nominated Vice-Patrons. One of these was Austen Chamberlain who would return to the Hall on several occasions, but specifically to attend the Tariff Reform League AGM in 1908 in support of his father Joseph Chamberlain's political initiative.

of Wales was also a late entry unlisted exhibitor with two non-competitive entries, one covering Liberia, the other France and Colonies. Other Royal exhibitors were the Heirs-apparent of Portugal and Siam, and Prince Gustav Adolf of Sweden. In their post-account of the exhibition *The London Philatelist* reported that Prince George of Wales, later to become the Duke of Kent, was a visitor to the show, as was Prince Albert 'accompanied by their tutor' who visited dealers' stalls 'making small purchases at each'. It is almost certain that part of the existing Royal Philatelic Collection, certainly the most important UK and Commonwealth collection in the world today, contains stamps purchased in the Hall at this exhibition, and subsequent ones, because several more important philatelic exhibitions were to follow that were visited by King George V, as he would become.

It would appear that the principal organisers and the dealers who took part in this event viewed it as a great success, but *Stamp Collectors' Fortnightly* in its June review showed that not everyone thought so. One visitor had written in and his letter was published as follows: 'I visited the Horticultural Hall on Saturday, May 26th, free day of course (normal admission 1s. (£4.47)), but, as I travelled all the way from Manchester, perhaps I could be forgiven for this. Upon entering I was at once loaded up with a quantity of literature. I then found myself roaming round amongst the greatest of the World's Postage Stamps. Now what are my impressions? It seems to me that could I but have had someone alongside me as I walked around, to point out and explain some of the Exhibits, I should have considered it the greatest of all Philatelic feasts. The

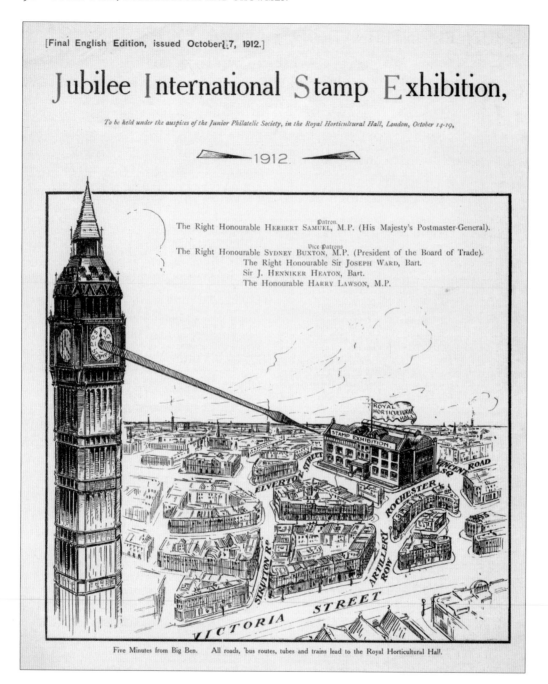

[Final English Edition, issued October 7, 1912.]

Jubilee International Stamp Exhibition,

To be held under the auspices of the Junior Philatelic Society, in the Royal Horticultural Hall, London, October 14-19,

1912.

Patron.
The Right Honourable HERBERT SAMUEL, M.P. (His Majesty's Postmaster-General).

Vice-Patrons.
The Right Honourable SYDNEY BUXTON, M.P. (President of the Board of Trade).
The Right Honourable Sir JOSEPH WARD, Bart.
Sir J. HENNIKER HEATON, Bart.
The Honourable HARRY LAWSON, M.P.

Five Minutes from Big Ben.   All roads, 'bus routes, tubes and trains lead to the Royal Horticultural Hall.

Graphic illustration from the Supplement of the 1862-1912 Jubilee International Stamp Exhibition showing that, 'All roads, 'bus routes, tubes and trains lead to the Royal Horticultural Hall!' In fact the position of the Hall is incorrect, as the entrance to the Hall faced onto Vincent Square, and not facing Big Ben, as shown.

knowledge that I was amongst so many rarities of the Stamp World and yet unable to make myself acquainted with their historical points, on the spot, was so tantalising, that I am afraid it lost me much of the Philatelic charm which I felt when entering the Hall.'

Lessons were learnt, and from this event emerged a man who would become one of the philatelic world's most important figures, Mr Frederick John Melville. He had started his interest in stamps (and journalism) at a very early age at Westminster School. After leaving school,

he received journalistic training from Sir Alfred Harmsworth (later Lord Northcliffe), the press baron who founded the *Daily Mirror* and the *Mail*, and these connections would remain and manifest themselves in many ways in his future life and activities. Indeed his first foray into both journalism and philately was in 1897 when he launched his one penny publication, *Stamp Collecting*. Then, in 1899, at the age of 17, he and his friends formed 'The Junior Philatelic Society' that would later become known as 'The National Philatelic Society', celebrating its

An enlarged reproduction of the "Ideal" Stamp which is being printed and perforated at the Jubilee International Stamp Exhibition.

An enlarged reproduction of the "Ideal" Stamp which is being printed and perforated at the Jubilee International Stamp Exhibition.

centenary in 1999. He had attended the 1906 Exhibition to give a lantern slide show on 'His Majesty's Mail' as part of the Calendar of Events and was made Chairman of the JPS Imperial Stamp Exhibition that took place in Caxton Hall in 1908. In the same year he became Editor of his new JPS journal that would become an enduring stamp lover's publication, the *Stamp Lover*. His deployed his skills as an exhibition organiser in earnest with the next

great philatelic event to take place in the Hall, the 1862-1912 Jubilee International Exhibition between 14-19 October 1912. This was billed as 'The largest and most international of its kind ever held in London or elsewhere with more than 200 philatelists of all nationalities' under the auspices of the Junior Philatelic Society, of which he was President. *The Times* claimed, 'The collection of stamps brought together is probably the largest ever shown, and is valued at

Set of six colour 1862-1912 Jubilee International Stamp Exhibition 'Ideal' commemorative postcards.

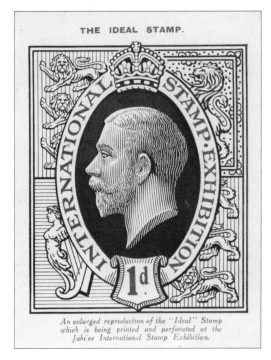

An enlarged reproduction of the "Ideal" Stamp which is being printed and perforated at the Jubilee International Stamp Exhibition.

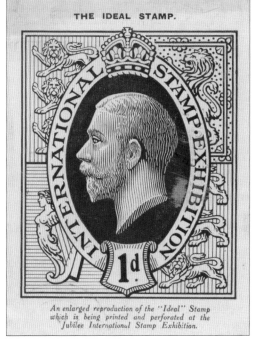

An enlarged reproduction of the "Ideal" Stamp which is being printed and perforated at the Jubilee International Stamp Exhibition.

Admission ticket to the 1923 London International Stamp Exhibition, organised by the Junior Philatelic Society, held in the Lindley Hall on 14-26 May 1923, 'With the compliments of Sefi, Pemberton and Co. Ltd', one of the stamp dealers on Stand 1.

£300,000 [£26.83 million]'. The exhibition was opened by the Postmaster General and Patron of the Exhibition, The Rt. Hon. Herbert Samuel, MP. One of the most important features was a model, but fully operational, stamp-making factory. The process involved paper making, stamp printing and perforation. A large Wharfedale printing press was part of this with a capacity to print 10 sheets of 240 stamps per sheet, per minute. According to Glenn H.

Block of four 1923 London International Stamp Exhibition commemorative mint stamps.

Morgan in his book, *British Stamp Exhibitions*, '24,000 "Ideal" stamps were produced at the show', and many remain today as collectable mementos of this exhibition. Fred Melville and his Junior Philatelic Society were back again on 14-26 May 1923 when the London International Stamp Exhibition was launched by them. Opened by the then Postmaster General, Sir William Joynson-Hicks, Melville had originally received an acceptance to his invitation for The Rt. Hon. Neville Chamberlain to open the exhibition some 20 months earlier when he then held the position of Postmaster General, but subsequently became the Prime Minister. HM King George V visited the exhibition on 18 May and spent nearly two hours there. Melville's work in connection with exhibitions brought him into regular contact with King George V, whose enthusiasm for philately is legendary. He always accompanied His Majesty on his inspection of exhibits at major exhibitions. Another Royal visitor was The Crown Prince of Sweden. Mr Leonard Wright's Orchestral Band played an extensive repertoire of music throughout, and the official banquet for the Exhibition was held at the famed *Hotel Cecil* on the Strand on 17 May. Melville also later became actively involved as Patron and adviser to several other notable exhibitions, especially the Schoolboy's Own Exhibitions that took place in the Hall from 1926. By 1930, he had secured the support of the *Daily Mail* and the Hon. Esmond Harmsworth, MP, opened this show on 31 December 1929. Esmond was Sir Alfred's brother.

In 1934, another landmark philatelic exhibition was held in the Hall called the International Air-Post Exhibition (APEX), when Fred Melville was the organising director on the Executive Committee. Only two international exhibitions concentrating on air-post had been held before; the first in Paris in 1930, and the second in Danzig in July 1932. Highlighting its international interest, Andrew, Prince of Russia visited this on the last day, and sent a postcard from the show to the Imperial Bank in Baghdad, Iraq, on 12 May. The first winged postmark had been created especially to use with it (applied to all mail that was sent

out from a special Post Office set up in the Hall) and the Marquess of Londonderry, the Secretary of State for Air (and also an honorary president), formally opened it on its first day, 7 May. This event was a real celebration of all post sent by air in one form or another. Pigeon post was celebrated when Lord Londonderry sent a 'pigeongram' message attached to the leg of a pigeon from the steps of the Hall to the Postmaster General, Sir Kingsley Wood, MP Other forms of air-mail by Zeppelins, balloons, gliders, catapults, aeroplane and sea-plane were celebrated, and six special postcards depicting some of the rarest and most curious exhibits had been produced. The first Autogiro Air Mail to be carried by its pilot, R. Brie, signed by his only passenger, James Davis, was flown over the original route of the first U.K. aerial post in 1911, between Windsor and London. Herr Gerhard Zucker displayed his Rocket that would create air mail history on 6 June that year when the first trial firing ever attempted on British soil with a mail-carrying

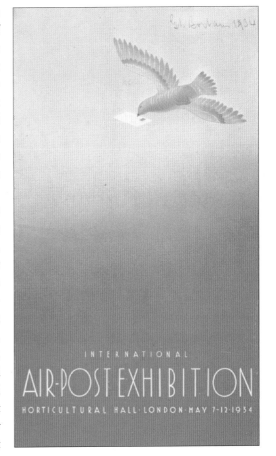

Official Catalogue of the 1934 International Air Post Exhibition (APEX), held in the Lindley Hall, 7-12 May 1934. The Exhibition was opened by the Rt. Hon. The Marquess of Londonderry, Secretary of State for Air (and also an honorary president) on 7 May 1934.

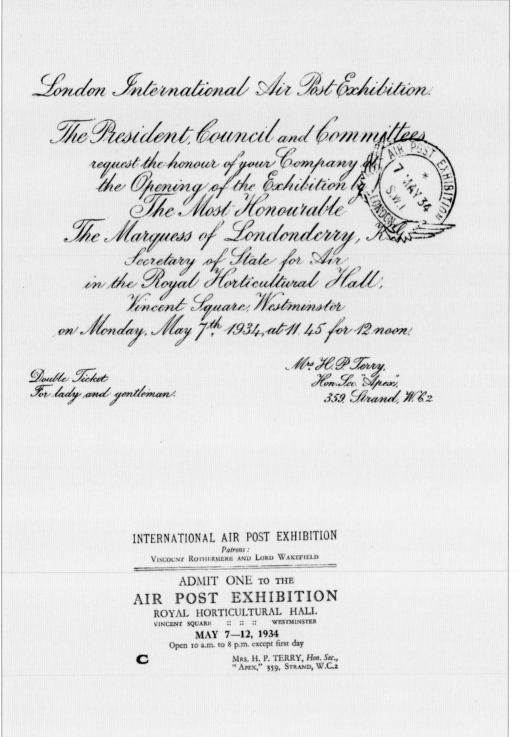

London International Air Post Exhibition.

The President, Council and Committees request the honour of your Company at the Opening of the Exhibition by The Most Honourable The Marquess of Londonderry, K.G. Secretary of State for Air in the Royal Horticultural Hall, Vincent Square, Westminster on Monday, May 7th 1934, at 11.45 for 12 noon.

Double Ticket
For lady and gentleman.

Mrs. H. P. Terry,
Hon. Sec. "Apex",
359. Strand, W.C.2

INTERNATIONAL AIR POST EXHIBITION
Patrons:
VISCOUNT ROTHERMERE AND LORD WAKEFIELD

ADMIT ONE TO THE
AIR POST EXHIBITION
ROYAL HORTICULTURAL HALL
VINCENT SQUARE :: :: :: WESTMINSTER
MAY 7—12, 1934
Open 10 a.m. to 8 p.m. except first day

C

MRS. H. P. TERRY, *Hon. Sec.,*
"APEX," 359, STRAND, W.C.2

LEFT *Admission tickets for the Official Opening and normal open days of the 1934 Air Post Exhibition, 7-12 May 1934.*

RIGHT *Set of six pairs of APEX commemorative stamps.*

RIGHT *An APEX postcard addressed to Baron Stackelberg, posted on 12 May 1934, signed by 'Andrew, Prince of Russia' who had visited the Exhibition.*

rocket successfully took place on the Sussex Downs with a payload of some 1,200 letters. It was fitting, therefore, that some of the world's most celebrated aviators visited the show, and also attended the official banquet held at the *Dorchester Hotel* on 9 May. Of particular note was that Monsieur Louis Bleriot was a Guest of Honour in commemoration of the 25th Anniversary of the first flight across the English Channel which he accomplished in 1909. Charles Rolls had followed him just over one year later with a double crossing when he also dropped mail over Sangatte, the first aeroplane letters addressed to the President of

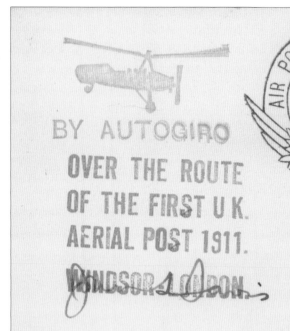

BY AUTOGIRO
OVER THE ROUTE
OF THE FIRST U.K.
AERIAL POST 1911.

WINDSOR — LONDON

Stand No. 12
"APEX"
Royal Horticultural Hall
Vincent Square
London

436

LA POSTE PAR PIGEONS

A bord de l' « Ariane »
22 juillet 1905

A l'occasion du grand lâcher effectué aujourd'hui dans la Manche, nous nous faisons un plaisir de vous adresser du large ce message par pigeon voyageur, en vous priant de le conserver comme souvenir de nos épreuves colombophiles de 1905.

LE MATIN.

MESSAGE PAR PIGEON

Concours Colombophile en Mer
Organisé par Le Matin

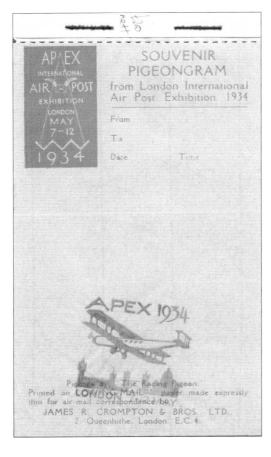

the Aéro Club de France. Bleriot was one of 12 Committee of Honour Aviators that included Sir Arthur Whitten Brown, Rear Admiral Richard E. Byrd, Sir Alan Cobham, Squadron Leader O.R. Gayford, Air Commodore Sir Charles Kingsford-Smith, J.A. Mollison and his wife, also known as Amy Johnson. Lord Rothermere, brother of the late Lord Northcliffe, was one of the two Patrons of APEX. It must be assumed that this choice was made, largely in recognition of the efforts he had made in the previous 25 years to stimulate the pioneers of mechanical flight to achieve what they had.

It would be March 1969 before another philatelic exhibition took place in the Halls, and this was the 16th STAMPEX, opened by Mr John Stonehouse, the last Postmaster General before the General Post Office (GPO) ceased to become a government department. STAMPEX continued to hold their annual show (bi-annual from 1984 with the British Philatelic Exhibition) in the RHS Halls until their 51st event in October 1995, after which

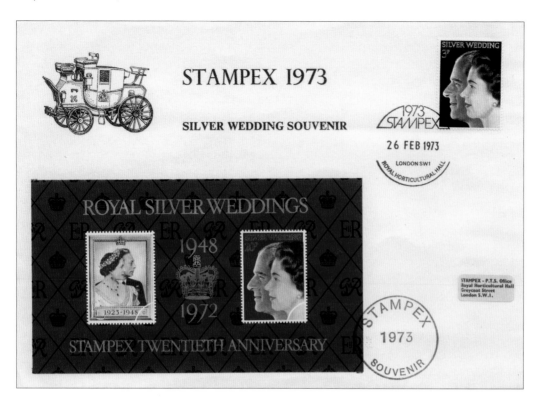

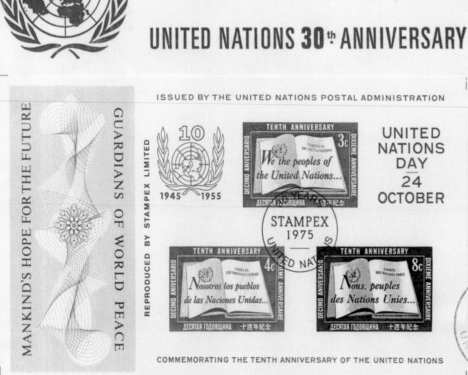

Selection of Commemorative First Day Covers for STAMPEX philatelic exhibitions in 1973, 1975, 1979 and 1984. These were able to be posted from either of the two Halls they were held in.

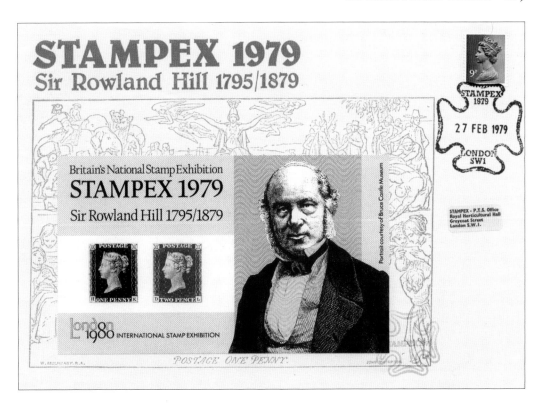

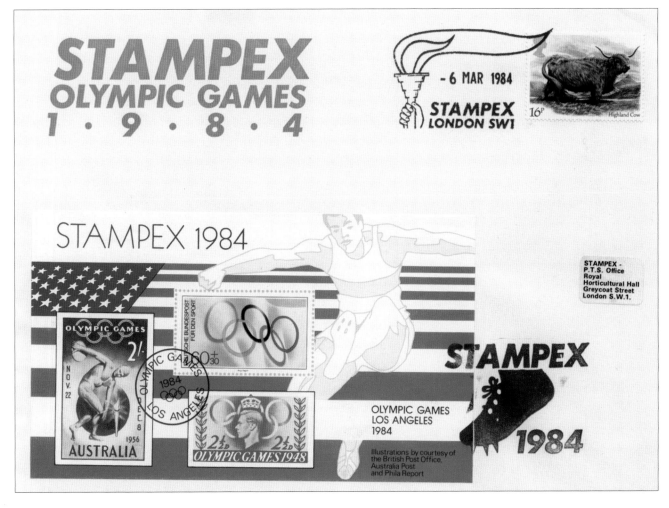

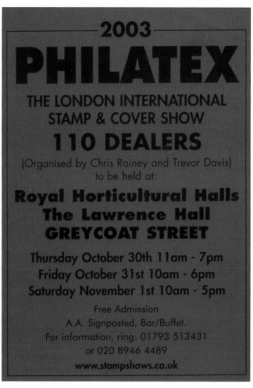

FAR LEFT   *Spring STAMPEX Catalogue held in both Halls on 25 February-1 March 1992. This was organised by STAMPEX Ltd, a wholly owned subsidiary of the Philatelic Traders' Society (PTS) that first inaugurated itself as a Limited Company on 14 September 1946.*

LEFT   *Promotional leaflet for the 2003 PHILATEX London International Stamp & Cover Show, held in the Lawrence Hall, on 30 October-1 November 2003.*

they abruptly moved to the Business Design Centre where this is still held. In its place came the 1st London Stamp & Postal History Fair held in the New Hall on 5-8 March 1997. This was organised by the late, and sadly missed, Trevor Davis with his business partner, Chris Rainey. It later became known as the London International Stamp & Cover Show and, finally, PHILATEX. This continues to be held bi-annually very successfully to the present day.

The Model Engineer

One of the most British and acclaimed areas of accomplishment at the turn of the 19th century was in the field of engineering, where its expertise in this area was manifest the whole world over, especially through the achievements of engineers such as William Murdoch, James Watt and George Stephenson. Of particular interest was the development of trains, boats and planes, but also all things involving engineering and the manufacture of its by-products, whether in the form of bridges, instruments or wireless. One man who harnessed this passion and created one of the most popular

and enduring shows for the British public was Percival Marshall, a small publisher who specialised in the field of model engineering. In January 1898 he published a new publication, *The Model Engineer and Amateur Electrician* and, in the same year, founded the first model engineering society in the UK, the Society of Model & Experimental Engineers (S.M. & E.E.), becoming its first President in 1911. On 22 October 1907 he successfully launched his new show, The Model Engineer, on the back of his magazine title in the Hall, and it continued to be held there every other year until the outbreak of the First World War in 1914. It re-started in 1922, and became an annual event in 1926 until the outbreak of the Second World War in 1939. It was re-established in 1946, and continued in the Hall until 1960. By 1961 overcrowding had become a problem and no suitable hall could be found for some years. However, after a short period it moved to a variety of London venues including Wembley Conference Centre, Olympia, and Ascot Racecourse. It continues to the present day, and in December 2010 the show was staged at Sandown Park in Surrey.

The Model Engineer and Electrician of 7 November 1907 described his first show as 'A brilliant success. Never has such a fine collection of models, such an excellent display of tools and materials, and such an interested and enthusiastic crowd of people been gathered together under one roof before'. Over 10,000 people had travelled from all over the country, and even from abroad to visit this show that concentrated on a series of hobbies and pastimes that were fervently practised by men in many households. One has to remember that, in the early days, many of the drills, files, casts, and the tools to make the models had to be made in a home workshop, where few homes had mains electricity. Gas engines had to be used to drive dynamos to provide electric lighting, and also drilling machines. Modellers had to prepare their own, including their initial design. There was no library of drawings, or plans to refer to, let alone internet access! So it was truly remarkable what these homespun engineers produced in terms of creativity and precision engineering. Percival Marshall himself acknowledged that he had known a doctor who had spent 13 years building 'a beautiful model of a locomotive'.

Further comment from the publication endorsed this when it reported. 'There were those who had passed long years in successful engineering work of every kind, and those on whose apprenticeship indentures the ink was scarcely dry. There were amateurs who had made models by the dozen, and amateurs who had never seen a model other than their own. Professors of engineering and other branches of applied science, naval and military officers, doctors, schoolmasters – and, indeed, people of every rank and calling, came, saw and admired. Those who knew what model engineering really meant went away with their approval more firmly established than before, while those who here made a first acquaintance with the model maker's art were impressed beyond all expectation. In securing public recognition of the real quality and value of model engineering, the Exhibition has, in fact, worked wonders.' Marshall also drew attention to the fact that the practice of making precision models was very important, and valuable, in perfecting design and construction for real-life prototypes, whether steamships, engines, hydroplanes, aeroplanes, locomotives, telescopes, or dynamos.

At the 1907 Show, one of the most prominent commercial exhibitors was A.W. Gamages Ltd, the famous store based in Holborn, London that displayed a wide range of models, both steam and electric. Racing yachts, complete motor boats, kites, wireless telegraphy sets, gas engines, rails and fittings were 'in profusion'. The first of successive highly competitive competitions in A, B and C Classes was held and 25 entries had been accepted. In Class A the first prize went to Mr John A. Barker for a beautifully finished model of a Stuart vertical compound engine. In Class B first prize was awarded to Mr Herbert Hildersley for his

Poster labels for The Model Engineer Exhibition for 1923 and 1924.

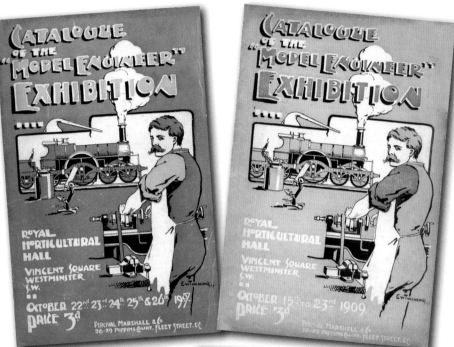

Catalogue covers for The Model Engineer Exhibition, first created and organised by Percival Marshall, held in both Halls between 1907 and 1955.

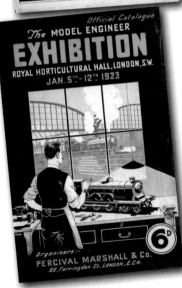

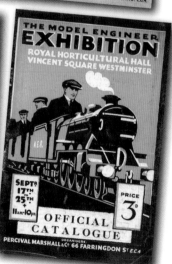

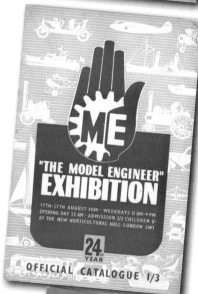

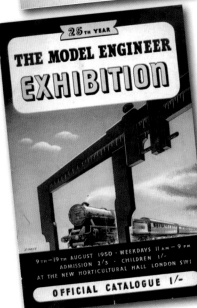

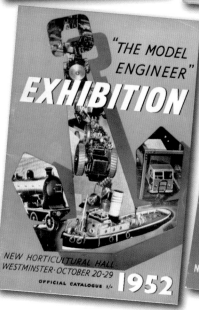

160-watt ironclad dynamo. In Class C the first prize went to Mr H.M. Savage for his 'magnificent model sea-going yacht *Muriel*'. Recognition was given to Mr Albert Lonsdale who had entered a small ironclad type dynamo, made entirely from scrap metal, without a lathe. It was also the first time that a model railway track would be assembled in the Hall but, by no means, the last. The railway connection was to remain a strong one, and a reflection of this was when Sir Josiah Stamp, Chairman of the London, Midland, and Scottish Railway opened the 19th show in 1935.

However, planes and boats were equally popular, and at the 1909 Exhibition over 50 model aeroplanes were on display showing prototype model engines that could fly them. Hitherto, reliance on their propulsion had been solely on the twisted bands of rubber that were fitted to them and this new prospect was an exciting development. This was fitting since this was also the show that Sir Hiram Steven Maxim had been invited to open, and he was presented with a silver model of his own record-breaking steam-propelled aeroplane flown 15 years earlier. Also there were working model steam and electric railways, wireless telegraphy in operation, model yachts and motor-boats, the 'Heptoic' Bioscope with the latest flying pictures, hundreds of interesting models, tools and scientific inventions. Throughout the exhibition, our old favourite, Herr Meny and his Blue Viennese Band, entertained the crowds who came in their thousands. However, it had been his White Viennese who had been present at the opening Exhibition in 1907. Just what the distinction was between them has proved difficult to discern.

Several generations of model railway enthusiasts would come to the Halls over the next 60 years and witness some of the finest displays ever mounted with legendary manufacturers such as Hornby and Bassett-Lowke among many others. Frank Hornby, a toymaker, had started his business in 1901 and would become one of the leading model train manufacturers of the 20th century until it began to hit the buffers in April 2000 when the appeal of model trains, boats and planes

had reached an all-time low from the young generation of the day. The Northampton company of Bassett-Lowke had been founded earlier by Wenman Joseph Bassett-Lowke in 1899 as a model railway equipment manufacturer including passenger carrying miniature railways, ship and industrial models. The company continued under this name until 1996, when it was sold to Corgi. It was Bassett-Lowke who provided the early model railway tracks and displays at Percival Marshall's show. The centrepiece of the shows was almost always the main track that was recorded in 1913 as being 76 feet in length with up to 14 locomotives on it. The way in which the track was laid and the power of the model locos meant that people could ride on the back of them, and in the 1930s more than 5,000 did at each show. W.J. Basset-Lowke was also a keen amateur photographer and cine enthusiast. Unique footage of his films taken at the 1924 and 1926 Model Engineer Exhibitions in The RHS Hall exist on a compilation video put together by, Rail Romances. The Model Railway Club attended the 1938 show as an exhibitor, as did several other regional clubs, and would later hold its own show in the RHS Halls from 1967-95. As an equally popular enthusiasts club, they were founded in 1910, 12 years after Marshall's new Society had been created.

ABOVE Daily Herald *photo of model aeroplane exhibitor outside the Lindley Hall arriving for the 17th The Model Engineer Exhibition, held 19-28 September 1935.*

ABOVE RIGHT *Photo of Lettice Holder, a friend and schoolboys, riding the railway track behind Aldington in the Lindley Hall at the 17th The Model Engineer Exhibition, held 19-28 September 1935. Miss Holder was the daughter of Terence Holder, well known in the large scale miniature railway field.*

BELOW RIGHT *Photo of Sir Josiah Stamp (Chairman of the London, Midland and Scottish Railway), driving a locomotive on the S.M.&E.E. track when he opened the 1935 exhibition. Sitting behind him are Percival Marshall with his sons Tim and Andrew, then James Crebbin and Arthur Dawson.*

At the 1913 Model Engineer Exhibition, an aerial with a range of about 100 miles was erected on the roof of the Hall to enable the demonstration of the latest types of wireless telegraphy, an early indication of the extreme interest and pro-active stance Marshall had in this new medium. He also helped those new to his beloved hobbies, by providing a permanently staffed and fully equipped 'Model Engineer Workshop' at his London headquarters, 66 Farringdon Street, London, EC4. Here, for very moderate fees, you could simply turn up when you liked, and learn whatever you wanted with the aid of a 'first-class' instructor who had at his disposal a wide range of lathes, planing, shaping and drilling machines, milling attachments and all kinds of metal-working tools.

In 1928, a new innovation that was to attract huge attention and discussion about our future way of life was the first British Robot, named Eric, who officially opened Marshall's 10th Exhibition. Made in aluminium and invented by Capt. W.H. Richards and Mr A.H. Reffell, the robot was able to rise from its seat, bow to an audience, and make a speech due to an electric motor and a system of pulleys and cables inside his body. The voice was that of a real person speaking through a wireless mechanism concealed in its throat. 'Eric' later toured Britain and the United States before returning to hold receptions during the 1929 Exhibition. Also at the 1928 show, Admiral Sir Richard Bacon proudly displayed his full-rigged line-of-battleship, Royal Albert, made to exact scale that took one year to make. At the Silver Jubilee Show in 1951, the star exhibit was a Churchill Tank and the 1st Miniature Racing Car Grand Prix was staged on 27 August, when Stirling Moss, Reg Parnell, and Bob Gerard – the top racing drivers of the day – were present and filmed by Pathé News.

The following year, in October 1952, HRH the Duke of Edinburgh was invited to officially open the 27th Show, just seven months prior to the coronation of his wife, HRH The Princess Elizabeth. He was presented with a model of HMS Magpie, the frigate he had commanded in the Mediterranean during the Second World War. He graciously lent this for display at the 1953 Exhibition, together with a model of the Royal Dragon class yacht Bluebottle. He was an enthusiastic visitor who had previously visited the Jubilee Exhibition held at the Imperial Institute in 1948 where he had driven Mr Linden's L.M.S. locomotive PRINCESS ELIZABETH. In 1953 he also rode the 'track', but also witnessed the amazing new central exhibit in the form of a mini racing car circuit almost 400ft in length, shaped like the Monza autodrome, with two parallel straights nearly 200ft long, a sharp loop-turn at one end and a flatter loop at the other, where precisely built model racing cars raced round between real trees. The famous maker of model

automobiles, Mr Rex Hays from Steyning in Sussex, planned the exhibit. The cars were beautiful models of about a foot in length replicating prominent Formula 2 machines – Ferrari from Italy, Gordini from France and H.W.M. from Britain. They achieved speeds of 30-40 mph and even their 'drivers' moved in their seats as they slid round in 'four-wheel drifts'. This was the first of four occasions I have been able to find when Prince Philip was invited to attend events in the RHS New Hall. The next time was on 23 May 1963 when he visited a Wildlife Exhibition sponsored by The Observer, in connection with the Council of Nature and National Nature Week when the famed naturalist and television personality, Armand Denis, displayed an African Marshall Eagle. Prince Philip returned the following year on 14 July in his capacity as President of the Fourth World Congress on the Prevention of Occupational Accidents to visit the International Industrial Equipment Exhibition for Health at Work, organised by the Royal Society for the Prevention of Accidents. His last visit was on behalf of HM The Queen, who had been invited by the

Royal Horticultural Society as their Patron, to mark the launch of its Bicentenary in the renamed Lawrence Hall on the occasion of their 16 February 2004 London Flower Show. The actual anniversary date was 9 March and this was celebrated by a reception at Hatchards Bookshop, Piccadilly, London where the RHS had been founded. I remember this well, as it was also the occasion when Dr Brent Elliott, the Society's Librarian and Archivist, launched his definitive book on the history of the Society.

2004 was also the Centenary of the original hall on Vincent Square and, in order to also celebrate this occasion, I organised a Centenary Exhibition (but held in the Lawrence Hall) as part of the RHS Bicentenary celebrations. This took place on 14-15 September. For many RHS Trustees and members this was a revelation, as material that I had uncovered and displayed was wholly unknown to them. The history of the Halls had simply been lost. I was lent a great deal of material by many who had risen to my challenge to support this unique exhibition. However, I felt particularly privileged to have been lent a superb model locomotive and tender that

RIGHT *Diploma of Merit awarded to W.A. Carter for 'An Electric Master Clock', signed by Percival Marshall, at the 6th The Model Engineer Exhibition, held in the Lindley Hall on 5-12 January 1923.*

LEFT *Photo of Showman's Traction Engine, 'A. Taylor – Electric Amusements' made by Mr A. Taylor at the 12th The Model Engineer Exhibition, held 4-13 September 1930 in the Lindley Hall.*

RIGHT *Medal awarded to W.A. Carter for 'general excellence' for his Steam Locomotive and Tender, Atlantic Type, at the 8th The Model Engineer Exhibition, held in the Lindley Hall on 17-25 September 1926.*

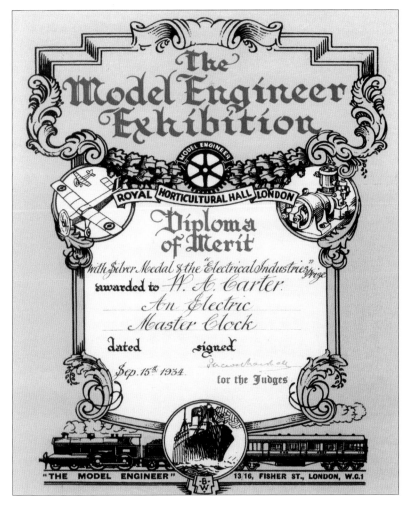

was still under construction in America when displayed! *The Times* reported that, 'in longitudinal cross-section, the model shows the works of the submarine in almost microscopic detail.' At the same event, Mr D.L. Butcher from Northamptonshire displayed a miniature of a 15th-century suit of armour that had taken him 10 years to complete. This had been entered into the Duke of Edinburgh's challenge trophy, the top award that model engineers strive to win. One can understand why when we learn that the parts for the suit of armour had all been hand beaten from sheet steel, amounting to 150 separate pieces in which had been drilled 800 holes, and the fixing of 400 tiny rivets to hold it all together. Overcoming his disability, blind ex-serviceman Mr T. Chamberlain of Reading had modelled a 10in. vertical stationary engine. Once again, *The Times* reported that, 'Every item of machining, drilling, tapping, milling, turning, and marking out was done by him from a Braille transcription of a blue print. He used micrometer and vernier caliper with Braille markings to achieve this.'

Orchestral Cage Birds

had been built by T.W. Averill of Alcester that had been exhibited at the very first Model Engineer Show in 1907. This was an exceptional example of the work model engineers carried out in replicating some of the finest locomotives the world has ever seen and took pride of place in my exhibition. It had been kindly lent by the Society that Marshall had founded, 116 years earlier, the S.M.E.E. Other exceptional examples were shown at the 1954 exhibition, opened by the Prince of the Netherlands, when Mr J.A. Brain of Glamorgan exhibited a model of the United States Navy atomic submarine, *Nautilus*, which

On 20 March 1906 the 18th London Cage Birds Association Show was held in the Hall for the first time. The noise that 700 barking terriers could make was clear but the noise made by over 2,000 cage birds was described as 'shrill'. The *Daily Express* reporting on the 1909 show described it as an 'Orchestra of Birds' continuing, 'As the number of birds increased the hall was filled with beautiful melodies and by twelve o'clock the great bird orchestra was heard at its best, with the nightingale as conductor.' Competitions were held to find the best songsters, mainly with Roller Canaries. Exhibitors would bring their birds of choice and enter them into either the novice, special and champion categories. Novices were allowed to accompany an organ to aid them but champions, who had already undergone training and lessons in singing, were not. Expert judges selected those with

Poster label for the 71st Crystal Palace National Show of Cage Birds, held in the Lawrence Hall on 19-21 January 1939. The Show had started in Crystal Palace, until it burnt down in 1936.

the greatest merit as in all competitions in whatever area.

The fascination for collecting exotic and rare birds, as well as simply keeping them in cages as songbirds, was practised by those who could afford them and, although the Society for the Protection of Birds had been formed in 1889 (its Royal Charter was gained in 1904), it had not made any real impact on these events. The primary concern of the

Society at this time, and the reason for its original formation, was to counter the trade in plumes taken from thousands of birds such as Egrets, Great Crested Grebes, Kittiwakes and Birds of Paradise for use in ladies' hats (the RSPCA, who also lobbied to change this, reported that, in 1898, one million egrets were killed in Venezuela alone). One of the rules of the Society was that, 'Lady-Members shall refrain from wearing the feathers of any bird not killed for purposes of food, the ostrich only excepted'. Adult birds were often shot or captured leaving their brood to die in their nests and this caused outrage among those who considered this an unacceptable price to pay for fashion. Travel and exploration in the 19th century by explorers, botanists, naturalists, archaeologists, game hunters and others had meant an extraordinary bounty of thousands of different species flooding into Britain,

Letter from Ramsden's Autumn Cage Bird Show requesting a tenancy in 1919.

CRYSTAL PALACE, SYDENHAM.

RAMSDEN'S AUTUMN CAGE BIRD SHOW,
CANARIES, MULES, BRITISH AND FOREIGN BIRDS,
AND TRADE EXHIBITION OF APPLIANCES, CAGES, FOODS, SEEDS, &c.
OCTOBER 27th, 28th and 29th, 1914.

SPECIAL FEATURES.—Full Prize Money Guaranteed. No Half Prize Money Rule. Classes for Champions,
Amateurs and Novices. £5 Limit Classes. Liberal Prize Money. Low Entry fee. Specialist Judges.

All communications must be made to
J. W. RAMSDEN,
~~41, Josephine Avenue, Brixton, London, S.W.~~

April 23 1919.

6 Wyatt Park Road
Streatham Hill. S.W.2.

25 APR 1919

The Secretary
    The Horticultural Hall.

Dear Sir
        Will you kindly let me have your terms for hiring the Horticultural Hall for the purpose of holding the national Cage Bird Show — Probable date last week in January or first week in February — Show to be open Tuesday, Wed & Thursday, Monday for entries to come in & Friday for clearing —
                        Yours faithfully
                            J. W. Ramsden

and the by-products of their interests were exploited ruthlessly. Together with butterflies, snakes and insects, Birds of Paradise and song birds from all over the world were collected and returned to be pinned, ensnared and caged for the pleasure of a large section of the Victorian and Edwardian public who could afford to do so. On 4 February 1922, *The Times* reported Sir Francis Younghusband saying that he had 'collected 57 different species of birds, specimens of mammals, fish, bees, and, he believed, two fleas during his 1921 Mount Everest Exhibition! Rhododendron seeds had also been collected and had been distributed to Kew, and the Royal Horticultural Society.' Sir Joseph Banks, a founder of the RHS, and President of the Royal Society, had much earlier epitomised the zeal for collecting all manner of specimens to bring back to Britain for scientific and other purposes. He is well known for his botanical and naturalist exploits while travelling with Captain Cook and the *Endeavour* during his circumnavigation of the world in 1768-7. Less known is the fact that he supplied rare specimens such as kangaroos for John Hunter, the famous surgeon who, at that time, was at the forefront of surgery, and who created what is now known as the renowned Hunterian Museum at the Royal College of Surgeons. However, it was in the late 1800s that RHS Vice-President Lionel Walter Rothschild, 2nd Baron Rothschild, Baron de Rothschild, son of Lord Nathan Rothschild, the banker and financier, began in earnest to develop his own collection that, at its height, included 300,000 bird skins, 200,000 birds' eggs, 2,250,000 butterflies, 30,000 beetles, as well as thousands of specimens of mammals, reptiles, and fishes. They formed the largest zoological collection ever amassed by a private individual.

The rare and beautiful King Bird of Paradise with its bright red plumage, and two elongated tail feathers, had a catalogue price of £1,000 (£89,430) at the 1907 Show. Another rare bird, the Trogan Bird of Paradise, with a similar price tag of £1,000 (£89,430) on it was exhibited at the 1908 Show – the first time this bird had been seen at any British show. Perhaps, it was not such a coincidence that the RSPB chose the RHS Hall to hold their Annual Meeting on 28 October 1908 not long before the London Cage Bird Association's December 1908 Show that had become a regular fixture at the Hall. However, at the 1909 Show the Rainbow Bunting from Mexico was also displayed for the first time ever in Britain as well as a rare and valuable Yellow-Winged Sugar Bird. Canaries and budgerigars were the most common birds of choice – the first budgerigar having brought in from Australia in 1840 by naturalist John Gould. However, these were not as common or cheap as they are now today and at the 1907 Show one canary had a price tag of £30 (£2,683) on it.

A slight deviation from this concentration on cage birds was the opening of the 1st Cage Birds and Aquaria Show in the New Hall on 13 and 14 December 1935. This was organised by G.B. Marshall of The Marshall Press Ltd, Milford Lane on the Strand. On display were about 3,000 entries of cage birds and over 400 glass tanks of cold water and tropical fish from exhibitors from around Britain. The Marshall Press published the only weekly paper devoted entirely to Bird Keeping called *Bird Fancy*, as well as 18 other titles from *Budgerigars for Beginners* to *White Canaries – How to Breed Them*.

By the time of the 1937 *Bird Fancy* Exhibition of Cage Birds organised by 'The Fanciers' Favourite Weekly Paper', these shows had grown to be huge. Budgerigars had by this time become the most popular and widely bred of all the cage birds. The reasons for this were several. They had proved to be hardy and did not succumb to the changeable climate in outdoor aviaries and they bred under these conditions very well with no special rearing foods required for their young. They were also available in a wide selection of bright and attractive colours and were easily trained as talking pets. Canaries were also very popular and 11 varieties of Canaries were exhibited from Border and Crested Canaries through to Lizard and Miniature Canaries. A very wide range of British Birds were also available. In the Hardbills category

were Goldfinches, Bullfinches, Greenfinches, Linnets, Redpolls, Siskins, Bramblefinches, Chaffinches, Yellow Buntings, Twite and Hawfinches. In the Softbills category were Nightingales, Stonechats, Woodlarks, Redstarts, Redwings, Fieldfares, Mistle-Thrushes, Ring Ouzels, Dippers, Shrikes, Waxwings and Woodpeckers amongst others. The Foreign Birds representation was truly international with all manner of 'Parrot-Like Birds', 'Seedeaters' and 'Insect, Fruit and Nectar Feeders'. The latter were described as 'living jewelled rainbows'. Exotic Humming Birds from South America, African Sunbirds, Bul-Buls and Fruitsuckers from Persia and India, the Bower and Bell Birds from Australia and Tanagers from North America were all there plus Hornbills, Toucans, Mynahs and Mocking Birds to name but a few.

At the 1949 76th 'Crystal Palace' Cage Birds National Championship Show staged in the New Hall, 5,000 birds were lined up like armies. Collectively, they were valued at over £100,000 (£2.67 million) and an Indian Mynah Bird cost £500 (£13,360). The Crystal Palace Show had to relocate, as did all of the other events held

Catalogue of the Bird Fancy Exhibition of Cage Birds, organised by G.B. Marshall, The Marshall Press Ltd, held in the Lawrence Hall, on 2-4 December 1937.

Photo of Audrey Hepburn with 'Hyacinth Macaw' at 76th Crystal Palace National Championship Show of Cage Birds, held in the New Hall on 17-23 January 1949.

there, following the disastrous fire of 1936 that raised it to the ground. It first came to the RHS Hall in 1939, and at that show white cockatoos performed acrobatics and tricks, such as shooting a gun, lighting a fire and dousing it with a tiny bucket! By 2003 the popularity of this national show had expanded so much that it was taking place at the NEC, Birmingham entitled, 'The National Cage and Aviary Birds Exhibition' under the ownership and direction of the publishing giant, IPC. The event industry publication, Meetings File, reported just before it that animal rights and protection group Animal Aid had denounced it as cruel and illegal claiming that 'three quarters of the 15,000 birds on sale at the show were captured in the wild using nets, baited cages or 'sticky bird lime' spread on branches of trees'. Action Aid had also claimed that three quarters of the birds caught died during transportation, and that selling pet animals in a public place was illegal. (In the autumn of 2010, the RSPB were still alerting its members and the general public of the fact that 1.4 million birds were being trapped illegally in Cyprus, and many hundreds of thousands more in Malta.) The fact is that keeping caged birds as pets came third in the rankings of pet ownership behind dogs first, and cats second. Keeping exotic fish was to become almost as popular. By the time of the 10th London Aquarium Show organised by the Federation of the British Aquatic Societies held in the RHS Hall on 29-31 October 1976, it was estimated that there were more than two million people in the UK who owned goldfish, or other exotic varieties of fish.

On 12 February 1940, Harold Clifford pleaded guilty at the Westminster Police Court to stealing a Green Border canary from the National Bird Show at the New Horticultural Hall, valued at £7 10s. (£360) He had been seen taking the bird, which had been awarded a first prize that day, from its cage, put it in his pocket and walked away. His defence was that a sudden impulse had come over him, and it was the same sort of impulse which might come over a stamp collector if he saw a blue Mauritius in front of him, or a jeweller on seeing a special piece of jewellery. The magistrate fined him £8 5s. (£396).

𝕸𝖎𝖑𝖎𝖙𝖆𝖗𝖞 𝕭𝖆𝖟𝖆𝖆𝖗

TO RAISE FUNDS FOR

REGIMENTAL ASSOCIATIONS & REGIMENTAL BENEFIT FUNDS OF REGIMENTS UNDER-TAKING STALLS, & FOR THE REGIMENTAL AGENCY

UNDER THE AUSPICES OF THE REGIMENTAL
———— AGENCY OF WHICH ————
H.M. THE KING IS PATRON
AND
H.R.H. THE PRINCESS LOUISE :: ::
DUCHESS OF ARGYLL :: IS PRESIDENT

WILL TAKE PLACE IN

THE ROYAL HORTICULTURAL HALL, VINCENT SQUARE

WESTMINSTER, S.W.

On 11th, 12th, and 13th DECEMBER 1913

IV

Before the Great War

It is true to say that in the years leading up to the 'Great War' the threat of war was ever present, and preparation for it became increasingly evident. This was reflected in some of the events staged in the Hall, both directly and indirectly.

Military Fundraising and Bazaars

On 12 April 1907, an at home and concert took place in the Hall, under the auspices of the Ladies' Association (Workroom Branch) of the Incorporated Soldiers' and Sailors' Help Society (later to become SSAFA in 1921) whose President was Princess Christian. The Ladies' Association had established workshops in Brompton Road three years before, and 72 'deserving' soldiers and sailors discharged as medically unfit for further service had been taught various trades to enable them to maintain themselves, either partly or completely. Then on 2 April 1908 they organised an exhibition and sale of the work made by disabled soldiers and sailors, under the patronage of HRH Princess Christian of Schleswig-Holstein. Major-General Lord Cheylesmore, Grenadier Guards, opened the exhibition. He had also played an active role in the foundation of The Westminster Children's Society in 1903, now known as the London Early Years Foundation; had been an alderman at Westminster City Council

and Mayor of Westminster in 1905 and 1906; became Chairman of London County Council in 1912 and was Chairman of the National Rifle Association. He died in 1925, and is commemorated by a monument by Edwin Lutyens in the Embankment Gardens, London that is inscribed, 'Soldier, Administrator, Philanthropist and Friend'. A flower market was also run by many 'well-known' ladies, including Lady Beatrice Pole-Carew. She would have been delighted to know that her grandson, Sir Richard Carew Pole, would become the Royal Horticultural Society's 10th President 94 years later to follow in her footsteps in the same Hall! The String Band of The Grenadier Guards played during the afternoon. The Rayleighs Dairies, Messrs Harrods and the United Kingdom Tea Company contributed their products and services free of charge towards the success of the exhibition. The SSAFA would also hold a fundraising event in the Hall, but not until almost a century later on 31 October 2006 when Air Chief Marshal Sir Jock Stirrup personally hosted a Forces Help Defence Industry Dinner and said, 'The proceeds of this evening will benefit SSAFA Forces Help and assist them in continuing their unique and special work.'

In December 1913, just eight months before the outbreak of the First World War,

Catalogue for the Military Bazaar, held 'Under the Auspices of the Regimental Agency' in the Lindley Hall on 11-13 December 1913.

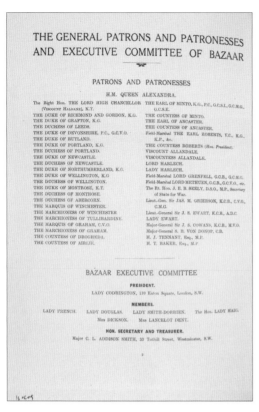

several events took place designed to support our military, and in particular the old soldiers who were poorly supported once they had left the Services, for whatever reason. One of the most extravagant and well represented was the Grand Military Bazaar held on 11-13 December 1913. This was held in order to raise substantial benefit funds for Regimental Associations and Regiments, under the auspices of The Regimental Agency, of which HM The King was patron and HRH The Princess Louise, Duchess of Argyll, was President. The Bazaar was opened by Prince Arthur of Connaught on the first day, Princess Louise declared it open on the second day and Field-Marshal The Earl Roberts opened it on the last day. These funds were used to help ex-soldiers in sickness, want or old age and Lord Roberts, in his opening address, had been particularly blunt in drawing attention to the fact that the country took scant heed of soldiers, or the class from which they were

LEFT *Inside front page of catalogue showing the General Patrons and Patronesses and Executive Committee for the Military Bazaar, held 'Under the Auspices of the Regimental Agency' in the Lindley Hall on 11-13 December 1913.*

BELOW *Commemorative Cover of Commando Association Day, held at the Lindley Hall, marking the 25th Anniversary of the Disbandment of Wartime Army Commando Units and the laying up of the Association's Battle Honour colours at Westminster Abbey, on 1 May 1971.*

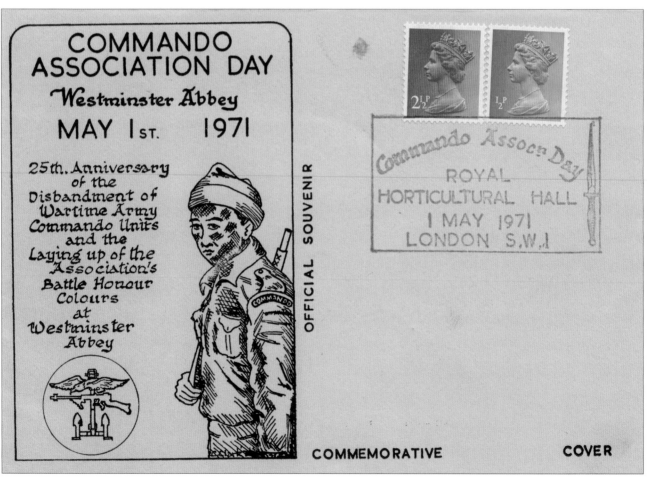

of Norfolk and St Albans. Interestingly, Field Marshal Francis Wallace Grenfell, 1st Baron Grenfell, who had been elected as the second President of the RHS earlier that year following Sir Trevor Lawrence's long tenure since 1885, was also shown as a patron. It would be natural to speculate about whether he had been instrumental in getting this important event staged in the RHS Hall. He would remain President until 1919 during the same period that King George V and Queen Mary were the Society's Royal Patrons.

Haldane had been appointed Secretary of State for War in 1905 in Henry Campbell Bannerman's administration and had implemented the Haldane Reforms, a wide-ranging set of reforms aimed at preparing the army for participation in a possible European war. In 1907 he formed the Territorial Army that was to become so important to the war effort at the start of the First World War. He was also instrumental in the setting up of the Advisory Committee for Aeronautics in 1909 that provided the fledgling aircraft industry in the United Kingdom with a sound body of science on which to base the development of aircraft for the next 70 years.

Seventeen of the nation's finest regiments took part, each with their own stall. These included The Brigade of Guards, The 4th. (Queen's Own) Hussars, The Royal Welsh Fusiliers, The 17th (Duke of Cambridge's Own) Lancers, The Duke of Cornwall's Light Infantry, Alexandra, Princess of Wales's Own (Yorkshire) Regiment and The Connaught Rangers. *The Times* reported that Queen Alexandra had 'presented a large number of articles to the stall of the Queen's (Royal West Surrey) Regiment.' The War Office were also there with a stall of their own and, undoubtedly, took the opportunity to re-affirm their view that the Hall would indeed be useful to them in the event of having to mobilise for war. Each stall had a Lady President and these included Princess Louise, the Duchess of Hamilton, Lady French, Lady Douglas, Lady Codrington and Lady Haig. Princess Louise and Princess Arthur of Connaught were selling at the Regimental Agency stall. Chelsea pensioners

ABOVE *Commemorative programme for the Soldiers, Sailors, and Air Force Association fundraising dinner held in the Lawrence Hall, on 31 October 2006.*

mainly drawn, once they had been discharged, disabled or were no longer able to continue. Those that were discharged after seven years Regular service were paid only 6d. (£2.10) a day and expected to live on this for the remaining five years serving in the Reserves.

The principal patron of the Bazaar was HM Queen Alexandra, but 42 Dukes, Duchesses, Marquisses and Marchionesses, Earls, Countesses, Viscounts, Lords and Ladies and senior military figures also lent their patronage, including The Lord High Chancellor (Viscount Haldane), Field Marshal Sir John French, Mr & Mrs Churchill, Princess Christian, Prince and Princess Alexander of Teck, Mr Balfour, the Duchess of Westminster and the Duchesses

were in attendance, as were a guard of men dressed in the uniforms of historic regiments of the past. A doll surgeon was also on hand who helped lots of children mend their dolls. Subsequent published accounts show that the event was a great success having raised almost £6,500 net (£545,675) taking into account all expenditure involved, including £86 6s. 8d. (£7,248) for the rent, lighting, heating, and cleaning of the Hall with a further £40 16s. 3d. (£3,426) for the salaries and wages of Hall staff, Commissionaires, Detectives and Police.

Four days after the Military Bazaar, Alice Princess Alexander of Teck staged a handicraft exhibition and fête in support of the scholarship fund of the Imperial Service College, Windsor, entitled 'Christmas in Fairyland'. A poster to promote this was drawn up by Lucy Atwell. In a letter to the editor of *The Times* on 9 October 1913, written from Henry III Tower, Windsor Castle, Alice explained that, 'The object of the scholarship fund is to offer scholarships at this school to the sons of officers of the Navy and Army and

Civil servants who through the exigencies of their calling are frequently unable to provide their children with an adequate education. I earnestly hope that by means of the Fête, further scholarships, which to my knowledge are urgently demanded, may be endowed.' The *Daily Express* offered £50 (£4,198) as prize money in the competition section and these were in six classes of needlework, lace, jewels and enamels, handmade toys, lamp and candle shades and Boy Scout crafts. The Hall was transformed into a forest of Christmas trees with booths that represented individual fairy tales. A life-sized Doll's House and kitchen was also featured where sweets were made and among those who supported this event were Princess Victoria of Schleswig-Holstein (she had been present at the opening of the Hall in 1904), Lady Edward Churchill, and Mrs Cubitt (wife of Henry Cubitt, whose grandfather was the famed architect, Thomas Cubitt). They had six sons but, tragically, three of them died in the Great War that was to follow shortly after this event.

A similar transformation of the Hall had taken place in December 1909 when the *Evening News* staged a Toy Fair promising 'free presents to every boy and girl under the age of 14 (by Father Christmas) and a chance to see the 100,000 articles to be given away to London's poor children, old soldiers and sailors at work'. Also present was Gulliver, 'a Giant over 7 feet high', Hop O' My Thumb, 'a diminutive Midget from Tiny Town' and Dusky, 'a live Teddy Bear' whose Eskimo attendant, according to *The Observer*, 'looked like Robinson Crusoe'. The Hall was filled with 'the most desirable and varied collection of toys ever seen' and free picture pantomimes with music were held at frequent intervals on each day. *The Observer* of 19 December reported, 'Here Joey, the Clown, is in serious and animated conversation with a tiny tot of four, while aged Pantaloon, his father, is mischievously inciting a small boy to pull the tail of a Teddy Bear who is stalking gravely past. In another corner the giant Gulliver hoists a little girl eight feet in the air so that she may get a better view of Punch's domestic difficulties. A bluff Beefeater, with a child clinging to either hand, leads the way to the Christmas tree, while a tiny damsel backs slowly down the crowded main "street" with mouth and eyes wide open in wrapt admiration of the Golliwog.'

Shooting Clubs and Competitions

One thing that was probably furthest from architect Edwin Stubbs's mind, and the RHS grandees when they considered the plans for their fine new hall, was that it should become a live small-arms shooting gallery but, on 24 and 25 June 1908, this is exactly what it did become, and may well have been used in the same way several years earlier by the Miniature Rifle Association. The incident itself is unique in the event history of the Hall (although .22 rifle competitions would be held regularly during Schoolboy's Exhibitions in the 1950s), but it also has an interesting place in the history of the lead-up to the First World War, and also what is now established as the National Small-bore Rifle Association.

The origins of this Association go back to the start of the second Boer War in 1899 when British forces found themselves frequently outmanoeuvred and outclassed in rifle-shooting skills. This brought about real concern from the populace back home who were worried that they would not be able to defend themselves adequately if they were invaded. Surprisingly, there were very few established rifle clubs using up-to-date weapons available to civilians, should the need arise. In 1900 The National Rifle Association that had been in existence since 1860 changed all that, because it gained the 'nomination of the War Office as the official medium for the recognition of Rifle Clubs'. This meant that civilians had the ability to train on service rifles, but small-bore rifles and ammunition was much more accessible and cheaper. Senior military figures also supported the view that it was just as relevant to train using small-bore than the larger calibre service rifles.

The primary supporter of this way of thinking was Major General Charles Edward

Luard, who had managed to gain support from many important figures but, most importantly, from a national hero in the form of Field Marshal Earl Roberts of Kandahar, Pretoria and Waterford, V.C. Roberts agreed to become the first President of a new organisation, The Society of Working Men's Rifle Clubs, in March 1901 based at 17 Victoria Street. A prominent supporter of this initiative was Rudyard Kipling who, at his Rottingdean home in Sussex, formed his own Rifle Club. In 1903, the Society merged with the British Rifle League to become The Society of Miniature Rifle Clubs and remained so until 1947 when it became The National Small-bore Rifle Association (N.S.R.A.) and is still known as such today. Luard continued as executive Chairman, but in 1906 became disillusioned with the way it was being run, resigned his position and went on to form The Patriotic Society that he felt was more in accordance with his own views, emphasising that 'shooting at stationary targets with no limit of time is only the elementary part of practical rifle shooting for war and that to enable the most useful results to be obtained from the magazine rifle of today [1906], and the automatic rifles of the near future, quick aiming and firing at disappearing targets requires to be well taught for twentieth century warfare'. His Patriotic Society was defined as 'an organisation for speeding the progress of rifle shooting throughout the United Kingdom by trying to persuade all men and boys of a suitable age to make themselves more skilful in the use of a rifle than any foreigner that might wish to make war on England' and, on 24/5 June 1908, he held an exhibition meeting at the RHS Hall to enhance this. This included rapid fire competitions for automatic and magazine rifles with prize money totalling £500 (£44,230), and was opened by Prince Alexander of Teck. There is no record of what the neighbours thought about this!

Eighteen months earlier Queen Alexandra had graciously provided and presented the 'The Queen's Cup' in the grounds of Buckingham Palace with Lord Roberts and many other important military figures and wealthy aristocrats for winners of County Rifle Competitions, a significant recognition of the drive being made to prepare civilians for future wars that would be sorely needed at the outbreak of the First World War. Three days after the competitions in the RHS Hall, the London Correspondent of *The Manchester Guardian* reported that, 'The visible patriotic element is provided by the employment of a number of non-commissioned officers and men of the Irish Guards in uniform as register keepers &c. but apart from this symbol there are no special features to distinguish the competitions, except that the targets are green with a brown bull's-eye and that a time limit is insisted on. The rifles mostly used are small-bore Martini's of the War Office pattern, except that there is one series for which the Winchester automatic miniature rifle is used. With this latter weapon an expert can get 14 shots in 17 seconds and make good shooting. The competitors included some keen boys and one or two hard-bitten specimens of the typical shooting man type – leather elbow pieces and all. Of course, there is a certain value in this miniature shooting from the musketry point-of-view, but it is overrated by enthusiasts, So far as the boys were concerned, one felt that a little healthy drill in the open air would be a more profitable exercise.'

At the Annual General Meeting of the S.M.R.C. held on 2 June 1908 Luard had severed his remaining link with the society by resigning from the Council and died three months later on 18 September 1908, shortly before his 69th birthday. A General Meeting of the Patriotic Society was subsequently held at the RHS on 14 October with Lord Leconfield presiding when they discussed the future of the Society. Captain Charles Elmhurst Luard, Charles Luard's eldest son, was present, as was Mr H.H. Twining, the Society's Treasurer, who confirmed that the Society's finances were not good and there was no apparent successor to be appointed. Colonel Charles Ward, MP moved an amendment that they should adjourn for a month to see if there was any possibility of amalgamating with the

Kent County Miniature Rifle Association. A further meeting was held at the RHS on 11 November presided over by Mr Sackville Creswell that agreed to wind up the Society. Captain Luard informed the meeting that the National Defence Association had agreed to take on the Society's work, as long as 100 or more of its members agreed to transfer their membership to them. This led to the Society's amalgamation with the S.M.R.C. Four of the six 'Patriotic Shields', handed over at that time, are still offered for annual competition to this day. Captain Luard was subsequently appointed to the Council of the S.M.R.C., thus continuing his father's involvement in this movement, until his untimely death in First World War action on 15 September 1914.

Photo of Madame Martina Sofia Helena Bergman Österberg (1849-1915), Founder of the first Physical Training College in England, founded 1885 on Ling's System, c.1900.

Physical Training – A Sound Mind in a Sound Body

Martina Sofia Helena Bergman Österberg was a remarkable Swedish lady who revolutionised the traditional methods of physical training for young girls and women in Britain but, more remarkably, the British Army and the other main Services mainly during a 20-year period leading up to the First World War. She was an independent and single-minded lady, and an early supporter of women's suffrage in Sweden, who had trained at the Royal Central Gymnastic Institute in Stockholm, following the then accepted and recognised scientific physical education methods of her fellow Swede and peer, Per Henrik Ling. After qualifying, she travelled extensively in Europe and devoted the rest of her life to teaching the Swedish System of Gymnastics to young women who could themselves, as instructors, pass it on to young children, in schools and other establishments, where it could be taught. She came to England and was appointed to the London Board of Education in 1881. In 1883 she gave a gymnastic and drill display to the Prince and Princess of Wales and their three young princesses at which the Prince acknowledged the performance, referring to the regiments of the Army, 'which might be proud of performing drill in the way which the boys have gone through today'. The following year she attended and spoke at the 1884 International Health Exhibition, held in the gardens of the Royal Horticultural Society in South Kensington. The experience she gained during the time she was in this post revealed the need to train teachers using the same methods, if her ambitions and work were to be furthered. However, the application of physical training itself was not her primary aim. Her objective was female emancipation: social, economic and spiritual freedom for women, enshrined under the maxim, 'A Sound Mind in a Sound Body'. She saw the advantages of creating a course that combined Swedish Gymnastics, anatomy, physiology, hygiene and massage with English Games like Cricket, Lawn Tennis and Fives as well as

Fencing, Swimming and Dancing. To this end she opened a college in Hampstead in 1885. Ten years later she expanded and moved to Dartford. She caused outrage amongst many less enlightened, or emancipated, women by discarding the traditional but restrictive corset. Instead, in 1892, she created what we now accept and recognise as the simple gymslip, or gym tunic as it was then called, a daring design of its day. She is also credited with having created the game of Netball that evolved at her college over 100 years ago as an offshoot of Basketball that she witnessed during her visits to America.

This College was the first of its kind and proudly proclaimed as 'The First Physical Training College in England'. The training that the young women were given there was applied across the country and internationally as far as Japan, the United States and to what were then known as the Colonies, as the recognised way to instruct children in physical training and drill. Luminaries of her college included E.R. Clarke, Captain of England's Lacrosse Team 1912-13, and later the 1964 Tokyo Olympic 800 metres Gold Medallist, Ann Packer. Rachael Heyhoe Flint, who captained the England Women's Cricket Team in July 1976, and herself an ex-student, had no fewer than seven Österberg-trained ladies in her team. Flint later became, and remains, Patron of the Bergman Österberg Union Archive.

As a means of spreading her influence and the importance of her physical training methods she staged 'Displays of Physical Culture' outside her college to professional and influential groups of people, including royalty, to make her system better known. Three of these were held in the RHS Hall on 17 and 24 June, and 1 July 1905. Further displays were held in each of the successive three years, at which Sir Henry Campbell Bannerman, the then Prime Minister; Princess Louise, the Duchess of Argyll (who was obsessed with physical fitness, even though she smoked heavily like her brother, King Edward VII), and the Headmaster of Eton, among many others attended. William Rickatson Dykes, the Royal Horticultural Society's future 17th Secretary, could also have

attended as he had been Master of Charterhouse School before he took up the appointment in 1920. It is also not surprising to hear that the Duchess attended one of Madame Österberg's displays. This was probably as much to do with the feminist views she was interested in, and shared with Madame, as well as her interest in physical fitness. These audiences were invited to see the high degree of skill, strength and self mastery that could be attained after two years of scientific physical training. Portable apparatus was especially constructed by Madame herself for the occasion.

Mme. Bergman Österberg's Physical Training College,
DARTFORD HEATH, KENT.

The first Physical Training College in England. Founded 1885 on Ling's System.

STUDENTS' DEMONSTRATIONS

Royal Horticultural Hall, Vincent Square, S.W.

June 17th, 1905.   Chairman:
THE RIGHT HON. LORD KINNAIRD.

June 24th, 1905.   Chairman:
COLONEL V. BALCK,
Head of the Military Department, Royal Central Institute of Gymnastics, Stockholm; Chief Organizer and Promotor of Out-of-Door Games and Sports in Scandinavia.

July 1st, 1905.   Chairman:
HIS EXCELLENCY BARON CARL BILDT,
Ambassador of Sweden in Great Britain.

ABOVE *Madame Bergman Österberg's Students' Physical Training College Demonstrations Programme, held in the Lindley Hall on 17 and 24 June, and on 1 July 1905.*

RIGHT *Photo of Madame Bergman Österberg's Students' Physical Training College Demonstrations, held in the Lindley Hall on 17 and 24 June, and on 1 July 1905.*

BELOW *Photo of Madame Bergman Österberg's Students' Physical Training College Demonstrations, held in the Lindley Hall on 17 and 24 June, and on 1 July. This is one of the very few photo's showing the original Minstrel's Gallery and clock at the far end of the Hall, that was demolished by a German bomb in June 1944.*

While this was having the desired effect on young women, young boys and men, especially in the Army, had continued to drill remorselessly and their physical education was based much more on the more traditional and German militaristic methods that had been introduced by Major Hammersley and his Army Gymnastic Staff (later to become the Army Physical Training Corps) in 1860. The development of physical education in Scandinavia did not pass unnoticed and the then Inspector of Gymnasia took a party of instructors to Sweden in 1882 to study the national system there, but the military authorities were not persuaded to make any change. Another abortive trip to Sweden, led by Colonel G.M. Fox, followed in 1890. However, by 1903 the Navy had become convinced of their methods and by 1906 the Army had also embraced the system advocated by Lieutenant Lankildd of the Danish Army. Interestingly, in 1908, the Board of Education, having seen the effect that Madame Österberg's methods through her college were having on young girls and women, and knowing that no alternative was being offered to men, took the opportunity of arranging a display for the benefit of school P.T. Instructors and men only. This was organised by the same Colonel G.M. Fox, this time as the Board of Education's recently appointed Inspector of Physical Training, and once again in the RHS Hall, on 8 and 18 July of that year. This was given by a team of Swedish gymnasts from the Royal Central Gymnastic Institute of Sweden (where Madame Österberg had originally trained) under the direction of its principal Director, Colonel Viktor Balck who had also been present at the 24 June 1905 display. On this occasion he and his team of gymnasts were visiting the 1908 London Olympics at the Great White Stadium, Shepherds Bush. The Board of Education stated clearly that 'such a display will prove of great interest and assistance to all who are interested in improving and developing the work of physical training throughout English schools and training colleges'. Unfortunately, this proved abortive and it did not convince them that they should change their methodology, even though Eton and Harrow schools had led

the way one year earlier. However, by 1911, when 30 students from Madame Österberg's Physical Training College in Dartford gave the opening performance to the Stratford-on-Avon Summer Festival, *The Times* reported that, 'Twenty years ago no one could have foretold that the methods of physical training introduced into England by this Swedish lady and others would upset the traditions of the British Army and modify some of the most stereotyped of its drill practices. Yet the incredible thing happened, and today Swedish gymnastics, largely because of what she began in the early '80s, are a commonplace of British bodily development.' Her college later changed to a trust she had set up to ensure it would carry on her work after her death, King George V and Queen Mary visited the college and witnessed her unique displays by her students on 28 February 1918. She would have been proud of that.

Sheila Cutler, an ex-student, and former Keeper of the Bergman Österberg Union Archive, recalls her time spent at the Österberg College. 'Forty four years after the event illustrated in this book, I became a student at Madame Österberg's College, now known as Dartford College of Physical Education. The internationally famous gymslip, designed by Madame, had been replaced by shorts and aertex blouses but most things remained much as she had planned. As nearly all of us had been taught by former students, as indeed they had too, traditions linked us directly to Madame Österberg herself: we were still known in the town as 'Madame's Girls'. I remember student life as a mixture of exhilaration and fear – perhaps this sounds shocking now. If one was not up to standard one had to go, and several did. It was exhausting physically and mentally with lectures beginning at 8.30 a.m. and work not officially over until 9.15 p.m. And what was the result? A very highly qualified Physical Educationalist, basking in the reflected glory of our Foundress, and very much in demand. This was perhaps best expounded in verse by Constance Braithwaite who was at the College in 1947 when she wrote,

At length these poor overworked, underclothed creatures,
Emerge in the sun fully qualified teachers.
They're top of the world and they do as they please
For to get them Headmistresses fall on their knees. *

* Reference: From a verse by Constance Braithwaite (1947) Printed in *The Bergman Österberg Union* magazine in 2008

Although I do not recall any prostrate Headmistresses, I worked in various day and boarding schools including one in Germany for the British Army of the Rhine. I ended my career as a Senior Lecturer at Digby Stuart College, a teacher training college, which is now part of Roehampton University … I also managed to include marriage and children. I hope Madame Österberg would have been satisfied.'

By contrast, 10 years earlier Charles Burleigh had requested nine days in the

Programme for the Children's Happy Evenings Association Inter-Branch Physical Competition, held in the Lindley Hall on 12 March 1913.

Children's Happy Evenings Association.

Patron ... HER MAJESTY THE QUEEN.

PRESIDENT—THE COUNTESS OF JERSEY.

Chairman—Lady WERNHER. | *Hon. Treasurer*—W. W. GRANTHAM,
Vice-Chairman—Colonel The EARL OF | Esq.
LONGFORD, K.P., M.V.O. | *Hon. Secretary*—Mrs. BLAND-SUTTON.

Inter-Branch Physical Competition.

Chairman—W. PETT RIDGE, Esq. | *Hon. Secretary*—Mrs. PERCY NOBLE.

District "B" Competition.

Convener—Miss SCHIFF.

Hon. Judges—THE VISCOUNT ACHESON, Major PIKE,
Mrs. KENDAL, Mrs. WORDSWORTH and Fraulein WILKE.
Boxing—Mr. B. J. ANGLE.

Royal Horticultural Hall, Westminster,

Tuesday, *March* 12th, 1912.

The Chair will be taken by Sir DOUGLAS STRAIGHT.

Class II.—DANCING.

Team No. 67	...	" Dancing "	...	...	... ... 24 Girls
Team No. 68	...	" Fancy Dancing "	...	...	... 12 Girls
Team No. 69	...	" Hornpipe "	...	...	... 24 Girls
Team No. 70	...	" Dancing "	...	...	... 24 Girls
Team No. 71	...	" Berolina Polka," " Trenchmole," " Nine-Pins," " Mountain March "		...	24 Girls
Team No. 72	...	" Swedish Dances "	...	...	... 24 Girls

Class I.—PHYSICAL DRILL

(with nothing in hands).

Team No. 73	...	" Physical Drill "	...	...	... 18 Boys
Team No. 74	...	" Physical Drill "	...	...	... 24 Boys
Team No. 75	...	" Physical Drill "	...	...	... 25 Boys

Class II.—PHYSICAL DRILL

(with something in hands).

Team No. 76	...	" Barbell Drill "	...	...	... 25 Boys
Team No. 77	...	" Physical Drill with Muskets "	...		25 Boys

Class VI.—SINGING GAMES.

Team No. 79	...	" Sleeping Flowers "	...	...	... 30 Girls
Team No. 80	...	" Singing Games "	...	...	... 32 Girls
Team No. 81	...	" Singing Games "	...	...	... 20 Girls

Class V.—DRILL (Various).

Team No. 82	...	" Bayonet Fighting Practice "	...	...	25 Boys
Team No. 83	...	" Marching "	...	...	... 20 Boys
Team No. 84	...	" Semaphore Signalling "	...	...	17 Boys

GOD SAVE THE KING.

Hall for displays of 'Assaults at Arms'. These highlighted the accepted German Gymnastic methods for men, together with boxing, fencing, wrestling, quarter-staff jousting and fire-escape life-saving demonstrations. Some demonstrations had colourful names such as, 'Prod & Slasher' and 'Cutting Mutton'! These had previously been held in St James Hall by the London Athletic Club. Other Athletic Clubs such as The Victoria Athletic Association of the Army & Navy Stores and the 'A' Division Athletic Club, Metropolitan Police that used the Hall on many occasions for their social reunions and dances could well have had Österberg-trained women instructors, but the men instructors tended to be ex-military personnel who had never had any exposure to the Swedish system.

Children regularly gave displays of 'drill' in the Hall as part of the various events staged by many clubs and organisations that they belonged to. On 5 May 1906 at the Industrial Exhibition of the Westminster Union of the Church of England Temperance Society, Princess Alexander of Teck opened the event, gave out prizes and watched children at their musical drill and Japanese maypole dances. On 20 March 1909, the London Girls' Club Union Drill Competition was held. HRH The Princess of Wales was its Patroness and had agreed to present the challenge shield and medals on this occasion. The LGCU dated from 1885 and was the creation of the Hon. Maude Stanley who founded the first Girls' Club at 59 Greek Street, Soho in 1880. In 1909 it comprised between 4,000 and 5,000 members, and organised annual musical drill competitions. In March 1910, the London Diocesan Church Lads' Brigade staged a Drill & Gymnastic Display, presided by Maj.-Gen. Codrington, C.B., commanding the London District and on 12 March 1912, The Children's Happy Evenings Association, whose Patron was Queen Alexandra and whose President was the Countess of Jersey, held one of their District 'Inter-Branch Physical Competitions; for boys and girls in the Hall. This was one of many held throughout the country, culminating in the Finals that were held in London's Guildhall in the presence of Princess Marie Louise of Schleswig-Holstein and the

Lord Mayor on 20 March. These competitions were split between boys and girls in various 'Classes'. The boys had to compete in Bayonet Fighting Practice, Semaphore Signalling, Boxing, Rifle Exercises and Physical Drill. The girls had Singing Games, Dancing, Action Songs, Fancy Marching and Physical Drill. It is noticeable from the programme of this event that every group of boys that took part in the final was trained by military personnel. None of the girls' trainers were, and it would be satisfying to think that, instead, many had been trained at Madame Österberg's College. On the occasion of their 'Silver Jubilee' held at the People's Palace on Mile-End Road, 5,000 Jewish children were treated to a wonderful tea and a pantomime performance. Each boy and girl received a cracker, a packet of chocolate, a Raphael Truck Christmas Card and a serviette memento with a picture of the Queen to remember their 'Happy Evening' with pride. Lord Rothschild, who had become the first Jew to take a seat in the House of Commons, sent bundles of holly to decorate the Hall. Ten years later, in 1922, the Hagodal Social Club of the Jewish Institute based in Mulberry Street, London, E1, and the East London Young Zionist League of Sandys Row, Middlesex Street, also in London, E1, booked the same Hall for their social dances.

On 26 and 27 November 1920, The Girls' Realm Guild of Service and Good Fellowship held a themed 'Gilbert and Sullivan' Fair and Bazaar in the Hall. The Guild had been founded in 1900 by the Bishop of London 'to aid girls of gentle birth, who may have unexpectedly to support themselves, to secure adequate training and work, and to promote service and good fellowship among girls.' This was their first event and HRH Princess Beatrice opened it on the first day. The Bishop of London opened the second day. The Hall was dressed with scenery from the Gilbert & Sullivan Operas (each stall represented one of their operas) and members of the famed Savoy Opera Company came from the Savoy Theatre and entertained. The Savoy Theatre had been built in 1881 and was renowned as the first public building in the world to be lit by Incandescent electric lights. Rupert D'Oyly Carte had taken a personal interest in the Fair and his wife, Lady Dorothy D'Oyly Carte, was a regular exhibitor of her dogs at the Ladies' Kennel Association Championship Shows in the same hall. Lady Gilbert took part of a stall and Herbert Sullivan sent a donation. Mrs Lloyd George, wife of David Lloyd George, had a stall of books. One of the Guild's successes had been to report that 'A.M.D. has obtained a post as teacher of Physical Culture with a salary of £250 [£9,483] a year, and she only completed her training two years ago.' Once again, it is tempting to speculate that she could have been an Österberg student. The last event staged by The Guild in the Hall was in 1923 when an 'All in a Garden' Fair was opened by Lady Carisbrooke.

Smoke and Smoking Events

While the evils of drinking were self-evident and organisations such as the Band Of Hope and Union and other temperance societies fervently campaigned their cause to offer a way out of this devastating addiction, especially among the poor, smoking was not recognised as such a danger, and was practised by the majority of the population in private, and in public in every theatre of life without any real consideration of the effect this was having on health. It would take many decades and generations for the realisation that smoking foreshortened and killed lives, before the medical profession, government and other influential bodies acted decisively to regulate the advertising of smoking and issue strong health warnings on the products themselves.

Paradoxically, smoke abatement was very much a 'live' topic of concern in 1905 and a Smoke Abatement Conference and Exhibition did take place in the Hall on 14 and 15 December that year. However, the principal topic under discussion, 'Factory and Trade Smoke Abatement', was not about smoke abatement from those working in the factories who smoked cigarettes inside them incessantly, but to do with black smoke from coal fires in factories that blackened towns and cities and dangerously reduced air quality across Britain. A great deal of debate seems to have centred around the protection of important public building and frescoes, but not so much on the health of the general public. There is also an almost frightening cadence of *déjà vu* here when one looks at the current climate change conferences and debates taking place that are still talking about the same difficulties involved with regulating emissions from factories and industry in the same terms, but over a century later. In order to help the conference delegates appreciate the points being made, afternoon visits were made to the South Metropolitan Gas Company's works on Old Kent Road and the Abbey Mills pumping station of the London Sewage Outfall Works!

And, two years later in 1907, the tobacco plant was revered and being actively promoted as a source of major trade and income. An expression of this, that could no longer be envisaged taking place now, was the 3rd International Tobacco Trades Exhibition dubbed, 'The Smokeries', first staged in the Hall on 20-5 April 1907 where, according to *The Observer*, 'every variety of tobacco and every quality of cigar was on view.' It went on to report that 'the originators of the exhibition (the journal *Tobacco*), obtained many varieties of commercial seed, which were placed in the hands of the Royal Botanical Society, Regent's Park, the Royal Horticultural Society, Westminster, and an Aberdeen society, with the result that plants have been cultivated so successfully as to inspire additional confidence amongst the Irish tobacco growers, who have just managed to pilot through the House of Commons a Bill extending throughout Ireland the privilege of tobacco cultivation.' Three years later in the Hall at the National Fruit Growers' Federation Meeting, held on 25 July 1910, it was agreed to ask the Chancellor of the Exchequer 'to insert in the Finance Bill this Session a provision allowing tobacco which had been denatured to be imported, for agricultural purposes, free of duty'. Ironically, Ireland would become the first country in the world to impose an outright ban on smoking in workplaces, but not until 29 March 2004. Alongside these leaf specimens on show in the Hall, proving that cultivation of tobacco was possible in the United Kingdom, were approximately 70 trade exhibitors, including the French and Turkish governments representing their own industries, Messrs Abdullah & Co. of New Bond Street (selling Turkish, Egyptian and Virginian cigarettes renowned for their bewitching Oriental flavour) and Messrs Morris's Grapevine Virginia Cigarettes at 10 for 3d. (£1.12), later to become Phillip Morris. Cigar manufacturers were also there, the most famous being the Havana firm of Uppman, selling their cigars at £1 (£89.43) each and £50 (£4,472) a box. King Edward VII was very partial to a good cigar and smoked them to the end. The more affordable ones at 2d.(75p) and 2½d. (93p) each from Messrs Sidney Pullinger, were also on offer. Cigarette-making machines were also there, demonstrating their ability to meet the insatiable need that existed for them at this point in time.

The exhibition ran again in March the following year in the Hall. On this occasion, *The Daily Express* reported that a lady from Bayswater had won a prize of 100 cigarettes per week for a year!! She probably lived to a ripe old age defying the trends for those who smoked heavily to become prone to lung and other forms of cancer, but it would still be 100 years before an outright smoking ban in all public places would be introduced in the United Kingdom. She may also have been interested later in 'smoker's teeth' that were being offered at the International Dental Society's Exhibition in the Hall four years later in September 1912. These were one of many sets of artificial teeth that could be bought to order, and were artistically hand-painted by experts to match existing nicotine stains! The *Daily Express* reported that 'sets of jet black ones were very fashionable in Siam, whereas the potentates of Northern India love plenty of bright colours such as sky blue, green and scarlet'. In keeping with the first medical, chemist and health exhibitions that had been staged at the RHS Hall, annual dental exhibitions under the excruciating name of the Society of Extractors and Adapters of Teeth, first took place in September 1909. After the war, in May 1921, the Tobacco Trades Exhibition was back in the Hall offering both men and women the opportunity to enter into 'smoking competitions', as if the war before it had not killed enough of the population by then. This prompted what was headed as, 'An Outspoken Protest' from an RHS Fellow in the form of a letter to *The Garden* magazine of 14 May 1921. Horace J. Wright wrote, 'I protest that the fountain head of British horticulture could be put to no baser use, and suggest that the body of Fellows should convey to the Council in emphatic terms the opinion that the Hall, which was built for horticulture, with hard-won horticultural money, shall not be hired out for any such depraved purposes.' He went on to say, 'There are those among the Fellows who are not in sympathy with the Hall being converted into a venue for dog and cat shows, at which neurotic women of fashion lavish more love and care on their over-pampered four-legged pets than they do their own children … When we reach women's smoking competitions however, I consider we reach the rock bottom of depravity.' The awful truth, however, was that the first Ladies and Gentlemen's Smoking Room (the first room in Europe where women could smoke in public) had been established as early as 1898 in the Midland Grand Hotel St Pancras Station, London. *The Times* Court Circular of 21 November 1915 also proudly announced that, 'The Queen yesterday sent to the Salvation Army a large package of cigars and cigarettes for distribution among wounded Belgian soldiers'. One hopes that they survived their war-wounds, and their self-inflicted ones. In 1923 and 1924, Messrs Lambert & Butler (Imperial Tobacco Co.) continued their association with the RHS Hall and held their staff dances there. In his 'Message to All Boys' at the 1930 *Daily Mail* Schoolboy's Exhibition, Lord Baden-Powell made his feelings known about this subject when he wrote, 'We badly need some training for our lads if we are to keep up manliness in the race instead of lapsing into a nation of soft, sloppy, cigarette

suckers'. Much later still in March 1947, The Maccabeans, a society of Jewish professional men who met to discuss matters of common import to the Jewish community in London, applied to hold a 'smoking concert' in the Hall. These had been very popular and held regularly in Gentlemen's Clubs and Hotels since well before the war when well-known artistes in the musical world appeared, men dressed in their 'smoking jackets', listened to the music, and … smoked! I can also remember very clearly my own habit of reaching out for the 'fag packet' upon first waking up in the morning in my billet at the All Arms Junior Leaders' Regiment in Tonfanau, Merionethshire, Wales at 16 years of age, as a boy soldier. Soldiers, Sailors, Airmen, and 'fags' have been as inseparable as they have been with their rifles for generations, and the tobacco industry thrived on it with brands such us Senior Service, Players Navy Cut, Corporal, Capstan, Viceroy, Marlboro, Lucky Strike, Pall Mall, and the throat rasping French brands of Gauloises and Gitanes.

Alcohol and the Temperance Movement

One of the first responses to the problems of excessive drinking in the 1800s was the formation of temperance societies. These usually had a Christian base and were initially composed of people who took a pledge to abstain from spirits, e.g. whisky, and be moderate in their consumption of other alcoholic drinks. However, social and domestic problems caused by excessive consumption of alcohol in society at that time were considerable and there was controversy as to whether moderate drinking of any alcoholic beverage was sufficient to tackle the problem.

In 1832 the 'Seven Men of Preston', including Joseph Livesey, signed a pledge to abstain totally from intoxicating beverages. The idea spread and temperance societies sprang up all over Britain, encouraging people to help deal with the problem of alcoholism by saying that they would no longer drink intoxicating beverages. This was known as

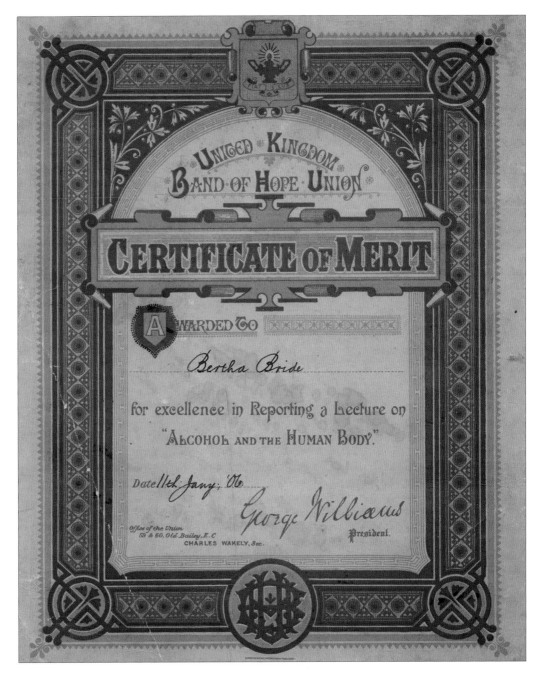

United Kingdom Band of Hope Union Certificate of Merit, awarded to Bertha Bride for excellence in Reporting a Lecture on 'Alcohol and the Human Body', dated 11 January 1906.

'signing the pledge', as individuals were invited to sign a promise. This movement was part of the Victorian Social Reform programme. In November 1847 the first meeting of this group took place in Leeds. About 300 children attended, 200 of whom 'signed the pledge' for the first time, the rest having already done so. The group became known as the 'Band of Hope'. The pledge of the Leeds Temperance Band of Hope was 'I, the undersigned, do agree that I will not use intoxicating liquors as a beverage'.

At around the same time other groups were starting the same kind of children's clubs and many of them took the name 'Band of Hope', together becoming the Band of Hope movement. The clubs grew rapidly and, although co-operating in local 'unions', operated as separate groups. In London there were several clubs, some within walking distance of each other yet operating individually. It became clear that they could be more effective if they worked together sharing resources, costs etc. and in 1855 the

UK Band of Hope Union was formed with Stephen Shirley as the first Secretary. The Band of Hope movement embraced all sorts of activities – it produced a children's hymn book, wrote children's songs, ran and started more children's clubs (the essence of the work), held bazaars, produced booklets, leaflets, magic lantern slide shows etc., sent qualified medical men to give lectures in schools, held competitions and festivals and crowned pageant queens every year. Queen Victoria became patron in 1897, the Jubilee year, and several celebrations were held. This included sermons preached in cathedrals, churches and chapels in all parts of the UK, headed by the Archbishops of Canterbury and Dublin.

The RHS Hall played host to many United Kingdom Band of Hope Union

Daily Mirror photo of Princess Alexander of Teck opening the Industrial Exhibition of the Westminster Union of the Church of England Temperance Society in the Lindley Hall on 5 May 1906.

Silver Band of Hope Union pendant c.1900.

Letter from the UK Band of Hope to the RHS for a tenancy in the Lindley Hall on 14 May 1919.

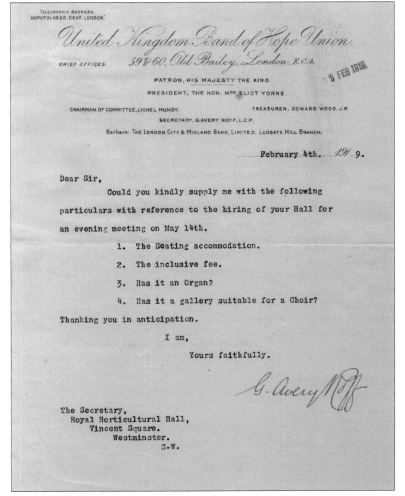

events beginning on 18-23 May 1907 with its National Bazaar, opened by the Duchess of Albany. The organisation, at this point in time, comprised 24,000 bands of hope with a membership of 3,000,000 children. Further social *soirées* were held annually until 1916. In 1995 it changed its name to Hope UK. With the increased use of illegal drugs, the Band of Hope had widened its field of education to include drugs other than alcohol. Its main emphasis now is on education and the traditions of pledge-signing and pageants of queens have long ago ceased.

Pure Foods

Today, we take for granted the fact that our food meets rigorous standards and scrutiny to ensure that what we are being sold is what we get and is nutritious. In Edwardian times this was not so, and on 18 November 1907 an exhibition entitled, 'Healtheries', the Pure Foods Exhibition opened at the Hall that exposed the fake foods that were being sold throughout Britain, mainly to the poor and lower-middle classes, sometimes with dangerous consequences to their health. Ironically, it was earlier in the same year that the 'Smokeries' Exhibition had taken place, and as diametrically opposed to each other in terms of health as one could get. By 23 May 1910, this became the International Pure Food and Allied Trades Exhibition, organised by A. Staines Mander, as already confirmed in an earlier chapter. Its brochure stated that. 'The Exhibition is designed to deal practically by a series of object lessons, with the great and growing evil of adulteration and contamination of our Food Supplies'. Thirty six patrons and honorary advisors were led by The Right Hon. Earl Hardwicke and included six JPs, three MPs, five Medical Officers of London Boroughs and the Principal of the National Training School of Cookery, Mrs E. Clarke. The Right Hon. Jesse Collins, MP, wrote: 'The Pure Food question is one of the utmost importance affecting the working and poorer classes. I heartily wish success in all reforms in that direction.' The displays horrified visitors with shocking examples of the way unscrupulous traders were duping the public, and this was reported widely in the press. However, it also brought a strident response and denial from the Federation of Grocers' Associations of the UK that saw this as a threat to their members.

Reporting on these on 22 May 1910, *The Observer* noted that, 'A seven-pound jar of jam, for instance, which is sold for the low price of 1s. 3d. (£5.47), is found on analysis to be innocent of any raspberries and currants. Their place is taken by mangolds (mangel-wurzels), turnips and beetroot, sweetened by a little glucose and saccharine. In order to add a touch of realism, sawdust is put in to represent the raspberry seeds.' It went on to say, 'In the cheap sweets bought by children many dangers lie hidden ... which have been known to contain the germs of lockjaw and cholera; and in others plaster of Paris is used to give the sweets stiffness.' The *Daily Mirror* reported other examples such as, 'Fish – raw Haddock, painted with creosote and Venetian red and, sold as 'smoked'; Cheap pastry – halfpenny tarts ... found to contain a large percentage of plaster of Paris and, flavoured with a poison, one drop of which would kill a dog; Pickles – diluted sulphuric acid, yellow chrome and vegetable refuse; Smoked sausages – the meat

is often mixed with creosote powder to give it a burnt flavour, while the skins are dyed red.' *The Times* reported that, 'In some cases, spirit of wine and sulphurous acid are used for mineral waters and limejuice, while tea, coffee and cocoa are 'faked' with a number of ingredients, including chicory, red oxide of iron, caramel, dried chestnuts, oak bark, Prussian blue, red ochre, chalk, and Venetian red.'

Almost as an afterthought, and having suitably frightened the reader with these shocking facts, the reporter did then confirm that the exhibition also displayed a large selection of really 'pure goods' prepared by high-class firms. One of the aims of the Pure Food and Health Society, run by the Ladies Grand Council whose President was Dowager Marchioness of Tweedale, was the provision of pure milk hostels, under the certification of the Society, to protect poor mothers from milk-borne diseases that were common, and often fatal, to young children. The Society was instrumental in helping bring about the Milk and Dairies (Consolidation) Act of 1915 although it was not until 1922 that the first really serious attempt to secure the production of safe and clean milk was made, and not until 1 January 1927 before The Public Health (Preservatives, etc., in Food) Regulations came into force.

V

Wartime and Beyond

Bleak Years

At the RHS Council Meeting on 26 November 1907 a letter had been read out from the Officer Commanding the troops in London asking for the use of the Hall, should mobilisation take place. This had clearly been a strategic contingency planning request made seven years before the outbreak of the First World War but, when the event became a reality in August 1914, the War Office changed their 'request' to a requisition order within weeks. They then did indeed use the Hall to bivouac troops prior to their departure for the Western Front until October of that year. The RHS was by no means alone in having its facilities requisitioned in this way. The Great White City buildings that had been used for so many of the large-scale colonial exhibitions were also requisitioned and used for troop mobilisation and deployment to the Western Front. Caxton Hall also had to be annexed

RIGHT *Special performance programme held at Daly's Theatre, Leicester Square, London in aid of Belgian war refugees on 16 September 1914. Daly's Theatre closed on 25 September 1937 and was later demolished and became the Warner Theatre. Its façade remains today and is known as Vue West End.*

FAR RIGHT *Derisory First World War postcard featuring the German Kaiser being flushed down the pan by the British John Bull, c.1914.*

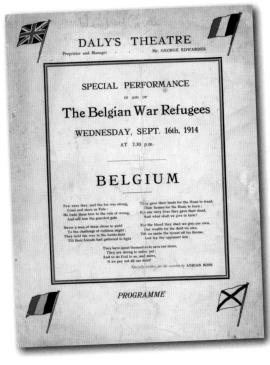

during mobilisation of the London Scottish Regiment because they did not have enough space to cope with the process from their HQ in Buckingham Gate. The London Scottish was one of the first Territorial Force battalions ordered to France and the first to see action in the First World War. The Duke of Argyll was honorary Colonel of the London Scottish Regiment between 1900 and 1914 and his wife, Princess Louise, Duchess of Argyll, was Colonel-in-Chief of the Argyll & Sutherland Highlanders from June 1911. After the War, their regimental dances were held periodically at the RHS Halls between 1920 and 1924.

The RHS had to hold many of their regular flower shows at other sites. In 1914 their May Spring Show was held at Chelsea Hospital and the Summer Shows at Holland Park and Royal Botanic Gardens, Kew, respectively. The Dahlia Society's Show was held at Crystal Palace. The emphasis on growing vegetables, rather than flowers, was also having an impact, even at this stage. At the 31 August RHS Show in the Hall, *The Times* reported that, 'Many nurserymen visiting the Horticultural Hall yesterday complained of the new vogue for digging up flower beds and lawns and planting vegetables in their place. One exhibitor said that his orders had fallen to less than half.' However, by the following year, the pace had quickened for the nation to produce more home-grown food, including vegetables, and the ever-innovative Mr Wareham-Smith from the *Daily Mail* organised a Home-Grown Food Exhibition and Competition that took place in the Hall on 22 September 1915. Prizes of £1,500 (£127,200) were offered to encourage home production of food during war-time and, 25,000 entries were received, as a result, ranging from 800 dozen new laid eggs, thousands of jars of preserved fruits, home-made honey and butter, to a great variety of vegetables in many classes. Much of the produce was subsequently sent to military hospitals. Sir Horace Plunkett, an Anglo-Irish Unionist, and later an Irish nationalist, had been a noted agricultural reformer and pioneer of agricultural co-operation in Ireland. His inspirational achievements in

enabling successful co-operative farming to take place in Ireland in equally difficult conditions and times had clearly influenced the *Daily Mail* to choose him to open the exhibition.

Ireland had gone through very tough times and The Gaelic League of London, whose main object was the promotion of Irish Industries, had held an annual exhibition of Irish Industries known as an 'Aonach' since 1906 in the RHS Hall. This had risen out of its movement to place their goods that included Irish lace and other homespun cottage industry products into the London

Letter from 10 Downing Street confirming that the War Office had no intention of taking the Lindley Hall for wartime purposes. Dated 12 December 1915.

marketplace, and had been hugely successful. In November 1911, *The Times* had reported that, 'in a four year period the value of Irish exports increased by nearly ten million pounds sterling, fully four-fifths of this trade being direct with England.' However, there were other motives for staging this, including the preservation of the Irish language and the distribution of propaganda leaflets and literature by 'Sinn Fein' that expressed the political conflict of time. Irish pipers played Irish airs and dancers gave demonstrations throughout. Admission was 6d. (£2.16). Sinn Fein, in the form of the Irish Republican Army (IRA), would make an unwelcome return to the RHS on 18 December 1973, when one of their Parcel Bombs exploded in the New Hall at 5.58 p.m. The Post Office had hired this as a Temporary Post sorting office, and the bomb injured six people working there. This was the second explosion of four in London on the same day injuring a total of 60 people. This was the beginning of a campaign over the Christmas period that saw 73 people injured by 24 bombs and explosive devices. The worst bomb exploded outside of a Home Office building in Westminster, when about 80lb of explosives packed into a stolen Ford car injured 54 people. The Post Office had hired the RHS

Halls as a Christmas post sorting office since December 1907. It would not be unreasonable to think that they chose the RHS Hall for this usage as a direct result of the previous year's 1906 International Philatelic Exhibition. It would also not be unreasonable to think that a subsequent consequence of this link was their choice of the RHS for their annual Post Office Orphan Homes Concerts that first came to the Hall in February 1909, and continued until 1938, when it also benefited GPO Widows.

In 1914, several important non-horticultural events had to be cancelled in September and October, including the first *Daily Express* Women and Their Work Show, the London Medical and the Universal Food & Cookery Exhibitions. The Surveyor's Institution and London University's Examinations, that had been held in the Hall almost annually since 1906 were also casualties of the change being forced upon the RHS. There was a brief respite, but in spite of a letter from the Prime Minister, Herbert Asquith, on 12 December 1915 that he had received an assurance from the War Office that 'there is no intention of taking the Hall of The Royal Horticultural Society', the War Office returned on 13 October 1916 to requisition the Hall for the next three years. This was then

Postcard of the London Scottish Regiment going into their trenches in the First World War in 1916.

55. LONDON SCOTTISH GOING INTO THEIR TRENCHES. OFFICIAL PHOTOGRAPH. CROWN COPYRIGHT RESERVED.

used to billet the Australian Imperial Forces prior to them being sent to active service on the Western Front and elsewhere. The Australian government had agreed to provide 20,000 troops to Britain at the start of the War and ended up supplying 322,000, of whom more than 280,000 were casualties with just under 60,000 dead. A poignant example of the early casualties was evident at the National Rose Society's Spring Show held on 16 April 1915 when war-wounded soldiers in bandages, and limping on crutches, were brought into this show by their nurses, and the flowers distributed to hospitals afterwards.

It was also during this period that sympathy and solidarity with Belgium and its soldiers manifested itself in many fund-raising events and special performances. One of these had been staged at one of London's most important theatres, Daly's Theatre just off Leicester Square, on 16 September 1914 billed as 'Special Performance in aid of The Belgian War Refugees' under the patronage of the War Refugees Committee whose president was HRH The Duchess of Vendôme and whose chairman was HRH Princess Christian of Schleswig-Holstein. Leading performers of the time, such as Phyllis Dare, Gertie Millar, Lily Elsie, Clara Butterworth, Adeline Genee danced, sang and recited a variety of excerpts from classical, traditional and nationalistic music, plays and operas. These ended with W.H. Berry singing the famous First World War song, 'It's a long, long way to Tipperary'. The Grand Finale included The London Welsh Choral Society, The London Welsh Male Choir and The Chorus from the Adelphi and Gaiety Theatres. They sang 'Land of Hope and Glory', The Belgian, Russian and Japanese National Anthems, The Marseillaise, Rule Britannia and God Save The King. The RHS had started its own War Relief Fund in 1915 and by March 1920 had raised £43,000 (£1.631 million). Lord Lambourne was president of the fund, Lord Grenfell past president (reflecting their presidencies of the RHS itself) and Lady Northcote was lady president. Sir Harry Veitch, who had been a member of the RHS Council until 1916, was honorary treasurer. Seeds and

TOP LEFT *Undated and unsigned letter from the Royal Horticultural Society to the Rt. Hon. Winston Churchill, MP, when he was Secretary of State for War, appealing to him to assist in regaining possession of their building in Vincent Square.*

BELOW LEFT *Letter from the Australian Imperial Force dated 19 June 1919.*

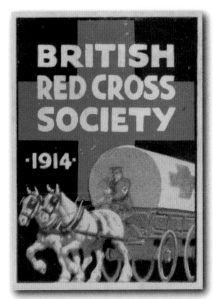

RIGHT *Poster labels for the British Red Cross Society dated 1914.*

garden mats to the value of £5,500 (£208,615) had been given to Belgium for the Yser region, in particular, that suffered during the Battle of Yser when the river had been deliberately flooded to impede the German's progress. France had received thousands of seeds and fruit trees. Serbia and Roumania had also been given thousands of tools and packets of seeds. Later, on 12 March 1925 at a meeting of the Garden Club in Mayfair, Lord Lambourne also supported the efforts of the *Le jardin de la France Devastée* (Garden League for Devasted France) that had been founded in 1920. Since that time they had sent over 1,200 garden tools and implements, large quantities of vegetable seeds, medicinal and other plants, and over 1,000 fruit trees.

The War Office intervention clearly meant that the established commercial lettings business that had been so successfully developed since 1904 had to stop, causing them and many other commercial organisations disruption and financial loss. This prompted a letter to be written by the RHS directly to the Secretary of State for War, the Rt. Hon. Winston Churchill, MP who was, of course, very familiar with the Hall, having attended events in them on a number of occasions. The letter implored him 'to assist us to regain the use of our building. We have not only already suffered considerable loss by its occupation, but are now suffering still further by its continued occupation, in that being compelled to decline all proposals for the renting of it on days on which we are not using it ourselves, we are providing a certainty of loss in the future from losing touch with our would-be clients who, unable to enter into a contract with us for any future date, are providing for themselves elsewhere, and will, we fear, become settled in other buildings to our great and permanent loss. [On 3 October 1912, Methodist Central Hall at the very bottom of Victoria Street had opened as a Church, Mission Hall and world administrative centre of Wesleyan Methodism. However, it soon also became an established and newly sought after venue that competed with the RHS Hall. The suffragettes were just one of the organisations that valued its prime Westminster location and

used it, as a result.] As an example, the Board of Trade is asking us to grant the use of our Hall in September next for a great Colonial grown Timber Exhibition – we do not like to decline so patriotic a movement, but under existing circumstances it is beyond our power to consent.' It went on to say that 'General Griffiths, at present in command of the Australians, sympathises with us, and would desire to carry out the promises of his predecessor made to us, we have every reason to know, but we believe that a little stimulus from yourself, Sir, might hasten movement.' Churchill's reply is not known, but the RHS did continue with their own flower shows, running these at the London Scottish Royal Volunteers Drill Hall in James Street and, of course, incurred hiring charges of their own until they could offset them against anticipated compensation. However, the War Office initially refused to do so and the RHS had to wait for a House of Lords ruling in their favour that the War Office was not above the law. On 13 June 1952, 44 years after he had first stepped into the RHS Hall and well after both World Wars, the recently re-elected Prime Minister, Winston Churchill, was back in the RHS Hall pictured watching some Siamese fighting fish when visiting the 5th Aquarium and Water Garden Exhibition (organised by the National Aquarists Society).

What had become clear in the 10 years that the RHS had operated the Hall for their own flower shows, and their third-party clients, was just how successful they had been in establishing their venue, and attracting such a wide range of events supported at the highest levels. Here we must also acknowledge, as did The Borough of Westminster Constitutional Association for its own reasons, the contribution that Mr Burdett-Coutts, MP for Westminster, had made during the 25 years since his election. This took the form of a Commemoration evening at the Hall on 18 November 1910. *The Times* reported that, 'He was the recipient of an illuminated address presented by men of all shades of opinion as a token of the admiration of the great services he has rendered to the constituency, the nation and the Empire.' Lord Onslow, who presided and made the

Photo of British Prime Minister, Winston Churchill, watching Siamese fighting fish at the 5th National Aquarium and Water Garden Exhibition, organised by the National Aquarists Society, held in the Lindley Hall from 10-16 June 1952.

presentation, said that, 'Mr Burdett-Coutts led the way to make Westminster the second place of importance, second only to London itself.' Had his late wife, the Baroness Angela Burdett-Coutts, still been alive, she would also undoubtedly have been proud. The strength and stability of the City Westminster as a business centre within London remains as important today, perhaps now even more so than its counterpart and historical rival, The City of London. However, the 'new kid on the block', London Eastside, has the potential to destabilise this position in the future,

depending on how this area will develop in the future, post 2012 London Olympics.

Before moving on to what were to become new horizons for the RHS and its Hall after the War (and new horizons for the British people also), one event that took place in the Hall on 14 June 1913, just 14 months prior to its outbreak on 4 August 1914, provides an illustration of just how much the long association with Germany – its Royal Family, culture and industry that had become so closely integrated with British culture – would change dramatically very soon after it.

The 25th anniversary of Kaiser Wilhelm II's Accession was on 17 June 1913 and, in Berlin, celebrations of his Jubilee were held in earnest by the Emperor and his Empress, and all members of the Prussian Royal Family. On the Pariser Platz, large signs proclaimed extracts from the Kaiser's speeches such as, 'My strength belongs to the world and to the Fatherland,' and 'Our future lies upon the water' and 'Berlin will yet be the most beautiful city in the World'. In Britain, this was celebrated by the German colony in London at the RHS Hall, just four days before it, with a lavish banquet and concert that included the band of the Grenadier Guards, organised by the German Athenaeum Club. Almost one thousand Germans living in London attended and the chair was taken by their Ambassador, Prince Lichnowsky. Dr Ernst Schuster, president of the colony, was also present. The Times reported that Dr Schuster gave an address to those present saying, 'that Germans were rejoicing in all parts of the world in commemoration of the fact that after a reign extending over a quarter of a century his Majesty was still in the prime of manhood.' He went on to express 'the hope that the present jubilee was merely a milestone on a long and beneficent journey. The weight of the voice of Germany during the last 25 years had constantly increased; it was heard with respect, because it was the voice of moderation and justice, because while firmly maintaining her own rights she gave due consideration to the rights of others.'

However, not all Germans were celebrating with the Emperor and notably absent from the Berlin Jubilee banquet and all other celebrations had been the Poles and the Socialists. The Times once again reported that at the Berlin banquet the President, Count Schwerin, had ended his own speech by ominously stating that, 'the Jubilee would, however, only be a lasting blessing if they carried from it the resolution to allow no one to rob them of their treasure, the Prussian Monarchy, or to diminish it.'

By 1914, in Britain, the atmosphere had changed completely and prompted by the strong belief that a German invasion was imminent the Daily Mail asked its readers not to trust German waiters and to ask to see their passports if they said that they were Swiss! The view was then held by many that resident Germans in London and England were thought to be a Fifth Column. My own grandfather, who had come to London from Bohemia in Austro-Hungary in 1900, and had set up a small restaurant called The Continental, in Holborn, was targeted by meat porters who were hell-bent on smashing all German and Austrian businesses (his name was Desensky) in spite of the fact that he had become a naturalised British subject and served on the Western Front during the First World War in the Middlesex Regiment. The Secret Service Bureau (precursor to MI5 and MI6) had been set up in 1909 in Victoria Street by an Irishman and Chief Detective at Scotland Yard, William Melville, under the code name 'M' – used by Ian Fleming in his James Bond novels. Melville discovered a German network of spies in 1912 that were allowed to carry on under observation until 1914, when they were then rounded up, crippling the German secret service operations in Britain at one stroke.

At 11 p.m. on the evening of 3 August 1914 a note was being prepared by Sir Edward Grey and his Foreign Office officials to deliver to Prince Lichnowsky, still Germany's Ambassador in London. It mistakenly began, 'The German Empire having declared war upon Great Britain'. In fact, the Germans had not done so. This was an incorrect declaration of war due to a Foreign Office blunder by failing to recognise the one-hour time difference between the two countries. However, by the time 4 August became so in both countries, England and Germany were at war with each other and Prince Lichnowsky had been handed back his passport ready to leave his German colony in London for good. Another twist of fate and irony was that, undoubtedly, some of those from London's German Colony who would have attended the Kaiser's Jubilee banquet in the RHS Hall would have been spies and later interned in several other famous London exhibition halls, namely, Olympia and Alexandra Palace that were used for that purpose during the war.

New Order/Women and Their Work

The rivalry between Lord Rothermere's new clutch of *Daily Mail* exhibitions, and those being organised by other newspapers took a new turn when the Beaverbrook-run *Daily* *Express* organised 'Women and their Work – An Exhibition of the Arts and Crafts of the Home Worker'. This was planned to take place in the RHS Hall in October 1914. However,

Poster label for the Daily Express Women and Their Work Exhibition. *This was meant to take place in the Lindley Hall on 23-30 October 1914, but was cancelled due to the outbreak of the First World War.*

due to the outbreak of the First World War, and the forced closure of the Hall, this was cancelled. It did take place the following year on 1-7 May 1915 under the patronage of HM Queen Alexandra. She visited the show on 3 May with Princess Victoria, but it was opened by Princess Arthur of Connaught. Mr Blumenfeld, the then Editor of the *Daily Express*, welcomed the Princess with Lady Carew, the Duchess of Wellington, Lady Bessborough, Lady Ancaster and Lady Cory. Admission was 5s. (£21.20) on opening day and 1s. (£4.24) after. The *raison d'être* of the Exhibition was based upon the notion that there were many women with 'clever ideas' scattered all over the country that would 'willingly turn over their ideas and diligence to a practical end' at home to generate some income for themselves. However, due to timidity, inexperience, or lack of knowledge, many excellent skills and products were not being realised for personal financial gain. The *Daily Express* felt that women in these situations should be helped to find outlets for their work.

The Clarion Press, based at 44 Worship Street, EC. London had already produced a dedicated Woman's Paper called, the *Woman's Worker*, but since its sister publication was entitled *The Clarion*, and unequivocally socialist, it was diametrically opposite to the right-wing conservative audience of the *Daily Express*, and the interpretation of 'Women's Work', also very different. However, it proudly claimed that 'it is the only Woman's Paper which assumes that its readers are not dolls or drudges, but WOMEN.' It went on to say that it contained 'bright and helpful articles for all classes of women workers; a record of the week's news specially affecting women's interests; a serial tale; stories and sketches, etc. etc.' My research has also produced an event entitled, 'Working Girls at Play', that had taken place in the Hall in 1910 and 27 May 1911. I have no specific information on this, and it could have been a precursor to the *Daily Express* event, but it could also have been something very different! However, it does seem very likely that the *Daily Express* show borrowed from the very successful Home Arts

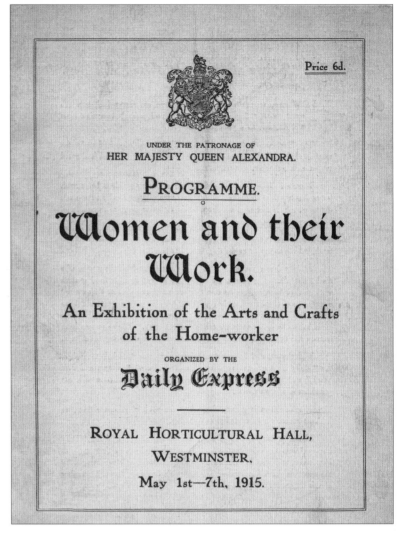

and Industries Exhibition, a similar event that had moved from the Royal Albert Hall to the RHS Hall in June 1908, and celebrated its 25th anniversary show one year later in May 1909, when Princess Christian of Schleswig-Holstein opened the show. This event also had Queen Alexandra as its Patron, and showcased her Sandringham cottage industries, which like the majority of other exhibitors also demonstrated their lace, embroidery, tapestries, and metal work. Certainly, it did not return to the Hall after 1909 and in 1914, under the patronage of Queen Alexandra, the annual Exhibition and Sale of Arts, Crafts and Industries took place at the Portman Rooms. However, the very first major exhibition to highlight women and their work in this way had taken place at Earl's Court in 1900 when The Woman's Exhibition was staged. This exhibition was

Programme for the, Women and Their Work. An Exhibition of the Arts and Crafts of the Home-worker, organised by the Daily Express, held in the Lindley Hall on 1-7 May 1915. The Exhibition was opened by HRH Princess Arthur of Connaught.

truly international and diverse in displaying woman in many guises from her traditional role as mother, nurse, and comforter to the way she fared in the fields of the applied and fine arts. There was a strong contingent of women from throughout Europe, especially Germany, Italy, France, Belgium, Holland, Spain, Switzerland, Austria and Hungary. Russia and America were also very much in evidence. Nine years later, in Olympia, a similar event entitled, Women of all Nations Exhibition of Arts, Crafts and Industries took place.

The Organising Committee of Women and their Work included representatives from the British and Irish Spinning and Weaving Industries, the Ladies' Army and Navy Club and the London Association for the Blind. Other organisations such as The Middlesex Hospital, the Self-Help Society, the West Central Flower Industry, the Ladies' Work Association and the Laurence Kirk Linen Industry, Scotland had stalls, as did the Agatha Stacey Homes, who displayed hand-made woollen hearthrugs, doormats, footmuffs, and other articles made by 'feeble-minded young women'. Lady Carew (grandmother of Sir Richard Carew Pole, who would become the 17th President of the RHS in 2001) was on Stall 21 with other Ladies

Poster label used on the back of an envelope advertising the Daily Express *Woman's Exhibition, held at Olympia, on 12-29 July 1922.*

displaying 'Pictures and Works of Art'. Mrs Ethel Morland on Stall No.9 exhibited her prize cats and kittens, and The Boué Sœurs, the renowned French fashion house that had not long opened a London base in 39 Curzon Street, London, staged a 'Great Exhibition by Living Mannequins' on 3 May. Champion Lady Fencers, pupils of the McPherson School of Fencing based at No.3, Victoria Street, gave a Display of Fencing. Much later, on 17 and 18 November 1930, the semi-final pools and final round of the Ladies' Foil tournament, competing for the Lady Louis Mountbatten Cup, was staged in the RHS New Hall. Miss Louise M.C. Ludolph, Certified Specialist for Breathing Gymnastics and Voice Culture gave a lecture on 'Breathing Gymnastics' and Madame Edith Grey-Burnand, a renowned soprano, and her orchestra, was in charge of the music and concert singing programme that ran throughout the period of the exhibition on every afternoon. Miss Elizabeth Clark gave a series of lectures, and entertained, endorsing the patriotic fervour needed at this time with titles such as 'Stories of Patriots and Heroes', and 'Stories of the Allied Nations'. Other lectures were given on 'Marriage or a Career', 'the War's Effect on Marriage and Women's Work', 'Electricity in the Service of the Home' and, 'Agriculture and Horticulture as a Profession for Women.' The Farrow's Bank for Women Knightsbridge Branch advertised in the Show Catalogue, and proudly proclaimed its Branch to be 'entirely controlled and worked by women'. The Ladies' Electric Sun Baths in Regent Street also advertised their Electrical Treatments, Vibro Treatment, and Light Baths for Ladies Only. The Fresh Air Fund took a whole page advert to promote their activities in enabling poor children to have a day in the country, or a fortnight at the seaside or a rural retreat. A 9d. (£3.18) donation would secure the former and 10s. (£42.40) for the latter. The Fund operated in London, and 42 of the United Kingdom's principal towns, where many children never saw beyond the urban squalor in which they lived. The Middlesex Hospital was represented on Stall 19. Following its success, this *Daily*

Express show was repeated in November that year at Prince's Skating Club, Knightsbridge, and transferred to Olympia in July 1922 as The Woman's Exhibition.

Perhaps the most interesting exhibitors of all at the 1915 event were Misses N.E. & R.A. Isaac of Dennington Park Road, N.W. who were on Stall 17, not because of what they displayed; sketch portraits, original drawings, jewellery, enamels, dyed and decorated woodwork and sculpture, but because two years later they were to become the organisers of a very similar exhibition in the Hall that was to become a standard bearer event for the applied arts industry, and held annually until 1937. The *Daily Telegraph* wrote of this event, 'What the Royal Academy is to Painters, this Exhibition would be to the craftsman'.

The 1st Applied Arts and Handcrafts Exhibition took place on 5-12 December 1924, organised by Misses Nellie E. and R.A. Isaac, and Mr H.J.C. Rowe of 26 Eastcastle Street, Oxford Circus, W1. Under the patronage of Princess Louise, Duchess of Argyll, Princess Arthur of Connaught, Princess Marie Louise and Princess Helen Victoria it was opened by Princess Marthe Bibesco, a well known

Romanian writer, hostess and socialite of the day, and a member of the *Académie Royale de Langue et de Littérature Française de Belgique* (coincidentally, the newly elected RHS Patron in that same year was Queen Marie of Romania who remained so until 1938). A special feature of European Modern Applied Arts was shown and admission was 1s. 3d. (£2.78) including tax. Exquisite and exclusive examples of pottery, glass, leatherwork, jewellery, decorative wood, fairy eggshell veneer, hand-weaving, photography, lacquer, stained glass, bookbinding, metal work, engraving, painting, lace and embroidery was on display. The predilection for using bird's feathers was still in evidence with feather lampshades said to give 'a most charming light'. Miss N. Isaac specialised in eggshell veneer, and her sister in jewellery. The second Applied Arts and Handcrafts Exhibition took place the following year on 4-11 December 1925 when Princess Louise, Duchess of Argyll was meant to have opened the Exhibition, but was prevented from doing so by what were then infamous, and thick, 'pea-soup' London fogs. In 1926 the Exhibition was opened by Lady Sassoon and in 1931 by one of the

Poster labels for the 6th, 7th and 8th Applied Arts and Handcrafts Exhibitions that took place in the Lindley Hall in 1928, 1929 and 1930 respectively. The 6th Exhibition was opened by the French Ambassador, M. De Fleuriau, and the 8th, opened by Lady Cynthia Mosley.

Nation's most loved actresses of the period, Gladys Cooper. (She had already been to the Hall twice before at least; once in 1913 when she attended the Fairyland Fête referred to earlier, and in 1920 when she was one of a number of theatrical celebrities, including Phyllis Monkton, Miss Marie Löhr and Mr Gerald du Maurier, who had taken part in a New Year's Eve Carnival Ball in aid of the After-Care Fund, whose patroness was Queen Alexandra. A special floor to accommodate 2,000 dancers had been laid at the 1920 event and boxes were booked by the officers of the Royal Horse Guards, the 2nd Battalion K.O.Y.L.I., the 1st Battalion East Lancashire Regiment and the 14th Brigade R.G.A.) At each show that continued until 1937, there were daily demonstrations by the varied artist craftsmen already described that took place in specially constructed miniature studios and workshops. Many of the artists who displayed at these exhibitions would have been pleased to have seen a recent resurgence of interest in their art forms, and one of them, a talented and internationally recognised studio potter during the 1920s, Stella Crofts, was the subject

Poster for the 9th National Federation of Women's Institutes Exhibition, held in the Lawrence Hall on 16-23 November 1938.

of a new exhibition of her work (principally of animals and birds) held in Gloucester in June/ July 2010.

As Tony Blair found out when he addressed the Women's Institute (WI) on 7 June 2000, the ladies that belong to it are not to be patronised nor taken lightly! And so it was from the very beginning when the National Federation of Women's Institutes (NFWI) first formed on 16 October 1917 with 137 existing WIs around the country. Lady Gertrude Denman was elected its first Chairman. With so many women having been aware of the Royal Horticultural Hall through its horticultural, handicraft, suffragette, political, and women-related events staged there, it is not surprising that they staged their second, 4th and 6th London Exhibition in the RHS Halls in May 1920, December 1939 and October 1947 respectively. It is also interesting to note that Sir Hubert Parry's famous music score of Blake's poem, that later became known as Jerusalem, was adopted as their hymn by the NFWI at their 1924 AGM, and continues to be sung at these meetings and others to this day. It was originally written specifically for a suffragette 'Fight for the Right' meeting at Queen's Hall, London in 1916.

Three of the NFWI London Handicraft and Home-craft exhibitions were also staged in the Hall in 1927 and 1935. Mr H.A.L. Fisher, who had become Minister of Education in 1916, and introduced significant reforms in the Education Act 1918, opened their second London Exhibition that included lecture demonstrations in crafts, drama by the British Drama League, and dancing. By 1935 the Hon. Frances M. Farrer was General Secretary, and at their handicraft exhibition that year in the New Hall 40 craftswomen demonstrated village industries. The Duchess of York opened the event and Queen Mary also paid a visit. At their 1938 Exhibition both Queen Elizabeth and Queen Mary visited on the opening day. Both were Institute members and paid their two shillings (£4.45) subscription every year. They were also both Presidents of the Sandringham WI. Mrs Neville Chamberlain also visited. In 1938, there were over 5,600 Institutes in

England and Wales with a membership of more than 310,000. Then, in 1947, the last of these events took place in the Hall, before moving to Olympia the following year when Queen Elizabeth opened it. She had also been Patron to the RHS with her husband, the future George VI, since 1936, although at that time they were still the Duke and Duchess of York. The NFWI did return on 9-10 October 1948 in the New Hall for their first 'Home Produce Exhibition'. This was part of a drive entitled 'Operation Produce', to augment the nation's food supplies when rationing was still in place post-war. Each NFWI member was asked to produce 10lb of food over and above her own needs, and everything that could be legally sold was done so at fixed prices. The produce that could not be sold was given to hospitals.

Fashion, Beauty and Health

In the two decades commencing 1990, the Royal Horticultural Halls built themselves a strong niche for hosting designer fashion shows. Luminaries of the fashion world, such as Alexander McQueen, Paul Smith, Wayne Hemingway of Red or Dead, Matthew Williamson, Ozwald Boateng, Gharani Strok, Elizabeth Walsh, Margaret Howell, Rafael Lopez, Warren Noronha, Shahid Sharif, Stella McCartney, and Frost & French helped establish their names in groundbreaking shows in the Halls. These were mainly held as part of London's hugely successful 'London Fashion Week' designer shows held annually in the Spring and Autumn. These were often seen as either special or quirky offshoots of the main event, but the fact was that they

Photo of the King's Consort, HM Queen Mary and Lady Denman, Chairman of the Federation, visiting the 9th National Federation of Women's Institutes Exhibition, held in the Lawrence Hall on 16-23 November 1938.

The Daily Mirror

THE MORNING JOURNAL WITH THE SECOND LARGEST NET SALE.

No. 1,767.   Registered at the G.P.O. as a Newspaper.   SATURDAY, JUNE 26, 1909.   One Halfpenny.

"THE DAILY MIRROR" FAIR OF FASHIONS WHICH OPENS TO-DAY: PHOTOGRAPH WHICH WON THE "FAMOUS WOMEN" COMPETITION.

To-day at 1.15 p.m. the Lady Mayoress, who will be accompanied by the Lord Mayor, will open *The Daily Mirror* Fair of Fashions at the Horticultural Hall, Vincent-square, Westminster. Next week the fair will be open from 10 a.m. till 10 p.m. each day, closing finally on Saturday, July 3. The Horticultural Hall is very conveniently situated, being within a few minutes' walk from St. James' Park Station on the Underground Railway. Victoria Station is also less than half a mile distant. Above is Isabella, the Nun, which, with a photograph of Rosalind, won the first prize of £50 in the famous women photograph competition. Both pictures are by Mr. Cavendish Morten, the well-known photographic artist. The competition was for persons in costume posing as well-known characters or representing famous pictures.

ABOVE Daily Mirror front page, dated 26 June 1909, promoting their Fair of Fashions, held in the Lindley Hall on 26 June-3 July 1909. Mr Wareham-Smith, Advertising Manager of the Daily Mail, who created the Ideal Home Exhibition, was its Director.

RIGHT Catalogue for the 2nd Junior Fashion Fair, organised by the National Children's Wear Association, held in the Lawrence Hall on 11-14 May 1953 (the first had been held at the Army & Navy Exhibition Halls on 4-7 November 1952). This Trade Fair was then held twice a year in the RHS Hall over a period between May 1953 and 3-6 October 1983.

provided unique and solus settings for up-and-coming designers to get themselves better known. I distinctly remember watching Alexander McQueen's inspired, spectacular, and controversial 1997 Spring/Summer collection, *Les Poupées*, displayed in the Lawrence Hall catwalk of water he had created. As the name implies, this collection was based on dolls. Debra Shaw wore the most extreme representation of this; a manacled structure restricting her movement that had been created to mimic the jerky movements of a marionette. Another model wore a beekeeper-type headdress full of butterflies flying around her head inside it.

However, it was as early as September 1978 when Prudence Lynn reported in her feature on the Men's Fashion scene in *The Times* that, 'Hived off this time from the might of the

MAB (Menswear Association of Great Britain) showing at Earl's Court, 18 of our brightest and best bloomed at the Horticultural Hall, Vincent Square under the green fingers of Ms Lynne Franks, a lady of amazing energy committed to the furthering of the fashion industry. She reckons, and she is probably right, that it will take four seasons to establish the alternative venue as the crucial spot for buyers to check into.' Franks had been involved with the London Menswear Collection but, sure enough in 1982 another show, Fashion and Beauty, took place in the Hall. A number of other fashion-related events and shows were staged subsequently by Fake, Jigsaw, French Connection, Principles, Harvey Nichols, Gant, Nicole Farhi, Miss Selfridge, Marks & Spencer, GFT, Margin, Billion Dollar Babes and Doll. The second showing of London Men's Fashion Week also took place in 1999, when designers such as D.A. Lilliard, All Saints and John Richmond wowed their audiences. Vivienne Westwood also took part in a charity event organised by IMG, and there were regular fabric sales by Colefax & Fowler, Jane Churchill, Manuel Canovas, Larsen and Osborne & Little. A fitting culmination to this activity was the 2007 British Fashion Awards, organised by The British Fashion Council that

NCWA

NATIONAL CHILDREN'S WEAR ASSOCIATION

welcomes you to the Fair

MAY 11th-14th, 1953

ROYAL HORTICULTURAL SOCIETY'S NEW HALL · S·W·1

were displayed by what they then called 'mannequins' in a specially constructed 'Theatre of Dress'. The most famous fashion houses of the day from London and Paris were there. Only one remains in its original form: Harrods. The others included Worth, Redfern, Martial et Armand, Ney Sœurs, Boué Sœurs, Mme. Arqua, Mme. Elinor Temple, Devereux, Maison Green, Grunwaldt, and Beer. Collectively, they supplied the most extravagant, exciting, revolutionary, and shocking designs of their period to the royalty of Europe, the rich and famous in the USA, and the aristocracy of Great Britain. Famous singers and actresses such as Lillie Langtry, Sarah Bernhardt, Nellie Melba and Jenny Lind favoured them in being able to create dresses and designs that would make sure that they would be forever remembered for the stars they were, and it is almost certain that many of them attended this new 'Fashion Fair'.

The House of Worth rose from small beginnings in Paris in 1858 when Charles Frederick Worth, an Englishman from Bourne, Lincolnshire, set up his first design partnership. He had first come to the attention of the fashion world with his prize-winning designs shown at the Great Exhibition of 1851 and the Exposition Universelle of 1855 in Paris. He secured the patronage of the Empress Eugénie, Napoleon III's wife, and became known as 'father of haute couture' and 'the first couturier'. Redfern were another of the most famous French fashion houses, based at the rue de Rivoli, Paris, and Paris was certainly regarded as the most important city of fashion, looked up to by the British. Interestingly, M. Redfern was asked about the possibility of the American designers setting up their own houses and ignoring Paris. (Many of them did, including the Boué sisters, whose signature lace lingerie and silver and gold textile collections were hugely expensive, but snapped up, nevertheless.) He is quoted by the *Daily Mirror* as replying, 'America is a very smart and up-to-date place, and its chief cities are in advance of those of Europe in many things; but in the matter of dress it is my belief that, from the artistic point of

took place on 27 November in the renamed Lawrence Hall, attended by the luminaries of the fashion world. Other events such as Junior Fashion Fair, a trade fair of children's clothes, had taken place twice a year over a 30-year period from May 1953. However, the earliest fashion show in the Hall had taken place in June 1909.

In keeping with the growing trend for national newspapers both to sponsor and organise exhibitions and events of their own, especially the *Daily Mail*, it was the *Daily Mirror* that, on this occasion, organised and promoted their spectacular 'Fair of Fashions'. This was held from 26 June to 3 July 1909, and opened by the Lady Mayoress, Lady Truscott, accompanied by the Lord Mayor. During the Fair, 36 masterpieces of costume from the principal costumiers of the world view, Paris will always lead the World.' French arrogance reigned supreme then, as now, but he was right! He would, undoubtedly, have made a similar comment about his French wines but, in this area, America and the New World certainly proved that they could eclipse the French and prick their arrogance, but not for another 90 years. However, one has to recognise that it had been an American, Gordon Selfridge, who had opened Selfridges in 1909 to great acclaim.

On the walls of the Hall were hung scores of portraits of living and famous women who had chosen their own heroines of history, art or fiction, and had been photographed as them. Joan of Arc was one. These caused a huge sensation and high value cash prizes were awarded to those judged to be the best three;

£50 (£4,423) for the 1st, £25 (£2,212) for the second, and £15 (£1,327) for the 3rd. Women and beauty were in vogue and, a year earlier on 4 May 1908, the *Daily Mirror* had organised an International Beauty Competition claimed as Britain's first national beauty contest, mainly in response to the Chicago Tribune's claim that the winner of the 1907 American Beauty Contest was 'the most beautiful woman in the world'. Over 15,000 women entered the British contest that was judged by a committee of distinguished artists. Ivy Lilian Close from Stockton-on-Tees was announced the winner and received a Rover car as her principal prize, but her portrait was also painted by Arthur Hacker and exhibited at the Royal Academy's 1908 summer show. She became a renowned beauty queen and film actress, described by the

Photo of mannequins modelling hand-painted silk gowns and parasols at the Daily Mirror Fair of Fashions, *held in the Lindley Hall on 26 June-3 July 1909.*

THE WINNER OF THE "DAILY MIRROR"
INTERNATIONAL BEAUTY CONTEST.
Published by C.W. Faulkner & Co Ltd, London E.C. Printed in England.

Postcard of the winner of the Daily Mirror *Fair of Fashions, Ivy Lilian Close from Stockton-on-Tees.*

Daily Mirror on her death as a 'Pioneer' who had also depicted figures from famous paintings in her husband's 1914 film, *Ivy's Elopement.*

In a strange paradox with both the location of the Fair at the Royal Horticultural Society's Hall, and a previous reference I have made about the use of bird's feathers for Lady's hats, the *Daily Mirror* proudly proclaimed that at their Fair it would be 'the first time in the history of fashion in London, that the use of artificial flowers made of feathers is to be introduced into millinery.' It went on to say, 'These feather flowers are so exquisite in colouring, and so perfect in form that at a short distance they cannot be distinguished from real blossoms.' The key to their success was that they could not be spoilt by the weather, and that they would also not fade from natural dyes, because the plumes were the natural colours of the plumage of the birds they came from. *The Mirror* was also quite brazen in explaining that the feathers came from exotic birds of brilliant plumage in Brazil. The artistic representations were, indeed, beautiful and exquisite, and likened to the skills of lace-makers in England, Ireland and the Continent. The ladies of the aristocracy, and those who could afford to do so, were as pre-occupied with the changing fashions that were being presented then, as today (and at the Royal Agricultural Hall

in Islington two years later, the Wholesale Drapery and Ladies Wear Exhibition the 'Rag Trade' were making sure that the retail shops and outlets in London met their demands). In the meantime, for those who were interested in the fashions of days gone by, they were treated to rare historical gems in the RHS Hall, such as a petticoat of Queen Anne, a court shirt made for Charles Dickens, an apron worn by

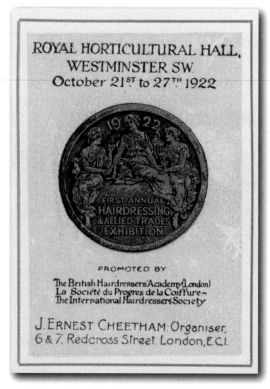

ROYAL HORTICULTURAL HALL,
WESTMINSTER S.W.
October 21ST to 27TH 1922

1922

FIRST ANNUAL
HAIRDRESSING
& ALLIED TRADES
EXHIBITION

PROMOTED BY
The British Hairdressers' Academy (London)
La Société du Progrès de la Coiffure -
The International Hairdressers Society

J. ERNEST CHEETHAM. Organiser,
6 & 7, Redcross Street. London, E.C.I.

Poster label for the First Annual Hairdressing & Allied Trades Exhibition, organised by J. Ernest Cheetham, held in the Lindley Hall on 21-27 October 1922.

Marie Antoinette, Ruffles made by the Nuns for the Young Pretender, and garments made with fish bones in the 14th century.

Then, in 1922, the 1st Annual Hairdressing & Allied Trades Exhibition took place on 21-7 October promoted by The British Hairdressers' Academy (London), *La Societé du Progres de la Coiffure* – The International Hairdressers' Society. This was organised by J. Ernest Cheetham who, later in May 1926, also launched in the Hall the 1st National Exhibition of Commercial Display.

Cheetham's hairdressing exhibition was a real *tour de force*, combining theatricality with trade expertise. It was Mrs Arthur Bourchier (Miss Violet Marion Kyrle Bellew) a prominent actress of the day, who said in her speech on opening the Exhibition, 'I

should like to emphasise the fact that such a grouping of hairdressing interests has rarely – if ever – been collected under one roof; at any rate, it is the first of its kind ever held in London.' It was also held to coincide with the 70th-birthday celebrations of one of the hairdressing world's great masters, the Frenchman, Marcel Grateau, who owed his success to a turn of events involving an earlier famous actress, Jane Hading. Grateau had invented the 'Marcel Wave' (a stylish wave given to the hair by means of heated curling irons) in 1872. This process, originally known as the 'Undulation Marcel', revolutionised the art of hairdressing all over the world, and remained in vogue for over fifty years. When he had styled Jane Hading's hair in this way, it generated enormous publicity which he duly capitalised on. It was, therefore, also fitting that he and his wife were received as guests of honour at the exhibition on 24 October, although Marcel was no stranger to London as he had been fêted at another international event entitled the 'Fête Marcel' in July 1908. This time, his visit to London and the exhibition was part of an even larger nine-day fête and exhibition that also took place in Luna Park (Port Maillot) in Paris. Marcel had already developed a permanent waving machine that was being used in hairdressing schools and parlours. Perms at that time were very expensive. He also developed other specialised hair waving equipment including hair curlers (1921), portable permanent hair wave machine (1923), perming pads (1925), an improved marcel iron (1927), curling pin (1927), hair waving device (1927,1928), flexible mica sheeting (1930), improved marcel iron (1932), adjustable marcel iron (1933), steam hair waving device (1933), croquignole permanent wave device (1935, 1937), permanent wave device (1935), barber's hair cutting clippers (1938), and a hair cleaning comb (1939). Although some of these patents were granted after Marcel's death in 1936, they were applied for years before.

The 28 October 1922 issue of *Hairdressers' Weekly Journal* covered the exhibition

Page from the Hairdresser's Weekly Journal issue dated 28 October 1922, showing Osborne, Garrett & Co. Ltd (known as 'Ogee'), displaying a wide selection of puffs on one of two stands at the show, held in the Lindley Hall on 21-7 October 1922.

HAIRDRESSERS' WEEKLY JOURNAL. [2132] OCTOBER 28, 1922

The Hairdressing and Allied Trades' Exhibition.

THE Horticultural Hall, Vincent Square, Victoria Station, wears many costumes during the year, because it is the temporary home of many exhibitions. On Saturday, October 21st, it was coiffured up for the occasion, and, truth to tell, the *tout ensemble* was very attractive. At the outset it must be understood that the hall affords something like 12,000 or more superficial feet of floor

space. A meagre show of goods would have looked vacuous and starved. On the other hand, a show of profuseness and plenty meant planking down thousands of pounds worth of property and expenditure of heaps of ready cash for stall structures. The latter of these propositions is what took place, and the show was the biggest and best that yet stands to the credit of the Trade.

Somewhere about forty stall-holders were there, and their exhibits included toilet requisites and luxuries, tools, apparatus and appliances for the saloon, postiche of all sorts, styles and shades, dyes by various makers, combs and brushes in great variety, permanent waving by different systems, wax figures in multitudinous numbers, and, in short, all the minutiæ of Trade stock and equipment.

Many of the "stands" were of considerable size, example, by the shape of the hall, there were some large alcoves, or recesses, standing outside the rectang outline of the main body of the hall, and these were able for demonstrations of waving or dyeing in presen of a large audience, with sitting accommodation spectators.

An efficient orchestra was in daily attendance, and th musical menu for each day covered a wide selection in a cl lively dances. The orchestra was accommodated in the centre of the Great Hall cular elevated band-stand in the centre of the Great Hall while the floor level around the same structure was by various exhibitors for the display of dressed wax figures set off to good effect, for these figures faced the entrance, and therefore arrested the gaze of every Even a Variety Theatre entertainment was catered for by the thoughtful Management and several well-known ar names appeared on the programme.

The JOURNAL was not crowded out; on the contrary was crowded in, for the JOURNAL's stall, though not large, was sufficient to keep the Trade Ogee

extensively with 11 pages devoted to all aspects of it, including the depiction of a wonderful selection of photos of the main stands from 'about forty stall-holders' that were there. These included 'toilet requisites and luxuries, tools, apparatus and appliances for the saloon, pastiche of all sorts, styles and shades, dyes by various makers, combs and brushes in great variety, permanent waving by different systems, wax figures in multitudinous numbers, and, in short, all the minutiae of Trade stock and equipment.' In the middle of the Hall was an ornate circular and elevated bandstand with a captivating display of dressed wax figures around it. Inside it, an orchestra played and a Variety Theatre entertained on a daily basis, including fashion parades of Court millinery and gowns from the well-known fashion house, Madam Louise. W. Clarkson exhibited some extraordinary 'modern and historical' wigs, ranging from the actual wig worn by George V when Prince of Wales at the Devonshire House Ball, to the long-flowing wig that covered Madame de Milo when she rode naked through the streets of Coventry as Lady Godiva. Many others were displayed, but also worthy of a mention was the wig worn by the recently deceased famous singer and comedienne, later dubbed, 'Queen of the Music Hall', Marie Lloyd, in a pantomime production called 'Little Boy Blue'. She had died on 8 October and her funeral, at which the procession included 12 cars of flowers with more than 100,000 people in attendance, had taken place only nine days before the opening of the exhibition.

Prominent within the exhibition were two stands by Osborne, Garrett and Co. Ltd, known as 'Ogee' with 'a charming array of puffs of every description, both small and large'. These items are now highly collectable and are also faithfully reproduced as newly fashionable items. They also displayed the then famous 'Eugene' hair waving machine, the 'Sterling' vibrator, Beyer's hair-dryer and Krauer's 'Hairometer' among many other items. Osborne and Garrett would return to the Hall on 24 October 1949, 27 years later, for what is believed to have been a social dance,

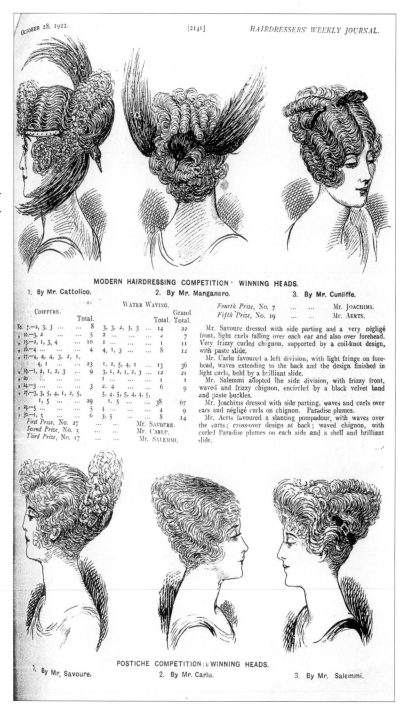

and Eugene Ltd would also book the Hall in 1927 and 1928 on a number of occasions for a dance and hairdressing competitions. Eugene were then based at 31 Dover Street, Piccadilly. L'Oreal also had a stand at the exhibition and displayed its 'harmless hair-dye called L'Oreal Henna Powder'. They also had Velouty de Dixor, a powder and cream combined used 'to beauty the hands and arms', and Eau Dixor – a depilatory. L'Oreal would return

Page from the Hairdresser's Weekly Journal *issue dated 28 October 1922, showing the 'Winning Heads' by Mr Cattolico, Mr Manganaro and Mr Cunliffe, held in the Lindley Hall on 21-7 October 1922.*

to the same Hall in their own right for their L'Oreal Collections Presentation, but not until 14 October 2002. On the Fisher and Co. stand could be found 'Pruh, this little article that removes unwanted hair, likewise Eydolash which is used for darkening the eye-lashes; also Deodel which prevents the odour of perspiration.' Ma Cherie proudly promoted 'a wonderful display of toilet articles, perfumes, colognes, face powders etc.' One of the leading lines on this stall was the 'pure plantation rubber strap for the bath, muscular development and body massage'. Mason Pearson displayed their wide range of beautiful brushes while Furs Unlimited gave a display of 'Rambit fur powder puffs of great interest to lady visitors, and their Rambit cosy slippers of nice soft rabbit fur were a dream of delight.' Probably the largest stand at the exhibition was Criscuolo and Co. that was conspicuous for a number of live tortoises that were 'at the threshold welcoming them in, to witness the display of raw hair, natural wavy hair, wax figures, transformations, bandeaux, tortoiseshell combs and brushes, hair ornaments, and toilet specialities; umbrellas and hand bags in tortoiseshell.' Quite what the tortoises felt about that we shall never know. Perhaps they graced the shelves of the next exhibition!

If they did, they did not have that long to wait as a Hairdressing Exhibition, organised by The Dorland Agency Ltd, was back in the Hall on 22-9 October 1926. This was the same organisation that organised the New Health Society's exhibition held on 7-14 November 1928. It would appear that no other hairdressing event was held in the Halls again until 1949, over 23 years later, and after the Second World War. This was an 'Open Competition' under the auspices of the General Association of Ladies Hairdressers and took place in the Old Hall on 7 November. Eight years later Ernest Schofield's British & Colonial Druggist (that had become British & Colonialist Trade Exhibitions Limited) organised the National Festival of Hairdressing Exhibition in the New Hall on 13-17 May 1957. This was followed by the International Hairdressing Exhibition

of Great Britain held in the New Hall on 25-8 March 1959, once again organised by British & Colonialist Trade Exhibitions.

All of these exhibitions, started by Cheetham's 1922 event were the precursors to new blockbuster consumer and trade hairdressing shows in the 1980s and '90s that ushered in new styles for new generations of men and women. One of these came to the RHS Halls on 6 September 2010, on the 10th Anniversary of the *Creative Head* 'Most Wanted' Hairdressing Awards, sponsored by the award-winning cutting edge publication, *Creative Head*. Similarly, the new consumer shows that rode on the back of popular BBC programmes, such as 'Clothes Show Live', and the 'Good Food Show', projected new lifestyle concepts and attracted new audiences. This had been partly due to the BBC and its commercial trading arm, BBC Enterprises, looking to exploit its products for commercial gain. I had witnessed this in 1988 when I returned again to work with Peter Anslow for the launch of the BBC Radio Show as its Sales Director. In effect, the BBC Radio Show held at Earl's Court was a 21st-birthday celebration of the launch of Radio One, and the renaming of the Light, Home and Third Programmes that became known as Radio 2, 3 and 4, but part-financed by commercial consumer electronics manufacturers, such as Memorex, JVC, and Panasonic who bought stands. Everyone from David Frost, to Frankie Howerd; The Archers to David Jacobs, and a very young Stephen Fry were there in a live radio broadcast show, attended by HRH Prince Edward.

Just as we have heard how Madame Österberg revolutionised the way physical training in private schools and the military services was applied in the late 19th and early 20th centuries through her Swedish system, and the dedicated Physical Training College she founded in Dartford, another lady, Mary Mollie Bagot Stack, made a similar, but longer-lasting and more far-reaching impact, much later in the 1930s. She too was influenced by another pioneer of the Modern Health Movement, Mrs Josef Conn, who specialised in remedial health exercises at her

WOMENS LEAGUE OF HEALTH AND BEAUTY

GREAT STUFF THIS, LASS!

Comic postcard of
the Women's League
of Health & Beauty,
c.1930.

After the First World War, in 1925, she opened her own school in Holland Park, the Bagot Stack Health School, and teamed up with Marjorie Duncombe. Marjorie had spent three years training at the Ginner Mawer School in Notting Hill Gate, London that had also based its training on the Greek cult of health, perfect proportion and beauty of the human form. This included exercises for every joint and muscle aiming at relaxation, mobility, poise, balance, strength and perfect co-ordination of the mind and body. As Duncombe explains in her book, *Dancing Fit*, published in March 2004, 'Ruby Ginner herself devised many dances and ballets that were staged in London theatres ... I was very proud to be one of the performers when Madame Pavlova was present in the audience.' And, 'Another annual performance was the matinée given in aid of the Sunshine Home for blind children. I remember the occasion well when Ninette de Valois, then just commencing her career, Karsavina and Phyllis Bedells were among the famous to be artists who gave up their time ... 'So, given this background, it was not surprising that, as well as remedial exercises, Bagot Stack and Duncombe taught expressive dance at their own new school. This led to the formation of The Women's League of Health & Beauty that Bagot Stack founded in YMCA premises in Regent Street in March 1930. Duncombe became its Principal, and its maxim was, 'Movement is Life'. It held its first, and hugely successful, public demonstration with 100 of its members in the Cockpit, Hyde Park, London on 12 June 1930 in front of 10,000 people who had come to witness it. The title, Health & Beauty would later be used by Billie Bristow of Pollen House, Cork Street, London, W1, when he organised and held the Health & Beauty Exhibition in the RHS Hall on 29 November-6 December 1935. Another movement, The Margaret Morris Movement, was filmed making a tableau

Conn Institute in London. These were based on a scientific system of Health Building that had its roots in the poise and balance known to the ancient Greeks. Mollie had had two dangerous operations before she reached eight years of age, and rheumatic fever before she was 16, so that when she met Conn, and learnt about her new theories about developing exercises for women, this fascinated her and gave her a new incentive to tackle her health issues in a different way. In fact, she enrolled at Conn's Institute in 1907, gained honours in every subject following graduation, and was offered a teaching post by Conn after it. Here the difference between Österberg and Bagot Stack becomes more apparent, because at this point Mollie's ambition was to allow her teaching to reach all of those who needed it most, not just an affluent minority. This she put into practice when she moved to Manchester to teach women mill workers the benefits of systematic exercise and after-work classes that re-invigorated them after a long hard day's work inside their mills. The word spread and demand for these grew.

Poster label for the
Health & Beauty
Exhibition, organised
by Billie Bristow, Cork
House, Pollen Street,
London W1, held in
the Lawrence Hall on
29 November-
6 December 1935.

The Margaret Morris Movement performing a tableau at the Health & Beauty Exhibition, organised by Billie Bristow, Cork House, Pollen Street, London W1, held in the Lawrence Hall on 29 November- 6 December 1935.

at the event. They would later team up in 1938 at the Royal Albert Hall with Bagot's League and the English Folk Dance & Song Society to perform jointly. The Health & Beauty Exhibition must have been an early forerunner of what would become another landmark show, and would first come to the RHS in May 1985 called, Mind Body Spirit. This had first been launched at Olympia in 1977 as the Festival of Mind and Body. 'Spirit' was added in 1980. Here again, we can refer back to Madame Österberg who, as you will recall, used the maxim, 'A Sound Body in a Sound Mind'.

However, the first time that the Women's League of Health & Beauty used the RHS Hall was on 18-20 May 1946 when they held a rehearsal for a large Rally and Demonstration that took place on 1 June at

Hyde Park and the Empire Pool, Wembley where there were 1,500 performers before an audience of 8,000. This was their first peacetime Rally, following the end of the Second World War. Mary Bagot Stack had died in 1935, but her drive to increase members and increase the League's profile had resulted in achieving 47,000 members by then. Subsequently, it gained the recognition of the Central Council of Recreative Physical Training (now the CCPR) by becoming affiliated with it in 1936, and Prunella Stack, Mary's daughter (who had taken over her mother's mantle and would become President designate in 1982) was invited to serve on the newly formed National Fitness Council for England and Wales in 1937. The following year, classes were started for the National Federation of Women's Institutes, and in 1938 the League took part in The Festival of Youth at Wembley Stadium when 900 members were among the 11,000 performers from a number of organisations in the presence of the King and Queen.

Then on 25 October 1947, once again in the RHS Hall, they opened their Autumn Season with a mass reunion class of some 900 members of the League who came from all over the country to do so. Prunella Stack (who had become Lady David Douglas-Hamilton) directed the members and put them through their paces. The New Hall continued to be used in this way by the League on 14 May 1949, then five times in 1950 in preparation for their 20th Anniversary Display and Reunion held in Wembley that year on 13 May, and finally on 24 October 1955 in preparation for their performance in the CCPR Festival of Movement and Dance, also at the Empire Pool, Wembley.

The League continued to grow and perform regularly at the Royal Albert Hall, Wembley and Hyde Park, as well as other locations, and at a variety of festivals and events. Prunella was pivotal in also developing its membership internationally, especially in Canada, South Africa and New Zealand. At The League's Diamond Jubilee, celebrated at The Royal Albert Hall in 1990, HM The Queen sent a message of congratulations, and in 1999 The League changed its name to The Fitness League. Mary Bagot Stack would have been proud to see how her organisation had flourished and developed, had she lived beyond her short 50-year lifetime. However, perhaps the most fitting footnote to this remarkable chapter of another pioneering woman's achievement is to record that Marjorie Duncombe, who had worked so hard with Mary as her Principal in the 1930s to drive the movement forward, celebrated her 100th birthday in 2004.

Photo of the Women's League of Health & Beauty opening its Autumn Season with a mass reunion class of 900, held in the Lawrence Hall on 25 October 1947.

Through Mind and Muscle

A collection of enamel badges worn by members of the Women's League of Health & Beauty. The badge with a black surround is inscribed on the reverse, 'Ida Dent, Life Member. No.164' from Sydney, Australia.

Having heard a lot about the pioneering achievements of women in the field of health and beauty, there were also some extraordinary men who brought their own strong beliefs and methods into practice, especially in the area of health and strength, for men from as early as 1909. *The Times* reported in their 2 March 1909 edition on Eugene Sandow and his Sandow System of Physical Culture practised in his own Institute, based in St James's Street, London, under the headline, 'Through Mind and Muscle to Health – Sandow and the New Medical Teaching'. Here again we find reference to the relationship between mind and body, this time more specifically the discovery of the transcendent action of Mind on Muscle and the reaction of Muscle on Mind. He was, in fact, a bodybuilder often referred to as 'The Father of Modern Bodybuilding', and devised the first major body-building contest which was held at the Royal Albert Hall in 1901, but he was much more than that. Sandow captured a mood for seeking new ways to gain and retain good health, without reliance on drugs.

The writer of *The Times* news item was clearly convinced of the Sandow System and effused, 'The present writer had hitherto regarded Mr Sandow as an exponent of muscularity, and had – in lamentable ignorance – imagined the Sandow System of Physical Culture to be nothing more than a means of developing abnormal strength at, perhaps, the expense of general health. How completely and absolutely this misapprehension was destroyed may be best realised by following the writer's steps, and visiting the Sandow Institute at 32a, St James's Street, where an interesting scene of activity, such as will be found nowhere else in the metropolis, is daily to be witnessed.' He referred to Sandow's publication, *Life is Movement* (the same phrase that Bagot Stack's League would use, in reverse, as its new maxim 21 years later) and went on to explain that, 'Sandow has been the first to recognise that the transformation of conditions of disease into those of health lies in action and operation of the mind upon and through the channels of the muscular organisation. Reliance upon drugs is happily giving place to more benign methods of cure. The modern physician may and does use drugs for specific purposes where a temporary effect is desired, but he has ceased to regard medicines as capable of yielding a permanent cure, and looks to other agencies to effect lasting good. Thus we find that such ills as Constipation, Insomnia, Neurasthenia, Indigestion, Anæmia, Obesity, are radically cured by Sandow's methods of physical exercises, whilst heart and lung and spinal troubles may be greatly alleviated and generally eliminated without any further treatments whatsoever.' Sandow was befriended by the likes of King George V, Thomas Edison and Sir Arthur Conan Doyle. He also became an internationally recognised figure, especially in the USA, where he toured for several years. By the time he left America, Sandow had earned more than a quarter million dollars, but died of a stroke at the age of 58 in 1925.

Another bodybuilder who had been apprenticed by Sandow in 1897, and was to become as legendary in this field of Health & Strength, was Monte Saldo. He claimed that his own method, called 'Maxalding', was 'the most convenient, the most simple, the most complete and the most effective method

of training for the health, physique and mentality' and his book of the same name was subtitled, *Nature's Way to Mental & Physical Fitness – For Health & Strength'*. The similarities to Sandow's methods were striking, but he became one of the most recognised and valued personal trainers of his time. Like Sandow and many other bodybuilders of that time, he had appeared in Strongman performances staged in a variety of theatres and venues. One of these was the Royal Aquarium Westminster on the site where Central Hall Westminster now sits. (This was a renowned London venue, opened in 1876 by the Duke of Edinburgh and boasted a conservatory, concert hall, art gallery, skating rink and restaurant. Strongman acts, circus acts, dog shows and billiard matches were but a few a few of the vast range of entertainments and activities offered in it.) Sandow was famous for introducing new and ground-breaking strongman acts such as in 1903 at the London Pavilion, when he supported a Darracq motor car full of passengers in what was known as 'The Tomb of Hercules' position. He was also an expert wrestler, co-founder of the famed Apollo-Saldo Academy in London's West End, and a prime mover in establishing the official governing bodies for amateur and professional

Poster labels for the New Health Society's Exhibitions in the Lawrence Hall on 7-14 November 1928 and 15-22 November 1929, respectively.

weightlifting in 1911. The Academy not only attracted the world's best wrestlers, but great athletes and sportsmen who also visited and trained there. Saldo then established a postal physical culture training system, while also still personally training a number of champion weightlifters, including Edward Aston, winner of the title 'Britain's Strongest Man' in 1911 and Jack Hayes, British 8 Stone Weightlifting Champion 1914. Needless to say, he regularly appeared on the covers of Health & Strength Magazine and was commissioned by them to write a book entitled, *How to Pose*. After the First World War his postal business became a worldwide enterprise, one of the most result-producing postal physical culture courses of all time, before Charles Atlas and his own similar courses many years later. However, in March 1926 he filed bankruptcy proceedings for himself and his Maxalding business, after which he then appears to have concentrated on giving lectures and touring with his son, Court Saldo, who continued to expound the Maxalding system and postal business, until his death in 1983. They were both present at a new health-led show at the RHS organised by another extraordinary man.

NHS

The New Health Society (NHS) introduces us to Sir William Arbuthnot Lane, Bart., C.B., M.S., F.R.C.S., who founded this in December 1925. He had been regarded as the best abdominal surgeon of his time, mainly associated with Guy's Hospital and The Hospital for Sick Children, Great Ormond Street. In fact, W.E. Tanner, who had been President of the Royal College of Surgeons in 1933, wrote in his book, *Arbuthnot Lane, His Life and Work*, published by Baillière, Tindall and Cox in 1946, 'Lane was acknowledged as the greatest surgeon of all time.'

Arbuthnot's New Health Society beliefs were not dissimilar to Sandow's and Saldo's, inasmuch as they were based on improving health, but the principles and wider objectives on which they were based were somewhat different. In Arbuthnot's own book, *Secrets of Good Health President of the New Health Society*, published by William Heinemann (Medical Books) Ltd, 1928, he states clearly his Society's three principal objects as: '1) The education of the public in diet and habits. 2) Efforts to promote the supply to the people of fruit, vegetables, and green food at a reasonable price, and 3) To encourage a return of a large proportion of the people to the land, making it possible by efficient education in intensive gardening, the care of cattle, and so on.'

In view of these primary objects it is, perhaps, not surprising that he chose The Royal Horticultural Society's Hall for the first of his own Society's national shows, The New Health Exhibition that took place in the aptly named New Horticultural Hall on 7-14 November 1928. He had already held a series of regional shows, complemented by monthly volumes of his New Health publication that had been a huge success reaching thousands of working-class men and women, eager to hear more about how they could improve their health. The Society was, in effect, the first organised body to deal with social medicine and, as such, an aspiring early model for today's NHS. His motto was, 'Prevention rather than cure' and for this he incurred the wrath of the British Medical Association and doctors at large. As Tanner commented in his book referred to earlier, 'Any attempt on the part of a medical man writing publicly about matters pertaining to public health was taboo, and could only be regarded as a method of self-advertisement. Nor was any guidance offered by the health authorities to a public utterly uninformed about the nature of disease and ill-health.' Rather than get struck off the BMA's register, which he came close to, he struck himself off.

However, he did have the early support of many influential people in high places, including Sir Arthur Stanley, Sir Horace Plunkett, Julian Huxley, H.S. Wellcombe, Dr John Kellogg, Ramsay MacDonald, the Rt. Hon. David Lloyd George, and the then Chief Medical Officer, Sir George Newman. If Arbuthnot Lane's New Health Society (NHS) could address these lofty ideals, it would help

Newman's government of the day. In 1912 a biennial health conference and exhibition (again organised by Ernest Schofield) had been held in the RHS Hall on 24-7 June. This was under the principal patronage of Princess Christian, but other prominent patrons included Lady Wantage, Lady Balfour of Burleigh and the Hon. Lady Acland. This event dealt with the health of infants, the health of boys and girls, public health and the care of the sick – evidence that these issues were certainly in need of attention at that time and, with the objective that this could lead to effective legislation to protect these vulnerable groups. Another link with the RHS was that Lady Balfour of Burleigh's husband, Alexander Bruce, 6th Lord Balfour of Burleigh, had been a Member of the RHS Council between 1906 and 1919.

What Arbuthnot Lane perceived at this period between the two world wars with the post-First World War slump and the Great Depression, was a fast degenerating community that was neglecting its health. Although life expectancy did continue to rise the early mortality death rate gap between the richest and the poorest was at its worst during this period, then regarded as the toughest economic and social period of the 20th century. (Alarmingly, a health report on BBC News on 23 July 2010 reported that the health inequality gap, between 1999 and 2007, was greater than between 1921 to 1939, suggesting that, 'health and wealth are directly linked and, unless we tackle the income gap, we could well see life expectancy actually starting to fall for the first time in the poorest areas.')

Arbuthnot Lane formed the Society expressly to change this and to produce a nation composed of healthy and active participants. In 1926, Lt. General Sir Matthew Fell had said that 35 per cent of army recruits failed their medicals carried out by recruiting officers because of the poor condition of their health. However, he also added that the actual failure proportion was far greater, due to many who were turned down simply on sight.

The way he felt he could change this was based on a combination of his own beliefs. Not surprisingly, perhaps, because of his vast experience and knowledge of human bowels and their condition, Arbuthnot Lane held the belief that the bowels were the key to good health, and considered constipation to be the cause of many ills of civilisation. In this respect, both Sandow and Saldo were of the same strong opinion. However, instead of health and happiness being able to be reached solely through mind and muscle he believed this could be achieved by all who maintained a hygienic regimen, assisted by the inclusion of a high-fibre diet (vegetables and bran cereal), regular outdoor exercise and sun-bathing. The 'Eat More Fruit' and better bread campaigns were largely as a result of his efforts (and this message is still being upheld strongly by the medical profession today). The *Daily Mail* was the first national newspaper that had helped him by taking the lead in supporting his NHS objectives. In October 1927, the NHS also exhibited at their Ideal Home Exhibition. In fact, the NHS were able, by means of the articles in the *Daily Mail* and elsewhere, to obtain the first Chair of Dietetics, which became part of London University, something he would never had been able to achieve had he remained a member of the BMA, and bound by its ethical committee rulings.

The Countess of Oxford and Asquith (wife of Herbert Henry Asquith, Prime Minister from 1908-16) opened the Exhibition, and the Queen of Norway paid an enthusiastic visit on the fifth day spending time at the National Child Adoption Society's stall. The President of the Sports Fellowship, Mr A.E. Gilligan spoke at the event but, perhaps, most interestingly Monte Saldo was present and delivered 10 lectures of his Maxalding physical culture methods that were demonstrated by his 17-year-old son, Court. These demonstrations were certainly in line with Arbuthnot Lane's key views on abdominal health, and Court ably demonstrated the Maxalding exercises that included the centralisation of the Abdominal Wall. There is also some evidence to confirm that Madame Clara Novello Davies, mother of Ivor Novello, also appeared with her famous Royal Welsh Ladies' Choir at this show (or on a separate occasion) as one of Saldo's advertisements states clearly that, 'Fifteen years after writing this letter Madame Davies appeared with her famous Welsh Choir at the Royal Horticultural Hall, Westminster, and Mr F.H.C. Woollaston presented a demonstration of Maxalding on the same programme.' The letter in question had been written by her to Saldo in 1915 when she was known as the foremost teacher of singing and elocution and said, 'It is my express wish that all who study with me should go to you too, as I find your system most helpful to my students.' This had been a wonderful testament for Monte, and the respiratory control exercises he also taught under his Maxalding method. In fact, she had applied to the RHS for a tenancy in her own right as early as June 1909 when she had requested a charitable rate, but was refused. By 1930, Madame Novello Davies had become a Vice-Patron of the Bachelor Girl's Exhibition that was held in the New Hall in 1930. In 1927, she and her renowned choir had only recently returned to Southampton on 8 August, following a 25,000-mile tour of South Africa where they had sung at 153 concerts in front of 250,000 persons. Not long before that, for eight months, they had also toured Canada and the United States. When Queen Victoria had still been alive Novello had had the honour of performing in front of her with her choir at Windsor Castle. Saldo had been a prime supporter of this new NHS exhibition. He wrote articles for Arbuthnot's publication and also took regular full-page advertisements in it. One wonders if he had been instrumental in getting Madame Davies and her choir there. The result was a unique blend of several cultural strands of what was perceived to be good for the health. By 1935, Madame Davies was shown as a Technical Advisor – Voice Production to the NHS. Sir William's Exhibition took place once again in the New Hall on 15-22 November 1929, but to my knowledge never re-appeared in that form, although they had discussed an exhibition for 1938. The New Health Society (NHS) was still going strong in 1936, and in 1934 ran its regular summer school in Malvern, which George Bernard Shaw attended and expressed a great deal of interest.

In breaking new ground and pushing boundaries, which the Society did, they were also controversial and often criticised. They were ridiculed when they called on employers to introduce the wearing of decent hygienic clothes to work that they saw as being shorts and open-necked shirts for men. However, they were involved in early research into the hygienic properties of textile fibres, yarns and fabrics that led to more suitable and healthy clothing being produced. At that time Jaeger were one of the main underwear and overwear manufacturer claiming their range of clothing to be 'hygienic'. The NHS also came under attack from the powerful National Temperance League, the National Union of Teachers and the Good Templar Grand Lodge when Sir William had advised the use of brandy for infants in direct contradiction to the government's educational syllabus on alcohol and hygiene. Further condemnation came from The Rev. Courtney Weeks who is reported in *The Times* of 11 April 1928 saying that, 'The New Health Society was a danger and menace to our national life. Sir William Arbuthnot Lane had put forward the theory that alcohol was infinitely more valuable than meat. I say that the two things are quite incomparable, for meat contains nitrogen, which is essential to the human body, and alcohol does not. The arguments of The New Health Society were based on obsolete science, and, as such, were a distinct menace in the light of modern scientific investigations as to the effect of alcohol.'

A report in *The Times* of 16 August 1927 gave another example of a dubious exercise that took place to support one of Arbuthnot's beliefs. It stated, 'Arrangements have been made for the opening in October, at the Sherwood Colliery, Mansfield, Notts., of a clinic for ultra-violet artificial sunlight treatment of pit-boys. The scheme, which has the consent and good will of the mine management will be organised by the New Health Society, acting in cooperation with the National Institute of Industrial Psychology and the Sunlight League.' The pit-boys of 14 to 16 years of age, and the younger children of miners were those that were

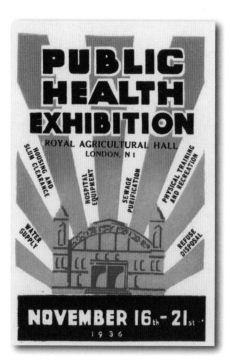

prone to rickets, teething convulsions and, 'ill-condition'. The object of the clinic was to 'demonstrate that the diseases and ailments which beset the industrial population owing to the scarcity of natural sunlight, actual and due to industrial occupation, may be arrested, and in time wholly eradicated, by artificial sunlight treatment.' Five pit-boys from the same Colliery were taken to the Swiss Alps for a fortnight by Lt. Col. G.S. Hutchinson on behalf of the New Health Society, the Sunlight League and the NIPIP, after which it was reported that the boys had gained weight, increased in height and expanded their chest measurements. Col. Hutchinson did not suppose that such developments were due alone to exposure to the actinic rays of the sun, however, he did state that 'there appears to be a wealth of evidence that it is the sun's actinic rays which are in large degree responsible for the results.' Two weeks in the Swiss Alps away from their mine pits must have been a real tonic for the boys, but an even greater shock when they had to return and disappear once again into the even more dangerous bowels of the earth to earn their living. However, the Society was also involved in recommending a system of periodical medical examinations

for doctor's patients, something that had been started in America by the Life Extension Institute of New York and had proved that the death rate had been reduced by 18 per cent as a result. There was no such system in place at this time in Britain.

Sir William and his New Health Society (NHS) had contributed to the long road of enlightenment, education, and change; ultimately to the formation of the National Health Service (NHS), launched on 5 July 1948. In my view he was one of many pioneers seeking to bring about change for the good, and should be given recognition for this, and as having been 23 years ahead of his time in many ways. In my view, he brought about immediate change when the first of many Public Health Congresses and Exhibitions were organised that spurred central and local government to consider their future approach to public health; the first having been held at the Royal Agricultural Hall on 19-24 November 1928, just five days after his own at the RHS! Their Patron was HM The King, and it was opened by the Rt. Hon. Neville Chamberlain, Minister of Health with 130 exhibitors. Their official report confirms that they received 800 delegates from 350 Local Authorities.

ABOVE *Poster labels for the 1932, 1936 and 1938 Public Health Congresses/ Shows, held in the Royal Agricultural Hall, London, on the dates shown.*

RIGHT *Advertisement for the Health & Strength Leaguers. This was a membership organisation run by Health & Strength Magazine.*

A National Health Society (NHS) had also been in existence since May 1872, but this had originally been founded as a Women's Society, 'for the cultivation of knowledge and practice of sanitary laws.' Another organisation, the National Council of Social Services (NCSS) that had been formed on 20 November 1919 well before the formal setting up of the Welfare State, celebrated its 60th birthday in the RHS Hall in November 1979 with a one-day exhibition depicting the role, work and interest of voluntary organisations, and was opened by HM The Queen. During its 60 years of existence, the NCSS had spawned significant voluntary organisations such as the Youth Hostels Association, the Citizens Advice Bureaux and Age Concern, but its primary role was in acting as the central co-ordinating and advisory body for all voluntary organisations in Britain at that time such as the Royal National Lifeboat Institution, the National Trust, The Girl Guides, Meals On Wheels and the blood donor schemes. Its then director, Nicholas Hinton, was quoted in 20 November issue of *The Times* as saying he was 'adamant that the voluntary sector should not be seen as providing an alternative Welfare State on the cheap'. He was also concerned that too much reliance on government subsidy could prove fatal in times of recession. At the time, some voluntary organisations were reliant on 80 per cent of their income coming from either central or local government. As I write this in 2010, following the new coalition government's appointment under David Cameron's premiership, we can see what he meant, and that philanthropy, self-help and self-reliance, as proffered by the likes of Sir William's New Health Society, are as important now as they were over a century ago.

The Health & Strength League, an active physical culture member's club set up by *Health & Strength Magazine* in 1906 whose motto was *Sacred Thy Body Even As Thy Soul*, booked the RHS Hall on 29 October 1949, and again in 1951 for their annual dances and membership gatherings. During the 1920s and 1930s, *Health & Strength Magazine* was selling 250,000 copies weekly, such was the desire to be healthy and fit. One can see how close the H&SL was to Sir William Arbuthnot Lane's beliefs that drew him to feature Monte Saldo in his exhibition when you read the advice imparted by the League's doctor in the pamphlet sent out to all new Leaguers. This stated clearly that 'the cause of 90 per cent of ailments can be narrowed down to one or more of the following: Taking insufficient exercise, living too much indoors, instead of outdoors, eating the wrong food, smoking too much, neglect of personal hygiene and inability to arrange daily routine so that there is time for relaxation and recreation as well as work.' The most interesting aspect of this for me, as I have commented earlier, is that smoking was still not seen as harmful to health in principle, but only in terms of the numbers of cigarettes smoked that were, in reality, never able to be properly quantified. For these generations of health and fitness pioneers and crusaders not to have given this more credence is an extraordinary commentary on the narrow approach they had then, and continued to have, for a very long time to come where this aspect of individual health was concerned.

The entry in H&SL's 1952 Annual reports that, 'For the 1951 Dance we returned to the venue that saw wild scenes of the 'Grimek' Leaguers Day in 1949 – the Royal Horticultural Society's Old Hall at Westminster. As our guests on this occasion, we had members of the celebrated Arsenal and Portsmouth Soccer clubs who at that time were the two leading first division clubs. It was a very jolly evening and everyone was sorry when it was finished.' Although there is no actual record of it, it is very likely that *Woolf Philips and the Skyrockets* orchestra played on both occasions. They were the London Palladium's resident band and normally provided music for the H&SL's events. These dances and social evenings always followed their Annual Displays when a series of what were originally termed 'Physical Excellence Displays' took place. A typical three-hour variety programme would include weightlifting, gymnastics, wrestling, strength feats, tumbling, single or duo hand balancing on blocks, chairs and poles; adagio, agility, club-swinging, chins, press-ups & dipping contests, strand pulling and agility team displays. In 1949 and 1951 these were held at the London Palladium. Each year, the titles of Mr and Miss Britain in the Senior Class and Junior Mr and Junior Miss Britain were also decided, and each received a large Silver Cup. The Leaguers also often staged impromptu cabaret at their dances that would have included some

of the above displays. One of the Leaguers who was present at both events in the Halls was Mr D.P. Webster who recalls that he went to one of these 'specifically to meet an Indian strongman called Monohar Aich so they could discuss his appearance at a similar event in Aberdeen, Scotland and also to compete with me in strand-pulling (chest expanders) which were popular at the time'. He went on to say that, 'Monohar did a weird act, walking with bare feet up a ladder of sharp swords and then lying on the top blade. He also had a sharp spearhead that he fastened to an iron rod. He secured the free end of the rod and put the point of the spear on his throat and walked forward until the spear bent under the pressure. His hands were free of the implement at all time.' By 1952 the 'Leaguers' had a membership of over 250,000 and Life Membership was 2s. 9d. (£3.18).

In 1951, as part of the Festival of Britain, the Royal Horticultural Hall was host to the British Sports & Games Fair between 28 July and 6 August, opened by Lord Luke. Ian St John Lawson Johnson, 2nd Baron Luke, had

ABOVE *Photo of two swimsuited young ladies receiving a shock soaking from an attendant, as they try out the latest Raleigh bicycles at the British Sports & Games Fair, held in the Lindley Hall on 28 July-6 August 1951. This was listed in the Health & Strength League's supplement during the Festival of Britain under the heading, 'Physique Contests and PC Shows'.*

ABOVE RIGHT *Photo of Arnold Dyson, Mr Universe of 1953, lifting two schoolboys on his weights in a demonstration of strength at the 27th National Schoolboy's Own Exhibition, held in both Halls on 31 December 1953-13 January 1954.*

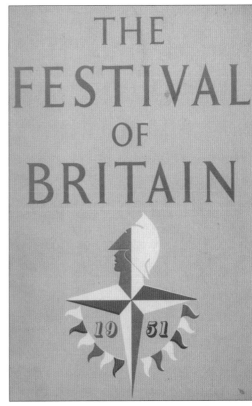

ABOVE FAR RIGHT
*Official book of the
1951 Festival of Britain
that took place in
London from 3 May to
the end of September
that year. Ten million
paid admissions were
recorded from the
six main exhibitions
during the five months.*

ABOVE *Metal
brooch of The Festival
of Britain, London,
that was held from
3 May to the end of
September 1951.*

become Chairman of Bovril on the death of his father, and later successfully also took over Marmite. His father would have been very aware of the RHS Hall; his company having exhibited there regularly since 1905 at most of the cookery, medical, nursing, health, schoolboys, model engineer, and other exhibitions staged there. Bovril was as strong a brand then as Coke or Nike have been since. Lord Luke produced a pamphlet on the part they had played in the Second World War, entitled *The War Story of Bovril*, illustrating the part they had played in supplying troops with their products to sustain them in their endeavours. He was also interested in all forms of sport and became a member of the International Olympic Committee in 1951. This Fair was listed under the programme heading of 'Physique Contests and PC Shows' by the Health & Strength Magazine, so this was obviously another occasion when dedicated exhibitions of physical culture took place that included performances of muscle control by men and ladies, strongman contests, gymnastic and acrobatic displays, and weight-lifting contests. At the 26th National

Schoolboy's Own Exhibition in 1953 Mr Universe, Arnold Dyson, was part of the show lifting two boys at a time on his weights. So, here was yet another way the RHS Hall was put to use in its long journey of experiential applications, and a very long way, I suspect, from the Society's founding fathers' original idea of how their Hall should be used.

As a footnote to this section, and perhaps to prove how pertinent this is, a young Royal, Prince William (son of Prince Charles and Princess Diana) was still performing a traditional role his Victorian and Edwardian counterparts had played so often and ably, in drawing attention to key social issues of the day by offering their support and patronage, when he gave a call to arms through the *London Evening Standard* to rid London of its deprivation and the dispossessed living in it. If you hadn't known the date of this report in 2010 you could have been forgiven for thinking this was about Dickensian London. *The Standard* reported that Prince William, acting as patron of Centrepoint, the leading charity for homeless people, said, 'I consider the Evening Standard's exposure

Don't let fatigue overtake you

In that all-important last spurt, fatigue is bound to beat you unless you have an extra reserve of energy.

That is the special value of Bovril. It gives more than muscular strength: Bovril has the remarkable power of building up resources of energy and strengthening endurance against the strain of any athletic contest.

No wonder so many champion athletes train on Bovril.

Take **BOVRIL** regularly

HENRY RICHARDSON, LTD., 4, Church Street, Greenwich, S.E.10

Wireless Telegraphy, Radio and Television

It is an established fact that the first Wireless Club in the country was formed in Derby in 1911. Prior to this, there had been an Association run by Percival Marshall's *Model Engineer*, and in the Society of Model & Experimental Engineer's 1997 publication, *100 Years of Model Engineering*, it states that, 'many model engineers were distracted from their models to experiment with wireless'. In 1913 the February issue of the *Model Engineer* carried a letter with a plea for other towns to start Wireless clubs. Correspondence ensued with several notable people of the day, resulting in the formation of numerous clubs, among them, the Birmingham Wireless Association, the Croydon Wireless and Physical Society, Northampton and Bristol Wireless Clubs. The London Wireless Club was formed on 5 July and re-formed as the Wireless Society of London on 10 October. In 1914, Nottingham formed a Wireless Club, and interestingly Hiram Percy Maxim, son of Sir Hiram Steven Maxim, co-founded the American Radio Relay League in May 1914. So, it can be seen that Percival Marshall was certainly instrumental, and influential, in the promotion and development of the rapidly growing interest in Wireless Telegraphy during this period. This led to what was billed as the 'First International Radio Exhibition and Wireless Convention' held on 2-3 September 1922 at Central Hall, Westminster. However, *The Times* in its report of the event on 4 September said, 'The many amateur enthusiasts and potential converts who visited it must have come away with an unsatisfied feeling. The exhibition, frankly, does not justify expectations and falls short of an adequate representation of either the magnitude or importance of this young industry. Many of the best-known names in the wireless world are absent. Here and there are freak applications of wireless principles to be seen but, little or no attempt has been made to illustrate the important part which wireless already plays in everyday life'. At this event, the MP, L'Estrange Malone, urged

of hidden poverty a call to arms for us all. This is a great city. However, the plight of the dispossessed in its many forms tarnishes it. For all the achievement of Londoners and the wonderful things that this city stands for, poverty, homelessness, lack of advantage for dispossessed young people continue to challenge us. It is up to us, not just politicians and charities, to answer this challenge – wherever, whenever and in whatever way, small or large, we feel we can.' He went on to say, 'Through my involvement with Centrepoint, and talking with the disadvantaged young people [Centrepoint] looks after, I feel I have an understanding of the many manifestations of poverty in this capital city. To spend night after night on the streets of London, in fair weather and foul, not knowing how to break out of a downward spiral of despair, would challenge the strongest amongst us. Whether it is sleeping, overcrowded housing, or spending your life in temporary accommodation, this spiral need not be unbreakable.'

Radio Society of Great Britain GB3RS card used at the International Radio Engineering and Communications Exhibition, organised by the Radio Society of Great Britain, held in the Lawrence Hall on 3 October 1968. The card was used by G2MI to confirm FONE QSO contact with the RSGB Exhibition Station at 14.18GMT that day. G2MI's call signal was G3TNO.

RADIO SOCIETY OF GREAT BRITAIN

GB3RS

International Radio Engineering
and Communications Exhibition
Royal Horticultural Society's New Hall London S.W.I.

wireless amateurs to form themselves into an association for the protection of their interests, in order to secure the maximum benefit from the broadcasting developments in the next year or two.

They took his advice and, on 11 November 1922, the Wireless Society of London was changed to the Radio Society of Great Britain (as it remains today) but, before this, just three weeks after the Central Hall event, the first All-British Wireless Exhibition & Convention of 55 stands representing all the principal British manufacturers and suppliers of instruments and accessories was held from 30 September to 7 October in the RHS Hall. This was organised by Bertram Day & Co. Ltd of Charing Cross SW1 under the auspices of the Wireless Society of London and affiliated societies. Like so many other exhibitions that would follow in the RHS Halls, this one was the pre-cursor and important start to a series of new national exhibitions dealing with key interests and developments of the day. In this case, the subject was wireless telegraphy that became known as radio and, shortly after, the introduction of television that would bring about dramatic change in communication, and social intercourse, just as the invention of the computer, internet

and electronic communication has today. In opening the Exhibition, Sir Henry Norman, MP announced that 'the difficulties that had delayed the institution of broadcasting had been overcome and that wireless broadcast from London would begin in a week or two, followed by Manchester and six other regional centres throughout Great Britain'. Sir Henry had been made Chairman of the War Office Committee on Wireless Telegraphy in 1912, and in 1920 was elected Chairman of the Imperial Wireless Telegraphy Committee, which drew up a complete wireless scheme for the British Empire. For a short period in 1910, he had also held a ministerial position as Assistant Postmaster General.

Sir Norman derided the view held by some that broadcasting was simply a new fad that would not last. He prophesied that broadcast wireless telephony was destined to become a natural part of everyone's social life, just as ordinary wireless telephony was. He also correctly predicted the time when a wireless set would be in the home of nearly every member of the community, and said that the final triumph would come when the King addressed the Parliaments of the Empire simultaneously by such means.

The Times reported that 'the exhibition itself was mainly necessarily technical' but that 'there were features to appeal to the popular imagination, particularly the demonstration stand, at which broadcast instrumental music, singing and speech were clearly received throughout each day'. One of the highlights was the reception of a broadcast on the last day of the exhibition made by the Prince of Wales, from York House to the Boy Scouts of Great Britain. The Gaekwar of Baroda visited on 4 October.

The success of this first exhibition was built on, and the 2nd Wireless Telegraphy Exhibition, once again organised by Bertram Day & Co. Ltd, was planned to be staged in the Hall from 27 September to 8 October 1923. However, this event was postponed, and amalgamated into The All-British Wireless Exhibition held at the White City on 8-21 November. Then, at the 1924 British Empire Exhibition the King's speech was relayed by the BBC to nearly seven million listeners who, for the first time, heard a monarch's actual voice over the wireless. The BBC was just 18 months old and still a tiny company, not a national corporation. Licensed by the Post Office, it transmitted to nine sites throughout the UK via its famous 2LO transmitter designed by H.J. Round' from its broadcast studio located in a top-floor office of Marconi House on the Strand, Central London. Famous 2LO 'firsts' included the first broadcast of the Armistice Day ceremony at the Cenotaph, the first election address by Prime Minister Ramsay MacDonald as head of the country's first Labour government, a description of the Carpentier-Lewis boxing match, and the first daily weather forecasts.

The 3rd All-British Wireless Exhibition was held on 27 September-8 October 1924 at the Royal Albert Hall, organised by the National Association of Radio Manufacturers when 55 manufacturers exhibited, and over 46,000 visitors attended. In 1925, the National Wireless & Radio Exhibition took place, again in the Royal Albert Hall, and then transferred to the New Hall, Olympia on 4-18 September the following year. In doing so, it more than doubled the previous attendance and in 1937

advertised nearly 300 stands. However, in 1931 a Radio Show organised by The Radio Manufacturers' Association was again held in the RHS Old Hall on 11-16 May and later still the Radio Components Manufacturers Association staged an exhibition in the New Hall on 7-14 March 1947.

The National Radio Exhibition continued to be held in Olympia, and became Radiolympia in 1936. It remained one of the most important public exhibitions until 1950 when it ended, but its beginnings were rooted at the RHS Hall, via the early experiments undertaken by Percival Marshall at his Model Engineer Exhibition.

On 10-16 October 1925, The Wireless, Arts and Handcrafts Exhibition organised by Arthur B. Dale of British Trades Exhibitions Ltd also took place in the RHS Hall. There were 109 exhibitors at this show and licence holders, by this time, had risen to 1½ million. John Logie Baird is rumoured to have given the first demonstrations of television at this show, and at Selfridges in London. This was followed in 1926 by public promotions of the television at the Army & Navy Stores in Victoria Street. Development was swift and the BBC began public transmissions of high-definition television to the London area in November 1936. The Science Museum responded quickly and arranged a special Television Exhibition which opened on 10 June 1937 and closed three months later on 21 September. Demonstrations of television reception were given on sets lent by eight leading manufacturers. These were carefully shrouded to conceal their maker's identity, to avoid accusations that the Museum was favouring one make over another. Many items of historical interest were also shown. The exhibition was seen by over a quarter of a million visitors during its three-month run by contrast with Radiolympia that, by comparison, had attracted 90,000 less visitors, with far greater publicity accorded to it, albeit that the Television Show had been free to enter and Radiolympia had not.

On 30 September 1967, what had been known up to that point as the Light Programme, changed to become Radios 1 and 2. The Third and Home Programmes became Radios 3 and 4, respectively. On 30 September, 21 years later, the BBC saw fit to celebrate their birthdays (and those of Local Radio), with a commercial exhibition and live performance under simple title of the BBC Radio Show. This was held at Earl's Court. As its Sales Director, I attended the Gala Banquet and after-dinner entertainment, The Radio Show Radio Show, a live performance (broadcast on Radio 2) that was presented by David Frost and featured radio luminaries such as Richard Murdoch, Frankie Howerd, Kit and the Widow, Rev. Roger Royle, The Week-Ending Team and a young Stephen Fry – all in the presence of HRH The Prince Edward. Today, Radio is still a strong medium, especially where local radio and stations that target specific audiences, such as Classic FM. In London, LBC had captured its own audience, and celebrated its 25th Anniversary in the Lindley Hall on 1-2 October 2003.

Shuttlecocks, Snooker and Skiing

The 30-years-run of the All England Badminton Championships at the RHS Hall from 1910 to 1939 is another one of those not infrequent surprises to figure large in the history of the RHS Hall on Vincent Square. The Badminton Association's first choice of venue had been none other than the headquarters of the London Scottish Rifles in London's Buckingham Gate (1899-1901). In 1902 they were at Crystal Palace and between 1903 and 1909 they had been at the London Rifle Brigades Headquarters, Bunhill Row, Islington. In March 1910 their 12th Championships came to the RHS Hall and stayed there for 30 years until 1939. However, as Bernard Adams explains in his book, The Badminton Story, 'At first, there were constant problems with the playing surface and the lighting. The original floor was white and slippery; in 1911 resin was applied to it, and it then became so sticky that players found it difficult to start quickly. In later years an extra wooden floor was specially constructed, but even that had its teething troubles. The playing conditions in the Championships at this stage were often less good than in some of the specially built badminton halls'. He went to explain that, 'One of the outstanding players of the period, G.A. Thomas always had difficulty in playing at the Horticultural Hall. He found the light a problem and this is partly why he never won an All England singles title before 1914.'

The arrangement by which they booked the Hall was novel and, possibly, the first time this had been agreed. Instead of a fixed lettings fee, the RHS agreed to charge them a mere £60 (£5,250) for a full three-day tenancy with half of the profits made up to £80 (£7,000) going to them also. The Championships were open to all to attend and The Badminton Gazette (the principal publication for the sport) reported in its March 1911 issue that 'the gate was well up to expectations; and even the enlarged stands were taxed to their utmost capacity on Saturday, when the crowds watching the finals must have been by far the biggest ever assembled round a badminton court. The attendance was, in fact, most satisfactory, and afforded the fullest proof of the enormous progress the game is making.' This must have been good news for the RHS and a vindication of the special contractual terms they had agreed to. However, much as the Badminton Gazette was writing as if there were huge attendances and support for the sport, Bernard Adams in his book dispels this notion by saying that, 'Reports on the sports pages of national papers had always been brief, and frequently cursory. Before 1914, players and officials had been glad of any attention in the press and there was a feeling that as the game grew in popularity coverage would increase. But by the mid-1920s enthusiasts began to feel that badminton was getting less than a fair deal. As early as 1926 an article in the Gazette had recognised the difficulty of securing adequate press coverage, and by 1934, the Badminton Association had also begun to be concerned.' It had been 'something of an event' when a long and informed article about badminton came out in the Evening Standard in March 1938, probably due to the fact that it was

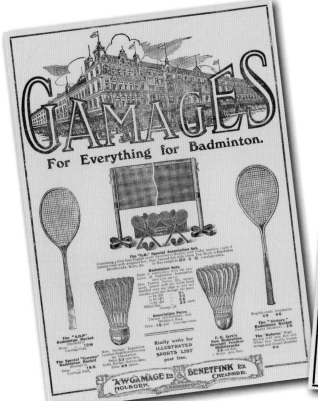

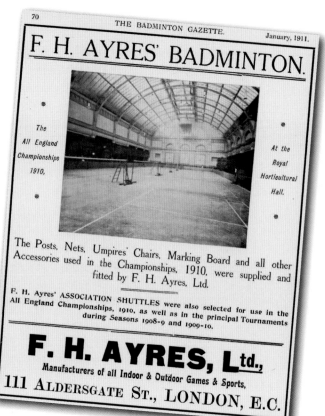

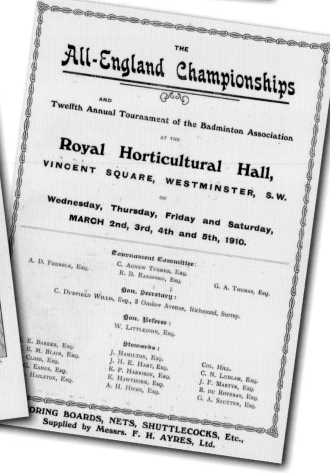

March, 1911. THE BADMINTON GAZETTE. 121

A GENERAL VIEW OF THE COURTS. Photo by London News Agency.

during these Championships that the Duchess of Gloucester, the first royal visitor to attend since it started on 4 April 1899, visited these in the Hall. There had also been jubilation when the BBC did a ten-minute radio commentary from the 1937 Championships, also in the RHS Hall. The difficulty of promoting the sport of Badminton continues to the present day, and in 2005 I remember securing a tenancy for what was going to be the Harris British Open Squash Championships, only for it to be cancelled when the sponsorship

Photos, Tournament Committee information, and advertisements for the Badminton Association 'All England Championships' from the Badminton Gazette, *the Official Organ of the Badminton Association, held in the Lindley Hall between 1910 and 1939.*

22 THE BADMINTON GAZETTE. April, 1910.

GENERAL VIEW OF THE ROYAL HORTICULTURAL HALL, WHERE THE ALL ENGLAND CHAMPIONSHIPS WERE HELD.

support failed. Unlike snooker, and later darts, that really took off and secured all-important television coverage, badminton and squash have remained somewhat in the shadows.

The last All England Badminton Championship to be held in the Royal Horticultural Halls was in 1939, and finally moved due to space constraints. It was due to move to Harringay Arena in 1940, but because of the outbreak of the Second World War this move was postponed until 1947. After the Second World War the Championships moved to Harringay Arena (1947-9), the Empress Hall, Earl's Court (1950-6), Wembley Arena (1957-93) and the National Indoor Arena, Birmingham (1994-).

Between 6 and 18 May 1946, one of the most important and remembered World Snooker Championships ever staged was held in the Old Hall. The final, between Joe Davis of England and Horace Lindrum of Australia, was also heard by a worldwide audience, including Australia, as the BBC made it the subject of a live broadcast on the radio. The commentators were Willie Smith, and Joyce Gardner who also acted as Commère. Joyce was no stranger to the world of professional billiards and snooker as she came with seven Championship titles to her name, and achieved the distinction of being the first woman to act in this capacity in the history of the game. It was also filmed by Movietone and Pathé. The event was the 15th World Snooker Championship of 1945-6. The very first world championship final had taken place at Camkin's Hall in Birmingham in 1927 and it was Joe Davis who had helped organise it. He also won the title, and went on to win another 14 world titles before arriving at the RHS Hall to play for, and win, his last. Interestingly, the match had been organised and sponsored by a billiard table manufacturer and retailer, William Jelks of W. Jelks & Sons, Ltd, 263-75 Holloway Road, London, N7. At that time, billiards was still the more popular of the two games, highlighted by the fact that there were only two entrants in 1931 World Snooker Championship, and the match took place in the back of a pub. Jelks saw his sponsorship of the Davis/Lindrum match as

Souvenir of the 15th World Snooker Championships, 1945-6, between Joe Davis of England, and Horace Lindrum of Australia, Organised and Presented by W. Jelks & Sons Ltd, 263-75 Holloway Road, London, N7, held in the Lindley Hall on 6-18 May 1946.

an opportunity to increase the awareness and recognition of snooker, not simply for altruistic reasons, but in order to make and sell more snooker tables, as well as those for billiards. However, in his Foreword to the souvenir programme produced for the event, Jelks begins with the statement, 'For the first time in history the World Snooker Championship is being staged in a manner befitting its importance and popularity. Hitherto, these Tests have been held in Halls where the seating accommodation has not exceeded the needs of little more than 200 people, and consequently thousands of devotees of the game have been denied the opportunity of witnessing and enjoying the great Snooker events.' He went on to say, somewhat prophetically, that, 'Snooker is destined to take its place among the top-line sports, and with this end in

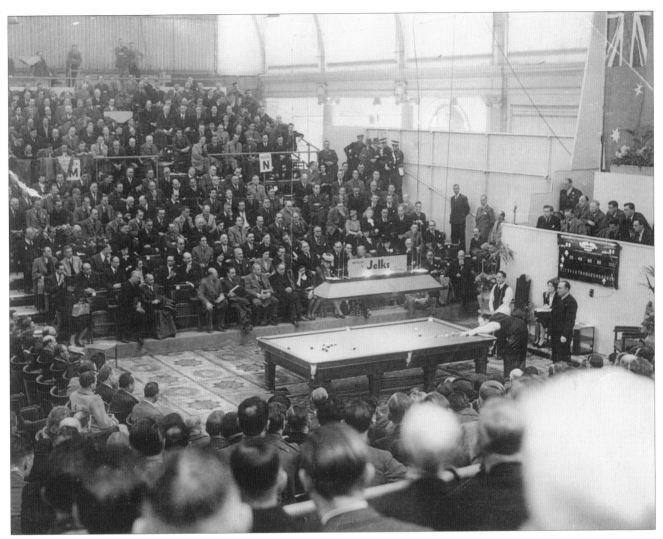

AND OVERLEAF
*Photos of the 15th
World Snooker
Championships, 1945-6,
between Joe Davis of
England and Horace
Lindrum of Australia.
Joyce Gardner, who
acted as one of the two
Commentators and
Commère, is pictured
with Davis and
Lindstrum. Organised
and Presented by W.
Jelks & Sons, Ltd,
263-75 Holloway
Road, London N7, the
Championships were
held in the Lindley Hall
on 6-18 May 1946.*

view I shall be glad to have the co-operation and help of all Snooker friends in shaping an aggressive policy of control and guidance for the benefit alike of coming professionals, both men and women, through Billiards Leagues and Clubs with Amateur County and Country Championships.' The Championship was run on behalf of the two governing bodies, the Billiards Association & Control Council (BA&CC). The Hall had to be blacked out, no mean feat when the entire span of the roof was glass, and this alone cost Jelks £400 (£12,684). In addition, as Davis recounted in his book, *The Breaks Came My Way*, he and Lindrum 'were insured for £3,000 [£31,710] to cover the risk of non-appearance.' Microphones were set up over the table to amplify the click of the balls. The entire Championship drew an attendance of 22,000 and there were regular attendances of 1,200 at each session paying 5s. to £3 (£7.93 to £95.13) a session. The box-office took £12,000 (£380,520) overall and sold some 8,000 programmes at 5s. (£7.93) each, made sweeter because the day before the Match the crippling entertainment tax of the day of 48 per cent was cut to 33.3 per cent! Davis won by 78 to 67 frames, and created a Championship record break of 136 for what was his 200th snooker century. Davis also wryly recalled in his book that, 'The final was a huge success. It was the only one of my fifteen snooker championships that made me any real money …' Davis retired after this from Championship matches, but there is an interesting postscript to this, not unlike the one I gave in an earlier chapter about Charles Rolls, and the demise of his Rolls-Royce Company. By an extraordinary quirk of fate, Davis's billiard table, the one provided by Jelks for the Championship Match, was sold in the same RHS Hall where his last final had been played on it, when a Sotheby's Sale of Rare Sporting Memorabilia was held there 33 years later on 6 December 1979. The table was expected to reach more than £10,000 (£42,300) before it was sold.

In 1984 I was lucky enough to work with a man called Peter Anslow, who can be credited with promoting the sport of skiing in this country by establishing the first consumer Ski Show. This was held in the RHS Old Hall on 5-9 September 1973, and also featured one of the first Dendix dry ski slopes to be used in an exhibition such as this that was managed by Sandown Park Ski School. Anslow's first International Ski Show had also secured vital sponsorship from the *Daily Mail*. Both its then Managing Director, Alwyn (Robbie) Robinson, and Editor, David English, were keen skiers, and primarily responsible for projecting the *Daily Mail* as 'the skier's paper'. This was complemented by the formation of the *Daily Mail* Ski Club and regular articles by their now legendary travel editor, Jill Crawshaw. Anslow, Robinson, and English all saw the huge potential for a new audience that would take up skiing for the first time and flock to new resorts in Europe and North America in the next two decades. As David English put it in his introduction to the first brochure, 'This is the first International Ski Show to be presented in Britain, so we are all making history here today'. He went on to say, 'But skiing is a sport which is constantly making history. New resorts, new equipment, new fashions, new records … and most of all new people; these are the ingredients

RIGHT Official Programme for the 1st International Ski Show, sponsored by the Daily Mail, *and opened by its Editor, David English, held in the Lindley Hall on 5-9 September 1973.*

of the most exciting sport in the world.' He was right and the show itself went on to reach pinnacles of success in the 1980s when Princess Diana responded to my invitation to her to open the 1986 *Daily Mail* International Ski Show. This increased attendance by 25 per cent, thus gaining huge publicity for the show, the sport and the *Daily Mail*.

The 2nd show grew substantially from the 27 exhibitors at the first show and consequently was transferred into the larger RHS New Hall where a much bigger Dendix dry ski slope was also able to be constructed. The 3rd show also took place there in 1975, when Denis Howell, the then Minister of Sport, was guest of honour, but in 1976 it had once again outgrown the space and transferred to the National Hall, Olympia. During the four years I was involved from 1984, the show took place in the Warwick Hall, Earl's Court. One of my most vivid recollections during this period was when what amounted to mini West End theatre productions, called 'Ski

Fantasias', were staged and choreographed by people such as Bruno Tonioli and Anthony van Laast, on the dry ski slope. In 1984, it was Tonioli of BBC Television's very much later 'Strictly Come Dancing' series that was the choreographer, and this was to the sound track of Michael Jackson's 'Thriller'. His 'Ski Fantasia' was certainly thrilling and magical with professional skiers dressed in zombie outfits performing 'aerials' out of traps and over jumps, as well as the whole troupe advancing down the slope in zombie formation backed by a super sound system that probably broke all health and safety rules. And, talking of health and safety, the 'Ski Fantasia' was sponsored during this period by Peter Stuyvesant Cigarettes! They put in around £150,000 to support this amazing show that drew thousands of people to Earl's Court to see it on a daily basis through the 10-day open period. Van Laast was already an established choreographer, but went on to great acclaim in many theatre, television, film and concert

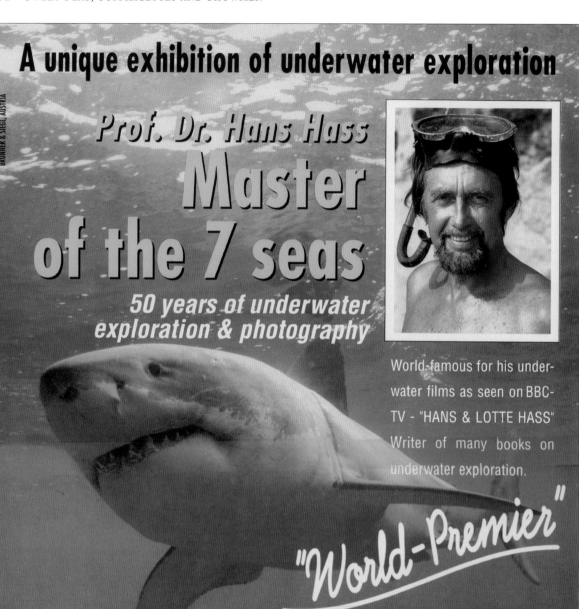

BRUNNER & SIEGL, AUSTRIA

A unique exhibition of underwater exploration

Prof. Dr. Hans Hass
Master of the 7 seas

50 years of underwater exploration & photography

World-famous for his underwater films as seen on BBC-TV - "HANS & LOTTE HASS" Writer of many books on underwater exploration.

"World-Premier"

© UNIVERSE PROMOTION / AUSTRIA

Come and visit at: **I N T E R N A T I O N A L**
DIVING SHOW
SUPPORTED BY THE DAILY MAIL
NEW HORTICULTURAL HALL
WESTMINSTER LONDON
16-20 JAN 1991

Open Times:
Wednesday - Friday:
12 noon till 9pm
Saturday - Sunday:
10am till 6pm

Admission:
£4 ADULTS,
£2.50 CHILDREN
(under 14)

productions not only as a choreographer, but as a director and stage manager, leading to him being awarded the MBE by Her Majesty The Queen for services to dance and choreography in 1999. Peter Anslow sold his show to the *Daily Mail*'s exhibition division in 1988, leading it to become Europe's largest consumer winter sports show, the Metro Ski and Snowboard Show in 2010 with its sister publication, The *Daily Mail Ski and Snowboard Magazine* as the UK's biggest selling winter sports magazine. This had started out as Ski International which I edited and produced for Peter Anslow in 1984. The

RHS Halls further helped this progression by hosting the very first skiboarding show in the Old Hall on 7-10 November 1996 called Board-X. The last exhibition I worked on with Peter and his team was the International Diving Show that was to have been held in the Old Hall on 16-21 January 1991, supported by the *Daily Mail*. Unfortunately, this was not able to be fulfilled, which was a great shame, as I had been to Austria and secured the agreement of one of the greatest icons of the diving fraternity, Hans Hass, to join us and display some of his remarkable early diving equipment and material.

VI

New Hall – New Events

New Hall

By the early 1920s the Vincent Square Hall had been found to be too cramped for the large-scale flower shows the Society was regularly holding. It had also become a bit shabby. On 15 November 1920 a letter is recorded as having been written to W.R. Dykes, the Secretary of the RHS, confirming a proposal to change the Hall into a 'very good picture theatre' at an outlay of £950 (£36,034) for conversion purposes. Profit was foreseen at £40 (£1,517) p.w. with weekly expenses of about £150 (£5,690). This offer, needless to say, was never taken up! However, £200 (£6,568) was spent in redecorating the Hall in 1921. In 1922, a housing committee was set up to report on accommodation, under the direction of C.T. Musgrave, Treasurer of the Society and a noted amateur gardener. Henry B. May, the nurseryman and grand old man of horticulture, then pushing 80, argued that the Society needed a second hall for exhibitions. The Vincent Square Hall had also increasingly been used for dances and social occasions for up to 1,250. Clubs, societies, political parties and commercial organisations were holding these more frequently, and looking for larger spaces, especially to entertain their staff and members, to hold reunions and celebrate anniversaries. His suggestion was at first unpopular, but soon the committee was examining sites in Regent's Park, the Embankment, and Greycoat Street, adjacent to the existing hall, as sites for a new building.

By November 1924 the Greycoat Street site had been decided upon (an underground link between the two halls was suggested, but rejected as too costly) and a Music and Dancing and Cinematography Licence for the New Hall was applied for. The decision not to build the underground link was one of the worst decisions ever made concerning the Halls. Had this been constructed, even at the undoubtedly high cost it would have been, the dividends would have been substantial. In the 17 years that I was at the RHS, one of the most difficult sales to make was in trying to sell both Halls together for one event. The problem was that, although they were very close, they were not linked. Had the link been there, a perfect combination and package would have ensured far greater success. It would also have been considerably easier to manage the 2,000 plus people that needed to leave the buildings away from very close proximity to our neighbours who ended up almost surrounding the Halls.

However, in 1924 the following particulars were given to the London County Council as part of the application: 'The premises are primarily required for the Horticultural Shows and Meetings of the Society, but the Lease of the premises will permit public or private meetings, concerts, entertainments, exhibitions and other functions. No stage performances are contemplated, nor are theatrical performances. The premises are, therefore, required for Exhibitions by the Society and others, Dancing, Banquets, Meetings and Displays, and Meetings of any sort confined to Members of the Society. 'An orchestra would be required for dancing and some entertainments and possibly at Banquets, and also professional entertainers might appear, but not in stage costumes.' Cinematograph displays were to be confined to lectures and demonstrations only. The application was opposed by none other than Miss Murray Smith, the same resident from St George's House in Vincent Square who had complained so often about the events that had taken place in the Vincent Square Hall. Messrs Cluttons, the Society's appointed property consultants and estate agents, pointed out in a letter that the New Hall was only going to be

used in the same way as the old one, so they didn't understand why a local resident should object, which given the previous circumstances, was exactly the reason why she was opposing it! The RHS brought out the big guns (Sir Henry Curtis Bennett KC – a name as prominent then as, say, Lord Goodman or Peter Carter-Ruck in more recent times) and the opposition was withdrawn. As part of the documentation for the licence application, the Society had to send in a list of the Hall bookings for 1924-6.

In July 1997 I had to go through a similar process when securing a Certificate of Lawful Use in conjunction with a Licence Application. This had become essential in fighting claims, or objections, that were being made by some residents that the original purpose of the Halls had been to hold the Society's horticulture-related shows, and not corporate functions, banquets, dances and other events. Because of the archive I had retrieved, I was able to show definitively that the type of events between

Photo of the laying of the foundation stone for the Lawrence Hall by Lord Lambourne, the 10th President of the RHS, on 10 October 1926.

Photo of the Lawrence Hall under construction in 1927, showing the structure of the parabolic arches.

1987 and 1997 in both Halls had certainly not been exclusively related to horticultural exhibitions and events. The event history of the Halls being depicted in this book shows that it was never thus, from the time the first Hall was built.

On 10 October 1926 Lord Lambourne, the then RHS President, laid the foundation stone for the 'New Hall' and by the end of the year the Music and Dancing and Cinematography Licence had been granted for it. The new exhibition hall had been designed by architects Murray Easton and Howard Robertson, and acclaimed as one of the best modern British buildings when it opened. However, as an American like Henry-Russell Hitchcock saw it at the time, it was, in fact, a Swedish building, for the splendid interior was closely modelled on the halls designed by Arvid Bjerke for the 1923 Gothenburg Exhibition with the great traverse arches translated from laminated wood to reinforced concrete construction. The Royal Horticultural Hall was, in fact, one of the supreme expressions of the dominant influence in Britain of modern Swedish architecture between the wars.

The Hall was formally opened by HRH Princess Mary on 26 June 1928 to a chorus of enthusiasm from the architectural press. Its use of reinforced concrete was seen as a significant advance in British architecture: 'Concrete has been taught to smile', said Morton Shand, and Verner Rees concurred: 'One has a sense that if this has happened, then other equally fitting and exciting forms are possible for other occasions.' The *Architecture & Business News* saw it as a revolutionary breakthrough in design and in 1929 the Hall received its ultimate accolade, a Gold Medal Award from RIBA.

Regrettably, the structure did not stay as sound as intended for very long. The first leaks in the roof were reported in August 1928, and on one night before the end of October no fewer than 41 leaks occurred. The Society's solicitor wrote to Easton and Robertson demanding that they rectify the matter and, after further experiments by Oscar Faber, the matter began to be resolved in the latter part of 1929. The difficulty of access for repairs continued to bedevil the maintenance staff, however, and eventually the panel system was

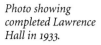

abandoned for a system of exposed radiators. (Twenty years later the roof was failing again, and a letter from the English Steel Corporation on 5 February 1947 pointed out that during their participation at The Worshipful Company of Shipwrights Exhibition on 5 February 1947 water was dripping onto their stand throughout!) Official contractors were appointed to deal with water and waste, and electricity supply and connection. The plumbers were appropriately named Messrs A. Smellie & Co. Ltd, 11 Rochester Row, SW1, and the electricians were Messrs Brooks & White, 10 Maclise Road, West Kensington, W14. Official caterers had also been appointed earlier in the original 'New Hall'. This was noted to be Iwan Kriens in 1926 to 1929, but probably from very much earlier because he was a key figure involved in the Universal Cookery Association and its Universal Cookery & Food Exhibition that was first held in our Hall in 1905. In 1930 he became Chairman of the Universal Cookery Association and one assumes that he must have had to relinquish his role with the Society to carry out his new duties. The Army & Navy Co-operative Society Ltd, Victoria Street, London SW1 took over the contract from 1929 until 1946.

As a result of the opening of the new New Hall, the original Hall on Vincent Square became known as the Old Hall and future contracts reflected this. They were coloured blue and grey to differentiate them from the original contracts that were all coloured grey. Rates for letting the respective halls were reviewed, although from January 1928 the Old Hall rate remained the same at £36 15s. (£1,696) per day to midnight, as it had been since 1922. The New Hall, Elverton Street rate was set at £78 15s. (£3,634) per day to midnight, and came into effect in June 1928.

Schoolboys, Schoolgirls and Bachelor Girls Reign

One the most popular, and successful national consumer shows of the 20th century, and certainly on a par with the Ideal Home Exhibition, was launched in the RHS Hall on 2 January 1926. This was the Schoolboy's Own Exhibition, a show that is as out of place now as a show about Kindles would have been then. However, this tapped into the post-war ascendancy of the Boy Scout movement, a need for the principal educational establishments across the land to keep alive traditional values, cling on to the fading Empire, and induce patriotism through service in the military. This event, the first of many that ran until 1968, took its name from *The Boy's Own Paper*. The event was conceived and organised by none other than our old friend, Ernest William Schofield of Kinematograph International Exhibitions Ltd (1913) who had, by then, moved to 46, Strand, WC2. *The Times* described the show as being where 'demonstrations are given of flying, wireless, engineering and motoring' and it was opened by Sir Sefton Brancker. Brancker

had been appointed Director of Civil Aviation in 1922, following a distinguished career in the Royal Flying Corps and, later, the Royal Air Force. He was also chairman of the Royal Aero Club's Racing Committee from 1921 to 1930 and was instrumental in introducing to them new and improved aircraft types such as the de Havilland Moth and Avro Avian. In his Patron's message in the 1930 Exhibition Catalogue, he wrote 'Aviation will be one of the greatest factors in the future of Great Britain, and of the British Empire … We must be strong in the air. Our future lies with the rising generation; and fortunately, the rising generation has already accepted aviation as a matter of course, and is only too anxious to learn all there is to know about it.' Nine years later, many of those schoolboys were in the air above the skies of Europe with his words ringing in their ears.

To begin with, Schofield's exhibition was very specifically aimed at the leading private schools of the day under the auspices of The

AND OVERLEAF
Catalogues for the Schoolboy's Own Exhibitions, held in both Halls during 1926-58, and in the National Hall, Olympia from 1959 to 1963. The Daily Mail *Schoolboy's and Girl's Exhibitions were held in the National Hall, Olympia, from 1964 to 1968.*

ABOVE *Admission ticket for 5 January 1956 to the 29th National Schoolboy's Own Exhibition.*

Private Schools Association. This included Charterhouse; The College, Bishop's Stortford; Perse School House Cambridge; and Caterham School whose headmasters each gave a message of support for the exhibition in the Year Book & Exhibition Guide. The leading message of support given in Schofield's first show catalogue was by the then Headmaster of Charterhouse School, Frank Fletcher, M.A. One can't help speculating whether the Society's 17th Secretary, William Rickaton Dykes, had been involved in some way, since before his RHS appointment he had only recently left Charterhouse where he had also been a Master. The initial aims and objects of the exhibition were 'to provide a place where certain sections of the term's work may be adequately displayed and demonstrated, and where the School Boy may see in concrete form certain branches of study which he has hitherto only had the opportunity to visualise.' A second aim was 'to encourage Citizenship and Patriotism; the love and care of Animals and Birds, and all forms of Handicraft.' The final aim was, 'to show under one roof everything used by, and of use to, the School Boy.' By 1939, Schofield had gathered a veritable Who's Who? of establishment figureheads, military heavyweights, sports personalities and celebrities from stage, screen and literary circles as patrons and advisers, as the event became more popular and established. However, his initial supporters were the influential educational associations and bodies, the Air Ministry, the Boy Scouts' Association, the RSPCA, the RSPB, and the Junior Philatelic Society. At this time also The Royal Horticultural Society's 10th President, Amelius Richard Mark Lockwood, 1st Baron Lambourne, MP for Epping Forest, was also Vice President of the RSPCA. Schofield chose as President for his show another luminary figure, Fred J. Melville, the founder of the Junior Philatelic Society. Melville had taken part in the 1906 International Philatelic Exhibition, organised the 1862-1912 Jubilee International Exhibition, the London International Stamp Exhibition in 1923, and would also become the organising director of APEX in 1934 – all significant philatelic shows that took place in the RHS Hall. Stamp collecting for boys was

Poster labels for the 1926-8 Schoolboy's Own Exhibitions, held in the Lindley Hall.

held to be an important and educational hobby, as popular then as boy bands are now.

At the 1927 exhibition, William Henry Grenfell, 1st Baron Desborough KG, GCVO, JP (a man whose credentials for opening such an event could surely not have been surpassed) duly opened it. Lord Desborough is reported in the 3 January edition of *The Times* as saying he 'believed that 20,000 boys had attended the first show and that it was expected to double with the present one'. Educated at Harrow School, and then Balliol College, Oxford, Grenfell (from the same Grenfell Buckinghamshire family as Field Marshal Francis Wallace Grenfell, 1st Baron Grenfell, who had acted as the 9th President of the RHS) became an athlete, sportsman, public servant and politician. He had been President of the Oxford University Boat and Tennis Clubs (and in the crew that won the 1878 Boat Race), climbed the Matterhorn three times, swam the Niagara rapids twice, rowed across the English Channel, and became President of the London Olympic Games in 1908. He had also been appointed as President to the Amateur Fencing Association (having won a silver medal in the team épée at the 1906 Athens Olympic Games), Marylebone Cricket Club, The Lawn Tennis Association, and the Thames Conservancy Board. He later also agreed to become one of the 22 leading patrons of this important new exhibition that, by the time of the 1939 exhibition, included national heroes and icons such as The Chief Scout – Lord Baden Powell (himself an ex-Charterhouse pupil), Sir John Reith (founder of independent public service broadcasting), Sir Malcolm Campbell (of Bluebird fame), Hugh Cecil Lowther, 5th Earl of Lonsdale (founder of the National Sporting Club; founder and first President of the A.A., and the man who donated the original Lonsdale Belts for boxing, and trophies for Darts) and A.A. Milne of Winnie the Pooh fame. It was inevitable, I suppose, that Lord Eustace Percy, who between 1924 and 1929 served as President of the Board of Education under Stanley Baldwin's government, was also a patron. It was also appropriate that Sir Charles Wakefield was included, as he was affectionately referred to as 'The Patron Saint of Aviation'. Just

as Percival Marshall had believed strongly that there was an important developmental role for models in arriving at real-life prototypes, so did Wakefield, and he channelled all his efforts into the development of aviation through his interest in aero models, working with Sir Sefton Brancker who had also become President of the Society of Model Aeronautical Engineers. He financed Sir Alan Cobham's return flight to Australia in 1926, and financially contributed to Amy Johnson's first solo flight to Australia by a woman in 1930.

However, he had started through interest in motor transport and developed lubricants for them. His trading name for them was Castrol. He supported Sir Henry Segrave's speed trials in Daytona and Miami, and presented the Wakefield Gold Trophy for the land speed record. He was a generous President of the Bethlem Royal Hospital, and a governor of St Thomas's and Bart's Hospitals. In 1937, together with his good friend, the Rev. Tubby Clayton, he set up the Wakefield Trust to help All Hallows by the Tower, Toc H, and good causes in the East End. The Trust continues to bear his name. He also served as Master of the Worshipful Company of Spectacle Makers that used the RHS Hall for its professional examinations between 1933 and 1935, and in 1937 an Optical Exhibition organised by the Association of Wholesale and Manufacturing Opticians was staged in the Hall. Toc H also used the Hall in 1931 and 1933, the latter for its annual Incorporated Festival. Toc H

Toc H enamel badge for their 1915-36 Anniversary. Toc H held their 1933 Festival in the Lawrence Hall on 10 December 1933.

began in 1915 during The First World War in Belgium. The Rev. Philip 'Tubby' Clayton, an Australian born army chaplain, established a rest and recreation centre near the battle lines. Its purpose was to provide basic comforts and refuge for the young men going to and from the front lines; a place to refresh the body and cheer the soul, where rank played no part. The organisation still does excellent work throughout the world today.

Overarching all of these, and acting as Honorary President of the 1939 Schoolboy's event and beyond, was Sir Harry Brittain, one of the most influential conservative and imperialist advocates of Tariff Reform who had formed the Tariff Reform League with Sir Cyril Arthur Pearson, founder of the *Daily Express*. Brittain had developed an early interest in journalism, and first became an assistant to Sir William Ingram, managing director of the *Illustrated London News*, but then worked on two of Pearson's papers, *The Standard* and the *Evening Standard*. He founded the Pilgrim's Society in 1902, an organisation that fostered closer ties and relationships with the United States of America. In 1909 he organised the first Imperial Press Conference, followed by the foundation of the Empire Press Union (later renamed the Commonwealth Press Union) that included over 1,500 newspapers and news agencies spread throughout the Commonwealth. He was also a keen supporter of the RSPB, and in 1925 was responsible for steering through Parliament the Protection of Birds Act (often also referred to as the 'Brittain Act').

An Advisory Committee had also been formed that included Robert Harding, the Editor of the *Boys' Own Paper* that had first been published in 1879, and continued until 1967. George Frederick Allison, Managing Director of Arsenal F.C., was also a member of it. He had famously been the BBC's principal football commentator from 1927 when the first FA Cup Final was played at Wembley Stadium that, only two years earlier, had housed the British Empire Exhibition. At this point, over 70 per cent of British households were without a radio of any kind, but in order to help the listener understand better what was taking place on the pitch, the

Radio Times published a graphic illustration of a football pitch that had been divided into a series of numbered squares. As Allison commentated on the progress of the match, his assistant would call out the number of the square where the ball was! Louis Charles Bernacchi was also on the Committee, and a household name at the time. He had joined the British Antarctic Exhibition in 1898 and later, in 1901-4, joined Captain Scott's National Antarctic Expedition on board the *Discovery* as a physicist. In 1938 he published his account of the latter under the title, the *Saga of the Discovery*.

For Schofield's 2nd exhibition in 1927, the Hall was laid out into sections. Six of these were: 'Airway Avenue, Handicraft Avenue, Book Worm Burrow, The Tuck Shop, Camera Corner and Harmony Corner'. Frankland & Frankland described themselves as 'musical merchandise', and were on Stand 26b on Harmony Corner. Advertising in the exhibition guide they posed the question, 'Can You Play The Ukulele?' The instrument had been made famous by George Formby who rose to fame with his cheeky songs, and was one of the most popular recording stars and performers during the 1930s through to the 1950s. Not the preferred musical instrument choice of today, but it was then, and you could buy one from their stand at 5s. each (£11.22). Standholders included Gieves Ltd of 21 Old Bond Street who proudly proclaimed themselves to be, 'Outfitters By Appointment to: Harrow School, Epsom College, Stubbington House, Fareham, St Piran's, Maidenhead, and Brighton College' among many others. The Royal Naval College Dartmouth were there recruiting for Cadets, and the Royal Air Force School of Technical Training were seeking apprentices. In the motor car racing section Mr J.W. Parry Thomas and his racing car 'Babs' were there, in which he had achieved a world-record speed of 170.624 mph in 21.099 seconds from a flying start at Pendine Sands, Carmarthenshire, on 28 April 1926. He would hold this record until February 1927 when Malcolm Campbell's latest 'Bluebird' model broke it, also on Pendine Sands. (In 1935, Campbell became the first man to break 300

Pin badge for Their Majesties King George VI and Queen Elizabeth's Coronation on 12 May 1937.

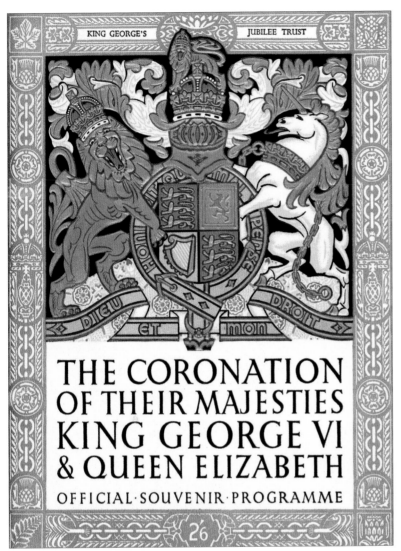

THE CORONATION
OF THEIR MAJESTIES
KING GEORGE VI
& QUEEN ELIZABETH
OFFICIAL·SOUVENIR·PROGRAMME

Official Souvenir Programme for the Coronation of Their Majesties King George VI and Queen Elizabeth distributed in London by Boy Scouts, who camped inside both Halls during 10-13 May 1937.

Shop, organised by Cadbury's of Bournville, Birmingham complemented by Schweppes Ltd who offered their non-alcoholic drinks of lemonade, ginger ale, ginger beer, lemon and orange squash, lime juice cordial, and cydrade. The Model Power Boat Association of Great Britain also exhibited and advertised two of the largest regattas ever held in the history of model power boats. In one of the Hall's Annexes were the Birmingham Small Arms Co. (BSA) where competitions were held on a daily basis with 'first-class B.S.A. Air Rifles' and in the other Annexe a Cine Camera Projection Room was operated by Kodak Ltd, Kingsway, WC2, where the latest Kodak No.2 Box 'Brownie' camera was available for 12s. 6d. (£28.06). Alternatively, the R.S.P.C.A. promised 'A few relics of some particularly bad cases of cruelty will be on view' on their stand 39a.

The Camping Club of Great Britain & Ireland, first formed in 1901, promoted its 'health-giving and invigorating pastime of camping', particularly for cyclists, motorists and caravanners, and first held one of their own reunion dances in the Old Hall on 17 February 1931. They continued to use the RHS for these during a 25-year period, right up to 1956.

The Boy Scout Movement was also very active, and a key part of the schoolboy's life. By 1910, the membership was claimed to be over 100,000. The first Scout event in the Hall had taken place on 15 June 1912, just five years after its foundation. This took the form of a display of drill. Further events, including many social and fundraising dances, were held by them and by the Girl Guides between 1926 and 1957. Olave, Lady Baden-Powell (who became Chief Guide for Britain in 1918) had also attended a Bazaar in the Hall in aid of the funds of the Alliance of Honour as part of the opening ceremonies on 7 December 1920. On that occasion, the Hall was decorated to represent the street of an old English town, where a historic pageant was also staged. In 1928, The Boy Scout Association was based at 25 Buckingham Palace Road. Two years later, Princess Mary, Countess of Harewood,

mph on land on Bonneville Salt Flats, Utah, and in 1939 broke another record by becoming the fastest man on water by achieving 141.74 mph. All his cars and boats were called 'Bluebirds'.) Also on hand were new settlement and farming opportunities in Dominion lands with The Australian Farms Training College and The 1820 Memorial Settlers Association of South Africa. Both organisations prepared and trained young graduates and public schoolboys to re-settle and maintain the dominant control of these vital areas for the continued benefit of the United Kingdom's trade interests.

The most famous bookshop in London, W. & G. Foyle Ltd in Charing Cross Road, and the most famous stamp shop in London, Stanley Gibbons Ltd in the Strand were also there, as was the all-important Tuck

WOVEN IN PURE SILK.

had played for England against Canada in the 1908 Olympic Games, Wilfred A. Johnson.

Not surprisingly, Percival Marshall's well-known and loved publication, 'The Model Engineer' and over 50 of his accompanying series of Popular Handbooks were on sale on Stand 1b together with, by now, many of his publishing company's other titles, such as 'The Model Railway News', Reliable Wireless Books, and 'Marshall's Practical Manuals'. These ranged from 'Screw Cutting Simply Explained' to 'Simple Experiments in Static Electricity' to 'Induction Coils For Amateurs' and 'Wireless Telegraphy Simply Explained.' Two other publications published by Marshall were available and these would, in their combined later form, lead to one of the most important publications of the 20th century. These were called 'Experimental Wireless Radio Call Book' and 'Experimental Wireless Radio Time Table'. The latter gave the times of transmissions, wave-lengths, call letters, and nature of messages of the regular transmitting stations of the world. It showed you at a glance what to listen to for at any hour of the day or night. As the advert for it said, 'Invaluable to all listeners and experimenters. Keep it handy to your set.' We still find *The Radio Times* invaluable today although, perhaps, not for long! Although not published by Marshall, *The Bazaar, Exchange & Mart*, that would later become simply *Exchange & Mart*, was also there in a very early form. Ebay would eventually replace its relevance and render it largely obsolete with the coming of the new internet medium, but for generations of people it was as popular and as widely used as Ebay, and other electronic marts such as Amazon are today.

By the time of the 1929 exhibition, it was clear that these events were being used as a showcase for the aviation industry's progress and development, something that we have noted in an earlier chapter was badly lacking before the war. On 18 December 1928 *The Times* reported in advance of the 1929 event that, 'The Air Ministry's exhibit will include the control car of the R33, the airship which broke away from her mast at RAF Pulham in Norfolk

President of the Girl Guides Association, laid the first stone on 23 May 1930 to open their new headquarters at 15-19 Buckingham Palace Road. By 1937, the Scouts had relocated to 66 Victoria Street. Then, between 10 and 13 May that year hundreds of Boy Scouts camped in both of the RHS Halls and used them as a base to fan out into the streets of London to sell the Official Coronation Programmes for King Edward VI. They were rewarded with a visit from their Chief Scout, Lord Baden-Powell, on the eve of the Coronation itself.

Ernest Schofield advertised, 'The Schoolboy's Own Summer Holiday Yachting Camp' under his personal supervision that included full tuition in Navigation, Sailing, Yacht Construction, Knotting and Reefing – all for £10 10s. for a full month (£471.35). Finally, seven of the leading sportsmen of the day made appearances on 5 January. These represented the sports of cricket, football and lacrosse, including the Captain of Surrey Cricket Club, P.G.H. Fender, the Captain of Arsenal F.C., Chas. M. Buchan, and the Captain of Middlesex Lacrosse team who

LEFT *Silk of Robert Stephenson Smyth Baden-Powell (1857-1941), educated at Charterhouse School and founder of the Scout Movement. He became Chief Scout of the World following the 1st World Scout Jamboree held at Olympia, 1920. In 1921, he was created a Baronet in the New Year Honours.*

ABOVE RIGHT *Photo of schoolboys on tank at the 24th Schoolboy's Own Exhibition held in both Halls on 1-13 January 1951.*

BELOW RIGHT *Photo of the Hon. Esmond Harmsworth, MP (son of Harold Sydney Harmsworth, who with his brother had been responsible for the rapid development and success of the Daily Mail), who opened the 10th Daily Mail Schoolboy's Own Exhibition on the steps of the Lawrence Hall on 31 December 1929.*

in the night of the 17/18 April 1920, and one of the latest fighting aeroplanes, a Woodcock, the two forming a striking proof of the enormous advance made in the conquest of air during the last few years.' Paradoxically, however, the R33 was constructed by the Sunbeam Motor Car Co. Ltd! This was also the first show at which Robots were exhibited, and these took the form of 'Robot Commissionaires' who directed enquirers to the various sections of the show. As has already been mentioned earlier, Eric, the first British Robot, had set the precedent by opening the 10th Model Engineer Exhibition only three months earlier. There were also demonstrations of wireless picture apparatus, a careers section, and the Schoolboy's Bisley, under the guidance of the Society of Miniature Rifle Clubs. It was also where a working model of John Logie Baird's TV system was on display.

In 1930, the *Daily Mail* became the main sponsor, and the Hon. Esmond Harmsworth

MP (son of Harold Sydney Harmsworth who with his brother had been responsible for the rapid development and success of the *Daily Mail*) opened the *Daily Mail* Schoolboy's Exhibition on the steps of the RHS New Hall where Rupert II, an ingenious Robot, also proved a great attraction. Esmond had taken control of the *Daily Mail* and General Trust Company in 1922 and became Chairman of Associated Newspapers in 1932 all the way through to 1971. He had also been one of the youngest MPs ever to be elected when in 1919 he became the Conservative MP for the Isle of Thanet. He also served as Aide-de-Camp to the Prime Minister at the Paris Peace Conference in the same year when the treaty of Versailles was signed. He had been educated in Eton, so everything that the Schoolboy's Own Exhibition represented would have been dear and familiar to him, coupled with the fact that here was another potential blockbuster exhibition that could help promote his newspaper, just as the other exhibitions that his family had become involved with were proving to be. The delights that awaited schoolboys (and the fathers who brought them) to the 1930 show were reported in the 4 January issue of *The Modern Boy*. Their Special Representative reported that, 'What is probably the finest model railway in the world has been arranged on one stand and, when you have feasted your eyes on this you can walk a few paces and inspect the Golden Arrow – the car in which Segrave made his record-breaking speed of 231 mph. Captain Campbell's mighty racing car, the Blue Bird is shown alongside Segrave's car, too. A little farther on you will see the fastest aircraft ever built-the Supermarine Rolls-Royce S6 in which Flight Lieut. Waghorn won the Schneider Trophy for Britain last September.' He also reported that, 'You can make your own (Recordavox) gramophone records of your own voice, for a small charge, and then take the records home to play them on your gramophone.' However, what also drew big crowds was the first public demonstration anywhere by John Logie Baird of Baird Television Development Company Ltd, 133 Long Acre, WC2, of his important invention, Noctovision. This allowed visitors to the exhibition in the Hall to witness the actual two-way transmission of moving pictures and sound between the Army & Navy Stores stand in the Hall, and their main building in Victoria Street on the Noctovisor screens set up in both locations. Selfridges also had a stand at this show and, in fact, later organised a Schoolboy's Exhibition of their own in their Palm Court on its 4th floor in January 1933. This followed on from the main exhibition held at White City when the King Edward's Hospital Fund for London (now known as The King's Fund) had a stand affording schoolboys the opportunity of an X-ray examination, and displaying the amputation knife used by Dr Watson at the Battle of Trafalgar. Returning to the aviation theme, Amy Johnson with her pilot husband James Mollison opened the Selfridges event on 9 January. Two days earlier, Amy had been awarded the Gold Medal of Honour of the League of Youth by Sir George Truscott, the acting Lord Mayor at Mansion House, so it was fitting that she was there to act as a beacon of aspiration for youth. Two months earlier, Amy had broken her husband's record for a solo flight to the Cape and, together, they would later become famous for their Atlantic crossing from Pendine Sands to Bridgeport, USA in their D.H. Dragon 'Seafarer' on 22 July that year. However, in spite of the extraordinary achievements of Amy Johnson, and other young women who were equally inspirational in breaking gender barriers, it was not until 1964 that it was felt necessary to include schoolgirls in the title of the show that changed to the *Daily Mail* Schoolboy's and Girl's Exhibition. Unfortunately, this was not to last long as its last show took place in 1968, never to reappear again. The Model Engineer outlasted it by almost half a century, and it is interesting to speculate why. One of the reasons I have heard, but cannot substantiate, is that towards the end it was being targeted by paedophiles. However, I also think that, when one looks at the exhibitors and exhibits towards the end of the 1960s, they were simply no longer as interesting or stimulating as they had been when inventions and cutting edge technologies were at the very beginning of their development. The new communication available to all through radio and television also made a huge difference. To the modern schoolboy in the 1960s, having emerged from the post-war depression, a more popular culture was developing; a cultural revolution was again in the air, and there was a need to re-invent, not rely on the ways of the past generations that had encompassed a fading Empire and two World Wars.

The exhibition had also gone through some transitions along the way. In 1931, the *Daily Mail* moved the show to Olympia. In 1932, the show had been mainly sponsored by the General Post Office (GPO) when it was entitled, the Young People's Telephone Exhibition, held at the Imperial Institute in Kensington. Opened by the Postmaster General, the show attracted 18,000 schoolchildren in the first five hours, and during its three-week open period recorded 328,000 visitors, a real indication of the interest in the telephone at that time. The Exhibition stayed at White City from 1933-5, and in 1934, Sir Harry Brittain is recorded as having opened it, and also communicated by wireless telephony with a group of 12 schoolchildren that had been flown over the site. After a brief return to the RHS Hall in 1935, the exhibition returned to the Imperial Institute and stayed there for the next three years, incorporating the National Treasures Exhibition in 1938 that, as part of the show, allowed access to the Science, Natural History and V&A Museums. The last event before the Second World War in January 1939 was held in the RHS Hall and, not surprisingly, was heavily biased towards promoting military hardware and reinforcing the armed services

and their prowess. Seven years then passed before the next one was staged, this time in Central Hall Westminster in 1947. However, from 1948 until 1958 it was held in the New Hall, or both RHS Halls, until it moved back again to Olympia in 1959.

In November 1930, Schofield's Kinematograph International Exhibitions Ltd (1913) did address the question of holding a similar event, specifically for young women, by also launching the Bachelor Girl's Exhibition in the RHS New Hall. Once again, he had secured an eclectic, but remarkable, list of all women patrons. These included Lady Brittain, Lady Houston, Lady Moore-Guggisberg, Lady Norah Bentinck (Vice-President), Daphne du Maurier (Lady Daphne Browning), Miss Lilian Baylis, Miss Jennie Lee and Mrs Marie Adelaide Belloc-Lowndes. Many had been active suffragettes, philanthropists, authors, politicians and pioneers of their times, and this event was seen as an important step in helping more women to recognise their true potential, and learn about careers that they could pursue, outside the confines of their husband's, brother's and men friend's realms of home and work. As if to reinforce how far they had come, a 'Woman's Chamber of Horrors' was created from relics lent by the then London Museum depicting a ducking stool, a scold's bridle and a whipping post – all used repressively against women in bygone days. Also on display were panes of glass that had been prised out of Holloway Prison,

Photo of schoolboy on the telephone speaking to the Chief of the Boy Scouts' Association in Ottawa, Canada – across 3,000 miles from the 10th Daily Mail *Schoolboy's Own Exhibition, held in the Lawrence Hall from 31 December 1929 to 8 January. 1930.*

THE
NATIONAL SCHOOLBOY'S OWN EXHIBITION
1957

This is to certify that . .

. . . .

visited the Royal Air Force Stand and met

. . . . .of the R.A.F. who

represented Great Britain at the Olympic Games

held in Melbourne, Australia, November 1956

XVI ᵀᴴ OLYMPIAD

and smuggled out by a suffragette when she had been incarcerated there at the height of the emancipation struggles.

A selection of prominent women gave talks about career possibilities every day during the nine days and Dame Muriel Talbot advised about migration. Lady Astor opened the show on the first day followed by Miss Betty Nuttall, Dame Louise McIlroy, Miss Margaret Bandfield and Miss Winifred Brown (who won the King's Cup Air Race), to name but a few. Of course, this was really aimed at the aristocratic and wealthy women of the day. However, it is interesting to note that *Burke's Peerage and Gentry*, the definitive list of aristocratic families and individuals, always listed male children first, because these were felt to be more important. Embarrassingly, in spite of all the changes in women's emancipation, recognition and progress throughout the 20th century, this was still taking place 184 years after it was founded, and only changed in 2010 when they also began to include illegitimate children. Not so bad, but still embarrassing, is the fact that it took 164 years before the Royal Horticultural Society elected the first woman onto its Council on 20 February 1968, and 206 years before the first woman President was elected on 1 July 2010. Respectively, these were Frances Perry, who had served as Chief Horticultural

Officer for Middlesex and a renowned authoress on horticulture, and Elizabeth Banks, DL, a landscape architect renowned for her pioneering work on both historic and contemporary gardens. Inga Grimsey became the Society's first woman Director General in 2007, but since the first time that the position of Director General had been created was in 1985

ABOVE LEFT *Photo of former King Peter of Yugoslavia and his son Prince Alexander wearing space suits as they prepare to enter the 'Space Machine' at the 27th National Schoolboy's Own Exhibition, held in both Halls on 31 December 1953-13 January 1954.*

ABOVE *Certificate issued at the 30th National Schoolboy's and Senior Students Own Exhibition by the RAF and signed by Dick Wheater, who represented Great Britain at the November 1956, Melbourne, Australia Olympics, held in both Halls on 31 December 1956-12 January 1957.*

LEFT *Poster label for the Bachelor Girl's Exhibition, held in the Lawrence Hall on 12-21 November 1930. Lady Astor, MP, opened the Exhibition.*

RIGHT *Letter
from Jessie Prior,
Organising Secretary
of the Bachelor Girl's
Exhibition to Dr Robert
Eric Mortimer Wheeler,
Curator of The London
Museum, dated
25 November 1930.
Dr Wheeler would later
become knighted in
1952 for his services to
archaeology, bringing
this science to the
attention of mass
audiences, through
his many appearances
on radio and
television programmes.*

with the appointment of Christopher Brickell, this cannot be compared in the same way.

The Bachelor Girl's Exhibition was short-lived in this form, but two Schoolgirls' Association Exhibitions did take place in 1949 and 1950, organised by J.P. Good (Exhibition) Ltd. The first one sought to illustrate life in the Women's Royal Army Corp (WRAC) as a serious career

option, because many women would not get the chance to marry. Dame Mary Tyrwhitt, the WRAC's first head, presided.

For the RHS, Schofield's Schoolboy's Own Exhibition, and Marshall's Model Engineer Exhibition were, each in their own right, as influential in marketing their facilities as the Universal Food and Cookery Exhibition had been in 1906. This was especially so given the completion of the New Hall on Elverton Street in 1928 that opened up new opportunities for larger exhibitions and events, as well as exposure to far greater audiences. Their duration, both lasting well into the 1960s, assured the status of the RHS as an important national venue in London. The Badminton Championships held over a 30-year period acted in a similar way. Many other sporting events have also been staged there but, in January 1935, the only boxing match ever to have taken place in the Halls was held in the Old Hall as part of the 15th Schoolboy's Own Exhibition. This was the London Schools Amateur Association Boxing Championships when, from 1,000 original entrants, 84 boys between 5st and 10st fought in 21 events. This was recorded by Pathé News and watched by a huge audience.

RIGHT *Photo of
Private Mary Poter of
Waterford, with some
of the dolls for the
Schoolgirl's Association
Exhibition, held in
the Lindley Hall on
2-24 August 1949.
The Exhibition
aimed to illustrate
life in the Women's
Royal Armoured
Corp (WRAC).*

Old Vic and Sadler's Wells

Lilian Baylis is, without doubt, remembered as the Grande Dame of the Old Vic and Sadler's Wells Theatres. She was the dominant force behind establishing the Old Vic as London's pre-eminent theatre house for her Shakespeare and Opera Companies that included some of the finest actors, actresses and singers in the land. She is also remembered for redeveloping Sadler's Wells and, as importantly, her role in the formation of the unique Vic-Wells partnership that introduced British Ballet to a sceptical world, in tandem with dramatic theatrical and operatic productions. It is no wonder that Ernest Schofield chose her to be a patron of his Bachelor Girl's Exhibition in 1930. She was an inspiration to women seeking to establish themselves in a male-dominated environment, and a match for any man. Her own involvement in the history of the RHS Halls is equally intertwined with the momentous events in the history of London theatre and British Ballet as, in 1925, she chose the RHS Hall for the first of six of her 'Old Vic Circle Twelfth

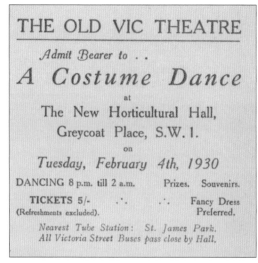

Night Costume Dances'. These were held on Shrove Tuesday each year, and were hugely successful, with more than one thousand of London's most famous thespians normally involved, all dressing up in theatrically-themed costume to be judged accordingly. Prizes were offered to the best and presented by Edith Evans, Sybil Thorndike, Baliol Holloway and Marie Ney, amongst others. Mr Sadler and his Orchestra entertained. What was special about them, in particular, was that the funds raised went directly into

Invitation cards and souvenirs for the Old Vic Circle 12th Night Costume Dances, held in the Halls from 1925 to 1930. These raised funds for the Sadler's Wells Development Fund that Lilian Baylis used to re-open Sadler's Wells Theatre, on 6 January 1931.

Baylis's Sadler's Wells Redevelopment Fund; the 1930 funds raised went specifically towards the stage equipment. The first three, from 1925 to 1927, were held in the Old Hall, and the last three up to 1930 were held in the Society's New Hall on Elverton Street. The late night noise restrictions that had been such a problem in the Old Hall were apparently no longer such an issue as dancing in the New Hall was allowed from 8 p.m. to 2 a.m. and tickets were 5s. (£11.54). A Char-a-banc Service was also available after the Dance from Samuelson's Saloon Coaches Ltd, 34 Victoria Street to London and the suburbs. But, while the New Hall did not have any residential property abutting it, or very close to it (something that would radically change in 1987 when Rowan House was built abutting the Hall, and later still in 1994 when Dencora Homes Ltd, and Barratt Harris Ltd, were allowed by Westminster City Council to demolish the commercial offices building of Assetts House to be replaced by 43 residential dwellings immediately facing the Hall in Elverton Street), more than one thousand revellers emerging into the streets at 2 a.m. would still have been noisy.

In the March 1926 issue of *The Old Vic Magazine*, reporting on the success of their 1925 Dance, it was noted that, 'Certainly, the audience had risen nobly to the organiser's plea for fancy dress, and arrived in such bewildering loveliness that the judges were almost afraid to enjoy themselves'. There were five main costume categories for men and women and these were: Most Beautiful, Jubilee of the Vic, Most Original, Most Beautiful Home-Made and Best Historical. The costume names were as interesting as the costumes themselves. Falstaff, Katherine of Aragon, Venetian Lady and Pompadour were to be expected, but others less so, like 3 O'clock in the Morning, Two British Workmen – Hall's Distemper and, Why Did I Kiss That Girl? The judging process took a very long time with over one thousand entries. In the 1927 Magazine, writing about the 1926 Dance, the editor referred to the actors and actresses

Past and Present Leads at 'Old Vic'
Sybil Thorndike.   Florence Saunders.   Florence Buckton.

who often had to make difficult journeys from the theatres they were performing at to join the dance in their chosen costumes. He commented, 'The judges would have liked to have known what became of the gentleman who had come thirty – or fifty or sixty – miles (accounts differ) to represent Pagliacci. The judges waited in vain for him in order to present him to Edith Evans; who surely made record time in coming from Hammersmith, where the curtain does not go down early on *The Beaux' Strategem*. Ernest Milton didn't have a fair start with *Daniel Deronda* at Kew, and gave up the race; but Marie Ney,

Postcard of past and present Old Vic Leading Ladies – Sybil Thorndike, Florence Saunders and Florence Buckton, c.1922.

with an unfamiliar shingle, made a surprise appearance on the judges' platform after *The Constant Nymph*. Wilfred Walter, with an orchid, Douglas Burbidge, as an immense Viking, Neil Curtis, as David Copperfield, were old friends who swam briefly into one's ken, and gave autographs. But nobody knows at what hour Edith Evans signed the last of John Garside's souvenir bookmarkers.' By 1930, the Dance had become a huge event that had luckily been able to move into the larger Hall, because even in 1925 ticket requests had had to be turned down and calls to move to the Royal Albert Hall had been made. It had also attracted a large number of organisations that both donated prizes and funds to the Development Fund.

Among these were Abdullah & Co. who gave a cabinet of their choice cigarettes, Mentmore Manufacturing Company offered

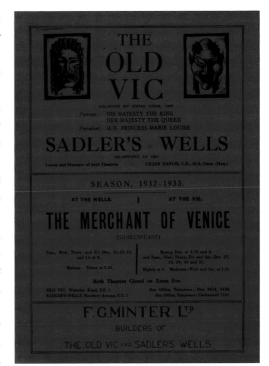

a Platignum desk set, Messrs, J.M. Dent & Sons gave the Larger Temple Shakespeare set, and Mr M. Vogler of 74, Oxford Street gave a permanent wave (of the hairdressing type)!

On 6 January 1931, Lilian Baylis had generated enough re-development funding and re-opened the Sadler's Wells theatre, appointing Ninette de Valois as its first Artistic Director. Ninette (real name Edris Stannus, born in County Wicklow, Ireland) had approached Baylis with her vision of creating an English school of ballet, attached to a theatre, where dancers could have real and constant stage experience. Baylis shared this vision and, as Baylis herself said in her Foreword to the book, *Ninette de Valois and the Vic-Wells Ballet* published in June 1934, 'I believe that we are on the threshold of a great renaissance of ballet in England; and that this renaissance will be characterised by the fact that English dancers, no longer hiding under foreign pseudonyms, will be acknowledged here, as they have been abroad, as truly fine exponents of the most difficult and comprehensive of all the arts.' Her words were prophetic as Ninette de Valois as artistic director, choreographer, and producer at the Vic-Wells Ballet, the only theatre school

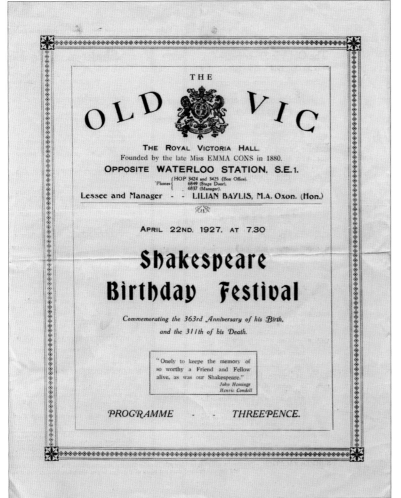

of ballet in Britain at the time, went on to establish The Royal Ballet, now one of the leading ballet companies in the world.

As Baylis continued to recount in the same Foreword as to how de Valois had started working with her, she said, 'She devised the dances in our operas and plays, with a scratch company rehearsed in odd corners, in bars and dressing rooms, and drew up her big scheme.' One of these very early performances was given at the last Old Vic Circle Twelfth Night Costume Ball held in the RHS New Hall on Shrove Tuesday 1930, as part of the cabaret for the evening. The occasion must have been wonderful and stimulating, surrounded by up to two thousand of England's finest theatrical, operatic and ballet-dancing artists, given also that she would become the new artistic director of Sadler's Wells in under a year. On 6 May 1974 during the Lilian Baylis Centenary Festival, a Gala Evening entitled, 'Tribute to the Lady', was staged in the Old Vic Theatre in front of its patron, HM Queen Elizabeth The Queen Mother, when a star-studded cast celebrated the life and work of this extraordinary woman who had started out at The Old Vic helping her aunt, Emma Cons, when it was still a temperance hall in 1898, called the Royal Victoria Hall. Among the cast were Sir Laurence Olivier, Dame Peggy Ashcroft, Paul Schofield, Robert Lang, Barbara Jefford, Nigel Stock and Barbara Leigh-Hunt. Special appearances were made by Dame Edith Evans, Dame Ninette De Valois, Dame Sybil Thorndike, Dame Flora Robson, Nigel Stock and Sir Ralph Richardson. As another footnote to this particular piece of history in the RHS Hall, I was instrumental in getting Sadler's Wells to use the Hall again 76 years later on 25 September 2006 to celebrate a unique evening to raise awareness and support for the Sadler's Wells Commissioning Fund when the historical references to the Hall were credited. Premier dance stars Matthew Bourne, Sylvie Guillem, Jonzi D, Akram Khan, Russell Maliphant, The Ballet Boyz, Wayne McGregor, Rambert Dance Company and Zenaida Yanowsky took part in what was entitled, 'Sadler's Wells Celebrates'.

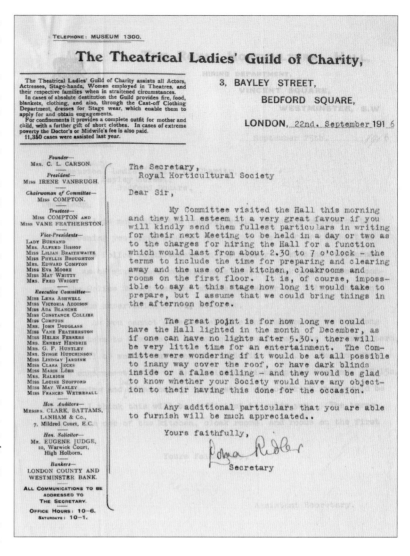

Holidays Camps and Cycling

On 18 February 1927, the first in a long series of holiday camp reunions and dances was held in the RHS Halls. This one was for the Civil Service Holiday Camps Ltd. Over the next 10 years many others were to follow their example and use the Halls to bring together hundreds of thousands of working class people and families that, through the invention of these affordable holiday camps, dramatically changed their lives in being able to enjoy relaxing seaside holidays with their children and families, away from their normal tiring, urban and city lives.

The earliest camp of all had been started in 1894, and was known as Cunningham Young Men's Holiday Camp, Douglas, on the Isle of Man. It was very basic, but the principles

ABOVE *Letter from Lorna Ridler, Secretary of The Theatrical Ladies' Guild of Charity, sent to the RHS Secretary on 22 September 1916 enquiring about a tenancy in the Hall. Miss Lena Ashwell was the sister of Roger Pocock, founder of the Legion of Frontiersmen who raised funds for them and, as an actress, organised large-scale entertainment for troops at the front during the First World War.*

THE NEW HALL, CAISTER HOLIDAY CAMP.

Postcards sent from Pakefield Hall and Caister Holiday Camps, dated August 1933 and September 1932 respectively. Pakefield Hall was close to Lowestoft, and Caister was in Caister-on-Sea, Great Yarmouth. Both Camps held their reunions and dances in the Halls from 1928 to 1937.

were sound, and others followed suit. The first Camp to become successfully established in a way that spurred on its followers further was the 'Socialist Caister-on-Sea Holiday Camp', near Great Yarmouth, started by John Fletcher Dodd in 1906; its name a clear indication that these were also born out of the social revolution that was taking place at the time to establish better lives for the working class, even if the accommodation was in tents, and the campers had to help out with the chores. (On 14 January 1929, when the Caister Holiday Camp used the New Hall for the first time for their reunion dance, the camp had become more permanent with wooden structures and recreational facilities.

SECTION OF DINING HALL, PAKEFIELD HALL HOLIDAY CAMP

GENERAL VIEW OF CAMP, PAKEFIELD HALL HOLIDAY CAMP

The St Martin's Guild of Fellowship from St Martin-in-the-Fields, close by, used Caister in August 1934, and would have become familiar with the Hall in February 1935 when their annual reunion social and dance took place.) This led to a number of Trades Unions, and the Civil Service establishing their own non-profit cooperative camps for their members. These were still the early days of holiday camps, long before the modern day versions and successors started by Harry Warner (whose first camp opened in 1931), Billy Butlin (in 1936) and Fred Pontin (in 1946).

On 20 January 1928, Maddieson's Hemsby Holiday Camp, also close to Great Yarmouth in Norfolk, booked its own dance and reunion at the Hall. 'Maddies' as it was affectionately referred to, was one of the many new commercial holiday camps that had begun to develop in the UK. H.J. (and H.R.) Maddieson established several other camps, including Littlestone-on-Sea, New Romney, Kent, that opened at Whitsun in 1931 ready to accommodate up to 150 people, and used the Hall for their very first reunion the next year on 30 January 1932. Other famous early Camps that used the Halls for their annual reunions

from 1929 to 1937 were the Pakefield Hall Holiday Camp, Lowestoft; The Jersey Holiday Camp at Portelet Bay; St Petersville Holiday Camp (that I have been unable to locate, but may also have been in Jersey or Guernsey); the Northney Holiday Camp, Hayling Island (this Camp was the second Camp to be opened by the Civil Service and later became the first ever Warner Holiday Camp, but was closed down and demolished in the early 1980s) and Brambles Chine Holiday Camp, Colwell Bay, Freshwater on the Isle of Wight. Harry Warner did also use the RHS Hall for his annual holiday camp reunion dances from November 1951 to November 1956 inclusive. Jersey, in the Channel Islands, was also a popular destination and three of their hotels also booked reunion dances in the halls. These were the *Sandringham Hotel, Columberie*, and Richard Binnington's *Chelsea Private Hotel* in St Helier.

Billy Butlin is the man that most people associate with

BELOW *Caister-on-Sea Holiday Camp commemorative medal struck by Walker & Hall Ltd showing portrait of its founder, John Fletcher Dodd, who established the Camp in 1906.*

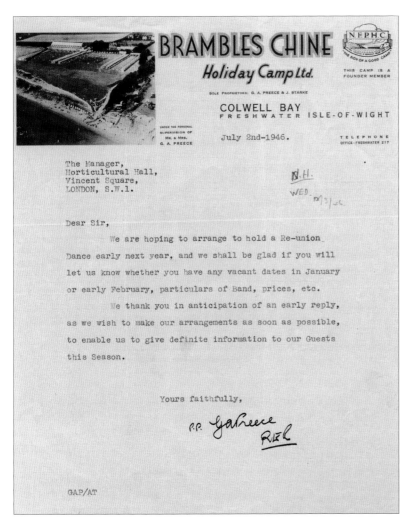

holiday camps, but his first camp was not opened until 11 April 1936 at Ingoldmells, adjoining Skegness. It was officially opened by Amy Johnson who, as has already been referred to, was the first woman to fly solo from England to Australia. An advertisement was placed in the *Daily Express* announcing the opening of the camp and inviting the public to book for a week's holiday, enclosing a ten-shilling (£2.68) registration fee. The advertisement offered holidays with three meals a day and free entertainment. A week's full board cost anything from 35 shillings to three pounds a week (£9.39-£156.66), according to the time of year. By the 1960s, over 100 holiday camps were registered and the later 1980s television programme, *Hi Di Hi*, gave testament to the affection of the British people for them.

Cycling had become an even more popular pastime by the time of the early holiday camp developments, and in keeping with the British bent for engineering and invention, people such as Claud Butler of Wandsworth; W.F. Holdsworth of Beckenham, Kent; F.H. Grubb of Twickenham; R.O. Harrison of Peckham were just a few of those pioneering new designs of bicycles that led to the first 'Light-Weight

ABOVE *Letter from Brambles Chine Holiday Camp, Isle of White, to RHS requesting a tenancy for a dance, dated 2 July 1946.*

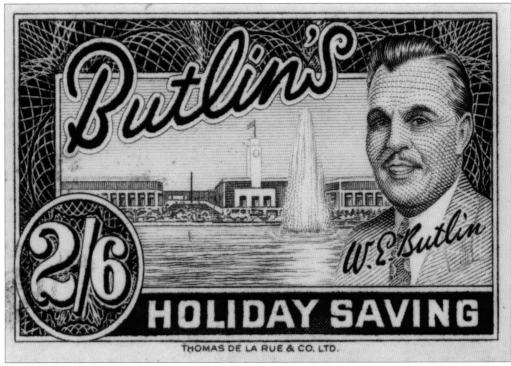

RIGHT *Post-Second World War Butlins Holiday Camp 2s. 6d. savings stamp.*

Cycling Exhibition including Hiking and Camping Equipment' that took place in the RHS Old Hall on 17-22 October 1932. This was organised by J.E. Holdsworth, brother of W.F. Holdsworth, Beckenham, Kent where they both lived. The following year it had already grown to relocate in the New Hall, and after the 4th Show in 1935 it moved to Olympia. At the 1934 Exhibition you could buy a Claud Butler cycle built to order from £7 17s. 6d, or a Hobbs Raceweight from £11 (£577.83) cash. The National Clarion Cycling Club, that had been formed in 1894, was also at this Exhibition, and held their own events at the RHS independently. The show catalogue stated that they were 'The Official Cycling Club of the National Workers' Sports Association.' Their motto was 'Peace through Sport' and at the time they had 5,000 members in 150 sections throughout Great Britain. One of the special exhibits on display at this show was the actual machine ridden by the German winner, Geyer, in that year's Tour de France. Mapmaker, John Bartholomew & Sons, was on hand to sell their indispensable and unmistakeable touring maps. Although neither the Cyclists' Touring

Club nor the National Cyclists' Union were present, the latter organisation had held fancy dress dances in the RHS Halls since 1912. The New Hall was booked for a similar reunion dance on 15 February in 1936, and in 1937 Claud Butler of Manor Street, London, SW4 signed a contract for a New Year's Dance in the New Hall on 31 December 1937.

ABOVE *Photo of woman demonstrating a cycle on the F.H. Grubb Ltd stand at the 4th Annual Lightweight Cycle Show, held in the Lindley Hall on 26 October- 2 November 1935.*

FAR LEFT *Poster label of the 3rd Annual Lightweight Cycle Show, held in the Lindley Hall on 27 October- 3 November 1934.*

LEFT *Catalogue for the 3rd Annual Lightweight Cycling Exhibition, organised by J.E. Holdsworth of Cycling Exhibitions Ltd, 99 Lennard Road, Beckenham, Kent, held in the Lindley Hall on 27 October- 3 November 1934.*

Showbands and Dancing

At all of these increasingly popular reunions and dances, the dance bands of the day would be booked. However, the music provided at the 1934 Lightweight Cycling Exhibition was provided by Decca Gramophone Co. Ltd on vinyl! On the programme of music for the exhibition were: Lew Stone and his Band, Roy Fox and his Band, The Alfredo Campoli Grand Orchestra, The Band of HM Grenadier Guards, Lilly Geynes and 20 Hungaria Girls, the Hastings Municipal Orchestra, the Berlin State Opera Orchestra, and Don Rietto and his Accordion Band. This was not the full list! There were scores of bands playing in the big hotels, clubs and restaurants across London and the big cities. Jazz was the predominant sound, but many other styles of music were being offered that had come from America, through to Germany. One of the best remembered and most highly acclaimed bands were Ambrose and his Orchestra run by Bert Ambrose who often had one of the most remembered vocalists with him, Sam Browne. But there were many others such as Billy Cotton and his Band who would later host his own radio show, the Billy Cotton Band Show every Sunday afternoon on the BBC Light Programme from 1949 to 1968. Cotton's familiar voice started each show with the cry 'Wakey-Wake-aaaay!' followed by the band's signature tune 'Somebody Stole My Girl'. As a boy, I remember these well. The show also ran on BBC Television from 1956 until 1965, although not always under the same name. Regular entertainers included Alan Breeze, Kathie Kay, Doreen Stephens and the pianist Russ Conway.

Jack Hylton's Band also rated as one of Britain's greatest show bands of the 1920s and 1930s as did Cecil & Leslie Norman and their Orchestra. Stan Greening and his Band, Billy Bissett and his Orchestra and Alfredo and his Band were other prolific bands that, as well as being resident at venues and clubs such as *The Savoy*, *The Mayfair Hotel* and *The Kit Kat Club*, found time to play at ballrooms, variety theatres and venues such as the RHS. Radio helped to broadcast them, but for the masses, the prolific recording of these artists by record companies onto black vinyl were eagerly bought, and still lovingly sought after and played by enthusiasts of their music today. These bands and their vocalists were the pop stars of their day and, just like today, everyone could identify them from each other from their individual styles and sounds. They were also loved by a very wide spectrum of social classes and age groups, and on 16 February 1924 A Grand 'Blues Night' Carnival Dance and Free Competition took place in the Hall on behalf of the East London Combined Appeal in aid of the National Institute for the Blind, organised by the National Dance Tune Organisation, 30 Bolsover Street, London W. (44 years later, the RNIB used the Old Hall for their Centenary Exhibition on 20-1 May 1968, opened by HM The Queen). In 1908 the 'A' and 'B' Divisions of the Athletic Club of the Metropolitan Police had held their regular dances and social events in Lyons Restaurant, Victoria Street. They also used the Grosvenor Club, Grosvenor Hall at 200 Buckingham Palace Road which had first opened on 7 October 1905 advertising Cinderella Dances with tickets priced at 1s. 6d. From 1921 until 1934 their 'A', 'B', and 'C' Division Athletic Clubs held their annual dances

Brass pin badge for the Dance Tune Association (D.T.A.) who organised a Grand 'Blues Night' Carnival Dance and Free Competition, held in the Lindley Hall on 16 February 1924.

LEFT *Programme of a Grand Dance for the Metropolitan Police 'A' Division Athletic Club, held in the Lindley Hall on 2 April 1925. On the reverse of the card was listed the Dance Programme that acted as a dance card to book your partners.*

LEFT *Photo of Herbert Morrison and his wife dancing in the Royal Horticultural Hall during The London Labour Party Reunion and Dance, on 30 January 1937. Herbert Morrison acted as Secretary of The London Labour Party that was then based at 12 Tavistock Place, Russell Square, WC1.*

Rt. Hon. Herbert Morrison, M.P.,
British Cabinet Minister.

at the New Hall. A Dance Card shows 22 dances listed with an interval in between. You could enter alongside them under the word 'Engagements' who you had engaged to dance with and take your pick from numbers such as 'Close in my Arms', 'Irish Memories', 'Mandalay', 'Lassie', or 'I Wonder what's become of Sally'. Some of the other organisations to regularly hold their dances in the Halls during this period were the Combined Cavalry 'Old Comrades' Association who held the annual reunion dances from 1925 (after their formation in 1924) to 1938, the Strand Corner House (also famously known as Lyons Corner House), the London Gardeners' Guild, the Victoria Athletic Association of the Army & Navy Stores, the London Galloway Association (in aid of the funds of The Royal Caledonian Schools), the Royal Antediluvian Order of Buffaloes (who raised funds for ambulances during the war), Harrods Producers Club, the Vacuum Oil Company Ltd (based at Caxton House, Westminster that eventually became Mobil), The Mullard Radio Valve Co., The United Dairies Co. (The Youdees Sports Club), the Junior Imperial and Constitutional League (received by Mr and Mrs Stanley Baldwin and by Lord and Lady Stanley), Gorringes (the prestigious drapery store at 75 Buckingham Palace Road), the The Old Contemptibles Association in 1933 and the London Labour Party, whose Secretary was Herbert Morrison (Peter Mandelson's grandfather). The Independent Labour Party International Reception on 24 September 1924 had its own band, the West End I.L.P. Orchestra. They played a mixture of One Steps, Fox Trots, Waltzs, and Lancers with titles such as, 'Pasadena', 'When the lights are low', 'If all the girls', and, 'Just a girl that men forget'!

MIDDLESEX DANCERS CLUB

Telephone:
HAMpstead 6406.

Organising Secretary: LEN JONES,
17 Cumberland Mansions,
West End Lane,
London, N.W.6

25th., June, 1946.

The Secretary,
Royal Horticultural Society,
Vincent Square,
Westminster, S.W.1.

Dear Sir,

We have been requested to write to you with regard to the hire of the Royal Horticultural Hall.

As you are probably aware, the majority of halls in London which cater for dancing are mainly run for, or patronised by, those who wish to indulge in what is termed "jiving, jitterbugging and swing".

We, in common with all Dancers Clubs, are interested, and work for, the advancement of strict Ballroom Dancing, and there is a great need in London for a Hall which will cater for these people, and although we are aware that your Society does not at present hold a licence for public dances, we wonder if there is any possibility of your Society applying for such a licence.

If so, we wonder if we might be given the opportunity of hiring the Hall regularly every Saturday evening, and

If the question of applying for such a licence has not been considered, may we be allowed to ask your Society if they would consider this question.

We are fully prepared, and indeed would welcome, any suggestion that we organise such weekly dances in close co-operation with your Society in the following ways:-

(a). Submitting our suggestions for the exact type of entertainment and "attractions" to be presented each week. Our willingness to modify such proposals should the Society not be in full agreement with them. (This would especially apply to any occasion where we might suggest a 'non-dancing' attraction.

(b). That an agreed proportion of the profits be given to the Society.

We hope the above proposals will prove our sincerity not only to forward Ballroom Dancing, but our desire to ensure that the good name of your Hall shall not in any way lowered.

Looking forward to hearing from you,

Yours sincerely,

Len Jones

Organising Secretary.

So popular were these that after the Second World War, in June 1946, the Middlesex Dancers Club were prompted to write to the RHS about a tenancy invoking their 'interest in advancing 'strict ballroom dancing' as against jiving, jitterbugging and swing that would not lower the good name of your Hall.' It was a forlorn hope to expect that this would make a difference to gaining a tenancy. The 'tone' of the Halls had already been 'lowered' many times by its regular clients that demanded the new American influences and Middlesex would have to wait for 'Strictly Come Dancing' in 2004 to redress the balance!

In the 1940s and '50s one band that became much sought after and popular was Cyril Stapleton & His Show Band. In fact, several 'short' films depicting them were made by Hammer Films!! At that time, Hammer did not simply make horror movies, but also 29-minute 'B' films for showing in cinemas between the main features. One of these was shot in the RHS Old Hall on 24 February–5 March 1955, entitled 'Cyril Stapleton and the Show Band' with Lita Rosa, Ray Burns and Bill McGuffie. A second film, also directed by Michael Carreras, was made in CinemaScope late in 1955 distributed to Odeon Cinema circuits called 'Just For You', and this could also have been filmed in the Hall. It was hosted by Cyril Stapleton & His Show Band and featured Big Band Sounds with guest artists Joan Regan and Ronnie Harris. Ted Heath & His Orchestra was another popular band that certainly played in the Halls during this period. Stapleton had joined Henry Hall and his BBC band in 1931 and played with him during the band's first broadcast. His own band's first broadcast did not take place until 1939, preceded by a long period of time working with Jack Payne's Orchestra. He later worked with the Jack Hylton Orchestra for a short period of time. After the Second World War he returned to playing symphonic music and was a member of the Philharmonia Orchestra, the National Symphony Orchestra and the London Symphony Orchestra. By 1947 he went back again to playing dance music with his own band and took a residence at an old haunt of his, Fisher's Restaurant, in New Bond Street. One of his singers was Dick James, the man who later became the legendary publisher of The Beatles' music. However, it was not until 1952, when the BBC Dance Orchestra changed to become the BBC Show Band that Stapleton's career really took off. He was appointed its conductor and his band's signature tune began with the words, 'Just For You', hence the name of the second film. His BBC shows attracted major British singing stars, as well as international heavyweights such as Frank Sinatra and Nat 'King' Cole. Stapleton helped launch many performers and singers from obscurity, one of whom was Matt Monro.

Pigeon Fanciers, Racers and Pigeongrams

In 1937, another sport and serious pastime introduced itself into the RHS Halls that was to become as regular and popular as the dog shows that had gone before. On 6 and 7 January that year, the National Pigeon Association and Marking Conference Ltd, of 33 Head Street, Halstead, Essex, organised a 'Fancy Pigeon Show' in the New Hall. This was the start of series of regular events that were held in both Halls until 6 January 1996.

However, this was not the first time pigeons had featured so prominently in the Halls as we have already seen from what took place at APEX, the London International Air-Post Exhibition. The significance of this event to warrant pigeons taking centre stage was their role as the carrier of 'Pigeon Post' with the specially produced Souvenir 'Pigeongrams' printed on 'WING MAIL' paper made expressly thin for air-mail correspondence by James R. Crompton & Bros. Ltd of 2 Queenhithe, London, EC4. The pigeon was supplied by *The Racing Pigeon*, the leading pigeon fanciers and racers publication of its day. Mrs F. W. Kessler of New York also sent her own pigeongram in the same way to Dr Philip G. Cole to announce his Grand Gold Medal award, won as a result of his exhibit. As Lord Londonderry had made clear in his opening speech, 'One of the earliest ways in which messages were transmitted by air was not by machinery at all, but by pressing into the service of mankind the wonderful homing instinct of

RIGHT *Catalogue for The 'Victory' Show (of Racing Pigeons), organised by* The People, *held at the Lindley Hall on 6-7 December 1946.*

the pigeon. Pigeons have been employed for this purpose throughout the ages, but you will see here some peculiarly striking instances of their use, as for example the exhibit of messages which were flown by pigeons out of the beleaguered city of Metz, and out of Paris during the great siege of 1870. Each tiny pellicule, which was so light that it could be attached to the bird's tail feathers, held an average of no less than 3,000 messages, and you will see here many of these messages in their original form.'

Seventy years later, on 14 September 2004, during the Bicentenary year of the RHS, and the Centenary year of the original Royal Horticultural Hall, I stood on the same steps and released a pigeon with the following message of congratulations on attaining its Centenary, and the opening of a unique Centenary Exhibition I had organised: 'Congratulations to the Royal Horticultural Halls on the opening of its 'Halls of Fame' – A Century of Exhibitions and Events Exhibition, during the RHS Bicentenary Year'. The man who provided the pigeon and helped me with this fitting celebration was Rick Osman. It was also fitting that he was there, because Rick's grandfather, W.H. Osman, had founded *The Racing Pigeon* in 1898 and his father, Colin Osman, had also held the position of Editor at it. As such, they were all prominent figures in the pigeon fancier's and racer's world. All three members of the family had organised their important Racing Pigeon shows in the RHS Halls and elsewhere. Colin had also released 1,000 pigeons outside the Royal Albert Hall on the occasion of the National Federation of Women's Institute's jubilee on 1 January 1965, and organised The Pigeon Olympiad at Alexandra Palace in the same year, the first to be held in Britain.

So, after the first Pigeon Show had taken place in January 1937, a Bird Fancy and Aquaria Exhibition was staged in the New Hall on 2 to 4 December that same year organised by G.B. Marshall of The Marshall Press Ltd, Milford Lane, Strand, London, WC2. Two years later Britain was at war, and The Royal Pigeon Racing Association (RPRA) on its website highlights

---

THE
"VICTORY" SHOW
(of RACING PIGEONS)

organised by

The People

in aid of the

Hospital for Sick Children, Great Ormond Street, London, W.C.1

at

THE HORTICULTURAL HALL,
VINCENT SQUARE, LONDON, S.W.

FRIDAY and SATURDAY, DECEMBER 6th, & 7th, 1946

JUDGES :

Temple Bros., Scarborough	Class 1 and 36
Doctor T. H. Rigg, Southport	,, 2
G. Sharrock, Haskayne	,, 3 and 23
W/Cdr. W. D . Lea Rayner	,, 4
F. Challinor, Wolverhampton	,, 5
W. T. Calver, Colchester	,, 6 and 31
J. Cheetham, Congleton	,, 7
E. C. Hardy, Weymouth	,, 8
S. A. Moon, Haywards Heath	,, 9 and 22
W. G. Burdett, Sheffield	,, 10
T. Millar, Alloa	,, 11 and 33
E. W. Steele, Sandringham	,, 12 and 32
J. Pitt Plymouth	,, 13
J. S. Hartridge, Leicester	,, 14 and 17
Norman Nickalls, Newmarket	,, 15
D. J. Morley, Port Talbot	,, 16
W. E. H. Dickin, Ellesmere	,, 18 and 34
Mrs. K. Tweddell, Tottenham	,, 19 and 20
Rudolf Ovesen and Rob Juul, Denmark ...	,, 21
J. W. Paulger, Staines	,, 24 and 25
Capt. J. S. Thompson, Denham	,, 26 and 27
F. W. Marriott, Birmingham	,, 28 and 29
Capt. J. Craiger, Tottenham	,, 30 and 35

NORMAN NICKALLS will Judge Birds for all Specials.

OFFICIAL CATALOGUE   1/- Each.

Show Secretary:
R. Ingham, "The People," 222/5, Strand, London, W.C.2.

NOTE:—The whole of the expenses in connection with the organising and running of the Show are paid by "The People." Each entry, each ticket, each donation, is a direct contribution to the Hospital and is handed over in the name of Racing Pigeon Fanciers of Great Britain.

the importance of the use of pigeons during the War as follows:

'At the outbreak of the War thousands of Britain's pigeon fanciers gave their pigeons to the war effort to act as message carriers. During the period of the war nearly a quarter of a million birds were used by the army, the RAF and the Civil Defence Services including the police, the fire service, Home Guard and even Bletchley Park. Pigeon racing was stopped, and birds of prey along the coasts of Britain were culled so that British pigeons could arrive home unhindered by these predators. There were tight controls on the keeping of pigeons and even rationing for pigeon corn. Homing pigeons were used not only in Western Europe by British forces, but also by American, Canadian, and German forces in other parts of the world during the war – Italy, Greece, North Africa, India and the Middle and Far East. One pigeon, GI Joe, saved the lives of thousands of British troops who were preparing to take an Italian town after the US Air Force had bombarded the Germans. However, the British forces found no resistance from the Germans and so entered the town unchallenged. Unfortunately the USAF was already en route to bomb the town, and with radio contact broken, GI Joe flew over a mile a minute (60 mph) back to the base. He arrived back just in time for the air raid to be called off before the USAF would have bombed our troops. All RAF bombers and reconnaissance aircraft carried pigeons and, if the aircraft had to ditch, the plane's co-ordinates were sent back with the pigeon to its RAF base, and a search and rescue operation was effected. Thousands of servicemen's lives were saved by these heroic birds that flew often in extreme circumstances. During the Second World War homing pigeons were seconded into the National Pigeon Service from Britain's fanciers, including one from the Royal Lofts. In fact one pigeon, Royal Blue, was the first pigeon to bring a message from a force-landed aircraft on the continent. On 10 October 1940 this young bird was released in Holland. He flew 120 miles in four hours 10 minutes reporting the information regarding the situation of the crew. After the war, the Dickin Medal was

instituted. Commonly known as the Animal VC, it was awarded to 53 animals including 32 homing pigeons including Royal Blue. Pigeons carried their messages either in special message containers on their legs, or small pouches looped over their backs. Quite often pigeons were dropped by parachute in containers to Resistance workers in France, Belgium and Holland. This was often quite precarious as it was a bumpy landing and very dangerous for the Resistance workers if they were caught with a British pigeon. Aircrew carried their pigeons in special watertight baskets and containers, in case the aircraft had to ditch into the sea. Pigeon lofts were built at RAF and army bases, but the mobile lofts had to be constructed so that they could move easily over land.'

Then on 26 and 27 January 1940 the national newspaper, *The People*, sponsored the first of many 'Victory' Racing Pigeon Shows in aid of the Great Ormond Street Hospital for Sick Children, The Children's Society

BELOW *Letter from W.H. Osman, Editor and Managing Director of The Racing Pigeon Publishing Co. Ltd, to the RHS, dated 27 June 1947, requesting a tenancy for a Pigeon Show on 8-10 January 1948.*

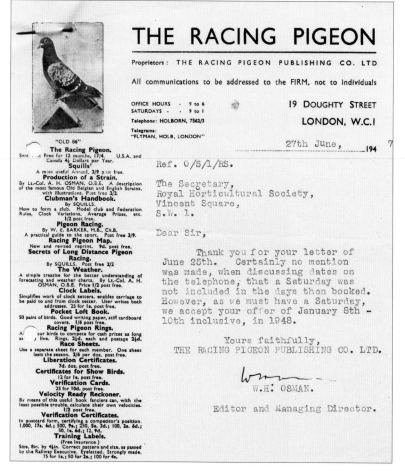

(the latter had originally been formed as The Church of England Incorporated Society for Providing Homes for Waifs & Strays, and had booked an early event in the Hall on 30 May 1916) and other charitable causes in the Old Hall. This Show took place only 'on the understanding that *The People* made the necessary arrangements with Messrs Edgingtons (also well known as flag makers) for the black-out of the Society's Old Hall and entrance, satisfactory to the Police wartime regulations.' It was also at this show that Sir Edward Campbell, acting in his capacity as PPS to Sir Kingsley Wood, Secretary of State for Air, announced that the government would remove their earlier ban on pigeon racing. In 2007, the British Parliament also banned pigeons racing from the mainland of continental Europe to Britain because of the risk of bird flu.

Just after the War, *The Racing Pigeon* organised the first of many of its own shows in the Old Hall, and this one took place on 11 and 12 January 1946. These shows also raised funds, specifically for the renowned Star & Garter Home for Disabled Soldiers, Sailors and Airmen on Richmond Hill in Surrey.

Pigeon Racing has long been a traditional sport of Royal family's and as the RPRA reminds us, 'both the Prince of Wales and Duke of York maintained teams of racing pigeons at Sandringham, and raced them successfully in both local and national events, and this continued when the Duke of York became King. The family tradition is maintained by our present monarch, Queen Elizabeth II, and the Royal Lofts are now well established at Sandringham'. Both the Kings of Belgium and Thailand were also enthusiastic racers in their day. The *Daily Express* reported in its 5 December 1964 edition that

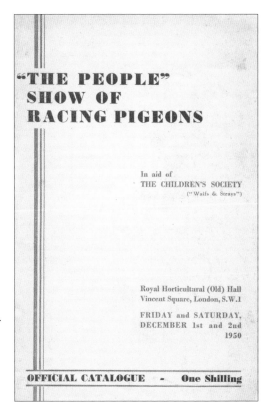

a pair of HM The Queen's birds had been entered into *The People*'s International Racing Pigeon Show in the Hall the day before, together with one owned by President Tito of Yugoslavia, and another from Prince Bernhard of the Netherlands. The Queen's Loft Manager was there as a show judge. Neither won, as it was a German bird that pipped all of these royal entrants to the prize! At the same show two years later, when funds were raised for The Children's Society, a similar disappointment was reported by *The Times* when four pigeons from the Queen's lofts were also beaten, this time by a Welsh entrant, out of more than 2,000 entries. Princess Alexandra opened *The Racing Pigeon*'s 'Old Comrades Show' in December 1969. As Patron of the Star and Garter Home, she met their President, governors and senior officers and also Colin Osman who, as *The Racing Pigeon*'s Editor, proudly announced that more than £18,500 (£236,060) had been raised to date, and that he expected to reach £20,000 for the Home by the end of the show. The Royal Loft manager and presidents of the major clubs in which HM The Queen flew her pigeons were also

LEFT *Photo of British and International Judges at* The People *International Show of Racing Pigeons, held in the Lawrence Hall on 2 December 1960.*

BELOW *Photo of Prizewinners at* The People *International Show of Racing Pigeons, held in the Lawrence Hall on 2 December 1960.*

RIGHT *Results Card for The 'Racing Pigeon' Old Comrades Show, held in the Lawrence Hall on 5-6 December 1969. HRH Princess Alexandra, opened the show that raised funds for the Star and Garter Home, Richmond, Surrey.*

THE "RACING PIGEON"
OLD COMRADES SHOW
Patron: H.R.H. Princess Alexandra

HORTICULTURAL HALL, 5th and 6th December, 1969

SIXTH

Class No. 22   Pen No. 3301
Ring No. RP 68 SG 509

Ron Bissett   Secretary

"OLD 86"

BELOW *Photo of The 'Racing Pigeon' Old Comrades Show, held in both Halls on 30 November-1 December 1985.*

present, as were representatives of the foreign judges and the secretaries of the International Federation and British Confederation.

Not so auspicious an occasion was their 5 December 1984 'Old Comrades Show' that, by then, had grown in size to take up both Halls. The *Daily Mirror* reported, 'Man rips off bird's head'. They went on to report that, 'A man tore the head off a live pigeon at a charity auction. Hundreds of bird lovers – including children

THE RACING PIGEON
OLD COMRADES SHOW

BEST IN SHOW 1984
SG83 00841, Wales 83S 1081, Shown by Eddie Gale of Brynna.

THE ROYAL HORTICULTURAL HALLS,
LONDON

SATURDAY, 30th NOVEMBER, 1985
SUNDAY, 1st DECEMBER, 1985

In aid of the Royal Star and Garter Home
for Disabled Ex-Soldiers, Sailors and Airmen, Richmond.

OFFICIAL CATALOGUE
WITH A FULL LIST OF ENTRANTS

75p.

collected its pedigree he began cursing. One official said: He kept screaming that he had been conned – which was completely untrue.' The man, who was not named, faced a disciplinary hearing by the Royal Pigeon Racing Association.

By 1985, the RPRA claimed that there were more than 3,000 racing pigeon clubs in the UK, with nearly a quarter of a million members. During the season, it was claimed that there could be as many as a million birds in the sky at one time. And large sums of money (up to £25,000 at that time) were paid for those birds that had proven pedigrees, and could be bred to produce winners. The major breeders of the day were investing in vast stud farms, especially in Norfolk, and these were reputed to be worth millions. Racing speeds from 30 mph to 70 mph were the norm, but some spectacular achievements had been recorded. 500 miles at 88 mph had been achieved in South Africa by one bird, but the world record was claimed by Sweden with a flight of 751 miles between dawn and dusk. The longest race in the world of over 1,000 miles was from Spain and Scotland and took five days.

– watched in horror as the bird fluttered round the stage, spurting blood, for several moments before it died. The man had just paid £30 (£74.70) for the pigeon ... but when he

Catalogue for The 'Racing Pigeon' Old Comrades Show, held in both Halls on 30 November-1 December 1985.

VII

More War – More Change

The Second World War had been declared on 3 September 1939, and almost all shows that had been booked in following this had to be cancelled, including the Society of British Aircraft Constructors who hoped to stage an exhibition of light plastic materials of aircraft parts. The *Battle of Britain* then took place less than three months from this intended event. However, from January 1940 some shows did take place, on the express understanding that they could meet the black-out conditions that had been imposed in London at that time. The 72nd Crystal Palace National Show of Cage Birds became the 1st National Cage Birds Show, organised by Cage and Aviary Birds and was held on 8-10 February raising funds for the Lord Mayor's Red Cross & St John Fund for the Sick and Wounded in the War. He attended on the second day and must have been delighted at the £10,000 raised as a result. The RHS planned to hold their own fundraising Sale for the same Fund on 24 to 26 September that same year but, in the event, it had to be held by post. This Sale resulted in the

papers of the distinguished garden designer, Gertrude Jekyll, being acquired for an American library. Significantly perhaps, a Concrete Hutting Exhibition also took place on 3 May 1940, organised by the Cement and Concrete Association. This must have been related to the War Effort and the need for protective and defensive concrete hutting structures throughout the land. Then in December 1940, the first of three occasions when bombs damaged the Halls took place. On this occasion a bomb nearly blew out the glass and doors on the Elverton Street frontage of the New Hall. In September 1941, the second bomb damage occurred to the New Hall, undoing all previous repairs from the first time it had been hit. The third bomb landed in June 1944 and resulted in damage to both Halls. The gable end of the Old Hall had to be rebuilt after the War, at a cost of over £4,000 (£126,840). This was when the distinctive 'Minstrel's Gallery' original feature was lost forever. Only a few photos taken during the Badminton Association's 'All England' Championships and several other early events have recorded this for us. From 1 October 1942, the Halls were occupied by the Territorial Army and Air Force Association of the County of London, the 193rd (101 LON.)

CATALOGUE
OF
THE ROYAL HORTICULTURAL
SOCIETY'S
RED CROSS SALE.

*The Royal Horticultural Society's Hall
Vincent Square London S.W.
Sept 24ᵗ 25ᵗ and 26ᵗ 1940.
This Catalogue admits to The Sale*

ABOVE LEFT
*Catalogue for the
fundraising Red Cross
Sale, organised by the
Royal Horticultural
Society, with a cover
designed by Oliver
Messel, to be held in
the Lindley Hall on
24-6 September 1940;
in the event was held
by post due to the
outbreak of the Second
World War.*

BELOW   *Letter from
H.L.M. Carter of
Poultry World, dated
2 August 1945, to Lt.
Col. F.R. Durham,
Secretary of the RHS,
concerning tenancy
details for the National
(Red Cross) Poultry
Show and the National
(Red Cross) Exhibition
of Cage Birds in the
Halls later that year.*

THE NATIONAL (RED CROSS) POULTRY SHOW
ROYAL HORTICULTURAL (New) HALL WESTMINSTER
IN AID OF THE RED CROSS AGRICULTURE FUND.
OCTOBER 24th-25th, 1945
Organised by "POULTRY WORLD," DORSET HOUSE, STAMFORD STREET, LONDON, S.E.I.
Telephone : WATerloo 3313
Telegrams : POULTANBIR, SEDIST, LONDON.

Organising Committee :
R. W. HADDON, C.B.E., Chairman
LORD GREENWAY, Deputy Chairman
Miss EUNICE L. KIDD
H. J. ANTHONY
H. D. BARLEY
F. W. BATCHELOR
R. BOTLOM
A. L. M. CARTER
N. H. FOX-BROCKBANK
W. E. GOLDING
KENNETH TH HAWKEY
G. P. ISHERWOOD
S. A. LEGG
Miss IAN MACDOUGALL
C. G. MAY
W. POWELL-OWEN
W. H. SILK
JIM SUTTON

HLMC/F/PW

2nd August, 1945

Lt.-Col. F. R.Durham, C.B.E., M.C.,
Royal Horticultural Society,
Vincent Square,
S.W.1.

Dear Col. Durham,

Re: National (Red Cross) Poultry Show
Oct. 24th & 25th and National (Red Cross)
Exhibition of Cage Birds, Nov.1st, 2nd & 3rd.

I enclose a copy of a letter I have received
from Mr. R. J. Reeves of Messrs. Beck & Pollitzer Ltd,
regarding his interview with Mr. Laker of the L.C.C.

Might I ask you to be so kind as to approach
the L.C.C. asking if they will, for the reasons stated
in Mr. Reeves' letter, waive the rules regarding the
fireproofing of stands provided the latter are heavily
treated with distemper.

Yours truly,

(H.L.M.Carter)
"POULTRY WORLD"

ALL COMMUNICATIONS TO DORSET HOUSE, STAMFORD STREET, LONDON, S.E.I

A.A. Battery, R.A. Home Guard. They were there to undertake anti-aircraft training, and, unlike during the First World War, the Halls were not requisitioned by the M.O.D. but let out commercially to them. This was on the understanding that it was 'subject to one month's notice on either side, and to be given only after the declaration of an Armistice or the end of the hostilities'. During almost all of December, both Halls were additionally used for Christmas postal sorting.

After the War, from January 1946, there was renewed vigour and hope, even though the country was suffering from post-war trauma, rationing and bomb sites were common in many cities. I remember them well in the 1950s when I was a boy, and also the disabled soldiers selling matchboxes and cigarettes on street corners. However, another spate of Championship Dog Shows were held, that displayed a continued reliance on our four-legged friends. A wide variety of breeds was paraded that included The Associated Sheep, Police & Army Dog Society, the English Shetland Sheepdog Club, the Afghan Hound Association, the United St Bernard Club and the British Chow Chow Club, among many others.

Trade Fairs and Exhibitions

In keeping with the traditional nature of how exhibitions are developed, there were those that were created to meet new demands, and those that grew out of these. The classic example given of the former is the Building Trades Exhibition started by Hugh Greville Montgomery, MP, at Earl's Court in 1895. This not only developed very successfully in its own right, leading to 'Interbuild' in the 1970s, and claimed by the still independent Montgomery Worldwide Group to be the largest specialised industrial trade show in Britain, but it is also true to say that it spawned a large number of even more specialised offshoots. The latter is certainly also true of Marshall's equally successful Model Engineer Show that spawned The Woodworker Show, in its own right, launched in

both RHS Halls on 6-10 November 1979. Another 10 exhibitions that were launched in the RHS Halls could easily have been direct offshoots from Montgomery's. These were, ROOFTECH, organised by the National Federation of Roofing Contractors; Flooring & Finishes; FENCEX; Wallpaper, Paint & Decorative Traders Fair; Decorative Lighting; European Do-It-Yourself Trade Fair; Natural Contract Furnishing & Interior Decorating; Manufacturing Boards & Decorative Surfaces; Hardware Trades Fair; Timber Build Exhibition organised by Industrial Trade Fairs; Commercial Flooring, and the Partitioning & Suspended Ceilings Industry Exhibition. Montgomery did also use the RHS for his Rubber Goods Exhibition, opened by Princess Louise, Duchess of Argyll, in the New Hall that ran from 30 November to 11 December 1928. An International Rubber & Allied Trades Exhibition had first been booked in the Old Hall on 21-6 September 1908 but, due to the event oversubscribing, it relocated to Olympia, and the RHS claimed £100 (£8,846) compensation for the cancellation, a not inconsiderable sum to lose in those days.

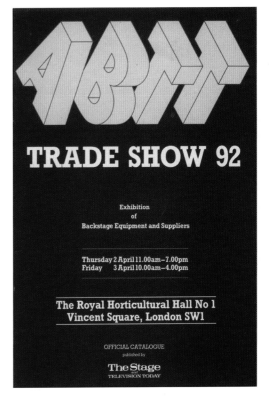

RIGHT *Catalogue for the Association of British Theatre Technicians (ABTT) Trade Fair, held in the Lindley Hall on 2-3 April 1992.*

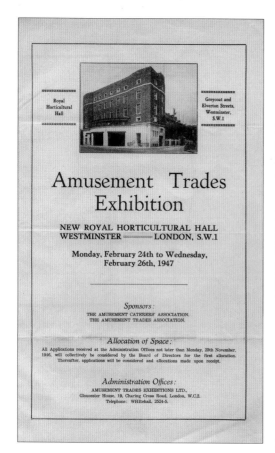

FAR LEFT *Invitation for applications from exhibitors to the 3rd Amusement Trades Exhibition, to be held at the Lawrence Hall on 24-6 February 1947.*

LEFT *Poster label for the Amusement Trades Exhibition, held in the Lawrence Hall on 6-8 March 1956.*

brightly coloured roundabouts and dodgems alternatively titled, 'Alice in Funland'); the Engineering Industries Association Exhibition; the British Carpet Exhibition; the Clothing Trade Factory Equipment and Accessories Exhibition; the London Dental Trades Exhibition, and the Optical Trade Exhibition (organised by the Association of Wholesale Manufacturing Opticians) were other new trade shows that took place in one or both Halls; the latter opened by Sir Alexander Fleming. The 39th Annual Exhibition of The Institute of Physics and The Physical Society Scientific Instruments & Apparatus was held for the first time in the New Hall on 25-8 April 1955. This ran until their 48th exhibition in January 1964, by which time they were using both Halls. These exhibitions covered spectacular achievements in atomic energy, space flight, and the electronic 'brain' among other subjects. The Oil and Colour Chemist's Association was formed in 1918, and staged an annual 'Technical Exhibition' that displayed the raw materials and equipment used in the paint, varnish and printing ink industries. This also highlighted the advances in materials, equipment and technology by suppliers with their consumers. They used the RHS Halls between 1954 and 1964 for their 6th-16th exhibitions.

The Shipwrights Exhibition; the 1st Welsh Industries Fair; the Gauge & Tool Makers Association Exhibition; the Amusement Devices and Trades Exhibition (for the latter the Hall was transformed into a funfair full of

LEFT *Poster label for the 6th London Regional Display of Products, Processes and Services of the Engineering Industry, organised by the Engineering Industries Association, held in the Lawrence Hall on 13-15 October 1953.*

Baking Trade Exhibitions have been held at the Halls since 10 January 1914 when the Hovis Bread Competition was staged, another good example of the splintering effect from larger exhibitions, as baking and bread were always represented at the early Universal Cookery & Food Exhibitions. In 1924 the first of 14 annual London Master Bakers and Confectionery Protection Society Exhibitions took place. The name, once again, reflects the protectionist culture that prevailed during this period, and immediately after the War. They resumed again in 1948 until 1952, this time organised by Mclaren & Sons. I have no record of these continuing until 1971 when they were then organised by the National Association of Master Bakers with the last one in our Halls taking place in October 1979 – a good run, nevertheless.

The 1960s was a period when young people kicked against the establishment and refused to accept what their parents had endured before. The exhibitions and events that were held, gave some indications to these changing times and the increased wealth and expectations from a new generation. Tastes for food, music, and fashion changed. New hobbies and pastimes also became fashionable and the world got smaller with the advent of cheaper air travel. DIY suddenly became necessary and concentration on the improvement of the home, all important and absorbing. Automation was sweeping in and computerisation with it. The 1st International Automatic Vending Machine Exhibition that started on 2-5 November 1959 was there to show us how easy it was to get Coca Cola from a machine at a railway station or at the airport at any time of the night or day. The 1st National Delicatessen Exhibition, started on 20-4 March 1961, told us that it was 'OK' to like salami and that we should cook with olive oil. There must have been strong approval as it ran for 19 years, eventually becoming DELEX '79, organised by Fairs & Exhibitions Ltd, 21 Park Square East, Regent's Park, London. The 1st Wallpaper, Print & Decorating Trades Fair ensured that the DIY retailers of the day would

be able to provide the most up-to-date patterns of wallpaper, prints and decorating 'gizmos' for us to renovate and redecorate our hitherto tawdry homes. Similarly the 1st Flooring & Finishes Exhibition, the Decorative Lighting Fair and Manufacturing Boards & Decorative Surfaces Exhibition together with the European Do-It-Yourself Fair would all help to improve the end result. In this new age of excess wealth and leisure time the Bookmakers' and Betting Shop Equipment Exhibition was there to improve the seedy Bookies' shops and

LEFT *Two poster labels for the Advertising Exhibition, organised by* The Advertising World/Weekly, *held in the Lindley Hall on 9-14 December 1912.*

LEFT *Photo of National Skateboard Trade Show, showing the 'King' of skateboards made by Thompson Sports that weighed 160 lbs, was 27 times the volume of a standard skateboard and cost £1,200. The Show was organised by Trades Exhibitions, Spring House, London, W2, held in both Halls, on 12-15 February 1978.*

RIGHT *Photo of In-Store Marketing Exhibition, organised by Centaur Exhibitions, held in the Lawrence Hall, c.1998.*

BELOW RIGHT *Poster label for HEATEX67, held in both Halls on 18-22 June 1967.*

BELOW *Poster label of the National Display Exhibition, organised by the Blandford Press, held in both Halls, on 20-4 September 1954.*

turn them into respectable establishments that could entice new clients. Promotions and incentives were becoming increasingly recognised tools for employers and businesses. The Premium Promotions & Sales Incentives Exhibition on 23-5 May 1967 in the New Hall was a small event by comparison with the many that would follow throughout the next 30 years, but the Advertising Exhibition, organised by *The Advertising World*, had been held in the Hall as early as 9-12 December 1912. In 1927, the London Advertising Exhibition & Convention was held in Olympia on 18-23 July 1927 (and strangely, the New Health Society had a stand there, although the connection must have been due to the fact that it was the Dorland Advertising Agency that organised the NHS shows). The First National Exhibition of Commercial Display organised by J. Ernest Cheetham was held in the RHS Hall on 22 May-3 June 1922, but that didn't prevent the same claim being made when the 1st National Display Exhibition and Convention organised by Blandford Press took place in both Halls on 20-4 September 1954.

With the advent of increasingly regular overseas travel to cheap European destinations such as Spain and Portugal, those with the means and inclination started to buy and develop homes in these emerging countries. Therefore, a new need was created and Michael Furnell created the New Homes Show (later to become the International New Homes Show)

on the back of his magazine, the *Homefinder and Homes Overseas*. He had started this show in 1956 in Westminster Central Hall and it first came to us in 1968, staying until 1979.

The RHS Halls, as I have mentioned before, have always been important seedbeds for new trade exhibitions and consumer shows. We have already heard of several that grew to become major international events, but a few more are also noteworthy. The National Aids for the Disabled Exhibition (NAIDEX) started by Naidex Conventions Ltd, 36 High Street, Sevenoaks, Kent, began life in the New Hall on 9-12 November 1977. It continues to this

National Display Exhibition

Royal Horticultural Society's New Hall Westminster S.W.1.

September 20 - 24

WE ARE EXHIBITING

Visit the Industrial Process Heating Exhibition

HEATEX 67

Royal Horticultural Halls Westminster SW1

June 19-22   Daily 10-6

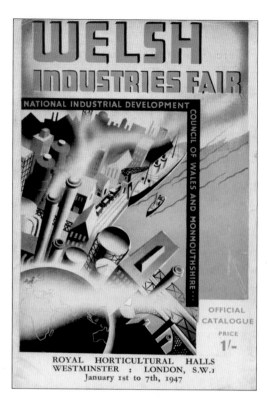

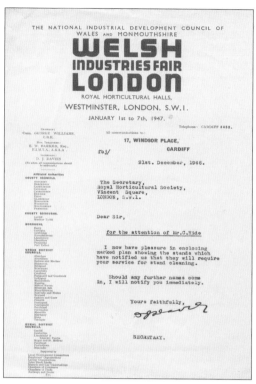

FAR LEFT   *Catalogue
for the Welsh Industries
Fair, organised by The
National Industrial
Development
Council of Wales and
Monmouthshire,
held in both Halls, on
29 December 1946-
12 January 1947.*

LEFT   *Letter from
D.J. Davies, Secretary
of the Welsh Industries
Fair to the Secretary
of the RHS, dated
21 December 1946,
concerning cleaning
arrangements for their
Fair in both Halls.*

day with not only a national show at the NEC, Birmingham, but one at London's ExCel that started in 2010. The 1st Christian Resources Exhibition, also still going strong nationally and regionally with exhibitions at Sandown Park, Telford and Peterborough, started in both halls on 6-9 February 1985. It was organised by Gospatrick Home of Argus Specialist Exhibitions Ltd, 1 Park View Road, Berkhamsted, Herts. He would come back to the Halls on 14-18 October to launch Research '96 (a joint partnership project with Centaur Exhibitions) in Hall 2, and had also been the man behind the launch of The Woodworker and Craft in Action in 1979 with his company Model & Allied Publications Ltd.

In 1965 Mack-Brooks Exhibitions Ltd began its own extraordinary development before becoming the Mack Brooks Exhibition Group it now is, organising international trade fairs and 'business to business' events and conferences around the World. On 11-14 February 1979 they launched the International Knitwear Fair in both Halls. This was an early precursor to the now also national and regional Knitting and Stitching Shows, now organised by Creative Exhibitions Ltd. However, the British Hosiery & Knitwear

Exhibition that was held in the New Hall on 29 February- 4 March 1960 was an even earlier version upon which future models were based. More recently, the first of several 'I Knit Day' knitting shows took place in the Hall on 6 September 2008. Then on 6-8 June 1978, the International Print Fair was launched in the New Hall by Brintex then still jointly owned by the Thomson Organisation and the Hemming Group, both heavily involved in publishing. Brintex are now one of the UK's leading exhibition organising companies with its flagship event, the London International Wine Fair taking place annually at ExCel. Finally, the Label, Labelling, Markings & Identification Industry Exhibition (LABELEX), organised for the first time by Labelex Ltd, 41 Southborough Road, Bickley, Kent in the Old Hall on 21-3 May 1980, has become LABELEXPO Europe claiming to be, 'The greatest label show on Earth' in 2009 with 24,169 visitors from 125 countries, now organised by the Tarsus Group.

Although Britain had won the Second World War, it was left in a depleted and exhausted state. For Wales, this was seen as an opportunity to regroup and represent what it could offer post-war for the benefit of

ABOVE   *Pin badge
to commemorate the
Coronation of Their
Majesties King George V
and Queen Mary.*

RIGHT   *Catalogue for
The Worshipful Company
of Shipwrights Exhibition,
and a Redheads leaflet
adverting their stand
No.18 at it, held in both
Halls, on 28 January-
8 February 1947.*

its people, its enterprises and its future. This manifested itself in the first Welsh Industries Fair to be organised and showcased in London. Previous Fairs, before the war, had always taken place in Cardiff. This took place in both of the RHS Halls from 1-7 January 1947. Organised by the National Industrial Development Council of Wales and Monmouthshire under the Chairmanship of Councillor George Williams, C.B.E., the Fair proved to be a huge success. *The Times* reported the day after the Fair had closed that 'Attendance exceeded 39,000 [over the seven days], and buyers came from all five continents'. They went on to say that, 'home and overseas orders totalled about £5,000,000'. Cllr Williams was so pleased with the results that he announced there would be a series of similar fairs throughout the United Kingdom, 'and we shall return to London before very long'.

Ships and Shipbuilding

In 1947, The Worshipful Company of Shipwrights was one of 78 City of London Companies or City Guilds, and the second largest in terms of membership. Its Permanent Master was King George VI, whose life had been steeped in the Royal Navy from boyhood, having served on a succession of men-of-war. Its desire to stage a Shipwrights Exhibition, only the third in its history, immediately following the Second World War, was clearly explained by Walter Pollock, Chairman of its Exhibition Committee in the Introduction to their Brochure and Catalogue. He said, 'It is appropriate that this exhibition should be held at the close of the Second World War which could not have been won without British designed, British built, British manned and British managed ships – upwards of 7,000 of them'. However, during the six years of the Battle of the Seas, about half the liners, numbering 1,300, were sunk. He went on to say, 'The exhibition is intended to reflect the enormous strides made in British ship construction for the Mercantile Marine throughout the World in general and in this country in particular, and for the Royal Navy.' However, one of the principal objectives of the exhibition was also to 'encourage young men of this country to take an interest in the art of naval architecture and the craft of shipbuilding.' To that end, several thousand free admission tickets were issued to apprentices and students. The Royal Horticultural Halls were chosen as the venue for this with the Old Hall serving as the Shipowners Hall and the New Hall serving as the Shipbuilders Hall.

For the RHS this was a major exhibition, the magnitude and importance of it not seen since the Universal Cookery & Food Association's first exhibition. Here, every major ship owner from the distinctive Cunard White Star, the Furness Lines (that included Houlder and Shaw Savill) to P&O, Orient Steam Navigation, Blue Funnel and British India Steam Navigation Co. were there. Representing the Shipwrights were the giants of shipbuilding from Thorneycroft of Southampton, John Redhead of South Shields, Swan, Hunter & Wigham Richardson of Newcastle-on-Tyne, Vospers of Portsmouth, Short Bros of Sunderland, Vickers-Armstrong of Barrow-in-Furness, Cammell Laird of Birkenhead, and John Brown of Clydebank, to name but a few. Charles Melville McLaren, 3rd Baron Aberconway, was a director of John Brown & Co. from 1939-85, Chairman from 1953-78, and President from 1978-85. He would later become the 14th President of the Royal Horticultural Society from 1961-84, but from 1931-53 his father, Henry Duncan McLaren, 2nd Baron Aberconway, had served as the 12th RHS President and had been Chairman of John Brown & Co. In 1927, he had also published a book entitled *The Basic Industries of Great Britain: Coal; iron; steel; engineering; ships. An historic and economic survey.* Once again, it is more than tempting to speculate that Charles had spoken to his father when he knew that the Shipwrights were looking for a venue for their exhibition in, even though he was not on the Exhibition Committee. However, a List of Supporters in the Show Brochure & Catalogue does credit John Brown, BSc, Marine Engineer, as being one of them. Other supporters listed also show

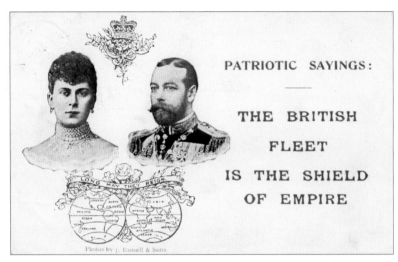

PATRIOTIC SAYINGS:

THE BRITISH
FLEET
IS THE SHIELD
OF EMPIRE

Photos by J. Russell & Sons.

the strong connections between this event and others staged in the Halls. The Gas Light & Coke Company was one, and Percival Marshall (listed as Editorial Authority) was another. Marshall didn't have a stand, but one of his most important exhibitors at his Model Engineer Exhibitions – Bassett-Lowke, Modelmakers of Northampton – did, and a great number of exhibits at the Shipwrights show were working models. The present-day website of '78 Derngate' that commemorates W.J. Bassett-Lowke, where he lived from 1917 makes it clear that 'he had begun making 'waterline' ship models in 1908. This type of model showing only the parts above the waterline was used in wartime as training aids for the Navy and Air Force. Yachts were also made to sail on boating lakes. Large shipping companies commissioned models of their luxury liners to display in their offices. Miniature railways were made for wealthy individuals and for exhibitions and resorts. The skilled model maker E.W. Twining formed Twining Models Ltd, which produced the highest quality architectural models with Bassett-Lowke Ltd.

In the 1914-18 war Bassett-Lowke Ltd made the gauges which tested the standard parts of guns. During the 1939-45 war a great variety of work was done. A method of training for aircraft recognition using mirrors was devised, and they produced training models of the sectional Inglis and later Bailey bridges. Perhaps the most important construction of this nature was the model of the floating Mulberry harbour, which was used to land troops in Normandy

Patriotic postcard pronouncing, 'The British Fleet is the Shield of Empire'. King George V was often referred to as 'Our Sailor King'. Both he and Queen Mary were Royal Patrons of the RHS; King George from 1910-36 and Queen Mary from 1910-53.

in 1944. Today, 78 Derngate, Northampton is not only open to the public to visit as the home of Bassett-Lowke, but for its renowned Rennie Mackintosh designs that were ordered by Bassett-Lowke for his revolutionary new house when he moved into it in 1926. I have to claim more than a passing interest in this house, as I knew it well between 1959 and 1979 when I lived exactly opposite it at *The Derngate Hotel* which my parents ran at that time.

Returning to the Shipwrights Exhibition, one of its other supporters was listed as the Gauge & Toolmakers' Association, and they had launched their first trade show in the New Hall one year earlier from 7-18 January. The Shipwrights Exhibition was opened by the Lord Mayor of London on 28 January and ran until 8 February. Sir Stafford Cripps, President of the Board of Trade, and other members of the government were present, as well as a large representation of the governments and shipping and shipbuilding industries of many countries. Underlying the event was an understated fear that Britain could lose its way and position as the hitherto undisputed leading naval force in the world if it didn't plan for the future, reposition and move forward. Unfortunately, the fact that the New Hall roof leaked badly at this event could not have helped that process. English Steel Corporation wrote to the RHS on 5 February 1947 reporting that 'the roof above our Stand has sprung a leak and a certain amount of water is dripping down on to our exhibits. We understand that arrangements have been made with the stand fitters, or other appropriate authority to repair this at the earliest moment, and shall be glad if you would let us have your confirmation that this matter has been attended to promptly as we are naturally anxious that our models should not be damaged in any way.' It's a letter that sends shivers down my spine when I read it because there have been many occasions when I recall that same roof failing, when water has come dripping onto stand holders underneath akin to some form of water torture.

On a more positive note to end this mariner's tale, Mr Christopher Cockerell, the British inventor of the Hovercraft, used the same Hall on 3 December 1964 when the 'Everyone By Hovercraft Exhibition' was staged. Working models of proposed 300 mph monorail hovercrafts were displayed, as well as land-based hovercrafts that would mimic those already being used on water. The Reception following the Centenary of the Royal Navy Submarine Service held at Westminster Abbey, at which the Duke of Edinburgh was present, was also held in this Hall on 2 November 2001. The International Maritime Organisation (IMO), the only UN executive agency based in the UK, and whose primary responsibility is the safety of ships, security, and the prevention of marine pollution from ships, also booked the renamed Lindley Hall for its plenary sessions and meetings in 2007 and 2008 while its South Bank Headquarters opposite the Houses of Parliament were being refurbished.

Darts Championships

Six months earlier, another major sporting event came to the RHS that was widely followed by the many who packed the Old Hall to watch. This was *The People* National Darts Teams Championship competing for the Lord Lonsdale Challenge Trophy fought between many pub teams from around the country. This first took place in July 1946 and stayed for the next seven years. *The People* had already enjoyed a very long and successful relationship with the RHS Halls via their Pigeon Shows, so it was natural they looked to the RHS again for a new series of events for them. During the 1948-9 Championship, nearly 30,000 men and women travelled by road and rail to follow the fortunes of their favourite teams. Famous entertainers such as Tessie O'Shea, with her trade mark Banjolele and song, 'Two Ton Tessie from Tennessee', and Jack Warner, then at the height of his stage and screen career, having just appeared in the film *The Blue Lamp* as PC George Dixon, entertained during the intervals. Odhams, the publishers of *The People*, rolled out their very own Odhams Press Band that gave 'performances

LEFT AND
RIGHT *Catalogue
front and back covers
for* The People
*National Darts Teams
Championships (Lord
Lonsdale Challenge
Trophy) 1948-9, held
in the Lindley Hall on
11 June 1949 and the
1952-3 Championships,
also held in the Lindley
Hall, on 27 June 1953.
The latter illustrates
well-known journalists,
writers, reporters,
forecasters, columnists,
and public figures that
wrote for* The People
*newspaper, including
E.H. Tattershall,
Britain's leading race
authority at the time.*

of popular music' under the direction of their conductor, George Thompson, and the George Mitchell Choir. The Grand-Final was fought between the Northern Counties Area Champions, Andrew Machine Construction Co. from Stockport, Cheshire and the Midland Counties Area Champions, the Braunston Gate Inn, Leicester. Then, in 1978 by a strange quirk of fate due to an electrician's strike at Wembley Conference Centre where the Winmau World Masters Darts World Finals presented by the British Darts Organisation had been booked to take place, they were switched at the last minute to be held in the Old Hall on 1-2 December 1978. Twenty-seven countries took part, and the event was televised by ITV World of Sport. In 1979 the 5th British Open Darts Championships were held in both Halls and returned again the following year. 150 dartboards were lined up side by side and a 50ft long bar was stocked with 20,000 pints of beer. A record 2,000 competitors, mostly from Britain, but some from 12 other countries attended. The total prize money on offer was £60,000. The event was televised and run by Mr Olly Croft, General

LEFT *Souvenir
Programme for the
Winmau World
Masters 78 World
Finals, organised
by the British Darts
Organisation, held in
the Lindley Hall on
1-2 December 1978
(and not at Wembley
Conference Centre
due to an
electrician's strike).*

Secretary of the British Darts Organisation, who was responsible for the sport becoming a recognised and professional sport. *The Times* reported on 5 January 1980 that, 'The man who put the game on the sports

map, Mr Croft, has seen dart-playing grow in 10 years to its present quota of 30-odd professionals and semi-professionals, who can earn up to £50,000 a year, the setting up of national teams, world championships and the influx of women. This year, women account for a quarter of the entrants.' Mr Croft returned once again in December 1990 to use both RHS Halls, when he brought the 17th British Open Darts Championships, organised by his BDO. These were televised by BSkyB and included 900 players from 12 countries, with all preliminary rounds played on 80 dart boards throughout the Halls, and the finals held on the main stage. This illustration is further evidence of the role the RHS Halls had played consistently throughout their event history in acting as one of London's most important 'seedbed' venues for new events, many of which became hugely popular, significant and important to so many groups of people across all areas of consumer, trade and political interest. Other sports-related events to have been staged at the Halls were *Daily Mail* Bridge Tournaments, Chess Championships and Bowling Tournaments.

Wine, Wine, and More Wine

Keeping to the theme of pleasurable activities, rather than trade, Universal Exhibitions Ltd hosted The Festival of Wine on 25 September 1951, just five days before the closing ceremony for the Festival of Britain. Whether this was connected to The Festival in any way is unclear. It was certainly the first Wine Festival to be staged at the RHS, but by no means the last. Perhaps, this was a reflection of the changing attitudes in post-war Britain to embrace more wine, rather than beer and ale. However, Australian wine, and the promotion of its benefits, had been exhibited as far back as 1884 at the International Health Exhibition. In the years to come, the Halls would become the home of many wine tasting events from the New World, especially as a result of a growing movement that changed the domination of the French, and surprised them in the process. The next one took place on 26-9 June 1971 in the New Hall, this time called the International Wine Marketing Exhibition, followed by WINEX (probably the same event re-branded) on 26 June in 1972. These were certainly early trailblazers for the major wine festivals and fairs

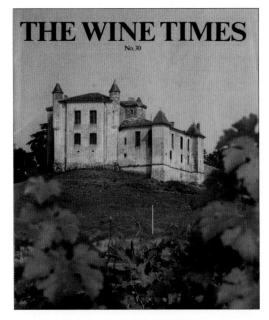

THE WINE TIMES
No.30

that would follow. A wine tasting event also took place in February 1976, and this was probably an early precursor to the first event organised by The Direct *Sunday Times* Wine Club founded by Harry (now Sir) Evans, Editor of the *Sunday Times* in 1979. The Club certainly held its annual Vintage Wine Festival in the same Hall on 26 March 1981, where it still continues today. *The Wine Times*, published by The Club in 1981 showed Jancis Robinson as its Editor, Derek Jewell and Tony Laithwaite as joint Chairmen, and Hugh Johnson (now OBE) as President. Twenty-eight years later Tony Laithwaite and his wife were selling around £350 million worth of wine, running what was claimed to be Britain's biggest wine company (and now the world's largest home delivery company), Direct Wines. Perhaps, it was also no surprise that Hugh Johnson, widely known as an authority and prolific author on wine, also became strongly connected with the RHS in 1975 when he acted as Editorial Director of the RHS Garden Magazine until 1989. Wine 'Tastings' from Spain, Chile, South Africa, California and Portugal were regularly held throughout the '90s at the RHS, especially in the Lawrence Hall (as it was renamed in 2001) as well as from France. All of these recognised the advantage of the wonderful light that the Halls offered to better enable their inspection of them.

Racing Cars and Bikes

We have already heard about some of the early pioneers of car manufacturing and motor racing that frequented the Hall. It is true to say that some of the most famous racing cars of their time, including Schneider Cup winners, came to both Halls throughout the long and exciting period of the Schoolboy's Exhibition. At the 29th National Schoolboy's and Senior Students Own Exhibition in 1955/1956 a model of the famous Supermarine, that travelled at 407 mph and won the Schneider Trophy that year, was on display. At the 23rd Exhibition in 1949/50 the *Daily Mail* snapped John Cooper pushing his new Cooper 1,000 into the Hall, where a mouth-watering selection of cars from 1903 to 1949 was on display. And, maybe in the same way we have seen that one thing, one contact, and one event leads to another, it could well be why the Old Hall became host to Britain's first annual Racing Car Show in 1960, organised by the British Racing & Sports Car Club. Britain's first official motor show had taken place at London's Crystal Palace, in January 1903. The show was organised by the Society of Motor Manufacturers and Traders (SMMT), the brainchild of Frederick Richard Simms who, together with Charles Harrington Moore, had also helped to found the Automobile Club (later to become the RAC) in 1897. Subsequently, the International Motor Exhibition was held annually at Olympia from 1905 to 1936 and led to what we all know as The British International Motor Show, which in 1978 moved to the NEC, Birmingham, only to return again to London (this time to Dockland's Excel) in 2008. The SMMT were primarily interested in the business of promoting their manufacturers and their industry to sell more cars.

Racing was a very different activity and interest, and the British Racing & Sports Car Club in 1959 had been buoyed by some spectacular Formula 1 wins by Jack Brabham at Monaco and the British Grand Prix, and by Stirling Moss at the Portuguese Grand Prix, the Italian Grand Prix, the New Zealand Grand

LEFT   The Wine Times, *the magazine of the Direct Sunday Times Wine Club, Winter 1981, No.30 issue, edited by Jancis Robinson with Hugh Johnson as President. The Festival took place in the Lawrence Hall on 26-7 March 1981, and is still taking place there in 2011.*

BRSCC Shield.

Catalogues and Guides for the 1960-3 Racing Car Shows, organised by the British Racing & Sports Car Club, held in the Halls for the first three, and in Olympia for the fourth. The one held in 1960 was the first of its kind and was opened by Earl Howe, BRSCC Patron, on 2 January 1960.

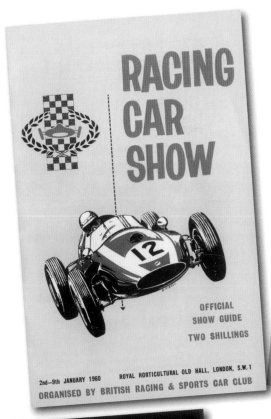

Prix, Goodwood, Silverstone International Trophy, and at Oulton Park. Bruce McLaren had also won the American Grand Prix. And in that year, no fewer than five of those wins were made with the undoubted car of the year, the Cooper-Climax. The Cooper was hailed as a triumph for British engineering, made even more remarkable given the cars were made in a small works in Surbiton by Charles and John Cooper.

It was fitting, therefore, that at this first show two of their cars, the ones in which Stirling Moss and John Arthur 'Jack' Brabham had won their GP Races, were positioned prominently in the Hall under the banner, 'Cars of the 1959 Champions' for all to see. Centre stage was the Formula 1 World Champion, Jack Brabham, who also drove for Cooper and went on to win the title in the following year. He won the title once more in 1966, but by then had left Cooper to found his own Brabham marque. Also on display in the Hall at the 1960 Show was a representative display of the cars of past, present and future.

Earl Howe, the Club's Patron, opened the show on 2 January 1960, although it was Club Treasurer, Ian Smith's idea to organise one. The Show attracted 40,000 visitors over the seven days. Deemed a huge success, this was the first of an annual show that returned the following year, and the one after, utilising both Halls until 1963 when it received welcome support in the form of the *Daily Express*, and moved to Olympia. As with so many successful shows that came to the RHS Halls, they often only stayed a few years before moving on to a venue that could offer them more space. Eventually, this show would become known as Autosport International run by Haymarket Exhibitions at the NEC, Birmingham, and the biggest event of its kind still running today. However, in 1968 the British Racing & Sports Car Club did hold their 9th show in both RHS Halls, once again. This time it was called AUTOSPEED '68, now under the presidency of John Cooper, but the *Daily Express* was no longer in support, and neither was the *Evening News* that had sponsored the previous year's event at Olympia. AUTOSPEED '68 was a

Programme for AUTOSPEED '68, presented by the British Racing & Sports Car Club, in both Halls, on 3-13 January 1968.

landmark show as Denis Howell, MP (then acting as Parliamentary Under Secretary of State Department of Education and Science) pointed out in his message in the show

Catalogue and Guide for The Specialist Sports Car Show and Accessory Supermarket, presented by the Daily Mail *and the British Racing & Sports Car Club, held in the Lindley Hall on 7-17 January 1970.*

Official Programmes for the Motorcycle Mechanics Racing & Sporting Motorcycle Shows held in both Halls from 1972 to 1979, and the 1984 Road 'n' Race Show.

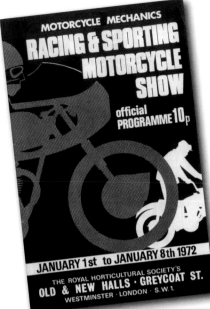

brochure. He said, 'There are many features of great interest to the motoring enthusiast at this show. Not least among them the 17 all-British vehicles on which 89 World, International and National Records were broken at the historic Sprint Attempts held at the RAF Station Elvington in October 1967.' John Cooper reminded everyone of the fact that their Club had been the first to stage an International Racing Car Show, and Ian Smith was still working hard on them acting as Show Director. Jack Brabham and Graham Hill had become Vice-Presidents and 25 championship Racing Cars were on display. A Junior Racing Car Club had been formed and was advertising that it would soon have its own circuit in Kent and a parade of Champions, starting with World Formula One Champion, Denny Hulme to Hot Car Boy Racer Simon Flangeplate appeared in the brochure. Pathé News once again covered the show with Paddy Hopkirk also featured. What is interesting to note is that, much later, it was reported that the SMMT had been concerned enough at the potential threat to their own show that they had banned the first Show in 1960, so that none of their motor manufacturing members, or component producers, could exhibit there.

The 10th Show returned to Olympia in 1969, but the BRSCC were back again in 1970, this time only in the Old Hall with a separate and more specialist show entitled, The Specialist Sports Car Show, and with sponsorship from the *Daily Mail*. Graham Hill, who had recently had an accident, attended this in his wheelchair. Shortly after this, on 5 February, another first took place in the Old Hall, this time led by Motor Cycle Mechanics Magazine, entitled the Racing & Sporting Motor Cycle Show. These shows lasted very much longer and, in their original form, for 12 years until 1981. In 1982, these became known as The Roadshow, until 1984 when the show became known as the Road 'n' Race Show. This was opened by Sir Hector Munro, MP, President of the Auto Cycle Union (ACU) where the 'Project Penetrator' (that was attempting to break the Land Speed Record of 211 mph set on British soil) was displayed. By now, with

upwards of 200 racing motor bikes converging onto the Halls (including Hells Angels who were regular visitors) any pretence of concern for ones neighbour's peaceful weekends would have been hard to sustain. Interspersed among these shows were also a number of Custom and Collectors' Bike Shows, Bike Marts and Grand London Auto Jumbles.

However, on 24 June 1966, another car-related first event took place that would lead to an even longer standing relationship with Coys of Kensington (now simply known as Coys), organisers of classic car auctions. This took place in the Old Hall, and was an auction of 45 veteran, vintage and post-vintage thoroughbreds, organised by the Antique and Classic Car Company of Mayfair. Two years later they were followed by Sotheby & Co. of 34 & 35 New Bond Street. The catalogue for this sale, and their second one in 1969, reveals an amazing selection of Veteran, Edwardian and Vintage Vehicles that would have been very familiar to all of the aristocratic families, royalty and leading figures of the Edwardian period we have been introduced to in the early chapters of my book. Many of these cars have been very familiar to me as I have watched them drive the London to Brighton run since I was a boy. However, for me, the most poignant item of the 1968 sale is one of the very last items listed in the catalogue, and not even a real motor car. It is listed under the heading, Model Cars, Ships and Locomotives. The caption describes it as item No. 277 Model Tram Car. An L.C.C. (London County Council) type open-top Tramcar, correctly enamelled in the colours of the time, powered by a 12-volt Garrard motor. The key to my interest was the caption underneath that says, 'This model was built by the vendor's grandfather and awarded a certificate of merit at the 1909 Model Engineer Exhibition.' I have

Enamel badges for the 1978, 1979 and 1981 Racing & Sporting Motor Cycle Shows, held in the Halls.

Catalogues for the 1968 and 1969 Sotheby's & Co. car auctions of Veteran, Edwardian and Vintage Vehicles and Post-Vintage Thoroughbreds Motoring Books, Accessories and Miscellanea, held in the Lawrence Hall on 24 and 23 October, respectively.

to say that this brought tears to my eyes, and is another strange quirk of fate that this was the second item Sotheby's had brought back to the RHS Halls to sell, where they had once resided so many years before. Eight years later, it was the turn of Bonham's, Montpelier Street, London, SW7, to bring to the Hall its auction of Post-War automobiles, 1947-67, to be sold on 21 September 1976, in aid of the Leukemia Research Fund, and attended by its Patron, The Duke of Kent.

So, taking us closer to the present-day period is the very strong association that the RHS Halls have had with Coys and their classic car auctions, founded in 1919 by Wilfred E. Coy, one of the world's truly innovative motoring and aviation entrepreneurs. Their rallying call for all enthusiasts and collectors until recently, was that 'We will travel anywhere in the world to obtain a classic motor car'. So on 13-15 January 1987 they held their first auction in the New Hall and they have continued to use the Halls up to the time of writing, over a period of 23 years, sometimes holding three or more auctions per annum. Some extraordinary cars have gone through the doors of both Halls. The ones that stand out for

me are Heavyweight Boxing World Champion Jack Dempsey's 1924 Rolls-Royce Silver Ghost Piccadilly Roadster, one of only four built, with Dempsey's the only one of three that survives. This was shown as Lot 217 in the 27 February 2007 Auction with an Estimate of between £150,000 and £170,000. The 1957 Cooper-Climax T43 Formula 2, once raced by Innes Ireland at Silverstone's International Trophy meeting, where he took first place in the first Formula 2 heat, would have been very familiar to all who had visited the 1st Racing Car Show in the Old Hall in 1960. This appeared as Lot 42 in the 25 February 1997 Auction with an Estimate of between £40,000 and £50,000. Back on 12 December 1990 Auction Lot 57 was an Aston Martin 1½ litre Short Chassis Le Mans with no estimate shown. This rare car was credited as having been the first Aston Martin to compete in the famous Mille Miglia and one of only three pre-war cars to do so. Eric Morecambe's 1974 Rolls-Royce Silver Shadow with personalised plates EM100 was sold for £35,650. Eric's widow, Joan, had put it for auction some years following his death in 1984. Harold Robbins' Jensen Interceptor

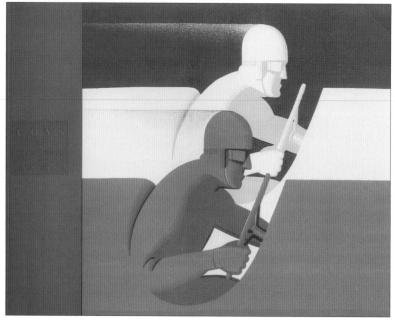

Catalogues for the 1997, 1998 and 1990 Coys of Kensington car auctions of important British and Continental Touring Cars; Veteran, Vintage and classic vehicles and historic sporting motor cars, held in the Lawrence Hall on 25 February 1997, 16 February 1998 and 12 December 1990, respectively.

was sold in July 1987, and 'Bergerac' (John Nettle's) 1947 Triumph Roadster, used in the first television series of the same name, was sold in February 1987. On 14 February 1990 a fine example of a 'cult car' was sold for £42,000. This was a 1967 Volvo P1800S owned from new by Roger Moore who used it during the making of his highly successful TV series, 'The Saint'. There have been many more that I could list, of course, but I will end with a car that has a particular resonance with me, again because of the man that owned it, another famous comedian I remember so well, Tony Hancock. This was a 1965 Aston Martin DB5 Convertible that sold on 14 February 1990 for £97,000.

Careers Start (or End) Here

During the 17 years I worked at the RHS I met an awful lot of people at external receptions and events that asked me the inevitable question most of us are asked, 'and where do you work?' When I told them, a surprising number would turn pale, and recall the fact that they had sat their professional or academic examinations in my Halls. Depending on whether this had been a positive experience for them, or not, either during the exam itself, or following it, the conversation resumed, or stalled. Having seen 1,000 people sitting at desks in regimented rows with strict invigilators watching over them with eagle eyes in the vast space that is the New Hall, I can understand why fear and panic drove many either to breakdown completely, or rush out in floods of tears. This was not helped by a pane of glass falling from the roof in the 1980s during one of these examinations. The need to call an ambulance during an examination tenancy was not uncommon.

The fact is that examinations have taken place in the Halls since 1905 when the first Office of Works Army, and gardening for Schoolteachers exam tenancies are recorded. The RHS Council Minutes of their 3 January meeting record that they decided to charge 50 guineas (£4,695) for this four-day tenancy and in July 1906 the University of London used the Hall for their Matriculation exams when they were charged £90 (£8,049). The latter was the first of almost annual tenancies that, bar 1916-20, went through to 1936, stopped until 1981, and resumed again up to 2004, often holding their exams three times a year. Other universities and colleges who have used the Halls for their own academic examinations have been King's College London, the University of Westminster and the University of Cambridge. The remaining and many organisations that have come to the Halls for this purpose have been professional organisations. The RHS held their own Public Parks exams from 1908-10 and School Teachers exams took place during the same period. However, the Surveyors' Institution (the forerunner of the Institution of Chartered Surveyors and then the Royal Institution of Chartered Surveyors (RICS), based at 12 Great George Street, Parliament Square, first used the Halls in 1909 and continued, bar a few breaks, until 1994. In 1915 the Incorporated Dental Society held their own exams (doubtless excruciating for some) and the National

Photo of examination taking place in the Lawrence Hall, c.1970.

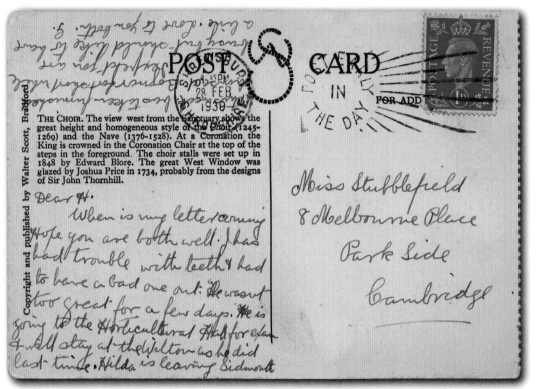

Postcard sent to Miss Stubblefield, Cambridge, dated 28 February 1939, referring to attendance at the Chartered Surveyors Institution exams held in the Lawrence Hall on 13-17 March 1939. Reference to 'The Wiltons' is the house on the corner of Vincent Square with Elverton Street, adjacent to the Lindley Hall.

Training School of Cookery started in 1931 (changing to the National Training College of Domestic Subjects in 1932) continued until 1935. Also in 1931, the Director of Lands and Accommodation, HM Office of Works placed their Civil Service examinations there, once again annually, through to 1950, and the Worshipful Company of Spectacle Makers held their exams for four years from 1933-6. One hopes that they were able to read their papers without any difficulty. The General Nursing Council for England and Wales began theirs in 1932 and the Royal College of General Practitioners (RCGP) in 1987. The General Medical Council, the Royal College of Physicians and the Royal College of Veterinary Surgeons came later in the first decade of the new millennium.

From this, a pattern can be seen whereby many of the examining bodies and organisations that used the Halls for these purposes were also using them for their exhibitions and other events separately. This certainly applied to the nursing, dental, optical and cookery exhibitions, but a further example is the Institute of Patentees who were based at 10 Victoria Street, SW1. They

held their Exhibition of Patents, also known as The Inventor's Exhibition, in the Old Hall on 15-17 February 1939. They then held their Institute of Patentees professional examinations in the same hall on 13-17 March that same year. Thirty years later they returned to launch LINPEX'69, the London International Inventions and New Products Show in the New Hall. They then returned again in 1970 when over 100 entries from Poland, Switzerland, France, Norway, South Africa and Great Britain were displayed. The show was extensively covered by Movietone and ITN Newsreel. The Association of Headmasters & Headmistresses of Home Office Schools were also based in Victoria Street, and ran The South of England Home Office Schools Exhibition in the New Hall on 19-21 May 1931, and this was opened by The Duke of York.

Hundreds and thousands of students, young and mature, have sat their professional examinations in these Halls. Hopefully, most of them are now enjoying successful careers as a result. They include lawyers, legal executives, barristers, chartered accountants, accounting technicians, auctioneers and valuers, revenue and rating officers, veterinary surgeons, doctors, physicians, nurses, chiropodists, podiatrists, stock brokers, prison officers, taxation officers, chartered surveyors, chartered insurers, chartered designers, chartered marketers, linguists, tour operators and European Union administrators. The Law Society booked the Halls for their own exams in the 1990s, and returned (perhaps out of nostalgia) to hold their 2009 Awards in the Lawrence Hall. There must have been a number of people at that function who had sat in the Hall under very different circumstances.

For a long time, these tenancies, and the type of business they represented, were either ignored, or shunned, by many traditional exhibition venues. The principal reason was that they brought no additional catering, stand fitting, electrical, or other ancillary income that was normally an important revenue stream in its own right, on top of the room hire charges. However, the flip side to this was that exam organisers often booked up to five years ahead, and one knew that the dates were firm. Exam dates are rarely changed; exhibitions and other events often are. With the booking confirmed, and deposits banked, you could relax and concentrate on securing other business around it. There was also minimal operational involvement by the Hall staff, minimal wear and tear, and outlay. During my time at the Halls, the business gained from examination tenancies never fell much below 17 per cent of total lettings revenue, so a hugely valuable contribution, and a consistently reliable base to work from. However, over a period of time many examination bodies, in an effort to cut their costs, made alternative arrangements either in-house, or with the increasingly active British Universities that marketed their vacant facilities during non-term times. Nevertheless, single flat uninterrupted spaces, like the ones offered at each of the RHS Halls, are hugely attractive because of the numbers of students that can be accommodated with the smaller number of invigilating staff required. That is why so many men and women up and down the land, and around the world, remember them.

Poster label for the Cinema Accessories and Musical Appliances Exhibition, organised by Ernest Schofield of Universal Exhibitions (Kinematograph International Exhibitions Ltd) of 22-4 Great Portland Street, London, W1, held in the Lindley Hall on 12-19 February 1921. This followed the larger and very successful Kinematograph Exhibition of 1913, held at Olympia, and from which they took their company name.

Film and TV Sets

One of the other non-conventional revenue streams to benefit the RHS Halls during the past 30 years was location filming. The Cinema Accessories and Musical Appliances Exhibition had taken place in the Hall as early as 1921; possibly one of Ernest Schofield's events under his Kinematograph Exhibitions Company. Location managers employed by film companies to seek out and find suitable venues, whether for a cinematic or television medium, knew that the distinctive art-deco features of the New Hall in particular (that by then had been renamed, the Lawrence Hall) could be used in a number of ways, and for a variety of scenes. So it is not surprising that the RHS Halls can be seen in a number of classic movies, as well as television dramas, documentaries, Christmas Specials, pop-videos and commercials.

Perhaps, the most well known of all of these was the BBC Ident of two acrobats suspended on swathes of red silk cloth high into the roof canopy of the Lawrence Hall. This was used by them for a full five-year period from 2002 to 2007 and always appeared just before the main News slot. I always wanted to be one of those

acrobats, and to be in a position to let everyone watching know that they were looking at the RHS New Hall, but sense prevailed! However, there was real excitement from my young female staff on 1 March 1997 when Partizan Films shot Robbie Williams's latest pop-video in the Old Hall (that by then had been renamed the Lindley Hall) called '*Old Before I Die*'. In the same vein, one of the earliest films to have been made using the Halls, other than the Cyril Stapleton films already referred to, was Alan Parker's (now Sir Alan) famous rendition of Pink Floyd's *The Wall*, shot in October 1981. Both Halls were used. The skinheads used for the rally sequences caused some consternation within the RHS. Bob Geldof, as Pink, was the central character, and Tin Blue Ltd, the film company that produced the film, used the New Hall to great effect in the first of three of the most dramatic portrayals of the Hall seen on film to this date. This was Pink's neo-Nazi rally and a rousing speech from the balcony. Geldof came back 11 years later with his independent television production company, Planet 24, co-founded by him, when Channel 4 Television's 10th Birthday Party was celebrated on 29 and 30 October 1992, and also on the occasion of their *Big Breakfast* first birthday party on 1 October 1993 when Paula Yates, Chris Evans, and Gaby Roslin also attended. Michael Grade was on hand to blow out the candles on the giant cake that took centre stage at their party, and Jools Holland and his band, among many other artists, performed.

Airports and train stations have also figured large in location manager's minds when they have looked at the Lawrence Hall, so it is not surprising to find the Hall being represented as Berlin Airport in Steven Spielberg's *Indiana Jones and the Last Crusade*, filmed by Lucas Films in the Hall in June 1988. However, scenes for the earlier *Indiana Jones and the Temple of Doom* in 1984 also featured the Hall. Sir Ian McKellen's contemporary version of 'Richard III' by Bayly/Paré Productions in February 1996 was the second occasion when the Hall was shown in all its glory: Sir Ian McKellen, again appearing in the Hall in contemporary neo-Nazi attire to receive

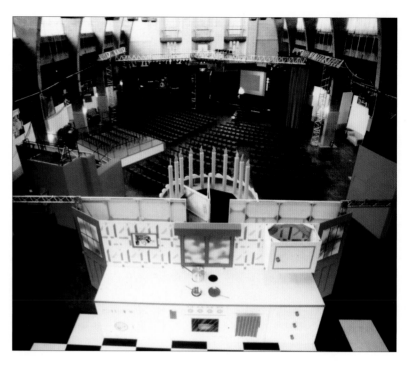

the adulation of his subjects as Richard III, revealed the true architectural splendour of this RIBA Gold Medal award-winning art-deco structure. The third depiction was Channel 4 TV's dramatisation, *Mosley and the Blackshirts* depicting the life of the British Union of Fascists Leader, Sir Oswald Mosley, produced by Alomo Productions. In particular, Mosley's 16 July 1939 rally, the world's largest indoor meeting of 30,000 that was held in Earl's Court, was shockingly recreated in the New Hall on 14 and 15 August 1997. This was so realistic that I received a call from the *Daily Telegraph* while the filming was taking place. They had received a call from a very concerned, and disgusted, neighbour who had seen what was taking place from a side door, and wanted the *Daily Telegraph* to report that the RHS were, among everything else that was taking place in the Hall, now allowing fascist rallies to take place! It is worth noting, in the context of the events that had taken place in the Halls, that Mosley's most prominent supporter was press baron Lord Rothermere, whose *Daily Mail* splashed the infamous headline 'Hurrah for the Blackshirts' on 15 January 1934. He was also backed by Vickers' boss, Lord Armstrong, car magnate Sir William Morris and extremist Tories.

ABOVE *Photo of Channel 4 TV's 10th Birthday Anniversary party and event, held in the Lawrence Hall on 29-30 October 1992.*

RIGHT *Photo of layout in the Lindley Hall for Bermuda Tourism's event, as part of their World Tour promotion. The floor was made to look like a swimming pool where bathers reclined around it, sipping exotic cocktails, and being entertained by Grace Jones.*

RIGHT *Catalogue for the 2007 Coys of Kensington Spring Classics car auction, held in the Lawrence Hall, on 27 February 2007, when the daring duo's 'Batmobile' was sold for £119,100.*

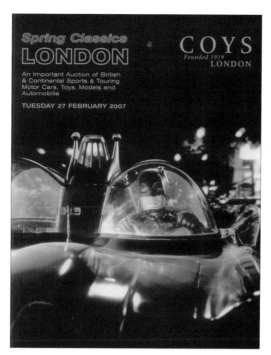

Sequences for the remake of *The Saint* with Val Kilmer by Paramount Films in 1997, Banshee Film's *Martha – Meet Frank, Daniel and Lawrence*, MGM's *Agent Cody Banks II*, and Quietus Production's *Children of Men* were just a few of the other feature films where the Halls were chosen. A documentary film about British Prime Ministers was also made in the 1980s when the main Council Room at 80 Vincent Square was used. It was an interesting piece of historical coincidence, given that Neville Chamberlain's father, Joseph Chamberlain, had been a past RHS Vice-President, and both father and son spent many hours in the Halls and Council Room deliberating about the Tariff Reforms and horticultural matters.

The television series of *Poirot* and *Marple*, and adverts for Carling Black Label, British

Midland, Levi Jeans, Savlon, Weetablix and Strongbow Cider have also used the Halls. Scenes for two BBC Christmas Specials have also been filmed in the New Hall. The *Only Fools and Horses Special* was filmed in 1996 (*Heroes and Villains*) and the *French and Saunders Celebrity Christmas Puddings* edition in 2002. In yet another twist of fate, Del Boy's famous 1972 Reliant Regal, affectionately known as 'Trotter Van', became Lot 237 at Coys *Spring Classics* Auction in the same Hall on 27 February 2007 with an estimate of £15,000-£20,000 on it. It came with a parking ticket, twine covering the roof-rack and a hand-written label on the corner of the windscreen reading, 'Tax in the post'. When the final hammer fell, it had sold for over double the estimate at £44,277. National Treasurer of the Reliant Owners Club, Peter Higgins, commented afterwards, 'Reliants are very collectable but I think that £44,277 must be the most ever paid for one'. This had taken part in the episode where they had driven to a fancy dress party dressed as Batman and Robin. Cue for another remarkable segue to Batman and Robin's Batmobile, also being offered at the same auction in the Hall directly from the world famous Cars of the Stars Museum, as Lot 241. No estimate was shown for this, but it sold for a not insignificant £119,100.

Speaking of stars, many have graced the Halls in various guises. One of the most memorable was Grace Jones performing an extraordinary set in the then renamed Lindley Hall that had been transformed into an exotic beach location, complete with bikini and shorts-clad sunbathers on sun loungers around an azure blue swimming pool projected onto the floor, during the British leg of the Bermuda Tourist Board's 2003/4 World Tour. Brian Ferry and Roxy Music played to a select audience invited to celebrate the Centenary of Montblanc International on 9 March 2006, once again in the renamed Lindley Hall. Clive Anderson will, I am certain, recall his visit to Reed Publishing's *The Grocer* Awards and Dinner Dance in the New Hall where he was Compère on 18 October 1995. Unfortunately, this will not be as positive as it should be, as both he and the event were stopped by Westminster City Council's 24 Hours Noise Team who had received complaints from neighbours.

VIII

Decline and Rejuvenation

Old Hall Crisis

In 1976, a report was commissioned and published on the future of the Old Hall, which was in a bad state of repair and in need of major renovation. The Society had gone through a very bad period culminating in 1970 with a serious deficit of £150,000 (£1.82 million) and Wisley Garden then a real drain on the Society's resources. Looking at the chronological event history in the Appendix will show quite clearly that, for at least a decade between the late 1960s and '70s, the hall bookings had become very thin. The Society, therefore, was not flush enough with funds to do anything about it and serious consideration was given to selling it. At a crisis Council Meeting, 13 Members of the Council were for selling it and only three against. The 3rd Baron Aberconway, Charles McLaren, the then 14th RHS President, managed to turn the decision round after a five-hour meeting. In early 1983 the restoration work began. It was completed just in time for the Society's Great Autumn Flower Show in September that year and cost £900,000 (£2.34 million), mainly spent on the roof that had been letting in water badly prior to the work. It is also indicative of the concern clearly being expressed as long ago as the late 1970s, that new branding was being considered for the first time since the

Brochure produced to combat the growing success of other London exhibition venues that were competing strongly for core exhibition business which had, hitherto, come to the RHS Halls. Central Hall, not far away, later also saw the value of using the Westminster branding, renaming their venue Central Hall Westminster. From 1991, the RHS Halls branding incorporated the tag line, 'In the Heart of Westminster' on all of its primary branding.

Old Hall had opened 84 years earlier. This was applied by Geoffrey Harvey who, as Assistant Secretary, had been appointed by Lord Aberconway to run Membership and Publications. He was already in charge of Chelsea and set about reversing the financial deficit that the Society had found itself in. The Royal Horticultural Halls changed to become

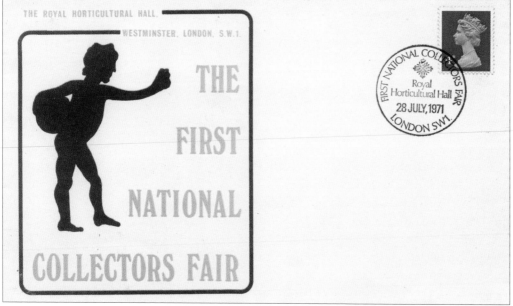

ABOVE *Commemorative First Day Cover for the RNIB Centenary Exhibition opened by HM The Queen, held in the Lindley Hall on 20-21 May, 1968.*

LEFT *Commemorative First Day Cover for the FIRST National Collectors' Fair, held in the Lindley Hall on 28-31 July 1971.*

RIGHT *Advertisement for the International New Homes Show, organised by Homefinder (1915) Ltd, and sponsored by Homes Overseas Magazine, held in both Halls, on 5-10 February 1974.*

the Westminster Exhibition Centre in order to compete more effectively with the many other venues that were increasingly competing for the same exhibitions. However, a special report by Eric Hart in *The Times* of 23 October 1978 compounded the negative views being expressed during this period by making it very clear that, 'The two aging Horticultural Halls (Westminster Exhibition Centre) are just not in the running …' He was comparing these with the much larger and better exhibition venues and facilities in mainland Europe, but, his use of the word 'aging' described the reality of situation.

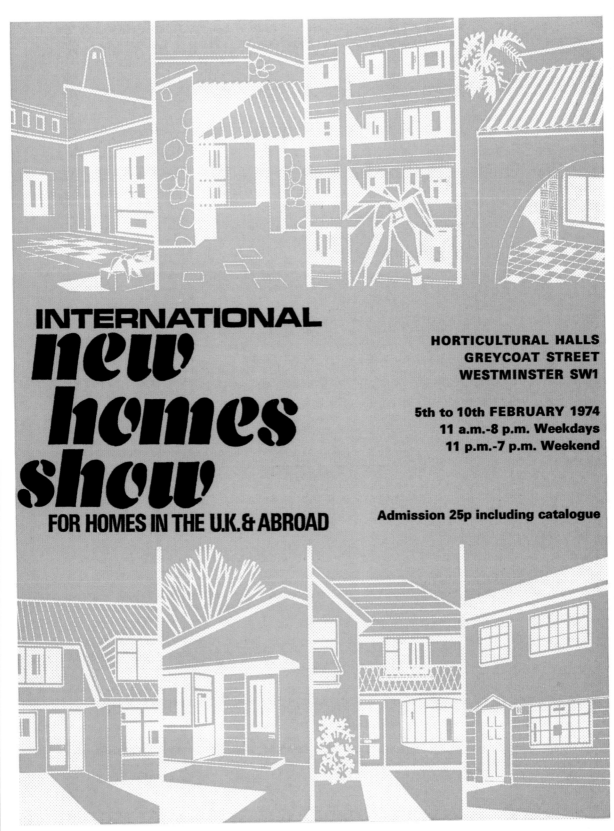

INTERNATIONAL
new homes show
FOR HOMES IN THE U.K. & ABROAD

HORTICULTURAL HALLS
GREYCOAT STREET
WESTMINSTER SW1

5th to 10th FEBRUARY 1974
11 a.m.-8 p.m. Weekdays
11 p.m.-7 p.m. Weekend

Admission 25p including catalogue

HHL Formation 1986

By the early 1980s, the regular RHS Westminster Flower Shows changed from their hitherto fortnightly frequency to monthly and, therefore, more space became available to sell to external clients with the additional pressure that this placed on the Society to sell the Halls. Then on 17 November 1986, the Society formed a wholly owned trading subsidiary called Horticultural Halls Limited (HHL) with Geoffrey Harvey as its first Managing Director. Prior to this, it had always been the Secretary's and Assistant Secretary's job to handle Halls bookings and tenancies, but now other activities required that the Halls be looked at independently, and the Society wished also to take advantage of the tax concessions that came as a result whereby they would no longer have to pay corporation tax on future profits made by Horticultural Halls Limited. A precedent had also already been set when RHS Enterprises Ltd had been formed earlier in May 1975 to encompass the retail and other commercial activities of the Society's Wisley Garden.

East Meets West

On 18-20 February 1914, the Hall was awash with colour from the East. This was in the form of valuable oriental carpets brought there to sell by Messrs I. Behar and The Anglo-Continental Co. Messrs Behar was from Constantinople, now Istanbul, and on sale were exquisite carpets valued then at £50,000, including one that had belonged to Napoleon.

On 7 December 1949, the Britain-China Conference Committee had met in the New Hall at a crucial time in Anglo-Sino relations during the Chinese Civil War, to give further consideration to Britain's lone recognition of China by the Attlee government, following

BELOW LEFT *Catalogue for the 62nd The Model Railway Club's International Railway Exhibition, held in both Halls, on 18-23 April 1987.*

BELOW *Official Guide to The Emperor's Warriors Exhibition, held in the Lindley Hall on 14 December 1987-20 February 1988. The Exhibition received over 250,000 visitors during the six weeks it was open.*

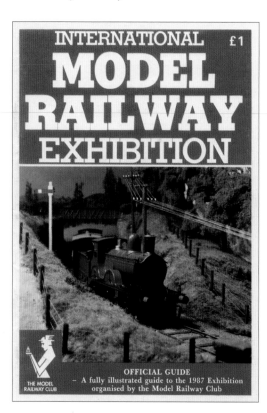

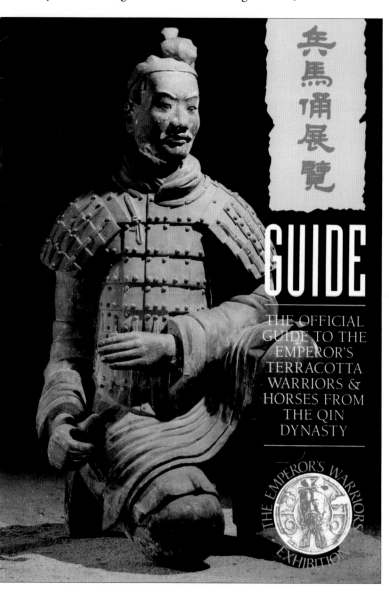

the proclamation of the People's Republic of China, and its capital in Peking, by Mao Zedong on 1 October 1949.

Thirty-nine years later China was the subject of one of the most successful consumer shows to take place in the Halls. This was the Emperor's Warriors Exhibition, when original Terracotta Army figures, horses, and other miscellaneous items were brought from China to the Old Hall for an exhibition that lasted from 14 December 1987 to 20 February 1988. The Army had been discovered by chance by villagers in 1974 at what has arguably become the most famous archaeological site in the world. The exhibition was organised by The Emperor's Warriors Exhibition Ltd, a private UK company, whose Chairman was David Arnell, in association with the Shaanxi Archaeological Overseas Exhibition Corporation from the People's Republic of China. Lord Boston of Faversham and the management of Television South plc assisted in the promotion of the event that resulted in over 250,000 people visiting the exhibition over the six-week period. This was not the first time that the Terracotta Army had come to the UK. The first time had been in 1981 when six warriors had been shown at Selfridges, London, as part of a marketing event called 'East Meets West'. Subsequently, the City of Edinburgh Museums and Art Galleries staged the first major display between 11 September and 1 November 1985 at the City of Edinburgh Art Centre. The event was co-sponsored by Mirror Group Newspapers, the *Scottish Daily Record*, and the *Sunday Mail*. Both displays in Edinburgh and London were identical. This comprised, two kneeling crossbowmen, one chariot horse, one cavalry horse, one standing crossbowman, one unarmoured soldier, one

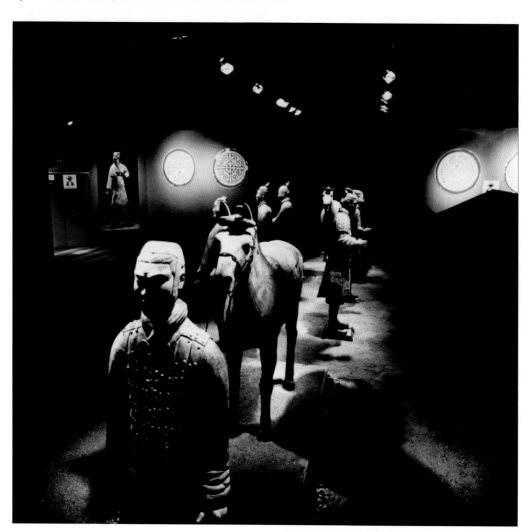

Photo of The Emperor's Warriors Exhibition in the Lindley Hall.

kneeling stable hand, two warriors in armour, one cavalryman, one armoured charioteer, and 21 miscellaneous items, i.e. Swords etc. The Warriors were insured at Lloyds for £15 million (£32.4 million) for the London event.

Twenty-six years later between 13 September 2007 and 6 April 2008, the British Museum staged a much more extensive exhibition of the Army that featured the largest group (120 pieces) of important objects relating to the First Emperor ever to be loaned abroad. This was sponsored by Morgan Stanley. The Warriors also appeared at the 1982 World's Fair in Knoxville, Tennessee, and have travelled all over the world to be displayed in several cities in the USA, the Netherlands, Malta, and Spain.

East also met West at the Japanese Traditional Handicrafts Demonstration and Exhibition (part of The Japan Festival in 1991)

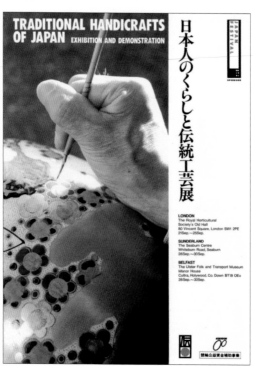

Catalogue for the Traditional Handicrafts of Japan Exhibition and Demonstration, as part of the Japan Festival, held in the Lindley Hall on 21-5 September 1991.

staged in the Old Hall on 21-5 September. Here, visitors were privileged to watch 12 skilled Japanese craftsmen and women work on, and display, their traditional handicrafts. These included exquisite Kimono dyeing, delicate Japanese rice paper, sublime earthenware dolls, intricate textile weaving, and fine silk braiding. In the centre of the Hall the traditional *Chanoyu* tea ceremony was performed for select visitors in a bamboo teahouse called a *Chashitsu*. Prince Charles was one of those who partook of this.

More Middle East than Far East was the 1986 exhibition entitled 'Riyadh: Yesterday and Today' that took place at the end of July 1986, where it was opened by Prince Salman in the presence of the Prince and Princess of Wales. It was the largest exhibition of its kind in London since the 1976 World of Islam Festival (See *Aramco World*, May-June 1976), and the public success of the previous event held in West Germany was repeated. According to Dermot Graham, who ran the exhibition company which acted as advisers to the Riyadh exhibition, it was the best-attended foreign exhibition ever held in Britain.

Computers, Gizmos, and Games

Between 1982 and 1992 saw a spate of new computer and computer technology shows. The first of these was the ZX Micro Computer Fair, dealing with Sir Clive Sinclair's new range of Sinclair machines, Spectrums in particular. The first of these took place on 21 August 1982. Over 27 of these were staged by Mike Johnson with the last being held on 9-10 December 1988. Sir Clive's infamous C5 was also separately demonstrated to the media in the Hall.

On 8-11 December 1983 the first of the BBC Micro & Electron User Shows over the next two years took place in the New Hall. The second one in 1984 saw 20,000 visitors coming to this event – 2,000 more than the first, reflecting the huge interest in the new age of computers. The next computer-focused show to come along and offer its wares was the 16 Bit Show, organised by Westminster

Exhibitions, on 12-14 January 1990 in both Halls. In the same year, and clearly reflecting the rapid changes taking place with IT and its hardware, two further events took place. The All Formats Computer Fair was organised by Bruce Everiss, and ran in the New Hall from 10 February 1990-14 March 1992. The BBC Acorn User Show was organised by Safesell Exhibitions in the New Hall, and ran only once on 7-9 September 1990.

Computer games have been almost exclusively the preferred form of entertainment for children for the past 35 years. This started in earnest with the creation of the ubiquitous 'Ping-Pong' game called simply 'Pong' by Nolan Bushnell who developed Atari in 1972. Nintendo produced a game called 'Go' in 1974, and the famous 'Game Boy' from Nintendo (the first handheld computer for playing games) would not be launched until 1989. However, in 1975 John Peake, Ian Livingstone, and Steve Jackson founded Games Workshop at 15 Bolingbroke Road, London. In September that year, they also launched an event called 'Games Workshop's Games Day' in the RHS Hall, and this was held annually until 1987. They came back once again many years later on 30 March 2002. Games Workshop was originally a manufacturer of wooden boards for games such as backgammon, mancala, Nine Men's Morris, and Go, which later became an importer of the U.S. role-playing game Dungeons & Dragons, and then a publisher of war games and role-playing games in its own right, expanding from a bedroom mail-order company in the process. From the outset, there had been a clear stated interest in print regarding 'progressive games', including computer gaming which led to the departure of traditionalist Peake in early 1976, and the loss of GW's main source of income. However, having successfully obtained official distribution rights to Dungeons & Dragons and other TSR (Tactical Studies Rules) products in the UK, and maintaining a high profile by running games conventions, the business grew rapidly. It opened its first retail shop in April 1978.

In early 1979, Games Workshop provided the funding to found Citadel Miniatures in Newark-on-Trent. Citadel would produce the metal miniatures used in role-playing and table-top war games. I remember buying these for my son! The Citadel name became synonymous with Games Workshop Miniatures, and continues to be a trademarked brand name used in association with them long after the Citadel company was absorbed into Games Workshop. For a time, Gary Gygax promoted the idea of TSR, Inc. merging with Games Workshop, until Steve Jackson and Ian Livingstone backed out. However, they went on to become hugely popular writers of the Fighting Fantasy adventure gamebooks. The first ever Fighting Fantasy gamebook, Warlock of Firetop Mountain, was originally published in 1982. It became an overnight bestseller, and went on to sell two million copies. The series 'captured the imaginations of a whole generation of teenage boys,' reached 59 titles and sold in excess of 15 million books around the world. In 2010, Wizard Books announced the return of the children's book sensation of the 1980s, Fighting Fantasy, and this is set to take over the world once again. Jackson himself credited the start of the phenomenon 'in 1980 at their Games Workshop's annual Games Day exhibition at the Royal Horticultural Hall in London'. Perhaps the most striking example of how important this period has become to our present-day generation is the value now being attached to these early (1980s) publications. Up for auction on Ebay on 30 May 2010 was a 1968 publication called Dungeons & Dragons TSR entitled, 'Up The Garden Path' with a starting price of £750. Using the 1986 National Garden Festival as its theme, this module was sold both at that Festival and at the 1986 Games Workshop Day RPG convention at the Horticultural Hall Saturday, on 27 September. This is one of the rarest, obscure, and most valuable TSR modules, mainly due to its extremely limited availability (only found at the Games Workshop convention) and a small print run speculated at 250-500.

Relaunch

In February 1991, I was brought in by Geoffrey Harvey in a newly created position as Sales & Marketing Manager to devise a new Marketing Strategy that could revitalise the Halls, reposition them, and derive greater profits for the Society. This new initiative followed another set of comprehensive reports that had been commissioned by the Society from Exhibition Consultants Ltd in September 1989, and from SGB Management Services on 20 November 1990. The reports made it clear that the Halls had again been losing ground in gaining new exhibitions because other facilities in London, especially the revamped Business Design Centre, which had started out as The Royal Agricultural Hall (and Olympia), had moved with the times and could offer more modern and flexible space. They also concluded that the Old Hall, in particular, was no longer large enough to be attractive to exhibition organisers, and that this should reposition itself to the corporate market for banquets, functions, product launches etc. My own Marketing Analysis, Report and Proposals dated 7 January 1991 re-iterated this, and also commented that the Old and New Halls were not the right names to carry on using if the Society was serious about converting this new market

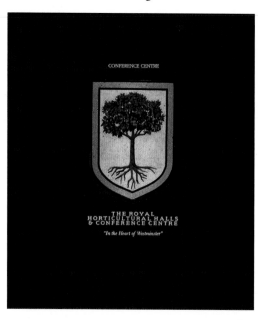

First dedicated brochure produced in 1993 for the newly created Conference Centre.

Newly created marketing brochure and inserts, following the 1991 upgrade, showing the re-branded 'Royal Horticultural Halls & Conference Centre' in the heart of Westminster. Note also the new use of Halls 1 and 2 from Old and New before.

to use its facilities. Trying to sell the 'Old Hall' was never going to be a marketer's dream come true, so I considered that my own recommendation to change both names to the geographical location names of the Vincent and Greycoat Halls was both timely and necessary. These were not accepted, but I did manage to get them renamed to Hall 1 and 2, although only for the commercial application through HHL. This was not terribly imaginative, but infinitely better than before. The RHS decided to continue using the original nomenclature for its flower shows, and those of its affiliated societies. It would be another 10 years before I could propose a further change and the

best solution that exists as I write this book, the Lindley and Lawrence Halls.

Following proposals that I put before the Society in the first months of my arrival, coupled with others, this culminated in a £1 million revamp of the Old Hall and, as importantly, a complete re-appraisal and refurbishment of the rooms that were a part of the New Hall. These had been utilitarian in aspect and every other way and, consequently, unsaleable for anything other than small amounts of token income. These were turned into a dedicated Conference Centre and the venue re-named again as The Royal Horticultural Halls & Conference Centre, this time with three distinctive, flexible and interchangeable products.

Brand-new and comprehensive marketing collateral was produced, and a major event industry re-launch was staged on 3 October that year, opened by the Lord Mayor of Westminster, Dame Shirley Porter, and Lord Pitt, Vice-President of the London Tourist Board and Convention Bureau. Robin Herbert, 15th President of the RHS, helped the Lord Mayor of Westminster, Dame Shirley Porter, cut the ribbon to open the new facilities; Lawrence Banks, in his

LEFT *Photo on the occasion of the official opening of the upgraded and refurbished Old Hall and Conference Centre, on 3 October 1991. Left to right in the front are: Robin A.E. Herbert, 15th President of the RHS; René Dee, Sales & Marketing Manager, Horticultural Halls Ltd; W. Lawrence Banks, Chairman of Horticultural Halls Ltd and Treasurer of the RHS; The Lord Mayor of Westminster, Dame Shirley Porter and Lord Pitt, Vice-President of the London Tourist Board and Convention Bureau. In the background to the right is Donald P. Hearn, Secretary and Finance Director of the RHS.*

capacity as Chairman of Horticultural Halls Ltd and Treasurer of the RHS, formed part of the welcome party. This was attended by over 150 primary exhibition, conference and events leaders. It was also the start of a major

transformation of the Society's facilities, which would bring in over £20 million contribution during the next 17 years.

I had already gained approval from the HHL Board to raise the prices in-line with

Thank you for inviting me to the first Christmas Fair of the year. What a good way to celebrate 90 years Events at the Royal Horticultural Halls. It just goes to show what can be achieved IN ANY EVENT and to ave at my fingertips e names of THE SUPPLIERS.

THE ROYAL HORTICULTURAL HALLS
& CONFERENCE CENTRE

"In the Heart of Westminster"

Special Events

*The Royal Horticultural Halls host balls,
corporate entertainment, product launches and a wide
variety of events in their two outstanding halls
in the heart of Westminster.*

ABOVE *Photo, and an invitation card signed by Sir Richard Branson at the launch of his Virgin Hong Kong Route, held in the Lindley Hall in conjunction with the Hong Kong Tourist Office, on 9-10 February 1994.*

RIGHT *The first 'Special Events' brochure produced in 1994 to attract more corporate events to the Halls.*

LEFT *90th Anniversary of the Lindley Hall photo, and brochure produced for the occasion. This was also promoted as the first Christmas Party of the year, held on 29 September 1994, and attracted many new exhibition industry buyers and influencers.*

the upgraded product and, once again in accordance with my original proposals, increased prices by over 50 per cent in two years (by 30 per cent in the first year). This did cause consternation among some of the then clients, and I did lose a few, but the Halls had been substantially undervalued and, in consequence, viewed as cheap. Three years later on 29 September 1994, another innovative promotional event took place in Hall 1. This was billed as the 'First Christmas Party of the Year' and also celebrated the Hall's 90th birthday. Organised by Cygnet Associates, it attracted 400 event and exhibition industry guests and buyers; 24 suppliers had been organised by Cygnet to support the event by donating their services free of charge and it was a huge success. This event also marked the launch of HHL's first Special Events brochure, which highlighted the new clutch of events coming to the RHS Halls. Richard Branson had launched his new Virgin Hong Kong route in Hall 1 on 9 and 10 February 1994, characteristically popping out of the head of the dragon at the end of a traditional dragon dance display arranged by the Hong Kong Tourist Office. Stonewall had held their annual party in the Lawrence Hall on 25 September 1993, and the costumes were amazing.

Lindley Hall and Lawrence Hall

Over the next 10 years the venue became highly visible, thoroughly established, and profits increased. I took over as Managing Director in 1996, and in the years that led up to the Millennium, regular investment was made to maintain and improve the Halls and the Conference Centre. However, due to the Society's need to modernise, and re-locate, the Lindley Library, which had become cramped, and difficult to house its valuable collection of books, a major restructuring of the Vincent Square headquarters was approved. Consequently, the Old Hall/Hall 1 closed on 15 August 1999; when it was formally re-opened on 20 March 2001, it had also been re-named The Lindley Hall, after John Lindley, whose newly configured Library had also been named after him. In changing the name of Hall 1, it had also become necessary to change the name of Hall 2 and this became known as the Lawrence Hall, after Sir William Lawrence, the Society's Treasurer at the time the Hall had been built, but not forgetting also the Society's 8th President, Sir Trevor Lawrence. A spectacular launch party, organised by First Protocol, took place in the Lindley Hall on 20 March 2001 accompanied by many exhibition, event and conference industry colleagues. During the event, funds were raised for the homeless charity, Crisis. The first event to be staged in it following the opening was the Corporate Hospitality Association's Annual Awards and Dinner on 23 March. From then on, with further key improvements that had been made to the Lindley Hall, it would increasingly host these types of corporate events. Due to the re-formatting of its space (it reduced in gross space by 24.8 per cent from 1,050m² to 790m²) its fate as a viable exhibition hall was sealed. The new events increasingly relied on a high quality of acoustic and catering being provided, so changes were also made to attract a select listing of top-of-the-range caterers to use our venue and to bring in their clients. So the trend that was started in the early 1990s by Geoffrey Harvey and Dorothy Burrows was continued by a new team, affectionately known as the 'A

ABOVE *Advertisement, c.1996, promoting the Halls for a variety of events showing previous examples.*

LEFT *Catalogue for the 3rd The Creative Show, organised by Centaur Exhibitions, held in both Halls, on 14-16 May 1996.*

member of the team. Fashion shows became regular events during each London Fashion Week. Events became more extravagant and technical. Car launches saw the new-look VW Beetle unveiled, as well as the Maserati Quattroporte and, in 2010, Lotus. Anniversary events rolled by, sophisticated receptions and dinners came. The three main political parties continued to use the Halls for their press launches, rallies and special conferences. In the Lawrence Hall, John Smith had been poignantly elected the new Labour Leader after Neil Kinnock at their Special Conference on 20 July 1992. On the dais with them were Michael Foot, James Callaghan, Margaret Beckett, Roy Hattersley, Bryan Gould, John Prescott, Jack Cunningham and Peter Mandelson. As a counterpoint to this, the Women's Conservative Party National Conference had been held in the same hall two years earlier on 3 June 1990. In October 2004, the world's most prestigious literary award, the MAN Booker Prize, was also staged there, and televised live to a BBC2 and BBC4 audiences. However, with these types of events came the realisation that more work needed to be done to this Hall, in particular, to address issues of improved acoustics, sound containment, better PA systems, greater operational flexibility and upgrades to the services. The Conference Centre was also tired and out of date. It was

Team', which included Susan Perry, Vivienne Scott, Marietjie Grose, Helen Jones and Maugie Lyons on the sales and administration side. On the operational side, these included Sam Dunthorne, Graham Curran, Roy Clarke, Roy Stone, Mourad Messari and Stuart Medhurst. George Long, acting in his often thankless task of having to marshall traffic in all weathers and conditions, and placate residents at the same time, is also fondly remembered as a stalwart

The Lindley Hall
Tuesday 20 March 2001

time for another major upgrade across all three facilities, and this was carried out to excellent effect. In our Spring 2007 Newsletter, I reported that, 'Our capital investment strategy (which included £1.2 million during the past year) has been entirely focused on achieving even greater flexibility, enabling us to operate as a truly multi-purpose venue. Given that the Halls were not designed for this purpose and are Grade II Listed, this has required particularly innovative thinking. The results have been remarkable and our greatly extended client base is a vindication of our efforts.'

ABOVE FAR LEFT
Commemorative brochure produced to celebrate the launch of the Lindley Hall (previously known as Hall 1, the Old Hall and the Royal Horticultural Hall), held there on 20 March 2001. Funds were raised for the homeless at this event through the charity, Crisis.

ABOVE AND LEFT
Photos of new Maserati car launch held in the Lindley Hall, on 19 June 2007.

LEFT   *Photo of Neil Kinnock, James Callaghan and Michael Foot at the Labour Party Centenary Celebrations, held in the Lawrence Hall, on 28 February 2000. They had also been there on 20 July 1992, when they attended the Special Conference of the Labour Party to elect John Smith the new Leader, following Neil Kinnock, and to elect Margaret Beckett as Deputy Leader.*

Mind Body Spirit and Healing Arts

This exhibition has already been referred to earlier, but its effect on present-day thinking has been as revolutionary as the early pioneers of alternative and natural ways of keeping healthy in mind, body, and spirit. When the show was first launched in 1977 at Olympia as the Festival of Mind and Body, Graham Wilson, its founder, would have had little idea what impact his show would have around the world. By the time it arrived at the RHS New Hall on 3-6 May 1985, it had become known as the First Festival of the Spirit: the former Mind Body Festival was held in Brighton's *Metropole Hotel* on 25-7 May in the same year. In one form or another, his Festival would continue in the New Hall for 25 years up to the time of writing, i.e.

2010. On 6 -8 November 1987 he launched the Psychic and Mystic Fair, once again in the Hall. The following year he launched Healing Arts at Kensington Exhibition Centre. On 24-8 May 1990 he launched The First Green Consumer Exhibition in the RHS Old Hall. Sadly, this was not repeated, even though the ticket entitled free entrance into the Festival for Mind Body Spirit in the adjacent Hall. However, it does tell us that he was again ahead of his time in wanting to bring to everyone's attention the important issues of renewable energy, deforestation, acid rain, river and sea pollution, ozone protection, and third-world implications. The 3rd Healing Arts Exhibition is first recorded taking place in the RHS New

RIGHT *Programmes for the 1993, 1995, 1998, 1999 and 30th Anniversary 2006 Mind Body Spirit Festivals, held in the Lawrence Hall. Front cover designs by Philip Cohen (1995, 1998 and 1999); Philip Cohen and Naki (2006).*

Hall later that year on 8-11 November 1990. This was to become his complementary and sister show to Mind Body Spirit for the next 15 years, closing finally in 2003 to be replaced by a rebranded version called, The Wellbeing Show, and opened by David Cameron, MP, in 2005.

In 1993, Wilson had claimed that, 'The Festival for Mind Body Spirit was the original event of this kind (alluding to the many others that were by now copying his show all around the world) and is the longest running and best attended new age festival in the world.' On the occasion of the 25th anniversary of the show in 2001 a special series of presentations and acknowledgements were made to Graham Wilson on the raised dais of the New Hall by many people who had benefited from the 25 years of his Festival in recognition of his achievement. They included many of the exhibitors, performers, speakers, healers, spiritualists, ecologists and practitioners of natural health that were changing the development of human consciousness where health, and healthy living was concerned. Also there to lend her personal, rather than professional, support was PR guru, Lynne Franks, herself a keen advocate of The Festival and all it stood for. My own contribution was small, but I did point out that, through his event, Wilson had brought into the lexicon of the English language the words Mind Body Spirit as a universally applied and recognised phrase that women's publications, and the media overall were using regularly, almost as a fixture, for reporting on alternative health for their readers. Wilson had not only held his show in London, but in Manchester, UK; Sydney Australia (1989-present); Melbourne, Australia (1992-present) and prior to Australia in New York (1979), Los Angeles (1982 and 1983), and San Francisco (1983), USA. It still continues under new owners in Australia, and in the Lawrence Hall, London.

This brought about a spate of smaller Mind Body Spirit or similarly termed events staged by other organisers, and these can now be found in many cities and towns throughout the world. It also spawned offshoots such as The Organic Food & Wine Festival, first staged in the RHS New Hall on 30 July-1 August 1999.

RIGHT *Poster labels for the 1922 and 1950 Photographic Fairs, held in each Hall, on 1-6 May and 12-17 May respectively.*

A Century of Photography

Photographic congresses and fairs have been held in the RHS Halls since 1910 when Lord Redesdale (whose daughters became known as The Mitford Sisters, and who had also been a Member of the RHS Council) opened the 1st Congress of the Professional Photographers' Association (P.P.A.) and the Photographic Arts & Crafts Exhibition on 9 April. Records show that they held eight of their 15 Congresses in the Hall between 1910 and 1930. The Photographic Arts and Crafts Exhibition was staged separately in the Hall on a number of occasions until 1933, and organised by Arthur C. Brookes of 'The Photographic Dealer'. Both the Congress and the Exhibition planned for 10-15 May 1926 were cancelled, due to the General Strike. At the 16th Congress of the P.P.A. held in the New Hall on 12-16 May 1930 when 'A Photographic Fair' was also held, a Play called 'Forward' written by Ben Elton was performed by members of the North London Centre of the P.P.A. on 13 May. A souvenir programme of the latter exists with corresponding photos of the performance included in it. A unique poster stamp also exists for this event. These poster stamps/labels, also often called Cinderella

RIGHT *Poster label for the Photographic Arts & Crafts Exhibition, organised by Arthur C. Brookes of 'The Photographic Dealer', that was to have been held in the Lindley Hall on 10-15 May 1926, but was cancelled due to the General Strike.*

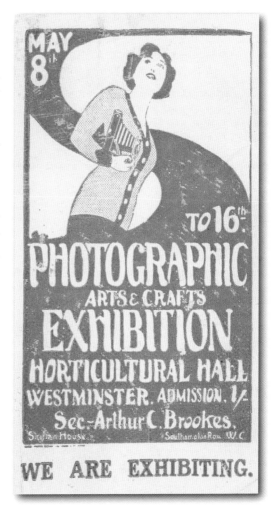

Stamps, were used by organisers of exhibitions and events such as these to advertise them. Separate ones were also printed for use by their exhibitors who would stick them on their letter or post card to let people know where and when they could see them. I have included almost all those known to have been printed for the RHS Hall events. Millions of others for other venues and events have been printed for similar purposes in Europe and across the world since the late 19th century, and were art forms in their own right. Many are now highly collectable, and expensive!

The first post-Second World War Photo Fair to take place in Britain was organised by British Organizers Ltd of 52 Grafton Way, London, W1 in the New Hall on 16-21 May 1955. British Organizers had been formed in 1920 by our old friend, Ernest Schofield, and between then and 1940 had been responsible for organising, or had been associated with, over 24 exhibitions all around the country. These included the London Medical, Chemist, Hospital, Nursing and Public Health events he had started, with the Schoolboys and Bachelor Girl's Exhibitions, the Cinema Accessories and Musical Appliances Exhibition, Simple Life, Wireless, Tobacco Trade, International Oil, Fish Trades, Modern Housekeeping, and Modern Homes.

The 1955 Photo Fair was also the first to have been staged in Britain for 25 years, and was opened by The Marquis of Ely. An Advisory Council existed of four leading photographic consumer and trade publications, the Photographic Importers' Association and the Photographic Dealers' Association. This was regarded as an important new exhibition that boosted the photographic industry, and was filmed by *Pathé News*. However, it would be another 15 years before another photography exhibition would take place in the Halls. This was called the Photography at Work Exhibition and was first staged in the New Hall on 15-18 June 1970. My records show that it was repeated in 1970, 1971, and 1975, but it could also have taken place in the intervening years. The next event to come to the RHS was one that would be held annually in the Old Hall for 24 years from 11 May 1986 to 23 May 2010,

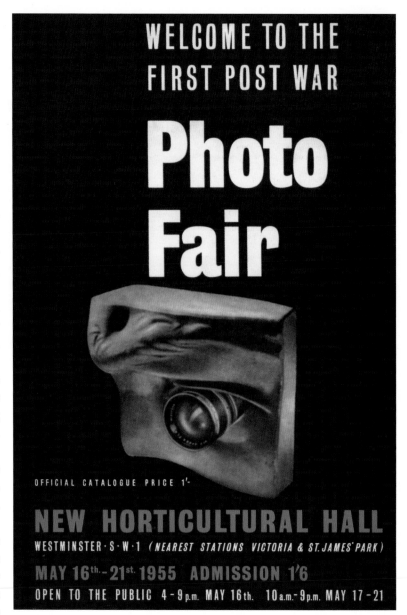

and looks likely to continue. This was first held in the Porchester Halls, London on 5 May 1985 and was called Photographica. At the time of writing, Photographica is the United Kingdom's largest photographic collectors' fair organised by a separate sub-committee of the Photographic Collectors' Club of Great Britain; a Club first formed in 1977. From those early beginnings the Club has grown into around 1,500 members located across Europe, America, Asia and Australasia. The Club imposes no restrictions on membership. The overwhelming majority of members are collectors but the Club also includes those who are involved in photographic history professionally including

Catalogue for the First Post War Photo Fair, held in the Lawrence Hall on 16-21 May 1955.

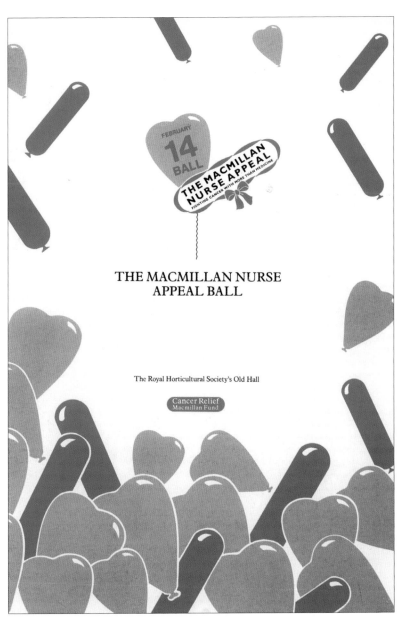

THE MACMILLAN NURSE
APPEAL BALL

The Royal Horticultural Society's Old Hall

Cancer Relief
Macmillan Fund

Programme for the Macmillan Nurse Appeal Ball, organised by Cancer Relief Macmillan Fund, held in the Lawrence Hall on 14 February 1992. Front cover designed by Harrison/Zulver.

some have found their way back, just like the model at the Sotheby's auction that I referred to earlier, but with secret images captured long ago. To round off this now extended century of photographic activity in the RHS Halls the Association of Photographers (AOP) Annual Awards took place in March 2005 and 2006 in the Lawrence Hall.

Adams Antiques (The Record Breaker)

I have given many examples of enduring exhibitions, fairs and events that have been strong fixtures in either, or both, of the Halls throughout the 106 years since the first 'New Hall' was built. In terms of duration, the London Medical Exhibition lasted longest from 1905 to 1962, albeit with some long breaks in between. The Model Engineer is the next longest from 1907 to 1960, also not continuously. The Badminton Championships can claim a virtual, 30-year continuity between 1910 and 1939. Junior Fashion Fair did run continuously for 30 years between 1953 and 1982, but with two events per year, making 60 continuous events in all. However, the event that breaks all records in terms of the number of events held in the Halls is the Adams Antiques Fair. Run by Matthew Adams, I was delighted to present him with a very good bottle of Champagne in July 2004, in recognition of what was then his 175th Fair in the Hall. Since then, he must have reached, if not exceeded two hundred. His first Fair had been held in April 1989, and he went on to establish his Sunday Antiques Fair as one of London's most popular, and well known, matching those of Portobello, Bermondsey and Camden. Matthew had started out by trading watches, bags, clothes and accessories between Tehran in Iran and Herat in Afghanistan to supplement a meagre teacher's income in Iran. On returning to England in 1979 he carried on trading by selling antiques and vintage fashion at the now defunct north London Swiss Cottage Market, and by 1980 had set up the thriving Stables Market in London's Camden Lock. In between dealing in antiques, textiles and vintage fashion both in London and America,

museum curators, dealers, publishers and practising photographers.

A typical Photographica Fair has around 200 tables offering everything from daguerreotypes and images, to brass and mahogany field cameras and Leica, through to old and new photographic books, collectable photographic accessories and supplies and tools for restoration. Photographica is also international in its stallholders and attendees. I have a fanciful notion that, during the time Photographica have held their fairs in the original RHS Hall where early shows in them saw the use of the very early cameras, magic lanterns and slides, optical toys, cine, kaleidoscopes and daguerreotypes, he has been running vintage fashion and retro events in London ever since, and now also runs a vintage fashion fair in Chelsea and Brighton called 'Frock Me!'

While on the subject of Fairs and Markets, it would be remiss of me not to also mention the Cancer Relief Macmillan Fund Christmas Market. This was first held in the Lindley Hall on 1-4 December 1988, and continued until 2008, after which it fell prey to the financial crises of the day. The established fixture, especially loved by all those ladies from Pimlico, Chelsea and Belgravia who liked to shop (as well as lunch), and who regularly supported this important charity, suddenly stopped coming. What had been the most important revenue-generating event in London for the Fund evaporated, together with the sponsorship that had supported it for so long. However, the Homes & Gardens Christmas Grand Sale was another similar event that raised funds for charity, this time in support of the Junior and Senior Leagues of Friends of the Royal Marsden NHS Trust. This had been started by Robert and June Torrance, and later similarly followed up by Noelle Walsh and David Heslam with their own 'Value for Money' event that was simply known as The Grand Christmas Sale.

Who Do You Think You Are?

We have recently become fascinated by the origins of famous personalities presented through the television series, Who Do You Think You Are? And rightly so. Delving into one's past to find out who one's ancestors are, what they got up to, whence they came, and discovering relatives you never knew existed before, can be both exhilarating and shocking; sad or funny; frustrating, or fulfilling. A catalyst for this show, that has generated an even greater interest in family history and genealogy than existed before, was the Family History Fair that was first organised by The Society of Genealogists in the Old Hall on 16 May 1993. Here, family history societies from all over the UK gathered to advise and help an army of mostly senior citizens who made their way to the Halls, keen

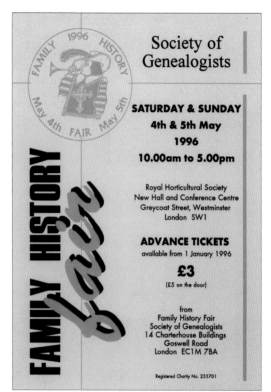

Programme for The 4th Family History Fair, organised by The Society of Genealogists, held in the Lawrence Hall on 4-5 May 1996.

to bridge long-standing gaps in their own family histories. But like time itself, the only thing that is constant, is change, and on 30 April 2004, the last show in the then Lawrence Hall took place before it moved to Olympia in 2005, where it became bigger, better supported (sponsored by Ancestry.com) and re-titled to WHO DO YOU THINK YOU ARE? Live, on the back of the TV series. The rest, they say, is history. In all, the Society of Genealogists had held their Family History Fair at the RHS on 12 occasions over 12 years, and seen the interest in it grow to the point where they had to move. I was personally sorry to see it go, as I had nurtured its early start with the then organisers, Marjorie Moore and Vivienne Lawrie. It is now billed as the largest family history and genealogy event in the world.

Answers on a Postcard

The link between postcards and family history is almost seamless, because so many collectors of cards are searching for their roots, whether these are in the towns or villages they and their ancestors lived in, or the actual buildings/dwellings themselves.

Commemorative postcard for the 1894/1994 Picture Postcard Centenary Exhibition, held in both Halls on 30 August–3 September 1994. Designed by Bill Kirkland and published by the Postcard Traders Association.

David and Maggie Davis have organised the BIPEX Picture Postcard Shows from the first event staged in the New Hall on 30 August-3 September 1994 up until the present time (11 events over 11 years in all). The first one was auspicious, since it celebrated the centenary of the postcard on 1 September 1894. They confirm that the main interest from UK collectors is for topographical cards where they can use them for family history purposes; the church where their grandparents were married, for example. David recalls that, 'At the 2010 Show, a customer bought a card of the village where he lives in Suffolk and told us that the old cottage shown thereupon was actually on the site of his house, and he had never known exactly what was on the site previously, and over the years, we have had people find postcards with pictures of themselves, or family members, that they were completely unaware of.' He went on to say, 'Visitors from overseas tend to be specific subject collectors (glamour artists, royalty, or trains, for example) rather than topographical collectors.'

During the time these have been organised on an annual basis, they have had exhibitors from 22 different countries and visitors from even more. Radio stations from across the

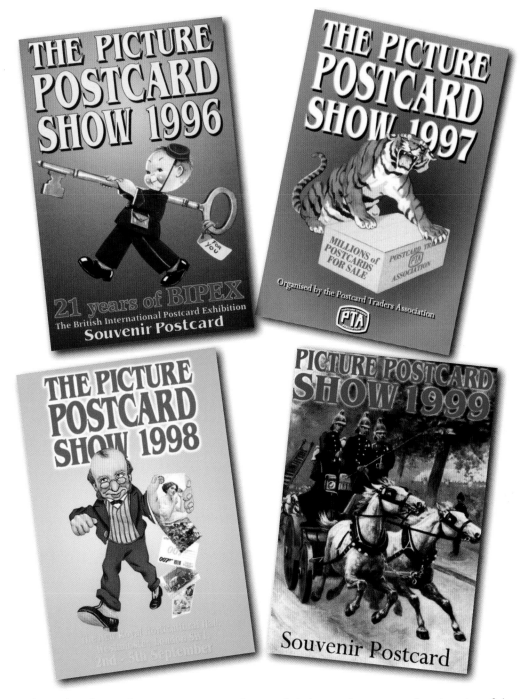

UK have also always shown an interest in the exhibition and set up live links from it, but also from as far as Australia.

A misconception, perhaps, is that postcards are cheap and almost 'two a penny'. Not so. Many special interest and scarce postcards can start easily at £20 and rise to the hundreds. The most expensive cards that have been sold (to David's knowledge) were a set of Antarctic exploration cards that gave the buyer little change from £20,000!

It is interesting to note that, in spite of the internet, there is still a great interest shown by people visiting live exhibitions, fairs, and events as these do give them the opportunity of seeing the complete range of subjects available on postcards. There is also nothing like actually seeing and feeling the card before purchase. The paradox is that the internet has, in fact, produced a new breed of collector who, once they have been hooked into buying on line, do eventually get out and visit these events.

IX

Horticultural Excellence, Sweet Peas and Floral Splendour

The RHS Today

As will have been evident, I have concentrated my book on the non-horticultural events in the Halls for the reasons already given. However, it would be remiss of me not to make reference to the exceptional and diverse range of flower, fruit, vegetable, plant and garden exhibitions that have been held in the Royal Horticultural Society's London halls from the very start. My own experience of them during my 17 years' tenure at these halls is full of wonderment at the skills shown by those who regularly transformed the Halls into vibrant vistas of colour, peaceful enclaves of dappled foliage, spiky and regimented landscapes of cacti, exotic orchid displays, and extraordinary line-ups of onions, potatoes, carrots, beetroot, parsnips, celery, apples and pears, to name but a few. I am a self-proclaimed non-horticulturalist (I don't even have a garden) but I do know that the art and science of horticulture requires great skill and application, and this was shown regularly at the London Shows staged by the RHS, and its many specialist and affiliated societies.

Sadly, these London Shows have now reduced in number to only four a year due to a variety of factors, some already referred to in earlier chapters relating to the licensing restrictions imposed by the Local Authority to abide by the Environmental Protection Act, and a self-imposed Good Neighbour Policy drawn up in the 1990s. However, this is not the first time the London Halls have been so little used by the RHS. In 1976, the Halls were only used on five occasions for flower shows, and four of these were in tandem with Affiliated Societies, and not in their own right.

In 2011, the RHS Shows planned will be the RHS London Plant and Design Show on 15 and 16 February; the RHS London Orchid Show and Botanical Art Show on 19 and 20 March; the RHS Great London Plant Fair on 29 and 30 March, and the RHS London Autumn Harvest Show on 4 and 5 October. The Camellia competition will also take place during the first two shows; the Daffodil and Rhododendron competitions during the third, and the fruit competition at the Autumn Show.

The heydays of the many affiliated and specialist societies that also regularly used these halls for their own shows have long passed, for similar reasons. This is in stark contrast to the position in 1985, when, according to Brent Elliott, in his book, *The Royal Horticultural Society – A History*

LEFT *Early RHS Vegetable Show being judged in the Lindley Hall, c.1910/15.*

1804-2004, he states that, 'By 1985 there were upwards of 2,000 affiliated societies'. I was a member of RHS Director General, Andrew Colquhoun's Working Party set up in early 2000 to look into the relationship between Affiliated Societies, Specialist Societies and the RHS. My report identified that within the previous 10 years the Chrysanthemum, Dahlia, British Orchid Growers' Association (BOGA), and Lily specialist societies had all booked the Halls independently for their own events at preferential and subsidised rates from the RHS, but that the Chrysanthemum and Dahlia Societies had both been forced to find other venues because of operational constraints. They had been used to arriving very early in the morning to set up their displays – sometimes also working through the night, and one of my three recommendations made in my paper was that this could not continue if the annual Exhibitions Licence issued by Westminster City Council that was required to operate the Halls was to be protected.

Brent Elliott covered the history of the Society's flower shows extensively in his book,

LEFT *Photo of Pumpkins and Chillies at an early Vegetable Show in the Lindley Hall, on 8 January 2007.*

not just in the London Halls, and not just from 1904 when the first Hall was built, so I am not going to attempt to repeat this. Nevertheless, in highlighting some of the flower shows that have taken place in London, it is also important to refer to the primary flower and horticultural shows that the Society stages across the country. The RHS Chelsea Flower Show is, without doubt, a world-renowned event, and the pinnacle of the horticulturalist's and garden aficionado's calendar; rightly so. The Hampton Court Palace Flower Show, RHS Show Tatton Park, and RHS Show Cardiff have certainly also established themselves as notable fixtures, and earned appropriate

RIGHT *Photo of The Big Lunch held in the Lindley Hall on 2 April 2009.*

RIGHT *Poster label of the RHS Spring Flower Show, Cardiff, held 18-20 April 2008.*

sobriquets to match. There are three other regional shows that the RHS are jointly involved in with other organisations. These are BBC Gardeners' World Live in Birmingham, and the Malvern Spring Gardening and Autumn Shows. The RHS is also a major publisher in its own right, publishing a large number of publications, from magazines, to books and videos. Three of the world's most respected gardening journals: *The Garden*, *The Plantsman* and *The Orchid Review* disseminate invaluable information to the Society's membership of *c.*360,000, and through national and international outlets on every subject relating to horticulture and gardening. The newly configured Lindley Library at Vincent Square is truly an exceptional resource for horticulturalists and gardeners alike. And then there are the Gardens. There can be few serious horticulturalists or gardeners that have not heard of, or visited, RHS Wisley Garden,

See us at the
Royal Horticultural Society's

RHS Spring Flower Show, Cardiff
18 – 20 April 2008
Tickets: 0870 040 0286
www.rhs.org.uk/flowershows

Surrey, with its recently added Glasshouse opened by HM The Queen on 26 June 2007, when I was also privileged to be there. This boasts the UK's first Root Zone – an interactive area where you can find out more about roots and the vital role they play. Equally splendid are its other gardens in Harlow Carr, North Yorkshire; Rosemoor, Devon, and Hyde Hall in Essex.

Horticultural Shows of the Past

Returning to the London shows, the first fortnightly RHS Westminster Flower Show to be held in its New Hall on Vincent Square was on 26 July 1904, just four days after the formal opening of the Hall. This show was held in conjunction with the National Carnation and Picotee Society when their annual competitions were also staged. The fortnightly shows were held on Tuesday for one day only until March 1913 when they became two-day shows, adding Wednesdays. The first Autumn Show of Roses held by the RHS in conjunction with the National Rose Society took place on 20 September 1904.

LEFT *Photo of Joan Collier admiring the carnations on display at the 'Flowers in Season' show at the Lawrence Hall on 2 April 1935.*

Then on 4-6 October, the 11th annual RHS Great Autumn Show of British-grown autumn fruits was staged, swiftly followed by the 1st National Potato Society Show held on 22 November. At the next show in 1905, the *Daily Mirror* reported that, 'specimens of the Eldorado, the most valuable variety of the potato in the world have just been exhibited. The exhibitor paid £40 for four small tubers weighing three-quarters of an ounce each.' This worked out at £477,000 per ton! The 1st RHS Colonial Exhibition of colonial fruit, and of preserved fruits and jam was on 13-14 December 1904. Exotic fruit, the Durian, Mangosteen and Christophine were on display at the 11th RHS Colonial Grown Fruits and Vegetable Exhibition on 13 June 1907. Donald Smith, 1st Baron Strathcona and Mount Royal, opened the 1908 Show. Lord Strathcona was a Scottish-born Canadian fur trader, financier, railroad baron and politician who became one of the leading supporters of British imperialism in London. Both the 3rd and 4th Barons Strathcona served on the RHS Council between 1939-41 and 1975-8, respectively.

BELOW *Invitation card to the National Chrysanthemum Society to attend the 1933 AGM in the Lindley Hall Restaurant.*

In 1905, the fortnightly RHS Show on 23 May also included the National Tulip Society, and later that year saw the Evening News Chrysanthemum League Show take place on 14 October. The League was a short-lived creation of the Evening News, presumed to be for the interested subset of its readers. The National Chrysanthemum Society began at Stoke Newington in 1846, and after a few changes of name it became the National Chrysanthemum Society in 1884, with its own show of the same name regularly taking place in the RHS Hall many years later. The Evening News was still involved in 1906, and many years later staged its own Garden Lovers' Flower Show in the New Hall on 4-5 July 1947. In the Foreword to their show catalogue for this event, they confidently stated, 'This year it is by way of being an experiment, but as there can be no question of its success, or the need for it, we look forward to the Evening News Garden Lovers' Show taking rank with the Royal Horticultural Society's Chelsea Spring Show, and the great late Summer Flower Shows of Southport and Shrewsbury, as one of the

National Chrysanthemum Society.

Secretary: CHARLES H. CURTIS, F.L.S., V.M.H., 5, Tavistock Street, W.C.2.

January 21st, 1933.

You are requested to attend the ANNUAL GENERAL MEETING of Members of the National Chrysanthemum Society, which will be held in the Restaurant, Royal Horticultural Hall (Old Hall), Vincent Square, Westminster, S.W.1, at 6.30 p.m., on Monday, February 6th, 1933.

Subscriptions for 1933 are now due.

PRIVATE VIEW.—Noon to One p.m.

NATIONAL ROSE SOCIETY
1914.

MEMBER'S TICKET.
(Transferable.)

THIS TICKET WILL ADMIT THE BEARER TO THE

AUTUMN ROSE SHOW

Which will be held in

The Royal Horticultural Hall, Vincent Sq., Westminster, S.W.,

On THURSDAY, 24th SEPTEMBER, at or after Twelve o'clock.

The Exhibition will be open till 7 p.m.

9441

This Ticket must be given up at the Entrance.

P.T.O

THE NATIONAL ROSE SOCIETY

Member's Transferable Ticket

THIS TICKET WILL ADMIT THE BEARER TO THE

1956 Summer Rose Show

TO BE HELD IN

THE ROYAL HORTICULTURAL SOCIETY'S HALLS
WESTMINSTER, S.W.1 (Nearest Station St. James's Park)
ON FRIDAY & SATURDAY, 29th & 30th JUNE, 1956

TIMES OF OPENING AND CLOSING

JUNE 29th   11 a.m. to 7 p.m.   (New and Old Halls)
JUNE 30th   10 a.m. to 5 p.m.   ·· (New Hall only)

THIS TICKET MUST BE
GIVEN UP AT ENTRANCE

H. EDLAND, Secretary

The Royal Horticultural Society's Tickets do not adm...

NATIONAL ROSE SOCIE...
1928.

MEMBER'S TICKET.
(TRANSFERABLE.)

This Ticket will admit the bearer to the

GREAT SHOW of NEW ROSES

Which will be held in the

Horticultural Hall, Vincent Square, Westminster, S.W1.,

ON

TUESDAY, JULY 24th, 1928.

The Show will open at 12.30 p.m. and close at 6 p.m.

THIS TICKET MUST BE GIVEN UP AT THE ENTRANCE.

COURTNEY PAGE, Hon. Secretary.

[P.T.O.

ABOVE *Member's tickets for the 1914, 1928 and 1956 National Rose Society Shows at both Halls.*

LEFT *Photo of young woman admiring a 1st Prize bowl of cut Roses at the Great Spring Show, held in the Lindley Hall on 25 April 1930.*

RIGHT *Catalogue for The* Evening News *Garden Lover's Flower Show, held in the Lawrence Hall on 4-5 July 1947.*

premier horticultural events of the year.' I have been unable to find any record of a subsequent show taking place! However, eight years later the Modern Gardening Exhibition took place in the New Hall on 25 and 26 February 1953. This was organised by Chase Protected Cultivation Ltd, who were based at 93, The Grange, Chertsey, Surrey, and had advertised in the 1947 Evening News Garden Lovers' Flower Show catalogue. This

must have been one of the first commercial gardening shows to be held in the Halls, other than those organised by the Society. They also had over 25,000 Members in 1947 belonging to their Chase Cloche Guild. They didn't return in 1954, and I have unable to find anything further about this event, or whether it was repeated elsewhere.

The Winter Carnation Show took place on 13 February 1906 with the 6th Annual

National Sweet Pea Society Show taking place on 5-6 July. The RHS Exhibition of Hyacinths took place on 31 March 1908 and the National Dahlia Society Show on 3 September that year. The 10th Annual National Sweet Pea Society Show was held on 13 July 1910 (the Society had been formed in March 1901, and a request for Sweet Peas to be shown at the RHS Rose Show was first agreed on 30 July in the same year). Sweet Peas were a particular favourite of Lord Northcliffe whose *Daily Mail* sponsored a Sweet Pea Competition offering a £1,000 (£86,550) prize for the best Sweet Pea in 1911. The winner was the Rev. D. Denholm Fraser, who published a book *Sweet Peas: how to grow the perfect flower* as a result. Sweet Peas were also one of only four flowers included for competitions at the Evening News 1947 Flower Show, also previously mentioned. The 1st National Hardy Plant Society's Show took place on 19 June 1912 and the Rhododendron Show on 27-30 May 1913. The National Gladiolus Society held their show on 1 October 1914 and the RHS Daffodil Show on 18 April 1915. Flowers, trees and fruit from a Persian garden valued at £3,000 (£254,400) were exhibited on 17 February 1914, but these had been in the form of a carpet when an exhibition of Eastern rugs and carpets was held, and at the 9 August 1921 RHS Council Meeting a tenancy was confirmed for the Guild of Blind Gardeners, although there is no record of when this took place.

Meanwhile, on 20-2 September, the Surrey Beekeepers' Association, who in an evolved form would later become regarded as a 'kindred society' of the RHS, held their annual show at Crystal Palace. The September issue of *The Chemist & Druggist* reported, 'the biggest display of honey and honey produce seen anywhere this year.' They had exhibited as early as 1884 as the British Bee Keepers Association at the International Health Exhibition in the same year. They first came to use the RHS Hall in 1937 with their 15th National Honey Show after Crystal Palace had burnt down within a month of their 1936 Show. Mr David Lloyd George had been a regular exhibitor, and had opened the 1936 Show. Mr James New, as a student at the

Catering College (next door to the RHS Hall) from 1935-8, and whose father, a 'Beekeeper', who won a medal at this show, recollected that he cooked 'teas' for exhibitors and the public at these Shows for 1s. per evening session. This was under the direction of Mr Iwan Kriens, a top Chef, and later President of The Universal Food & Cookery Association, but who was then acting as a caterer to the RHS and its clients. The National Honey Show returned in 1937 and 1938. The Hall was unavailable in 1939, and the Second World War then intervened. Consequently, they did not return again until September 1949. They had tried to hire the Hall in 1947, and had requested a discount but the RHS did not consent to this. They returned each year until 1954, however, this show had to be cancelled, due to bad weather that summer having affected the bee's production. Billed by the 7 August issue of *The Times* that year as, 'the biggest affair of its kind in the world, as a rule attracting about 2,000 entries' the show had never been cancelled before. Caxton Hall in Westminster became their next principal venue until it closed down in 1983. [see inset box]. The National Honey Show returned to the RHS eventually in 1990. Unfortunately, they became a victim of the steep increase in rates from 1992, and 1991 was the last time they used the Hall.

> Caxton Hall had, as referred to earlier, famously hosted many suffragette meetings and a very wide variety of other events from disparate organisations of the day. During the Second World War it was used by the Ministry of Information for Press Conferences given by Winston Churchill and his ministers. From 1933-77 many thousands of couples were married at Caxton Hall in the Westminster Registry Office including Sir Anthony Eden, Ingrid Bergman's third marriage, Elizabeth Taylor's marriage to Michael Wilding, Peter Sellers, Roger Moore, Diana Dors (twice), George Harrison and Ringo Starr.

Set of poster labels for the Royal International Horticultural Exhibition, held at the Royal Hospital Gardens, Chelsea, on 22-30 May 1912. This was, in effect, the start of the Royal Horticultural Society's most enduring horticultural event, The Chelsea Flower Show.

Postcard of Carters Prize Exhibit of Kales etc at the RHS Show, held at the Lindley Hall on 25 May 1916.

In a lecture at the RHS Vegetable Show on 26 September 1911, Mr Herman Senn talked on 'Salads – Subjects for, and their Preparation'. As previously mentioned in an earlier chapter, Senn gave regular lectures on cookery subjects, especially on the subject of the use of vegetables in cooking, and the RHS would publish several of his articles in connection with its wartime work on domestic food production. He was asked to join a Vegetable Show Committee, formed by Sir Austen Chamberlain when acting as Chancellor of the Exchequer, and with Lord Lambourne, the RHS President at the time. The *Daily Mail* had organised a Home-Grown Food Exhibition in the Hall opened by Sir Horace Plunkett on 22 September 1915, and seven years later, after the War, staged the *Daily Mail* Imperial Fruit Show at the Crystal Palace on 25 October-4 November 1922.

Allotments Rule

In today's environment of heightened ecological and environmental consciousness, allotments have become *de rigueur*, and waiting lists for them have become as long as the early days of golf club memberships were. There is a desire by our frenetic, stress-laden, and computerised lifestyles to return to our roots. The desire to return to organic and, seemingly, more healthy food has also driven our desire to shun mass produced food. The cost of food has also prompted many in unstable situations to return to the land and cultivate their own. During the First World War allotments became hugely important, but were then, understandably, driven by real and urgent needs to produce as much home-grown food as possible. Brent Elliott again explains in his book that, 'The Society's work on vegetables suddenly took on national importance. As early as February 1915, the Society had issued press statements on the importance of private gardens growing vegetables, and it began that year to issue pamphlets on fruits and vegetables for the home garden, fruit bottling, and vegetable cookery.' The government promoted a scheme to encourage allotments, and the Society supported this. Evidence of this movement to promote allotments and gardens for home-grown food production continued well after the war, and into the Second World War. Lord Lambourne, the Society's President, attended the Gardeners' (Livery) Company ladies' dinner at the Grocers' Hall in the presence of the Lord Mayor and Lady Mayoress and the Sheriffs on 14 March 1923. He was quoted by *The Times* the next day as having said that, 'the Gardeners' Company had done a great deal in the way of allotments, and the coming exhibition in 1924 would probably afford the company and his society an opportunity of working together and showing to the world at large what two ancient institutions could do in helping horticulture.' The Gardeners' primary objective was 'to promote the art and practice of good gardening throughout the country', but especially in the City of London and the London area, and this remains the case to the present day. The 1924 show was duly held on 4-6 September.

LEFT *Menu for the Royal International Horticultural Exhibition Banquet held at the Lindley Hall on 24 May 1912. The catering was provided by Messrs Searcy, Tansley & Co. Ltd, now known as Searcys.*

LEFT *Schedule of Classes and Handbook, 1938, for the 17th Annual London Allotments and Gardens Show of Vegetables, Fruit Flowers, Honey and Preserves held at the Lawrence Hall on 3 September 1938.*

The London Gardens Guild, and The London and District Allotments and Garden Society all held shows in the halls on subjects such as town gardening, fruit and vegetable growing through the 1920s and early '30s. At the 6th London Allotments and Garden Society Show in 1927, Lord Lambourne opened it. The Minister of Agriculture sent a message pointing out that there was no part of the country where greater benefits could be derived from allotments and gardens than in London. David Lloyd George also made it clear in his foreword, that the allotment holders of the country had made a magnificent

response to the national appeal, and that they should not be squeezed out of existence now. The Secretary of the society highlighted the fact that there were 'about 50,000 allotment-holders around London, and a large waiting list.' The London Gardens Guild & Garden Society annual Fruit, Flower & Vegetable Show held in the New Hall on 25-9 August 1931 judged over 3,000 entries from those with gardens in London's Council Housing Estates. The Horticultural Society of the Ministry of Agriculture & Fisheries, based at 10 Whitehall Place, SW1 also ran annual Fruit, Flower & Vegetable Shows in the Old and New Halls between 1931 and 1939. The Gas Light & Coke Co., that had exhibited in the Hall at several non-horticultural shows since 1906, also formed its own Horticultural Society and ran a Vegetable & Flower Show in the New Hall on 26 July 1930. In between this activity, the RHS and its affiliated societies ran their own shows and the Iris Society Flower Show was opened by the French Ambassador

in the Old Hall on 6 June 1929. The 6th RHS Cherry & Soft Fruit Show opened in the New Hall on 16 July 1929. The 1st Annual Show of the Alpine Garden Society took place in the Old Hall on 8 and 9 May 1930, and the Cactus & Succulent Society of Great Britain staged their own show in the Old Hall on 20 June 1933. The London Gardens Society, based at 47 Whitehall, SW1 ran its own Summer Show of Flowers in the Old Hall on 24-5 July 1936 and, thereafter, each year up to 1939. The Civil Service Horticultural Federation (based at the Metropole Building, Nothumberland Avenue, SW1) Fruit, Flower & Vegetable Show was held in the New Hall on 9 July 1937, and thereafter also ran up to 1939. The Future of Gardens and Gardening had been the subject of a conference by the Institute of Landscape Architects, chaired by Sir William Lawrence, in the New Hall on 15 April 1931. One suggestion was that a new feature for all future large gardens should contain, as an essential element of the plans,

ABOVE *Photograph of BBC Radio 4's Gardeners' Question Time panel during their 2,000th programme held live in the Lindley Hall on 1 November 1992. The panel was chaired by Clay Jones and the speakers were Dr Stefan Buczacki, Sue Phillips, Fred Downham and Daphne Ledward.*

LEFT *Photograph of Martin Slocock, Chairman of Horticultural Halls Ltd, presenting Clay Jones, Chairman of BBC Radio 4's Gardeners' Question Time with a gleaming watering can, on the occasion of their 2,000th programme held in the Lindley Hall on 1 November 1992.*

a landing place for aeroplanes. This did not appear to have got off the ground! However, what was transmitted across the airwaves from the Society's Hall in 2000, was the first of several Gardeners' Question Time programmes to be broadcast from an RHS site. The anecdote that links this to my earlier references concerning allotments is that the very first Gardeners Question Time, broadcast on 9 April 1947, took a panel of expert gardeners along to answer questions from members of the Smallshaw Allotments Association.

Floral Splendour

Floral display and arrangement for its own sake, rather than for reasons of cultivation and propagation, fuelled a long-running saga of contentious debate within the RHS over a long period of time as to whether this warranted recognition by the RHS, or not. Brent Elliott deals with this admirably in his book. Suffice to say here that the key event that led to flower arranging becoming organised as a movement in its right took place on 16-17 July 1952 when The Flower Academy Exhibition took place in the New Hall. The London Floral Decoration Society had been one of four clubs and societies that organised this. The following year, they staged their own show in the Old Hall on 29 June-1 July and again in the Old Hall on 21-3 June 1954. They subsequently changed their name to become the National Floral Arrangement Society and staged annual shows in the RHS Halls through to 1961, when the Flower Arrangement Association of London and Overseas staged a show in the Old Hall on 6 December. There appears to be a gap after this, but they re-appeared on 21 July 1965 as the National Association of Flower Arrangement Societies of Great Britain (NAFAS) with their Festival, 'This Sceptr'd Isle'. Many years earlier, on 24 October 1933, an Exhibition of South African Wild Flowers had been opened by Princess Alice, Countess of Athlone, in the Old Hall. This was fitting, since she had been the Vicereine to her husband who

had acted as the Governor-General of the Union of South Africa from 1924-31. At the 1933 Rhododendron Show displays of 20ft specimens from the Himalayas were the attraction. In 1935, an RHS Exhibition of Paintings & Drawings of Plants, Flowers & Gardens took place and an RHS Ornamental Flowering Trees and Shrubs Conference was held in the New Hall on 26-9 April 1938.

The Second World War disrupted inter-War normality but, on 25 September 1945, the 3rd Royal Air Force Fruit and Vegetables Show took place in the New Hall. During the Second World War, the RAF had cultivated around 6,330 acres of surplus land to produce food for their own consumption. Post-war Britain slowly built itself back up and the RHS continued to develop with it through highs and lows of development and change, to become what it is today. Undoubtedly, one of its most successful recent projects has been its involvement with 'Britain in Bloom', the national horticultural competition first held in 1963 by the British Tourist Board. The RHS first became involved in 1990 with the then organisers, the Tidy Britain Group. From 2002 it has organised the competition by itself with the support of heavyweight sponsors such as B&Q and Shredded Wheat. 'Britain in Bloom' encompasses 12 English regions, as well as Scotland, Wales, Northern Ireland, Isle of Man, Jersey and Guernsey. Because of the area that is covered, judging usually takes place over two years in two stages. Sixty-seven participants compete across 13 categories, of which seven are for towns, cities and urban groups with five categories covering villages and coastal communities, and one for high achievers from any category. All who reach the UK Finals are aiming to earn the highest recognition for their efforts, a gold medal, and possibly be awarded the title of category winner. Floral displays play an important part in the contest, but the 'Bloom' title is now, perhaps, misleading: in recent years the competition has increasingly assessed how all sectors of the local community are managing their local environment, enabling a real sense of civic pride for them. It is commonly accepted that the concept for 'Britain in Bloom' was taken from a French competition that originally resulted from the orders of President Charles de Gaulle to brighten up the country after the war. This French competition was first called 'Fleurissement de France' in 1959, but has since been renamed as the 'Concours des villes et villages fleuris'.

London Hall Visits by the Society's Royal Patrons

References to the visits by Their Majesties King Edward VII and Queen Alexandra to the Halls have already been made in earlier chapters, as have references for HM King George V. Not all have been documented, but at the RHS Flower Show on 29-30 June 1920, Queen Mary, accompanied by Princess Mary, paid a informal visit to this show on the first day and was received by the Society's 10th President Lord Lambourne, and by Mr W.R. Dykes, the Society's 17th Secretary. Queen Mary was Patron of the RHS from 1910-53. She returned to pay a visit to another of the Society's flower shows on 13 March 1923. On that occasion she was accompanied by Sir George Holford, one of the Society's Vice-Presidents. Mary, Princess Royal was patron from 1928-65.

Queen Elizabeth (the Queen Mother) as RHS patron from 1936-2002 was one of the Royal Family's most active and regular visitors, not only to the London Shows, but to the Society's Gardens and Chelsea. Her brother, Sir David Bowes-Lyon, served on Council at various periods between 1934 and 1961, served as the Society's 13th president from 1953-61 and as Treasurer from 1948-53. From what I have been able to find out, Queen Elizabeth's first visit to an RHS Flower Show in the Halls was on 6 March 1951, when she opened the first RHS Spring Orchid Show. She returned on 2 July 1976 to visit the National Rose Society Show in the New Hall, accompanied by Queen Ingrid of Denmark, and again on her own the following year to the same show. Brent Elliott makes no reference to the Society's current patron, Queen Elizabeth II, having paid any visits to the London Hall for any of its own flower shows, although *The Times* reported on 6 April 1960 that she had, 'for the first time, exhibited plants before a committee of the RHS'. This was at the Society's two-day show that had opened the day before on 5 April. Four varieties of *Camellia Japonica* were displayed, and three of them, 'Pink Champagne,' 'Mrs D.W. Davis,' and 'Tomorrow' – received awards of merit. As Duchess of York, Queen Elizabeth the Queen Mother had visited the Old Hall as early as 3 November 1931 when she attended the 9th Applied Arts and Handcrafts Exhibition, and brought her daughter with her, our present Queen, who I have been told bought a small zebra foal from ceramic sculptor, Stella Crofts, at her stand.

Postcard of HM Queen Elizabeth II, c.1953, and a present day Royal Patron of the Royal Horticultural Society. Her Majesty has been a Royal Patron of the Society since 1952, following the death of her father, King George VI, who had been a Royal Patron since 1936. Queen Elizabeth II (the Queen Mother), had also become a Royal Patron in 1936, and remained so until her death in 2002. HRH Mary, Princess Royal, also acted as a Royal Patron from 1928-65, partly during HM The Queen's own term as a Royal Patron.

X

Personal Recollections

During the 17 years I was at the RHS there were a number of events, situations, and circumstances that stand out, each for different reasons. I would like to end my journey through almost 11 decades of the Society's event, and social history in its Halls with a few of these. Before doing so, I have to thank all of those that supported me throughout my time there managing and repositioning these Halls which became recognised as one of London's leading event venues in the face of increasingly strong competition. My task in transforming the tired and financially underperforming Halls when I first arrived was made easier by their advice and support. I am going to refrain from individually naming them all because there are too many, but they include my staff, my respective Chairmen who kept me on the straight and narrow, members of my Board, and the many officers and executives of the RHS throughout, especially Donald Hearn, who acted as Secretary and Finance Director from 1989-2001. My book is dedicated to the late Geoffrey Harvey, the first Managing Director of the RHS Halls, whom I succeeded. Christopher Bricknell, the Society's first Director General, who served from 1985-93, referred to him as 'a much valued colleague and friend for many years … and was certainly one of the great stalwarts that progressed the RHS during his time with The Society'. I also owe him a debt of gratitude for having given me the opportunity to take on the mantle I did, at a time when my own personal situation was very difficult.

Millennium Crisis

The next two entries involve crisis and suffering, both in name and nature. In 2000, the homeless charity, Crisis, approached me to see if I would support a Millennium Party for 700 of London's homeless. I agreed to do so, and to be personally involved in it, and be present on the night. The event was originally opposed by local residents, and had to go through a Westminster Council Hearing for a decision that was supported by local Councillors, the Police and me. HRH Princess Anne and her husband, Commander Tim Lawrence, visited the party before they sailed down the Thames on their way to the Dome Millennium Party. The Lord Mayor of Westminster was also in attendance to meet HRH. He got short shrift from a man who wanted to know why he had come to their party, but had never come to see him on the streets where he had been all year! It was an extraordinary party, an extraordinary way to have celebrated the Millennium, and not without incident. In the end, it had to be stopped at 3 a.m. rather than going on throughout the night, as originally planned.

7/7 Crisis

On the Sunday afternoon of 10 July 2005, I received a call at my home from one of my staff who passed me to a senior police officer in the Metropolitan Police. He was in our Lindley Hall wanting to move in there and then to relocate what had been named the 7th July Family Assistance Centre. This had been set up immediately after 7 July London bombings that killed 52 people and injured more than 770. Westminster City Council, as the Local Authority, and the Metropolitan Police had been caught unawares, and did not have a contingency venue to use that was ideal for this purpose. They had immediately requisitioned The Queen Elizabeth The Queen Mother Sports Centre in Vauxhall Bridge Road. The principal reason for doing so was to provide a facility that would meet the needs of the families and victims of the London bombings. The Sports Centre was not ideal for their purposes, and in looking for a better venue they had been recommended to contact me. I was asked if I would come up from Brighton immediately by taxi so I could deal with this, which I did. When I arrived a plan had already been drawn up of how it would look, and I was told that this was being sanctioned at the highest level, via the Office of the Deputy Prime Minister, leaving me in no doubt that I should allow this to proceed, without formality or contract (the following day, the Prime Minister, Tony Blair, announced in the House of Commons that the Centre would be moving from the Sports Centre to the RHS Halls on 12 July). Overnight, they set up a new, more appropriate Centre that would stay there until 21 August. Fortunately, we were not overly booked and were able to relocate, and rebook events we already had. This Centre was the first of its kind to be set up in Britain and was the basis for considerable further debate and future policy decision making on them. A video entitled, 'Messages from 7/7' was produced by the Metropolitan Police, which I contributed to, and which featured footage of the Centre in the Lindley Hall in operation. The Centre operated as a

multi-faith and multi-agency, visited by Tessa Jowell, and the then Mayor of London, Ken Livingstone. Subsequently, in March 2006, I was asked by the Metropolitan Police and Cabinet Office to present to country-wide Local Authority representatives at the Cabinet Office's Emergency Planning College in York. This was part of a series of courses entitled 'Family Assistance Centres', with the principal aim, 'To enable delegates to develop plans and management strategies to implement the Humanitarian Assistance in Emergency Guidance on Establishing Family Assistance Centres.' In short, these were to ensure that, if any future man-made or natural disaster of the same magnitude, or more, befell any major city in the UK, the Local Authority concerned would be prepared with a contingency plan already in place. When the 7 July bombings had taken place not only was there no prior experience to inform development, but there had been no forward planning because the guidance document on humanitarian assistance was still being drafted, was not in the public domain, and had not been seen by the emergency responders. New non-statutory guidance was later issued by the Rt. Hon. Tessa Jowell, MP, acting in her capacity as Minister for Humanitarian Assistance when it was also explained that the usage of the name, Family Assistance Centre, had been changed to Humanitarian Assistance Centre.

The Westminster Connection

I hope that it will have been apparent from what I have already illustrated in previous chapters that the location of the RHS Halls in Westminster has always been an important thread, binding it to its potential clients and other external interests. This was also recognised by several other primary venues in Westminster as early as 1994 when Malcolm Miller from Church House Conference Centre and I discussed the formation of a Westminster venues marketing collective that could promote itself to buyers, both to refer

Photo of The Westminster Collection Showcase, held in the Lindley Hall, on 12 October 2006.

and retain the business within, rather than lose it to other parts of London, or elsewhere. However, this first attempt did not get off the ground for a number of reasons, and it would not be until nine years later that a second attempt was made by me and Lacy Curtis-Ward who had, by then, taken over from Malcolm at Church House. This time agreement was reached to form the group under the name I had coined for it, The Westminster Collection (TWC). Its first members were the RHS, Church House Conference Centre, Central Hall Westminster, *The Rochester Hotel*, City Inn Westminster and One Whitehall Place. It grew organically under my Chairmanship until August 2008 when it became formally constituted as a Not For Profit Limited by Guarantee Company with a board of five directors. Under this configuration I became Chairman of the Board, and also CEO. The Collection grew rapidly thereafter to include over 50 of the leading venues in the City of Westminster, supported by both Westminster City Council and Visit London. Its mission was agreed early on: 'To be recognised as the leading business tourism marketing collective in Westminster for venues and events' and this has already been achieved. Underpinning this were three core values, one of which was

in 'understanding that our strength is both our individual and collective attributes'. To this end I also created a 'Showcase' event, at which all members would be able to promote themselves equitably to potential buyers. These early Showcases were held in the Lindley Hall.

As I write this book, the Collection grows from strength to strength. Wider recognition and support is being given by Westminster City Council in support of the work TWC does in strengthening Westminster's brand and status, as the World's leading business tourism destination, enhanced by The Westminster Destination Guide, also conceived by me in 2007 that is offered by Visit London as one of its seven official Event Planner's Guides.

Unsurprisingly, many of the venues that are now members of TWC are historically intertwined with the RHS by dint of some of the early events that took place in the Halls. The Royal College of Surgeons with the New Health Society and medical exhibitions/ conferences; RICS with their very early exams as the Institution of Surveyors, and Central Hall with regular crossovers of events between us including The Model Railway Club exhibitions, STAMPEX, and many others. Central Hall is particularly famous for having held the first session of the newly configured United Nations General Assembly, convened on 10 January 1946, following in the wake of the failed League of Nations. Two years later, on 17 January 1948, the RHS New Hall was the location for the United Nations Association National Appeal Committee's first Dance and Auction that had the Mayor of the City of Westminster and many of the London Metropolitan Mayors in attendance. The film star, Miss Barbara White, gave away prizes! The Methodist Association of Youth Clubs (M.A.Y.C.) Council London Weekend Celebration events were also held in the New Hall between 1953 and 1957. The Royal Aeronautical Society (now based at No.4 Hamilton Place) were involved with the 1907 Travel Exhibition and Model Engineer Exhibitions, and the Institution of Civil Engineers, also known as One Great George Street, were involved in the Model Engineer Exhibitions. The National Liberal Club, also known as One Whitehall Place and St Stephen's Constitutional Club, would have been where their respective political party members would have met (and still do) to discuss campaigns, meetings, and receptions, many of which took place in the Halls. One Queen Anne's Gate was the home of Sir Edward Grey, but is now a conference centre and meetings facility and the Royal United Services Institute (RUSI) is where high level discussions on most matters of a military nature were discussed, including the physical training methods of the British Army when Madame Österberg was proposing her own to them.

Chocolate Galore

In 1997, I managed to persuade my board that we should not only manage the Halls, but also run events to generate more profit and maximise their occupancy (something I had included in my original 1991 proposals). A separate subsidiary company, HHL Events Ltd, was formed to deal with these and a number of events were planned and held. Unfortunately, these were short-lived. However, the 1st and 2nd International Festivals of Chocolate, both held in the

Lawrence Hall, were conceived by me, but run as a joint partnership with Touchwood Exhibitions Ltd on 27-9 November 1998 and 3-5 December 1999. Apart from claiming to have the world's largest chocolate bar (9½ feet long weighing more than a ton) and young girls choosing to bathe in chocolate, this event (the 2nd Festival) is particularly memorable because of the fact that a full-sized chocolate replica of Alain Prost's Formula 1 Racing Car that I had located at an earlier festival in Paris, and which I had arranged to be displayed at my own, arrived from France by truck shattered into hundreds of pieces. On 2 December 1999, the *Evening Standard* reported the story as a '£40,000 meltdown! Disaster as full-size chocolate Grand Prix car smashes into hundreds of pieces on lorry.' The maker of the car, French *chocolatier* Pascal Guerreau was devastated when he arrived from Paris separately to see it, but the simple truth was that the car had not been packed properly to withstand the bumpy ride. It had taken Guerreau more than 400 hours to make the 600kg sculpture, and had been made from the same moulds for the actual AP01 car that Alain Prost had managed the year before. Guerreau managed to work on it before the

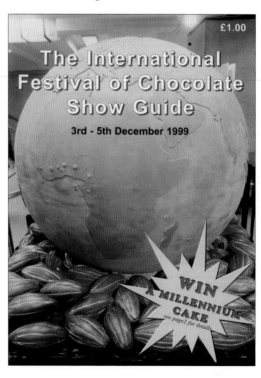

Catalogue for the 2nd International Festival of Chocolate, held in the Lawrence Hall, on 3-5 December 1999.

Photo of The International Festival of Chocolate held in the Lawrence Hall on 27-9 November 1998.

BELOW   *Photo of life-sized replica of Alain Prost's Formula 1 racing car made with chocolate, with its creator, French chocolatier, Pascal Guerreau.*

show opened and put a fair chunk (or should that be chunks) of it back to achieve a good resemblance of the car, and it was positioned, as originally intended, centre stage alongside Prost's actual car. In fact, in the end, the damaged car caused more interest than had it been intact!

The International Festival of Chocolate had been conceived to bring to the British public the very best chocolate that one could buy from around the world. It was strongly supported by The Chocolate Society and luminaries from the world of real chocolate such as Chantal Coady from Rococo in London's King's Road. Chocolate cookery demonstrations and Forums & Tastings took place at the Demonstration Theatre in the Hall by other aficionados and experts such as renowned chocolate maker, Gerard Ronay.

Jayne-Stanes, Director of Culinary Arts, Chocolate Evangelist and author of *Chocolate*, was there, as was Craig Sams, co-founder of Green & Black's, Clair Clark, Head Pastry Chef at Claridge's (and one of Britain's finest *chocolatiers*), Nicola Porter, co-founder of The Chocolate Society, Eric Deblond, Executive Chef at *The Four Seasons Hotel* and food writer, Steven Wheeler.

Exhibitors came from as far afield as Mexico, the Middle East, Sweden, Italy, Belgium, and France. However, mainly because of the very high sugar taxes that were imposed on those chocolate manufacturers who wanted to distribute their specialised products in Britain, but could not afford to do so, the opportunity to develop the event further as a consumer show did prevent it from becoming the success it deserved to be. Certainly, the public response to it was emphatically positive. One day, perhaps, there will be another opportunity to revive this event because there are some extraordinary chocolate manufacturers around the world that are being prevented from presenting their excellent products to a British market due to these largely protectionist taxes.

Party Time

In the early part of 1994 Bentley's Entertainments, run by Peregrine Armstrong-Jones, approached me about a tenancy in the then named Hall 2 for his client, Intercapital Brokers. It would be a 1960s themed party. A party it certainly was, and those members of staff from Intercapital Brokers who came to it on 1 July that year will, I'm sure, remember it well, and wonder if they will ever see anything like it again in this current period of austerity. It certainly is the most extravagant and cleverly designed event I have ever seen staged in either of the Halls during my tenure. It is also the only occasion I have known when a two-tier construction was built in the Hall using its height to full effect. No other organisation has ever done this before, or since (other than during the 1952 Silver Jubilee Schoolboy's Exhibition

Above *Photo of Intercapital Broker's 1960s themed party, organised by Bentley's Entertainments, held in the Lawrence Hall on 1 July 1994.*

when a 36ft tower was built for young boys to jump off in a simulated Red Devils parachute jump). 1960s music and *The Bootleg Beatles* rocked, 1960s fashion models displayed, 1960s DJs compèred, and Hell's Angels bikers revved their bikes outside. Centre stage was

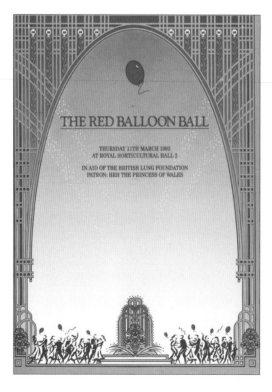

THE RED BALLOON BALL

THURSDAY 11TH MARCH 1993
AT ROYAL HORTICULTURAL HALL 2

IN AID OF THE BRITISH LUNG FOUNDATION
PATRON: HRH THE PRINCESS OF WALES

Left *Programme for The Red Balloon Ball, organised by The British Lung Foundation, held in the Lawrence Hall on 11 March 1993.*

ABOVE *Photo of the Anderson Consulting Dinner Dance, held in the Lawrence Hall on 19 March 1994. This was organised by The Finishing Touch who themed the Hall as a cruise ship.*

an extraordinary and giant-sized psychedelic octopus with arms waving and light beaming from its eyes. Bentley's did come back to us with a few more of their exceptional events, but nothing ever compared with their first. In 2009, Peregrine celebrated the 25th anniversary of when he first established Bentley's Entertainments in 1984. During that time he had organised some of the most prestigious, lavish, and unique events for his clients worldwide. These included the wedding of David and Victoria Beckham, a BOND mission weekend on the ski slopes of Gstaad, the Civil Ceremony of Sir Elton John and David Furnish, a 'Pirates of the Caribbean' week in Barbados, the wedding of Elizabeth Hurley to Arun Nayar, the World Cup Full Length & Fabulous Ball 2006, and the Royal Wedding of Peter Phillips to Autumn Kelly.

Photo of red-carpet entrance to the Lindley Hall for a series of Mask Entertainment Christmas themed corporate events in 1991. These included, Bank Credit Suisse, Price Waterhouse, Bank of Bilbao, BUPA, and Philips and Drew. The Corinthian Casuals Football Fundraising Ball was also held here in 1991. Since the changes made to the building in 2000, the front entrance is no longer able to be used in the same way.

Exhibition and Events Industry
Show Time

Having been an exhibition and conference organiser who became a multi-purpose venue owner, and subsequently became involved in most other areas of what is known as the Meetings, Incentives, Conferences and Exhibitions (MICE) industry, including corporate hospitality, I knew it was essential that the RHS Halls positioned themselves prominently within these sectors. One of the ways to do this was to become a main sponsor of a new MICE event. SHOW'95, conceived by Gordon Holt, Managing Director of Show Management Services Ltd, and staged in the New Hall on 12 and 13 January 1995, drew the exhibition industry together in a way that had not been done before, although MICE industry events had been staged before.

Indeed, as far back as 1979, Exhibition '79 was staged on 3-5 July in both RHS Halls, following its first appearance at Wembley Conference Centre on 8-10 February 1978. This event was organised by Network, based at Market Hill, Buckingham, and well before what has now become the main industry event in the UK, CONFEX, that was first launched by Blenheim Exhibitions in 1984 at the Barbican.

Catalogue for SHOW '95, organised by Show Management Services Ltd, held in the Lawrence Hall on 12-13 January 1995.

Subsequently, MICE '87 (Meetings Industry Charity Event) took place in the RHS New Hall. This was inaugurated by Rob Spalding, Peter Longbottom, John Jones, Nic Mayne and others, supported by M&IT Magazine and held on 14-16 May 1987. I have also found a reference to a MICE'84, but am unsure if that took place in the RHS Hall, or elsewhere.

For SHOW '95, a steering committee had been formed to develop this that, apart from SMS Ltd and the Halls, consisted of the Incorporated Society of British Advertisers (ISBA), the late Mike Agostini of The Exhibitor Club, Peter Cole of Exhibition Bulletin, and Paul Rouse, Editor of Conference and Exhibition Fact Finder. The Exhibitor Club had already established their regular programme of events in our recently developed Conference Centre where the legendary Mike Agostini would tackle his evening talks and presentations with memorable relish and gusto! In the Show Catalogue, Bryan Montgomery, acting in his capacity as President of *Union des Foires Internationales*, the world association for exhibition organisers, hall owners, and specialist trade associations, wrote the Foreword (spelt Forward) and reminded everyone that his own company would soon celebrate the centenary of their first exhibition, the Building Exhibition, that I have referred to earlier.

SHOW '95 was a success, and repeated as SHOW '96 the following year using both Halls, before it moved on to the Business Design Centre when it later became known as EVENT, then lost ground and faded away. The same sponsors supported SHOW '96 with

Photo of the Royal Horticultural Halls & Conference Centre 'A' Sales Team on their stand at CONFEX, Earl's Court, London, c.1994. From left to right in red are, Helen Jones, Maugie Lyons and Susan Parry. The lady in the middle was receiving a Certificate for the 'Most Productive Agent' and a bottle of Champagne.

additional support from Haymarket Business Publications. Of interest to all who have watched the development of London's newest exhibition centre, and latterly the launch of London's new International Convention Centre (ICC) at ExCel in Docklands, is that ExCel first exhibited themselves with their early development plans, and a model of what ExCel might look like when built, at this show on their stand No. 272. The London Docklands Development Corporation selected London International Exhibition Centre Ltd (LIECL) as the preferred developer. Ian Shearer was then heading up this initiative, and the current CEO, Kevin Murphy, was also there separately, chairing one of the innovative '39 Steps of Effective Exhibiting' sessions entitled, 'Preparing your company for the exhibition', but in his then capacity as Exhibition Director of EMAP Business Communications. The 39 Steps of Effective Exhibiting was a force in itself, and one that was physically presented by Keith Reading of SMS Ltd in the form of an ambitious feature in Hall 1; verbally in the form of a wide ranging seminar and conference programme, and as a dedicated publication of the same name. The overall result was probably the most concentrated and educational programme ever staged for the benefit of potential exhibitors, and the principles behind it became a template upon which future industry organisations, such as the Association of Exhibition Organisers (AEO), would rely for many years to come. The 74-page publication, written by Gillian Cartwright, had a cover price of £5 on it and was on sale at the show. Trevor Foley, who would become a prominent figure and driving force in uniting industry associations to become what is now known as the Event Industry Association (EIA), was also there, but employed then with the Audit Bureau of Circulation. He had been my client for some time before, holding many of his own training seminars in the Conference Centre.

There has been substantial change in the last twenty years with many MICE organisations having either rebranded, regrouped or disappeared due to market conditions and changed priorities. One organisation that has stayed the course, and celebrates its 40th anniversary in 2011, is the Association of Conference Organisers (ACE).

They first formed in 1971 at 71 Portland Place, and Peter Cox became their first Secretary General. However, the longest running MICE publication still in circulation today, *Exhibition Bulletin*, is 63 years old. Now published by Mash Media, its first issue was published in November 1948 by The London Bureau, run by Peter Cole.

A Centenary Marked

The launch of the Royal Horticultural Society's Bicentenary was marked at their London Show in the Lawrence Hall on Monday, 16 February 2004, when HRH The Duke of Edinburgh attended. 2004 was, of course, also the Centenary of the Lindley Hall, and I marked this with a Centenary Exhibition, held in the Lawrence Hall on

Front cover of Conference & Exhibition Fact Finder June 2002 Supplement that depicts the iconic ident used by BBC Television. This was filmed by 2AM Films on 21-3 March 2002 and used by the BBC for a five-year period.

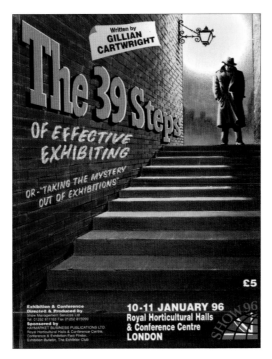

Booklet entitled, The Thirty Nine Steps of Effective Exhibiting – or taking the mystery out of exhibitions, *written by Gillian Cartwright, and produced for SHOW '96 in both Halls, on 10-11 January 1996.*

14 and 15 September during the Society's Great Autumn Show. This was supported by a number of RHS Members who responded to my call to arms made in *The Garden* when they let me have their own recollections of non-horticultural events that they had either visited as children, or participated in later.

Much of the material that I had painstakingly gathered for this display during the previous five years had never been seen before by long-standing members and trustees of the RHS,

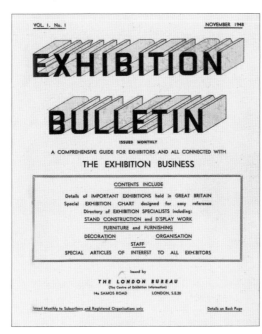

Cover of the first Exhibition Bulletin issued by The London Bureau (the Centre of Exhibition Information) in November 1948.

because not a great deal of the archives for these activities had been retained or documented. Certainly, no other person had revealed the true extent of their use before then. This was the moment I knew that a book should be written to record this as an integral part of the Society's history. It has taken me a further six years to achieve this, but in that time I have managed to find out a lot more and fill in many of the gaps that existed. My Appendix listing the events that have taken place in the century since 1904 must be one of the most complete, if not the most complete, record of any London venue over this period of time. By having done so, I have achieved what I set out to do: to reveal just how active and important the Halls have been to the RHS as a matter of record and interest. I have been fascinated and spurred on by the rich tapestry laid in front of me at every turn, as I learnt more about the men and women with drive, ambition, innovation and courage that changed the social conditions, attitudes, industry, art, and culture of Britain during that period, through the events they staged and took part in, in these Halls.

A Crystal Ball

As I write this we are still in an unstable and difficult situation, whereby a spending review by the new coalition government has already led to stringent 'austerity cuts' and the necessity for 'cutting out waste' – the new bywords of government and business. This has had a very real impact on venues in London and elsewhere, especially those that have relied strongly on the Public Sector to date. The RHS is no exception to this, but because of its ability to be multi-purpose, and flexible – something I recognised to be important from the time of my arrival in 1991, and something that shines through from the illustrations of its history that I have given in this book, it has been able to weather many storms, including recessions and closures.

Whatever the advances made in new technologies, face to face meetings, fairs, exhibitions, shows and events will continue to be important and necessary. The advent of virtual exhibitions was announced with great

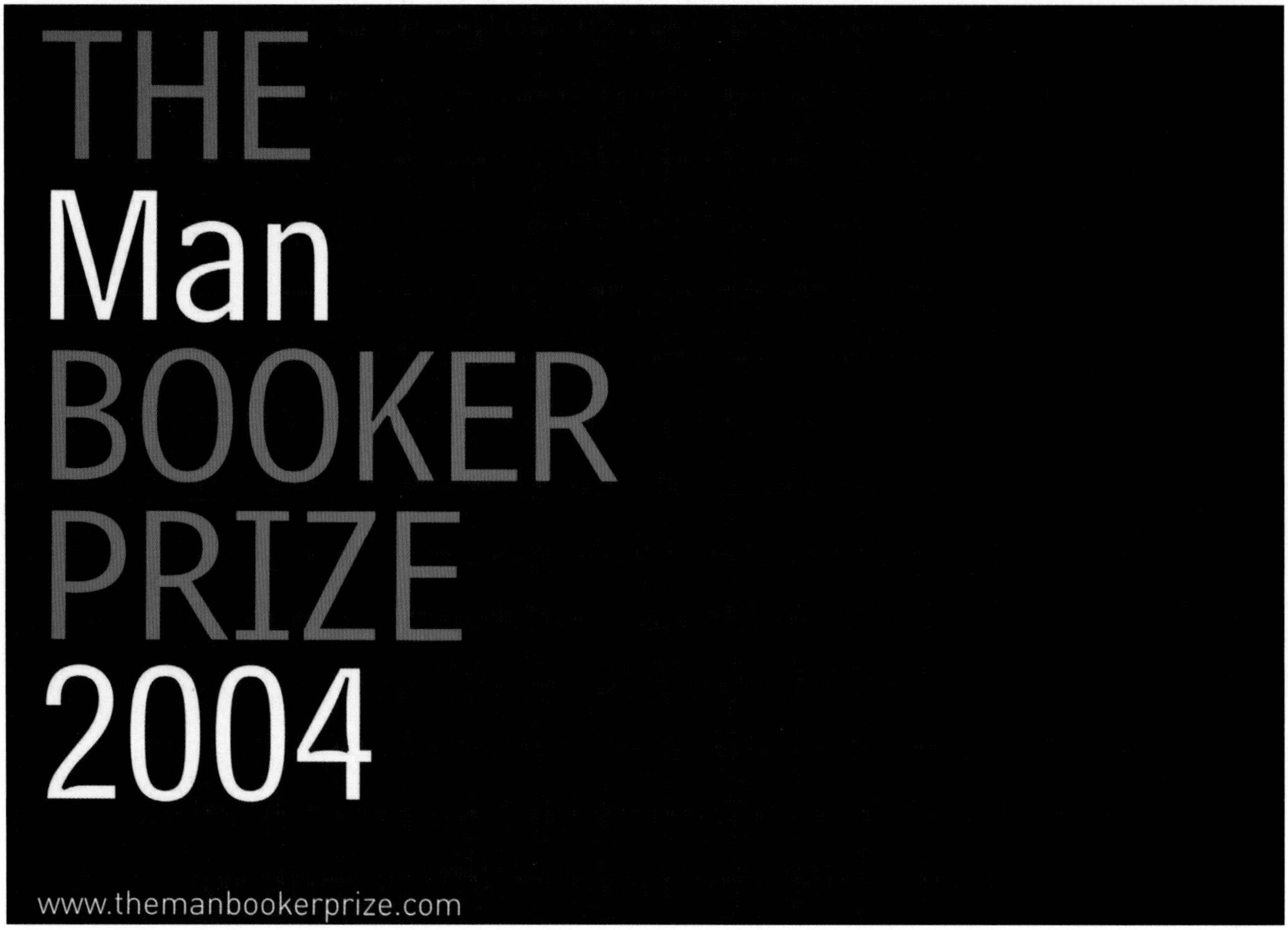

THE Man
BOOKER
PRIZE
2004

www.themanbookerprize.com

Programme for the Man Booker Prize 2004 Awards, held in the Lawrence Hall on 19-20 October 2004.

fanfares by many who proclaimed the end of actual exhibitions, but this has not taken place. There is a place for both. What is also clear is that history shows that the principal consumer and trade themes for events and exhibitions are repeated, albeit re-packaged accordingly. Whether these are better, deemed to be progressive, or whether we have learnt very little and repeat, or compound, our mistakes is up for debate. Once again, the illustrations given in my book give some indicators.

So venues, in all their shapes and sizes, have become increasingly necessary for these diverse business and leisure events to be staged in. Location is also hugely important and central London is very much a preferred location for many.

Paradoxically, it can also have a negative value. The downside is often that venues located in central London are also in close proximity to residential property, causing conflict when late night or noisy events take place. They are also increasingly expensive, not just to hire, but to get to and service. In many cases residential property has been allowed to develop all around them, subsequent to when they were more isolated, and when road access was also more straightforward. This has certainly been the case with the RHS, when, in spite of strong and repeated representations made to Westminster City Council at the time not to build more residential property, this was ignored. A great deal of my time while at the RHS was spent placating the residents around the Halls, regularly addressing sound containment, road and traffic management, access and exit systems and adjusting the type of events we could accommodate to safeguard the necessary annual licences required that were regularly contested by our residents at Westminster City Council Licence Hearings.

The pendulum began to change shortly before I left and now as I write this in the grip of business downturns, Westminster City

Photo of Rick Osman and the author, René Dee, at the Centenary Celebration for the Lindley Hall standing in the Lawrence Hall with a model locomotive, lent by the S.M. & E.E., that had been first displayed at the 1907 Model Engineer Exhibition.

Royal
Horticultural
Society
200 YEARS

The President and Council

request the pleasure of the company of

Rene Dee

*at a Preview of the Society's London Show
to mark the launch of the RHS Bicentenary
attended by HRH The Duke of Edinburgh KG, KT
in the Lawrence Hall, Greycoat Street, London SW1*

on Monday 16th February 2004

R.S.V.P. by 23rd January 2004
The Secretary
The Royal Horticultural Society
80 Vincent Square, London SW1P 2PE

6.00 pm – 8.00 pm
Please arrive by 5.30pm
Lounge suit

Please present this card at the entrance

RIGHT *Invitation to attend the RHS Flower Show on 16 February 2004 to mark the occasion of the Society's Bicentenary. This was held in the Lawrence Hall, attended by HRH The Duke of Edinburgh, on behalf of HM The Queen, Royal Patron of the RHS.*

LEFT   *First day cover posted from Buckingham Palace on 25 May 2004 to commemorate the Royal Horticultural Society Bicentenary Celebration, 1804-2004.*

Council have begun to give more recognition to the value of business and business tourism, in the form of venues such as the RHS Halls, versus wholesale submission to the needs of their residential community. This may change again, but as long as a balance is maintained giving recognition to each other's needs and legal rights, the Halls should be able to continue to serve their diverse community. However, wider scenarios exist. In the past 10 years there

FAR LEFT   *Leaflet commemorating the Horticultural Halls Centenary Exhibition that was held in the Lawrence Hall during the Royal Horticultural Society's Bicentenary Celebration on 14-15 September 2004.*

LEFT   *Centenary birthday card sent to Horticultural Halls from the RHS Publishing Department in 2004.*

have been a number of 'new' venues that have come 'on stream' in the marketplace. Many of these have always been there in their capacity as headquarter buildings; galleries (even Courts of Justice) for whatever institution or body they represent, but have never marketed themselves in this way. Many witnessed the boom years when corporate hospitality, exhibitions and events thrived, and took strategic decisions to invest in substantial refurbishments and redevelopment to take advantage of this. Now that they have, coupled also with substantial new hotel stock coming into the market, there is greater competition than ever, and with no real growth for events in these facilities during the past two years (2009 and 2010) in particular, they will face a long road to achieve the returns on investment they banked on. The RHS and others also face substantial maintenance costs with their buildings that are periodically 'worn-out' through age and use.

Taking into account all of these factors, one of the options open to the RHS and others (and a few have already taken this route) is to divest themselves of the property altogether, thereby also reducing the environmental issues that the RHS Halls have increasingly had to deal with, and relocate outside London where costs are substantially lower. This remains a real option, and so the recording of their history becomes even more important.

A Day in the Life

When Brent Elliott's definitive history of the RHS was published in 2004 he gave me a copy inscribed with the words, 'For René, now it's your turn.' I took up his challenge, and started this book by comparing an exhibition and event Hall with a theatre, remarking that without the events inside them, including the people and sub-texts behind them, they are simply lifeless buildings. I hope that I have succeeded in bringing them to life for you and have revealed their context within our social, political, religious and military history that reflects such a striking diversity and richness of interests, culture, thinking, attitudes, and individuals.

Brent Elliott ended his own chapter on the Royal Horticultural Halls in his 2004 History of the RHS with a piece I wrote for the RHS internal staff magazine *Grassroots* in January/ February 2002. I end mine in the same way, as I believe it is a fitting 'tongue-in-cheek' ending to all those involved in managing event venues, conjuring up images of the Circus, the drama of theatre, the frenetic activity that so often takes place, and the fear of the knife-edge.

The telephone rings. The walkie-talkie crackles. The mobile interrupts. Dawn breaks on Horticultural Halls. Organic debris and life-healing crystals are being cleared from the Halls where the Mind Body Spirit Festival has just died. The Conference Centre opens to a babble of intense and high tensile speakers. Delegates jostle. The coffee is late. The flowers are the wrong colour. Another table is required. The speech is in the third cubicle on the right in the Gent's Loos, at the M4 Granada Service Station just past Swindon. The neighbours would like a word. So would the visitor who has collected a Marks & Spencer jacket but claims a Gucci. It's too hot; please open the windows. It's too cold; please turn up the heating. Excuse me but those delegates look like builders: when did you say the Hall had reopened? Can you please move the Great Autumn Show to fit in a 10-day Korean Trade Fair on semi-conductors? The Heavy Metal Music Convention is coming to the Lindley, but don't tell the DG. The Countryside Alliance rally of 2,000 starts outside the Library at 10 a.m. but don't tell the Librarian. We need an extra breakout room. Can we use the DG's office? We will need to build through the night, and by the way, we will be flying trapeze artists from your girders, but don't tell the Facilities Manager. How many Centurion tanks can I fit into the Lawrence Hall? When are you going to build a tunnel between the two Halls?

The Show goes on. 'Roll up, Roll up'

END

Photo of Jane's Police Awards held in the Lawrence Hall on 13 November 2008, showing the splendid architectural features of this RIBA Gold Award Art-Deco structure at its best.

Bibliography

Adams, Bernard, *The Badminton Story* (London: British Broadcasting Association, 1980)

Allwood, John, *The Great Exhibitions* (London: Studio Vista, 1977)

Arbuthnot Lane, William, *Secrets of Good Health ... President of the New Health Society* (London: William Heinemann, 1928)

Bagot Stack, Mrs, *Building the Body Beautiful ... The Bagot Stack Stretch-and-Swing System* (London: Chapman and Hall, 1938)

Ball, Eric E., *100 Years of Model Engineering ... A History of the Society of Model & Experimental Engineers* (S.M. & E.E, 1997)

Davidson, Rob and Rogers, Tony, *Marketing Destinations and Venues for Conferences, Conventions and Business Events* (Oxford: Elsevier, 2006)

Davis, Joe, *The Breaks Came My Way* (London: W.H. Allen, 1976)

Davy, M.J.B., *Handbook of the Collections Illustrating Aeronautics – 1 HEAVIER-THAN-AIR AIRCRAFT* (London: H.M. Stationery Office, 1935)

Duncombe, Marjorie, *Dancing Fit ... Memoires by Marjorie Duncombe* (Centenarian): Marjorie Duncombe, 2004)

Elliott, Brent, *The Royal Horticultural Society...A History 1804-2004* (Chichester: Phillimore, 2004)

Eucharistic Congress Sectional Meetings Sub-Committee, *Report of the Nineteenth Eucharistic Congress, held at Westminster from 9th to 13th September 1908* (London: Sands, 1909)

Furnell, Michael, *National Philatelic Society Centenary Handbook* (London: National Philatelic Society, 1999)

Glanfield, John, *Earls Court and Olympia ... From Buffalo Bill to the 'Brits'* (Stroud: Sutton, 2003)

Hamilton, Cicely and Baylis, Lilian, *The Old Vic* (London: Jonathan Cape, 1926)

Hobhouse, Hermione, *The Crystal Palace and the Great Exhibition ... A History of the Royal Commission for the Exhibition of 1851* (London: Athlone Press, 2002)

McKellen, Ian, *William Shakespeare's Richard III ... A Screenplay Written by Ian McKellen & Richard Loncraine* (London: Doubleday, 1996)

Mackenzie, Midge, *Shoulder to Shoulder* (Borzoi/Alfred A. Knopf, 1975)

May, Jonathan, *Madame Bergman Österberg ... Pioneer of Physical Education and Games for Girls and Women* (London: Harrap, 1969)

Morgan, Glen H. and Wilson, Graham M., *British Stamps Exhibitions – A Priced CD Catalogue of Sheets, Cards, Labels and Presentation Packs* (London: Glen H. Morgan & Graham M. Wilson, 2010)

Neatby, Kate, *The Artists of the Dance Number Eleven … Ninette de Valois and the Vic-Wells Ballet* (London: British-Continental Press, 1934)

Percival, Alicia C., *About Vincent Square* (London: Vincent Square Residents' Association, 2007)

Pocock, Geoffrey A., *One Hundred Years of The Legion of Frontiersmen … Soldiers, Spies and Counter Spies, Sacrifice and Service to the State* (Chichester: Phillimore, 2004)

Sabey, Alan D., *British Empire Exhibition Wembley 1924-1925 Publicity Labels* (London: Cinderella Stamp Club and Glass Slipper, 1994)

Tanner, W.E., *Arbuthnot Lane, His Life and Work* (London: Bailliére, Tindall and Cox, 1946)

The Institute of Physics and the Physical Society, *Handbook of Scientific Instruments … 1963 Exhibition* (London: The Institute of Physics and The Physical Society, 1963)

Tindall, Gillian, *The House by the Thames … and the people who lived there* (London: Chatto & Windus, 2006)

Worshipful Company of Shipwrights, *Shipbuilding and Ships … Papers Read at the Worshipful Company of Shipwrights Exhibition* (London: The Worshipful Company of Shipwrights, 1947)

APPENDIX

Event History, 1904-2004

1904

8 March: RHS Council unanimously decided to name the new hall, 'The Royal Horticultural Hall'.

3 May: Letting circular for the Hall approved by RHS Council.

22 July: The New Hall opened by HM King Edward VII and HM Queen Alexandra, accompanied by HRH Princess Victoria.

26 July: First Fortnightly RHS Westminster Flower Show held four days after opening.

9 August: First formal Hall Applications to hire the Hall received.

6 September: RHS Council agreed to the Conditions and Regulations and Charges for Letting the Hall. First bookings then accepted on the basis of these.

20 September: 1st Autumn Show of Roses held by the RHS in conjunction with the National Rose Society.

4-6 October: 11th annual RHS Great Autumn Show of British-grown autumn fruits.

18 October: RHS Council reported that the London Coliseum had approached the RHS to be allowed to 'piece and fix stage scenery in the Hall'.

22 November: 1st National Potato Society Show.

23 November: St Margaret's Musical Society Concert.

13 December: RHS Council agreed on this date 'to allow political and other meetings to be held in the Hall, irrespective of party, creed etc.'

13-14 December: 1st RHS Colonial Exhibition of colonial fruit and of preserved fruits and jam.

1905

3 January: Army Examinations.

20 January: 65th Choral Concert by the Bach Choir.

10 March: St Margaret's Musical Society 'Grand Sacred Concert'.

30-1 March: 2nd RHS Colonial Exhibition of colonial grown fruits, vegetables and other products.

6 April: Ladies' Kennel Association Championship Dog Show.

11 April: Westminster Constitutional Association Meeting.

22-6 April: 11th Chemist Society Exhibition.

2-5 May: 16th Universal Cookery & Food Exhibition.

c.May: RHS Colonial Growers' Fruit Show.

16 May: Liberal Social Council Reception.

23 May: RHS Fortnightly Flower with The National Tulip Society.

24 May: The Magpie Madrigal Society Concert.

31 May: Magpie Madrigal Society Concert.

5 June: St Margaret's Musical Society 'Grand Operatic Concert'.

17, 24 June: Madame Bergman Österberg Display of Physical Culture.

1 July: Madame Bergman Österberg Display of Physical Culture.

2 July: Westminster Chapel, Buckingham Gate – Sunday Service.

8 July: Queen's Westminster Volunteers Banquet.

9, 16, 23, 30 July: Westminster Chapel Sunday Service.

6, 13 August: Westminster Chapel Sunday Service.

15 August: RHS Fortnightly Flower Show.

20, 27 August: Westminster Chapel Sunday Service.

3, 10, 17 September: Westminster Chapel Sunday Service.

15 August: RHS Fortnightly Flower Show.

12 September: RHS Fortnightly Flower Show.

21 September: 2nd RHS Autumn Show of Roses.

24 September: Westminster Chapel Sunday Service.

2-6 October: 1st London Medical Exhibition.

10-12 October: The RHS British Fruit Show and Conference.

14 October: *Evening News* Chrysanthemum League Show.

21 October: Trafalgar Day celebrations – Musical celebrations held in the Hall.

24 October RHS: Fortnightly Flower Show.

22 November: RHS Colonial Growers' Fruit Show.

23-4 November: 2nd National Potato Society Show.

28 November: St Margaret's Musical Society Grand Patriotic Concert.

8 December: Winter Show of Pet and Other Dogs.

12-15 December: Smoke Abatement Conference & Exhibition.

1906

13 February: Winter Carnation Show.

15 February: Independent Labour Party Reception.

21 February: 'English Ladies' Orchestral Society Concert.

20 March: 18th London Cage Birds Association Show.

22 March: RHS Colonial Growers' Fruit Show.

30 March: 4th Annual French Bulldogs, Griffons Bruxellois and Pekingese Championship.

17 April: RHS Fortnightly Flower Show.

23-7 April: 12th Chemist Society Exhibition.

5 May: Industrial Exhibition of the Westminster Union of the Church of England Temperance Society.

9 May: Liberal Social Council 'At Home' Reception.

16 May: Magpie Madrigal Society Concert.

17 May: The Annual Meeting of the National Anti-Vivisection Society.

23 May-1 June: International Philatelic Exhibition.

6 June: RHS Colonial Fruit Show.

14-15 June: A Grand Bazaar and Floral Fête.

20 June: Exhibition of Table Decorations &c.
23 June: Madame Bergman Österberg Display of Physical Culture.
28-30 June: Reformatory and Refuge Union Jubilee Exhibition of children's work.
5-6 July: 6th Annual National Sweet Pea Society Show.
17 July: RHS Flower Show.
19 July: Labour Party Inter-Parliamentary Reception.
c.July: 1st University of London Examinations.
13 September: 15th Annual London Bulldog Society Championship Show.
19 September: The National Rose Society's Autumn Show.
20-2 September: *Evening News* Chrysanthemum League Flower Show.
1-5 October: 2nd London Medical Exhibition.
19-20 October: 18th London Cage Bird Association Show.
27 October: Independent Labour Party (Great Britain) Reception.
20 November: RHS Flower and Fruit Show.
22 November: Demonstration in support of Women's Suffrage by Keir Hardie of I.L.P.
27 November-1 December: 17th Universal Cookery & Food Exhibition.
28 November: The Art of Omelet Making – Demonstration Lecture by C. Herman Senn.
2 November: 1st The Gaelic League of London 'Aonach'.
7 December: Pet Dog Society Show.
4 December: RHS Colonial Growers' Fruit Show.
13-14 December: 3rd National Potato Society Show.
17-19 December: The Gaelic League of London 'Aonach'.

1907

1 January: Wimbledon and District Canine Association Dog Show.
8 January: RHS Flowers and Fruit Show.
10-11 January: Southern Counties Cat Club Show.
15-16 January: National Terrier Club Championship Show (*see Daily Express* article, 16 January).
22 January: RHS Flowers and Fruit Show.
23 January: W.S.P.U. women only meeting prior to 1st Women's Parliament.
26 January: Dance in aid of the Orphanages of the Teachers' Union.
31 January: St Margaret's Musical Society Concert.
12 February: RHS Flowers and Fruit Show.
5 March: RHS Flowers and Fruit Show.
8 March: Victoria League Committee 'At Home' Reception.
13 March: 'At Home' Reception – General Committee of the South African Products.
19 March: RHS Flowers and Fruit Show.
23 February-16 March: South African Products Exhibition.
9 April: Ladies' Kennel Association Dog Show.
11 April: 5th Annual French Bulldog, Griffon Bruxellois and Pekingese Clubs Championship Show.
12 April: Soldier' and Sailors' Help Society – Ladies' Association 'At Home' and Concert.
16 April: RHS Flowers and Fruit Show.
20-5 April: 3rd 'Smokeries' International Tobacco Trades Exhibition.
1 May: Magpie Madrigal Society Concert.
6-10 May: 13th Chemists' Exhibition.
18 May-8 June: Travel Exhibition.
31 May: Pomeranian Club Championship Show.
13 June: RHS Colonial Grown Fruits and Vegetable Exhibition.
22 June: Madame Bergman Österberg Display of Physical Culture.
c.July: 7th Annual National Sweet Pea Society Show.
8 July: Pekingese Club Championship Show.
9 July: RHS Summer Show at Holland Park.
c.July: 2nd University of London Examinations.
16 July: 7th Annual National Sweet Pea Society Show.
18 July: The Empire Education Fund Exhibition.
23 July: RHS Flowers and Fruit Show.
24 July: National Carnation Society's Show.

6, 20 August: RHS Flowers and Fruit Show.
4, 17 September: RHS Flowers and Fruit Show.
19 September: 16th Annual London Bulldog Society Championship Show.
21 September: 70th anniversary celebration of the Royal Oak Benefit Society.
24 September: 4th Annual Autumn National Rose Society Show.
26-8 September: The 5th Gaelic League of London Irish Exhibition.
1 October: RHS Flowers and Fruit Show.
7-11 October: 3rd London Medical Exhibition.
15 October: RHS Flowers and Fruit Show.
17-19 October: RHS Show of British-grown fruits.
22-6 October: 1st *Model Engineer* Exhibition.
31 October: Ladies' Kennel Association, Incorporated Dog Show.
5-9 November: 18th Universal Cookery & Food Exhibition.
11 November: RHS Flowers and Fruit Show.
14 November: Llanelli Choral Society Concert.
18 November: 1st 'Healtheries' Pure Foods Exhibition.
26 November: RHS Flowers and Fruit Show.
28-9 November: RHS Colonial Grown Fruits and Vegetables Exhibition.
4-5 December: Sale of Work in aid of Home and Foreign Missions.
6 December: 19th London Cage Bird Association Show of British and Foreign Birds.
10 December: RHS Flowers and Fruit Show.
13 December: Pet Dog Society Dog Show.
16 December: Bazaar and Concert in aid of the Nursing Sisters of the Poor.
18-20 December: The Gaelic League of London 'Aonach'.
21 December: Bazaar in aid of The Sisters of the Poor.
c.December: Hall and basement let to Government's Post Office.

1908

1-2 January: Wimbledon Canine Association Show.
8-9 January: The Southern Counties Cat Club Show.
c.January: An Aonach (Fair), Gaelic League of London.
2 January: Wimbledon and District Canine Association Dog Show.
4 January: 1st Band of Hope and Union event.
13 January: RHS Public Parks Examination.
RHS Flowers and Fruit Show 14 January
National Terrier Club Championship Show 16 January
London Girls Club Union Church Dance 18 January
Grand Lodge 20 January
23 January: The National Women's Social and Political Union Suffragette Meeting.
25 January: Dance in aid of the Orphanages of the Teachers' Union.
3 February: United Kingdom Band of Hope Union Annual soirée.
7 February: Tariff Reform League Annual Meeting & Conference.
11 February: RHS Flowers and Fruit Show.
c.February/March: 'Assaults at Arms' displays.
17 March: RHS Flowers and Fruit Show.
9-14 March: *Daily Mail* Exhibition of British and Irish Lace.
20-8 March: 4th International Tobacco Trades Exhibition.
30 March: Tar-Spraying Demonstration by the Tar Road Syndicate in Vincent Square.
31 March: RHS Exhibition of Hyacinths.
1 April: RHS Spring Carnation and Winter Flowering Carnation Society.
2 April: Soldiers' and Sailors' Help Society Exhibition.
7 April: Old English Sheepdog Club Championship Show.
8 April: 6th Annual Joint Championship Show of Bouledogues Français, Griffons Bruxellois, Pekingese and Pomeranians.
28 April: RHS Exhibition of Flowers and Plants.
29 April: Schoolteachers &c Examinations.
29 April: Watch Tower Bible Society (Jehova's Witnesses).
4-8 May: 14th Chemist Society Exhibition.
12 May: RHS Flowers and Fruit Show.
14 May: Invalid Children's Association.

18-23 May: The National Bazaar for the United Kingdom Band of Hope Union.

22 May: Pekingese Club Championship Show.

26 May: Annual Royal National Tulip Society's Member's Exhibition.

26 May: RHS Temple Show where the Queen visited.

26 May: Children's Aid Society

Pomeranian Club Championship Show 28 May

28 May: Annual Meeting of the Women's Unionist and Tariff Reform Association.

11-12 June: RHS Colonial-Grown Fruit, Vegetables and Preserves Show.

13-16 June: University of London Matriculation Examinations.

17-20 June: 24th Home Arts and Industries Exhibition.

23 June: RHS Flowers and Plants Show.

24-7 June: Patriotic Society Exhibition.

c.July: 8th Annual National Sweet Pea Society Show.

7 July: St Margaret's Musical Society Concert.

8 July: Displays of Swedish Drill by Colonel Fox.

9-16 July: University of London Examinations.

18 July: Madame Bergman Osterberg's demonstrations of Swedish Drill.

21 July: RHS Flowers and Plants Show.

22 July: Carnation Society Show.

24 July: 8th Annual National Sweet Pea Society Show.

4, 18 August: RHS Flowers and Plants Show.

1 September: RHS Flowers and Plants Show.

3 September: National Dahlia Society Show.

9 September: Archbishop of Westminster's Conference.

10-13 September: 19th Eucharistic Congress.

15 September: RHS Flowers and Plants Show.

17 September: National Rose Society Autumn Flower Show.

21-6 September: International Rubber Exhibition & Allied Trades Exhibition.

18 September: 4th Annual National Rose Society Autumn Show.

29 September: RHS Flowers and Plants Show.

5-9 October: 5th London Medical Exhibition.

14 October: The Patriotic Society – General Meeting.

15 October: RHS Flowers and Plants Show.

15-16 October: 15th RHS Annual Exhibition of British Grown Fruits.

20-4 October: Robert Browning's Settlement and Bazaar.

27 October: RHS Flowers and Plants Show.

28 October: Annual Meeting of the Royal Society for the Protection of Birds.

3-7 November: 19th Universal Cookery & Food Exhibition.

10 November: RHS Flowers and Plants Show.

11 November: Patriotic Society general meeting.

12-13 November: Sale of Christmas presents in aid of foreign missions.

12 November: 17th Annual London Bulldog Society Championship Show.

15-17 November: The Gaelic League of London 'Aonach'.

18 November: Chow Chow Club Championship Show.

24 November: RHS Flowers and Plants Show.

26 November: 12th Annual RHS Colonial Fruit Show opened by Lord Strathcona.

27 November: British Optical Association.

4-5 December: London Cage Bird Association Show.

8 December: RHS Flowers and Plants Show.

9 December: 5th Perpetual Flowering Carnation Society Show.

11 December: Pet Dog Show.

22 December: RHS Flowers and Plants Show.

28 December: Ragged School Union and Shaftesbury Society Colonial Dinners.

1909

c.January: St Margaret's Choral Society.

1 January: Wimbledon and District Canine Association Dog Show.

9 January: 4th London Clarion Van Committee – social reunion.

11 January: RHS Public Parks Examination.

14 January: Southern Counties and Midland Counties Cat Clubs' combined show.

26 January: RHS Flowers and Plants Show.

28 January: Church Army Friend's of the Poor.

30 January: The Union of Women Teachers (UWT) Dance.

1 February: United Kingdom Band of Hope Union Annual soirée.

c.February: 1st Post Office Orphan Homes Concert.

6 February: WSPU Meeting.

8 February: National Fruit Growers' Federation Annual Meeting.

9 February: RHS Flowers and Plants Show.

10 February: Women's Freedom League – A Lecture on Some Economic Aspects of the Women's Suffrage Movement by Reginald John Campbell.

16 February: Four-day Socialist demonstration including the Socialist Democratic Party, the Independent Labour Party, the Labour Representation Association and the Right to Work Committees.

18 February: 1st Primrose League (St George's Habitation) General Meeting.

23 February: RHS Flowers and Plants Show.

9 March: RHS Spring Flower Show.

13 March: Union of Clerk's Dance.

c.March: 1st Surveyors Institution Examinations.

17, 24 March: High Class Cookery Demonstrations.

18 March: Annual prize-giving display of St Gabriel, Pimlico, Company of the London Diocesan Church Lads Brigade.

20 March: London Girls' Club Union Drill Competition.

23 March: RHS Flowers and Plants Show.

24 March: 5th Perpetual Flowering Carnation Society Show.

6 April: RHS Flowers and Fruit Show.

7, 21 April: High Class Cookery Demonstrations.

20 April: RHS Flowers and Plants Show.

22 April: 7th Annual Joint Championship Show of Bouledogues Français, Griffons Bruxellois, Pekingese and Pomeranians.

29 April: Annual Meeting of the Society for the Propagation of the Gospel.

29 April: Cookery Demonstrations.

5 May: United Kingdom Band of Hope Union Annual soirée.

6 May: Cookery Demonstrations.

10-15 May: 15th Annual Chemists' Exhibition.

20-4 May: 25th Home Arts and Industries Association Exhibition.

26 May: High Class Cookery Demonstrations.

27 May: Pekingese Club Championship Show.

2 June: High Class Cookery Demonstrations by Mr Iwan Kriens, G.C.A. and other Chefs under the direction of Mr C. Herman Senn, G.C.A.

8, 10, 18 June: RHS Flowers and Plants Show.

14-17 June: University of London Matriculation Examinations.

22 June: RHS Flowers and Plants Show.

26 June-3 July: The *Daily Mirror* Fair of Fashions.

8-15 July: University of London Examinations.

20 July: RHS Flowers and Fruit Show.

21 July: Perpetual Flowering Carnation Society Show.

23 July: 9th Annual National Sweet Pea Society Show.

28-9 July: *The Garden* Show.

3 August: RHS Flowers and Fruit Show.

c.August: Office of Works Military Exams.

17 August: RHS Flowers and Fruit Show.

31 August: RHS Flowers and Fruit Show.

6-10 September: Society of Extractors and Adapters of Teeth Annual International Dental Exhibition.

14 September: RHS Flowers and Fruit Show.

16 September: 6th Annual National Rose Society Autumn Show.

18-27 September: Baptist Missionary Society Exhibition.

28 September: RHS Flowers and Fruit Show.

5-9 October: 5th London Medical Exhibition.

12 October: RHS Flowers and Fruit Show.

15-23 October: 2nd *Model Engineer* Exhibition organised by Percival Marshall.

26 October: RHS Flowers and Fruit Show.

28 October: 18th Annual London Bulldog Society Championship Show.

2-6 November: 20th Universal Cookery & Food Exhibition.

9 November: RHS Flowers and Fruit Show.

11-12 November: Annual Sale of Work and Christmas Presents in aid of church work at home and abroad.

16-20 November: The Gaelic League's 7th 'Aonach' and Irish Industrial Exhibition.

23 November: RHS Flowers and Fruit Show.

24 November: Ladies' Kennel Association Dog Show.

26-8 November: London Cage Bird Association Exhibition.

28-30 November: British Columbia Exhibition charged £30.

1 December: RHS Colonial Show.

7 December: RHS Flowers and Fruit Show.

8 December: Perpetual Flowering Carnation Society Show.

10 December: Pet Dog Society Dog Show.

15-24 December: *Evening News* Toy Fair.

1910

5 January: South-Western Dog Society Dog Show.

10 January: RHS Public Parks Examination.

11 January: RHS Flowers and Fruit Show.

13-14 January: Southern Counties Cat Club Show.

20 January: London County Council (L.C.C.) Tramway Concert.

22 January: 5th London Clarion Van Committee Social Reunion.

25 January: RHS Flowers and Fruit Show.

29 January: Teachers' Orphanage Dance.

31 January: United Kingdom Band of Hope Union Social soirée.

8 February: RHS Flowers and Fruit Show.

10 February: Post Office Orphan Homes Concert.

10 February: Women's Freedom League.

15 February: Sir David Gill lectures on astronomy in aid of Cape Town Mission.

22 February: RHS Flowers and Fruit Show.

23 February: National Fruit Growers' Federation Annual meeting.

25 February: St Margaret's Musical Society concerts.

2-5 March: 12th Badminton Association 'All-England Championships'.

8-9 March: RHS Spring Bulb Show.

11, 18 March: London Diocesan Church Lads' Brigade Drill & Gymnastic Display.

20-1 March: Surveyor's Institution Examinations.

22 March: RHS Flowers and Fruit Show.

23 March: Stour Valley Garden and School Exhibition of English early-grown fruits and vegetables.

5 April: RHS Flowers and Fruit Show.

5 April: Inaugural meeting to appoint a committee of management to discuss the holding of an International Horticultural Exhibition in London in 1912.

6-10 April: 1st Congress of the Professional Photographers' Association.

27 April: School Teachers' Examination.

28-30 April: 3rd Annual Nursing & Midwifery Conference & Exhibition.

3 May: RHS Flowers and Fruit Show – Auricula and Primula Show.

6 May: HM King Edward VII dies.

10-19 May: 16th Annual Chemists' Exhibition.

23-8 May: International The Pure Food and Allied Trades Exhibition.

31 May: 8th Annual Joint Championship Show of Bouledogues Français, Griffons Bruxellois, Pekingese and Pomeranians.

4 June: Working Girls At Play.

7 June: RHS Flowers and Fruit Show.

9 June: 8th Perpetual Flowering Carnation Society Show.

9 June: Anti-Vivisection Society.

14 June: Miss James' Drill Display.

*c.*June: University of London Examinations.

21 June: RHS Flowers and Fruit Show.

23-4 June: Girls' Friendly Society Conversatzione.

28 June: Bulldog Club Incorporated Championship Show.

*c.*July: University of London Examinations.

13 July: 10th Annual National Sweet Pea Society Show.

*c.*July: *The Garden* Show for one day.

19 July: RHS Flowers and Fruit Show.

22 July: Office of Works Military Examinations.

25 July: National Fruit Growers' Federation Meeting.

26 July: Annual National Carnation and Picotee Society Show.

29 July: Lyons Co. Dinner.

16 August: RHS Flowers and Fruit Show.

5-9 September: Society of Extractors and Adapters of Teeth Annual International Dental Exhibition.

13 September: RHS Flowers and Fruit Show.

15 September: 7th Annual National Rose Society Autumn Show.

20-3 September: Office of Works Military Examinations.

27 September: RHS Flowers and Fruit Show.

28 September: 1st National Vegetable Society Exhibition.

3-7 October: 6th Annual London Medical Exhibition.

11 October: RHS Flowers and Fruit Show.

13-14 October: RHS Autumn Show of British-Grown Fruits.

25 October: RHS Vegetable and Flowers Exhibition.

27 October: 19th Annual London Bulldog Society Championship Show.

1-5 November: 21st Universal Cookery & Food Exhibition.

8 November: RHS Flowers and Fruit Show.

10-11 November: Annual Sale of Work and Christmas Presents in aid of church work at home and abroad (Home and Foreign Missions).

18 November: The Borough of Westminster Constitutional Association.

18-21 November: The Gaelic League of London 'Aonach'.

22 November: RHS Flowers and Fruit Show.

23 November: Ladies' Kennel Club, Incorporated Dog Show.

25-8 November: 22nd Annual London Cage Birds Association Show.

1-3 December: RHS Colonial Fruits Exhibition.

6 December: RHS Flowers and Fruit Show.

6 December: The Cooking of Vegetables lecture by Mr C. Herman Senn.

9 December: Pet Dog Society Championship Show.

13 December: Perpetual Flowering Carnation Show.

15 December: Joint Championship Show of Chow Chow Club and Pekingese Club.

16 December: Army & Navy Male Nurses' Co-operative Jumble Sale, 'At Home'.

1911

5 January: South-Western Dog Society Show.

11 January: Pekingese Dog Show.

14 January: 6th London Clarion Vans.

19 January: Southern Counties Cat Club Show.

23 January: National Fruit Growers' Federation Council Meeting.

26 January: St Margaret's Philharmonic Society's Concert.

31 January: RHS Flowers and Fruit Show.

6 February: UK Band of Hope Union.

14 February: RHS Flowers and Fruit Show.

15 February: United Temperance Council.

16 February: Post Office Orphan Homes Concert.

22-5 February: 13th Badminton Association 'All-England Championships'.

28 February: RHS Flowers and Fruit Show.

4-11 March: Vegetarian Exhibition.

14 March: RHS Spring Bulb Show.

18 March: London Girls' Club Union musical drill competition.

21-4 March: Surveyors Institution Examinations.

30 March: 9th Annual Joint Championship Show of Bouledogues Français, Griffons Bruxellois and Pekingese.

4-7 April: 4th Annual Nursing & Midwifery Conference & Exhibition.

11 April: RHS Flowers and Fruit Show.

15 April: The London Cab-drivers' Union mass meeting.

24 April: London Diocesan Girls Union.

25 April: RHS Flowers and Fruit Show.

1 May: Mr Twining.

3 May: Pentecostal League.

4 May: Magpie Madrigal Society Concert.

15-19 May: 2nd Congress of the Professional Photographers' Association.

23 May: Bulldog Club Incorporated Championship Show.

27 May: Working Girls at Play!

6 June: RHS Flowers and Fruit Show.

8 June: Coronation Bazaar in aid of the National Blind Relief Society.

10-15 June: London University Examinations.

20 June: RHS Flowers and Fruit Show.

22-3 June: Admiralty.

1-8 July: London University Examinations.

11-12 July: 11th Annual National Sweet Pea Society Show.

18 July: RHS Flowers and Fruit Show.

25 July: Annual National Carnation and Picotee Society Show.

19-22 September: Office of Works.

26 September: RHS Vegetable Show. Mr Herman Senn talked on, 'Salads – Subjects for, and their Preparation'.

2-6 October: 7th London Medical Exhibition.

10-11 October: RHS Autumn Fruit Show.

13-21 October: 3rd *Model Engineer* Exhibition.

25 October: Westminster Chapel Social Gathering.

31 October-4 November: 22nd Universal Cookery & Food Exhibition.

9-10 November: Annual Sale of Work and Christmas Presents in aid of church work at home and abroad (Home and Foreign Missions).

14-18 November: The Gaelic League of London 'Aonach'.

22 November: Ladies' Kennel Association Dog Show.

23-5 November: London Cage Bird Society's Show.

6 December: National Blind Relief Society.

8 December: Pet Dog Society Championship Show.

14 December: Pekingese Club Championship Show.

16 December: Women's Liberal Federation Meeting.

19-26 December: Post Office Christmas sorting.

1912

4 January: South-Western Dog Society Show.

11-12 January: Southern Counties Cat Club Show.

16 January: Pekin Palace Dog Association Show.

20 January: London Girls' Club Union.

23 January: RHS Flowers and Fruit Show.

25 January or 1 February: St Margaret's (Westminster) Choral Society Concert.

27 January: Teachers' Orphanage Dance.

29 January: United Kingdom Band of Hope Union Soirée.

30 January: Concert in aid of the Nursing Sisters of the Poor of Westminster.

30 January: Madame Blanche Marchesi's concert.

31 January-2 February: Special Conference of the Manchester Unity Independent Order of Oddfellows Friendly Society.

3 February: National Cyclists' Union Dance.

6 February: RHS Flowers and Fruit Show.

12-17 February: A Historical Pageant of Non-conformity.

20 February: RHS Flowers and Fruit Show.

28 February-2 March: 14th Badminton Association 'All-England Championships'.

7 March: Women's Social & Political Union.

8 March: Pimlico Brigade.

9 March: London Girls' Club Union musical drill competition.

12 March: The Children's Happy Evenings Association Inter-Branch Physical Competition.

20 March: Post Office Orphans Homes Concert.

21-2 March: 12th Perpetual Flowering Carnation Society Show.

22 March: Griffon Club Show.

25-9 March: Surveyors Institution Examinations.

4-12 April: Photographic Arts & Crafts Exhibition.

8-9 April: Police Minstrels Concert.

16-17 April: RHS Daffodil Show.

19 April: French Bulldog Club Show.

23-6 April: 5th Annual Nursing & Midwifery Conference & Exhibition.

30 April: RHS Flowers and Fruit Show with National Auricula and Primula Society.

9-13 May: 3rd Congress of the Professional Photographers' Association together with …

3-11 May: … a Photographic Arts & Crafts Exhibition.

14 May: RHS Tulip Show.

16 May: 10th Annual Joint Championship Show of Bouledogues Français, Griffons Bruxellois and Pekingese.

17-18 May: Police Minstrels Concert.

24 May: Horticultural Exhibition Banquet.

6 June: St Margaret's Choral Society Concert.

15 June: Boy Scouts Display.

18 June: RHS Flowers and Plants Show.

19 June: 1st National Hardy Plant Society's Show.

24-8 June: Biennial Health Conference and Exhibition.

30 June: Nursing Sisters of the Poor.

2-4 July: RHS Summer Show – Holland House.

*c.*July: 12th Annual National Sweet Pea Society Show.

23 July: Annual National Carnation and Picotee Society Show.

2-7 September: International Dental Exhibition.

12 September: Autumn National Rose Society Show.

16-20 September: Box-Making Machinery Exhibition.

30 September-4 October: 8th London Medical Exhibition.

14-19 October: The 1862-1912 Jubilee International Stamp Exhibition.

29 October-2 November: 23rd Universal Cookery & Food Exhibition.

8 November: 21st Annual London Bulldog Society Championship Show.

12-16 November: The Gaelic League of London 'Aonach'.

20-3 November: Annual Sale of Work and Christmas Presents in aid of church work at home and abroad.

26 November: Ladies' Kennel Club Show.

28-30 November: London Cage Bird Society's Exhibition.

6 December: Pet Dog Society Championship Show.

9-12 December: Advertising Exhibition.

18 December: Pekingese Club Championship Show.

19-26 December: Post Office Christmas sorting.

1913

14 January: South Western Dog Society Show.

16-17 January: Southern Counties Cat Club Show.

21 January: RHS Flowers and Plants Show.

23 January: W.S.P.U. Meeting.

25 January: Teachers' Orphanage Dance.

27 January: United Kingdom Band of Hope Union Soirée.

28 January: W.S.P.U. Meeting with Mrs Emmeline Pankurst in the chair.

30 January: Pekin Palace Dog Association's Show.

1 February: London Cyclists' Union Fancy Dress Dance.

4-5 February: RHS Flowers and Plants Show – Spring Bulbs.

6 February: Conservative and Unionist Women's Franchise Association.

6 March: Post Office Orphan Homes Concert.

8 March: London Girls' Club Union Musical Drill Competition.

11 March: Baker & Sons supper.

26 February-1 March: 15th Badminton Association 'All-England Championships'.

26 March: Ladies' Kennel Club Championship Show.

7-11 April: 4th Congress of the Professional Photographers' Association together with …

4-12 April: … a Photographic Arts & Crafts Exhibition.

15 April: Daffodil Show.

22-5 April: 6th Annual Nursing & Midwifery Conference & Exhibition.

29 April: RHS Auricula and Primula Show.

1 May: National Rose Society Spring Show.

3 May: Girls' Club Union.

6-8 May: Women's Liberal Federation Annual Council Meeting.

9 May: Pet Dog Championship Show.

14 May: RHS Tulip Show.

23 May: 11th Annual Joint Championship Show of Bouledogues Français, Griffons Bruxellois and Pekingese.

27-30 May: Rhododendron Show.

5 June: Bulldog Incorporated Championship Show.

7-12 June: London University Examinations.

14 June: The German Colony in London banquet to celebrate the Kaiser's jubilee.

18 June: Westminster Boy Scouts.

24-8 June: Roads Exhibition (in conjunction with the 3rd International Road Congress).

5-12 July: London University Examinations.

17-18 July: 13th Annual Sweet Pea Society Show.

26 August: RHS Flower and Plant Show.

1-6 September: International Dental Exhibition.

9 September: Hermann Senn Lecture on Vegetables.

11-12 September: Autumn National Rose Society Show.

c.September/October: 9th The London Medical Exhibition.

10-18 October: 4th *Model Engineer* Exhibition organised by Percival Marshall.

29 October-1 November: 24th Universal Cookery & Food Exhibition.

6 November: 22nd Annual London Bulldog Society Championship Show.

10-15 November: The Gaelic League of London 'Aonach'.

21-4 November: Annual Sale of Work and Christmas Presents in aid of church work at home and abroad.

25 November: Ladies' Kennel Association Dog Show.

26-8 November: London Cage Bird Society's Exhibition.

3 December: Perpetual Flowering Carnation Society Winter Show.

5 December: Pet Dog Society Championship Show.

11-13 December: Grand Military Bazaar and Christmas Fair.

16 December: Imperial Service College, Windsor, Bazaar.

17-18 December: 'Christmas in Fairyland' Fête.

1914

3 January: The London Clarion Van's 9th Annual New Year Re-Union Dance, Concert and Whist Drive.

6 January: Pekin Palace Dog Association Show.

8 January: Southern Counties Cat Club 'Westminster' Grand Championship Show.

10 January: Hovis Bread Competition.

15 January: Pekingese Club Championship Dog Show.

24 January: Teachers' Dance.

31 January: National Cyclists' Union Dance.

2 February: UK Band of Hope Union.

12 February: National Union of Women's Suffrage Society.

18-20 February: Messrs I. Behar and The Anglo-Continental Co. Compulsory Sale of Valuable Oriental Carpets.

27 February: Conservative & Unionist Women's Franchise Association.

3-7 March: 16th Badminton Association 'All-England Championships'.

12 March: Post Office Homes Concert.

14 March: Annual Musical Drill Competitions of the London Girls' Club Union.

15-16 March: RHS Daffodil Show.

16 March: Surveyors Institution Examinations.

28 March: Simple Life Exhibition.

3 April: National Sweet Pea Society.

16-17 April: Daffodil Show.

23 April: National Rose Society's 2nd Spring Show

27 April-1 May: 7th Annual Nursing & Midwifery Conference & Exhibition.

5 May: RHS Tulip Show.

11-15 May: 5th Congress of the Professional Photographers' Association together with a Photographic Arts & Crafts Exhibition.

20 May: 12th Annual Joint Championship Show of Bouledogues Français, Griffons Bruxellois and Pekingese.

22 May: Rhododendron Show.

24 May: Empire Day.

26 May: Rhododendron Show.

8 June: London University Examinations.

13 June: St Stephen's Church Concert.

18 June: English Folk Dance Society Demonstrations.

20 June: 20th *Daily Herald* League Grand Re-Union & Dance.

4 July: London University Examinations.

16 July: 14th Annual National Sweet Pea Society Show.

4 August: Outbreak of the First World War. From the outbreak of the war on 4 August to October, the Hall was used as a bivouac for soldiers on their way to the front, although records show differently.

12 August: National Hardy Plant Society.

c.August/September: Red Cross Cookery Demonstration.

24 September-3 October: 10th London Medical Exhibition.

24 September: Autumn Rose Show organised by the National Rose Society.

1 October: National Gladioli Society.

2 October: National Blind Relief Society.

23-30 October: *Daily Express* Women's Work Show. A Unique Poster Stamp depicts this.

5 November: The Ladies' Kennel Club Dog Show.

6-10 November: Gaelic League Exhibition.

17-20 November: Annual Sale of Work in aid of church work at home and abroad, organised by Home and Foreign Missions.

21 November: Sheet Metal Workers Concert.

24 November: 23rd Annual London Bull Dog Society Championship Show.

25-7 November: London Cage Bird Society's Show.

2 December: National Carnation & Picotee Society – Perpetual Flowering Carnation Show.

4 December: Pet Dog Society Championship Show.

19 December: Post Office Comptroller, Christmas Post sorting.

c.December: War Office. Use of Hall. Fusiliers.

1915

2 January: The London Clarion Van's 10th Annual New Year Re-Union Dance, Concert and Whist Drive.

12 January: St Edward's Convent.

14 January: Southern Counties Cat Club.

25 January: United Kingdom Band of Hope Union.

27 January: Pekingese Club Dog Show.

30 January: National Cyclists' Union Dance.

15 February: National Hardy Plant Society.

2 March: Hardy Plant Society.

4 March: Post Office Homes Concert.

9 March: RHS Spring Flower Show.

22 March: Surveyors Institution Examinations.

16 April: National Rose Society's Spring Show.

20 April: 13th Annual Joint Championship Show of Bouledogues Français, Griffons Bruxellois and Pekingese.

23 April: London & Provincial Pekingese Dog Club.
23 April: Toy Dog Society Championship Show.
27 April: National Auricula Society's Show.
1-7 May: Women and their Work – An Exhibition of the Arts and Crafts of the Home Worker.
18-22 May: 8th Annual Nursing & Midwifery Exhibition.
19 May: Horticultural Teachers' Association.
27 May: Sheet Metal Workers Concert.
10 June: Bulldog Club Incorporated Championship Show.
12 June: London University Examinations.
25 June-1 July: The National Road Conference and Exhibition.
15 July: London University Examinations.
16 July: 15th Annual National Sweet Pea Society Show.
20 July: National Carnation Picotee Society.
21 July: Incorporated Dental Society Examinations.
27 August: Incorporated Dental Society Exhibition.
20 September: Associated Newspapers Ltd (possible Bridge contest).
22-4 September: The *Daily Mail* Home-Grown Food Exhibition.
8 October: 10th The London Medical Exhibition – (cancelled).
11-12 November: National Chrysanthemum Society.
23 November: RHS Flower Show.
24 November: 2nd Sale of Work in Aid of Church Work at Home & Abroad, Home and Foreign Missions.
3 December: Pet Dog Society Championship Show.
8 December: Perpetual Flowering Carnation Society Show.
9 December: London Cage Birds Show.
14 December: Great Joint Terrier Championship Show.
20 December: Post Office Comptroller – Christmas postal sorting.
31 December: Horticultural Benefit Society Annual.
c.December: War Office. Use of Hall. Yeomanry.

1916

6 January: Southern Counties Cat Club (deposit forfeited).
11 January: RHS Flowers Show.
13 January: National Gundog Show Society Championship Show.
19 January: Pekingese Club Championship Show.
25 January: RHS Flowers and Fruit Show.
27 January: National Cat Club Show.
29 January: UK Band of Hope Union.
31 January: Knight Sarrey & Co. (storing).
8 February: RHS Spring Flower Show.
15 March: Wisbech & District Fruit Growers.
18 March: Post Office Homes Concert.
29 March: Perpetual Flowering Carnations.
17 April: Fruit Growers' Federation.
18 April: RHS Daffodil Show.
4 May: 14th Annual Joint Championship Show of the French Bulldog Club of England and the Griffon Bruxellois Club.
24 May: Horticultural Teachers' Association.
30 May: Church of England Incorporated Society for Providing Homes for Waifs & Strays.
1 June: Bulldog Club Incorporated Championship Show.
28-9 June: RHS Sale of Flowers and Plants in aid of the Red Cross.
5 July: Horticultural Trade Association.
1 August: RHS Dry Bulb Show.
14 September: Horticultural Teachers' Association.
21 September: Wounded Soldiers for Tea, &c.
6 October: 16th Annual National Sweet Pea Society Show.
12-21 October: 10th The London Medical Exhibition – (cancelled).
13 October: The War Office formally requisitioned the Hall during the First World War for use by the Australian Imperial Forces to billet its troops prior to being sent to the front.
9 November: The National Chrysanthemum Society Flower Show.
6 December: National Perpetual Carnation Society.
8 December: National Rose Society Autumn Show.
31 December: Horticultural Benefit Society Annual.

1917-18

11 November: Hall occupied and in use by the Australian Imperial Force.

1919

11 February: RHS Winter Vegetable Show.
13 October: The Hall was returned to the Society by the War Office.

1920

19 January: National Terrier Club Championship Show.
20 January: The Fox Terrier Club's 38th Championship Show.
17 February: Pekingese Club Championship Show.
2-6 March: 17th Badminton Association 'All-England Championships'.
25 March: Ladies' Kennel Association Incorporated Dog Show.
16-24 April: 6th Congress of the Professional Photographers' Association together with a Photographic Fair.
27 April: RHS Show of Roses, Auriculas and Primulas.
15 May: 2nd National Federation of Women's Institutes London Exhibition.
26 May: The Great Joint Terrier Club Championship Show.
27 May: Wire Fox Terrier Association Championship Show.
1 June: Herts. and Middlesex Canine Club Championship Show.
9-10 June: Fair in aid of Our Dumb Friends' League.
15 June: RHS Flower Show.
29-30 June: RHS Flower Show.
c.July: 20th Annual National Sweet Pea Society Show.
23 September: National Rose Society's Autumn Show.
24 September-20 October: 25th Universal Cookery & Food Exhibition.
12 October: Mayflower Pageant.
18-19 November: 27th Sale of Work in Aid of Church Work at Home & Abroad, Home and Foreign Missions.
23 November: Ladies' Kennel Association Incorporated Dog Show.
26-7 December: Gilbert & Sullivan Fair and Bazaar.
7-11 December: Bazaar in aid of the funds of the Alliance of Honour.
31 December: New Year's Eve Carnival Ball in aid of the After-Care Fund.

1921

19 January: National Terrier Club Championship Show.
12-19 February: Cinema Accessories and Musical Appliances Exhibition.
1-5 March: 18th Badminton Association 'All-England Championships' Annual Tournament.
10 March: Joint Championship Show held by the French Bulldog Club of England and The Pekingese Club.
25 March: The Victoria Athletic Association of the Army & Navy Stores Dance.
18-22 April: 7th Congress of the Professional Photographers' Association together with a Photographic Fair organised by Arthur C. Brookes.
2-6 May: Tobacco Trades Exhibition.
24 May: The Championship Great Joint Terrier Show.
25 May: The Championship Bulldog Club Show.
30 May: Regent Athletic Club Dance.
11-16 June: University of London Examinations.
24 June: Alsatian Wolf Dog Club Championship Show.
2-9 July: University of London Examinations.
c.July: 21st Annual National Sweet Pea Society Show.
c.July: French Commercial Office in Great Britain had to ask the RHS to be relieved of a one week tenancy in July due to the 'trade depression'. It was agreed to only charge them £117.10.
22 September: National Rose Society Show.
29 September: Christian Science Lecture.
1 October: 'A' Division Athletic Club, Metropolitan Police Dance.
22 October: The Victoria Athletic Association of the Army & Navy Stores Dance.

22 October: Pomeranian Club Dog Show.

8 November: Thomas Cook Dance.

c.November: 28th Sale of Work in Aid of Church Work at Home & Abroad, Home and Foreign Missions.

16-18 November: International Potato Conference and Exhibition.

22 November: Ladies' Kennel Association Show.

6-8 December: National Utility Poultry Society's Show.

10 December: The London Union of Training College Clubs Dance.

15 December: A' Division Athletic Club, Metropolitan Police Dance.

1922

4 January: The Victoria Athletic Association of the Army & Navy Stores Dance.

7-14 January: 5th *Model Engineer* Exhibition.

18 January: J. Lyons & Co. Shops Dept. Dance.

21 January: London Gardens Guild Dance and Lecture on Town Gardening.

24 January: The National Terrier Club Championship Show.

28 January: The London Union of Training College Clubs Whist Drive.

4 February: National Cyclists' Union Dance and Reunion.

6 February: The Strand Corner House Dance.

8 February: York Mansion Restaurant Dance in aid of the Westminster Hospital.

9 February: Headquarters London Scottish Regiment Dance.

10 February: The Association of Ex-Service Civil Servants Dance.

11 February: The London Clarion Van's Fellowship Reunion.

19-23 February: 26th Universal Cookery & Food Exhibition.

2 March: Messrs Gorringes' of 75 Buckingham Palace Road, Dance.

7-11 March: 19th Badminton Association 'All-England Championships' Annual Badminton Tournament.

16 March: J. Lyons & Co. Ltd Dance.

17 March: 'A' Division Athletic Club, Metropolitan Police Dance.

18 March: The London Union of Training College Clubs Dance/Whist Drive.

21 March: The British Carnation Society Flower Show.

23 March: The National Print Workers Social & Sports Alliance Dance and Whist Drive.

24 March: Regent Athletic Club (Wages Dept) Strand Hotels Ltd Dance.

31 March: Messrs Lambert & Butler (Imperial Tobacco Co) Dance.

4-7 April: 12th Annual Professional Nursing & Midwifery Conference & Exhibition.

21 April: The Kinematograph Sports Association (Wardour Films) Fancy Dress Dance.

22 April: 'A' Division Athletic Club, Metropolitan Police Dance.

22 April: Pomeranian Club Championship Show.

1-6 May: Photographic Fair.

11-20 May: Ecclesiastical Art & Furniture Exhibition.

22 May-3 June: The First National Exhibition of Commercial Display.

10-15 June: University of London Examination.

17 June: Stepney Philanthropic Society Dance in aid of the Jewish Orphan Homes, West Norwood.

19 June: The Pekinese Club & French Bulldog Club of England Show.

1-8 July: University of London Examination.

c.July: 22nd Annual National Sweet Pea Society Show.

6 September: The National Dahlia Society Flower Show.

7/8 September: The French Bulldog Club of England Dog Show.

15 September: 'A' Division Athletic Club, Metropolitan Police Dance.

21 September: The National Rose Society Autumn Rose Show.

30 September-7 October: 1st All-British Wireless Exhibition and Convention.

6 October: Toy Spaniel Club Championship Show.

13 October: 'A' Division Athletic Club, Metropolitan Police Dance.

21-7 October: First Annual Hairdressing & Allied Trades Exhibition.

1 November: The Victoria Athletic Association of the Army & Navy Stores Dance.

2 November: 'A' Division Athletic Club, Metropolitan Police Dance.

3 November: London Telephone Service Swimming Association Dance.

4 November: District Traffic Office GPO South Dance.

6 November: The 'Youdees' (United Dairies) Social & Sports Club Dance.

7 November: A.B.C Sports Club Dance.

8-11 November: 29th Sale of Work in Aid of Church Work at Home & Abroad, Home and Foreign Missions.

16-17 November: The National Chrysanthemum Society Show.

18 November: Hagodal Social Club, Jewish Institute Dance.

20 November: The National Print Worker Social & Sports Alliance Dance.

21-3 November: The Girls' Realm Guild 'All in a Garden' Fair.

25 November: The Regent Athletic Club, The Strand Hotel Ltd Dance.

29 November-1 December: Our Dumb Friends' League Bazaar.

2 December: The London Union of Training College Clubs Dance/Whist Drive.

5-7 December: The National Utility Poultry Society Pullet Show.

7 December: Pomeranian Club Championship Show.

9 December: The Victoria Athletic Association of the Army & Navy Stores Dance.

14 December: 'A' Division Athletic Club, Metropolitan Police Dance.

15 December: Headquarters London Scottish Regiment Headquarters Dance.

16 December: A.B.C. Sports Social Club Dance.

19 December: First Church of Christ Scientist-Christian Science Lecture.

23 December: East London Young Zionist League Dance.

30 December: H. Prior, Dance in aid of The Royal Antediluvian Order of Buffaloes Orphanage.

1923

1 January: National Print Workers London Social & Sports Alliance – Dance.

5-12 January: 6th *The Model Engineer* Exhibition.

18 January: 'A' Division Athletic Club, Metropolitan Police Dance.

19 January: Kent County Rugby Football Union Dance.

20 January: The T.O.T. Philharmonic Society and London General Omnibus Company (L.G.O.C.) Underground Railways Dance.

23 January: The National Terrier Club Championship Dog Show.

25 January: J. Lyons & Co. Shops Dept. Dance.

26 January: A.B.C. Sports Club Dance.

29 January: The London Union of Training College Clubs Dance/Whist Drive.

1 February: Headquarters London Scottish Regiment Dance.

3 February: The National Cyclist's Union Dance.

7 February: Westminster Hospital Dance.

10 February: The Arubian Company Limited Dance.

13 February: RHS Rhododendron Show.

15 February: 'A' Division Athletic Club, Metropolitan Police Dance.

17 February: The London Clarion Van's Committee Reunion.

19 February: National Print Workers London Social & Sports Alliance Dance.

20 February: Maison Lyons Dance.

23 February: The Regent Athletic Club, The Strand Hotels Ltd Dance.

24 February: The Victoria Athletic Association of the Army & Navy Stores Dance.

6-10 March: 20th Badminton Association 'All-England Championships' Annual Badminton Tournament.

13-14 March: RHS Flower Show.

15 March: 'A' Division Athletic Club, Metropolitan Police Dance.
16 March: The 'Youdees' (United Dairies) Social & Sports Club Dance.
17 March: National Amalgamated Approved Society Dance
20-2 March: Mr Robert Soloman Fair and Ball.
24 March: The London Union of Training College Clubs Dance/ Whist Drive.
4 April: Pug Dog & London & Provincial Pug Dog Club Show.
7 April: Messrs Lambert & Butler (Imperial Tobacco Co) Dance.
14 April: The Victoria Athletic Association of the Army & Navy Stores Dance.
17 April: War Charities Extension Scheme Dance.
18 April: 'A' Division Athletic Club, Metropolitan Police Dance.
20 April: The National Rose Society Flower Show.
27 April: The French Bulldog Club of England Dog Show.
30 April: The Cabdrivers Benevolent Association Concert.
10 May: 'A' Division Athletic Club, Metropolitan Police Dance.
14-26 May: The Junior Philatelic Society London International Stamp Exhibition.
28 May-9 June: The Colonial & Continental Church Society Exhibition of the Society's Work.
14-23 June: Rev. G.A. Hope Westminster Missionary Exhibition of the Society for the Propagation of the Gospel.
28 June: St Vincent's Orphanage – Girl Guides Display.
30 June-7 July: University of London Examinations.
c.July: 23rd Annual National Sweet Pea Society Show.
21 August: RHS Flower Show.
5 September: The National Dahlia Society Flower Show.
6-8 September: The London Gardens Guild Fruit and Vegetable Show.
19-21 September: The National Rose Society Flower Show.
27 September-8 October: 2nd Wireless Telegraphy Exhibition.
11 October: 'A' Division Athletic Club, Hyde Park Police Station Dance.
13 October: A.B.C. Club Dance.
22-6 October: 27th Universal Cookery & Food Exhibition.
1-2 November: The National Chrysanthemum Society Flower Show.
3 November: 'A' Division Athletic Club, Hyde Park Police Station Dance.
6-9 November: 30th Sale of Work in Aid of Church Work at Home & Abroad, Home and Foreign Missions.
10 November: The Victoria Athletic Association of the Army & Navy Stores Dance.
16 November: The Vacuum Oil Company Ltd Dance.
17 November: The National Cyclists' Union Dance.
20 November: The Kensington Canine Society Dog Show.
22 November: The 'Youdees' (United Dairies) Social and Sports Club Dance.
23 November: Kinematograph Sports Association, Wardour Films Ltd Dance.
24 November: London Telephone Toll Exchange Dance.
28-30 November: Our Dumb Friends' League Bazaar.
12 December: 56th London Division Dance, Concert and Re-union.
13 December: 'A' Division Athletic Club, Hyde Park Police Station Dance.
14 December: Headquarters London Scottish Regiment Dance.
15 December: The Victoria Athletic Association of the Army & Navy Stores Dance.
22 December: Messrs Elliote Brothers (London) Ltd Reception, Concert and Dance.
29 December: Royal Antediluvian Order of Buffaloes Dance.
31 December: A.B.C. Club Dance.

1924

4-11 January: 7th The Model Engineer Exhibition.
17 January: 'A' Division Athletic Club, Hyde Park Police Station, Dance.
19 January: The London Clarion Van's Committee Re-union.

22 January: National Terrier Club Championship Show.
24 January: Messrs Lyons (Shops Dept.) Dance.
25 January: Kinematograph Sports Association, Wardour Films Ltd Dance.
26 January: London Union of Training College Clubs Dance/Whist Drive.
31 January: The GPO Widows and Orphans Christmas Hamper Fund Dance.
6 February: The 'Youdees' (United Dairies) Social & Sports Club Dance.
7 February: Headquarters London Scottish Regiment Dance.
8 February: The Vacuum Oil Co. Ltd Dance & Whist Drive.
9 February: National Cyclists' Union Dance.
14 February: 'A' Division Athletic Club, Hyde Park Police Station, Dance.
16 February: A Grand 'Blues Night' Carnival Dance and Free Competition.
21 February: Royal Antediluvian Order of Buffaloes Dance.
22 February: Harrods Producers Club Dance.
23 February: The Victoria Athletic Association of the Army & 4-8 March Navy Stores Dance.
4-8 March: 21st Badminton Association 'All-England Championships' Annual Tournament.
14 March: Kinematograph Sports Association, Wardour Films Ltd Dance.
15 March: National Amalgamated Approved Society Dance.
17 March: 'A' Division Athletic Club, Hyde Park Police Station, Dance.
19 March: The French Bulldog Club of England Dog Show.
22 March: London Union of Training College Clubs Dance/Whist Drive.
27 March: The British Carnation Society Carnation Show.
29 March: Messrs Lambert & Butler, Imperial Tobacco Co. Dance.
31 March-4 April: Bakery Exhibition organised by The London Master Bakers' and Confectioners' Protection Society.
The National Rose Society Rose Show 10-11 April
23 April: Electrical Trades Union & Electricity Supply Commercial Association Dance.
24 April: 'A' Division Athletic Club, Hyde Park Police Station, Dance.
25 April: Pug Dog & London & Provincial Pug Dog Club Show.
26 April: The Victoria Athletic Association of the Army & Navy Stores Dance.
28 April: Messrs Finnigans Dance.
1 May: Westminster Labour Party – May Day Dance.
21 May: Pomeranian Club Championship Show.
31 May-20 June: University of London (South Kensington) Examinations.
10-11 July: 24th Annual National Sweet Pea Society Show.
4-6 September: The London District Allotments & Gardens Society Show Fruit and Vegetable Show.
10 September: The National Dahlia Society, Dahlia Show.
27 September: Independent Labour Party International Reception and Dance.
11 October: The Victoria Athletic Association of the Army & Navy Stores Dance.
16 October: 'A' Division Athletic Club, Hyde Park Police Station Dance.
25 October: The Cyclists' Touring Club Dance and Whist Drive.
27 October: John James Keen – Dance in aid of King's College Hospital.
6-7 November: The National Chrysanthemum Society Autumn Show.
8 November: The Victoria Athletic Association of the Army & Navy Stores Dance.
11-14 November: 31st Sale of Work in Aid of Church Work at Home & Abroad, Home and Foreign Missions.
15 November: York Mansions Restaurant Dance in aid of Westminster Hospital.

20 November: 'A' Division Athletic Club, Hyde Park Police Station Dance.

21-2 November: The London Labour Party, Labour Fair and Dance.

25-7 November: The National Utility Poultry Society Pullets Show.

28 November: Griffon Bruxellois Club Dog Show.

29 November: London Union of Training College Clubs Dance.

5-12 December: 1st Applied Arts and Handcrafts Exhibition.

18 December: A' Division Athletic Club, Hyde Park Police Station Dance.

20 December: GPO Widows and Orphans Christmas Hamper Fund Dance and Whist Drive.

31 December: 'A' Division Athletic Club, Hyde Park Police Station Dance.

1925

1 January: Miss Podolsky, Arcos Ltd (Entertainments Committee) Dance.

6 January: The Old Vic Theatre (Royal Victoria Hall) – Old Vic Circle Twelfth Night Dance.

9 January: The Mullard Radio Valve Co. Dance.

15 January: The London Clarion Reunion Committee Dance.

16 January: The Vacuum Oil Company Ltd Dance and Whist Drive.

17 January: The National Cyclists' Union Dance.

22 January: St Martin's Guild of Fellowship Dance.

23 January: Trunk and EC Districts (London Telephone Service) Carnival Committee GPO South Dance.

24 January: The London Labour Party Dance.

29 January: The United Dairies Co. (The Youdees Sports Club) Dance.

31 January: London Union of Training College Clubs Dance.

3 February: 1st annual Winter Show of the Alsatian League of Great Britain.

5 February: 'A' Division Athletic Club – Hyde Park Police Station Dance.

7 February: The Victorian Athletic Association Dance.

16-20 February: 28th Universal Cookery & Food Exhibition.

3-7 March: 22nd Badminton Association 'All-England Championships' Annual Tournament.

11 March: Pug Club and London and Provincial Pug Club Show.

12 March: 'A' Division Athletic Club – Hyde Park Police Station Dance.

13 March: Harrods Producers Club Dance.

14-20 March: The London Master Bakers & Confectioner's Protection Society Bakery Exhibition.

21 March: National Amalgamated Approved Society Dance.

26 March: The British Carnation Society – Carnation Show.

28 March: London Union of Training College Clubs Dance.

1 April: The Westminster Labour Party Dance.

2 April: 'A' Division Athletic Club, Hyde Park Police Station, Dance.

4 April: Messrs Kearley & Tonge Dance.

18 April: The City of Westminster Philanthropic Society, Caxton Hall, SW1, Dance.

24 April: The National Rose Society Rose Show.

29 April: The French Bulldog Club of England Dog Show.

1 May: The Westminster Labour Party Dance.

19-28 May: Modern Housekeeping Exhibition.

2-5 June: University of London Examinations.

13-19 June: University of London Examinations.

3 July: St Vincent's Orphanage, Carlisle Place, SW1, Girl Guides Display.

4-11 June: University of London Examinations.

16-17 July: 25th Annual National Sweet Pea Society Show.

4-5 September: The London and District Allotments & Gardens Society Show Fruit and Vegetable Show.

9 September: National Dahlia Society Show.

3 October: 'A' Division Metropolitan Police Athletic Club, Hyde Park Police Station, Dance.

10-16 October: Wireless, Arts and Handcrafts Exhibition.

22 October: Griffin Athletic Club, Dulwich Village, Dance.

24 October: The Cyclists' Touring Club Dance.

26 October: John James Keen Dance.

29 October: 'A' Division Metropolitan Police Athletic Club, Hyde Park Police Station, Dance.

31 October: London Galloway Association Dance.

5-6 November: National Chrysanthemum Society Autumn Show.

7 November: 1st Combined Cavalry 'Old Comrades' Association Reunion Dance.

9 November: A.B.C. Sports Club, 17 Camden Road, NW1, Dance.

11-12 November: 32nd Sale of Work in Aid of Church Work at Home & Abroad, Home and Foreign Missions.

14 November: The Victorian Athletic Association Dance.

19 November: 'A' Division Metropolitan Police Athletic Club, Hyde Park Police Station, Dance.

24 November: United Dairies Social and Welfare Council Reception and Dinner.

26 November: The City of Westminster Philanthropic Society, Caxton Hall, SW1, Dance. (This Dance was cancelled due to the death of Queen Alexandra.)

28 November: London Union of Training College Clubs Dance.

4-11 December: 2nd Applied Arts and Handcrafts Exhibition.

16-28 December: South Western District Post Office – Christmas postal work.

1926

2-8 January: 1st The Schoolboy's Exhibition.

14 January: 'A' Division Athletic Club, Hyde Park Police Station Dance.

16 January: The London Labour Party Dance.

19 January: Organisation for the Maintenance of Supplies Concert.

21 January: Messrs J. Lyons & Co. Ltd (Shops Dept) Dance.

23 January: The London Clarion Re-Union Committee Reunion and Dance.

28 January: St Martin's Guild of Fellowship Dance.

30 January: London Union of Training College Club Dance.

6 February: 'A' Division Athletic Club, Hyde Park Police Station Dance.

12 February: York Mansions Restaurant, Petty France, SW1, dance in aid of the funds of Westminster Hospital.

13 February: The National Cyclists' Union (London Centre) Dance.

16 February: The Old Vic (Royal Victoria Hall) Miss Lilian Baylis, Old Vic Circle Costume Dance.

18 February: Widows and Orphans Christmas Hamper Fund, Inland Section GPO Sports London Dance and Whist Drive.

19 February: A.B.C Sports Club Dance.

20 February: The Victorian Athletic Association Dance.

2-6 March: 23rd Badminton Association 'All-England Championships' Annual Tournament.

11 March: 'A' Division Athletic Club, Hyde Park Police Station, Dance.

14-18 March: The London Master Bakers' & Confectioners' Protection Society Bakery Exhibition.

20 March: The Combined Cavalry 'Old Comrades' Association Dance.

25 March: 'A' Division Athletic Club, Hyde Park Police Station Dance.

27 March: London Union of Training College Club Dance.

30 March: The French Bulldog Club of England Dog Show.

5 April: East London Scout Settlement Dance.

8 April: Lecture given by Mr J. Easton, of Messrs Easton and Robertson, the Architects of the planned New Horticultural Hall.

14 April: Pug Club and London and Provincial Pug Club Shows.

15 April: The British Carnation Society Show.

23 April: The National Rose Society Show (28 Victoria Street).

24 April: The Rhododendron Society Show.

29 April: 'C' Division Athletic Club, Vine Street Police Station, Dance.

30 April: The Association of Ex-Service Civil Servants (3 Victoria Street) Dance.

1 May: National Amalgamated Union of Shop Assistants & Clerks May Day Rally and Dance.

10-15 May: Photographic Arts & Crafts Exhibition organised by Arthur C. Brookes of The Photographic Dealer (both were cancelled due to the General Strike).

18 May: King Charles Spaniel Club Dog Show.

4-11 June: Applied Arts and Handcrafts Exhibition.

26 June: The Girl Guides Association (East London Division) Fundraising Entertainment.

3-10 July: University of London Examinations.

c.July: 26th Annual National Sweet Pea Society Show.

23 July: The National Rose Society Show.

3-4 September: The London and District Allotments & Gardens Society Fruit and Vegetable Show.

8 September: The National Dahlia Society Show.

10-11 September: The National Rose Society Show.

17-25 September: 8th The Model Engineer Exhibition.

2 October: The Association of Ex-Service Civil Servants Dance.

7 October: Griffin Athletic Club (Dulwich Village, SE) Dance.

9 October: 'A' Division Athletic Club, Hyde Park Police Station Dance.

14 October: The City of Westminster Philanthropic Society Dance.

15 October: The Mullard Radio Valve Co. Dance.

16 October: St Martin's Cycling Club, Islington, N1, Dance.

22-9 October: Hairdressing Exhibition.

4-5 November: National Chrysanthemum Society Flower Show.

c.November: London Galloway Association Dance in aid of Royal Caledonian Schools.

8 November: John James Keen Dance in aid of King's College Hospital.

9-11 November: 33rd Sale of Work in Aid of Church Work at Home & Abroad, Home and Foreign Missions.

13 November: The Victoria Athletic Association Dance.

18 November: 'A' Division Athletic Club, Hyde Park Police Station Dance.

19 November: The Combined Cavalry 'Old Comrades' Association Dance.

20 November: King Edward Building Sports Association GPO, EC1, Dance.

23 November: Pro Patria Day Nurseries (24 Bruton Street, W1) Jumble Sale and Bazaar. Bazaar in aid of the South Islington Day Nursery.

25-6 November: Our Dumb Friends' League Bazaar.

27 November: London Union of Training College Clubs Dance.

3-10 December: 4th Applied Arts and Handcrafts Exhibition.

16-28 December: South Western District Post Office Christmas postal work.

1927

1-7 January: 2nd The Schoolboy's Own Exhibition.

13 January: 'A' Division Athletic Club, Hyde Park Police Station Dance.

15 January: The Cyclists' Touring Club Dance.

20 January: St Martin's Guild of Fellowship Dance and Whist Drive.

22 January: The London Clarion Reunion Committee Reunion and Dance.

26 January: East London Scout Settlement Dance.

29 January: London Union of Training College Clubs Dance.

27 January: Widows and Orphans Christmas Hamper Fund (Inland Section GPO) Dance and Whist Drive.

2 February: The Alsatian League & Club of Great Britain Championship Dog Show.

5 February: 'A' Division Athletic Club, Hyde Park Police Station Dance.

9 February: Eugene Ltd Dance and Hairdressing Competition.

10 February: Messrs Lyons & Co. Ltd (shops dept), 59 Shaftesbury Ave, W1, Dance.

11 February: The Worker's Travel Association Ltd (Transport House, Smith Square, SW1) Social and Dance.

12 February: The Victoria Athletic Association Dance.

14 February: Inauguration of 'The Ginger Club' at a birthday party given by George Lansbury, MP (Lansbury's Labour Weekly) Social and Dance.

15 February: Miss Lilian Baylis (The Old Vic, Royal Victoria Hall) The Old Vic Costume Dance.

16 February: C.W. Harris of York Mansions Restaurant (Petty France, SW1) Dance.

17 February: 'C' Division Athletic Club Vine Street Police Station Dance.

18 February: The Civil Service Holiday Camps Ltd Dance.

28 February-5 March: 24th Badminton Association 'All-England Championships' Annual Tournament.

11 March: The Distillers' Co. Ltd Dance.

13-18 March: The London Master Bakers & Confectioners Protection Society Exhibition.

19 March: 'A' Division Athletic Club, Hyde Park Police Station Dance.

24 March: The United Dairies (Youdees) Social and Sports Club Dance.

26 March: London Union of Training College Clubs Dance.

29-30 March: The British Carnation Society Flower Show.

2 April: 'A' Division Athletic Club, Hyde Park Police Station Dance.

9 April: The Combined Cavalry 'Old Comrades' Association Dance.

22 April: The National Rose Society Show.

30 April: 'C' Division Athletic Club, Vine Street Police Station.

3-4 May: 2nd The Rhododendron Society Show.

13-21 May: Photographic Arts & Crafts Exhibition Fair.

26-8 May: 1st Hospitals and Institutions Exhibition.

30 May: The French Bulldog Club of England Dog Show (cancelled).

2 June: The Iris Society Flower Show.

10 June: Westminster Hospital Dance in aid of the Hospital (deposit forfeited and cancelled).

11-17 June: University of London Examinations.

30 June: The Bergman Österberg Physical Training College Gymnastic Display. (This event was cancelled and £3 13s. 6d. deposit forfeited.)

7-8 July: 27th Annual National Sweet Pea Society Show.

15 July: The National Rose Society Show.

23 July: The Gas Light & Coke Company Horticultural Society, at 84 Horseferry Road, SW1 – Vegetable and Flower Show.

1-3 September: The 6th London Allotments & Gardens Society Fruit and Veg Show.

9-10 September: The National Rose Society Show.

14 September: The National Dahlia Society Show.

17-24 September: 9th The Model Engineer Exhibition.

1 October: 'A' Division Athletic Club, Cannon Row Police Station Dance.

4-7 October: National Federation of Women's Institutes Home Crafts Exhibition.

8 October: The Knight's of St Columba Dance.

13 October: 'C' Division Athletic Club, Vine Street Police Station W1.

14-15 October: Labour Fair & Dance organised by the London Labour Party

24 October: John James Keen – Dance in aid of King's College Hospital.

28 October: The Mullard Radio Valve Co. Ltd Dance.

29 October: London Association of Old Scholars' Clubs Dance.

3-4 November: The National Chrysanthemum Society Show.

5 November: London Galloway Association Dance.

8-10 November: 34th Sale of Work in Aid of Church Work at Home & Abroad and Foreign Missions.

12 November: Combined Cavalry 'Old Comrades' Association Dance.

17 November: 'A' Division Athletic Club, Cannon Row Police Station.

19 November: The Victoria Athletic Association Dance.

23-4 November: Our Dumb Friends' League Fair.

26 November: London Union of Training College Clubs Dance.

c.November: The New Health Society's Exhibition.

2-9 December: 5th Applied Arts and Handcrafts Exhibition.

15 December: 'C' Division Athletic Club, Vine Street Police Station, W1.

16-27 December: South Western District Post Office – Christmas postal work.

31 December: London Clarion Fellowship Reunion and Dance.

1928

7-13 January: 8th Schoolboy's Own Exhibition – Old Hall.

20 January: 1st Maddieson's Hemsby Holiday Camp – Old Hall.

21 January: London Labour Party Dance – Old Hall.

25 January: Claude Fisher, Boy Scouts Association – Old Hall.

26 January: 'C' Division Athletic Club Vine Street Police Station – Old Hall.

28 January: London Union of Training College Clubs (Teachers' Dance) – Old Hall.

2 February: Alsatian League & Club of Great Britain Dog Show – Old Hall.

4 February: National Cyclists' Union Dance – Old Hall.

17-18 February: Mr Douglas Cator, St Matthew's Westminster School – Old Hall.

21 February: Miss Lilian Baylis of The Old Vic, The Old Vic Circle Costume Dance – Old Hall.

22 February: Eugene Ltd, 31 Dover Street, Dance and Hairdressing Competitions – Old Hall.

24 February: C.W. Morris, York Mansions Restaurant, Dance – Old Hall.

25 February: 'A' Division Athletic Club, Metropolitan Police Dance – Old Hall.

5-10 March: 25th Badminton Association 'All-England Championships' Annual Tournament– Old Hall.

16 March: Eugene Ltd, 31 Dover Street, Dance and Hairdressing Competitions – Old Hall.

18-23 March: London Master Bakers' Exhibition (London Master Bakers' and Confectioners' Protection Society) – Old Hall.

19-23 March: Annual Drapery Exhibition – New Hall.

24 March: London Union of Training College Clubs Teachers' Dance – Old Hall.

29 March: 'C' Division Athletic Club Vine Street Police Station Dance – Old Hall.

31 March: A.C. Gosling (Hon. Secretary) Combined Cavalry 'Old Comrades' Association Dance – Old Hall.

7 April: GPO Widows and Orphans Christmas Hamper Fund Dance & Whist Drive – Old Hall.

20 April: The National Rose Society Show – Old Hall.

26-7 April: The British Carnation Society Show – Old Hall.

1 May: 1st Show of the Rhododendron Association – Old Hall.

5 May: The Society of Our Lady of Good Counsel Jumble Sale – Old Hall.

10-22 May: Associated Newspapers.

26 May-1 June: 2nd Hospitals & Institutions Exhibition.

8 June: The Iris Society Flower Show – Old Hall.

9-15 June: University of London Exams – Old Hall.

26 June: 4th RHS Annual Flower Show for Amateurs – Old Hall.

c.July: 28th Annual National Sweet Pea Society Show – New Hall.

19-20 July: The British Carnation Society Show – Old Hall.

24 July: Great Show of New Roses, organised by the National Rose Society – Old Hall.

28 July: The Gas Light & Coke Co. Horticultural Society Vegetable and Flower Show – Old Hall.

10 August: British Gladiolus Society Flower Show – Old Hall.

30 August-1 September: The London Allotments & Gardens Show Society Fruit and Vegetable Show – Old Hall.

7-8 September: The National Rose Society – Old Hall.

12 September: The National Dahlia Society Show – Old Hall.

15-22 September: 10th *The Model Engineer* Exhibition – Old Hall.

17-24 October: The International Exhibition of Garden Design and Conference – New Hall.

31 October: The National Sweet Pea Society Annual Meeting.

1-2 November: The National Chrysanthemum Society Show – Old Hall.

3 November: The Cyclists' Touring Club Dance – Old Hall.

6-8 November: 35th The Sale of Work in Aid of Church Work at Home & Abroad, Home and Foreign Missions – Old Hall.

7-14 November: The New Health Exhibition – New Hall.

10 November: The London Galloway Association, Royal Caledonian Schools Annual Scottish Carnival Dance – Old Hall.

13 November: RHS Flower Show – Old Hall.

15-16 November: Our Dumb Friends' League Christmas Fair – Old Hall.

16 November: National Union of Conservative & Unionist Associations.

17 November: London Union of Training College Clubs (Teachers' Dance) – Old Hall.

23 November: The Mullard Valve Radio Co. Ltd Dance – New Hall.

24 November: London Association of Old Scholars' Clubs Dance – Old Hall.

24 November: 9th Church of Christ Scientist Christian Science Lecture – New Hall.

30 November-11 December: Rubber Goods Exhibition organised by Hugh Greville Montgomery – New Hall.

30 November-7 December: The 6th Applied Arts and Handcrafts Exhibition – Old Hall.

12-15 December: The British Fur Rabbit Society Rabbit & Fur Show – Old Hall.

15 December: Combined Cavalry 'Old Comrades' Association Dance – New Hall.

17-27 December: South West District Post Office Christmas sorting– Old Hall.

11 Dates: Horticultural Trades Association – Old Hall.

Date Unknown: United Horticultural Benefit Provident Society – Old Hall.

1929

29 December '28-5 January '29: 9th Schoolboy's Exhibition – New Hall.

8-11 January: University of London Examinations– Old Hall.

12 January: London Labour Party Dance – Old Hall.

14 January: 1st Caister Holiday Camps Reunion Dance – New Hall.

19 January: London Clarion Club Dance – Old Hall.

23 January: Boy Scouts Association – Old Hall.

26 January: GPO Widows and Orphans Christmas Hamper Fund – Old Hall.

31 January: Alsatian League & Club of Great Britain Championship Show – Old Hall.

2 February: London Union of Training College Clubs Dance – Old Hall.

12 February: Miss Lilian Baylis of the Old Vic, The Old Vic Theatre Costume Dance (Shrove Tuesday) – New Hall.

4-9 March: 26th Badminton Association 'All-England Championships' Annual Tournament – Old Hall.

5 March: 6th London Master Bakers' Exhibition – New Hall.

15 March: C.W. Morris, York Mansions Restaurant Dance – Old Hall.

16 March: 'A' Division Athletic Club Metropolitan Police Dance – Old Hall.

18-22 March: 19th Annual Professional Nursing, Midwifery & Public Health Exhibition and Conference – New Hall.

18-22 March: Liberal Campaigns Department – Old Hall.

23 March: London Union of Training College Clubs Dance – Old Hall.

12 April: Catholic Truth Society – Old Hall.

16 April: Studley College Fundraising Event– Old Hall.

19 April: The National Rose Society – Old Hall.

16-31 May: Home Arts & Industries Association Exhibition – Old Hall.

4-7 June: University of London Examinations – Old Hall.

6 June: The Iris Society's Show – New Hall (opened by French Ambassador).

c.June: 1st Annual British Delphinium Society Show – New Hall.

1-4 July: University of London Examinations – Old Hall.

11 July: Amateur Flower Show.

c.July: 29th Annual National Sweet Pea Society Show – New Hall.

16 July: 6th RHS Cherry & Soft Fruit Show – New Hall.

23 July: The National Rose Society – Old Hall.

24 July: 1st General Meeting of The Roads Beautifying Association – Old Hall.

27 July: The Gas Light & Coke Co. Horticultural Society Vegetable and Flower Show – Old Hall.

6-7 September: London Allotment & Garden Show Society – New Hall.

7-14 September: 11th The Model Engineer Exhibition – Old Hall.

13-14 September: The National Rose Society's Autumn Show – New Hall.

11 September: National Dahlia Society Annual Show – New Hall.

8-9 October: RHS Annual Fruit and Vegetable Show – New Hall.

2 November: Junior Imperial and Constitutional League Reception and Dance – New Hall.

2 November: Brewer F.E. – Old Hall.

6-7 November: 36th Sale of Work in Aid of Church Work at Home & Abroad, Home and Foreign Missions – Old Hall.

7-8 November: National Chrysanthemum Society Annual Show – New Hall.

8-22 November: 1st Bachelor Girl's Exhibition.

9 November: Combined Cavalry 'Old Comrades' Association Dance – Old Hall.

11 November: National Society of Operative Printers' Assistants – Old Hall.

13-14 November: Our Dumb Friends' League Bazaar – Old Hall.

15-22 November: The New Health Society's Exhibition – New Hall.

16 November: The London Galloway Association Dance – Old Hall.

19 November: RHS Flower Show and Walnut Competition – Old Hall.

20-1 November: The British Carnation Society Annual Show – Old Hall.

26 November-6 December: The 7th Applied Arts and Handcrafts Exhibition – Old Hall.

29 November: Mullard Radio Valve Co. – New Hall.

4 December: Mystery Ball – New Hall.

9 December: The Universal Cookery & Food Association event organised by Iwan Kriens – Old Hall.

11-14 December: The British Fur Rabbit Association Rabbit & Fur Show – Old Hall.

16-27 December: South West District Post Office Christmas sorting– Old Hall.

1930

31 December '29-8 January '30: 10th Daily Mail Schoolboy's Own Exhibition – Old and New Halls.

11 January: Annual Reunion of the Labour Party and Dance – Old Hall.

14-17 January: London University Examinations – Old Hall.

18 January: London Clarion Club Dance – Old Hall.

18 January: 2nd Maddieson's Hemsby Holiday Camp – New Hall.

22 January: Roland House Settlement Dance – Old Hall.

25 January: GPO Widows and Orphans Christmas Hamper Fund Dance and Whist Drive – Old Hall.

4 February: Miss Lilian Baylis, Old Vic, The Old Vic Costume Dance – New Hall.

6 February: Alsatian League & Club of Great Britain Championship Show – Old Hall.

8 February: National Cyclists' Union – Old Hall.

15 February: 2nd Caister Holiday Camps Reunion Dance – New Hall.

15 February: Combined Cavalry 'Old Comrades' Association Dance – Old Hall.

21 February: Westminster Hospital – New Hall.

22 February: London Rover Council – New Hall.

24 February: Lyons Corner House Sports Club Dance – Old Hall.

3-8 March: 27th Badminton Association 'All-England Championships' Annual Tournament – Old Hall.

3-7 March: 20th Annual Professional Nursing, Midwifery & Public Health Exhibition & Conference – New Hall.

1-4 April: 7th London Master Bakers' Baking Trades Exhibition – New Hall.

25 April: National Rose Society Great Spring Show – Old Hall.

29-30 April: 3rd Rhododendron Association Annual Show – New Hall.

30 April: Lyons Corner House Sports Club Dance – Old Hall.

8-9 May: 1st Annual Show of the Alpine Garden Society – Old Hall.

12 May: 'A' Division Athletic Club Metropolitan Police Dance – Old Hall.

12-16 May: 16th Congress of the Professional Photographers' Association together with a Photographic Fair – New Hall.

21-30 March: 39th Chemists' Exhibition.

22-31 May: Home Arts & Industries Association Exhibition – Old Hall (cancelled).

3-6 June: London University Examinations – Old Hall.

26 June: 2nd Annual British Delphinium Society Show – New Hall.

3 July: 'Signs of the Times' pageant and ball held in aid of Queen Charlotte's Maternity Hospital Rebuilding Fund – New Hall.

7-10 July: London University Examinations – Old Hall.

8 July: 30th Annual National Sweet Pea Society Show – New Hall.

11-12 June: Iris Society's Show – Old Hall.

15 July: RHS Flower Show – New Hall.

15-16 July: National Carnation and Picotee Society Show – Old Hall.

18 July: Ministry of Agriculture & Fisheries Horticultural Society – Old Hall.

22 July: National Rose Society – New Hall.

26 July: Gas Light & Coke Co. Horticultural Society Vegetable & Flower Show– New Hall.

7-15 August: 9th International Horticultural Congress – Old Hall.

c.August: RHS Flower Show.

29-30 August: London Gardens Guild Annual Exhibition – New Hall.

4-13 September: 12th The Model Engineer Exhibition – Old Hall.

5-6 September: London Allotment & Garden Show Society – New Hall.

11-12 September: National Dahlia Society Annual Show – New Hall.

19-20 September: National Rose Society – New Hall.

11 October: London Co-operative Society – New Hall.

20-4 October: 1st Medical Exhibition organised by the British & Colonial Druggist Co. Ltd – New Hall.

21 October: The Roads Beautifying Association Annual Meeting – Old Hall.

1 November: Combined Cavalry 'Old Comrades' Association Dance – Old Hall.

1 November: Chelsea Boarding Estate – New Hall.

12-13 November: 37th Sale of Work in Aid of Church Work at Home & Abroad, Home and Foreign Missions – Old Hall.

12-21 November: 1st or 2nd Bachelor Girl's Exhibition, organised by Kinematograph International Exhibitions, Ltd (1913) – New Hall.

15 November: The London Galloway Association Dance in aid of Royal Caledonian Schools – Old Hall.

17-18 November: Semi-final pools and final round of the Ladies' Foil tournament competing for the Lady Louis Mountbatten Cup – New Hall.

18-20 November: Our Dumb Friends' League Christmas Fair – Old Hall.

25 November-5 December: The 8th Applied Arts and Handcraft Exhibition, Old Hall.

26-7 November: The British Carnation Society's Autumn Show – New Hall.

16-27 December: South West District Post Office, Christmas Sorting – Old Hall.

1931

5 January: The Alsatian League & Club of Great Britain Championship Show – Old Hall.

6-8 January: Director of Lands and Accommodation, HM Office of Works, King Charles Street, Whitehall Civil Service Examinations – New Hall.

10 January: The London Labour Party Dance – Old Hall.

12-13 January: Institute of Landscape Architects – New Hall.

12-16 January: University of London Examination – Old Hall.

15 January: The London Co-operative Society Ltd, Dance and Social – New Hall.

17 January: The London Clarion Fellowship Re-union Committee Dance – Old Hall.

17 January: 3rd Maddieson's Hemsby Holiday Camp, near Great Yarmouth Dance – New Hall.

21 January: Roland House (Scout Settlement) Dance in aid of the East London Scout Settlement (Rowland House and Boy's Hostel) – Old Hall.

27 January: British Carnation Society AGM – New Hall.

31 January: The National Cyclists' Union (London Centre) Dance – Old Hall.

5 February: The Alsatian League & Club of Great Britain Winter Championship Show.

7 February: The Combined Cavalry 'Old Comrades' Association Dance – Old Hall.

9 February: The National Society of Operative Printers' Assistants (NASOPA) Dance – Old Hall.

12 February: Knights of St Columba Dance – Old Hall.

14 February: GPO Widows and Orphans Christmas Hamper Fund Dance – Old Hall.

17 February: Toc H, London Area, 47 Francis Street, SW1, Festival.

17 February: The Camping Club of Great Britain & Ireland Dance – Old Hall.

21 February: George N. Kemp (Hon. Secretary) London Rover Committee (Boy Scouts Association) – New Hall.

2-7 March: 28th Badminton Association 'All-England Championships' Annual Tournament – Old Hall.

2-6 March: 21st Annual Professional Nursing, Midwifery & Public Health Exhibition & Conference – New Hall.

14-21 March: Bakers' Exhibition organised by the London Master Bakers' & Confectioners' Protection Society – New Hall.

17 March: 'A' Division Police Athletic Club Dance – Old Hall.

18 March: Sir Ernest Petter, 22 Grosvenor Place, London, SW.

8-9 April: 2nd Annual Show of The Alpine Garden Society – Old Hall.

12 April: 7th Model Railway Exhibition – Old Hall.

14-15 April: The British Carnation Society Show – Old Hall.

15 April: The Future of Gardens and Gardening by the Institute of Landscape Architects.

21-2 April: RHS Daffodil Show – New Hall.

24 April: The National Rose Society Show – New Hall.

25 April: The Masses Stage & Film Guild.

28-9 April: The Rhododendron Association Show – New Hall.

11-15 May: 40th Chemists' Exhibition.

19-21 May: The South of England Home Office Schools Exhibition – New Hall.

11-16 May: Radio Show organised by The Radio Manufacturers' Association- Old Hall.

1-5 June: University of London Examination – Old Hall.

9-10 June: The Alpine Garden Society Show – Old Hall.

9-10 June: The Iris Society Flower Show – New Hall.

23 June: Amateurs' Flower Show.

25 June: The British Delphinium Society Show – New Hall.

25 June: The Westminster Congregational Church Reception – Old Hall.

29 June-3 July: The National Training School of Cookery Examinations – Old Hall.

4-9 July: University of London Examination – Old Hall.

8-9 July: 31st Annual National Sweet Pea Society Show – New Hall.

10 July: The Horticultural Society of the Ministry of Agriculture & Fisheries Fruit, Flower & Vegetable Show – New Hall.

14-15 July: The National Carnation & Picotee Society Show – Old Hall.

17 July: The National Rose Society Show – New Hall.

25 July: The Gas Light & Coke Company Vegetable & Flower Show– New Hall.

11-12 August: The International Exhibition of The British Gladiolus Society Show – Old Hall.

25-9 August: London Gardens Guild Annual Flower Show Society Fruit, Flower & Vegetable Show – New Hall.

3-12 September: 13th *The Model Engineer* Exhibition – Old Hall.

10-11 September: The National Dahlia Society Show – New Hall.

18-19 September: The National Rose Society Show – New Hall.

10 October: S.D. Prain, Aberfeldy Hotel, St Helier, Jersey, C.I., Dance – New Hall.

19-23 October: London Medical Exhibition– New Hall.

27-8 October: The Independent Labour Party (34 Victoria Street, SW1) – New Hall.

31 October: Chelsea Boarding Establishment Dance – New Hall.

5-6 November: The National Chrysanthemum Society Show – New Hall.

7 November: The Combined Cavalry 'Old Comrades' Association Dance – Old Hall.

7-20 November: 2nd Modern Housekeeping Exhibition organised by British Organizers.

9 November: The National Society of Operative Printers' Assistants (NATSOPA) Dance – Old Hall.

10-12 November: 38th Sale of Work in Aid of Church Work at Home & Abroad, Home and Foreign Missions – Old Hall.

14 November: The London Galloway Association Dance – Old Hall.

17-19 November: Our Dumb Friends' League Fair – Old Hall.

18-19 November: Director of Lands & Accommodation, HM Office of Works Customs & Excise Examinations – New Hall.

24 November-4 December: The 9th Applied Arts and Handcrafts Exhibition – Old Hall.

2 December: Director of Lands and Accommodation, HM Office of Works Civil Service Examinations – New Hall.

8-9 December: The Dockland Settlements Sale of Work – Old Hall.

16-28 December: South Western District Post Office Christmas postal work – Old Hall.

1932

12-15 January: The University of London Examinations – Old Hall.

16 January: 4th Maddieson's Hemsby Holiday Camp, near Great Yarmouth Dance – New Hall.

16 January: The London Clarion Fellowship Reunion Committee Dance – Old Hall.

23 January: 1st Pakefield Hall Holiday Camp, Lowestoft Dance – Old Hall.

23 January: 1st Jersey Holiday Camp (Portelet Bay, Jersey, C.I.) Dance – New Hall.

30 January: The *Sandringham Hotel* (St Helier, Jersey C.I.) Dance – New Hall.

30 January: 1st Littlestone-on-Sea Holiday Camp, New Romney Reunion Dance – Old Hall.

6 February: The London Rover Committee (Boy Scouts Association) Dance – New Hall.

6 February: The National Cyclists' Union (London Centre) Dance – Old Hall.

29 February-5 March: 29th Badminton Association 'All-England Championships' Annual Tournament – Old Hall.

13 February: The GPO Widows and Orphans Christmas Hamper Fund Dance – Old Hall.

20 February: The Combined Cavalry 'Old Comrades' Association Dance – Old Hall.

20 February: 3rd The Holiday Camp-Caister-on-Sea, near Great Yarmouth Dance – New Hall.

29 February-4 March: 22nd Annual Professional Nursing, Midwifery & Public Health Exhibition & Conference – New Hall.

12 March: The Camping Club of Great Britain & Ireland Dance – Old Hall.

15-18 March: Bakers' Exhibition organised by the London Master Bakers' & Confectioners' Protection Society – New Hall.

17 March: 'A' Division Athletic Club Cannon Row Police Station Dance – Old Hall.

1 April: Emilio Scala, Hamilton Lodge, Honour Oak Road, Forest Hill – New Hall.

5-6 April: The Alpine Garden Society Show – Old Hall.

12-13 April: The London Gardens Guild Flower Show – Old Hall.

16 April: The GPO Widows and Orphans Christmas Hamper Fund Dance– Old Hall.

22 April: The National Rose Society Show – New Hall.

29 April: Frederick T. Goldsmith, 46 Dorset Mews, Wilton Street, SW1, dance in aid of Westminster Hospital – New Hall.

3-4 May: The Rhododendron Association Show – New Hall.

10-11 May: The General Nursing Council for England and Wales Examinations – Old Hall.

23-7 May: 41st Chemists' Exhibition organised by the British & Colonial Druggist Co. Ltd – New Hall.

7-8 June: The Alpine Garden Society Show – Old Hall.

9-10 June: The Iris Society Show – New Hall.

28 June: RHS Amateur Gardener's Show – New Hall.

30 June: The British Delphinium Society Show – New Hall

1 July: The National Training College of Domestic Subjects Examinations – Old Hall.

4-7 July: The University of London Examinations – New Hall.

15 July: The Horticultural Society of the Ministry of Agriculture and Fisheries Show of Fruit, Flowers & Veg – Old Hall.

15 July: The National Rose Society Show – New Hall (cancelled).

19-20 July: The National Carnation & Picotee Society Show – 2/3 Old Hall.

19-20 July: The Alpine Garden Society Show – 1/3 Old Hall.

1-10 September: 14th *The Model Engineer* Exhibition – Old Hall.

2-3 September: The London Allotments and Gardens Show Society Fruit, Flower and Vegetable Show – New Hall.

13-14 September: The National Dahlia Society Show – New Hall.

16-17 September: The National Rose Society Show – New Hall.

17-21 October: 3rd Medical Exhibition – New Hall.

17-22 October: 1st Light-Weight Cycle Show including Hiking and Camping Equipment – Old Hall.

29 October: The *Sandringham Hotel*, Columberie, Jersey C.I. Reunion Dance – Old Hall.

29 October: Richard Binnington Chelsea Private Hotel, 11 Gloucester Street, St Helier, C.I., Dance – New Hall.

1-2 November: The National Chrysanthemum Society Show – New Hall.

5 November: The Combined Cavalry 'Old Comrades' Association Dance – Old Hall.

7 November: The National Society of Operative Printers' Assistants Dance – Old Hall.

8-10 November: 39th Sale of Work in Aid of Church Work at Home & Abroad, Home and Foreign Missions – Old Hall.

12 November: The London Galloway Association Dance – Old Hall.

16-17 November: Our Dumb Friends' League Fair – Old Hall.

7-13 November: 7th National Federation of Women's Institutes, Handcrafts Exhibition – New Hall.

22 November-2 December: The 10th Applied Arts and Handcrafts Exhibition – Old Hall.

23-4 November: The British Carnation Society Show – New Hall.

29 November: The Ladies' Kennel Association Dog Show – New Hall.

6 December: HM Office of Works Civil Service Examinations – New Hall.

16-28 December: South Western District Post Office Christmas postal work – Old Hall.

31 December: The National Cyclist's Union Dance – Old Hall.

1933

10-13 January: The University of London Examinations – Old Hall.

14 January: The GPO Widows and Orphans Christmas Hamper Fund Dance – Old Hall.

14 January: 5th Maddieson's Hemsby Holiday Camp near Great Yarmouth Dance – New Hall.

1 February: Messrs Joseph Lyons & Co. Ltd (Teashop Social Section, Lyons Club) Dance – New Hall (cancelled).

28 January: The London Clarion Fellowship Reunion Committee Dance – Old Hall.

4 February: 2nd Pakefield Hall Holiday Camp Dance – New Hall.

11 February: The London Rover Committee Dance – Old Hall

18 February: The Combined Cavalry 'Old Comrades Association' Dance – Old Hall.

25 February: 2nd Littlestone-on-Sea Holiday Camp, New Romney Dance – Old Hall.

25 February: 4th The Holiday camp Caister-on-Sea Dance – New Hall.

6-11 March: 30th Badminton Association 'All-England Championships' Annual Tournament – Old Hall.

4 March: The Old Contemptibles Association Concert and Dance – New Hall.

17 March: 'A' Division Metropolitan Police Athletic Club, Cannon Row Police Station Dance – Old Hall.

14-16 March: Bakers' Exhibition organised by The London Master Bakers' & Confectioners' Protection Society – New Hall.

18 March: The Camping Club of Great Britain & Ireland Reunion & Dance – Old Hall.

27-31 March: 23rd Nursing & Midwifery Exhibition – New Hall.

4-5 April: The Alpine Garden Society Show – Old Hall.

11-12 April: The British Carnation Society Show – Old Hall.

21 April: The National Rose Society Show – New Hall.

2-3 May: The Alpine Garden Society Show – Old Hall.

2-3 May: The Rhododendron Association Show – New Hall.

8 April: The London Gardens Guild Flower Show – Old Hall.

6-9 June: The University of London Examinations – Old Hall.

10-11 June: The Society of St Vincent de Paul (66 Victoria Street), Centenary Meetings – New Hall.

13 June: The Worshipful Company of Spectacle Makers Examinations– Old Hall.

13-14 June: The Iris Society Show – New Hall (cancelled).

20 June: The Cactus & Succulent Society of Great Britain Show – Old Hall.

26-7 June: Mr Douglas Cator (13 Westminster Mansions, SW1) Sale of Work in aid of the Westminster Belgravia and Pimlico Association for Women's Welfare – Old Hall.

29 June: The National Sweet Pea Society Show – Old Hall.

29 June: The British Delphinium Society Show – New Hall.

3-6 July: The University of London Examinations – Old Hall.

10-12 July: The National Training College of Domestic Subjects Examinations – Old Hall.

14 July: The Horticultural Society of The Ministry of Agriculture & Fisheries Fruit, Flowers & Vegetables Show – Old Hall.

18-19 July: The National Carnation & Picotee Society Show – Old Hall.

31 August-9 September: 15th *The Model Engineer* Exhibition – Old Hall.

1-2 September: The London Allotments & Gardens Show Society Fruit, Flowers and Vegetable Show – New Hall.

5-6 September: The National Dahlia Society Show – New Hall.

8-9 September: The London Gardens Guild Flower Show – New Hall.

15-16 September: The National Rose Society Show – New Hall.

25-9 September: 42nd Chemists' Exhibition – New Hall.

10-11 October: The General Nursing Council for England & Wales Examinations- Old Hall.

16-20 October: 4th Medical Exhibition – New Hall.

24 October: Exhibition of South African Wild Flowers – Old Hall.

30 October: Messrs J. Lyons & Co. Ltd (The Trocadero) Dinner – New Hall.

4 November: The Combined Cavalry 'Old Comrades' Association Dance – Old Hall.

7-9 November: 40th Sale of Work in Aid of Church Work at Home & Abroad, Home and Foreign Missions – Old Hall.

9-10 November: The National Chrysanthemum Society Show – New Hall.

11 November: The GPO Widows and Orphans Christmas Hamper Fund Dance – Old Hall.

13 November: The National Society of Operative Printers' Assistants – Old Hall.

15-16 November: Our Dumb Friends' League Fair – Old Hall.

16-22 November: 2nd J.E. Holdsworth Light-Weight Cycle Show including, Hiking and Camping Equipment – New Hall.

18 November: The London Galloway Association Dance – Old Hall.

30 November-1 December: The British Carnation Society Show – New Hall.

28 November-9 December: The 11th Applied Arts and Handcrafts Exhibition.

29 November: The Ladies' Kennel Association Dog Show.

4-5 December: HM Office of Works Civil Service Examinations – New Hall.

8 December: The Worshipful Company of Spectacle Makers Examinations – New Hall.

10 December: Toc H Incorporated Festival – New Hall.

27 December: South Western District Post Office Christmas Postal Work – Old Hall

30 December: The National Cyclists' Union Dance – Old Hall.

1934

1 January: Government Minor & Manipulative Grades Association Dance – Old Hall.

6 January: Combined Cavalry 'Old Comrades Association' Dance – Old Hall.

9-12 January: University of London Examinations – Old Hall.

13 January: The Widows and Orphans Christmas Hamper Fund Dance – Old Hall.

13 January: Gaumont British Picture Corporation Ltd Dance – New Hall.

13 January: 6th Maddieson's Hemsby Holiday Camp Dance – New Hall.

3 February: 3rd Littlestone-on-Sea Holiday Camp Dance – Old Hall.

10 February: The London Rover Committee Dance – Old Hall.

10 February: 3rd Pakefield Hall Holiday Camp Dance – New Hall.

17 February: 5th Caister-on-Sea Holiday Camp Dance – New Hall.

24 February: The Camping Club of Great Britain & Ireland Dance – Old Hall.

24 February-2 March: The London Master Bakers' & Confectioners' Protection Society Bakers' Exhibition – New Hall.

5-10 March: 31st Badminton Association 'All-England Championships' Annual Tournament – Old Hall.

6-7 March: RHS Flower Show – New Hall.

17 March: 'A' Division Athletic Club Cannon Row Police Station Dance – Old Hall.

24 March: Combined Cavalry 'Old Comrades Association' Dance – Old Hall.

4-5 April: The Alpine Garden Society Flower Show – Old Hall.

7 April: The London Gardens Guild Flower Show – Old Hall.

13 April: The National Rose Society Flower Show – New Hall.

1-2 May: The Alpine Garden Society Flower Show – Old Hall.

1-2 May: The Rhododendron Association Flower Show – New Hall.

7-12 May: 'APEX' The International Air-Post Exhibition – Old Hall.

25 May: The North London District of the Manchester Society of Oddfellows Dance – New Hall.

5-8 June: University of London Examinations – Old Hall.

7-8 June: The Iris Society Flower Show – New Hall.

16, 18, 21 June: The Worshipful Company of Spectacle Makers Examinations – Old Hall.

23 June: Lambert & Butler Ltd Dance – Old Hall.

27 June: The Queen's Institute of District Nursing (members meeting) – Old Hall.

29 June: The British Delphinium Society Flower Show – New Hall.

2-5 July: University of London Examinations – Old Hall.

2-6 July: The National Training College of Domestic Subjects (examinations) – New Hall.

10-11 July: The National Sweet Pea Society Flower Show – Old Hall.

13 July: The National Rose Society Flower Show – New Hall.

13-14 July: The National Carnation & Picotee Society Flower Show – Old Hall.

20 July: The Horticultural Society of the Ministry of Agriculture & Fisheries – Fruit Flowers & Vegetables Show – Old Hall.

24 July: The Cactus & Succulent Society of Great Britain Cactus Show – Old Hall.

30-1 August: The London Allotments & Gardens Show Society Fruit & Vegetable Show – New Hall.

3 September: The National Dahlia Society Flower Show – New Hall.

6-15 September: 16th *The Model Engineer* Exhibition – Old Hall.

7-8 September: The London Gardens Guild Flower Show – New Hall.

14-15 September: The National Rose Society Flower Show – New Hall.

24-8 September: 43rd Chemists' Exhibition – New Hall.

15-19 October: 5th London Medical Exhibition – New Hall.

27 October-3 November: 3rd J.E. Holdsworth – Light-Weight Cycle Show including, Hiking and Camping Equipment – Old Hall.

24 October: The Personal Service League (Meeting) – Old Hall.

27 October: The London Group of the 'Holiday Fellowship' (Re-union) – New Hall.

7-9 November: 41st Sale of Work in Aid of Church Work at Home & Abroad, Home and Foreign Missions – Old Hall.

8-9 November: The National Chrysanthemum Society Flower Show – New Hall.

10 November: The London Galloway Association Dance in aid of Royal Caledonian Schools – Old Hall.

13-15 November: Our Dumb Friends' League (Fair) – Old Hall.

16 November: The National Society of Operative Printers' Assistants Dance – Old Hall.

17 November: The GPO Widows and Orphans Christmas Hamper Fund Dance – Old Hall.

29 November: The Dockland Settlements Dance – New Hall.

28 November-8 December: 12th Applied Arts and Handcrafts Exhibition – Old Hall.

12-13 December: The Worshipful Company of Spectacle Makers Examinations – Old Hall.

17, 19 December: The Worshipful Company of Spectacle Makers Examinations – New Hall.

15-27 December: South Eastern District Post Office (Christmas Post sorting) – Old Hall.

29 December: The National Cyclists' Union Dance – Old Hall.

1935

26 December '34-5 January '35: 15th Schoolboy's Own Exhibition – London Schools Amateur Association Boxing Championships – Old Hall.

8-11 January: The University of London Examinations – Old Hall.

19 January: Miss Sadie Cheesman, The Central Women's Organisation Committee Dance – Old Hall.

19 January: 7th Maddieson's Hemsby Holiday Camp Dance – New Hall.

26 January: George S. Griffiths, The London Rover Committee Dance – Old Hall.

2 February: 4th Littlestone-on-Sea Holiday Camp Dance – Old Hall.

9 February: 4th Pakefield Hall Holiday Camp Dance – New Hall.

9 February: GPO Widows and Orphans Christmas Hamper Fund Dance – Old Hall.

16 February: 6th The Holiday Camp – Caister-on-Sea Dance – New Hall.

16 February: 1st St Petersville Holiday Camp Ltd Reunion Dance – Old Hall.

25 February-1 March: 34th Universal Cookery & Food Exhibition – New Hall.

23 February: Combined Cavalry 'Old Comrades' Association Dance – Old Hall.

4-9 March: 32nd Badminton Association 'All-England Championships' Annual Tournament – Old Hall.

11-15 March: 25th Annual Professional Nursing, Midwifery & Hospitals Exhibition & Conference – New Hall.

16 March: The Camping Club of Great Britain & Ireland Reunion & Dance – Old Hall.

22-3 March: The Gas Light Sports Association Staff Arts and Crafts Exhibition – Old Hall.

26-8 March: The London Master Bakers' & Confectioners' Protection Society Bakers' Exhibition – New Hall.

2-3 April: The RHS Flowers in Season Show – New Hall.

6 April: The London Gardens Society Spring Exhibition – Old Hall.

9-10 April: The British Carnation Society Show – Old Hall.

12 April: The National Rose Society Show – Old Hall.

30 April-1 May: The Rhododendron Association Show – New Hall.

30 April: The Alpine Garden Society Show – Old Hall.

18-25 May: The Co-operative Wholesale Society Ltd Exhibition – Both Halls.

4-7 June: The University of London Examinations – Old Hall.

6-7 June: The Iris Society Show – New Hall.

15 June: Miss Carter, The Carter School of Dancing, 1 Buckingham Palace Gardens, Buckingham Palace Road, SW1. Dancing Display – Old Hall.

21 June: The Civil Service Horticultural Federation Horticultural Show – Old Hall.

22, 24, 27 June: The Worshipful Company of Spectacle Makers Examinations – Old Hall.

27-8 June: The National Training College of Domestic Subjects Examinations – Old Hall.

27 January: The British Delphinium Society Show – New Hall.

2-3 July: The Cactus & Succulent Society of Great Britain Show – Old Hall.

4-5 July: The National Training College of Domestic Subjects Examinations – Old Hall.

8-11 July: The University of London Examinations – Old Hall.

9-10 July: The Horticultural Society of The Ministry of Agriculture & Fisheries, Fruit, Flower and Vegetable Show – New Hall.

23-4 July: The National Carnation & Picotee Society Show – Old Hall.

13-14 August: The British Gladiolus Society Show – Old Hall.

29-31 August: The London Allotments & Gardens Show Society Fruit, Flower and Vegetable Show – New Hall.

3-4 September: The National Dahlia Society Show – New Hall.

6-7 September: The London Gardens Society, 47 Whitehall, SW1 – Old Hall.

9-10 September: The Alpine Garden Society Show – Old Hall.

13-14 September: The National Rose Society Show – New Hall.

19-28 September: 17th *The Model Engineer* Exhibition – Old Hall.

23-7 September: 44th Chemists' Exhibition – New Hall.

15-17 October: RHS Exhibition of Paintings & Drawings of Plants, Flowers & Gardens.

21-5 October: 6th Medical Exhibition – New Hall.

26 October-2 November: 4th Annual Lightweight Cycle Show organised by J.E. Holdsworth of Cycling Exhibitions Ltd – Old Hall.

2 November: The London Group of The Holiday Fellowship Reunion – New Hall.

6-7 November: 42nd Sale of Work in Aid of Church Work at Home & Abroad, Home and Foreign Missions – Old Hall.

6-7 November: National Chrysanthemum Society Show – New Hall.

9 November: The London Galloway Association Dance – Old Hall.

13-20 November: 8th National Federation of Women's Institutes Handcraft Exhibition – New Hall.

11 November: The National Society of Operative Printers' Assistants Dance – Old Hall.

13-14 November: Our Dumb Friends' League Christmas Fair – Old Hall.

16 November: Combined Cavalry 'Old Comrades' Association Dance – Old Hall.

19-20 November: The British Carnation Society Show – Old Hall.

23 November: The GPO Widows and Orphans Christmas Hamper Fund Dance – Old Hall.

23 November: 1st The Northney Holiday Camp (Hayling Island Ltd) Dance – New Hall.

29 November-6 December: Health & Beauty Exhibition – New Hall.

5 December: 5th Pakefield Hall Holiday Camp Dance – Old Hall.

7-11 December: The Worshipful Company of Spectacle Makers Examinations – Old Hall.

13-14 December: 1st Bird and Aquaria Show – New Hall.

15-27 December: South Eastern District Post Office Christmas postal work – Old Hall.

1936

4 January: Messrs Ambrose Wilson Ltd (60 Vauxhall Bridge Road) Dance – Old Hall.

11 January: Central Women's Organisation Committee – Old Hall.

11 January: Messrs Carreras Ltd Dance– New Hall.

14-17 January: The University of London Examinations – Old Hall.

18 January: 8th Maddieson's Hemsby Holiday Camp Dance – New Hall.

18 January: GPO Inland Section, the Widows and Orphans Christmas Hamper.

Fund Dance – Old Hall.

1 February: 5th Littlestone-on-Sea Holiday Camp Dance – Old Hall.

8 February: 1st Brambles Chine Holiday Camp, Freshwater Isle of Wight, Reunion Dance – Old Hall.

15 February: The National Cyclists' Union Ltd (London Centre) Dance – New Hall.

15 February: The London Labour Party, Reunion and Dance – Old Hall.

21 February: 2nd The Northney Holiday Camp (Hayling Island) Ltd Dance – Old Hall.

22 February: Combined Cavalry 'Old Comrades' Association Dance – Old Hall.

22 February: 6th The Caister-on-Sea Holiday Camp Ltd (Great Yarmouth) Dance – New Hall.

7 March: 6th Pakefield Hall Holiday Camp (Pakefield, Lowestoft) Dance – New Hall.

2-7 March: 33rd Badminton Association 'All-England Championships' Annual Tournament – Old Hall.

13 March: The International Friendship League (13 Tavistock Square, WC1), Dance – Old Hall.

16-20 March: The Chartered Surveyors' Institution (12 Great George Street) Examinations – New Hall.

14 March: The Camping Club of Great Britain & Ireland Dance – Old Hall.

24-6 March: The London Master Bakers' & Confectioners' Protection Society Exhibition – Old Hall.

4 April: The London Gardens Society Spring Exhibition – Old Hall.

7-8 April: The Alpine Garden Society Flower Show – Old Hall.

21-2 April: The British Carnation Society Show – Old Hall.

24 April: The National Rose Society Show – New Hall.

28-9 April: The Rhododendron Association Show – New Hall.

11-14 May: London County Council, County Hall Examinations – Old Hall.

13 May: Association of Parks Superintendents – Old Hall.

13-16 May: Association of Dental Manufacturers & Traders of the UK Exhibition – New Hall.

19-21 May: Directorate of Lands & Accommodation, HM Office of Works Examinations – Both Halls.

27 May: Roads Beautifying Association Exhibition – New Hall.

2-5 June: The University of London Examinations – Old Hall.

4-5 June: The Iris Society Flower Show – New Hall.

10, 15, 16 June: The Worshipful Company of Spectacle Makers Examinations – Old Hall.

20 June: City of Westminster Boy Scouts Association Scout Display – Old Hall.

23-4 June: The Cactus & Succulent Society of Great Britain Show – Old Hall.

2 July: The National Sweet Pea Society Show – Old Hall.

2 July: The British Delphinium Society Show – New Hall.

6-9 July: The University of London Examinations – Old Hall.

14 July: Horticultural Society of the Ministry of Agriculture & Fisheries, Flowers, Fruit and Vegetables Show – New Hall.

14-15 July: The National Carnation & Picotee Society Show – Old Hall.

24-5 July: The London Gardens Society Summer Show of Flowers – Old Hall.

1 September: The Alpine Garden Society Show – Old Hall.

4-5 September: The London Allotments & Gardens Show Society, Fruit, Flower and Vegetable Show – New Hall.

8 September: Annual Autumn Show of the British Bee-Keepers' Association – Old Hall.

8-9 September: The National Dahlia Society Show – New Hall.

11-12 September: The National Rose Society Show – Both Halls.

17-26 September: 18th *The Model Engineer* Exhibition – Old Hall.

21-5 September: 45th Chemists' Exhibition and Empire Drug Trade Mart – New Hall.

1 October: The Civil Service Horticultural Federation Show of Flowers, Fruit & Vegetables – New Hall.

10 October: The International Friendship League Dance – Old Hall.

13 October: Directorate of Lands and Accommodation (HM Office of Works) Examinations – Old Hall.

19-23 October: 7th International Medical Exhibition organised by the British & Colonial Druggist Ltd – New Hall.

31 October: The Combined Cavalry 'Old Comrades' Association Dance – Old Hall.

31 October: The London Group of the Holiday Fellowship Reunion – New Hall.

3-5 November: 43rd Sale of Work in Aid of Church Work at Home & Abroad, Home and Foreign Missions – Old Hall.

5-6 November: The National Chrysanthemum Society Show – New Hall.

10-12 November: Our Dumb Friends' League (72 Victoria Street) Fair – Old Hall.

14 November: The London Galloway Association (Royal Caledonian Schools) Dance – Old Hall.

18-19 November: The Hospital for Sick Children, Great Ormond Street. Bazaar in aid of the Reconstruction Fund – New Hall.

21 November: The GPO Widows and Orphans Christmas Hamper Fund-Inland Section Dance – Old Hall.

24-5 November: The British Carnation Society Show – Old Hall.

27 November: The League of Mercy (12 Whitehall) Children's Market & Toy Fair in aid of Hospitals – New Hall. Opened by HRH Duchess of Gloucester. ITN Newsreel exists for this Fair.

28 November-10 December: 14th Applied Arts and Handcrafts Exhibition organised by Nellie E. Isaac of 26 Eastcastle Street, Oxford Circus, W1 – Old Hall.

11 December: Mrs Cecil Raphael of 10 Eaton Gate, SW. Dance in aid of Queen Charlotte's Hospital – New Hall.

12-13 December: 2nd Bird and Aquaria Show (organised by The Marshall Press Ltd) – New Hall.

16-28 December: Christmas Postal Work, South Eastern District Post Office – Old Hall.

1937

*c.*December '36/January '37: 17th Schoolboy's Own Exhibition held at Imperial Institute.

2 January: Messrs Ambrose Wilson Ltd (60 Vauxhall Bridge Road, SW1) Staff Party – Old Hall.

6-7 January: The National Pigeon Association and Marking Conference Ltd, 'Fancy Pigeon Show'.

16 January: The Workers' Travel Association Ltd Dance – New Hall.

20-2 January: The *Daily Mail* (Associated Newspapers) Bridge Contest – New Hall.

23 January: Messrs Carreras Ltd Dance – New Hall.

23 January: Mr Douglas T. Watson of 77 Gresham Street, EC2, Dance – Old Hall.

28 January: HM Office of Works Civil Service Examinations – Old Hall.

14-15 February: 1st Hardware Trades Fair organised by Universal Exhibitions Ltd – New Hall.

31 January-4 February: Optical Exhibition organised by The Association of Wholesale and Manufacturing Opticians, 69-73 Cannon Street, EC4 – New Hall.

30 January: The London Labour Party (Herbert Morrison) Reunion and Dance – Old Hall.

6 February: 2nd Brambles Chine Holiday Camp Ltd, Colwell Bay, Freshwater, Isle of Wight, Reunion Dance – Old Hall.

12 February: Marks & Spencer Ltd Dance (Michael House, 82 Baker Street, W1) – New Hall.

13 February: GPO Widows and Orphans Christmas Hamper Fund Dance – New Hall.

14-19 February: The London Master Bakers' & Confectioners' Protection Society Bakers' Exhibition (13th entry) – Old Hall.

18 February: London Transport (Country Omnibuses) Sports Association Dance – New Hall.

18, 19 February: The *Daily Mail* (Associated Newspapers) Bridge Contest – New Hall.

20 February: Campers Ltd of 101 Hatton Garden, EC1, Dance – New Hall.

20 February: The Combined Cavalry 'Old Comrades' Association Dance – Old Hall.

23 February: The National Society of Operative Printers' Assistants – Old Hall.

1-5 March: 27th Hospitals, Nurses, Midwifery & Public Health Exhibition & Conference – New Hall.

1-6 March: 34th Badminton Association 'All-England Championships' Annual Tournament – Old Hall.

13 March: The Camping Club of Great Britain & Ireland – Reunion and Dance – Old Hall.

15-19 March: The Chartered Surveyors' Institution Examinations – New Hall.

18 March: HM Office of Works Civil Service Examinations – Old Hall.

21 March: The London Sunday School Society Pageant – Old Hall.

30 March-3 April: 13th The Model Railway Club's Exhibition at Central Hall, Westminster.

1 April: HM Office of Works Civil Service Examinations – Old Hall.

3 April: The London Gardens Society Spring Exhibition- Old Hall.

23 April: The National Rose Society Flower Show – New Hall.

27-8 April: The British Carnation Society Show – Old Hall.

29 April: Royal Arsenal Co-operative Society Ltd Dance – New Hall.

30 April: The Great West Road Coronation Ball– New Hall.

4-6 May: The Rhododendron Association Flower Show – New Hall.

10-13 May: The Boy Scouts Association.

19-20 May: The General Nursing Council for England and Wales Examinations – Old Hall.

24-8 May: The Association of Dental Manufacturers of the UK Exhibition – Both Halls.

22-3 June: The Cactus & Succulent Society of Great Britain Show – Old Hall.

30 June-1 July: Southwark Catholic Rescue Society Golden Jubilee Exhibition of Handcrafts and Dairy Work – Old Hall.

1 July: The British Delphinium Society Show – New Hall.

6-7 July: The Alpine Garden Society Show – Old Hall.

9 July: The Civil Service Horticultural Federation Fruit, Flowers and Vegetables Show – New Hall.

13-14 July: The National Carnation & Picotee Society Show – Old Hall.

16-17 July: The London Gardens Society Summer Flower Exhibition – New Hall.

17-18 July: The British Gladiolus Society Show – Old Hall.

3 August: The *Daily Mail* (Associated Newspapers) Bridge Contest – New Hall.

31 August-3 September: 15th The National Honey Show – Old Hall.

3-4 September: The London Allotments and Gardens Show Society, Fruit, Flowers and Vegetables Show – New Hall.

7-8 September: The Alpine Garden Society Show – Old Hall.

7-8 September: The National Dahlia Society Show – New Hall.

10-11 September: The National Rose Society Autumn Flower Show – New Hall.

16-25 September: 19th *The Model Engineer* Exhibition – Old Hall.

3-4 October: 44th Sale of Work in Aid of Church Work at Home & Abroad, Home and Foreign Missions – Old Hall.

5-6 October: HM Office of Works Civil Service Examinations – New Hall.

18-22 October: 8th London Medical Exhibition Organised – New Hall.

4-5 November: The National Chrysanthemum Society Show – New Hall.

7-13 November: 15th Applied Arts and Handcrafts Exhibition organised – Old Hall.

17-18 November: Our Dumb Friends' League Fair – Old Hall.

19 November: Mrs Cecil Raphael of 10 Eaton Gate, SW, Dance in aid of Queen Charlotte's Hospital – New Hall.

20 November: The London Galloway Association Dance in aid of The Royal Caledonian Schools – Old Hall.

23-4 November: The British Carnation Society Show – Old Hall.

27 November: The Greater World Christian Spiritualist Association Christmas Fair – Old Hall.

30 November-1 December: Social Services Exhibition in aid of the Civil Service Social Service Associations work in the distressed areas – Old Hall.

2-4 December: Bird Fancy Exhibition of Cage Birds – New Hall.

9 December: The National Union of Conservative and Unionist Associations, Metropolitan Area, Women's Committee Dance – New Hall.

10 December: London Business Houses Amateur Sports Association Dance – New Hall.

15-28 December: South Western District Post Office Christmas postal work – Both Halls.

31 December: Claude Butler of Manor Street, London, SW4, Dance – New Hall.

1938

28 December '37-8 January '38: 18th Schoolboy's Own Exhibition with National Treasures Exhibition held at the Imperial Institute, South Kensington, London.

15-21 January: Domestic Services Exhibition – Both Halls.

24 January: Messrs Carreras Ltd Dance – New Hall.

29 January: HM Office of Works Civil Service Examinations – Old Hall.

31 January: The London Labour Party (Herbert Morrison) Reunion and Dance – Old Hall.

14 February: GPO Widows and Orphans Christmas Hamper Fund Dance – Old Hall.

28 February-5 March: 35th Badminton Association 'All-England Championships' Annual Tournament – Old Hall.

7 March: 28th Annual Hospitals, Nursing, Midwifery & Public Health Conference & Exhibition organised by *Nursing Mirror & Midwives Journal* – New Hall.

14 March: The Camping Club of Great Britain & Ireland – Reunion and Dance – Old Hall.

16-20 March: The Chartered Surveyors' Institution Examinations – New Hall.

7 March: Amusement Trades Exhibition– New Hall.

2 April: HM Office of Works Civil Service Examinations – Old Hall.

4 April: The London Gardens Society Spring Exhibition- Old Hall.

14-19 April: London County Council, County Hall Examinations – Old Hall.

26-9 April: RHS Ornamental Flowering Trees and Shrubs Conference – New Hall.

11-14 May: The Boy Scouts Association London Scout Office – Both Halls.

1 June: Civil Service Clerical Association Examinations – New Hall.

28-9 June: Mrs J. Bosanquet – Old Hall.

17-18 July: The London Gardens Society Summer Flower Exhibition – New Hall.

3-4 September: The London Allotments and Gardens Show Society, Fruit, Flowers and Vegetables Show – New Hall.

11-12 September: The National Rose Society Flower Show – Old Hall.

15-24 September: 20th *The Model Engineer* Exhibition – Old Hall.

25 September-1 October: National Honey Show – Old Hall.

4-5 October: 45th Sale of Work in Aid of Church Work at Home & Abroad, Home and Foreign Missions – Old Hall.

6-7 October: HM Office of Works Civil Service Examinations – Old Hall.

17-21 October: 9th Chemists' & London Medical Exhibition organised by the British & Colonial Druggist Co. Ltd – New Hall.

18-20 October: Mrs Hornby – Old Hall.

31 October: The London Group of The Holiday Fellowship Reunion – New Hall.

5-6 November: The National Chrysanthemum Society Show – New Hall.

12 November: Rustington Lido Dance – Old Hall.

18-19 November: Our Dumb Friends' League Fair – Old Hall.

*c.*December: Radiological Exhibition – Central Hall Westminster.

5-8 December: London Association Certified Accountants Exams – Old Hall.

16-23 November: 9th National Federation of Women's Institutes Handcraft Exhibition – New Hall.

15-28 December: South West District Post Office Christmas Postal Sorting – Both Halls.

31 December: Claude Butler of Manor Street, London, SW4, Dance – New Hall.

Date Unknown: Guild of Trade Horticulturalists – New Hall.

Date Unknown: Horticultural Trades Association – New Hall.

Date Unknown: Great Ormond Street Hospital – New Hall.

Date Unknown: British Auto Machine Manufacturers – New Hall.

1939

31 December '38-14 January '39: 19th Schoolboy's Own Exhibition organised by School Equipment Camp and Boy's Own Exhibitions Ltd – Old Hall.

19-21 January: S.A. Legg, Crystal Palace, SE19, The 71st Crystal Palace National Show of Cage Birds – New Hall.

23-6 January: HM Office of Works Civil Service Examinations – Old Hall.

28 January: Messrs Carreras Ltd – New Hall.

4 February: Cornelius A. Joyce of Palace Hotel, Bloomsbury Street, WC1. Display by the City of Westminster Boy Scout Association – Old Hall.

11 February: Radio Rentals Ltd Dance – Old Hall.

13-17 February: 29th Annual Hospitals, Nursing, Midwifery & Public Health Conference & Exhibition – New Hall.

15-27 February: Exhibition of Patents organised by the Institute of Patentees inc. 10 Victoria Street, SW1 – Old Hall.

27 February: Lyons Coventry Street Corner House Staff Dance (2,000) – Old Hall.

3 March: Donald Van den Bergh Ltd Annual prize giving and Dance of the 53rd (City of London) A.A. Brigade R.A. (T.A.) – New Hall.

6-11 March: 36th Badminton Association 'All-England Championships' Annual Tournament – Old Hall.

13-17 March: The Chartered Surveyors Institution Examinations – New Hall.

13-17 March: Institute of Patentees Examinations – Old Hall.

18 March: The Camping Club of Great Britain & Ireland Reunion and Dance – Old Hall.

25 March: London Rover Committee Dance (Scouts) – Old Hall.

26 March: Exhibition of Spring Flowers and Children's Paintings organised by The London Gardens Society – Old Hall.

28-9 March: The British Carnation Society Show –New Hall.

28-9 March: The Alpine Garden Society Show – Old Hall.

1 April: The London Gardens Society Spring Exhibition – Old Hall.

17-19 April: London County Council Education Office Department, The County Hall, General Grade Examinations – Old Hall.

20-1 April: The National Rose Society Flower Show – Old Hall.

25-6 April: The Alpine Garden Society Show – Old Hall.

2-3 May: The Rhododendron Association Show – New Hall.

9-10 May: Territorial Army & Air Force Association – Both Halls.

10-11 May: Mrs A. Croxton of 32 Buckingham Palace Road, SW1, to hold a Westminster Market and Fair of Food and Wine, in aid of The Westminster Hospital re-building Fund – New Hall.

16-19 May: Mrs Charles Wintour, The Grange Cottage, St Michaels, Tenterden, Kent, to hold an Antique Caledonian Market in aid of the 'Service Fellowship Association' – Old Hall (cancelled).

23-4 May: Territorial Army & Air Force Association – Both Halls.

30-1: May Territorial Army & Air Force Association – Both Halls.

13-14 June: Territorial Army & Air Force Association – Old Hall.

20-1 June: The Cactus & Succulent Society of Great Britain Show – Old Hall.

23 June: The British Delphinium Society Show – New Hall.

23 June: The National Sweet Pea Society Show – Old Hall.

24 June: Alpine Garden Society Show – Old Hall.

27-8 June: Territorial Army & Air Force Association – Old Hall.

4-5 July: Territorial Army & Air Force Association– Old Hall.

4-5 July: RHS Fortnightly Flower Show and annual Lily Show dinner – New Hall.

11-12 July: Territorial Army & Air Force Association – Old Hall.

15 July: Territorial Army & Air Force Association – Old Hall.

18-19 July: The National Carnation and Picotee Society Show – Old Hall.

29-30 August: The Alpine Garden Society Show – Old Hall.

1 September: First World War declared.

1-2 September: The London Allotments and Gardens Show Society, Fruit, Flowers and Vegetables Show – New Hall (cancelled).

5-6 September: The National Dahlia Society Show – New Hall (cancelled).

7-16 September: The 21st *Model Engineer* Exhibition – Old Hall (cancelled).

8-9 September: London Gardens Society Summer Exhibition – New Hall (cancelled).

16-17 September: London Gardens Society Summer Exhibition – New Hall.

19-20 September: The National Chrysanthemum Society Show – New Hall (cancelled).

22, 26 September: The Civil Service Horticultural Federation (Metropole Building, Northumberland Avenue, SW1). Show of Flowers, Fruit and Vegetables – New Hall (cancelled).

22-3 September: The National Rose Society Flower Show – New Hall (cancelled).

24 September: Alpine Gardens Society Show – Old Hall (cancelled).

26 September: The Civil Service Horticultural Federation (Metropole Building, Northumberland Avenue, SW1). Show of Flowers, Fruit and Vegetables – New Hall (cancelled).

27 September: British Carnation Society Show –New Hall (cancelled).

29-30 September: The London Gardens Society Show – New Hall (cancelled).

16-20 October: 10th Chemists' & London Medical Exhibition – New Hall (cancelled).

24-6 October: The British Carnation Society Show – Old Hall (cancelled).

28 October: The London Group of the Holiday Fellowship Reunion Dances – Both Halls (cancelled).

2-3 November: The National Chrysanthemum Society Show – New Hall (cancelled).

7-10 November: 46th Sale of Work in Aid of Church Work at Home & Abroad – Old Hall (cancelled).

10-21 November: Imperial Fruit Show and Conners Exhibition – Both Halls (cancelled).

22-24 November: Our Dumb Friends' League Fair – Old Hall (cancelled).

13 December: 4th The Women's Institutes Exhibition – New Hall.

15-27 December: South Eastern District Post Office Christmas Sorting – Old Hall.

14-27 December: South Western District Post Office Christmas Sorting – New Hall.

1940

15-21 January: S.A. Legg, Crystal Palace, SE19. The 72nd Crystal Palace National Show of Cage Birds – New Hall.

26-7 January: Racing Pigeon Show in aid of charity sponsored by *The People* – Old Hall.

8-10 February: 1st National Cage Birds Show on behalf of the Lord Mayor's Red Cross & St John Fund for the Sick and Wounded in the War – New Hall.

9 March: The Camping Club of Great Britain & Ireland Reunion and Dance – Old Hall (cancelled).

11-15 March: The Chartered Surveyors' Institution Examinations – New Hall (cancelled).

12-16 March: Annual Hospital, Nursing, Midwifery & Public Health Conference & Exhibition – New Hall (cancelled).

8-12 April: Annual Hospital, Nursing, Midwifery & Public Health Conference & Exhibition – New Hall.

3 May: Concrete Hutting Exhibition organised by Cement and Concrete Association – New Hall.

24 May: The Society of British Aircraft Constructors Ltd Exhibition of Light Plastic Materials of Aircraft Parts – Old Hall (cancelled).

20-9 June: 11th London Medical Exhibition – (cancelled).

28-9 June: The National Rose Society Show – Both Halls.

24-6 September: The RHS Red Cross & St John Sale – Old Hall.

12-28 December: South West and South East Districts, Post Office – Both Halls.

c.December: First of three occasions when bomb damage occurred to the Halls. On this occasion a bomb nearly blew out the glass and doors on the Elverton Street frontage of the Lawrence Hall.

1941

27 February: RHS Flower Show.

c.September: Second bomb damage to Lawrence Hall undoing all previous repairs.

16 September: RHS Flower Show resumed after no shows took place in August. This ran in conjunction with the National Dahlia Society and the National Chrysanthemum Society.

13-29 December: South West and South East Districts, Post Office Christmas/war postal.

c.December: Sorting – Both Halls.

Date Unknown: Horticultural Club – New Hall.

1942

Second World War – No external exhibitions listed.

Territorial Army & Air Force Association of the County of London

From 1 October 193rd (101 LON.) A.A. Battery, R.A. Home Guard occupied the New Hall for anti-aircraft training. This was, 'subject to one months notice on either side and to be given only after the declaration of an Armistice or the end of the hostilities'. (This was a normal letting unlike during the First World War when the War Office had requisitioned the Hall).

South West and South East Districts, Post Office – Both Halls

Christmas/war postal sorting

1943

All Year: No external exhibitions listed. Hall occupied by the Home Guard.

Territorial Army and Air Force Association – New Hall.

19 July-18 August: Ministry of Works – Directorate of Lands & Accommodation Civil Service Examinations – New Hall.

14-28 December: South West and South East Districts, Post Office – Both Halls.

Christmas/war postal sorting.

Date Unknown: Horticultural Club – New Hall.

1944

No external exhibitions listed. Hall occupied by the Home Guard – All Year.

Territorial Army and Air Force Association – New Hall.

c.June: Third bomb damage sustained to both Halls that resulted in the gable end of the Lindley Hall having to be rebuilt after the war, at a cost of over £4,000.

10-28 December: South West and South East Districts, Post Office – Both Halls.

Christmas/war postal sorting.

1945

15-18 January: Farm Crop Driers' Association – Old Hall.

22 June: Air Ministry Civil Defence Stand-Down Social – New Hall.

25 September: 3rd Royal Air Force Fruit and Vegetables Show – New Hall.

24-5 October: National (Red Cross) Poultry Show – New Hall.

30 October: New Zealand Forces Dance – New Hall.

9 November: New Zealand Forces Dance – New Hall.

1-3 November: National (Red Cross) Show of Cage Birds – Old Hall.

14 November: Ministry of Works – Directorate of Lands & Accommodation Civil Service Examinations – New Hall.

17 November: Manchester Unity Odd Fellows Dance – Old Hall.

27 November: Ministry of Works – Directorate of Lands & Accommodation Civil Service Examinations – New Hall.

9 November-1 December: The 'Victory' Show of Racing Pigeons – Old Hall.

7-9 December; 2nd National (Red Cross) Show of Cage Birds – Old Hall.

12-28 December: South West and South East Districts, Post Office Christmas sorting – Both Halls.

1946

4 January: Association of Ex-Civil Servants Dance – Old Hall.

7-18 January: 1st Gauge & Tool Makers' Association Exhibition – New Hall.

11-12 January: Racing Pigeon Show sponsored by *The Racing Pigeon* – Old Hall.

16-17 January: '2nd Fancy Pigeon' Show organised by National Pigeon Association & Marketing Conference Ltd – Old Hall.

23 January: Air Ministry Civil Defence, Reunion Social Dance – Old Hall.

27 January-2 February: National Show of Cage Birds – Old Hall.

5-8 February: 2nd Amusement Devices & Trades Exhibition – New Hall.

9-10 February: Chase Cultivation Ltd – Old Hall.

26 February-4 April: Solid Smokeless Fuels Federation Dance – Old Hall.

5 April: Great West Road Industries Dance – New Hall.

8 April: Air Ministry, Reunion of ex-Halton aircraft apprentices – Old Hall.

10 April: Ministry of Aircraft Production Recruiting Council – Old Hall.

6-18 May: 15th World Snooker Championship, 1945-6 – Old Hall.

8 May: Ministry of Supplies and Aircraft Production (Scoffin) – New Hall.

18-20 May: Women's League of Health & Beauty – New Hall.

6 June: Ministry of Works Social and Athletic Club Dance – Old Hall.

28 June: National Rose Society Show – Old Hall.

6 July: 1st Pioneer Model Racing Car Club – Old Hall.

6 July: Wimbledon & District Canine Society Dog Show – New Hall.

11 July: National Rose Society Show – New Hall.

17-18 July: 1st *The People* National Darts Teams Championship – Old Hall.

22 July: Mrs Emmeline Sylvia Pankhurst wrote to request a tenancy in the Old Hall.

29-30 July: London County Council Exams – Old Hall.

22-31 August: 21st *The Model Engineer* Exhibition – New Hall.

5 September: The Associated Sheep, Police & Army Dog Society Championship Show – Old Hall.

17 September: National Chrysanthemum Society Centenary Exhibition – Old Hall.

20 September: National Rose Society Show – Old Hall.

28 September: National Union of Printing, Bookbinding & Paper Workers' Dance – New Hall (Printing Machine Branch).

28 September: Pioneer Model Racing Car Club – Old Hall.

1-2 October: Middlesex Federation of Women's Institutes Exhibition – Old Hall.

12 October: Holiday Fellowship Ltd Reunion Dance – New Hall.

15 October: Florist Telegraph Delivery Association Dance – Old Hall (deposit forfeited).

15 October: English Shetland Sheep Dog Club Championship Show – Old Hall.

15 October: Poodle Club Championship Show.

17 October: London Cocker Spaniel Society Championship Show–Old Hall.

22-4 October: The National Poultry Show – New Hall.

26 October: Decca Records Co. (Dance) – Old Hall.

29 October: Wimbledon & District Canine Society Dog Show – New Hall.

30 October: Harrods Ltd Social Club Dance – Old Hall.

5-6 November: National Chrysanthemum Society Show – New Hall.

11-16 November: The 1st National Small Live Stock Exhibition, National Championship Show – Old Hall.

11-25 November: The 12th London Medical Exhibition – New Hall.

19 November: International Poodle Club Championship Show – Old Hall.

23 November: Union of Post Office Workers Dance – Old Hall.

26 November: The British Chow Chow Club Championship Show – Old Hall.

27 November: The Keeshond Club Championship Show (Mrs Anderson) – Old Hall.

30 November: The Pathfinders Reunion Dance organised by The RAF Pathfinders Association Ltd – New Hall.

6-8 December: 3rd National Cage Birds sponsored by *Poultry World* – New Hall.

6-7 December: The 'Victory' Show of Racing Pigeons – Old Hall.

11-28 December: London Postal Region – Both Halls.

Date Unknown: British Legion Dance.

1947

29 December '46-12 January '47: The National Industrial Development Council of Wales and Monmouthshire (1st Welsh Industries Fair in London) – Both Halls.

4-11 January: 20th Schoolboy's Own Exhibition (organised by School Equipment, Camp and Boy's Own Exhibitions Ltd) – Central Hall Westminster.

13-19 January: National Championship Show of Cage Birds – New Hall.

17-18 January: 'Old Comrades Show' organised by *The Racing Pigeon* – Old Hall.

20 January: Pioneer Model Racing Car Club – New Hall.

21-2 January: Wimbledon & District Canine Society – Both Halls.

28 January-8 February: Worshipful Company of Shipwrights Exhibition – Both Halls.

22 February: Association of Engineering Ship Manufacturing Draughtsmen – Old Hall.

24-6 February: 3rd Amusement Trades Exhibition – New Hall.

24 February: Pioneer Model Racing Cars – Both Halls.

26 February: Dachshund Club Championship Show (James Pye Dog Shows) – Old Hall.

27 February: Associated Sheep, Police & Army Dog Society Championship Show – Old Hall.

28 February: 13th Championship Show of The Scottish Terrier Club – Old Hall.

1 March: Pioneer Model Racing Cars – Both Halls.

7-14 March: Radio Components Manufacturers Association Exhibition – New Hall.

8 March: Artists International Association – Old Hall.

22 March: British Alsatian Association Championship Show – New Hall.

25 March: London Cocker Spaniel Society Championship Show – New Hall.

29 March: Pioneer Model Racing Car Club – Old Hall.

8 April: Chinese Chow Chow Club Championship Show – Old Hall.

9 April: Championship Shows for The Southern Dachshund Association, Gordon Setter Association, Irish Wolfhound Club, Elkhound Club, Pyrenean Mountain Dog Club of Great Britain and the International Poodle Club – New Hall.

10 April: Wimbledon & District Canine Society – Both Halls.

3 May: Pioneer Model Racing Car Club – Old Hall.

7 May: Wire Fox Terrier Association Championship Show – Old Hall.

8-25 May: *British Bulletin of Commerce Exhibition* – Old Hall.

14 May: Mrs S.F. Kearns Dog Show. Combined Show by Southern Dachshund Association, G.S.A Irish Wolfhound Club and Elkhound Society – Old Hall.

7 June: *The People* Darts Final – Old Hall.

7 June: King's Royal Rifle Corps Association Dance – New Hall.

10 June: Afghan Hound Association Championship Show – New Hall.

10 June: United St Barnard Club Championship Show.

10 June: Borzoi Club Championship Show.

10 June: Saluki or Gazelle Hound Championship Show.

10 June: British Chow Chow Club Championship Show.

11 June: The Southern Cairn Terrier Club Championship Show – Old Hall.

14 June: Pioneer Model Racing Car Club – Old Hall.

26-7 June: The National Rose Society Summer Show – Both Halls.

4-5 July: The *Evening News* Garden Lovers' Flower Show – New Hall.

15-16 July: 2nd *The People* National Darts Teams Championship – Old Hall.

19 July: Pioneer Model Racing Car Club – Old Hall.

20 July-10 August: *News of the World* Ltd – unknown event – Old Hall.

10 August: Corsetry Underwear Exhibition –- New Hall (deposit forfeited).

11-28 August: Co-op Wholesale Society – Old Hall.

20-30 August: 22nd *The Model Engineer* Exhibition – New Hall.

19 September: Gold Coast Students' Union – Old Hall.

26 September: Scottish Terrier Club Championship Show.

26 September: Sealyham Terrier Breeders' Association Championship Show.

29 September: Association of Conservative Clubs.

30 September: Great Joint Dachshund Association Championship Show.

1 October: The British Samoyed Club Championship Show – Old Hall.

1 October: Keeshond Club Championship Show.

2 October: London Cocker Spaniel Society Championship Show.

11 October: Workers Travel Association Ltd Dance – New Hall.

15 October: International Poodle Club Championship Show – Old Hall.

15 October: Dachshund Club Championship Show.

26 October: Women's League of Health & Beauty – New Hall.

28-30 October: 6th National Federation of Women's Institutes Exhibition – New Hall.

c.October: *British Bulletin of Commerce* – (deposit forfeited).

1-10 November: National Championship Show of Cage Birds – New Hall.

5-6 November: *The People* Pigeon Show.

8-13 November: Ministry of Works – Directorate of Lands & Accommodation Civil Service exams.

10-24 November: 13th Medical Exhibition (organised by British & Colonial Druggist Co. Ltd).

17-22 November: 2nd National Small Live Stock Association – Old Hall.

19 November: International Poodle Show (James Pye Dog Shows) – Old Hall.

26 November: Associated Sheep, Police and Army Dog Society Championship Show.

26-8 November: 'Old Comrades Show' – Old Hall.

27-8 November: St John's Ambulance Brigade Competition – New Hall.

4-6 December: 4th National Cage Birds sponsored by *Poultry World* – New Hall.

9 December: Pioneer Model Racing Cars – New Hall.

c.December: London Postal Region.

1948

1-10 January: 21st Schoolboy's Own Exhibition – New Hall.

3 January: Pioneer Model Racing Car Club (H.J. Lamb) – Old Hall.

8-10 January: *The Racing Pigeon* Publishing Company Pigeon Show – Old Hall.

12-18 January: Championship Show of Cage Birds – Old Hall.

17 January: United Nations Association National Appeal Committee Dance & Auction – New Hall.

20 January-9 February: 2nd Gauge & Tool Makers' Association Ltd – New Hall.

19-27 February: 4th Amusement Trades Exhibition – New Hall.

21 February: J. Miller Ltd – Old Hall.

27 February: Houses of Parliament Sports Social Club Dance – Old Hall.

28 February: Pioneer Model Racing Car Club – Old Hall.

6 March: Camping Club of Great Britain Dance – Old Hall.

8-25 March: *British Bulletin of Commerce* – Old Hall.

12 March: 1st Entry as RICS – Royal Institute of Chartered Surveyors' Examinations – New Hall.

27 March: London & Home Counties Old Time Dancing – New Hall.

27 March: Pioneer Model Racing Car Club – Old Hall.

2 April: Central British Fund for Jewish Relief Dance – New Hall.

6-8 April: Ministry of Works – Directorate of Lands & Accommodation examinations – Old Hall.

10 April: Pioneer Model Racing Car Club – Old Hall.

15 April: London Cocker Spaniel Society Dog Show – Old Hall.

24 April: Old Coldstreamers Association Dance – Old Hall.

24 April: Rifle Brigade Association Dance – New Hall.

18-25 May: *British Bulletin of Commerce* – Old Hall.

9-30 May: The British Carpet Exhibition: guide to British carpet manufacturers and patterns, organised by the Carpet Manufacturers Executive Committee – New Hall.

15 May: The King's Royal Rifle Corps Association Dance – Old Hall.

22 May: Pioneer Model Racing Car Club – New Hall.

4-5 June: 3rd *The People* National Darts Teams Championship – Old Hall.

8-14 June: 1st Aquarium and Water Garden Exhibition organised by the National Aquarists Society – Old Hall.

12 June: Pioneer Model Racing Car Club – New Hall.

16 June: Nordic Breeds Society Championship Dog Show – Old Hall.

26 June: James Pye Dog Show – New Hall.

26 June: Queens Royal Regiment Old Comrades Association Dance – Old Hall.

28-9 June: Ministry of Works – Directorate of Lands & Accommodation examinations – New Hall.

10 July: Pioneer Model Racing Car Club – New Hall.

18-28 August: 23rd *The Model Engineer* Jubilee Exhibition – New Hall.

31 August-2 September: 15th London Master Bakers' Exhibition – Old Hall.

13-14 September: National Chrysanthemum Society Show – New Hall.

17 September: RAF Association Dance – Old Hall.

18 September: British Alsatian Association Dog Show – Old Hall.

27-9 September: The London Dental Trade Exhibition – New Hall.

8-23 October: *British Bulletin of Commerce* – Old Hall (cancelled).

9 October: Association of Cinematograph & Allied Technicians – Old Hall.

9-10 October: National Federation of Women's Institutes Home Produce Exhibition – New Hall.

16 October: Pioneer Model Racing Car Club – Old Hall.

26 October: British Legion Dance – New Hall.

27 October: J.Y.B. Decorators Ltd – Old Hall (cancelled).

30 October: Royal Army Service Corps Association Dance – New Hall.

4-5 November: National Chrysanthemum Society Show – New Hall.

6 November: People's Dispensary for Sick Animals Dance – Old Hall.

6 November: Pioneer Model Racing Car Club – New Hall.

8-22 November: 14th Medical Exhibition, British & Colonial Druggist Co. Ltd – Both Halls.

12 November: British Legion Dance – New Hall.

12 November: G.H. Zeal – Old Hall.

13 November: Royal Tank Regiment Dance – Old Hall.

16 November: Pioneer Model Racing Car Club – New Hall.

18 November: Union of Post Office Workers Dance – Old Hall.

20 November: British League of Racing Cyclists' Dance – Old Hall.

22-4 November: Ministry of Works – Civil Service Examinations – Old Hall.

25 November: Metropolitan Police Club Dance – New Hall.

26 November: Old Coldstreamers Dance – Old Hall.

27 November: London Conservative Union Dance – New Hall.

2-4 December: 5th National Exhibition of Cage Birds (and Aquaria) – New Hall.

2-6 December: *The People* Pigeon Show – Old Hall.

8-28 December: London Postal Region Christmas postal sorting – Both Halls.

31 December: London & Home Counties Old Time Dancing Clubs New Years' Eve Dance – Old Hall.

1949

28 December '48-17 January '49: 22nd Schoolboy's Own Exhibition – New Hall.

1 January: General Sir William Slim Park Hill Cycling Club – Old Hall.

8 January: Neville Ltd H.W. – Old Hall.

15 January: London Labour Party Dance – Old Hall.

17-23 January: 76th Crystal Palace National Championship Show of Cage Birds, *Poultry World* – New Hall.

19 January: Ministry of Works – Directorate of Lands & Accommodation Civil Service Examinations – Both Halls.

22 January: Pioneer Model Racing Cars – Both Halls.

9 February: Pioneer Model Racing Cars – Both Halls.

18-25 February: 5th Amusement Trades Exhibition – New Hall.

7-9 March: Ministry of Works – Directorate of Lands & Accommodation.

*c.*March: Civil Service Examinations – Both Halls.

19 March: Pioneer Model Racing Cars – Both Halls.

2 April: London Musical Comp. Festival.

8 April: BBC Club Dance.

21 April: London Cocker Spaniel Society Dog Show – Old Hall.

23 April: *The Times* Companionship Club Dance.

24 April: International Poodle Show – Old Hall. Organised by The Poodle Club.

7 May: Pioneer Model Racing Cars – Both Halls.

9 May: Ralph Reader Ltd (Dance) – Old Hall.

14 May: Women's League of Health & Beauty – New Hall.

14-28 May: *British Bulletin of Commerce* – Old Hall.

20-1 May: Chartered Institute of Secretaries Examinations – New Hall.

11 June: 4th *The People* National Darts Teams Championship – Old Hall.

13 June: Ralph Reader Ltd Dance – Old Hall.

14-20 June: 2nd Aquarium and Water Garden Exhibition organised by the National Aquarists Society – Old Hall.

16 July: Pioneer Model Racing Cars – Both Halls.

18-20 July: Ministry of Works – Directorate of Lands & Accommodation Civil Service Examinations – Both Halls.

2-23 August: 1st Schoolgirl's Association Exhibition – Old Hall.

17-27 August: 24th *Model Engineer* Exhibition – New Hall.

26-7 August: London Electricity Sports Association – Old Hall.

31 August: Scottish Terrier Club Championship Show – New Hall.

31 August: Sealyhan Terrier Breeders' Association Championship Show – New Hall.

30 August-2 September: 16th Bakers' Exhibition organised by Maclaren & Sons Ltd – Old Hall.

6-7 September: RHS Flower Show.

16-22 September: National Honey Show – Old Hall.

1 October: The People's Republic of China proclaimed in Beijing.

6-8 October: Middlesex County Show organised by Middlesex County Education Committee – New Hall. Pathé Newsreel exists.

7-8 October: North London District Amalgamated Bakers – Old Hall.

11 October: The Poodle Club Championship Show – Old Hall.

12 October: Championship Show of Cage Birds – New Hall.

12-13 October: Bertrams C. Zarifi – New Hall.

13 October: London Cocker Spaniel Society Dog Show – Old Hall.

15 October: King's Royal Rifle Corps Association – Old Hall.

17 October: London Labour Party – Old Hall.

22 October: Royal Marines Association – New Hall.

22 October: Covent Garden Social Club Dance – Old Hall.

24 October: Osbourne Garrett & Co. Ltd Dance – Old Hall.

28 November-4 December: National Championship Show of Cage Birds – New Hall.

29 October: Health & Strength League 'Grimek' Leaguers Day Dance – Old Hall.

7 November: General Association of Ladies Hairdressers Open Competition – Old Hall.

14-18 November: 15th Medical Exhibition (British & Colonial Druggist Co. Ltd) – New Hall.

12 November: Old Coldstreamers Association – Old Hall.

19 November: Covent Garden Social Club Dance – Old Hall.

21-4 November: Institute of Chartered Accountants – Old Hall.

22-4 November: 2nd Engineering Industries Association Exhibition – New Hall.

25 November: London Symphony Orchestra (Committee Rooms).

26 November: W.T. Henlys Telegraph Works – New Hall.

1-3 December: 6th National Exhibition of Cage Birds (and Aquaria) – New Hall.

1-5 December: The People Pigeon Show – Old Hall.

7 December: Britain-China Conference Committee – New Hall.

8 December: National Union of Printers Dance – Old Hall.

9-28 December: London Postal Region – Christmas post sorting – Both Halls.

British Legion, Lloyds – New Hall (deposit forfeited).

1950

31 December '49-14 January '50: 23rd Schoolboy's Own Exhibition – New Hall.

20 January: Pews A. & J. – New Hall.

4 February: W. Melhuish Ltd – Old Hall.

7 February: Women's League of Health & Beauty – New Hall.

10-17 February: 6th Amusement Trades Exhibition – New Hall.

10 February: Home Counties Conservative Association – New Hall.

c.February: The Fabian Society.

16-20 February: Gas Light Sports Association – Old Hall.

18 February: Pioneer Model Racing Car Club – Both Halls.

25 February: Women's League of Health & Beauty – New Hall.

28 February: Sir A. Levenson Taylor – New Hall.

4 March: Camping Club – New Hall.

4-10 March: RICS Examinations – Old Hall.

11 March: Whippet Club Championship Show – Old Hall.

11 March: Women's League of Health & Beauty – New Hall.

15 March: Wimbledon and District Canine Society – Old Hall.

23 March: BBC Club Dance – New Hall.

25 March: Pioneer Model Racing Car Club – Both Halls.

27-9 March: Directorate of Lands & Accommodation Civil Service Exams – New Hall.

29 March: The Dachshund Club Championship Show – Old Hall.

30 March: International Poodle Club Championship Show – Old Hall.

c.March: Treasury Sports & Social Club – Old Hall (deposit forfeited).

12 April: Women's League of Health & Beauty – New Hall.

22 April: Ministry of Labour Staff Association Dance – New Hall.

25 April: Women's League of Health & Beauty – New Hall.

29 April: Rifle Brigade Association Dance – Old Hall.

10 May: Southern Dachshund Club Championship Show – Old Hall.

11 May: London Cocker Spaniel Society Dog Show – Old Hall.

11 May: Wimbledon District Canine Society Dog Show – New Hall.

13 May: The 'Great Met' Ltd – New Hall.

12-17 May: Strive & Bowden, Photographic Fair – New Hall.

18-20 May: Chartered Institute of Secretaries Examinations – New Hall.

24 May-3 June: 2nd Schoolgirls Association Exhibition – New Hall.

9-10 June: 5th The People National Darts Teams Championship – Old Hall.

13-19 June: 3rd Aquarium and Water Garden Exhibition organised by the National Aquarists Society – Old Hall.

17 June: Pioneer Model Racing Car Club – Both Halls.

22 June: Austin Reed Ltd Dance – Old Hall.

24 June: Association of Portland Cement Manufacturers – New Hall.

15 July: Pioneer Model Racing Car Club – Both Halls.

24-8 July: Sixth International Congress of Radiology – Both Halls.

9-19 August: 25th Model Engineer Exhibition – New Hall.

30-1 August: 17th Bakers' Exhibition by Maclaren & Sons. Ltd – Old Hall.

2 September: Queen Alexandra R.A.N.C. Association – Old Hall.

2 September, 2 October: Pioneer Model Racing Cars – Both Halls.

7 September: Wire Fox Terrier Association Championship Show – Old Hall.

3-6 October: 50th Chemists' Exhibition (British & Colonial Druggist Co. Ltd) – New Hall.

30 September: Printing Machine Branch N.U.P.W. – Old Hall.

13 October: Scottish Terrier Club Championship Show – Old Hall.

14 October: Royal Marines Association Dance – New Hall.

14 October: King's Royal Rifle Corps Association – Old Hall.

23 October: The Poodle Club Championship Show – Old Hall.

28 October: Barnet Hatfield West Canine Society – Old Hall.

15-16 October: 3rd Display of Engineering Industries Association.

c.September: National Honey Show – Old Hall.

30 October/18 January: London Labour Party Reception – The Fabian Society – Both Hall.

3-6 November: London Electricity Sports & Social Association – Old Hall.

7-8 November: Amalgamated Union of Operative Bakers – Old Hall.

10 November: Metropolitan Police Athletics Association – New Hall.

15-18 November: Clothing Trade Factory Equipment and Accessories Exhibition – Old Hall.

11 November: C. Zarifi – New Hall.

20-4 November: 16th The London Medical Exhibition – New Hall.

27-9 November: Directorate of Lands & Accommodation Civil Service Exams – Old Hall.

20-5 November: Royal Sanitary Institute – Old Hall.

1-2 December: The People Show of Racing Pigeons – Old Hall.

9 December: National Council for Animal Welfare – Old Hall.

9-27 December: London Postal Region (Christmas sorting) – Both Halls.

10 December: Scottish Country Dancing – Old Hall.

c.December: Old Coldstreamers Association – Old Hall (deposit forfeited).

1951

1-13 January: 24th Schoolboy's Own Exhibition organised by British Organizers Ltd – Both Halls. Pathé Newsreel of this Show exists including showing the cockpit of a 600mph Meteor fighter. ITN Newsreel also exists showing Vampire Jet and Sir Basil Embry talking to Aircraftmen.

30 January-11 February: 7th Amusement Trades Exhibition – New Hall. A model of Battersea Pleasure Gardens was displayed at this event.

c.February: Festival of Wine organised by Universal Exhibitions– Old Hall.

12-19 February: British Electrical Development Association – Old Hall.

13 February: Pioneer Model Racing Car Club – New Hall.

24 February: Camping Club of Great Britain – New Hall.

28 February: Pioneer Model Racing Car Club – New Hall.

1 March: London Welsh Association – Old Hall.

6 March: RHS Flower Shows – The Queen visited these.

9 March: Industrial Recreational Services – New Hall.

10-16 March: RICS Exams – Both Halls.

24 March: Pioneer Model Racing Car Club – New Hall.

29 March: International Poodle Club Championship Show – Old Hall.

7 April: London & Home Counties International Sequence Dance – New Hall.

7-13 April: RICS Exams – Old Hall.

9 April: Industrial Recreational Services – New Hall.

10 April: Pioneer Model Racing Car Club – New Hall

11 April: Dachshund Club Championship Show organised by James Pye Dog Shows – New Hall.

28 April: Rifle Brigade Club – Old Hall.

15-25 May: 3rd Gauge & Tool Makers' Association Ltd Exhibition – New Hall.

16 May: The Great Dane Club Championship Show – Old Hall.

16 May: Wimbledon & District Canine Society Dog Show – New Hall.

17 May: Fox Terrier Club Championship Show – Old Hall.

25-6 May: Royal Sanitary Institute – Old Hall.

28 May-1 June: Institute of Chartered Accountants Examinations – Old Hall.

2 June: Pioneer Model Racing Car Club – New Hall.

8-9 June: 6th *The People* National Darts Teams Championship – Old Hall.

14-16 June: 4th Aquarium and Water Garden Exhibition – Old Hall.

19 June: Girl Guides Association – Old Hall.

29 June: National Rose Society's Summer Show – Both Halls.

2 July: British Dental Association – Metropolitan Branch – New Hall.

3-6 July: British Dental Association – Metropolitan Branch – Old Hall.

10 July: British Dental Association – Metropolitan Branch – Old Hall.

10 July: Roads Beautifying Association AGM – New Hall.

16-21 July: Optical Trade Exhibition – Both Halls.

24-5 July: 16th Kensington Kitten & Neuter Cat Club – New Hall.

28 July-6 August: British Sports & Games Fair – Old Hall.

16-19 August: 5th National Honey Show – Old Hall.

22 August-1 September: 26th *Model Engineer* Silver Jubilee Exhibition – New Hall.

22 August: 6th United and British Boxer Club Festival and Championship Show – Old Hall.

23 August: Scottish Terrier Club Championship Show – Old Hall.

28 August: RHS Flower Show – Old Hall.

7 September: West Indian Students Union – Old Hall.

25 September-3 October: The Festival of Wine – Old Hall.

29 September: National Union of Printing & Paper Workers – New Hall.

c.September: 51st Chemists' Exhibition – New Hall (deposit forfeited).

13 October: King's Royal Rifle Corps Association – Old Hall.

13 October: London Society of Compositors – New Hall.

16-17 October: 4th London Regional Display of Engineering Industries Association – New Hall.

24 October: Poodle Club Championship Show – Old Hall.

29 October-1 November: The British Dental Trade Exhibition – Both Halls.

26-9 October: Institute of Chartered Accountants in England & Wales Examinations – New Hall.

5-7 November: Institute of Municipal Treasurers & Accountants Examinations – Old Hall.

8 November: British Red Cross Society – Old Hall.

10 November: Health & Strength League Dance – Old Hall.

19-23 November: 17th The London Medical Exhibition – New Hall.

24 November: Commando Association – Old Hall.

28 November: Warner's Holiday Camps – New Hall.

7-8 December: *The People* Pigeon Show – New Hall.

c.December: London Postal Office, Christmas Sorting – Both Halls.

1952

31 December '51-12 January '52: 25th National Schoolboy's Own Exhibition Silver Jubilee – Both Halls.

19-21 February: 8th Amusement Trades Exhibition – New Hall.

22 February: London Coastal Coaches – Old Hall.

1 March: Camping Club of Great Britain & Ireland – New Hall.

15-21 March: RICS Examinations – Both Halls.

27 March: International Poodle Club Championship Show – Old Hall.

28-9 March: Electrical Engineers Exhibition organised by the Association of Supervisory Electrical Engineers – New Hall.

29 March-4 April: RICS Examinations – Old Hall.

9 April: The Dachshund Club Championship Show – Old Hall.

25-6 April: National Coal Board – Old Hall.

5-9 May: Institute of Municipal Treasurers & Accountants Examinations – Old Hall.

17 May: Southern Dachshund Association Championship Show – Old Hall.

19-22 May: Institute of Chartered Accountants Examinations – Old Hall.

24 May: Empire Day Movement – Old Hall (Empire Day).

26-30 May: Institute of Chartered Accountants Examinations – Old Hall.

31 May-2 June: Plymouth Brethren – K.J. Price – Old Hall.

6-7 June: 7th *The People* National Darts Teams Championship – Old Hall.

10-16 June: 5th Aquarium and Water Garden Exhibition – Old Hall.

12 June: Rifle Brigade – Old Hall.

20 June: London Transport (Central Road Services) Sports Committee – Old Hall.

29-30 July: 17th Kensington Kitten & Neuter Cat Club – New Hall.

20 August: 7th United and British Boxer Club Championship Show – Old Hall.

30 August: Bakers' Exhibition (Maclaren & Sons) – Old Hall.

22 September-3 October: 52nd Chemists' Exhibition (British & Colonial Druggist Co. Ltd) – Old Hall.

16 October: National Honey Show Ltd – Old Hall.

10 October: The Poodle Club Championship Show – Old Hall.

11 October: London Transport Services Club – New Hall.

14-15 October: 5th London Regional Display, Engineering Industries Association – New Hall.

25 October: HOC-Down Clubs – Old Hall.

20-9 October: 27th *The Model Engineer* Exhibition – New Hall.

6-8 November: Clothing Trades Exhibition – Old Hall.

4-7 November: 1st Junior Fashion Fair at the Army & Navy Exhibition Halls.

12 November: British Red Cross Society – Old Hall.

22 November: Hoc-Down Clubs – Old Hall.

26 November: Warner's Holiday Camps – New Hall.

27-9 November: National Council for Animals Welfare – Old Hall.

17-21 November: 18th The London Medical Exhibition – Both Halls.

2-3 December: The National Cat Club's 56th All Breeds Championship Cat Show – Old Hall.

4-8 December: *The People* Pigeon Show – New Hall.

5 December: Elliott Bros. – Old Hall.

6 December: International Dancing Masters' Association – Old Hall.

*c.*December: London Postal Region, Christmas sorting – Both Halls.

*c.*December: Tenport Trading Co. – New Hall (deposit forfeited).

*c.*December: Sixth International Congress on Accounting – Both Halls (deposit forfeited).

*c.*December: British Parentcraft Exhibition – New Hall (deposit forfeited).

1953

31 December '52-10 January '53: 26th National Schoolboy's Own Exhibition – Both Halls.

17 January: J. Thompson – Old Time Dance – Old Hall.

27-9 January: 9th Amusement Trades Exhibition – Old Hall.

24 January: Industrial Recreational Services – New Hall.

25 January: Infantile Paralysis Fellowship – New Hall.

2 February: Southern Counties Cat Club Show (Mrs Williams) – Old Hall.

20 February: Shell Mex BP Ltd – New Hall.

21 February: Camping Club of Great Britain & Ireland – New Hall.

25-6 February: Modern Gardening Exhibition – New Hall.

7-13 March: RICS Examinations – Both Halls.

23-7 March: 1st Factory Equipment Exhibition – New Hall.

21-7 March: RICS Examinations – Both Halls.

4 April: Webb A.E. I.D.M.A. – Old Hall.

8 April: Dachshund Club Championship Show – Old Hall.

17 April: Scottish Reel Club – Old Hall.

18 April: Rifle Brigade Club & Association – New Hall.

18 April: Commando Association – Old Hall.

11-13 May: Chartered Institute of Secretaries Examinations – Old Hall.

11-14 May: 2nd Junior Fashion Fair – New Hall.

18-24 May: Institute of Chartered Accountants Examinations – Old Hall.

22 May: Inns of Court – Regt. – New Hall.

23 May: Plymouth Brethren – New Hall.

30 May: London Caledonian Games Association – Old Hall.

30 May: Sydney Thompson? – New Hall.

3 June: United and British Boxer Club Championship Show – Old Hall.

6 June: Old Coldstreamers Association – Old Hall.

11-13 June: 6th Aquarium and Water Garden Exhibition – Old Hall.

*c.*June: Glass Industries (Grimaldi) – Old Hall (deposit forfeited).

15-19 June: London Coronation Choir – New Hall.

27 June: 8th *The People* National Darts Teams Championship – Old Hall.

29 June-1 July: London Floral Decoration Society – Old Hall.

20-1 July: London County Council Examinations – Old Hall.

22-3 July: Conveyencer Fork Trucks Ltd – Old Hall.

30-1 July: 18th Kensington Kitten & Neuter Cat Club's 'Coronation Kitten & Neuter Show' – Old Hall.

1-3 August: The Society of St Vincent de Paul – Both Halls.

19-29 August: 28th *The Model Engineer* Exhibition – New Hall.

7-10 September: 53rd Chemists' Exhibition – British & Colonial Druggist Co. Ltd – Old Hall.

1 October: Siamese Cat Club Show – Old Hall.

9 October: Coronation Championship Cat Show Governing Council of the Cat Fancy All Breeds– New Hall.

10 October: The Poodle Club Championship Show – James Pye – Old Hall.

13-15 October: 6th London Regional Display of Products, Processes and Services of the Engineering Industry – New Hall.

13-17 October: National Honey Show – Old Hall.

18-26 October: Clothing Trades Exhibition – Old Hall.

24 October: The 9th London M.A.Y.C. (Methodist Association of Youth Clubs) Council London Weekend Celebration – New Hall.

30 October: Davis Gas Stove Company – New Hall.

3-6 November: 3rd Junior Fashion Fair – Old Hall.

5-7 November: National Chrysanthemum Society Show – New Hall.

11 November: Croydon Cat Club – Old Hall.

16-20 November: 19th The London Medical Exhibition – New Hall.

19-21 November: National Council for Animal Welfare – Old Hall.

23-7:November Institute of Chartered Accountants Examinations – Old Hall.

27 November: Warner's Holiday Camps Ltd – Reunion and Dance – New Hall.

28 November: Vickers-Armstrong Ltd – Dance – Old Hall.

*c.*November: Poodle Club – Old Hall.

3-7 December: *The People* Pigeon Show – New Hall.

5 December: Printing Machine Branch N.U.P.B. and P.W. – Old Hall.

9 December: The National Cat Club's 57th All Breeds Championship Cat Show – Old Hall.

10-28 December: London Postal Region – Christmas Postal Sorting – Both Halls.

12 December: British Red Cross Society – Old Hall.

12 December: Bertram & Co. Ltd – (Caterers) – Old Hall.

1954

31 December '53-13 January '54: 27th National Schoolboy's Own Exhibition – Both Halls.

9-16 January: 2nd National Stamp Exhibition held at Central Hall, Westminster.

16 January: West African Students Union – Old Hall.

23 January: Industrial Recreational Services – New Hall.

January/February: North Thames Gas Board – Old Hall.

2 February: 50th Southern Counties Cat Club Championship Show – Old Hall.

5 February: London Fire Brigade – Old Hall.

9-11 February: 10th Amusement Trades Exhibition – New Hall.

19-27 February: Arts & Crafts Exhibition – Old Hall

20 February: Camping Club of Great Britain – New Hall.

7 March: 150th Anniversary of the founding of the RHS.

22-6 March: 2nd Factory Equipment Exhibition – Both Halls.

*c.*March: 6th Technical Exhibition organised by the Oil & Colour Chemists' Association – Old Hall.

10-14 May: 4th Junior Fashion Fair – Old Hall.

17-28 May: 4th Gauge and Toolmaker's Association Exhibition – New Hall.

17-28 May: Institute Chartered Accountants Examinations – Old Hall.

29-30 May: British Youth Festival Committee – Old Hall.

10-12 June: 7th National Aquarium Exhibition – Old Hall.

18 June: Catholic Overseas Club – Old Hall.

21-3 June: London Floral Decoration Society – Old Hall.

17 July: Wiggins Teape Sports Club Dance – Old Hall.

30 July: 19th Kensington Kitten & Neuter Cat Club – Old Hall.

18-28 August: 29th *The Model Engineer* Exhibition – New Hall.

7 September: Herts. & Middlesex Cat Club Show – Old Hall.

15 September: National Chrysanthemum Show.

20-4 September: 1st National Display Exhibition and Convention – Both Halls.

27 September: Kensington Kitten & Neuter Cat Club – Old Hall.

27-30 September: 54th Chemists' Exhibition – Old Hall.

8 October: Siamese Cat Club – Old Hall.

9 October: The 10th London M.A.Y.C. Council London Weekend Celebration – New Hall.

9 October: The Poodle Club Show Championship Show – Old Hall.

12-15 October: 7th Engineering Industries Association Exhibition – New Hall.

13-17 October: National Honey Show – Old Hall (cancelled).

17-25 October: Clothing Trades Exhibition – Old Hall.

25-9 October: The British Dental Trade Exhibition – New Hall.

1-5 November: 5th Junior Fashion Fair – Old Hall.

23-6 November: X-Ray Apparatus Association – Old Hall.

c.November: London Caledonian Games Association – Old Hall.

c.November: N.U.P.B. and P.W. – Old Hall.

c.November: Middlesex Federation of W.I. – Old Hall (deposit forfeited).

15-19 November: 20th The London Medical Exhibition – New Hall.

9-10 November: Croydon Cat Club Championship All-Breed Cat Show – Old Hall.

11 November: British Red Cross Society – Old Hall.

18-20 November: National Council for Animals Welfare Exhibition – Old Hall.

23 November: The Harrodian Club Dance – New Hall.

26 November: Warners Holiday Camps Reunion Dance – New Hall.

29 November-8 December: The Budgerigar Society Club Show – Old Hall.

29 November-11 December: The Boy Scouts Association in conjunction with The London Scout Council.

8 December: The National Cat Club's 58th All Breeds Championship Cat Show – Old Hall.

18 December: Announcement of John Murray Easton, Architect, winning the R.I.B.A. Gold Medal for Architecture in 1955.

c.December: *The People* Racing Pigeon Show – New Hall.

c.December: The London Postal Region Christmas Sorting – Both Halls.

1955

31 December '54-13 January '55: 28th National Schoolboy's and Senior Student's Own Exhibition – Both Halls.

8-15 January: 3rd National Stamp Exhibition held at Central Hall, Westminster.

20-9 January: International Holidays & Sports Exhibition – Old Hall.

1-3 February: 11th Amusement Trades Association Exhibition – New Hall.

3 February: Southern Counties Cat Club Show – Old Hall.

19 February: British National Carnation Society Show.

15-17 March: 7th Technical Exhibition organised – Old Hall.

24 February-5 March: Hammer Film Productions (Cyril Stapleton) – Old Hall.

28 February-4 March: 1st Stationery & Book Trades Fair – New Hall.

28 February-4 March: Handcrafts & Hobbies & Allied Trades Fair – Old Hall.

28 March: Caterers Bertram & Co. – Old Hall.

c.March: Toc H. Inc. Festival – Old Hall.

25-8 April: 39th Annual Exhibition of The Institute of Physics and The Physical Society Scientific Instruments & Apparatus – New Hall.

9-13 May: 6th Junior Fashion Fair – Old Hall.

16-21 May: 1st Post-War Photo Fair organised by British Organizers – New Hall.

20-2 May: National Flower Arrangement Society – Old Hall.

13 June: 8th National Aquarium Exhibition – Old Hall.

18-21 July: International Water Supply Exhibition – New Hall.

28 July: 20th Kensington Kitten & Neuter Cat Club – Old Hall.

17-27 August: 30th *The Model Engineer* Exhibition and the Exhibition of Inventions – New Hall.

23 September: Herts. & Middlesex Cat Club – Old Hall.

4 October: RHS Autumn Fruit and Vegetable Show.

6-7 October: Siamese Cat Club – Old Hall.

8 October: The Poodle Club – Old Hall. (This was the last dog show to take place in the Halls since the first one on 6 April 1905, 51 years before.)

10-15 October: 8th Engineering Industries Association Exhibition – New Hall.

11 October: British Red Cross Society Dance – Old Hall.

12 October: J. Lyons & Co. Dance – Old Hall.

16-24 October: Factory Managers Clothing Association Exhibition – Old Hall.

22 October: The 11th London M.A.Y.C. Council London Weekend Celebration – New Hall.

24 October: Women's League of Health & Beauty – New Hall.

31 October-4 November: 7th Junior Fashion Fair – Old Hall.

11 November: Croydon Cat Club Championship Cat Show – Old Hall.

14-18 November: 21st The London Medical Exhibition – New Hall.

17-19 November: Racing Pigeon Publishing Co. Pigeon Show – Old Hall.

24-6 November: National Council for Animals Welfare – Old Hall.

28 November: Warner's Holiday Camps Reunion Dance – New Hall.

1-4 December: *The People* Pigeon Show.

7 December: The National Cat Club's 59th All Breeds Championship Show – New Hall.

15 December: Southern Counties Cat Club – Old Hall.

c.December: London Postal Region Christmas Post Sorting – Both Halls.

c.December: 150th Anniversary of 'I' Battery Royal Horse Artillery – New Hall.

Date Unknown: English Speaking Union and English Society.

Date Unknown: Universal Exhibitions Ltd – Old Hall (deposit forfeited).

Date Unknown: Office Management Association – Old Hall.

Date Unknown: Insurance Institute of London Examinations – Both Halls.

Date Unknown: Institute of Chartered Accountants Examinations – Old Hall.

Date Unknown: National Chrysanthemum Society Show.

Date Unknown: National Rose Society Show.

Date Unknown: Gardeners' Royal Benevolent Society Show.

Date Unknown: British Delphinium Society Show.

Date Unknown: British Iris Society Show.

Date Unknown: Organisation for Succulent Plant Study.

Date Unknown: National Dahlia Show.

Date Unknown: British Gladiolus Society Show.

Date Unknown: N. Thames Gas Board Dance – Old Hall (deposit forfeited).

Date Unknown: Lep Transport Dance – New Hall.

1956

31 December '55-14 January '56: 29th National Schoolboy's and Senior Student's Own Exhibition – Both Halls.

31 January: Southern Counties Cat Club – New Hall.

6-10 February: 2nd Stationery & Book Trades Fair – Both Halls.

15 February: J. Edgington & Co. – Old Hall.

22-4 February: 2nd Hardware Trades Fair – Both Halls.

6-8 March: 12th Amusements Trades Exhibition – New Hall. A unique poster stamp exists for this event.

1-2 July: The National Rose Society Summer Show – Both Halls.

1-2 May: RHS Fortnightly Flower Show with British Iris Society.

1-2 May: British Delphinium Society.

1-2 May: National Sweet Pea Society.

1-2 May: British National Carnation Society.

20-2 March: 8th Technical Exhibition, Oil & Colour Chemists Association – New Hall.

23-7 April: 8th Junior Fashion Fair – Old Hall.

14-17 May: 40th Annual Exhibition of The Institute of Physics and The Physical Society Exhibition of Scientific Instruments & Apparatus – Both Halls.

28 July: 21st Kensington Kitten & Neuter Cat Club – Old Hall.

22 August: Herts. & Middlesex Cat Club – Old Hall.

22 August-1 September: 31st *The Model Engineer* Exhibition – New Hall.

9 September: The National Rose Society Autumn Show – Both Halls.

8-13 October: 9th Engineering Industries Association Exhibition – New Hall.

20 October: The 12th London M.A.Y.C. Council London Weekend Celebration – New Hall.

24 October: British Red Cross Society – Old Hall.

29 October-2 November: 9th Junior Fashion Fair – Old Hall.

3-4 November: National Flower Arrangement Society – Old Hall.

7 November: Croydon Cat Club Championship Cat Show – Old Hall.

12-16 November: 22nd The London Medical Exhibition – New Hall.

22-3 November: Warners Holidays Camps Ltd – Reunion Dance – New Hall.

c.December: London Postal Region Christmas Postal Sorting – Both Halls.

Date Unknown: Camping Club of Great Britain & Ireland – New Hall

Date Unknown: National Cat Club – New Hall.

Date Unknown: National Dahlia Society Show.

Date Unknown: RICS Examinations – Old Hall.

Date Unknown: Imperial Chemical Industries – Old Hall.

Date Unknown: J. Edgington & Co. – New Hall.

Date Unknown: National Flower Arrangement Society – Old Hall.

Date Unknown: Racing Pigeon Publishing Co. Ltd – Pigeon Show – Old Hall.

Date Unknown: National Council For Animals Welfare – Old Hall.

Date Unknown: The People Pigeon Show – New Hall.

Date Unknown: National Chrysanthemum Society Show.

Date Unknown: British Gladiolus Society Show.

Date Unknown: Alpine Garden Society.

1957

31 December '56-12 January '57: 30th The National Schoolboy's and Senior Student's Own Exhibition – Both Halls.

29-31 January: 13th Amusements Trades Exhibition – New Hall.

13-15 February: 3rd National Stationery & Book Trades Fair – Both Halls.

25 February-1 March: 3rd Hardware Trades Fair by Universal Exhibitions Ltd – Both Halls.

9-15 March: RICS Examinations – Old Hall.

12-14 March: 9th Technical Exhibition, Oil & Colour Chemists Association – New Hall.

25-8 March 41st Annual Exhibition of The Institute of Physics and The Physical Society Scientific Instruments & Apparatus – Both Halls.

8-11 April: 4th National Display Exhibition organised by Blandford Press – New Hall.

29-30 June: The National Rose Society Summer Show – Both Halls (deposit forfeited).

13-17 May: 10th Junior Fashion Fair – Old Hall.

13-17 May: National Festival of Hairdressing Exhibition – New Hall.

20 June: Wiggins Teape Sports and Social Club Dance – New Hall.

8-11 July: Grocery and Provisions Trades Fair – New Hall.

20 July: 22nd Kensington Kitten & Neuter Cat Club Show – Old Hall.

24-31 July: Boy Scouts Association – Old Hall.

16 August: Lep Transport (Hardware Trade) – New Hall.

21-31 August: 32nd The Model Engineer Exhibition – New Hall.

c.September: LABELEX – New Hall.

7 September: National Dahlia Society Show.

11-12 September: The National Rose Society Autumn Show – Both Halls.

17 September: Herts. & Middlesex Cat Club Show – Old Hall.

24-5 September: RHS Great Autumn Show – Both Halls.

27 September: National Chrysanthemum Society Show.

c.October: The 13th London M.A.Y.C. Council London Weekend Celebration – New Hall.

c.October: 10th Engineering Industries Association Exhibition – New Hall.

4-8 November: 11th Junior Fashion Fair – Old Hall.

12-14 November: 4th Technical Exhibition – New Hall.

13 November: Croydon Cat Club Championship Cat Show – Old Hall.

18-22 November: 22nd The London Medical Exhibition – New Hall.

24-7 November: 1st International Radio Hobbies – Old Hall.

28 November: National Cat Club's 61st All Breed Championship Show – New Hall.

7 December: The People International Show of Racing Pigeons – New Hall.

Date Unknown: The North Thames Gas Board – Old Hall.

Date Unknown: Lep Transport (Hardware Trade) – New Hall.

Date Unknown: National Floral Arrangement Society – Old Hall.

Date Unknown: National Sweet Pea Society.

Date Unknown: British National Carnation Society.

Date Unknown: Factory Managers Clothing Association Exhibition – Old Hall.

1958

31 December '57-11 January '58: 31st National Schoolboy's and Senior Student's Own Exhibition – Both Halls.

28-30 January: 14th Amusement Trade Exhibition – New Hall.

10-14 February: 4th National Stationery & Book Trades Fair – Both Halls.

24-8 February: Hardware Trades Fair – Both halls and with Central Hall Westminster.

11-13 March: 10th Technical Exhibition – New Hall.

24-7 March: 42nd Annual Exhibition of The Institute of Physics and The Physical Society Scientific Instruments & Apparatus – Both Halls.

5-9 May: 12th Junior Fashion Fair – Old Hall.

24 May: Empire Day (Last time it was called so. In 1959 it became known as British Commonwealth Day).

9-12 June: Grocery, Provisions & Self Service Exhibition – Both Halls.

c.June: The National Rose Society Summer Show – Both Halls.

16 August: 23rd Kensington Kitten & Neuter Cat Club Show – Old Hall.

20-30 August: 33rd The Model Engineer National Models Exhibition – New Hall.

c.September: LABELEX – New Hall.

c.September: The National Rose Society Autumn Show – Both Halls.

3-7 November: 13th Junior Fashion Fair – Old Hall.

10-14 November: 23rd The London Medical Exhibition – New Hall.

26-9 November: 2nd International Radio Hobbies Exhibition – Old Hall.

6 December: The People Show of Racing Pigeons – Old Hall. The Old Contemptibles.

1959

7-9 January: Villiers Group of Companies Diamond Jubilee Exhibition – Both Halls.

19-22 January: 43rd Annual Exhibition of The Institute of Physics and The Physical Society – Scientific Instruments & Apparatus – Both Halls.

28 January-7 February: Catering Trades Fair – Old Hall.

3-5 February: 15th Amusement Trades Exhibition – New Hall.

16-20 February: 5th National Stationery & Book Trades Fair – Both Halls.

17-19 March: 11th Technical Exhibition – New Hall.

25-8 March: International Hairdressing Exhibition of Great Britain – New Hall.

27-30 April: Corrosion Exhibition – New Hall.

c.May: 14th Junior Fashion Fair – Old Hall.

26 June: The National Rose Society Summer Show – Both Halls.

15-18 June: 6th National Display Exhibition – New Hall.

29 July: 24th Kensington Kitten & Neuter Cat Club Show – Old Hall.

25 August: 1st Schools Equipment Exhibition – New Hall.

26 August: Herts. & Middlesex Cat Club Show – Old Hall.

c.September: The National Rose Society Autumn Show – Both Halls.

21-31 October: 44th Motor Show – Earl's Court.

2-5 November: 15th Junior Fashion Fair – Old Hall.

2-5 November: 1st International Automatic Vending Machine Exhibition – Old Hall.

16-20 November: 24th The London Medical Exhibition – New Hall.

17 November: Croydon Cat Club Championship Cat Show – Old Hall.

9 December: National Floral Arrangement Society Annual Exhibition – Old Hall.

25-8 November: 3rd International Radio Hobbies Exhibition – Old Hall.

4 December: *The People* International Show of Racing Pigeons – Old Hall.

1960

31 December '59-9 January '60: 34th 'Model Engineering National Models Exhibition' – New Hall. (This was the last show held at the Halls.)

2-9 January: 1st Racing Car Show (organised by the British Racing & Sports Car Club), opened by Earl Howe – Old Hall.

18-21 January: 44th Annual Exhibition of The Institute of Physics and The Physical Society Scientific Instruments & Apparatus – Both Halls.

1-5 February: National Cleaning & Maintenance & Floor Trades Exhibition &Conference – Old Hall.

2-4 February: 16th Amusement Trade Exhibition – New Hall.

15-17 February: Industrial & Commercial Refrigeration Exhibition – Old Hall.

15-18 February: 2nd International Automatic Vending Machine Exhibition – New Hall.

1 March: Gas at Work in Industry Exhibition – Old Hall.

29 February-4 March: British Hosiery & Knitwear Exhibition – New Hall.

15-17 March: 12th Technical Exhibition – New Hall.

28 March-1 April: 6th National Stationery & Allied Trades Fair – Both Halls.

5-6 April: RHS Flower Show at which The Queen exhibited her Camelias.

30 May: National Floral Arrangement Society Show.

9-12 May: 16th Junior Fashion Fair – Old Hall.

20-3 June: 1st Laboratory Apparatus & Materials Exhibition – New Hall.

1-2 July: National Rose Society of Great Britain Summer Rose Show – New Hall.

28 July: 25th Kensington Kitten & Neuter Cat Club Show – Old Hall.

12-13 August: British Gladiolus Exhibition and Competition – Old Hall.

23-4 August: Home Heating and Winter Comfort Exhibition – New Hall.

30-1 August: RHS Flower Show – Old Hall.

9-10 September: National Rose Society of Great Britain Autumn Rose Show – New Hall.

31 October-3 November: 17th Junior Fashion Fair – Old Hall.

14-18 November: 25th The London Medical Exhibition – New Hall.

23-6 November: 4th International Radio Hobbies Exhibition – Old Hall.

2 December: *The People* International Show of Racing Pigeons – New Hall.

1961

31 December '60-7 January '61: 2nd The Racing Car Show (organised by the British Racing & Sports Car Club) - Both Halls.

16-20 January: 45th Annual Exhibition of The Institute of Physics and The Physical Society Scientific Instruments & Apparatus – Both Halls.

31 January-2 February: 17th Amusement Trade Exhibition – New Hall.

6 February: Comfort In The Home Exhibition organised by the Gas Council.

6-9 March: 13th Technical Exhibition – Both Halls.

20-3 March: Meat Machinery, Processing & Handling Exhibition – Old Hall.

20-4 March: 1st National Delicatessen Exhibition – New Hall.

1-4 May: 18th Junior Fashion Fair – Old Hall.

15-19 May: 3rd International Automatic Vending Exhibition & Conference – New Hall.

16-18 May: Modern Pharmacy Exhibition – Old Hall.

19-22 June: 2nd Laboratory Apparatus & Materials Exhibition – New Hall.

30 June-1 July: National Rose Society of Great Britain Summer Rose Show – New Hall.

29 July: 26th Kensington Kitten & Neuter Cat Club Show – Old Hall.

12-13 August: British Gladiolus Exhibition and Competition – Old Hall.

15-16 August: RHS Flower Show – Old Hall.

19-25 August: New TV Show – New Hall.

30 August: Herts. & Middlesex Cat Club Championship Shows – Old Hall.

30 August: RHS Flower Show – New Hall.

5-6 September: National Dahlia Society's Show.

8-9 September: National Rose Society of Great Britain Autumn Rose Show – New Hall.

17-19 October: 1st Engineering Industries Association Engineering Display – New Hall.

17-19 October: 1st National Security Exhibition – Old Hall.

30 October-2 November: 19th Junior Fashion Fair – Old Hall.

13-17 November: 26th London Medical Exhibition – New Hall.

22-5 November: 5th International Radio Hobbies Exhibition – Old Hall. Organised by the Radio Society of Great Britain. Mr Henry Loomis, director of *Voice of America* opened the exhibition.

7 December: *The People* International Show of Racing Pigeons – New Hall.

6 December: Flower Arrangement Association of London and Overseas – Old Hall.

1962

30 December '61-6 January '62: 3rd The International Racing Car Show (organised by the British & Racing Car Club) – Both Halls.

1-13 January: 35th National Schoolboy's and Senior Student's Own Exhibition – National Hall, Olympia.

15-19 January: 46th Annual Exhibition of The Institute of Physics and The Physical Society Scientific Instruments & Apparatus – Both Halls.

30 January-1 February: 18th Amusement Trade Exhibition – New Hall.

26 February-1 March: 14th Technical Exhibition – Both Halls.

12-16 March: 2nd Delicatessen Exhibition – Both Halls.

16-24 March: 9th STAMPEX held at Central Hall, Westminster.

26 March: 1st CENTRA International Congress and Exhibition – Old Hall.

26-9 March: Meat Machinery, Processing & Handling Exhibition – New Hall.

7-10 May: 20th Junior Fashion Fair – Old Hall.

14-17 May: Education Supplies and Equipment Exhibition – New Hall.

25 July: 27th Kensington Kitten & Neuter Cat Club Show – Old Hall.

7-8 September: National Rose Society Autumn Show.

16-18 October: Engineering Industries Association Engineering Display – New Hall.

29 October-1 November: 21st Junior Fashion Fair – Old Hall.

12-16 November: 27th The London Medical Exhibition – New Hall (last show in the Halls).

12-16 November: Wallpaper, Paint & Decorating Trades Fair – Old Hall.

20-2 November: 1st London Bookmakers & Betting Shop Equipment Exhibition – Old Hall.

1963

c.December '61-c.January '62: 4th The International Racing Car Show (organised by the British Racing & Sports Car Club) and sponsored by the *Daily Express* – Olympia.

28 December '62-10 January '63: 36th *Daily Mail* Schoolboy's & Senior Student's Own Exhibition – Both Halls.

14-17 January: 47th Annual Exhibition of The Institute of Physics and The Physical Society Scientific Instruments & Apparatus – Both Halls.

24 January: 58th Southern Counties Cat Club Show – Old Hall.

29-31 January: 19th Amusement Trades Exhibition – New Hall.

11-14 February: International Industrial Lubrication Exhibition – New Hall.

25 February-1 March: 3rd Delicatessen Exhibition – Both Halls.

11-14 March: 15th Technical Exhibition – Both Halls.

25-8 March: Meat Machinery & Butchers' Supplies Exhibition – New Hall. Organised by Trade & Technical Exhibitions Ltd; Dorset House, Stamford Street, London, SE1.

8-11 April: Aluminium for Architects Exhibition – New Hall.

6-9 May: 2nd Junior Fashion Fair – Old Hall.

17-24 May: Wildlife Exhibition sponsored by *The Observer* – Both Halls.

6 June: British Iris Society's Show – Old Hall.

24 June: Security Exhibition – New Hall.

9 July: The British Carnation Society's Show – Old Hall.

27 July: 28th Kensington Kitten & Neuter Cat Club Show – Old Hall.

1-4 October: Flooring and Finishes Exhibition – New Hall.

8-31 October: 23rd Junior Fashion Fair – Old Hall.

15 October: Engineering Industries Association Exhibition – New Hall.

11-14 November: 2nd London Bookmakers & Betting Shop Equipment Exhibition – Old Hall.

1964

6-9 January: 48th Annual Exhibition of The Institute of Physics and The Physical Society Scientific Instruments & Apparatus – Both Halls.

18 January: 59th Southern Counties Cat Club Show – Old Hall.

20-3 January: Diecasting & Precision Metal Moulding Exhibition – New Hall.

28-30 January: 20th Amusement Trade Exhibition – New Hall.

5 February: RHS Flower Show – Old Hall.

4-15 February: 'Comfort in the Home' Exhibition (organised by the Gas Board) – New Hall.

11-13 February: London Master Bakers Exhibition – Old Hall.

13-16 April: Meat Machinery & Butchers Supplies Exhibition – New Hall.

2-6 March: 4th Delicatessen Exhibition – New Hall.

10 March: RHS Daffodil Show – New Hall.

16-19 March: 16th Technical Exhibition – Both Halls.

21-4 April: 1st National Angling Show – Old Hall.

27-30 April: 24th Junior Fashion Fair – New Hall.

13-17 July: International Industrial Equipment Exhibition for Health at Work organised by the Royal Society for the Prevention of Accidents – Both Halls.

25 July: 29th Kensington Kitten & Neuter Cat Club – Old Hall.

11-12 August: RHS Flower Show – Both Halls. Included British Fuchsia Society Show.

2-5 November: 25th Junior Fashion Fair – Old Hall.

16-19 November: 3rd Bookmakers & Betting Shop Equipment Exhibition – Old Hall.

19 October: Fireplaces Fair – New Hall.

3 December: Everyone By Hovercraft Exhibition – New Hall.

4 December: *The People* International Racing Pigeon Show.

1965

c.December '64-c.January '65: 6th The Racing Car Show – Both Halls.

28 December '64-9 January '65: 38th *Daily Mail* Schoolboy's and Girl's Exhibition (organised by the *Daily Mail*) – National Hall, Olympia.

6-7 January: Churches, Schools and Youth Clubs Exhibition – Both Halls.

16 January: 1st National Pets Club Show – New Hall.

c.February: 'Olympiad' Pigeon Show – New Hall.

26-8 January: 21st Amusement Trade Exhibition – New Hall.

30 January: 60th Southern Counties Cat Club Show – Old Hall.

8-11 February: 1st National Stationery & Allied Trades Fair – New Hall.

c.March: 5th Delicatessen Exhibition – New Hall.

22-6 February: DISPOSEX '65 (Disposable Equipment Exhibition) – New Hall.

8-11 March: International Industrial Lubrication Exhibition – New Hall.

22-5 March: Lighting Exhibition sponsored by the Electric Light Fittings Association – New Hall.

5-8 April: European Do-It-Yourself Trade Fair – New Hall.

11-15 May: 2nd National Angling Exhibition – Old Hall.

26-9 April: 26th Junior Fashion Fair – New Hall.

29-30 June: RHS Flower Show – New Hall.

21 July: National Association of Flower Arrangement Societies of Great Britain Festival 'This Sceptr'd Isle' – New Hall.

31 July: 30th Kensington Kitten & Neuter Cat Club – Old Hall.

24-7 August: National Model Show – New Hall.

12-14 October: Engineering Industry Association Engineering Display – New Hall.

25-8 October: 27th Junior Fashion Fair – New Hall.

9-11 November: 4th Bookmakers & Betting Shop Equipment Exhibition – Old Hall.

15-18 November: Storage Exhibition – New Hall.

22-5 November: Lighting Exhibition – New Hall.

3 December: *The People* International Racing Pigeon Show – New Hall.

1966

27 December '65-8 January '66: 39th *Daily Mail* Schoolboy's and Girl's Exhibition – National Hall, Olympia.

6-11 January: Churches, Schools and Youth Clubs Exhibition – Both Halls.

11-14 January: 1st National Contract Furnishing & Interior Décor Exhibition – Both Halls.

22 January: 61st Southern Counties Cat Club Show – Old Hall.

25-7 January: 22nd Amusement Trades Exhibition – New Hall (last year at the RHS).

1-3 February: Automatic Laboratory Techniques Exhibition – ALTEX – Old Hall

12 February: Croydon Cat Club Championship Cat Show – Old Hall.

1-4 March: Food Hygiene and Quality Control Exhibition – Old Hall.

c.March: 6th Delicatessen Exhibition – New Hall.

14-17 March: Stationery & Office Equipment Trade Fair – Both Halls.

28-31 March: Bio-Medical Exhibition & Symposium – New Hall.

25-8 April: 28th Junior Fashion Fair – New Hall.

20-1 May: Home Economics Conference & Exhibition – New Hall.

20-3 June: Decorative Lighting Fair – New Hall.

24 June: Antique and Classic Car Company of Mayfair Auction – Old Hall.

26-7 July: RHS Flower Show and British Fuchsia Society – Old Hall.

30 July: 31st Kensington Kitten & Neuter Cat Club – Old Hall.

19-23 September: Manufacturing Boards & Decorative Surfaces Exhibition – New Hall.

4-7 October: International Clean Air Exhibition – New Hall.

18-20 October: Engineering Industries Association Engineering Exhibition – New Hall.

12-19 November: National Hobbies Exhibition – Old Hall (organised by Trades Exhibitions Ltd).

31 October-3 November: 29th Junior Fashion Fair – New Hall.

2 December: *The People* International Racing Pigeon Show – New Hall.

1967

27 December '66-10 January '67: 40th *Daily Mail* Schoolboy's and Girl's Exhibition – Empire Hall, Olympia.

14 January: *The Racing Pigeon* Old Comrades Pigeon Show – New Hall.

14-27 January: National Churches, Schools and Youth Clubs Exhibition – Both Halls.

4 February: 62nd Southern Counties Cat Club Show – Old Hall.

9-18 February: Record Retailers & Allied Trades Exhibitions RECORD '67 – New Hall. Organised by Trades Exhibitions Ltd (Ronald Hugh Maloney). This show was cancelled and the RHS took Trades Exhibitions to court and won a claim against them for £768 in lost rental with £22 4s. 6d. awarded for costs.

28 February-3 March: Carton & Case Making Exhibition & Conference CARTONEX – New Hall.

18 March: Croydon Cat Club Championship Cat Show – Old Hall.

25-31 March: 42nd The Model Railway Club's Exhibition – New Hall.

10-14 April: 7th Delicatessen International Exhibition – New Hall.

23-5 May: Premium Promotions & Sales Incentives Exhibition – New Hall.

7-8 June: British Iris Society Show – Old Hall.

19-22 June: Industrial Process Heating Symposium and Exhibition, HEATEX '67 – Both Halls.

29 June-1 July: Arms and Armour International – New Hall.

24-7 July: National Self-Service Laundry and Coin Operated Dry Clean Exhibition – New Hall.

29 July: 32nd Kensington Kitten & Neuter Cat Club Show – Old Hall.

6-7 September: Royal National Rose Society Show – New Hall.

27-30 September: Radio Engineering and Communications Exhibition – New Hall.

2-5 October: Drink Trades Marketing Exhibition – New Hall.

17-19 October: Engineering Industries Association Engineering Exhibition – New Hall.

23-6 October: 31st Junior Fashion Fair – Old Hall.

26 October: Sotheby's & Co. Auction of Veteran, Edwardian and Vintage Vehicles and Post-Vintage Thoroughbreds Motoring Books, Accessories and Miscellanea – New Hall.

3-4 November: National Chrysanthemum Society Show – Old Hall.

7-9 November: 5th or 6th Betting Shops and Gaming Equipment Exhibition – Old Hall.

13-16 November: Engineering Inspection & Control Exhibition & Conference – INSPEX – Both Halls.

1968

3-13 January: AUTOSPEED '68 presented by the British Racing & Sports Car Club – Both Halls.

27 December '67-6 January '68: 41st *Daily Mail* Schoolboy's and Girl's Exhibition – Empire Hall, Olympia.

27 January: 63rd Southern Counties Cat Club Show – Old Hall.

c.February: *Homefinders* New Homes Show – New Hall.

13-15 February: Automatic Laboratory Techniques Exhibition – ALTEX – Both Halls.

23 March: Croydon Cat Club Championship Cat Show – Old Hall.

8-15 April: 43rd The Model Railway Club's Exhibition – New Hall.

9-10 April: Alpine Garden Society's Show – Old Hall.

c.April: 8th Delicatessen Exhibition – New Hall.

22-5 April: 32nd Junior Fashion Fair – Old Hall.

14-15 May: National Angling Show – New Hall. Mr Heath opened the show.

20-1 May: RNIB Centenary Exhibition – Old Hall. Opened by HM The Queen.

6 June: British Iris Society's Show – Old Hall.

25-6 June: National Sweet Pea Society and Delphinium Society Shows – Old Hall.

27 July: 33rd Kensington Kitten & Neuter Cat Club – New Hall.

10-11 September: Royal National Rose Society Show – New Hall.

13-14 September: National Chrysanthemum Society's Show – Old Hall.

17-18 September: National Dahlia Society Show – Old Hall.

2-3 October: International Radio Engineering and Communications Exhibition – New Hall.

21-4 October: 33rd Junior Fashion Fair – Old Hall.

30 October: London Bakers' Exhibition – Alexander Palace.

24 October: Sotheby's & Co. Auction of Veteran, Edwardian and Vintage Vehicles and Post-Vintage Thoroughbreds Motoring Books, Accessories and Miscellanea – New Hall.

1969

6-11 January: 1st LINPEX '69 – London International Inventions and New Products Show – New Hall.

29 January: 64th Southern Counties Cat Club Show – Old Hall.

31 January-7 February: Racing and Sporting Motorcycle Show – Old Hall.

12-18 February: *Homefinders* New Homes Show – New Hall.

5-13 March: 16th STAMPEX Philatelic Exhibition – New Hall. Opened by Mr John Stonehouse as the last Post Master General before the GPO ceased to be a government department. This was the first of the STAMPEX exhibitions that stayed with the RHS until October 1995 when it moved to the Business Design Centre.

18-19 March: RHS Flower Show – Both Halls

22 March: Croydon Cat Club Championship Cat Show – Old Hall.

24 March: Stone Industries Exhibition – New Hall.

c.April: 9th Delicatessen Exhibition – New Hall.

21-4 April: 34th Junior Fashion Fair – New Hall.

1 July: National Sweet Pea Society and Delphinium Society Shows – Old Hall.

26 July: 34th Kensington Kitten & Neuter Cat Club Show – Old Hall.

12-13 August: RHS Summer Flower Show – New Hall.

18-23 August: 44th The Model Railway Club's Exhibition, 'The National Model Railway Show' – New Hall.

3-4 September: National Dahlia Society Show – New Hall.

12-13 September: National Rose Society's Autumn Show – New Hall.

16-17 September: National Chrysanthemum Society Show – Old Hall.

c.October: 35th Junior Fashion Fair – New Hall.

23 October: Sotheby's & Co. Auction of Veteran, Edwardian and Vintage Vehicles and Post-Vintage Thoroughbreds Motoring Books, Accessories and Miscellanea – New Hall.

5-6 December: *The Racing Pigeon* Old Comrades Pigeon Show – New Hall.

1970

3 January: 65th Southern Counties Cat Club Show – Old Hall.

7-17 January: The Specialist Sports Car Show and accessory supermarket, presented by the *Daily Mail* and The British Racing & Sports Car Clubs Ltd – Old Hall.

5 February: STATIONDEX '70 – Stationery Exhibition – New Hall.

5 February: 1st *Motorcycle Mechanics*, Racing & Sporting Motorcycle Show – Old Hall.

c.February: *Homefinders* New Homes Show – New Hall.

3-4 March: Confectionery, Tobacco and Allied Trades Fair – Both Halls.

3-7 March: 17th STAMPEX Philatelic Exhibition – New Hall.

21 March: Croydon Cat Club Golden Jubilee Championship Cat Show – Old Hall.

c.April: 10th Delicatessen Exhibition – New Hall.

20-3 April: 36th Junior Fashion Fair – Old Hall.

31 May-4 June: LINPEX '70, 2nd London International Inventions and New Products Exhibition sponsored by the Institute of Patentees and Investors – New Hall.

15-18 June: Photography at Work Exhibition – New Hall.

1 August: 35th Kensington Kitten & Neuter Cat Club Show – Old Hall.

2-3 September: National Dahlia Society Show – New Hall

11 September: National Chrysanthemum Society's Show – New Hall.

15-16 September: National Rose Society's Show – New Hall.

19-22 October: International Radio Engineering and Communications Exhibition – New Hall.

19-22 October: 37th Junior Fashion Fair – New Hall.

3-4 November: National Chrysanthemum Society's Show – Old Hall.

4-5 December: *The Racing Pigeon* Old Comrades Pigeon Show – New Hall.

1971

2-9 January: 2nd *Motorcycle Mechanics*, Racing & Sporting Motorcycle Show – New Hall.

16-20 January: Leather Goods, Luggage and Handbag Fair – New Hall.

28 January: 66th Southern Counties Cat Club All Breeds Championship Cat Show, New Hall.

8-13 February: *Homefinders* New Homes Show – New Hall.

1-6 March: 18th STAMPEX Philatelic Exhibition – New Hall.

20 March: Croydon Cat Club Show – Old Hall.

28-9 March: RHS Flower and Garden Equipment Show – New Hall.

10-13 April: Incentive Marketing and Premium Exhibition – New Hall.

29 April: 11th Delicatessen Exhibition – New Hall.

24-7 April: 38th Junior Fashion Fair – New Hall.

1 May: Commando Association Day – New Hall.

16-18 May: London Meat Trades Fair – New Hall.

13-16 June: Engineering Design Show – New Hall.

14-17 June: Photography at Work Exhibition – New Hall.

26-9 June: International Wine Marketing Exhibition (WINEX) – New Hall.

7-8 July: RHS Flower Show attended by Princess Alexandra.

28-31 July: FIRST National Collectors Fair – Old Hall.

31 July: 36th Kensington Kitten & Neuter Cat Club Show – New Hall.

2-6 October: London Bakers' Exhibition – New Hall.

16-19 October: 39th Junior Fashion Fair – Old Hall.

8-15 November: Children's Book Show – Old Hall.

19-22 November: British Sports Trade Fair – Both Halls.

3-4 December: *The Racing Pigeon* Old Comrades Pigeon Show – New Hall

1972

1-8 January: 3rd *Motorcycle Mechanics*, Racing & Sporting Motorcycle Show – Both Halls.

27 January: 67th Southern Counties Cat Club All Breeds Championship Cat Show – New Hall.

c.February: *Homefinders* New Homes Show – New Hall.

28 February-4 March: 19th STAMPEX – New Hall.

21-3 March: Automatic Laboratory Techniques Exhibition – New Hall.

18 March: Croydon Cat Club Show – Old Hall.

c.April: 12th Delicatessen Exhibition – New Hall.

c.April: 40th Junior Fashion Fair – Both Halls.

26 June: International Wine Marketing Exhibition (WINEX) – New Hall.

31 July: 37th Kensington Kitten & Neuter Cat Club All Breed Premier Show, New Hall.

30 August: National Dahlia Society Show – New Hall.

2-6 October: London Bakers' Exhibition – New Hall.

16-19 October: 41st Junior Fashion Fair – Old Hall.

17-22 October: Home Brew '72 (1st Home Brewing and Winemaking Exhibition) – Old Hall.

11 November: The National Chrysanthemum Society's Chrysanthemum Show – New Hall.

1973

6-13 January: 4th *Motorcycle Mechanics*, Racing & Sporting Motorcycle Show – Both Halls.

6-11 February: International New Homes Show – New Hall.

26 February-3 March: 20th STAMPEX – New Hall.

28 March: 68th Southern Counties Cat Club All Breeds Championship Cat Show, New Hall.

c.April: 13th Delicatessen Exhibition – New Hall.

9-12 April: 42nd Junior Fashion Fair – Both Halls.

28-31 July: 38th Kensington Kitten & Neuter Cat Club Show – New Hall.

5-9 September: The International Ski Show – Old Hall.

c.September: 1st Early Musical Instrument Exhibition – New Hall.

1-4 October: 43rd Junior Fashion Fair – Both Halls.

11 November: 6th Aquarium Show presented by the Federation of British Aquatic Societies and the Final of the Federation's Championship Trophy Competitions – Old Hall.

18 December: IRA Parcel Bomb explodes at Temporary Post sorting office in New Hall. It went off at 5.58 p.m. and injured six people. This was the second explosion of four in London on the same day injuring a total of 60 people. This was the start of a campaign over the Christmas period 'that saw 73 people injured by 24 bombs and explosive devices. The worst bomb exploded outside of a Home Office building in Westminster, when about 80lb of explosives packed into a stolen Ford car injured 54 people'.

1974

5-12 January: 5th *Motorcycle Mechanics* Racing & Sporting Motorcycle Show – Both Halls.

5-10 February: International New Homes Show – Both Halls.

25 February-2 March: 21st STAMPEX – New Hall.

16 March: 69th Southern Counties Cat Club All Breeds Championship Cat Show, New Hall.

c.April: 14th Delicatessen Exhibition – New Hall.

25-8 March: 44th Junior Fashion Fair – Both Halls.

14 July: 39th Kensington Kitten & Neuter Cat Club All Breed Premier Show – New Hall.

30 September-3 October: 45th Junior Fashion Fair – Both Halls.

11-14 November: 7th Aquarium Show – Old Hall.

27 November-1 December: The 2nd *Daily Mail* International Ski Show – New Hall.

1975

4-11 January: 6th *Motorcycle Mechanics* Racing & Sporting Motorcycle Show – Both Halls.

5-10 February: International New Homes Show – Both Halls.

24 February-1 March: 22nd STAMPEX – New Hall.

17-20 March: Photography At Work Exhibition – New Hall.

c.April/May: 15th Delicatessen Exhibition – New Hall.

*c.*March/April: 46th Junior Fashion Fair – Both Halls.

*c.*July: 40th 'Ruby Anniversary' Show of Kensington Kitten & Neuter Cat Club – New Hall. (This was also the 25th Anniversary of using the Halls.)

*c.*September: 2nd Early Musical Instrument Exhibition – New Hall.

*c.*September: 1st Games Workshop's Games Day Exhibition organised by Steve Jackson and Ian Livingstone who went on to become hugely popular writers of the *Fighting Fantasy* adventure gamebooks – New Hall.

13-16 October: 47th Junior Fashion Fair – Both Halls.

25-9 November: The 3rd *Daily Mail* International Ski Show – New Hall.

1976

10-17 January: 7th International Racing & Sporting Motorcycle Show – Both Halls.

5-7 February: Wine Tasting – Old Hall.

6-11 February: International New Homes Show – New Hall.

24-8 February: 23rd STAMPEX – New Hall.

9-10 March: RHS Flower Show – Old Hall.

4-8 April: 48th Junior Fashion Fair – Both Halls.

13-14 April: RHS Spring Flower Show – Both Halls.

*c.*April/May: 16th Delicatessen Exhibition – New Hall.

2 July: National Rose Society Show – New Hall.

10-11 August: RHS Summer Flower Show – Both Halls. British Gladiolus Society Jubilee International Exhibition in the Old Hall.

*c.*September: Games Workshop's Games Day Exhibition organised by Steve Jackson and Ian Livingstone – New Hall.

21 September: Bonham's Auction of Post-War thoroughbred cars 1947-67 – Old Hall.

28-9 September: RHS Autumn Show – Both Halls.

17-21 October: 49th Junior Fashion Fair – Both Halls.

29-31 October: 9th London Aquarium Show – Old Hall.

1977

7-15 January: 8th International Racing & Sporting Motorcycle Show – Both Halls.

*c.*February: International New Homes Show – Both Halls.

1-5 March: 24th STAMPEX – New Hall.

15-16 March: RHS Spring Flower Show – Both Halls.

21-4 March: 50th Junior Fashion Fair – Both Halls.

*c.*April or May: 1st Festival of Mind and Body held in Olympia.

19-20 April: RHS Spring Show – Both Halls.

16-19 May: 17th Delicatessen International Exhibition – New Hall.

1-2 July: The Royal National Rose Society – Old Hall.

*c.*September: Games Workshop's Games Day Exhibition organised by Steve Jackson and Ian Livingstone – New Hall.

14-17 September: 3rd Early Musical Instrument Exhibition – New Hall.

5-6 October: London Bakers' Exhibition – New Hall.

11-12 October: RHS Autumn Show – Both Halls.

16-20 October: 51st Junior Fashion Fair – Both Halls.

27-30 October: 10th Aquarium Show – Old Hall.

1-2 November: RHS Late Autumn Show – Old Hall.

9-12 November: National Aids for the Disabled Exhibition NAIDEX – New Hall.

1978

7-14 January: 9th International Racing & Sporting Motorcycle Show – Both Halls.

25-9 January: London New Year Gift Show – Old Hall.

*c.*February: International New Homes Show – Both Halls.

12-15 February: National Skateboard Trade Show – Both Halls.

18-19 April: RHS Spring Show – Both Halls.

28 February-4 March: 25th STAMPEX – New Hall.

12-16 March: 52nd Junior Fashion Fair – Both Halls.

*c.*May: 18th Delicatessen Exhibition – New Hall.

21-4 May: Business to Business Exhibition – Old Hall.

6-8 June: International Print Fair – New Hall.

1 July: The Delphinium Society Golden Jubilee Show – Old Hall.

*c.*August: 43rd Kensington & Kitten Neuter Cat Club Show – New Hall.

17-20 September: London Menswear Collection Exhibition – Old Hall.

*c.*September: Games Workshop's Games Day Exhibition organised by Steve Jackson and Ian Livingstone – New Hall.

10-11 October: RHS Autumn Flower, Fruit and Vegetable Show – Both Halls. The Alpine Society celebrated their 50th anniversary.

15-19 October: 53rd Junior Fashion Fair – Both Halls.

14-28 November: The Great Stovevent – Old Hall.

1-2 December: Winmau World Masters Darts Tournament presented by the British Darts Organisation – Old Hall.

5-7 December: UK Automatic Testing Exhibition – Both Halls.

1979

6-14 January: 10th International Racing & Sporting Motorcycle Show – Both Halls.

19-21 January: 5th British Open Dart Championships directed and supervised by the British Darts Organisation – Both Halls.

28-31 January: London New Year Gift Show –Both Halls.

6-8 February: London Catering Fair – New Hall.

11-14 February: International Knitwear Fair – Both Halls.

*c.*February: International New Homes Show – Both Halls.

27 February-3 March: 26th STAMPEX – New Hall.

18-22 March: 54th Junior Fashion Fair – Both Halls.

25 March: Catering Trade Exhibition – Old Hall.

14-17 May: 19th Delicatessen Exhibition DELEX '79 – New Hall.

3-5 July: Exhibition '79 – Both Halls.

*c.*September: Games Workshop's Games Day Exhibition organised by Steve Jackson and Ian Livingstone – New Hall.

13-15 September: 4th London Exhibition of Early Musical Instruments – New Hall.

3-4 October: London Bakers' Exhibition – New Hall.

14-18 October: 55th Junior Fashion Fair – Both Halls.

6-10 November: 1st Woodworker Show – Both Halls.

13-16 November: 1st Craft in Action Exhibition – New Hall.

20 November: National Council of Social Service (NCSS) 60th birthday exhibition on the work, interests and role of voluntary organisations.

4-8 December: Breadboard Exhibition (Home Electronics) – Old Hall.

6 December: Sotheby's Sale of Rare Sporting Memorabilia including the Billiards table of the legendary snooker player, Joe Davis, who had won his last final in the same Hall in May 1946, before retiring.

1980

4-6 January: 6th British Open M.Y. Dart Championships directed and supervised by the British Darts Organisation – Both Halls.

12-20 January: 11th London Racing & Sporting Motorcycle Show – Both Halls.

27-30 January: London New Year Gift Show – Both Halls.

5-7 February: London Grocers Show – Old Hall.

5-9 February: 27th STAMPEX – New Hall.

3-5 March: National Mail Order Merchandise Show – Both Halls.

16-20 March: 56th Junior Fashion Fair – Both Halls.

5-9 April: International Exhibition of Self-Sufficiency – Both Halls.

22-4 April: Laboratory Equipment Exhibition LABWARE – Both Halls.

11-14 May: Confectionery, Tobacco & Newsagents' Exhibition – New Hall.

20-2 May: London Catering Fair – Both Halls.

21-3 May: Label, Labelling, Markings & Identification Industry Exhibition LABELEX – Old Hall.

*c.*September: Games Workshop's Games Day Exhibition organised by Steve Jackson and Ian Livingstone.

10-11 September: 1st National Federation of Roofing Contractors Exhibition ROOFTECH – New Hall.

30 September-2 October: London Shopfitting Equipment & Services Exhibition – New Hall.

12-16 October: 57th Junior Fashion Fair – Both Halls.

*c.*October: 2nd The Woodworker Show.

2-4 December: UK Automatic Testing Exhibition – Both Halls.

1981

10-18 January: 12th London Racing & Sporting Motorcycle Show – Both Halls.

21 January: ECFMG examinations – New Hall.

25-8 January: London New Year Gift Show – New Hall.

25 January: Antiques Trade Fair (ATF) Antiques Fair – Old Hall.

29 January: DOE Examinations – Old Hall.

1 February: ATF – Old Hall.

9-11 February: Law Society Examinations – Old Hall.

10-12 February: London Catering Fair – New Hall.

24-8 February: 28th SUPER STAMPEX – Both Halls.

8-11 March: 58th Junior Fashion Fair – Both Halls.

26-7 March: 1st *Sunday Times* Wine Festival – New Hall (organised by Direct *Sunday Times* Wine Club, New Aquitaine House, Paddock Road, Reading).

22-5 March: Careers '81 – Both Halls.

29 March: Fish Catering Trades Exhibition – Old Hall.

2-8 April: CII Examinations – Both Halls.

9-12 April: 1st Windsurfing Show – Old Hall.

19 April: ATF – Old Hall.

10 May: ATF – Old Hall.

11-13 May: Institute of Taxation Examinations – Old Hall.

19-21 May: London Refrigeration & Air Conditioning Exhibition – New Hall.

19-21 May: London Printing Trade Exhibition – Old Hall.

24 May: ATF – Old Hall.

30-1 May: Collectors' Bike Show – Both Halls.

1-5 June: Institute of Chartered Secretaries Examinations – Old Hall.

3-5 June: LABELEX '81 – New Hall.

10 June: ICRF – New Hall.

8-10 June: CIBEA Exams – Old Hall.

14 June: ATF – Old Hall.

15-19 June: London University Exams – Old Hall.

16-17 June: RHS Early Summer Flower Show – New Hall.

18-24 June: Law Society Examinations – Old Hall.

18-24 June: College of Law Exhibitions – New Hall.

20-6 June: College of Law Examinations – Old Hall.

28 June: ATF – Old Hall.

1 August: 46th Kensington and Kitten Neuter Cat Club's 'Royal Celebration Show' to mark the wedding of HRH the Prince of Wales to Lady Diana Spencer – New Hall.

2 August: ATF – Old Hall.

23 August: ATF – Old Hall.

6 September: ATF – Old Hall.

8-14 September: Citizens' Band Show.

26-7 September: Games Workshop's Games Day Exhibition – New Hall.

27 September: ATF – Old Hall.

29 September-3 October: 5th Early Musical Instrument Exhibition – New Hall.

11-14 October: 59th Junior Fashion Fair – Both Halls.

20-2 October: London Publicans Show – Old Hall.

20-5 October: 3rd The Woodworker Show – New Hall.

25 October: Grand London Auto Jumble – Old Hall.

26-30 October: Tin Blue Ltd Alan Parker's/Pink Floyd's 'The Wall' – Both Halls.

31 October: ATS '81 Bazaar – Old Hall.

1 November: ATF – Old Hall.

2-4 November: Institute of Taxation Examinations – Old Hall.

6-8 November: Craft Fayre – Old Hall.

11-15 November: Breadboard Exhibition (Home Electronics) – New Hall.

14 November: British Deaf – Old Hall.

17-20 November: ABPG – New Hall.

22 November: ATF – Old Hall.

28-9 November: *The Racing Pigeon* Old Comrades Show – Both Halls.

4-11 December: Association of Certified Accountants Examinations – Old Hall.

13 December: ATF – Old Hall.

14-17 December: Institute of Chartered Accountants Examinations – New Hall.

16 December: Christmas Gardner's Market – Old Hall.

19-20 December: 1st Solstice Festival & Yuletide Fair – Old Hall.

1982

8-17 January: The Roadshow – Both Halls.

20 January: ECFMG Examinations – New Hall.

24 January: ATF – Old Hall.

31 January-3 February: LIGEX '82 London Grocers' Exhibition – New Hall.

31 January: ATF – Old Hall.

5-12 February: Law Society Examinations – Old Hall.

23-8 February: 29th SUPER STAMPEX – Both Halls.

5 March: Rugby Union Dance – New Hall.

7-10 March: 60th Junior Fashion Fair – Both Halls.

19-21 March: Custom Bike Show – New Hall.

21 March: ATF – Old Hall.

23-7 March: London Beauty & Fashion – Old Hall.

25-6 March: 2nd *Sunday Times* Wine Festival – New Hall.

28 March: ATF – Old Hall.

30 March-2 April: CII Examinations – Old Hall.

1-7 April: CII Examinations – New Hall.

4 April: ATF – Old Hall.

5 April: CII Examinations – Old Hall.

20-2 April: LABWARE '82 – Both Halls.

25 April: Auto Jumble – Old Hall.

29 April-3 May: Windsurfing Show – Old Hall.

9 May: ATF – Old Hall.

10-12 May: Institute of Taxation Examinations – Old Hall.

18-20 May: Partitioning & Suspended Ceilings Industry Exhibition – New Hall.

22 May: CB Dance – Old Hall.

23 May: ATF – Old Hall.

30-1 May: Beer Festival – Old Hall.

3-6 June: London Beer Festival – New Hall.

5-24 June: London University School Examinations – Old Hall.

20-8 June: Law Society Examinations – Both Halls.

29 June-1 July: National Federation of Roofing Contractors Exhibition ROOFTECH'82 – Both Halls.

4 July: ATF – Old Hall.

18 July: ATF – Old Hall.

31 July: 47th Kensington Kitten & Neuter Cat Club Show – New Hall.

14-18 August: 1st European Festival of Model Railways EUFMO – New Hall.

21 August: 4th ZX Micro Fair – New Hall.

21 August: ATF – Old Hall.

22 August: Bike Mart – Old Hall.

6 September: 88th Season of Henry Wood Promenade Concerts – Old Hall. (The first UK performance of Pierre Boulez's *Réspons*.)

8-9 September: VQE Examinations – Both Halls.

25-6 September: Games Workshop's Games Day Exhibition – New Hall.

26 September: ATF – Old Hall.

3-6 October: 61st Junior Fashion Fair (the last show held with us) – Both Halls.

19-24 October: 4th The Woodworker Show – Both Halls.

31 October: Grand London Auto Jumble – Old Hall.

1-3 November: Institute of Taxation Examinations – Old Hall.

6 November: 1st LOTS organised by London Omnibus Traction Society – Old Hall.

7 November: ATF – Old Hall.

10-14 November: Breadboard '82 (Home Electronics) organised by – Old Hall.

21 November: ATF – Old Hall.

27-8 November: *The Racing Pigeon* Old Comrades Show – Both Halls.

29 November-1 December: Examinations – Old Hall.

30 November-1 December: Enigma Filming – New Hall. Pink Floyd's 'The Wall'.

3-10 December: Association of Certified Accountants Examinations – Old Hall.

12 December: ATF – Old Hall.

13-16 December: Institute of Chartered Accountants Examinations – New Hall.

15 December: Christmas Gardeners' Market – Old Hall.

18-19 December: 2nd Solstice Festival & Yuletide Fair – Old Hall.

18 December: 5th ZX Micro Fair – New Hall.

1983

7-9 January: London Home Computer Show – Old Hall.

11 January: Filming – Old Hall.

16 January: Antiques Trade Fair organised by Step-In Management Services – Old Hall.

19-23 January: The Roadshow '83 – New Hall.

26 January: ECFMG Examinations – New Hall.

30 January: Antiques Trade Fair organised by Step-In Management Services – Old Hall.

1-3 February: London Catering Fair – New Hall.

15-20 February: 30th SUPER STAMPEX – Both Halls.

25-7 February: Lambeth Chess Congress – Old Hall.

26 February: 6th ZX Micro Fair – New Hall.

5-6 March: 3rd *Sunday Times* Wine Festival – New Hall.

16 March: Budget Forum – Old Hall.

20 March: Fish Catering Trades Exhibition – Old Hall.

22-4 March: Institute of Quantity Surveyors Examinations – Old Hall.

3 April: Antiques Trade Fair organised by Step-In Management Services – Old Hall.

5-13 April: Chartered Insurance Institute Examinations – Old Hall.

30 April-1 May: Rhododendron Show – New Hall.

8 May: Grand London Auto Jumble – Old Hall.

9-11 May: Institute of Taxation Examinations – Old Hall.

15 May: Antiques Trade Fair organised by Step-In Management Services – Old Hall.

18-20 May: LIBMUSEX – Old Hall.

5 June: Antiques Trade Fair organised by Step-In Management Services – Old Hall.

6-10 June: Institute of Chartered Surveyors Examinations – Old Hall.

19 June: Antiques Trade Fair organised by Step-In Management Services – Old Hall.

20-1 June: The Rating and Valuation Association Examinations – Old Hall.

3 July: Antiques Trade Fair organised by Step-In Management Services – Old Hall.

5-6 September: Law Society Examinations – Old Hall.

11 September, 2 October: Antiques Trade Fair organised by Step-In Management Services – Old Hall.

18-23 October: 5th The Woodworker Show – Both Halls.

5 November: London Omnibus Traction Society Show (LOTS) – Old Hall.

5 November: Games Workshop's Games Day Exhibition – New Hall.

6 November: Antique Trades Fair – Old Hall.

10-13 November: PUSM Event – Old Hall.

18-20 November: 6th Early Music & Classical Music Exhibition – Both Halls.

27 November: Auto Jumble – Old Hall.

3-4 December: 'Old Comrades' Pigeon Show organised by *Racing Pigeon* – Both Halls.

8-11 December: 1st The *BBC Micro & Electron User* Show – New Hall.

10-16 December: Association of Certified Accountants Examinations – Old Hall.

12-15 December: Institute of Chartered Accountants Examinations – New Hall.

18 December: Antiques Trade Fair organised by Step-In Management Services – Old Hall.

1984

13-16 January: Road 'n' Race Show – New Hall.

6-11 March: 31st SUPER STAMPEX – Both Halls.

*c.*March: 4th *Sunday Times* Wine Festival – New Hall.

25 March: Antiques and Collectors Fair (ATF) – Old Hall.

29 March-1 April: 2nd *The Electron & BBC Micro User* Show – New Hall.

*c.*June: ROOFTECH '84 –Both Halls. (This was the last time they used the RHS.)

28 July: 49th Kensington Kitten & Neuter Cat Club Show – New Hall.

1-2 September: Games Workshop's Games Day Exhibition – New Hall.

11-12 September: National Chrysanthemum Society's Show – Both Halls.

19-20 September: RHS Great Autumn Show – Both Halls.

30 September-3 October: Home Improvement Show – Old Hall.

9-10 October: RHS Flower, Fruit and Vegetable Show – Both Halls.

16-22 October: British Philatelic Exhibition (STAMPEX) – Both Halls (130 dealers).

28 October: Grand London Auto Jumble – Both Halls.

21 November: RHS Flower Show – Old Hall.

26-8 November: National Careers Exhibition – Old Hall.

5 December: 'Old Comrades' Pigeon Show organised by *Racing Pigeon* – Both Halls.

6-9 December: 3rd *The Electron & BBC Micro User* Show – New Hall.

16 December: Antiques and Trade Fair – Old Hall.

1985

6-9 February: 1st Christian Resources Exhibition – Both Halls.

26 February-3 March: 32nd SUPER STAMPEX – Both Halls.

*c.*March: 5th *Sunday Times* Wine Festival – New Hall.

20-3 March: Centenary International Orchid Conference – Old Hall.

30-1 March: 4th *The Electron & BBC Micro User* Show – New Hall.

10-11 April: RHS Spring Flower Show – Old Hall.

28 April: Antiques and Trade Fair – Old Hall.

3-6 May: First Festival of Spirit – New Hall. (Launched at Olympia in 1977 as the Festival of Mind and Body. It added 'Spirit' in 1980 and was at Olympia until 1984. Mind Body Festival moved to the Brighton Metropole on the 25-7 May.)

2 June: Antiques and Trade Fair – Old Hall.

22 June: 15th ZX Micro Fair – New Hall (for users of Sinclair machines).

6-7 August: RHS Summer Flower Show – Both Halls.

*c.*July/August: 50th 'Golden Anniversary' Show of Kensington Kitten & Neuter Cat Club.

1 September: Antiques and Trade Fair – Old Hall.

10-11 September: 1st Joint Royal National Rose Society and National Chrysanthemum Society Show – Both Halls.

17-19 September: RHS Great Autumn Flower Show – Both Halls.

22 September: Antiques and Trade Fair – Old Hall.

24-6 September: Timber Build Exhibition – Both Halls.

28-9 September: Games Workshop's Games Day – New Hall.

15-20 October: British Philatelic Exhibition (BPE) – Both Halls.

30 October-1 November: Liquids Handling in Offshore, Petroleum & Shipping Industries Exhibition – WORLDFLOW – Both Halls.

26-7 November: RHS Winter Flower Show – New Hall.

c.November: 7th Early Music & Classical Music Exhibition – Both Halls.

30 November-1 December: 'Old Comrades' Pigeon Show organised by *The Racing Pigeon* – Both Halls.

4-7 December: Westminster Christmas Antiques Fair – Old Hall.

14 December: 16th ZX Micro Fair – New Hall.

1986

5-8 February: 2nd Christian Resources Exhibition – Both Halls.

4-9 March: 33rd SUPER STAMPEX – Both Halls.

16-18 March: 5th *The Electron & BBC User* Show – New Hall.

11 May: 2nd Photographica – Old Hall.

23-6 May: 11th Festival of Mind Body Spirit – New Hall.

c.March: 6th *Sunday Times* Wine Festival – New Hall.

29 March-3 April: 61st The Model Railway Club's International Model Railway Exhibition – Both Halls.

c.July: The Riyadh (State of Qatar) Exhibition – Old Hall.

27 September: Games Day RPG Convention hosted by Games Workshop.

14-19 October: British Philatelic Exhibition (BPE) – Both Halls.

17 November: Horticultural Halls Limited incorporated as a wholly owned trading subsidiary of the RHS to enable profits to be covenanted to it without tax penalties.

c.December: 1st Westminster Antiques Fair.

13 December: 21st ZX Micro Fair – New Hall.

1987

13-15 January: 1st Coys of Kensington Classic Car Auction – New Hall.

10-11 January: 1st International Record Fair – Old Hall.

3-5 February: 2nd Coys of Kensington Classic Car Auction – New Hall.

18 January: ATF Consumer Antique Fair – Old Hall.

20-1 January: EC Farming Examinations – Old Hall.

21-9 January: French Connection Fashion Show – Old Hall.

27-8 January: RHS Flower Show – New Hall.

30-1 January: 22nd ZX Micro Fair – New Hall.

3-5 February: 3rd Coys of Kensington Classic Car Auction – New Hall.

3-11 February: Law Society Examinations – Old Hall.

15 February: ATF Consumer Antique Fair – Old Hall.

16 February: Fruit of the Loom Filming for advertisement – Old Hall.

24-5 February: RHS AGM and Lecture – Old Hall.

24-5 February: RHS Flower Show – New Hall.

3-8 March: 34th Spring STAMPEX (BPE) Stamp Fair – Both Halls.

11-13 March: Financial Training Exams – New Hall.

14-15 March: British Orchid Growers' Association – Flower Show – Old Hall.

17-18 March: RHS Flower Show – New Hall.

20-2 March: 7th *Sunday Times* Wine Festival – New Hall.

21 March: International Record Fair – Old Hall.

22 March: ATF Consumer Antique Fair – Old Hall.

1-2 April: Retail Newsagents Trade Exhibition – Old Hall.

2 April: Levis – Location Filming – New Hall.

7-8 April: RHS Flower Show – Both Halls.

9-14 April: Chartered Insurance Institute Examinations – Both Halls.

18-23 April: 62nd The Model Railways Club's International Model Railway – Both Halls.

28-9 April: RHS Flower Show – New Hall.

27-8 April: Specialist Growers' Market Consumer Flower Show – Old Hall.

5-6 May: Royal College of General Practitioners Examinations – Old Hall.

8-10 May: 6th *BBC Micro User* Computer Exhibition – New Hall.

10 May: 3rd Photographica – Old Hall.

11-13 May: Institute of Taxation Examinations – Old Hall.

14-16 May: MICE '87 (Meetings Industry Charity Event) – New Hall.

18-22 May: Incorporated Society of Auctioneers & Valuers Examinations – Old Hall.

21-5 May: 12th Mind Body Spirit Festival – New Hall.

30 May: 23rd ZX Micro Fair – New Hall.

31 May: ATF Consumer Antique Fair – Old Hall.

31 May: Location Filming – New Hall.

1-5 June: Institute of Chartered Secretaries & Administrators Examinations.

6-12 June: Chartered Association of Certified Accountants Examinations – New Hall.

10-12 June: Financial Training Examinations – Old Hall.

16-17 June: RHS Flower Show – New Hall.

15-18 June: Association of Accounting Technicians – Old Hall.

21 June: ATF Consumer Antique Fair – Old Hall.

27-8 June: International Record Fair – Old Hall.

1-8 July: College of Law Examinations – Both Halls.

14 July: RHS Members Lecture – Old Hall.

14-15 July: RHS Flower Show – New Hall.

19 July: ATF Consumer Antique Fair – Old Hall.

24-5 July: 52nd Kensington Kitten & Neuter Cat Club Show – New Hall.

11-12 August: RHS Flower Show – Both Halls.

21-3 August: 1st Ellis Brigham Retail Sports Equipment Sale – Old Hall.

22 August: 24th ZX Micro Fair – New Hall.

27-31 August: National Dahlia Society Flower Show – New Hall.

1-2 September: National Dahlia Society Flower Show – New Hall.

7-8 September: RHS Flower Show – Old Hall.

7-8 September: Chrysanthemum Show – New Hall.

16-17 September: RHS Flower Show – Both Halls.

22-7 September: 35th Autumn STAMPEX (BPE) Stamp Fair – Both Halls.

6-7 October: RHS Flower Show – Both Halls.

9-11 October: Games Workshop's Games Day Exhibition – New Hall.

10 October: Affiliated Societies Members Conference – Old Hall.

17-18 October: Arcadia '87, Trade Fair for Amusements Trades Industry – New Hall.

18 October: ATF Consumer Antique Fair – Old Hall.

21-2 October: FENCEX '87, Building Trade Fair – Old Hall.

27-8 October: RHS Flower Show – New Hall.

26-7 October: Royal College of General Practitioners Examinations – Old Hall.

30-31 October: 8th London Exhibition of Early Musical Instruments – New Hall.

30 October: Financial Training Professional Examinations – Old Hall.

31 October: London Omnibus Traction Society Consumer Hobby Exhibition – Old Hall.

2-4 November: Institute of Taxation Examinations – Old Hall.

6-7 November: National Chrysanthemum Society Flower Show – New Hall.

6-8 November: Psychic & Mystic Fair organised by New Life Designs – Old Hall.

13-15 November: 7th *BBC Micro User*, Computer Show – New Hall.

15 November: ATF Consumer Antique Fair – Old Hall.

24-5 November: RHS Flower Show – New Hall.

27-9 November: Direct Design Exhibition – New Hall.

4-11 December: Chartered Association of Certified Accountants Examinations – New Hall.

12 December: 25th ZX Micro Fair – New Hall.

13 December: ATF Antique Fair – New Hall.

14-31 December 87: Chinese Terracotta Warriors Exhibition – Old Hall.

15-16 December: Stock Exchange Examinations – New Hall.

1988

1 January-20 February: Chinese Emperors Warriors Exhibition – Old Hall.

17 January: ATF Antique Fair – New Hall.

6 February: RHS Flower Show – New Hall.

7 February: ATF Antique Fair – New Hall.

16 February: 4th Coys of Kensington Auction of Veteran, Vintage and Classic Vehicles – Old Hall.

23-4 February: RHS Flower Show – New Hall.

1-6 March: 36th Spring STAMPEX (BPE) Stamp Fair – Both Halls.

12-13 March: British Orchid Growers' Association – Old Hall.

12-18 March: Tunisia Week Tourism Show – New Hall.

15-18 March: Financial Training Examinations – Old Hall.

19-20 March: Bowls Alive Bowling Tournament – Old Hall.

22-3 March: RHS Flower Show – New Hall.

25-7 March: 8th British Gem and Minerals Show – Old Hall.

25-7 March: 8th *Sunday Times* Wine Festival – New Hall.

1-8 April: 63rd The Model Railway Club's International Model Railway Exhibition – Both Halls.

12-13 April: RHS Flower Show – Both Halls.

14-20 April: Chartered Insurance Institute Examinations – Both Halls.

19-25 April: 1st Westminster Antiques Fair – Old Hall.

23-9 April: SASMEX Trade Exhibition – New Hall.

27 April: MIND Charity Conference – Old Hall.

4-5 May: RHS Flower Show – Both Halls.

9-11 May: 4th Photographica Camera Show – Old Hall.

11-15 May: 8th *BBC Micro User* Computer Exhibition – New Hall.

12 May: ALAPG – Old Hall.

18-22 May: Direct Design & British & Continental Furniture Show – New Hall.

25-31 May: 13th Festival of Mind Body Spirit – New Hall.

29 May: ATF Antique Fair – Old Hall.

3-9 June: Association of Accounting Technicians Examinations – Old Hall.

7-10 June: Financial Training Examinations – New Hall.

11 June: 26th ZX Micro Computer Exhibition – New Hall.

12-17 June: London University Examinations – Old Hall.

13-14 June: University of Cambridge Examinations – New Hall.

15-17 June: Lucas Films Location Filming *Indiana Jones & The Last Crusade* – New Hall.

18-22 June: RHS Flower Show – New Hall.

20-22 June: St Martin's School of Art and Fashion, Fashion Show – Old Hall.

1-4 July: Artists' Materials Exhibition – New Hall.

3 July: ATF Antique Fair – Old Hall.

5-8 July: College of Law Examinations – Old Hall.

5-13 July: College of Law Examinations – New Hall.

19 July: RHS Members Lecture – Old Hall.

19-20 July: RHS Flower Show – New Hall.

26 July: 5th Coys of Kensington Sale of Important and Sporting Vehicles – Old Hall.

29-30 July: 53rd Kensington Kitten & Neuter Cat Club Show – New Hall.

31 July: ATF Antique Fair – Old Hall.

16-17 August: RHS Flower Show – Both Halls.

18-24 August: Seniig & Co. Location Filming – New Hall.

30-1 August: National Dahlia Society – New Hall.

1-4 September: 2nd Ellis Brigham, Sports Equipment Sale – Old Hall.

5-6 September: Rhododendron Show – New Hall.

11 September: ATF Antique Fair – Old Hall.

21-2 September: RHS Flower Show – Both Halls.

27 September-2 October: 37th Autumn STAMPEX (BPE) Stamp Fair – Both Halls.

11-12 October: RHS Flower Show – Both Halls.

24-5 October: Royal College of General Practitioners Examinations – Old Hall.

28 October: Financial Training Examinations – Old Hall.

29 October: London Omnibus Traction Society Exhibition – Old Hall.

30-1 October: RHS Flower Show – New Hall.

30 October: ATF Antique Fair – Old Hall.

4-5 November: Institute of Taxation Examinations – Old Hall.

3 November: 1st Cancer Relief Macmillan Fund Christmas Market – Old Hall.

9-13 November: 9th *BBC Micro User* Computer Exhibition – New Hall.

24 November: National Union of Students Conference/Rally – New Hall.

29 November: RHS Awards Presentation – Old Hall.

29-30 November: RHS Flower Show – New Hall.

1-4 December: 1st Christmas Gift Fair organised by Cancer Relief Macmillan Fund – Old Hall.

1-5 December: Direct Design & British & Continental Furniture Show – New Hall.

5-8 December: Association of Accounting Technicians Examinations – Old Hall.

8 December: Palace Productions – New Hall.

9-10 December: 27th ZX Micro Computer Fair – New Hall.

11 December: ATF Antiques Fair – Old Fair.

13-16 December: Financial Training Examinations – Old Hall.

16 December: *The Economist* Conference and Exhibition – New Hall.

31 December: Lord of Mayor of Westminster's Party, Private Function – Both Halls.

1989

29 January: Antiques Trade Fair organised by Step-In Exhibitions – Old Hall.

1-2 February: 8th *Sunday Times* Wine Festival – Old Hall.

7 February: Babyware Exhibition – New Hall.

7-15 February: The Law Society Examinations – Old Hall.

11-12 February: Pin Table '89 organised by Alan Goldsmith Ltd – New Hall.

13-14 February: 6th Coys Auction of Veteran, Vintage & Classic Vehicles – New Hall.

28 February-5 March: 38th Spring STAMPEX (BPE) – Both Halls.

17-18 March: 9th Wine Festival – organised by the Direct *Sunday Times* Wine Club – New Hall.

c.April: 1st Adams Antique Fair organised by Matthew Adams – Old Hall.

21 March: NUT – Old Hall.

25-30 March: 64th The Model Railway Club's International Model Railway Exhibition – Both Halls.

1 April: Alternative Micro Show – New Hall.

1-2 April: 9th British Mineral & Gem Show organised by Earth Science Promotions – Old Hall.

3-7 April: Royal Institute of Chartered Surveyors Examinations – Old Hall.

12-19 April: The Insurance Institute of London Examinations – Both Halls.

18-20 April: Chance Entertainment – Old Hall.

20-3 April: Westminster Antiques Fair organised by Penman Antiques Fairs – Old Hall.

7 May: 5th Photographica '89 – Old Hall.

8-10 May: The Institute of Taxation Examinations – Old Hall.

14 May: 2nd Adams Antiques Fair – Old Hall.

18-21 May: Direct Design & British Contemporary Furniture Exhibition – New Hall.

23-5 May: Institute of Legal Executives Examinations – Old Hall.

25-9 May: 14th Festival for Mind Body Spirit organised by New Life Designs – New Hall.

29 May-1 June: Car Clinic – Old Hall.

2-9 June: University of London Examinations – Old Hall.

6-9 June: Financial Training (London) Ltd Examinations – New Hall.

10-16 June: The Chartered Association of Certified Accountants Examinations – Both Halls.

19-23 June: Association of Accounting Technicians Examinations – Old Hall.

25 June: 3rd Adams Antiques Fair – Old Hall.

4-12 July: College of Law Examinations – Both Halls.

24 July-15 September: Tale of Two Cities (to mark the Bicentenary of the French Revolution) organised by Manorial Research plc – Old Hall.

24 July: Auction of Vintage, Veteran & Classic Vehicles organised by Coys – New Hall.

29 July: 54th Kensington Kitten & Neuter Cat Club Show – New Hall.

1-4 September: 3rd Sports Sale organised by Ellis Brigham Ltd – New Hall.

22-4 September: Photo Video Show organised by City Camera Exchange – New Hall.

24 September: 4th Adams Antique Fair – Old Hall.

26-7 September: Coppas Films (location filming) – New Hall.

27 September-3 October: Direct Sale organised by Goldsmith Company – Old Hall.

29-30 September: 9th London Exhibition of Early Musical Instruments – New Hall.

2-4 October: Royal Institute of Chartered Surveyors Examinations – New Hall.

17-22 October: 39th STAMPEX (BPE) organised by Stampex Ltd – Both Halls.

24-6 October: Institute of Legal Executives Examinations – Old Hall.

25 October: TV Production – New Hall.

27 October: RISVI – New Hall.

27 October: Financial Training (London) Ltd Examinations – Old Hall.

28 October: Annual Transport Spectacular Bazaar organised by the London Omnibus Traction Society – Old Hall.

29 October: 5th Antiques Trade Fair – Old Hall.

30-1 October: Royal College of General Practitioners Examinations – Old Hall.

5 November: Record Convention organised by Sound Publishing – Old Hall.

6-8 November: Institute of Taxation Examinations – Old Hall.

10-13 November: International Partnership Fair organised by The Trust for Education & Development – Both Halls.

13-14 November: Christmas Gift Fair organised by Cancer Relief Macmillan Fund – Old Hall.

19 November: 6th Adams Antiques Fair – Old Hall.

21 November: Royal Institute of Chartered Surveyors Examinations – Old Hall.

22-3 November: Wavetrade organised by Focus Events – New Hall.

25-6 November: Homebrew organised by Collins' Consultants – Old Hall.

30 November: Food & Drink Co. – Old Hall.

5 December: 7th Coys Auction of Veteran, Vintage and Classic Vehicles – New Hall.

4-8 December: Association of Accounting Technicians Examinations – Old Hall.

14 December: Council of Legal Education Examinations – New Hall.

17 December: 7th Adams Antiques Fair – Old Hall.

31 December: Lord of Mayor of Westminster's Party, Private Function – Old Hall.

31 December: New Years Eve Ball Brittanic Investments – New Hall.

1990

12-14 January: 16 Bit Show organised by Westminster Exhibitions – Both Halls.

21 January: 8th Adams Antiques Fair – Old Hall.

27-8 January: Drawing Office Material Manufacturers & Dealers Association Ltd (DOMMDA) – Old Hall.

1-5 February: 1st Colefax & Fowler Sale – Old Hall.

1-8 February: The Law Society Examinations – New Hall.

10 February: All Formats Computer Fair organised by Bruce Everiss – New Hall.

11 February: 9th Adams Antiques Fair – Old Hall.

14 February: 8th Coys Auction of Veteran, Vintage & Classic Vehicles – Both Halls.

27 February-4 March: 40th Spring STAMPEX (BPE) – Both Halls.

7 March: The Council of Legal Education Examinations – New Hall.

16-17 March: 10th *Sunday Times* Wine Festival – New Hall.

17 March: Play by Mail Convention – Old Hall.

18 March: 10th Adams Antiques Fair – Old Hall.

23-5 March: What Video Camcorder User Show – Both Halls.

4-11 April: The Insurance Institute of London Examinations – Both Halls.

10 April: Abbey National AGM – Old Hall.

14-19 April: 65th International Model Railway Exhibition – Both Halls.

27 April: Institute of Actuaries Examinations – Old Hall.

29 April: 11th Adams Antiques Fair – Old Hall.

2-6 May: Westminster Antiques Fair organised Penman Antiques Fairs – Old Hall.

8-9 May: The Royal College of General Practitioners Examinations – Old Hall.

10-12 May: Filming – Old Hall.

13 May: 6th Photographica – Old Hall.

14-16 May: Institute of Taxation Examinations – Old Hall.

20-2 May: 12th Adams Antiques Fair – Old Hall.

24-8 May: The First Green Consumer Exhibition organised by New Life Designs – Old Hall.

24-8 May: 15th Festival for Mind Body Spirit organised by New Life Designs – New Hall.

1-15 June: University of London Examinations – Old Hall.

5-8 June: Financial Training (London) Ltd Examinations – New Hall.

9-10 June: All Formats Computer Fair – New Hall.

12 June: ABTA Examinations – New Hall.

18-22 June: Association of Accounting Technicians Examinations – Old Hall.

23 June: Conservative Women's National Conference – New Hall.

24 June: Antiques Fair organised by Adams Antiques Fairs – Old Hall.

28 June-1 July: 16 Bit Show organised by Westminster Exhibitions – Both Halls.

3-11 July: College of Law Examinations – Both Halls.

12 July: BP Exploration Britoil plc Party – Old Hall.

28 July: 55th Kensington Kitten & Neuter Cat Club Show – New Hall.

4-5 August: All Formats Computer Show organised by Bruce Everiss – New Hall.

1-2 September: All Formats Computer Show organised by Bruce Everiss – New Hall.

2 September: 13th Adams Antiques Fair – Old Hall.

7-9 September: BBC Acorn User Show – organised by Safesell Exhibitions – New Hall.

7-9 September: 4th Sports Sale organised by Ellis Brigham Ltd – Old Hall.

21-3 September: Autumn Photo Video Show organised by City Camera Exchange – New Hall.

26-7 September: National Cancer Week Event – Old Hall.

29 September: National Shoe Repair Exhibition – New Hall.

29 September: Small Press Group Exhibition – Old Hall.

30 September: 14th Antiques Fair organised by Adams Antiques Fairs – Old Hall.

2-3 October: Royal Institute of Chartered Surveyors Examinations – Both Halls.

16-21 October: 41st Autumn STAMPEX (BPE) organised by Stampex Ltd – Both Halls.

23-5 October: Institute of Legal Executives Examinations – Old Hall.

26 October: Financial Training Company Examinations – Old Hall.

27 October: Annual Transport Spectacular organised by London Omnibus Traction Society – Old Hall.

28 October: 15th Antiques Fair organised by Adams Antiques Fairs – Old Hall.

29-30 October: Royal College of General Practitioners Examinations – Old Hall.

1-3 November: National Honey Show – Old Hall.

4 November: All Formats Computer Show organised by Bruce Everiss – New Hall.

5-7 November: Institute of Taxation Examinations – Old Hall.

8-11 November: 3rd Healing Arts organised by New Life Designs – Old Hall.

11 November: 1st Record Convention – Old Hall.

12-13 November: Royal Institute of Chartered Surveyors Examinations – New Hall.

13-14 November: Christmas Market organised by Cancer Relief Macmillan Fund – Old Hall.

16-18 November: Global Partnership '90 organised by The Trust for Education and Development – New Hall.

19-20 November: 16th Antiques Fair organised by Adams Antiques Fairs – Old Hall.

25 November: Antiques Fair organised by Adams Antiques Fairs – Old Hall.

30 November-4 December: Furniture Exhibition – Old Hall.

3-7 December: Association of Accounting Technicians Examinations – New Hall.

12 December: 9th Coys Auction of Important Historic and Sporting Cars – New Hall.

15 December: Wedding Reception organised by Miss L. Hussian – New Hall.

16 December: 17th Antiques Fair organised by Adams Antiques Fairs – Old Hall.

22 December: All Formats Computer Show organised by Bruce Everiss – New Hall.

28-9 December: 17th British Open Darts Championships organised by the British Darts Organisation – Both Halls.

31 December: New Years Eve Celebration organised by Youth Music for the World – Both Halls.

1991

4 January: Location filming by KM Films Ltd – New Hall.

6 January: 18th Antiques Fair organised by Adams Antiques Fairs – Old Hall.

23-6 January: 2nd Colefax & Fowler Fabric Sale – Old Hall.

2 February: Play by Mail Convention organised by the British PBM Association – Old Hall.

2 February: All Formats Computer Fair organised by Bruce Everiss – New Hall.

3 February: 19th Antiques Fair organised by Adams Antiques Fairs – Old Hall.

6-8 February: *Government Purchasing* Exhibition – New Hall.

5-13 February: The Law Society Examinations – Old Hall.

26 February-3 March: 42nd Spring STAMPEX (BPE) organised by Stampex Ltd – Both Halls.

16 March: School Fair '91 organised by the London Tourist Board – Old Hall.

17 March: 20th Antiques Fair organised by Adams Antiques Fairs – Old Hall.

20 March: 10th Coys Auction of Veteran, Vintage & Classic Vehicles – New Hall.

23 March: All Formats Computer Fair organised by Bruce Everiss – New Hall.

24 March: Record Convention organised by P. & J. Promotions – New Hall.

30 March-4 April: 66th The Model Railway Club's International Model Railway – Both Halls.

11-17 April: The Insurance Institute of London Examinations – Both Halls.

19-20 April: 11th *Sunday Times* Wine Festival – New Hall.

21 April: 21st Antiques Fair organised by Adams Antiques Fairs – Old Hall.

24-8 April: Westminster Antiques Fair organised by Penman Antiques Fairs.

4 May: Spring Transport Spectacular organised by the London Omnibus Traction Society – Old Hall.

5 May: 22nd Antiques Fair organised by Adams Antiques Fairs – Old Hall.

7-8 May: Royal College of General Practitioners Examinations – Old Hall.

12 May: 7th Photographica – Old Hall.

13-15 May: The Institute of Taxation Examinations – Old Hall.

21-3 May: The Institute of Legal Executives Examinations – Old Hall.

23-7 May: 16th Festival for Mind Body Spirit – New Hall.

31 May-14 June: University of London Examinations – Old Hall.

2 June: 23rd Antiques Fair organised by Adams Antiques Fairs – Old Hall.

11-14 June: Financial Training (London) Ltd Examinations – New Hall.

17-21 June: Association of Accounting Technicians Examinations – Old Hall.

23 June: Comic Fair organised by Mr Rob Barrow – Old Hall.

25 June: 11th Coys Auction of British & Continental Touring Cars – Old Hall.

30 June: 24th Antiques Fair organised by Adams Antiques Fairs – Old Hall.

Halls closed for refurbishment during July, August and re-opened on 15 September.

16-18 August: Motor Cycle Show organised by Mead Speed of Newport Pagnell, Bucks. (Originally booked but did not take place because of Hall closure.)

15-20 September: 43rd Autumns STAMPEX (BPE) organised by Stampex Ltd – Both Halls.

21-5 September: Traditional Handicrafts of Japan (part of The Japan Festival) – Old Hall.

3 October: Official re-launch of the Royal Horticultural Society's Halls following a £1 million refurbishment and facelift and a re-branding exercise. This included the transformation of the rooms in the New Hall to a modern Conference Centre facility and a new corporate identity to The Royal Horticultural Halls & Conference Centre. Just prior to this it had been called the Westminster Exhibition Centre. The re-launch was organised by René Dee, the then Sales & Marketing Manager for Horticultural Halls Limited with The Lord Mayor of Westminster, Dame Shirley Porter and Lord Pitt, Vice-President of the London Tourist Board and Convention Bureau formally opening the new facilities. The event was attended by over 150 primary exhibition and conference industry leaders.

31 October-2 November: National Honey Show opened by David Maclean MP, Minister For Food – Old Hall. (This was the last time the NHS used the RHS.)

26-9 September: 4th Healing Arts – New Hall.

8-10 November: 10th The London International Exhibition of Early Music – New Hall.

14-16 November: European Model Railway Exhibition – CONTEX organised by Peco Publications of Beer, Seaton, Devon – Old Hall.

11 December: 12th Coys Auction of British & Continental Touring Cars – Old Hall.

Date Unknown: Price Waterhouse Christmas Dinner Dance.

Date Unknown: Bank Credit Suisse Christmas Dinner Dance.

Date Unknown: BUPA Christmas Dinner Dance.

Date Unknown: Bank of Bilbao Christmas Dinner Dance.

Date Unknown: Philips and Drew Christmas Dinner Dance.

Date Unknown: The PGA Annual Tour Dinner.

Date Unknown: The Producers Alliance to Cinema and Television Dinner Dance.

Date Unknown: Corinthian Casuals Football Club Fundraising Ball.

1992

18 January: All Formats Computer Fair – New Hall.

19 January: 1st Antique Dolls Fair (organised by Judy Bebber) – Old Hall.

19 January: 25th Adam's Antique Fair – New Hall.

23-5 January: Lloyds (Howard Evans, Business Briefings) – New Hall.

28-9 January: RHS Flower Show – New Hall.

1 February: African Cultural Evening (organised by Ivy Frimpong) – New Hall.

1-2 February: 3rd Colefax and Fowler Fabric Sale – Old Hall.

4-12 February: The Law Society Examinations – New Hall.

8 February: The British PBM Association, Play By Mail Convention – Old Hall.

9 February: 26th Adams Antique Fair – Old Hall.

13 February: By Word of Mouth Charity Ball – Old Hall.

14 February: The Macmillan Nurse Appeal Ball – Old Hall.

14 February: Cultural Event (Mr B.A. Miga) – New Hall.

18 February: RHS AGM – Old Hall.

19 February: RHS Lecture – Old Hall.

18-19 February: RHS Flower Show – New Hall.

21 February: 'About Last Night' Valentine's Ball – Old Hall.

21 February: 44th Spring STAMPEX (BPE) – Both Halls.

7-8 March: RHS British Orchid Growers' Association – Old Hall.

7-8 March: RHS Flower Show – New Hall.

14 March: All Formats Computer Fair (Mr Bruce Everiss) – New Hall.

17-18 March: 13th Coys of Kensington Car Auction – New Hall.

14 –15 March: Harvey Nichols – Clothing Sale – Old Hall.

20 March: Iranian New Year Celebration (organised by Iranian Embassy) – Old Hall.

20-1 March: 12th *Sunday Times* Wine Festival (Wine Club) – New Hall.

22 March: 27th Adams Antique Fair – Old Hall.

28-9 March: P. & J. Promotions – Record Convention – New Hall.

2-3 April: 1st ABTT (Association of British Theatre Technicians) Trade Fair – Old Hall.

7-8 April: RHS Flower Show – Both Halls.

9-15 April: Chartered Insurance Institute of London Examinations – Both Halls.

18-22 April: 67th The Model Railway Club's International Model Railway Exhibition (organised by Hobby Publicity Ltd) – Both Halls.

28-9 April: RHS Flower Show – New Hall.

26 April: 28th Adams Antique Fair – Old Hall.

30 April-3 May: Penman Antiques Westminster Fair – Old Hall.

6 May: Royal College of General Practitioners Examinations – Old Hall.

7-8 May: 1st The Museums and Heritage Show – New Hall.

9 May: Spring Transport Spectacular, London Omnibus Traction Society – Old Hall.

10 May: 29th Adams Antiques Fair – Old Hall.

12-13 May: The Institute of Taxation Examinations – Old Hall.

16 May: All Formats Computer Fair (Mr Bruce Everiss) – New Hall.

16 May: Australian Wine Centre Wine Festival – Old Hall.

18 May: 8th Photographica – New Hall.

19-21 May: Institute for Legal Executives Examinations – Old Hall.

21-5 May: 17th Festival for Mind Body Spirit – New Hall.

24 May: Antique Doll Fair – Old Hall.

25-7 May: Bartle Bogle Hegarty, Advertising Agency 10th Birthday Dinner/Dance – Old Hall.

1-12 June: University of London Examinations – Old Hall.

9-12 June: Financial Training (London) Ltd Examinations – New Hall.

16-17 June: RHS Flower Show – New Hall.

15-19 June: Association of Accounting Technicians Examinations – Old Hall.

21 June: 30th Adams Antiques Fair – Old Hall.

23-4 June: 14th Coys of Kensington Car Auction – New Hall.

26-7 June: Homes and Gardens Show – Old Hall.

28 June: Comic Fair (organised by Mr Rob Barrow) – Old Hall.

1-8 July: College of Law Examinations – New Hall.

12 July: 31st Adams Antique Fair – Old Hall.

14 July: RHS Lecture – Old Hall.

14-15 July: RHS Flower Show – New Hall.

15-18 July: 15th Coys of Kensington Classic Car Auction – Old Hall.

20 July: Special Conference of the Labour Party to elect John Smith as the new Labour Leader and Margaret Beckett as his Deputy following Neil Kinnock – New Hall.

25 July: 57th Kensington Kitten & Neuter Cat Club Show – Old Hall (last event in the RHS Hall).

11-12 August: RHS Flower Show – New Hall.

30 August: 32nd Adams Antique Fair – Old Hall.

1-2 September: Dahlia Flower Show – New Hall.

3-6 September: 6th Ellis Brigham Sports Equipment Sale – Old Hall.

5-6 September: Toy Soldiers Fair – New Hall.

7-11 September: Facilities Management Trade Exhibition – New Hall.

15-16 September: RHS Flower Show – Both Halls.

17 September: The National Society for Epilepsy Operatic Evening – Old Hall.

19 September: Small Press Group, Publishing Fair – Old Hall.

19-20 September: Record Fair – New Hall.

20 September: 33rd Adams Antique Fair – Old Hall.

23-5 September: Flexible Training Showcase opened by Gillian Shepherd – Old Hall.

23-8 September: 5th Healing Arts Exhibition – New Hall.

27 September: Antique Dolls Fair – Old Hall.

30 September: 16th Coys of Kensington Auction of Sports & Touring Cars – Old Hall.

3-7 October: 34th Adams Antiques Fair – Old Hall.

6-7 October: RHS Flower Show – New Hall.

13-18 October: 45th Autumn STAMPEX (BPE) Stamp Fair – Both Halls.

22-8 October: Chartered Insurance Institute Examinations – Both Halls.

27-9 October: Institute of Legal Executives Examinations – Old Hall.

29-30 October: Channel 4 Television 10th Birthday Party – New Hall.

30 October: Financial Training Examinations – Old Hall.

31 October: London Omnibus Traction Society Hobby Fair – Old Hall.

1 November: 35th Adams Antique Fair – Old Hall.

3-4 November: RHS Flower Show – New Hall.

2-4 November: Institute of Taxation Examinations – Old Hall.

6-7 November: Chrysanthemum Show – New Hall.

10 November: Royal Institute of Chartered Surveyors Examinations – New Hall.

11 November: 5th Cancer Relief Macmillan Fund Charity Fundraising Show – New Hall.

12-14 November: 1st *Homes and Gardens* Grand Furnishings Show – Old Hall.

24-5 November: RHS Flower Show – New Hall.

23-4 November: Elegant Homes Exhibition – Old Hall.

26-9 November: Photo Video Show – New Hall.

27-8 November: You and Your Family Exhibition – Old Hall.

29 November: 2nd Antique Dolls Fair – Old Hall.

30 November: 36th Adams Antiques Fair – Old Hall.

1-3 December: Association of Accounting Technicians Examinations – New Hall.

2-5 December: Penman Westminster Antique Fair – Old Hall.

9 December: 17th Coys of Kensington Classic Car Auction – New Hall.

8 December: University of Westminster Examinations – Old Hall.

10-12 December: Mask Entertainment, Christmas Dinner Dance – Old Hall.

13 December: 37th Adams Antique Fairs – New Hall.

15-16 December: Mask Entertainment, Christmas Dinner Dance – Old Hall.

1993

17 January: 3rd Antique Dolls Fair – Old Hall.

26-7 January: RHS Flower Show – New Hall.

24 January: 38th Adams Antique Fairs – Old Hall.

25-31 January: 4th Colefax and Fowler Fabric Sale – Old Hall.

14 February: 39th Adams Antique Fairs – Old Hall.

14-18 February: 1st Commercial Flooring Exhibition – New Hall.

15-18 February: Design and Art Directors Association Exhibition – Old Hall.

23-4 February: RHS AGM and Lecture – Old Hall.

23-4 February: RHS Flower Show – New Hall.

2-7 March: 46th Spring STAMPEX (BPE) Stamp Fair – Both Halls.

13-14 March: British Orchid Growers' Association – Old Hall.

11 March: The Red Balloon Ball in aid of the British Lung Foundation Annual Fundraising Dinner Dance – New Hall.

16-17: March RHS Flower Show – New Hall.

15-17 March: Elegant Homes Exhibition – Old Hall.

19-21 March: 13th *Sunday Times* Wine Festival – New Hall.

22 March: 18th Coys of Kensington Auction of British & Continental Collectors' Cars – Old Hall.

28 March: 40th Adams Antique Fair – Old Hall.

1-2 April: Royal Institute of Chartered Surveyors Examinations – Old Hall.

3-4 April: Record Fair – New Hall.

4 April: Antique Dolls Fair – Old Hall.

10-14 April: 68th The Model Railway Club's International Model Railway Exhibition (organised by Hobby Publicity) – Both Halls.

17 April: London Marathon Pasta Party – New Hall.

20-1 April: RHS Flower Show – Both Halls.

22-8 April: Chartered Insurance Institute Examinations – New Hall.

25 April: 41st Adams Antique Fair – Old Hall.

27-30 April: 2nd Association of British Theatre Technicians' Trade Fair – Old Hall.

5 May: Royal College of General Practitioners Examinations – Old Hall.

8 May: London Omnibus Traction Society Hobby Fair – Old Hall.

9 May: 9th Photographica Camera Show – New Hall.

10-12 May: Institute of Taxation Examinations – Old Hall.

10-14 May: The Live Show Exhibition – New Hall.

13 May: European Community Examinations – Old Hall.

15 May: Australian Wine Tasting – New Hall.

16 May: 1st Family History Fair organised by The Society of Genealogists – Old Hall.

18-19 May: 2nd Museums and Heritage Show – New Hall.

22-31 May: 18th Festival for Mind Body Spirit organised by New Life Designs – New Hall.

23 May: 42nd Adams Antique Fair – Old Hall.

1-3 June: 1st Professional Fundraising Exhibition – Old Hall.

4-18 June: London University Examinations – Old Hall.

8-11 June: Financial Training Examinations – New Hall.

14-17 June: 1st *Government Computing* Exhibition and Conference – New Hall.

20 June: 43rd Adams Antique Fair – Old Hall.

24-7 June: Westminster Antiques Fair – Old Hall.

21-7 June: 5th Colefax and Fowler Fabric Sale – New Hall.

*c.*July: 1st Dedicated Conference Centre brochure produced.

6-8 July: Guardian Student Expo Fair – Old Hall.

6-14 July: College of Law Examinations – New Hall.

11 July: 44th Adams Antique Fair – Old Hall.

20 July: RHS Lecture – Old Hall.

20-1 July: RHS Flower Show – New Hall.

11-13 August: RHS Flower Show – New Hall.

30-1 August: National Dahlia Society Flower Show – New Hall.

29 August: 45th Adams Antique Fair – Old Hall.

1 September: National Dahlia Society Flower Show – New Hall.

2-5 September: 7th Ellis Brigham Sports Equipment Sale – Old Hall.

8 September: 19th Coys of Kensington Auction of Sports & Touring Cars – Old Hall.

8-9 September: International Record Fair – New Hall.

14-15 September: RHS Flower Show – Both Halls.

19 September: 46th Adams Antique Fairs – Old Hall.

25 September: Special Press Group, Publishers Trade Show – Old Hall.

25 September: Stonewall Anniversary Party – New Hall.

26 September: Antique Dolls Fair – Old Hall.

1 October: 'The Big Breakfast' 1st Anniversary Party – New Hall.

5-6 October: RHS Flower Show – Both Halls.

12-17 October: 47th Autumn STAMPEX (BPE) Stamp Fair –Both Halls.

20-1 October: French Wine Tasting – Old Hall.

20-7 October: Chartered Insurance Institute Examinations – New Hall.

22-3 October: The Dental Systems Supplies Association Annual Trade Fair – Old Hall.

26-8 October: Institute of Legal Executives Examinations – Old Hall.

30 October: London Omnibus Traction Society – Old Hall.

30-1 October: RHS Flower Show – New Hall.

31 October: 47th Adams Antique Fair – Old Hall.

1-3 November: Institute of Taxation Examinations – Old Hall.

2-3 November: RHS Flower Show – New Hall.

5-6 November: Chrysanthemum Society Flower Show – New Hall.

9 November: Royal Institute of Chartered Surveyors Examinations – New Hall.

10-11 November: 6th Cancer Relief Macmillan Fund Charity Fundraising Event – New Hall.

13 November: 11th International Early Music Show, Musical Instruments Show – New Hall. (Organised by the Early Music Shop, Bradford, Yorks. Last time with the RHS.)

14 November: 48th Adams Antique Fairs – Old Hall.

17 November: Portland Hospital Private Reception – Old Hall.

18-20 November: 2nd *Homes and Gardens* Grand Furnishings Show – New Hall.

23-4 November: RHS Flower Show – New Hall.

26 November: Department of Environment Staff Conference – New Hall. This was a briefing by John Gummer, M.P., to his staff prior to them relocating from the three towers in Westminster to Docklands.

28 November: 4th Antique Dolls Fair – Old Hall.

2-5 December: Westminster Antiques Fair – Both Halls.

1-6 December: 6th Healing Arts Exhibition – New Hall.

6-10 December: Association of Accounting Technicians Examinations – Old Hall.

12 December: 49th Adams Antique Fair – Old Hall.

15 December: 20th Coys of Kensington Classic Car Auction – Old Hall.

17-18 December: RHS Flower Show – New Hall.

1994

18-19 January: Performance Industry Trade Show LIVE – New Hall.
25-6 January: RHS Flower Show – New Hall.
23 January: 50th Adams Antique Fair – Old Hall.
25-9 January: 5th Colefax and Fowler Fabric Sale – Old Hall.
29-30 January: International Record Fair – New Hall.
6 February: 5th Antique Dolls Fair – Old Hall.
9-10 February: Virgin Atlantic Hong Kong Route Launch – Old Hall.
12 February: Filipino Women's Association Fundraising Function – Old Hall.
15-17 February: 2nd Commercial Flooring Exhibition – New Hall.
13 February: 51st Adams Antique Fair – Old Hall.
22-3 February: Boum Balls Student Ball – Old Hall.
22-3 February: RHS Flower Show – New Hall.
22 February: RHS AGM and Lecture – Old Hall.
1-6 March: 48th Spring STAMPEX Stamp Fair – Old Hall.
1-6 March: 48th Spring STAMPEX Stamp Fair – New Hall.
8-10 March: Spanish Wine Tasting – New Hall.
12-13 March: British Orchid Growers' Association Flower Show – Old Hall.
12-13 March: RHS Flower Show – New Hall.
14-15 March: Witan Investments AGM and Reception – Old Hall.
19 March: Andersen Consulting Dinner Dance – New Hall.
21 March: 21st Coys of Kensington Classic Car Auction – Old Hall.
27 March: 52nd Adams Antique Fair – Old Hall.
2-6 April: 69th International Model Railway Exhibition – Both Halls.
12-13 April: RHS Flower Show – Both Halls.
14-17 April: 14th *Sunday Times* Wine Festival – New Hall.
17 April: Antique Dolls Fair – Old Hall.
21-2 April: 3rd Association of British Theatre Technicians Trade Fair ABTT – Old Hall.
24 April: 53rd Adams Antique Fairs – Old Hall.
25-30 April: Westminster Antiques Fair – Old Hall.
29-30 April: RHS Flower Show – New Hall.
1 May: Westminster Antiques Fair – Old Hall.
1-4 May: RHS Flower Show – New Hall.
3-4 May: Royal College of General Practitioners Examinations – Old Hall.
5-6 May: French Wine Tasting – Old Hall.
7 May: London Omnibus Traction Society Hobby Fair – Old Hall.
7-8 May: 2nd Family History Fair – Old Hall.
8 May: 10th Photographica Camera Show – Old Hall.
9-11 May: Institute of Taxation Examinations – Old Hall.
12 May: John Smith dies.
9-13 May: 1st The Creative Show Exhibition – New Hall.
14 May: Australian Wine Tasting – New Hall.
17-18 May: 3rd Museum and Heritage Show – Both Halls.
21-30 May: 19th Mind Body Spirit Festival – New Hall.
22 May: 54th Adams Antique Fair – Old Hall.
1-2 June: 2nd Professional Fundraising Exhibition – Old Hall.
11-12 June: Record & CD Collectors' Fair – New Hall.
15 June: 22nd Coys of Kensington British & Continental Touring Cars Auction – Old Hall.
15-16 June: 2nd *Government Computing* Exhibition and Conference – New Hall.
18-22 June: RHS Flower Show – New Hall.
19 June: 55th Adams Antique Fairs – Old Hall.
20-4 June: Association of Accounting Technicians Examinations – Old Hall.
25-6 June: Allen and Hanbury Pharmaceuticals – Both Halls.
1 July: Intercapital Brokers '1960s' Private Party (organised by Bentley's Entertainment) – New Hall.
3 July: Antique Dolls Fair – Old Hall.
4 – 6 July: Design and Art Directors Design Trade Fair – Old Hall.

10 July: 56th Adams Antique Fair – Old Hall.
19-20 July: RHS Flower Show – New Hall.
19 July: RHS Lecture – Old Hall.
16 – 17 August: RHS Flower Show – New Hall.
28 August: 57th Adams Antique Fair – Old Hall.
30 August – 3 September: The 1894/1994 Picture Postcard Centenary Exhibition – Both Halls.
4 September: Antique Dolls Fair – Old Hall.
6-7 September: National Dahlia Society Flower Show – New Hall.
13-14 September: RHS Flower Show – Both Halls.
15-18 September: 8th Ellis Brigham Sports Equipment Sale – Old Hall.
17-18 September: Record & CD Collectors' Fair – New Hall.
20 September: 23rd Coys of Kensington British & Continental Touring Cars Auction – Old Hall.
21-2 September: Information Technology in Local Government – New Hall.
24 September: Special Press Group, Publishing Fair – Old Hall.
25 September: 58th Adams Antique Fair – Old Hall.
29 September: 90th Anniversary Party for Old Hall – Old Hall.
4-5 October: RHS Flower Show – Both Halls.
6 October: The Foyer Federation Conference – New Hall.
11-16 October: 49th Autumn STAMPEX Stamp Fair – Both Hall.
20 October: 24th Coys of Kensington Classic Car Auction – Old Hall.
19-26 October: Chartered Insurance Institute Examinations – New Hall.
23 October: 59th Adams Antique Fair – Old Hall.
25-7 October: Institute of Legal Executives Examinations – Old Hall.
29 October: London Omnibus Traction Society Hobby Fair – Old Hall.
30-1 October: RHS Flower Show – New Hall.
31 October: Institute of Taxation Examinations – Old Hall.
1-2 November: Institute of Taxation Examinations – Old Hall.
1-2 November: RHS Flower Show – New Hall.
3-6 November: Chrysanthemum Flower Show – New Hall.
7-8 November: 7th Cancer Relief Macmillan Fund Charity Fundraising Event – New Hall.
9-14 November: 7th Healing Arts Exhibition – New Hall.
13 November: 60th Adams Antique Fair – Old Hall.
15-16 November: Jigsaw Fashion Show – Old Hall.
15-19 November: 3rd *Homes and Gardens* Shows – New Hall.
20-3 November: RHS Flower Show – New Hall.
24-7 November: SAGA Holidays Festival Promotion – New Hall.
25 November: Ultimate Experience Christmas Party – Old Hall.
26 November: SAGA Holidays Reception – Old Hall.
27 November: 6th Antique Dolls Fair – Old Hall.
28-31 November: Westminster Antiques Fair – Old Hall.
1 December: 25th Coys of Kensington Historic Collectors' Car Auction – New Hall.
1-4 December: Westminster Antiques Fair – Old Hall.
9-10 December: RHS Flower Show – New Hall.
7-9 December: Association of Accounting Technicians Examinations – Old Hall.
11 December: 61st Adams Antique Fair – Old Hall.
15-16 December: Effective Business Events Christmas Party – New Hall.
15-17 December: Events Etc Christmas Parties – Old Hall.

1995

8 January: Racing Pigeon Show – Old Hall.
12-13 January: Show '95 – New Hall.
17-18 January: The Live Show – New Hall.
19-20 January: Exhibition Partnership – Old Hall.
17-21 January: 6th Colefax and Fowler Fabric Sale – Old Hall.
24-5 January: RHS Flower Show – New Hall.

22 January: 62nd Adams Antique Fair – Old Hall.

24 January: 26th Coys of Kensington British & Continental Touring Car Auction – Old Hall.

26-8 January: Fabric Sale – Old Hall.

29 January: International Record Fair – New Hall.

5 February: 7th Antiques Dolls Fair – Old Hall.

12 February: 63rd Adams Antique Fair – Old Hall.

15-16 February: Design Week – New Hall.

21 February: RHS AGM and Lecture – Old Hall.

21-2 February: RHS Flower Show – New Hall.

28 February-5 March: 50th Spring STAMPEX (including AUSTRAPEX) Stamp Fair – Both Halls.

8-9 March: Spanish Wine Fair – New Hall.

11-12 March: RHS Orchid Show – Old Hall.

14-15 March: RHS Flower Show – New Hall.

11 March: Witan Investments AGM and Reception – Old Hall.

18-19 March: 15th *Sunday Times* Wine Festival – New Hall.

19 March: 64th Adams Antique Fair – Old Hall.

21-2 March: Canadian/USA Bus Exhibition – New Hall.

21 March: 27th Coys of Kensington Historic Collectors' Cars Auction – Old Hall.

26-8 March: Brown Goods Industry Show – Old Hall.

25-6 March: Collectors' Fair – New Hall.

29 March: Brox Corporation AGM – Old Hall.

29 March: National Union of Teachers' Conference and Rally – New Hall.

31 March-1 April: *Woman's Journal* – New Hall.

2 April: Antique Dolls Fair – Old Hall.

3-7 April: Chartered Insurance Institute Examinations – New Hall.

4-7 April: 4th Association of British Theatre Technicians – Old Hall.

11-12 April: RHS Flower Show – Both Halls.

13-19 April: 70th International Model Railway Exhibition – New Hall (last event held).

23 April: 65th Adams Antique Fair – Old Hall.

23 April: 11th Photographica Camera Show – New Hall.

26-9 April: Annual Exhibition of The Society of Amateur Artists – New Hall.

24-6 April: Energy Efficiency Housing '95 – Old Hall.

2-3 May: RHS Flower Show – New Hall.

2-3 May: Royal College of General Practitioners Examinations – Old Hall.

4-5 May: University College, London Examinations – Old Hall.

6-7 May: 3rd Family History Fair – New Hall.

9-11 May: Institute of Taxation Examinations – Old Hall.

12-13 May: World Conference Travel, BA Promotion – Old Hall.

13 May: Australian Wine Tasting – New Hall.

14-18 May: 2nd The Creative Show organised by Centaur Exhibitions – Both Halls.

20-9 May: 20th Mind Body Spirit Festival – New Hall.

21 May: 66th Adams Antique Fair – Old Hall.

25 May: Alternative Science Conference – Old Hall.

31 May-1 June: 3rd Professional Fundraising Exhibition – Old Hall.

5-16 June: London University Examinations – Old Hall.

6-9 June: The EXE Software Developers Show – New Hall.

10-11 June: International Record Fair – New Hall.

12-15 June: 3rd *Government Computing*, Exhibition and Conference – New Hall.

20-1 June: RHS Flower Show – New Hall.

18 June: 67th Adams Antique Fair – Old Hall.

20-1 June: Open Media TV Production – Old Hall.

27 June: 28th Coys of Kensington Historic Collectors Cars Auction – Old Hall.

4-6 July: Design and Art Directors Design Trade Fair – Old Hall.

7 July: Grandfield AGM – Old Hall.

15-19:July RHS Flower Show – New Hall.

16 July: 68th Adams Antique Fair – Old Hall.

17-18 July: RHS Lecture – Old Hall.

1-2 August: Red Rooster Films Filming – 'Red or Dead' fashion show – New Hall.

12-16 August: RHS Flower Show – New Hall.

27 August: 69th Adams Antique Fair – Old Hall.

30 August-2 September: 2nd Picture Postcard Show – New Hall.

3 September: Antique Dolls Fair – Old Hall.

5-6 September: National Dahlia Society Flower Show – New Hall.

12-13 September: RHS Flower Show – Both Halls.

16-17 September: International Record Fair – New Hall.

17 September: 70th Adams Antique Fair – Old Hall.

19 September: 29th Coys of Kensington Historic Motor Cars Auction – Old Hall.

18-21 September: Information Technology in Local Government – New Hall.

21-4 September: 9th Ellis Brigham Sports Equipment Sale – Old Hall.

3-4 October: RHS Flower Show – Both Halls.

10-15 October: 51st Autumn STAMPEX Stamp Fair – Both Halls.

17-18 October: Reed Publishing 'The Grocer' Awards & Dinner and Dance – New Hall.

19-22 October: Operation Bumblebee Police Roadshow – Old Hall.

19-22 October: Rural Crafts Craft Fair – New Hall.

23-7 October: Chartered Insurance Institute Examinations – New Hall.

24-6 October: Institute of Legal Executives Examinations – Old Hall.

27-8 October: Buckland Dix and Wood Coin Fair – Old Hall.

30-1 October: RHS Flower Show – New Hall.

29 October: 71st Adams Antique Fair – Old Hall.

1 November: 30th Coys of Kensington Classic Car Auction – Old Hall.

4-5 November: Chrysanthemum Show – New Hall.

4-5 November: The London Astronomy Show – Old Hall.

6 November: 8th Cancer Relief Macmillan Fund – New Hall.

6-8 November: Institute of Taxation Examinations – Old Hall.

9-12 November: 8th Healing Arts Exhibition – New Hall.

12 November: 72nd Adams Antique Fairs – Old Hall.

14-18 November: 4th *Homes and Gardens* Show – Old Hall.

16 November: Peabody Trust Reception – Old Hall.

21-2 November: RHS Flower Show – New Hall.

25 November: World Wildlife Fund Fundraising Promotion – Old Hall.

26 November: 8th Antique Dolls Fair – Old Hall.

27-30 November: GFT Clothing Show – Old Hall.

29-30 November: CIPFA Examinations – New Hall.

1-4 December: GFT Clothing show – Old Hall.

4-8 December: HPICM Product Launch – New Hall.

10 December: 73rd Adams Antique Fair – Old Hall.

11-12 December: RHS Flower Show – Both Halls.

14 December: 31st Coys of Kensington Classic Car Auction – Old Hall.

1996

6 January: Pigeon Show – Old Hall (last show to take place with the RHS).

10-15 January: SHOW '96 – Both Halls. (This was the first time ExCel displayed its new facility that had not yet been built.)

16-20 January: 7th Colefax and Fowler Fabric Sale – Old Hall.

23-4 January: RHS Flower Show – New Hall.

21 January: Australian Wine Tasting – Old Hall.

27 January: International Record Fair – New Hall.

28 January: 74th Adams Antique Fair – Old Hall.

30 January: 32nd Coys of Kensington Classic Car Auction – Old Hall.

1-5 February: Gorgeous Films, Sir Ian McKellen's *Richard III* – New Hall.

4 February: 9th Antique Dolls Fair – Old Hall.

11 February: 75th Adams Antique Fair – Old Hall.

20-1 February: RHS Flower Show – New Hall.

20 February: RHS AGM and Lecture – Old Hall.

29 February: International Record Fair – New Hall.

5-7 March: Spanish Wine Tasting – New Hall.

6-10 March: British Orchid Growers' Association Flower Show – Old Hall.

12-13 March: RHS Flower Show – New Hall.

11-12 March: Witan Investments AGM and Reception – Old Hall.

14 March: 33rd Coys of Kensington Classic Car Auction – Old Hall.

14-16 March: 16th *Sunday Times* Wine Fair – New Hall.

17 March: 76th Adams Antique Fair – Old Hall.

19-20 March: Network Fair – New Hall.

21-4 March: French Property Exhibition – Old Hall.

27-8 March: 4th Museum and Heritage Show – New Hall.

27-8 March: HM Prison Service Examinations – Old Hall.

31 March: Automobile Association Conference – Old Hall.

1-3 April: Energy Effective Housing – New Hall.

9-11 April: 5th Association of British Theatre Technicians – Old Hall.

13-17 April: RHS Flower Show – Old Hall.

13-17 April: RHS Flower Show – New Hall.

20 April: London Marathon Carbo Carnival – New Hall.

21 April: 77th Adams Antique Fair – Old Hall.

21 April: 12th Photographica Camera Show – Old Hall.

22-6 April: Chartered Insurance Institute Examinations – New Hall.

30 April-1 May: RHS Flower Show – New Hall.

1 May: 34th Coys of Kensington Classic Car Auction – Old Hall.

4-5 May: 4th Family History Fair – New Hall.

7-9 May: Royal College of General Practitioners Examinations – Old Hall.

14-16 May: 3rd The Creative Show – Both Halls.

18-27 May: 21st Mind Body Spirit Exhibition – New Hall.

19 May: 78th Adams Antique Fair – Old Hall.

25 May: Australian Wine Tasting – Old Hall.

1-4 June: Paramount Pictures Filming, *The Saint* feature film – New Hall.

1-14 June: University of London Examinations – Old Hall.

12-13 June: 4th *Government Computing* Exhibition and Conference – New Hall.

19-20 June: 4th Professional Fundraising Show – Old Hall.

23 June: 79th Adams Antique Fair – Old Hall.

28 June: Research Services Anniversary Dinner Dance – New Hall.

29 June: International Record Fair.

4-7 July: Jamaica Expo – New Hall.

9-13 July: Osborne and Little Fabrics Sale – Old Hall.

14 July: 80th Adams Antique Fair – Old Hall.

14 July: Cadbury's Strollerthon – New Hall.

23-4 July: RHS Flower Show – New Hall.

23 July: RHS Lecture – Old Hall.

8 August: Chartered Insurance Institute Examinations – New Hall.

20-1 August: RHS Flower Show – New Hall.

25 August: 81st Adams Antique Fair – Old Hall.

28-31 August: 3rd Picture Postcard Show – New Hall.

1 September: Antique Dolls Fair – Old Hall.

5 September: Chartered Insurance Institute Examinations – New Hall.

7-8 September: National Dahlia Society Flower Show – New Hall.

17-18 September: RHS Flower Show – Both Halls.

20-2 September: 10th Ellis Brigham Retail Sports Equipment Sale – Old Hall.

26-8 September: British Mycological Society Centenary Conversazione, 'FUNGUS 100' – Old Hall.

29 September: 82nd Adams Antique Fair – Old Hall.

3 October: 35th Coys of Kensington Classic Car Auction – New Hall.

3 October: Chartered Insurance Institute Examinations – Old Hall.

8-9 October: RHS Flower Show – Both Halls.

10-13 October: Rural Crafts Craft Fair – New Hall.

13 October: 83rd Adams Antique Fair – Old Hall.

14-18 October: Chartered Insurance Institute Examinations – Old Hall.

14-18 October: Research '96 Exhibition – New Hall.

22-4 October: Institute of Legal Executives Examinations – Old Hall.

27-31 October: Design '96 Exhibition organised by Centaur Exhibitions – New Hall.

1-3 November: London Astronomy Show – Old Hall.

2 November: International Record Fair – New Hall.

5-6 November: RHS Flower Show – New Hall.

4-6 November: Institute of Taxation Examinations – Old Hall.

7 November: Chartered Insurance Institute Examinations – New Hall.

7-10 November: Board-X 1st Skiboarding Show – Old Hall.

8-9 November: Anglo Latin American Foundation Fundraising Event – New Hall.

10-11 November: 9th Cancer Relief Macmillan Fund Fundraising Event – New Hall.

12-17 November: 9th Healing Arts Exhibition – New Hall.

17 November: 84th Adams Antique Fair – Old Hall.

18-23 November: 5th *Homes and Gardens* Show – New Hall.

20-3 November: Hispania Eurofair – Old Hall.

24 November: 10th Antique Dolls Fair – Old Hall.

24-7 November: RHS Flower Show – New Hall.

1-2 December: GFT Clothing Show – Old Hall.

3 December: 36th Coys of Kensington Classic Car Auction – New Hall.

5 December: Chartered Insurance Institute Examinations – New Hall.

9-10 December: RHS Flower Show – Both Halls.

15 December: 85th Adams Antique Fair – Old Hall.

1997

6-10 January: 1st King's College Examinations – New Hall.

9 January: Chartered Insurance Institute Examinations – Old Hall.

14-18 January: 8th Colefax and Fowler Fabric Sale – Old Hall.

21-2 January: RHS Flower Show – New Hall.

19 January: 86th Adams Antique Fair – Old Hall.

20-2 January: University of Westminster Examinations – Old Hall.

24-6 January: Independent Travellers World Exhibition – Both Halls.

28-9 January: What's New in Landscaping – New Hall.

1 February: International Record Fair – New Hall.

2 February: 11th Antique Dolls Fair – Old Hall.

6 February: Chartered Insurance Institute Examinations – New Hall.

9 February: 87th Adams Antique Fairs – Old Hall.

12-15 February: Inspirations – Old Hall.

18-19 February: RHS Flower Show – Both Halls.

22 February: Guides Associations – New Hall.

c.February: Alexander McQueen Spring/Summer Collection (*Les Poupées*) – New Hall.

23 February: 88th Adams Antique Fair – Old Hall.

25 February: 37th Coys of Kensington Classic Car Auction – Old Hall.

26-7 February: Network Fair Careers Exhibition – New Hall.

1 March: Partizan Filming – Robbie Williams *Old Before I Die* Pop Video – Old Hall.

2-3 March: Liberal Democrats Election Rally – Old Hall.

5-8 March: 1st London Stamp & Postal History Fair – New Hall (later to become known as The London International Stamp & Cover Show and finally PHILATEX. Organised by Trevor Davis and Chris Rainey, this show successfully replaced STAMPEX after they left abruptly in 1995!)

8-9 March: RHS Orchid Show – Old Hall.

13-15 March: PACE Government Exhibition – Old Hall.

18-19 March: RHS Flower Show – New Hall.

16 March: 89th Adams Antique Fair – Old Hall.

17-18 March: Witan Investments AGM and Reception – Old Hall.

19-22 March: MIATEX Exhibition – Old Hall.

20-2 March: Computing Careers Exhibition – New Hall.
23-6 March: 5th Museum and Heritage Show – New Hall.
25 March: College of Law Examinations – Old Hall.
28-30 March: London Tackle Show – New Hall.
1-3 April: 6th Association of British Theatre Technicians – Old Hall.
1-3 April: Wines from Spain – New Hall.
6 April: Antique Dolls Fair – Old Hall.
7-11 April: Chartered Insurance Institute Examinations – Old Hall.
8 April: Liberal Democrats Election Rally – New Hall.
15-16 April: RHS Flower Show – Both Halls.
17-20 April: 17th *Sunday Times* Wine Fair – New Hall.
20 April: 13th Photographica – Old Hall.
21-2 April: Nestle Torque d'Or Cuisine Fair – Old Hall.
26-30 April: RHS Flower Show – New Hall.
2-3 May: 5th Family History Fair – New Hall.
6-8 May: Royal College of General Practitioners Examinations – Old Hall.
6-9 May: King's College Examinations – New Hall.
12-16 May: King's College Examinations – New Hall.
18 May: 90th Adams Antique Fair – Old Hall.
19-22 May: King's College Examinations – New Hall.
20-2 May: 5th Professional Fundraising Show – Old Hall.
24 May-1 June: 22nd Mind Body Spirit Festival – New Hall.
27-9 May: King's College Examinations – Old Hall.
2-13 June: London University Examinations – Old Hall.
7 June: International Record Fair – New Hall.
12-13 June: Banshee, *Martha Meets Frank, Daniel & Lawrence*, feature film – New Hall.
18-19 June: 5th *Government Computing* Exhibition & Conference – New Hall.
18 June: VFN – Old Hall.
20 June: COL – New Hall.
22 June: 92nd Adams Antique Fair – Old Hall.
24-5 June: RHS Flower Show – New Hall.
25-6 June: 5th Professional Fundraising Show – Old Hall.
2-3 July: Design & Art Directors Advertising Awards – Old Hall.
2-3 July: RNPS – New Hall.
6-7 July: Jamaica Expo – Both Halls.
13 July: 93rd Adams Antique Fairs – Old Hall.
22-3 July: RHS Flower Show – New Hall.
22 July: RHS Lecture – Old Hall.
18-22 July: King's College Examinations – Old Hall.
19-20 August: RHS Flower Show – New Hall.
24 July: 94th Adams Antique Fairs – Old Hall.
14-15 August: Alomo Productions, *Mosley & The Blackshirts*, Channel 4 TV docu-drama – New Hall.
26-9 August: King's College Examinations – Old Hall.
27-30 August: 4th Picture Postcard Show – New Hall.
7 September: 12th Antique Dolls Fair – Old Hall.
7 September: The Dahlia Society Flower Show – New Hall.
9-11 September: WOSA – New Hall.
16-17 September: RHS Flower Show – Both Halls.
19-21 September: 11th Ellis Brigham Sports Equipment Sale – Old Hall.
25-7 September: London Brewers' Festival organised by the Association of London Brewers and Licensed Retailers – Old Hall.
26-8 September: Country Style Crafts Fair – New Hall.
28 September: 95th Adams Antiques Fair – Old Hall.
4 October: International Record Fair – New Hall.
7-8 October: RHS Flower Show – Both Halls.
10-12 October: Rural Crafts Exhibition – New Hall.
12 October: 96th Adams Antiques Fair – Old Hall.
15-17 October: 1st Market Research Exhibition – Both Halls.
19 October: TB – Old Hall.
21 October: 38th Coys Classic Car Auction – New Hall.
21-4 October: Chartered Insurance Institute Examinations – Old Hall.

28-30 October: The Design Show organised by Centaur Exhibitions – New Hall.
28-9 October: Institute of Legal Executives Examinations – Old Hall.
1-2 November: Practical Astronomy Show – Old Hall.
3-5 November: Institute of Taxation Examinations – Old Hall.
4-5 November: RHS Flower Show – New Hall.
8-9 November: Chrysanthemum Society Flower Show – New Hall.
10 November: 10th Cancer Relief Macmillan Fund Fundraising Event – New Hall.
13-16 November: 10th Healing Arts Festival – New Hall.
16 November: 97th Adams Antiques Fair – Old Hall.
20-2 November: 6th *Homes & Gardens* Christmas Market – Both Halls.
23 November: 13th Antique Dolls Fair – Old Hall.
25-6 November: RHS Flower Show – New Hall.
28-30 November: Link House – New Hall.
3 December: 39th Coys Classic Car Auction – New Hall.
5-7 December: Christmas Fair – Old Hall.
9 December: RHS Lecture – Old Hall.
9-10 December: RHS Flower Show – New Hall.
14 December: 98th Adams Antiques Fair – Old Hall.

1998

12 Adams Antiques Fairs throughout the year
*c.*January: 9th Colefax & Fowler Clothing Sale – Old Hall.
*c.*March: 2nd London Stamp & Postal History Fair – New Hall.
2 March: 40th Coys Auction of Important British and Continental Touring Cars – New Hall.
*c.*March: 6th Museums & Heritage Show – New Hall.
*c.*April: 7th ABTT Trade Show.
*c.*April: British Midland Commercial.
*c.*April/May: 18th *Sunday Times* Wine Fair – New Hall.
*c.*May: 6th Family History Fair – New Hall.
10 May: 14th Photographica – Old Hall.
23-31 May: 23rd Mind Body Spirit Festival – New Hall.
17-18 June: 6th *Government Computing* Exhibition – New Hall.
2-5 September: 5th Picture Postcard Show – New Hall.
*c.*September: 12th Ellis Brigham Sports Equipment Sale – Old Hall.
25 September: Antonio Berardi Fashion Show as part of London Fashion Week – Old Hall.
26 September: 41st Coys Auction of Important British and Continental Touring Cars – New Hall.
*c.*September: ITV Autumn Programme Schedules Launch – Old Hall.
25-8 October: London Remainder Book Fair – New Hall.
12-15 November: 11th Healing Arts Festival – New Hall.
*c.*November: 11th Cancer Relief Macmillan Fund Christmas Market – New Hall.
27-9 November: The International Festival of Chocolate – New Hall.
6 June: Vickers EGM – Old Hall.

1999

12 Adams Antiques Fairs throughout the year
*c.*January: 10th Colefax & Fowler Clothing Sale – Old Hall.
15 February: London Men's Fashion Week – Both Halls.
3-6 March: The London International Stamp & Cover Show – New Hall.
*c.*March: 7th Museums & Heritage Show – New Hall.
*c.*April: 8th ABTT Trade Show.
9 May: 15th Photographica – Old Hall.
*c.*April/May: 19th *Sunday Times* Wine Fair – New Hall.
*c.*May: 7th Family History Fair – New Hall.
22-31 May: 24th Mind Body Spirit Festival – New Hall.

16-17 June: 7th *Government Computing* Exhibition – New Hall (last show at RHS).

30 July-1 August: The 1st Organic Food and Wine Festival – New Hall.

13-15 August: The T.A.G. Sale organised by Michael Roosen – Old Hall (this was the last event to take place in the Old Hall before it closed for refurbishment. When the Hall re-opened it was re-named the Lindley Hall and the New Hall was renamed to the Lawrence Hall).

1-4 September: 6th Picture Postcard Show – Lawrence Hall.

c.September: 13th Ellis Brigham Sports Equipment Sale – Old Hall.

16-17 October: 7th London Wedding Show organised by Jeff Nyman – Lawrence Hall.

28-30 October: PHILATEX – Lawrence Hall.

11-14 November: 12th Healing Arts Festival – Lawrence Hall.

c.November: 12th Cancer Relief Macmillan Fund Christmas Market – Lawrence Hall.

3-5 December: The 2nd International Festival of Chocolate – Lawrence Hall.

31 December: Millennium Party for 700 of London's homeless, organised by 'Crisis' – Lawrence Hall.

2000

The Old Hall closed for refurbishment all year except for three days in November when the Institute of Taxation held their examinations in the Hall. The Hall was not finished and water came through the roof!

10-14 January: King's College Examinations – Lawrence Hall.

18-22 January: 11th Colefax & Fowler – Lawrence Hall.

25-6 January: RHS Flower Show – Lawrence Hall.

28-30 January: 14th Ellis Brigham Ski Grab Sale – Lawrence Hall.

15-16 February: RHS Flower Show – Lawrence Hall.

19 February: CD & Record Fair – Lawrence Hall.

20 February: 123rd Adams Antiques Fair – Lawrence Hall.

23-4 February: 8th Museums & Heritage Show – Lawrence Hall.

25 February: Peter Kerr Associates Paul Weiland Film Company – Lawrence Hall (Weetabix film commercial).

28 February: Labour Party Centenary Celebration organised by the National Trade Union and Labour Party Liaison Committee – Lawrence Hall.

2-4 March: PHILATEX 2000- Lawrence Hall.

5 March: 124th Adams Antiques Fair – Lawrence Hall.

14-15 March: RHS Flower Show – Lawrence Hall.

18-19 March: Orchid Show – Lawrence Hall.

20-2 March: Wines From Spain – Lawrence Hall.

26-7 March: California Wine – Lawrence Hall.

4-6 April: 9th ABTT – Lawrence Hall.

11-12 April: RHS Flower Show – Lawrence Hall.

13-16 April: 20th *Sunday Times* Wine Club – Lawrence Hall.

25-6 April: RHS Flower Show – Lawrence Hall.

30 April: 125th Adams Antiques Fair – Lawrence Hall.

2-3 May: Royal College of General Practitioners Exams – Lawrence Hall.

5-7 May: 8th Family History Fair – Lawrence Hall.

12-13 May: Record Fair – Lawrence Hall.

14 May: 16th Photographica – Lawrence Hall.

15-19 May: King's College London Examinations – Lawrence Hall.

20 May: Australian Wines – Lawrence Hall.

21 May: 126th Adams Antiques Fair – Lawrence Hall.

22-4 May: King's College London – Lawrence Hall.

23-31 May: 25th Mind Body Spirit Festival – Lawrence Hall.

9 June: King's College London Examinations – Lawrence Hall.

1 June: 127th Adams Antiques Fair – Lawrence Hall.

12-15 June: Institute of Chartered Accountants Examinations – Lawrence Hall.

20-1 June: RHS Flower Show – Lawrence Hall.

25-6 June: The Picture Business Live – Lawrence Hall.

30 June-2 July: Gant USA American Sportswear Sale – Lawrence Hall.

3-6 July: Food From Spain – Lawrence Hall.

7-8 July: 15th Ellis Brigham Hiking Boots Sale – Lawrence Hall.

9 July: 128th Adams Antiques Fair – Lawrence Hall.

11 July: Royal College of Veterinary Surgeons – Lawrence Hall.

13-14 July: Chartered Insurance Institute Examinations – Lawrence Hall.

26-30 July: Organic Food and Wine Festival – Lawrence Hall.

12 August: Record Fair – Lawrence Hall.

21-5 August: King's College Examinations – Lawrence Hall.

30 August-2 September: 7th Picture Postcard Show – Lawrence Hall.

3 September: 129th Adams Antiques Fair – Lawrence Hall.

4-6 September: Wines of Chile – Lawrence Hall.

8-13 September: RHS Flower Show – Lawrence Hall.

15-17 September: 16th Ellis Brigham Ski Grab Sale – Lawrence Hall.

23-5 September: Ciana – Lawrence Hall.

26-9 September: Employee Benefits Exhibition – Lawrence Hall.

3-4 October: RHS Flower Show – Lawrence Hall.

8 October: 130th Adams Antiques Fair – Lawrence Hall.

9-12 October: Dudley London Business Show – Lawrence Hall.

13-15 October: London Wedding Show – Lawrence Hall.

16-20 October: Chartered Insurance Institute Examinations – Lawrence Hall.

23-4 October: Members – Lawrence Hall.

25-6 October: PHILATEX – Lawrence Hall.

31 October-1 November: RHS Flower Show – Lawrence Hall.

2 November: National Mentoring Consortium – Lawrence Hall.

4 November: Record Fair – Lawrence Hall.

5 November: 131st Adams Antique Fair – Lawrence Hall.

6 November: 13th Macmillan Cancer Relief Fund Christmas Event – Lawrence Hall.

7-13 November: 13th Healing Arts – Lawrence Hall.

14-18 November: Grand Christmas Sale – Lawrence Hall.

20-3 November: PR Showcase – Lawrence Hall.

27-9 November: Gant UK Clothing Sale – Lawrence Hall.

30 November-4 December: GFT Great Britain Clothing Sale – Lawrence Hall.

5-9 December: Nicole Farhi Clothing Sale – Lawrence Hall.

12-13 December: RHS Flower Show – Lawrence Hall.

14-15 December: Just Communicate ref: BT – Lawrence Hall.

17 December: 132nd Adams Antiques Fair – Lawrence Hall.

18 December: Transport for London – Lawrence Hall.

2001

8-12 January: King's College Examinations – Lawrence Hall.

13-17 January: RHS Flower Show – Lawrence Hall.

21 January: 133rd Adams Antiques Fair – Lawrence Hall.

22-5 January: Wines of Australia – Lawrence Hall.

26-8 January: 17th Ellis Brigham Ski Grab Sale – Lawrence Hall.

29 January: Dewynters plc – Lawrence Hall.

30 January –3 February: 12th Colefax & Fowler Fabric Sale – Lawrence Hall.

9-14 February: RHS Flower Show – Lawrence Hall.

17-19 February: Margaret Howell Fashion Show – Lawrence Hall.

23-4 February: CD & Record Fair – Lawrence Hall.

25 February: 134th Adams Antiques Fair – Lawrence Hall.

26-7 February: California Wines – Lawrence Hall.

28 February-3 March: PHILATEX – Lawrence Hall.

5-8 March: 9th Museums & Heritage – Lawrence Hall.

15-18 March: Orchid Show – Lawrence Hall.

19-21 March: Wines from Spain – Lawrence Hall.

20 March: Formal re-opening and launch party of the refurbished Lindley Hall from what it was called before, i.e. The Old Hall, after 18 months closure. The event was organised by First Protocol and raised funds in aid of the homeless charity, Crisis. Six events took place before this in often difficult conditions.

These were the Institute of Taxation Exams, the Chartered Insurance Institute Exams, the Ellis Brigham Ski Sale, two RHS Flower Shows and the Paul Smith Fashion Show. The first official event following the re-launch was the Corporate Hospitality Association Annual Awards and Dinner on 23 March.

23 March: CHA Awards Dinner – Lindley Hall.

25 March: 135th Adams Antiques Fair – Lawrence Hall.

27-8 March: BBC Autumn Programme Launch – Lindley Hall.

6-11 April: RHS Flower Show – Both Halls.

15 April: 136th Adams Antiques Fair – Lawrence Hall.

18 April: City Financial Communication – Both Halls.

19-22 April: 21st *Sunday Times* Vintage Festival – Lawrence Hall.

23-6 April: Chartered Insurance Institute Examinations – Lindley Hall.

25-30 April: RHS Flower Show – Lawrence Hall.

1-2 May: Royal College of General Practitioners Examinations – Lawrence Hall.

4-6 May: 9th Family History Fair – Lawrence Hall.

7-12 May: King's College Examinations – Both Halls.

13 May: 17th Photographica – Lawrence Hall.

14-19 May: King's College Examinations – Both Halls.

19 May: Australian Wine Fair – Lindley Hall.

20 May: 137th Adams Antiques Fair – Lawrence Hall.

21 May-1 June: King's College Examinations – Lindley Hall.

24 May-4 June: 26th Mind Body Spirit Festival – Lawrence Hall.

5-9 June: 1st STEPS Spanish Travel Trade Show – Lawrence Hall.

5-6 June: Valencia Tourism Presentation – Lindley Hall.

7-8 June: Balearic Islands Tourism Organisation – Lindley Hall.

10 June: 138th Adams Antiques Fair – Lawrence Hall.

11-14 June: Institute of Chartered Accountants Examinations – Lawrence Hall.

12-16 June: Nicole Farhi Clothing Sale – Lindley Hall.

15-18 June: The Art of Okibana Exhibition – Lawrence Hall.

23-7 June: Flower Show – Lawrence Hall.

25-7 June: RHS AGM Lecture – Lindley Hall.

28 June: British Design & Art Directing – Lindley Hall.

28 June: Christ Redeemers Friends Trust –Lawrence Hall.

29-30 June: Cyprus Tourism Organisation Travel Show – Lindley Hall.

29 June-1 July: GANT UK Clothing Sale – Lawrence Hall.

9-10 July: Royal College of Veterinary Surgeons Examinations – Lawrence Hall.

15 July: 139th Adams Antiques Fair – Lawrence Hall.

16-17 July: Chartered Insurance Institute Examinations – Lawrence Hall.

23-6 July: Institute of Chartered Accountants Examinations – Lindley Hall.

29 July: 40th Coys of Kensington – Lawrence Hall.

20-31 August: King's College Examinations – Lindley Hall.

29 August-1 September: 8th Picture Postcard Show – Lawrence Hall.

2 September: 140th Adams Antiques Fair – Lawrence Hall.

3-5 September: Wines of Chile – Lawrence Hall.

8 September: CD & Record Fair – Lawrence Hall.

10-13 September: Institute of Chartered Accountants Examinations – Lindley Hall.

14-19 September: RHS Flower Show – Both Halls.

20 September: Elizabeth Walsh Fashion Show – Lindley Hall.

20-1 September: Matthew Williamson Fashion Show – Lawrence Hall.

21-3 September: 18th Ellis Brigham Ski Sale – Lindley Hall.

3-4 October: Toy & Game Exhibition – Lindley Hall.

5-10 October: RHS Flower Show – Both Halls.

12 October: PricewaterhouseCoopers – Lindley Hall.

14 October: 141st Adams Antiques Fair – Lawrence Hall.

15-18: October Chartered Insurance Institute Examinations – Both Halls.

22-3 October: Royal College of General Practitioners Examinations – Lawrence Hall.

24-7 October: PHILATEX – Lawrence Hall.

30 October: Central Council for Physicians Examinations – Lindley Hall.

2 November: The Centenary of The Royal Navy Submarine Service- Lawrence Hall.

4 November: 142nd Adams Antiques Fair – Lawrence Hall.

5-6 November: 14th Cancer Relief Macmillan Fund Christmas Market – Lawrence Hall.

5-7 November: Institute of Taxation Examinations – Lindley Hall.

7-12 November: 14th Healing Arts Festival – Lawrence Hall.

8-9 November: European Tour Operators Association – Lindley Hall.

13-17 November: Grand Christmas Sale – Lawrence Hall.

23-5 November: Gant UK Clothing Sale – Lawrence Hall.

27 November-1 December: Nicole Farhi Clothing Sale – Lindley Hall.

29 November: Department of Culture – Lawrence Hall.

6-23 December: Elegant Days Christmas Parties – Lindley Hall.

7 December: RHS London staff Christmas Party organised by René Dee with party planners, Elegant Days, in the Lindley Hall. This was the first time that a proper Christmas Party for RHS staff had been organised and was a huge success, establishing a precedent for future years.

5-7 December: Goldman Sachs Venetian themed party – Lawrence Hall.

10-13 December: Institute of Chartered Accountants Examinations – Lawrence Hall.

16 December: 143rd Adams Antiques Fair – Lawrence Hall.

17 December: BPP Law School Examinations – Lawrence Hall.

2002

7-11 January: King's College Examinations – Lawrence Hall.

13 January: 144th Adams Antiques Fair – Lawrence Hall.

18-23 January: RHS Flower Show – Lawrence Hall.

21-2 January: Chartered Insurance Institute Examinations – Lindley Hall.

24-7 January: 19th Ellis Brigham Ski Grab Sale – Lindley Hall.

27 January: Shahid Sharif – Lawrence Hall.

28-31 January: Australia Tasting Day – Lawrence Hall.

2-3 February: 145th Adams Antiques Fair – Lindley Hall.

10 February: 146th Adams Antiques Fair – Lawrence Hall.

12-16 February: 13th Colefax & Fowler Clothing Sale – Lawrence Hall.

17-20 February: RHS Flower Show – Lawrence Hall.

20-1 February: Inca Productions, Gharani Strok Fashion Show – Lindley Hall.

23 February: CD & Record Fair – Lawrence Hall.

25-6 February: California Wine – Lawrence Hall.

27-8 February: The Industrial Society – Lawrence Hall.

27 February-2 March: PHILATEX – Lawrence Hall.

3 March: 147th Adams Antiques Fair – Lawrence Hall.

4-7 March: 10th Museums & Heritage – Lawrence Hall.

4-9 March: Whisky Live – Lindley Hall.

9-13 March: RHS Flower Show – Lawrence Hall.

11-13 March: Witan AGM – Lindley Hall.

14-15 March: European Commission Examinations – Lindley Hall.

14-17 March: RHS Orchid Show – Lawrence Hall.

18-20 March: Spanish Wine – Lawrence Hall.

21 March: Sodexho Reception – Lindley Hall.

21-3 March: 2AM Films, BBC ident filming – Lawrence Hall.

23-4 March: 148th Adams Antiques Fair – Lindley Hall.

30 March: Games Workshop – Lindley Hall.

31 March: 149th Adams Antiques Fair – Lindley Hall.

2-4 April: Food from Spain – Lawrence Hall.

6-10 April: RHS Flower Show – Both Halls.

12-14 April: 22nd *Sunday Times* Wine Club – Both Halls.

15-16 April: Chartered Insurance Institute Examinations – Lawrence Hall.

20-4 April: RHS Flower Show – Lawrence Hall.

23-4 April: Wines of Portugal – Lindley Hall.

29 April: Costa del Sol Tourist Board – Lindley Hall.

30 April-1 May: Royal College of General Practitioners Examinations – Lindley Hall.

25 April-2 May: STEPS 2002 – Lawrence Hall.

3-5 May: 10th Family History Fair – Lawrence Hall.

6-23 May: King's College London Examinations – Lawrence Hall.

12 May: 18th Photographica – Lawrence Hall.

13-15 May: Institute of Taxation Examinations – Lindley Hall.

16-31 May: King's College Examinations – Lindley Hall.

19 May: 150th Adams Antiques Fair – Lawrence Hall.

24 May-4 June: 27th Mind Body Spirit Festival – Lawrence Hall.

5-6 June: German National Tourist Office Promotion – Lawrence Hall.

7-8 June: Gant UK Limited Clothing Sale – Lawrence Hall.

9 June: 151st Adams Antiques Fair – Lawrence Hall.

10-13 June: Institute of Chartered Accountants Examinations – Lawrence Hall.

11-15 June: Nicole Farhi Clothing Sale – Lindley Hall.

14 June: BPP Law School – Lindley Hall.

25-6 June: RHS AGM Meeting – Lindley Hall.

27 June: Whole Life Expo Limited – Lawrence Hall.

4-5 July: ANTOR 50th Anniversary Dinner – Lindley Hall.

8 July: Channel 4 Staff Meeting – Lawrence Hall.

9-11 July: BBC – Both Halls.

14 July: 152nd Adams Antiques Fair – Lawrence Hall.

15-16 July: Chartered Insurance Institute Examinations – Lawrence Hall.

22-5 July: Institute of Chartered Accountants Examinations – Lawrence Hall.

15-19 August: TAG Sale organised by the Trading Arts Group Ltd – Lawrence Hall.

16-30 August: King's College Examinations – Lindley Hall.

21 August: Channel 4 Television – Lindley Hall.

28-31 August: 9th Picture Postcard Show – Lawrence Hall.

7 September: CD & Record Fair – Lawrence Hall.

8 September: 153rd Adams Antiques Fair – Lawrence Hall.

9-12 September: Institute of Chartered Accountants Examinations – Lawrence Hall.

12-18 September: RHS Flower Show – Both Halls.

19-22 September: 20th Ellis Brigham Ski Grab Sale – Lindley Hall.

23-6 September: Employee Benefits Exhibition – Both Halls.

26 September: Relish Family Trip – Lindley Hall.

29 September: 154th Adams Antiques Fair – Lawrence Hall.

3 October: 41st Coys of Kensington – Lawrence Hall.

2-3 October: Toy & Game Exhibition – Lindley Hall.

4 October: Westminster Kingsway College Graduation Parade – Lindley Hall.

5-9 October: RHS Flower Show – Both Halls.

10 October: Relish Family Trip – Lindley Hall.

11 October: Theme Traders – Lawrence Hall.

13 October: 155th Adams Antiques Fair – Lindley Hall.

13-15 October: L'Oreal – Lindley Hall.

14-16 October: Chartered Insurance Institute Examinations – Both Halls.

21-2 October: Royal College of General Practitioners Examinations – Lindley Hall.

21 October: Quebec Government Office Promotion – Lawrence Hall.

30 October-2 November: PHILATEX – Lawrence Hall.

3 November: 156th Adams Antiques Fair – Lawrence Hall.

4-5 November: 15th Macmillan Cancer Relief Fund Christmas Market – Lawrence Hall.

4-6 November: Institute of Taxation Examinations – Lindley Hall.

6-11 November: 15th Healing Arts Festival – Lawrence Hall.

12 November: Relish Family Trip – Lindley Hall.

15 November: Black Police Officers Association – Lawrence Hall.

16-20 November: RHS Flower Show – Lawrence Hall.

22-4 November: Gant UK Clothing Sale- Lawrence Hall.

22 November: European Commission Examinations – Lindley Hall.

24-6 November: Principles Fashion Show – Lindley Hall.

27 November: Utell International – Lindley Hall.

25-30 November: Grand Christmas Sale – Lawrence Hall.

2 December: Royal College of Veterinary Surgeons Examinations – Lindley Hall.

5 December: 42nd Coys of Kensington – Lawrence Hall.

3-7 December: Nicole Farhi Clothing Sale – Lindley Hall.

7 December: BBC – French & Saunders Filming – Lawrence Hall.

9-12 December: Institute of Chartered Accountants Examinations – Lawrence Hall.

9-11 December: King's College Examinations – Lindley Hall.

15 December: 157th Adams Antiques Fair – Lawrence Hall.

16 December: RHS Christmas Party – Lindley Hall.

18 December: Interaction Event Management – Lindley Hall.

2003

9-10 January: University and Colleges Admission Services Examinations – Both Halls.

13-17 January: King's College Examinations – Lawrence Hall.

14 January: Elan Promotion – Lindley Hall.

15 January: Global Graduates Training – Lindley Hall.

16 January: Sopexa Wine Tasting – Lindley Hall.

18-22 January: RHS Flower Show – Lawrence Hall.

20-1 January: Chartered Insurance Institute Examinations – Lindley Hall.

26 January: 158th Adams Antiques Fair – Lindley Hall.

28 January-1 February: 14th Colefax & Fowler Clothing Sale – Lawrence Hall.

31 January-2 February: Headmount Ltd (Business in the Community) – Lindley Hall.

3-6 February: Australia Day – Lawrence Hall.

8 February: CD & Record Fair – Lindley Hall.

10-13 February: 11th Museums & Heritage Show – Lawrence Hall (last show with us).

15-19 February: RHS Flower Show – Lawrence Hall.

19 February: Elizabeth Walsh Fashion Show – Lindley Hall.

23 February: 159th Adams Antiques Fair – Lawrence Hall.

26 February-1 March: PHILATEX – Lawrence Hall.

1-5 March: RHS Flower Show – Lawrence Hall.

6-8 March: Whisky Live – Lindley Hall.

7-16 March: European Orchid Conference – Both Halls.

17-19 March: Wines From Spain – Lawrence Hall.

20 March: Ethnic Minorities Group – Lawrence Hall.

23 March: 160th Adams Antiques Fair – New Hall.

25-6 March: California Wine – Lawrence Hall.

2-3 April: STEPS 2003 – Lawrence Hall.

7-8 April: Chartered Insurance Institute Examinations – Lawrence Hall.

7-8 April: Wines of Portugal – Lindley Hall.

9-10 April: Chartered Insurance Institute Examinations – Lindley Hall.

10-13 April: 23rd *Sunday Times* Wine Fair – Both Halls.

24 April: National Mentoring Consortium – Lawrence Hall.

26-30 April: RHS Flower Show – Both Halls.

1, 2-6, 7 May: University College London Examinations – Lindley Hall.

2-4 May: 11th Family History Fair – Lawrence Hall.

8-10 May: International Conferences – Both Halls.

11 May: 19th Photographica – Lawrence Hall.

12-14 May: Institute of Taxation Examinations – Lindley Hall.

12-22 May: King's College Examinations – Lawrence Hall.

18 May: 161st Adams Antiques Fair – Lawrence Hall.

19 May-6 June: King's College Examinations – Both Halls.

24 May: The Great Australian Wine Tasting.

25 May-1 June: 28th Mind Body Spirit Festival – Lawrence Hall.

6-7 June: Gant UK Clothing Sale – Lawrence Hall.

7 June: CD & Record Fair – Lindley Hall.

8 June: 162nd Adams Antiques Fair – Lawrence Hall.

9-12 June: Institute of Chartered Accountants Examinations – Lawrence Hall.

9-13 June: Chartered Institute of Marketing Examinations – Lindley Hall.

17-19 June: ABTT – Both Halls.

22-4 June: MGM Productions – *Agent Cody Banks* feature film – Both Halls.

24 June: Chartered Society of Design Examinations – Lindley Hall.

25 June: RHS AGM – Lindley Hall.

25-9 June: Next Step – Lawrence Hall.

7 July: Royal College of Veterinary Surgeons Examinations – Lawrence Hall.

8-9 July: British Design & Art Direction – Lindley Hall.

9-11 July: Westminster Kingsway College Graduation Ceremony – Lindley Hall.

13 July: 163rd Adams Antiques Fair – Lawrence Hall.

14-15 July: Chartered Insurance Institute Examinations – Lawrence Hall.

14-15 July: BBC Annual Report – Lindley Hall.

19 July: Westminster Central Hall – Lawrence Hall.

21-4 July: Institute of Chartered Accountants Examinations – Lawrence Hall.

28 July: 43rd Coys of Kensington – Lawrence Hall.

29 July: RHH Client Evening – Lindley Hall.

13 August: Royal College Physicians Examinations – Lindley Hall.

18-29 August: King's College Examinations – Lindley Hall.

27-30 August: 10th Picture Postcard Show – Lawrence Hall.

2-4 September: Hardware Support Exhibition – Lawrence Hall.

2-4 September: Funny Films, *Fat Slags* TV Production – Lindley Hall.

7 September: 164th Adams Antiques Fair – Lawrence Hall.

8-11 September: Institute of Chartered Accountants Examinations – Lawrence Hall.

10-12 September: BT Broadband Challenge – Lindley Hall.

12-17 September: RHS Flower Show – Both Halls.

18 September: BMW Concerto – Lindley Hall.

19-20 September: 21st Ellis Brigham Sports Sale – Lindley Hall.

21-3 September: Frost & French Fashion Show – Lindley Hall.

22 September: Rafael Lopez Fashion Show – Lawrence Hall.

23-5 September: Warren Noronha Fashion Show – Lawrence Hall.

27 September: CD & Record Fair – Lindley Hall.

28 September: 165th Adams Antiques Fair – Lawrence Hall.

30 September-3 October: 43rd Coys of Kensington – Lawrence Hall.

1-2 October: LBC Radio 25th Anniversary Party – Lindley Hall.

3 October: Westminster Kingsway College Graduation Ceremony – Lindley Hall.

4-8 October: RHS Flower Show – Both Halls.

10-12 October: Direct Wines – Lawrence Hall.

13-14 October: Royal College of General Practitioners Examinations – Lawrence Hall.

16-18 October: Society of Chiropodists & Podiatrists Examinations – Both Halls.

19 October: 166th Adams Antiques Fair – Lawrence Hall.

20-3 October: Chartered Insurance Institute Examinations – Both Halls.

24-6 October: Home Spain – Lawrence Hall.

28-30 October: College of Law Examinations – Lindley Hall.

30 October-1 November: PHILATEX – Lawrence Hall.

3-5 November: Institute of Taxation Examinations – Lindley Hall.

3-4 November: 16th Cancer Relief Macmillan Fund Christmas Market – Lawrence Hall.

5-10 November: 16th Healing Arts Festival – Lawrence Hall (last show named as such).

6-7 November: Transport for London – Lindley Hall.

11-15 November: The Luggage & Accessories Show – Lawrence Hall.

14-20 November: Marks & Spencer Collective Fashion Launch – Lindley Hall.

17-22 November: Grand Christmas Sale – Lawrence Hall.

23-5 November: RHS Flower Show – Lawrence Hall.

27 November: Business Services Association – Lindley Hall.

27-30 November: Gant UK Limited Clothing Sale – Lawrence Hall.

1 December: Royal College of Veterinary Surgeons Examinations – Lindley Hall.

4 December: 44th Coys of Kensington – Lawrence Hall.

7 December: 167th Adams Antiques Fair – Lawrence Hall.

8-11 December: Institute of Chartered Accountants Examinations – Lawrence Hall.

2004

7 January: King's College Examinations – Lindley Hall.

8-9 January: Universities and Colleges Admissions Service Examinations – Lawrence Hall.

11 January: 168th Adams Antiques Fair – Lawrence Hall.

12-16 January: King's College Examinations – Lawrence Hall.

15 January: Sopexa Wine Tasting – Lindley Hall.

17-21 January: RHS Flower Show – Lawrence Hall.

19-20 January: Chartered Insurance Institute Examinations – Lindley Hall.

21 January: General Medical Council Examinations – Lindley Hall.

22-5 January: Maserati Car Launch – Lawrence Hall.

22 January: Institute of Linguistics Examinations – Lindley Hall.

26 January: Piccadilly Jim Productions, *Sailor*, P.J. Woodhouse – Lawrence Hall.

27-31 January: 15th Colefax & Fowler Clothing Sale – Lawrence Hall.

30-1 January: 22nd Ellis Brigham Ski Grab Sale – Lindley Hall.

1-4 February: Australia Day Tasting – Lawrence Hall.

2-4 February: Fisher Productions – Lindley Hall.

5-7 February: Australian Life – Lawrence Hall.

10 February: Conservative Central Office Press Launch – Lindley Hall.

12 February: Sopexa Wine Tasting – Lindley Hall.

13-18 February: RHS Flower Show – Lawrence Hall.

15-16 February: Paul Smith Fashion Show – Lindley Hall.

17-27 February: Hong Kong Trade Development Council – Lindley Hall.

22 February: 169th Adams Antiques Fair – Lawrence Hall.

23-4 February: California Wine – Lawrence Hall.

25-8 February: PHILATEX – Lawrence Hall.

28 February: CD & Record Fair – Lindley Hall.

4-6 March: Whisky Live – Lindley Hall.

6-10 March: RHS Flower Show – Lawrence Hall.

11-14 March: RHS Orchid Show – Both Halls.

15 March: Inns of Court School of Law Examinations – Lindley Hall.

15 March: Wines from Spain – Lawrence Hall.

21 March: 170th Adams Antiques Fair – Lindley Hall.

22-3 March: Recruitment International – Lindley Hall.

24 March: London Fashion Forum – Lawrence Hall.

25-8 March: 24th *Sunday Times* Wine Fair – Both Halls.

29 March: Conservative Central Office Press Launch – Lindley Hall.

29 March-2 April: STEPS 2004 – Lawrence Hall.

1 April: Thomas Cook – Lindley Hall.

3-7 April: RHS Daffodil Show – Both Halls.

10 April: Khurram Shamsee – Lindley Hall.

11 April: 171st Adams Antiques Fair – Lindley Hall.

14 April: Royal College of Physicians Examinations – Lindley Hall.

16-18 April: By Word of Mouth-Bahmitzvah – Lindley Hall.

16 April: Inns of Court School of Law Examinations – Lawrence Hall.

19-22 April: Chartered Insurance Institute Examinations – Lawrence Hall.

20-1 April: Wines of Portugal – Lindley Hall.

23-7 April: College of Law Examinations – Lindley Hall.

27-9 April: Food from Spain – Lawrence Hall.
28 April-5 May: University College London Examinations – Lindley Hall.
30 April: 12th Family History Show – Lawrence Hall.
4-5 May: Royal College of General Practitioners Examinations – Lawrence Hall.
9 May: 20th Photographica – Lawrence Hall.
10-12 May: Institute of Taxation Examinations – Lindley Hall.
10-20 May: King's College London Examinations – Lawrence Hall.
13 May-4 June: King's College Examinations – Lindley Hall.
16 May: 172nd Adams Antiques Fair – Lindley Hall.
22 May: Great Australian Wine Tasting – Lindley Hall.
24 May-1 June: 29th Mind Body Spirit Festival – Lawrence Hall.
2 June: King's College Examinations – Lawrence Hall.
3-6 June: Gant UK Clothing Sale – Lawrence Hall.
7-10 June: Institute of Chartered Accountants Examinations – Lawrence Hall.
9-11 June: Chartered Institute of Marketing Examinations – Lindley Hall.
13 June: 173rd Adams Antiques Fair – Lindley Hall.
14 June: Bloomberg Recruitment Fair – Lindley Hall.
15-17 June: ABTT – Both Halls.
18-20 June: French Property Exhibition – Lawrence Hall.
26-30 June: BBC – Both Halls.
30 June-1 July: RHS AGM – Lindley Hall.
5 July: Royal College of Veterinary Surgeons Examinations – Lawrence Hall.
6-7 July: Adidas Olympic Team Kit Launch – Lindley Hall.
11 July: 174th Adams Antiques Fair – Lindley Hall.
12-17 July: Chartered Insurance Institute Examinations – Lawrence Hall.
13 July: General Medical Council Examinations – Lindley Hall.
20-2 July: Institute of Chartered Accountants Examinations – Lawrence Hall.
21-2 July: Blue Creative Communication – Lindley Hall.
28 July: Royal College of Physicians Examinations – Lindley Hall.
16-27 August: King's College Examinations – Lindley Hall.
31 August-4 September: 11th Picture Postcard Show – Lawrence Hall.
3-5 September: Austravel – Lindley Hall.
7 September: Specialist Schools Trust – Lindley Hall.
14-15 September: RHS Flower Show – Both Halls.
14-15 September: Centenary Exhibition of Royal Horticultural Halls – Lawrence Hall.
16 September: General Medical Council Examinations – Lawrence Hall.
17-18 September: 23rd Ellis Brigham Ski Grab Sale – Lindley Hall.
19 September: 175th Adams Antiques Fair – Lindley Hall.

19-20 September: Paul Smith Fashion Show – Lawrence Hall.
21-3 September: Hardware Support Exhibition – Lawrence Hall.
21 September: Royal College of Physicians Examinations – Lindley Hall.
30 September: 45th Coys of Kensington – Lawrence Hall.
2-6 October: RHS Flower Show – Both Halls.
11-14 October: Chartered Insurance Institute Examinations – Lawrence Hall.
18-19 October: Royal College of General Practitioners Examinations – Lindley Hall.
19-20 October: Man Booker Prize – BBC – Lindley Hall.
27-30 October: PHILATEX – Lawrence Hall.
27-9 October: College of Law Examinations – Lindley Hall.
1-3 November: Institute of Taxation Examinations – Lindley Hall.
2 November: National Mentoring Consortium – Lawrence Hall.
3-8 November: 1st Wellbeing Show (previously known as Healing Arts) – Lawrence Hall.
7 November: 151st Adams Antiques Fair – Lindley Hall.
9 November: General Medical Council Examinations – Lindley Hall.
8-9 November: 17th Macmillan Cancer Relief Fund Christmas Market – Lawrence Hall.
9-13 November: RHS Flower Show – Lawrence Hall.
18-21 November: Gant UK Clothing Sale – Lawrence Hall.
22-7 November: Grand Christmas Sale – Lawrence Hall.
28 November: 176th Adams Antiques Fair – Lindley Hall.
29 November: King's College Examinations – Both Halls.
30 November: Royal College of Veterinary Surgeons Examinations – Lindley Hall.
1 December: 46th Coys of Kensington – Lawrence Hall.
1-23 December: The Ultimate Experience Corporate Christmas Parties – Lindley Hall.
6-9 December: Institute of Chartered Accountants Examinations – Lawrence Hall.

NB. The dates and information given above have been compiled by the author from a number of sources that include: RHS archives, correspondence, show catalogues, trade directories, leaflets, posters, digital website references, *The Times* online (and other national, regional and local newspapers), magazines, periodicals, newsreels, poster labels, postcards, ephemera and books. These may not all be reliable or 100 per cent accurate so they are provided as the best information known to the author to date, and a basis for further research, if required. The author has concentrated on revealing the non-horticultural events that have never before been published in this form. While some RHS Flower Shows and other horticultural events have been listed, not all are. A full listing of the horticultural shows and events held by the RHS and its affiliated societies in the Halls can be found in its Lindley Library archives at 80 Vincent Square, London, SW1P 2PE.

Index

Index compiled by Auriol Griffith-Jones.

Note: Page numbers in *italics* refer to illustrations